Thomas Murphy has lectured on industrial relations in University College Dublin since 1979. He has held appointments at executive level in industrial relations and personnel management in the semi-state sector, and was one of the founders of *Industrial Relations News*. He has written widely on trade union organisation at company level, and on the impact of employment law on the practices of employers and trade unions.

Professor Bill Roche is Dean of the Michael Smurfit Graduate School of Business at University College Dublin and Director of Research in the Faculty of Commerce. He has published extensively on human resource management and industrial relations and his publications include a book and a range of articles on working time. Professor Roche is academic editor of the series Irish Studies in Management.

Irish Studies in Management

Editors:

W.K. Roche
Graduate School of Business
University College Dublin

David Givens
Oak Tree Press

Irish Studies in Management is a new series of texts and research-based monographs covering management and business studies. Published by Oak Tree Press in association with the Graduate School of Business at University College Dublin, the series aims to publish significant contributions to the study of management and business in Ireland, especially where they address issues of major relevance to Irish management in the context of international developments, particularly within the European Union. Mindful that most texts and studies in current use in Irish business education take little direct account of Irish or European conditions, the series seeks to make available to the specialist and general reader works of high quality which comprehend issues and concerns arising from the practice of management and business in Ireland. The series aims to cover subjects ranging from accountancy to marketing, industrial relations/human resource management, international business, business ethics and economics. Studies of public policy and public affairs of relevance to business and economic life will also be published in the series.

CONTENTS

CONTRIBUTORS

Teresa Brannick is a Senior Research Associate of the Business Research Programme at the Graduate School of Business, University College Dublin.

Nuala Butler is a practising lawyer and lectures on Employment Law in the Graduate School of Business, University College Dublin. She is former vice-chairperson of the Employment Appeals Tribunal.

Linda Doyle is Personnel Officer with Securicor Ltd. She is a former lecturer in the Department of Industrial Relations, University College Dublin.

John F. Geary is a lecturer in the Department of Industrial Relations, University College Dublin.

Patrick Gunnigle is Head of the Department of Personnel and Employment Relations, University of Limerick.

Fintan Hourihan is a Press/Information Officer with the Association of Secondary Teachers Ireland. He is former industrial correspondent with Industrial Relations News Report.

Aidan Kelly is a Professor of Business Administration in the Faculty of Commerce, University College Dublin. He is a former Dean in the Faculty of Commerce.

Anthony Kerr is a lecturer in the Faculty of Law, University College Dublin.

Brendan MacPartlin is a lecturer at the National College of Industrial Relations.

Michael McGinley is a lecturer in the Department of Industrial Relations, University College Dublin.

Michael Morley is a lecturer in the Department of Personnel and Employment Relations, University of Limerick.

Thomas Murphy is Acting Head of the Department of Industrial Relations, University College Dublin.

William K. Roche is Dean of the Graduate School of Business and Director of Research in the Faculty of Commerce, University College Dublin.

Thomas Turner is a lecturer in the Department of Personnel and Employment Relations, University of Limerick.

INTRODUCTION

The field of industrial relations (IR) has a critical bearing on economic performance and a range of social and political concerns. The character of industrial relations is an obvious influence of the degree of success with which businesses compete or attain their key objectives. But the way in which industrial relations are conducted will also influence employees' experience of work; their views as to fairness of pay and salary levels, and their attitudes to the exercise of managerial authority. The handling of industrial relations in general, and of pay bargaining in particular, has also become a major concern of governments in Ireland, as elsewhere.

This is a revised edition of the original text which was first published in 1994. Two of the chapters from the earlier edition have been replaced by three new chapters dealing with the management of Industrial Relations practices in multinationals and the emergence of a new IR agenda. This text seeks to present to students, professional practitioners and the general reader, detailed and authoritative readings on the core concerns of Irish industrial relations practice. All contributors to the book possess considerable professional experience of the field, whether as lecturers, researchers, lawyers, industrial relations journalists, managers or trade unionists.

The publication of the text also reflects the growth, in recent years, in the numbers of people studying industrial relations at university level and in professional, business, executive and trade union courses. The paucity of suitable teaching material, which addresses Irish concerns and issues directly, has been a major acknowledged weakness of Irish industrial relations education for many years. Too often teachers and students have been forced to rely upon texts with little direct bearing on the Irish experience. With the publication of the present work, it is hoped that the features of Irish industrial relations, and the forces which influence Irish practice, may be better understood than heretofore.

It is important to outline the approach we have taken in shaping the book. We have sought to produce a book with several major distinguishing features. First, we were concerned that current issues and practice in Irish industrial relations should be understood in their proper historical context. It seems to us that the key to understanding major concerns in Irish industrial relations, some of them perhaps distinctive to the Irish experience, is to be found in a proper appreciation of the development of practices, institutions and approaches over time. Often, as a number of chapters will bear out, such an understanding of current issues also requires a familiarity with aspects of Irish economic, political and legal history.

Second, we have also been concerned to apply to the Irish case aspects of theory which have informed the study of industrial relations internationally. While in many respects, Irish historical developments have shaped Irish practice in important and distinctive ways, what also stands out is the degree to which those involved in Irish industrial relations have faced similar pressures, constraints and options to those faced in the industrial relations experience of other countries, especially in the European Union. An appreciation of what may be distinctive in Irish industrial relations, need not, and cannot, stand divorced from an appreciation of common pressures and experiences across different countries. Therefore, the critical application of bodies of ideas used to understand developments in industrial relations internationally adds to our understanding of Irish institutions and practices.

Third, contributors have been encouraged to take full account of relevant research studies and to draw on relevant primary statistical and documentary data. It is gratifying to note that as the number of scholars engaged in industrial relations has increased in recent years, the volume of research on Ireland has been growing. A number of contributors have been able to draw extensively and instructively on existing research. In some areas, however, there remains a dearth of good basic research. It is hoped that the body of research on Irish industrial relations will continue to grow. Ultimately, research, above all, holds the key to an understanding of practice.

Finally, we have asked contributors to provide comprehensive reviews of current and recent developments in their subject areas. The reader should be able to turn to the book for an account of current practice and major concerns in all the subject areas encompassed by the contributions.

Little elaboration is necessary regarding the themes we have chosen to provide focus for the book: they are the central concerns of industrial relations internationally. The contributions are of generally uniform length, but we have permitted some exceptions. There seemed little purpose in applying a rigid formula with respect to length in the case of contributions dealing, for example, with the historical evolution of Irish industrial relations since the middle of the nineteenth century. In the same way, the book's longest chapter seeks to provide a detailed treatment of pay determination in Irish industrial relations in the context of developments in state strategy and the politics of industrial relations. The closely intertwined areas of collective bargaining over pay and government postures towards industrial relations are of such importance as to merit extended and detailed treatment.

It is our belief that the publication of this book demonstrates the current vibrance and importance of the field of industrial relations in Ireland. In the universities and colleges, the number of students studying industrial relations and allied fields continues to grow. Major current developments, especially European integration and the growth of international competition, will continue to put the spotlight on industrial relations in Ireland and demand a new level of awareness and understanding of how Irish industrial relations operates and how the field may be changing.

It seems to us fitting that the book should issue from the Department of Industrial Relations at University College, Dublin. The Department at UCD pioneered teaching and research in industrial relations in Irish third-level education. The present book draws heavily on research conducted by UCD academics in areas like union growth and organisation, strikes, trade union law, industrial relations in the public sector and the development of management practice.

It is one of the pleasures of editorship to thank colleagues and friends who have made valuable contributions to the completion of the book. A number of people helped with drafts and the preparation of the final manuscript of the first edition including John Byrne, Linda Doyle, Noelle Donnelly, Fiona Walsh, Fionnuala McCarthy (editorial assistant to the series) and Majella Fahy. Marian Murphy helped with earlier drafts and the preparation of the final manuscript in respect of this revised edition. She was helped in this by Linda Dowling. We wish to express our thanks and appreciation to all of them.

We wish, in particular, to thank David Givens of Oak Tree Press for his faith in the project from its inception; his patience and determination in guiding the work to completion, and his professionalism in turning a complex manuscript into an integrated text.

Tom Murphy and Bill Roche

Graduate School of Business
University College Dublin
January 1997

CHAPTER 1

INDUSTRIALISATION AND THE DEVELOPMENT OF INDUSTRIAL RELATIONS*

William K. Roche

THE LIBERAL THEORY OF INDUSTRIALISM AND INDUSTRIAL RELATIONS

This chapter is concerned with the development of Irish industrial relations over a period of nearly a century. It considers the changing character of relations between employers and employees in Ireland in the context of four central theoretical concerns of the dominant post-war theoretical approach to industrial-relations change in industrial nations: the so-called liberal theory of industrialism. In essence, liberal theory focuses on the impact of industrialisation on long-run change in management strategy and the character of trade union activity. The process of industrialisation is assigned primary importance in shaping industrial relations. The chapter finds little evidence in Irish experience that a clearly identifiable "logic of industrialism" shaped the behaviour of managements, unions or the state during the course of industrial and economic development. The actual effects of industrial and economic trends on industrial relations are shown to be considerably more complex and contorted than allowed for in liberal theory. The outcomes of some processes of change identified by the liberal position are found not to be as predicted. Few secure secular trends in employer, union and government activity can be identified. Instead of inexorable sociological processes and trends, what sometimes stands out in the Irish experience is the impact of unusual circumstances, the continuing relevance of options and the complexity of patterns of change.

The central concerns of the liberal theory of industrial relations can be divided into one set of propositions concerning the effects of unions and employers on the "take-off" into industrialisation and three further sets of propositions concerning the effects, following

take-off, of long-term development towards an increasingly industrialised society. The major arguments regarding take-off and secular
change can be stated as follows:

1. Worker and union militancy and radicalism peak early in the
   course of industrialisation and represent a protest against social
   dislocation occasioned by the rigours of industrial organisation
   and urban life. The faster the pace of industrialisation, the more
   severe the disjuncture with traditional patterns of life and the
   greater the degree of militancy with which workers respond (Kerr
   et al., 1973: 218–9; Lipset, 1969: ch. 6). Industrial technology and
   its supposed "imperatives" are attributed major, indeed almost
   exclusive, importance in influencing trends in behaviour and organisation. Other concomitants of industrialisation, such as the
   development of markets, growing regional and international economic interdependence, and the effects of business cycles, have
   virtually no place in liberal theory. The impact of take-off is, however, believed to be compounded by the social and political circumstances in which it is achieved. Of particular importance in this
   respect is the *sequencing* of "national, political and industrial
   'revolutions' in a country relative to the rise of the labour movement" (Dunlop, 1958: 313 and ch. 8; Kahn-Freund, 1972: 39–40;
   Commons, 1932: 683; Sturmthal, 1951; Kendall, 1975; Lorwin,
   1954). Similarly, it is noted that the social divisions of rural society may "carry over" into industrial society through pre-capitalist
   traditions of militancy which continue to influence newly-recruited
   industrial workers and their unions.[1]

The three remaining sets of propositions of the liberal theory are addressed to long-run change in industrial relations.

2. Sustained employer resistance to union recognition and collective
   bargaining results in union demands becoming utopian and eventually revolutionary. The prospect of a spiral of politicisation, in
   which employer resistance and union militancy reinforce each
   other, leads in most national cases to a revision of employer strategy. A class compromise of a kind is achieved which allows a
   "containment spiral" to take effect. The waning of employer resistance reduces significantly the "intensity" of industrial conflict.
   What Kerr calls the "glacial impact" of institutionalised compromise gradually transforms industrial relations. By degrees, the
   exercise of industrial authority comes to be shared between managers and managed. A "constitutional approach" to the governance

of work replaces confrontation. Following an early decline in the intensity of industrial conflict comes a long-run decline in the *level* of industrial conflict (Ross and Hartman, 1960).

The progressive development of a "constitutional approach" to the governance of the workplace — the elaboration of a "web of rules", or the emergence of "industrial citizenship", as the process is sometimes described — is the guarantor of long-run social integration and economic stability (Kerr, 1955; Slichter, Healy and Livernash, 1960; Flanders, 1970). Pluralist industrial relations strategy involves a rejection of "monism" or "unitarism". Efforts at total control of employees' attitudes to employment are viewed as superfluous and damaging (Kerr, 1955: 167; Fox, 1966).

3. Geographical and social mobility increase in response to economic development, the spread of educational opportunity and the gradual growth of occupations requiring higher levels of skill (Kerr et al., 1973: chs. 1 and 8). Class structures decompose and give way to social structures in which people's identities in the labour market are formed no longer on the basis of class allegiance but on the basis of occupation or "status position". Occupational identities and interests cannot be accommodated in large "inclusive", multi-occupational unions. In consequence, general and industrial unions experience long-run decline at the expense of more "exclusive" types of trade unions, such as craft and occupational unions (Kerr et al., 1973: 274). Trade unions lose the capacity to act in concert in pursuit of the common interests of all workers.

4. Changes in social stratification and the institutionalisation of industrial conflict result in the scaling-down of trade union objectives. The very idea of labour organisations as "component parts of class movements urging programmes of total reform" ceases to have meaning (Kerr et al., 1973: 274). Politics and industrial relations become distinct spheres of activity, responding, as it were, to their own cycles. Cleavages in industry and politics arise around different issues. Political parties originating on the left open out to embrace issues not traditionally polarised in terms of a left–right split and, as a result, the interests of unions and "progressive (socialist, labour) parties" diverge (Dahrendorf, 1959: 267–318). The state continues to be powerful and active, but operates as an honest broker, overseeing the "rules of the game", and protecting civil liberties in a society dominated by interest organisations.[2]

These propositions have had a major impact on thought regarding the development of relations between employers and employees in western industrial nations. For adherents of the liberal canon, they are no less applicable to Third World, Asian and east European nations (Kerr et al., 1973). It will be argued in this chapter that the development of Irish industrial relations confounds liberal theory in a number of major respects. The shortcomings of the liberal position will be examined by reviewing the Irish experience against each of the four sets of propositions in turn. In addition to testing the liberal propositions in the Irish case, this chapter is concerned to advance alternative, and more empirically grounded, explanations of the forces that have shaped industrial relations in Ireland.

WORKING-CLASS MILITANCY IN SOCIOLOGICAL CONTEXT: 1900–22

In the period from about 1907 to 1920 unionisation first became a mass economic and social force in Ireland. Prior to the early twentieth century, only skilled craftsmen working in the towns and cities of the eastern, southern, and western seaboards had attained significant levels of sustained union organisation. The majority of these craftsmen were members of Irish branches of several of the formidable British "new model" unions (Clarkson, 1926; Keogh, 1982: ch. 2). It was a British trade union activist, James Larkin, who set off the avalanche of unionisation which began in 1907. The Irish Transport Union (later, the Irish Transport and General Workers' Union) was founded by Larkin in 1909, following a dispute with his own union, the British National Union of Dock Labourers. The ITGWU was to be at the centre of the remarkable transformation of Irish industrial relations in the years to 1920. The sequence of events during this period need only be considered here in outline.

The membership of unions affiliated to the Irish Trade Union Congress rose from about 30,000 in 1894 to 250,000 in 1920. The Irish Transport alone reached a membership level of over 100,000 by 1920 (Greaves, 1982).

In very rough terms, total trade union membership in that year represented about 25 per cent of wage earners. From the incomplete statistical data available on strike trends, it is clear that a major strike wave occurred during the period, with particularly high levels of strike participation registered during the years 1917–20 (Fitzpatrick, 1980). From the many descriptive studies of strikes during the period, it is clear that industrial conflict was of unique intensity compared with subsequent strike waves (O'Connor, 1988; Greaves, 1982; Lysaght, 1982).

The period as a whole can be divided into two sub-periods, each characterised by a distinct cycle of unionisation and militancy. In the first period, covering the years from 1907 to the Dublin lockout of 1914, the self-styled syndicalist ITGWU concentrated on gaining membership and recognition in the towns and cities of the "maritime economy" that had been the bulwarks of craft unionism. The urban membership drive of the nascent general union was centred on relatively mature working-class occupational communities of dockers, transport workers, millers and engineering workers. This drive for membership and also recognition met with concerted employer resistance, and resulted in a series of major lockouts, culminating in the great Dublin lockout of 1914, which all but destroyed the ITGWU. In the years 1914–17 the union was virtually dormant. The years to 1920 witnessed the second cycle of unionisation and militancy, this time focused on rural areas, and in particular on agricultural labourers. The rank-and-file militancy of this second cycle showed signs of social radicalism. Land seizures and factory occupations became common. These initiatives were encouraged by the widespread collapse of civil order during the Anglo-Irish War. From 1919, attempts by employers to cut wages also spurred workers into militant action. The rhetoric and sometimes the tactics of trade union militancy were influenced by the Bolshevik revolution (Mitchell, 1974: 141–2; Lysaght, 1982; Fitzpatrick, 1977: ch. 7).[3]

As outlined above, liberal theory attributes major importance to the traumas associated with the takeoff into industrialisation in explaining the tendency for "worker protest to peak early in the course of industrialisation and decline in intensity thereafter" (Kerr et al., 1973: ch. 6). However, the intense strike wave and worker militancy in Ireland in the years 1907–20 cannot meaningfully be regarded as a response to economic and social dislocations resulting from industrialisation. In many of the towns and rural areas in which working-class militancy was particularly intense, takeoff into industrialisation in any real sense had yet to be attained or re-attained. In other areas with a more developed industrial base, militancy arose in a context of industrial stagnation or decline.

The standard indicators of levels of industrialisation presented for Ireland and other European countries in Tables 1.1 and 1.2 indicate that in the 1890s and early 1900s overall levels of industrial employment and non-agricultural employment in Ireland were on a par with continental European countries, though well behind Great Britain, the world's "first industrial nation". The regional penetration of industrialisation in early twentieth century Ireland was nonetheless very uneven. The heaviest concentration of industrial employment was found in the northeast, centred on Belfast. Generally, levels of industrial employment were lower in the late nineteenth and early twentieth centuries than they had been in the early nineteenth century (Booth, 1902; Cullen, 1972).

TABLE 1.1: PERCENTAGE OF TOTAL WORKFORCE IN AGRICULTURAL EMPLOYMENT IN IRELAND AND OTHER EUROPEAN COUNTRIES, 1891–1971

	Ireland	Great Britain	France	Italy	Sweden
1891	44.2*	10.4	40.3	59.4 (1901)	53.9
1901	44.6*	7.7	41.8	59.4	49.8
1911	43.0*	8.1	42.7 (1906)	55.5	45.6
1926	51.3	6.0 (1931)	38.3	47.3 (1931)	35.4 (1930)
1951	39.6	5.0	27.2 (1954)	40.0	20.3
1961	35.2	3.6	20.3 (1962)	28.2	13.8
1971	25.4	2.5	12.2 (1975)	16.3	8.1

* Irish data for 1891–1911 relate to all Ireland.

Sources: Data for European countries derived from Flora et al. (1983). Data for Ireland for 1891 derived from Coyne, ed. (1902: 65) and for 1901 and 1911 from the Census of Population for Ireland 1911, General Report, occupational tables.

TABLE 1.2: PERCENTAGE OF TOTAL WORKFORCE IN INDUSTRIAL EMPLOYMENT IN IRELAND AND OTHER EUROPEAN COUNTRIES, 1891–1971*

	Ireland	Great Britain	France	Italy	Sweden
1891	27.2	44.5	28.1	23.7	14.4
1901	32.6	45.6	30.0	23.7	19.7
1911	33.8	44.6	29.5	26.8	24.7
1926	14.5	46.1	33.0	29.4	30.9
1951	24.4	49.2	35.7	30.4	40.6
1961	25.5	47.4	38.5	39.4	45.1
1971	31.5	42.2	34.7	42.2	40.3

* Time points as in Table 1.1.

Sources: As in Table 1.1.

The available evidence suggests that the pace of output growth in Ireland over the period since the middle of the nineteenth century was slower than in any other European country (Kennedy et al., 1988: ch. 1). Thus, in many parts of Ireland, the nineteenth century and early 1900s witnessed "deindustrialisation". The 1890s saw the beginnings of an economic revival of this shrinking industrial base (Cullen, 1972). The circumstances of the First World War rendered uneven the fortunes of different sectors of Irish industry between 1914 and 1920.

Sectors that could take advantage of war contracts prospered, as did parts of the food industry, but sectors that had relied heavily on imported raw materials or on export-markets were adversely affected (Riordan, 1920).

The relevant point here is that, even in the absence of reliable indicators of aggregate industrial output, liberalism's social dislocation theory is clearly redundant in explaining the intense worker militancy of early twentieth century Ireland. No severe disjuncture in living or working conditions was experienced by Irish industrial or agricultural workers such as might explain the extreme intensity of the industrial and class conflict of the period. An alternative explanation for the "peaking of worker protest" and the course of union militancy in Ireland in the years 1907–20 can be found in the interaction of three sets of factors: first, the two cycles of economic activity in industrial and agricultural Ireland; second, the progress of the Anglo-Irish War and the associated near collapse of civil order in rural areas; and third, the response of employers and farmers to attempts by the unskilled to unionise.

The early success of Larkin and his Irish Transport Union in organising urban workers occurred against the background of industrial revival (Cullen, 1972). While the numbers employed in manufacturing generally continued to fall in the period 1891–1911, employment rose in occupations in transport and communications, which represented the early focus of unionisation. The rate of growth in occupations in the census classification of "general labourers" was only about one-third of that achieved over the period 1841–81 (Booth, 1902; *Census of Population*, 1891; 1909; 1911). This might suggest that a combination of economic revival and slow-down in the growth of the labour supply at the base of the occupational structure contributed to the first cycle of unionisation and militancy in urban areas.

The second cycle of unionisation and militancy from about 1917 to 1920 occurred against an economic background of wartime food shortages, spiralling inflation and sharply falling real wage levels. In such conditions, workers developed an intense conviction that employers and shopkeepers were profiteering by creating artificial shortages and by hoarding goods (Fitzpatrick, 1977; O'Connor, 1988). Workers in urban-based industries faced highly uneven economic conditions, but the net employment situation in the towns appears to have been poor throughout the War. The position of agricultural la-bourers was more conducive to unionisation and militancy. Rural workers faced problems of inflation and relative deprivation similar to those faced by workers in the towns. However, soaring agricultural prices during the First World War led to a boom in farming. Rural labour markets were thus generally tighter than those in the towns, especially following the imposition of compulsory tillage, backed by legal minimum wages, between 1917 and 1919. The growth of agricultural trade unionism was dramatic. By the end of 1919 agricultural labourers had become the single biggest membership category of the Irish Transport, accounting for just under 30 per cent of the total union membership (Greaves, 1982: 259). More generally, the Irish Transport enjoyed spectacular membership growth and quickly became by far the largest trade union in Ireland, although its progress was very uneven geographically (Kenny, 1985; Fitzpatrick, 1977: 247).

"Modern" or revisionist explanations of the spectacular, but geographically uneven, rise in the unionisation of agricultural labourers usually stress the importance of the rise in tillage acreage. Because tillage is more labour-intensive than pastoral farming, an increase in tillage acreage is understood to have increased the demand for labour. This in turn is taken to have enhanced the bargaining power and confidence of agricultural workers, and increased their propensity to unionise and press claims on farmers (Fitzpatrick, 1977: ch. 7; Kenny, 1985: ch. 3). The revisionist position among historians and historical geographers tends, at the same time, to down-play the role of resurgent nationalism in legitimising the strongly republican ITGWU and enhancing its attractions to wage earners (see esp. O'Connor, 1988). The participation of the union's acting general secretary, James Connolly, in the 1916 Rising and his subsequent execution, gave the union a symbolically powerful place in the pantheon of Irish revolutionary martyrdom. During the Anglo-Irish War, union officials were actively engaged in the independence movement. The union participated in a series of major political strikes and in a campaign against conscription (Mitchell, 1974). The potency of nationalism among rank-and-file trade unionists was apparent in a wave of

breakaway activity by the Irish branches of British trade unions during
and after the Anglo-Irish War.

A statistical assessment of the relative influences of these economic and socio-political factors on working-class organisations and
militancy is presented in Roche (1992). These results, admittedly tentative due to the shortcoming of the data available, underscore the
role of socio-political factors, like traditions of agrarian radicalism
and Sinn Féin activism, in explaining differences between counties in
the branch penetration of the ITGWU. The role of increased tillage
acreage, or the intensity of tillage farming, emerges as a considerably
less straightforward or direct influence on inter-county differences in
ITGWU organisation's success than proposed in the "revisionist" historical tradition.[4] The significance of variations between counties in
the scale of the agricultural labouring class, occupied on large commercial farms, in explaining differences in levels of trade union organisation, is also confirmed in the statistical analysis (Roche, 1992).

Given the shortcomings of the available data, the results of the
statistical exercise must obviously be regarded as tentative. Nonetheless, by integrating them with the historical record, a number of conclusions can be drawn regarding the roots of unionisation and working-class militancy in Ireland in the early decades of the century. The
pace, character or process of industrialisation is not directly relevant
to an understanding of the scale and intensity of worker militancy
during the period 1907–20. The most militant sections of the urban
working class were those working and living in relatively mature
communities in the main cities and towns of the maritime economy.
The most highly organised and militant agricultural workers were
labourers on larger commercial farms who had probably become reconciled to their status as an agricultural proletariat. The growth of
trade unionism in town and country thus reflected the mediate influence of dispositions formed by stable social arrangements, rather
than putative processes of social dislocation or "anomie". The demands of Irish workers during this period give no hint of any atavis-
tic rejection of industrial or commercial economic relations. What is
striking, rather, is the precocious nature of much of the militancy of
the period, considering that the great majority of the workers involved had little tradition of trade unionism (see, for example,
O'Connor, 1988 and Cronin, 1979: ch. 5).

On the other hand, liberal theory's emphasis on the role of employer resistance in spurring working-class militancy is broadly consistent with the record in Ireland. After the first intense set-piece
confrontations with new unionism in the towns, employers appeared

to accept, however grudgingly, that union recognition and collective bargaining could not be fought off indefinitely. Employer resistance to the rudiments of collective bargaining was also intense in rural Ireland from 1918 to 1920. This probably contributed to the volatility, violence and intermittent radicalism of rank-and-file militancy in the countryside. Here the onset of the postwar slump in agricultural prices from late 1920 defused rural class struggle by undermining working-class power and confidence. So a spiral of politicisation failed to take hold in Irish industrial relations, in part because working-class insurgency in the face of intense employer militancy was not sustained for sufficiently long to have critically transformed the sociopolitical values of workers.

In sum, then, cyclical recovery in the urban economy, followed by the abnormal economic and social conditions of wartime in urban and rural economies alike, gave rise to economic conditions conducive to unionisation and militancy. The proximate economic influences on the surge of unionisation between 1917 and 1920 appear to have been those that affected more or less all agricultural labourers: in particular, the prosperity of employers, a general tightening of labour markets, inflation and stagnant or falling real wages. Legal provision for guaranteed minimum wages was also important in that it provided the ITGWU with a prop in its dealings with farmers and cast the union in the role of custodian of public policy (Greaves, 1982: ch. 10). From the data available, variations between counties in unionisation appear not to have been affected in any direct or simple way either by the scale of tillage farming or the growth in tillage acreage.

In addition, the subsidiary liberal idea of effects is useful in a number of respects in appreciating the distinctiveness of Irish industrial relations. The geographical pattern of unionisation appears to have been influenced by nineteenth century traditions of rural agitation and by contemporary nationalist political mobilisation. More generally, the sequencing of industrialisation and unionisation in Ireland was unusual owing to the influence of British institutions and ideas. At independence, trade unionism in Ireland was organised along lines similar to British trade unionism, in spite of the dramatic difference between the two countries in levels of industrial and economic development. Strong craft and occupational unions coexisted with industrial and general unions in a fragmented trade union system. The occurrence of the national revolution was to fragment Irish trade unionism further by causing a wave of breakaway activity in the Irish branches of virtually all of these types of British unions.

The simultaneity of national revolution and mass unionisation contributed both to the emergence and containment of social radicalism in the period 1917–20, and at the same time to the marginalisation of the Labour Party in the formative period of Irish politics. The land seizures and factory occupations were spurred by the political upheaval of the Anglo-Irish War and Civil War and the virtual collapse of civil order over much of the country. Radicalism was also contained by the balance of class forces in the national revolution. The revolutionary political élite sought to contain class conflict during the struggle for independence, initially to promote united insurgency, and later to placate farming and business interests and maintain the status quo (Strauss, 1951: 265; Laffan, 1985: 205). In this they were aided by the successors of Larkin and Connolly and the leaders of the Irish Labour Party and Trades Union Congress. In general, labour leaders during the period 1917–20 drew back from rank-and-file militancy, using their energies instead to build and consolidate trade union organisation.

In deference to the strength of the nationalist movement, and constrained by the weakness of party organisation at constituency level, the Labour Party failed to contest the first election held in 1918 under universal adult suffrage. This election ultimately led to the establishment of the independent Irish State. The Civil War, which began shortly after the truce in 1922 and continued into 1923, set the mould of party politics in Ireland. By mobilising support around the national question, the parties drew electoral support from across the class structure.

The critical formative influences on Irish industrial relations are thus to be found in the interaction of mediate influences that imply social dispositions formed in a context of stability rather than dislocation, influences arising from cyclical and wartime economic conditions, and the kind of sequence effects viewed by liberal theory as little more than subsidiary influences on the impact of industrialisation.

TRENDS IN "EXCLUSIVE" AND "INCLUSIVE" TRADE UNIONISM

Liberal theory predicts a secular rise in the membership shares of craft and occupational unions at the expense of general and industrial unions. This trend gradually attenuates unions' inclination or capacity to act in concert to achieve common objectives. In short, liberal theory argues from trends in organisation to trends in union strategy, predicting a secure future for trade unions, but the end of "trade union movements".

The level of trade union "density" attained by Irish unions increased from less than 20 per cent in the 1920s to a peak of over 60 per cent in 1980 (Roche and Larragy, 1989: 22). Short- and medium-term fluctuations around this rising secular trend can be attributed to business cycle and institutional influences on unionisation (Roche and Larragy, 1990). The membership of Irish unions also became occupationally and industrially more diverse over this period. Of particular sociological interest, however, are trends in the distribution of this growing level of union membership across unions along the continuum from "inclusive" to "exclusive" unionism. General unions are the most inclusive of all unions in aspiring to organise the "entire working class" or workforce, whereas pure craft and professional unions are the most exclusive in restricting membership to trained members of the craft or profession. Often craft and professional unions impose barriers to entry in order to restrict labour supply. They also try to "police" the work of members to preserve the "integrity" of the craft or profession against encroachment by other occupations. Between these extremes of union character fall unions of more or less inclusive membership and ambition. Industrial unions and unions organising workers engaged in broadly similar or "allied occupations" — possibly in different industries — are closest to general unions. Unions of single occupations are closest to pure craft and professional unions, differing perhaps only in their inability to exercise closure over entry to the occupation, or to control the boundaries of the jobs done by their members.

Table 1.3 presents the distribution of union membership across unions grouped into these three broad types at ten-year intervals since 1930. Data for 1985 are also presented, as this is the most recent year for which reliable data can be obtained.[5] The terms "quasi-industrial" unions and "ex-craft" unions are used in the tables to indicate that not all industrial unions aspire to complete organisation of their industrial domain, and that many craft unions, though originating in organisations restricted solely to apprenticed tradesmen, have "opened" and admitted semiskilled workers over time. This point is elaborated later. The table indicates that the share of total union membership organised by general unions remains by far the largest of any union type. General unions, quasi-industrial unions, and unions organising allied occupations combined, in 1985 still organised 68 per cent of all Irish trade union members — more than double the combined share of craft and occupational unions.

TABLE 1.3: PERCENTAGE DISTRIBUTION OF UNION MEMBERSHIP BY
ORGANISATIONAL TYPE*

	General Unions	(Quasi-) Industrial and Allied Occupational Unions	(Ex-) Craft and Occupational Unions
1930	38.4	30.8	30.8
1940	46.0	27.1	26.9
1950	54.8	20.9	24.2
1960	56.8	19.5	23.7
1970	52.3	19.6	27.7
1980	49.5	20.7	29.8
1985	45.2	22.5	32.3

* The membership of a small number of unions of indeterminable status has
been omitted. Rows may not sum to one hundred due to rounding.

Source: Dues Data Series on Ireland.

If the level of membership accounted for by inclusive unions is inconsistent with liberal theory, the "trend" in membership shares might
still be interpreted as providing it with some support. The period covered by the data appears to break down into two distinct sub-periods.
During the first, from the 1930s to about 1960, the trend favours general unions.

The share of the intermediate union types declines sharply, as
does that of craft and occupational unions. From then on, however,
the share of intermediate types fluctuates around a fairly level trend;
the share of general unions declines and that of occupational and
craft unions (in fact, of occupational unions alone) rises. On closer
inspection, however, the support provided by these data is far from
compelling.

First of all, the unions classified by type in Table 1.3 have themselves undergone significant change. General unions have in practice
become progressively more general or inclusive over time. Their ambition to organise workers of all industries and occupations is closer
to their actual achievement in recent years than in the past. The 45 per
cent of trade union membership accounted for by general unions in
1985 is much more heterogeneous in occupational and industrial
terms than the 57 per cent organised in 1960. It follows that the inclusive unions have been capable of accommodating an increasingly
diverse membership, whereas the prediction of Kerr and his associ-
ates was that occupational identities would become increasingly un-

manageable in unions of this type. A similar trend holds at the other end of the organisational spectrum, at least for craft unions. A major trend among craft unions for many years has been to engage in mergers, where necessary, with contiguous craft unions. As a result, many craft unions are now in reality conglomerate organisations of craft workers and unskilled workers in related job territories. Thus, the rising share held by craft and occupational unions since the 1960s masks the growth of occupational diversity within at least some unions of this type. A final problem concerns the allocation of unions to the typology. Any typology of union type or character inevitably gives rise to difficult cases, and in the typology of Tables 1.3 and 1.4 the difficult cases arise in the occupational unions category. Several unions defined in the breakdowns of Tables 1.3 and 1.4 as occupational unions might arguably be better defined as industrial unions. The Irish Bank Officials' Association is a case in point.

The IBOA organises the great majority of officials in Irish banks, from entry grade up to and including management levels. Thus, it might be regarded as an industrial union of all bankers. However, the IBOA does not attempt to organise manual and craft workers in the industry, and has long adopted an exclusive strategy which has until recently involved remaining outside the ICTU and avoiding alliances with blue-collar unions. So it seems more valid to define the union as an exclusive occupational union. At the same time, the vertical integration of different levels of the same occupation in IBOA, and in other similar unions, means that unions in the occupational category range from small civil service grade associations, representing only workers at the same level in the public service, to much wider ranging occupational unions taking in all grades from the bottom to the top of a particular profession. In other words, the changing distribution of membership shares across inclusive and exclusive unions masks growing internal occupational and industrial diversity across nearly the whole range of union types — a trend inconsistent with liberal theory's predictions.

A second reason for caution in interpreting organisational trends as favouring these predictions is that there seems nothing inexorable about the overall trend towards occupational unions since the 1960s. Of particular relevance in this respect has been the upsurge in recent years of merger activity involving occupational unions. A notable example is the declared intention of three separate unions of teachers and a union of lecturers to consider merger into one industrial union for education; an interim federal organisation of teaching unions has already been formed. Again, significant numbers of civil service grade unions and staff associations are merging into increasingly conglomerate unions in the public sector. These currently comprise such a significant share of the "closed" unions category that the outcome of their merger activities may decisively affect the future overall trend. Finally, the merger in 1990 of the Irish Transport and General Workers' Union and the Federated Workers' Union of Ireland into the self-styled "super union", SIPTU, has resulted in new recruitment and organisation campaigns which could lead to a revival in the membership share of general unions.

TABLE 1.4: PERCENTAGE DISTRIBUTION OF UNION MEMBERSHIP BY ORGANISATIONAL TYPE (EXCLUDING GENERAL UNIONS)*

	(Quasi-) Industrial	Applied Occupations	Occupational	(Ex-) Craft
Blue-collar Unions				
1930	36.0 (6)	9.1 (7)	1.3 (2)	53.2 (50)
1940	28.2 (7)	14.3 (7)	0.9 (4)	56.6 (50)
1950	25.2 (5)	13.6 (7)	0.0	61.2 (44)
1960	22.4 (4)	16.4 (8)	0.0	61.2 (42)
1970	14.9 (4)	20.9 (8)	2.4 (2)	61.8 (26)
1980	9.3 (3)	17.9 (7)	2.6 (1)	70.2 (22)
1985	7.8 (3)	19.2 (7)	2.9 (1)	70.0 (16)
White-collar Unions				
1930	31.8 (6)	22.9 (8)	45.2 (16)	
1940	40.8 (5)	19.4 (11)	39.8 (25)	
1950	33.9 (5)	20.8 (10)	45.2 (34)	
1960	30.5 (5)	21.0 (11)	48.4 (40)	
1970	22.0 (7)	24.3 (13)	53.7 (43)	
1980	13.6 (5)	34.1 (12)	52.1 (38)	
1985	12.2 (5)	34.9 (13)	52.9 (33)	

* Percentages express the shares held by different types of unions of total blue-collar and white-collar union memberships for the years shown (the membership of general unions being excluded from these totals). Rows may not sum to one hundred due to rounding. Membership of a small number of unions of indeterminable status has been excluded. Figures in parentheses show number of unions in each category.

Source: As for Table 1.3.

One last reason for scepticism regarding the long-run sociological significance of the overall organisational trend since the 1960s emerges if we consider white-collar and blue-collar unions separately (omitting general unions from the analysis). This is done in Table 1.4. The table indicates that within the blue-collar group the most salient trend is the decline of quasi-industrial unionism. This has not occurred through organisational disintegration, resulting from the conflicting pressures exerted by a diverse membership, but typically because the unions affected suffered from the long-run decay of their industrial domains. An example is the Irish Shoe and Leather Workers' Union, which transferred to the ITGWU when the Irish leather industry collapsed in the wake of increased international competition. More important is the trend among white-collar unions, where occupational unionism appears to have reached a plateau and the major development is the sharp growth of conglomerate unions of allied occupations. Given that the white-collar workforce is destined for future relative growth, and that recent merger activity appears to reinforce the trend apparent in the table, the prototypical union form may well be the large conglomerate and not Kerr's narrow craft, occupational and professional union. It is also significant in this respect that some major white-collar unions of this type have become so diverse, for example, the Manufacturing, Science and Finance Union, that they are increasingly described as general unions or "white-collar general unions".

Several further features of the trend in union organisation in Ireland bear comment in regard to the question of fragmentation. The first is the long-run decline which has occurred in the number of unions relative to the number of union members. In 1930, in the region of 100 unions and associations organised about 104,000 workers. In 1985, 83 unions and associations organised 500,000 workers. Also relevant is the level of organisational concentration. The share of membership held by the top five unions in 1980 was 56 per cent — the same level of concentration as in 1930, though a drop from the high point of 63 per cent reached in the 1960s. In terms of the predictions of liberal theory, organisational concentration might be expected to have undergone secular decline as an outcome of growth in occupational and grade-based unionism. The "monopoly" of the Irish Congress of Trade Unions as the peak federation of Irish unions is likewise relevant in considering trends in organisational cohesion. ICTU–affiliated unions have organised in the region of 90 per cent of trade union members since the federation was re-established in 1959, following a 1945 split which led to the establishment of two rival federations. Attempts by white-collar unions to establish a separate white-collar federation have had little effect on ICTU's monopoly: the vehicle of white-collar exclusivism, the Irish Conference of Professional and Service Associations, has remained ineffectual.

One secular trend that has gone contrary to any tendency towards fragmentation is the declining share of union membership organised by unions with headquarters in the United Kingdom — "British unions", in the parlance of the Irish trade union world. The British–Irish divide has long been a source of deep conflict in collective bargaining and policy-making within the ICTU. Most British unions are philosophically opposed to centralised, national wage bargaining and particularly to tripartite agreements involving government. The preference of most British unions for "free collective bargaining" contrasts with the more pragmatic approach of Irish unions. The share of British union membership in total membership, and commensurately the influence of British unions on the policies of the Irish labour movement, have declined steadily over time. In 1930 about 30 per cent of Irish trade union members were represented in British unions, compared with 14 per cent in the mid-1980s. The declining membership share of British unions can be accounted for in part by the prolonged influence of nationalism. Nationalist sentiment appears to have both encouraged secession by the Irish branches of British unions and retarded their membership growth (Roche, forthcoming).

What, then, may be emphasised is the degree to which the Irish case deviates from the liberal pluralist prediction of an increasingly sectionalist trade unionism, fragmented by occupational interests, and progressively less capable of conceiving of itself as a "movement" transcending the immediate priorities of its many component groups. Though already fragmented by the circumstances of their early development, Irish unions have had sufficient capacity for concerted action to enter centralised wage agreements in 19 of the 29 "wage rounds" which have occurred since 1946. Four such agreements have formally involved government in tripartite deals. The objectives of the ICTU in centralised tripartite bargaining have included "wage solidarism", tax reform, employment creation and the preservation and extension of social policy. The degree to which these objectives have been attained is a subject of continuing trade union and academic debate. And it cannot be denied that the fragility of cohesion in the trade union movement and the limited authority of the ICTU have been evident in such centralised bargaining (Roche, 1987a; Hardiman, 1988). Yet the evolution of trade union organisation in the course of industrialisation has not rendered it impossible, or progressively more difficult, for unions in Ireland to act in a concerted manner, or to pursue policies which are in significant respects class-oriented. The ideal of trade unions as components of a social movement has not altogether disappeared; it remains a compelling ideal, albeit one that meets with variable support from different types of trade unions and different trade union leaders. Though the alliances of unions involved in centralised bargaining have always been contingent and thus insecure, they have nonetheless pursued social democratic objectives that challenge market outcomes in the common interest of working people. Acting concertedly to influence macro-economic and social policy, unions in Ireland have retained a pivotal influence over the granting or withholding by employees of consent to government policy. Some 60 years after the Irish State first began actively to promote industrialisation, unions still debate the mission of their organisations. Though no longer engaging in militant class insurgency, they are still capable of creating alliances which transcend narrow occupational interests. The future of such alliances is open and not predetermined by an inexorable "logic of industrialism".

That no clear trends towards "exclusive" trade unionism or progressive fragmentation can be identified in the Irish case points to a number of weaknesses in liberal theory's grasp of the effects on union organisation and strategy of industrialisation and economic development. The departure of craft unions from exclusive organisational strategies and the growing prominence of unions of allied occupations can be attributed in part to the effects on union policies of technological and industrial change. Changing technology in many instances blurred established lines of demarcation between crafts and other occupations, making it more difficult for exclusive unions to control job boundaries and thus to restrict these jobs to their members. If the work traditionally done by union members can be allocated to semi-skilled workers, or to the members of other craft or occupational unions, a union may be forced to respond by trying to organise the potential substitute workers. This can then result in the merger of craft unions into a craft conglomerate; in the admission of semiskilled workers; or in the addition of allied non-craft occupations to a core craft membership.

Another force linked with economic development but going counter to fragmentation is the state's policy of encouraging trade union "rationalisation". The impetus behind this policy is the belief that union multiplicity encourages inter-union conflict and compromises economic growth. A series of legislative initiatives by successive Irish governments has addressed this issue. It has been made progressively more difficult for groups of workers to establish new unions. As well as encouraging newly unionising occupational groups to opt for representation in existing unions, this policy has also made it harder for disaffected groups to secede from unions in order to set up more exclusive organisations. State policy favouring large inclusive unions also gave unions like the Irish Transport an advantage in organising the new workforces of incoming multinational companies. The process of change within unions themselves is further inimical to fragmentation and exclusivism. Much of liberal writing on change in trade unions has focused on how processes of "union maturation" transform unions from militant organisations to "sleepy bureaucracies" (Lester, 1958). Other effects of "maturation" should also be recognised. As unions become more concerned to represent members "professionally", introducing to this end an increasing range of services and "selective incentives", the size-threshold for financial viability probably rises. Craft and occupational unions tend to be small, and such unions are particularly vulnerable to financial pressure arising from membership setbacks, inflation and relative improvements in the services and benefits offered by larger unions. Unlike larger organisations, they may be unable to scale-down administrative overheads to weather financial difficulties. Financial vulnerability to merger with predatory inclusive organisations has long been a weakness of exclusive unions, and such vulnerability has probably increased with the general "professionalisation" of union activities.

The overall conclusion must therefore be that the prediction of an inexorable drift towards exclusive unionism lacks validity in the Irish case. Irish trade unions remain capable of operating in concert as a "movement". The impact of industrial and technological development on trade union structure and strategy has been more complex than grasped by liberal theory. The future, with respect both to trade union structure and strategy, is open rather than predetermined.

THE DEVELOPMENT OF PLURALIST INDUSTRIAL RELATIONS PRACTICES

The conduct of industrial relations in Ireland has evolved more or less along "liberal pluralist" lines, but the outcome of liberal pluralist practices has not been as predicted. Little development in industrial relations institutions or practices occurred in the new Irish State until after the Second World War. During the period of intense industrial and social conflict from 1907 to 1920 Irish employers were already retreating from dogmatic opposition to the unionisation of the unskilled, and were pragmatically accommodating to collective bargaining (O'Connor, 1988). Through its membership of the International Labour Organisation, independent Ireland was bound by resolutions concerning the right to freedom of association and the promotion of collective bargaining. The Irish Constitution of 1937 granted citizens the right to "form" associations and unions.

The establishment of the Labour Court in 1946 was a watershed in Irish industrial relations. The Court was established to provide a facility for conciliation or adjudication in industrial disputes. It was philosophically disposed towards encouraging the spread of collective bargaining, and intervened early in disputes over union recognition in a number of industries. While the Labour Court was beginning to foster a pluralist model of "good industrial relations" in the private sector, collective bargaining was also gaining acceptance in the public services. As a result of developments from the late 1940s, civil service unions and associations gained recognition as representative organisations in conciliation and arbitration schemes.[6] As unionisation increased, a system of collective bargaining emerged which was dominated by multi-employer and multi-union bargaining units. Wage bargaining came to be heavily influenced by a series of recurring economy-wide "wage rounds". In establishing an economy-wide "orbit of coercive comparison" for wage rises, the industrial bargaining structure virtually "took wages out of competition" across the entire economy.

Certain elements of pluralist industrial relations were thus in place early in the State's history, while other elements evolved slowly but progressively. From the 1960s state development agencies successfully followed a policy of encouraging foreign companies to adapt to local practices. Many incoming international firms concluded "preproduction" agreements with unions covering recognition and procedural arrangements for the conduct of industrial relations.[7] The "constitutional" approach to the governance of the workplace entered a new phase during the 1960s and 1970s with the professionalisation of personnel and industrial relations management. Up to then, except in large enterprises, industrial relations activity was mostly conducted at industry level. It was at that level that wage bargaining was concentrated and there was little more to industrial relations. From the 1960s, workplace bargaining and associated policies and procedures began to be elaborated, and enterprise-level industrial relations assumed growing importance.

Table 1.5 indicates the increase which occurred in the number of professional personnel managers and departments. In a survey of 141 manufacturing companies in 1984 Murray (1984: 21) found that 74 per cent of companies had a personnel function. Compared with the situation in the mid-1960s, when only 4 per cent of companies had a personnel executive reporting to the company's chief executive, in 1984 the head of personnel was directly accountable to the top manager in 84 per cent of companies with a personnel function; and 24 per cent of personnel directors had a seat on company boards. Further, almost 90 per cent of companies claimed to have a written personnel policy. So-called "comprehensive agreements", covering pay, conditions and procedures, became more common and fixed-term agreements became standard (McCarthy et al., 1975). Management education in personnel and industrial relations also expanded in universities, third-level colleges and professional institutes like the Irish Management Institute and the Institute of Personnel Management. The canons of "good industrial relations" taught in higher education and professional bodies were stridently pluralist in character.

TABLE 1.5: THE GROWTH OF PROFESSIONAL PERSONNEL MANAGEMENT

A. *Estimated national totals of personnel managers in firms with different levels of employment (1964 and 1973)*

	Employing Less than 100	Employing 100-499	Employing over 500	All Firms
1964	21*	16*	53	90
1973	93*	135*	155	383

B. *Estimated number of firms with designated personnel office, 1981–82, in different sectors*

Manufacturing/industrial (including construction)	550
Financial	70
Other services/distribution etc.	150
Total	770

*Estimates are likely to be imprecise because of survey sampling errors. Very small firms (less than 20 employees in 1964 and less than 25 employees in 1975) were excluded from the surveys.

Sources: Data for 1964 and 1973 are derived from results reported in Gorman et al. (1975: 36-9). Data for 1981–2 are derived from Institute of Public Administration (1982).

Studies conducted during the 1970s and 1980s indicated that techniques of "rational" personnel and industrial administration — such as selection, training, employee appraisal, disputes and grievance procedures — were by then extensively used (Gunnigle and Shivanath, 1988; Keating, 1987; Murray, 1984; Wallace, 1981; Gorman et al., 1975). During the 1960s, in contrast, they were seldom used even in large companies (Tomlin, 1966: ch. 15). Productivity bargaining, some of it certainly spurious, also became common during the 1960s and 1970s (McCarthy, 1982; O'Brien, 1981). The growth of professionalisation and rationalisation was encouraged by the main employers' industrial relations body, the Federated Union of Employers (FUE) (later the Federation of Irish Employers, now IBEC). The Federation followed a policy of broadly supporting collective bargaining in companies where some degree of unionisation had occurred. During the 1960s and 1970s, FUE increased its level of penetration of Irish business and developed an extensive set of services for member firms (Committee of Inquiry on Industrial Relations, 1981: ch. 4; O'Brien, 1987).

The evidence that a process of extensive and intensive professionalisation and rationalisation in the management of Irish industrial relations gathered pace during the 1960s and 1970s is thus compelling. The changes which occurred at the level of the firm endorsed the basic principles of liberal pluralism. Collective bargaining remained the cornerstone of professional industrial relations and personnel management. The new techniques and practices were implemented with a view to rationalising collective bargaining, and often to extending its scope. By the end of the 1970s pluralism's "constitutional approach to the governance of work" reigned almost supreme in Irish industrial relations.

The question that then arises is what effect these changes had on industrial relations and on the policies of trade unions. There is no simple answer to this question. But what can be suggested is that a number of trends and developments indicate that the consequences of professionalisation, in all its forms, have been a good deal more complex than is presumed in the liberal pluralist model. The liberal pluralist claim that the "intensity" of industrial conflict peaks early in the course of industrialisation and declines thereafter can be accepted as a reasonable portrayal of the course of such conflict in Ireland. Employers' gradual and pragmatic acceptance of trade unionism, and unions' withdrawal from militant class insurgency, during the period from 1907 to the early 1920s defused the intensity of conflict in Irish industrial relations. But of particular interest here is whether the establishment and development of pluralist and professionalised industrial relations practices led to a long-run decline in industrial conflict. One obviously critical indicator of any such trend is the record of strike activity.

An analysis of the long-run trend of strike activity is presented in Roche (1992: 314–7). The analysis indicates that over the period from 1922 to date, the level of industrial action has fluctuated sharply in a cyclical manner, reflecting the overall state of the economy and degree of buoyancy in the labour market. However, no compelling evidence of a long-term trend could be identified in employees' strike behaviour. There was no clear decline in employees' willingness to go on strike when viewed over a long period of time.

What also clearly emerges is that levels of industrial conflict failed to respond in any significant degree to the professionalisation of industrial relations at workplace level. The rise in strike participation and working days lost during the 1960s and 1970s occurred in spite of the rising incidence of procedures for conflict avoidance and the growing resort to the conciliation and investigation services of the Labour Court. In addition, a diverse repertoire of other sanctions apart from strikes became evident in industrial relations during this period — for example, go-slows, overtime bans, bans on flexible working, refusal to work co-operatively and so on. It is difficult to identify with certainty trends in their occurrence but in many large organisations, like ESB, such sanctions both became more common and were deployed with greater sophistication. Murray's 1984 survey of manufacturing found that the incidence of non-strike forms of industrial action was triple the incidence of strikes (Murray, 1984: 8); and an exploratory study, based on the reportage of such tactics in a specialist industrial relations news periodical during the 1980s, also concluded that there appeared to have been an increase in the level of sophistication with which non-strike sanctions were deployed (Moore, 1988).

The growing formalisation of wage bargaining structures also had economic effects that were unanticipated in liberal theory. Research on wage rounds during the 1960s suggested that the system of wage fixing had become almost entirely unresponsive to market signals and conditions. Prevailing microeconomic and macroeconomic conditions seemed to have little effect on wage determination, in comparison with the "micropolitical" dynamic enjoined by inter-union relations and the determined use of collective organisation (McCarthy et al., 1975). Wage pressure on direct labour costs began to rise from the 1960s, and so too, it appears, did pressure for concessions on a range of fringe benefits and conditions of employment. The scope of collective bargaining also began to widen to encompass allowances of various kinds (Hardiman, 1988: 155–8). To the traditional union policy of claiming wage-round increases and the maintenance of relativities were added an opportunistic seizing of bargaining opportunities wherever they arose and an entrepreneurial flair for creating such opportunities where none had existed before. Orbits of coercive comparison also began to widen as blue-collar groups for the first time pursued parity of pay and conditions with white-collar workers (Roche, 1981). In this context, disillusionment set in among employers with some of the most "progressive" techniques of the period, and with productivity bargaining in particular.

Some of the consequences of pluralist industrial relations practices have been as expected and intended. Pluralist systems of industrial authority have afforded employees greater job protection, reduced their vulnerability to arbitrary or capricious management decisions, and provided them with a means of voicing grievances. Professionalisation along pluralist lines has also given companies greater predictability in respect of wage costs, and greater stability in the intensity with which work is performed. By routinising and even ritualising industrial conflict through procedures, the parties to industrial relations have defused its intensity and volatility. Pluralist practices have also made it possible to build up a body of precedents regarding equity in wage determination. However, other consequences of pluralist professionalisation seem at variance with the expectations of liberal theory. Worker grievances and industrial conflict have proved to be "durable". Attempts to democratise and constrain the exercise of managerial authority have expanded the bargaining agenda of unions and have probably encouraged worker "entrepreneurship". The development of wage-bargaining structures has resulted in the suppression of market signals. In short, while some, though not all, of the anticipated effects of pluralism have been achieved, other effects, scarcely considered by liberal theory, have probably had no less an impact on industrial relations. And these unintended consequences, as well as the unrealised effects of pluralism, point to weaknesses in liberal theory. In this theory, the various forms of joint regulation are viewed primarily as providing a series of channels for "draining away" conflict and worker dissent. This view neglects entirely the complex ways in which institutions can interact with day-to-day industrial relations to heighten awareness of bargaining opportunity and, as it were, "create their own supply" of grievances and demands. The idea that professional management and its institutional supports can contain or reduce worker militancy or "pushfulness" ignores a number of problems. The establishment of procedures for conflict avoidance appears often to result in a tactical use of such procedures during the course of disputes. Far from commanding normative commitment, the various stages and levels associated with procedural agreements are often viewed in an instrumental way. Procedure is frequently exploited tactically as a resource for furthering a dispute; and procedural rules can be ignored by either side, as the occasion demands (see Murray et al., 1984; Wallace and O'Shea, 1987). The adoption by managers of a more professional and strategic approach to containing industrial action may evoke a similar response on the part of unions and their members. This can result in a widening of the repertoire of methods of industrial action. The more sophisticated employees become in responding to management professionalism, the more they may resort to methods that are acknowledged by managers to be very difficult to counter: for example, a tacit refusal to work flexibly, or a withdrawal of goodwill. By establishing committees, tribunals, representatives and channels for processing claims, pluralist forms of industrial relations can foster worker opportunism and — "entrepreneurship". By encouraging orderly and stable union organisation at the level of the enterprise and the workplace, professional managers may strengthen their "adversaries" and their capacity to pursue claims effectively. In elaborating a web of rules in the workplace, pluralist forms of industrial relations may institutionalise job boundaries and demarcations. Career-ladders and rights of access to jobs and promotional opportunities are usually highly regulated by collective agreements, as are wage relativities between different grades. In these ways pluralist practices further compound the bureaucratic organisation of work.

If pluralist practices can in this way "build up codified work rules" which intensify bureaucracy, they may also "erode social norms" which facilitate organisational integration and the control of work by managers. It is now widely recognised that productivity bargaining serves often to heighten bargaining awareness and to encourage an instrumental attitude to work. By focusing attention on the wage effort bargain, productivity bargaining may encourage employees, in effect, to "ration" work effort and sell it at the margin. In the same way, where a strong predisposition develops among employees to trade work effort marginally, aspects of effort which may in the past have been offered "free" — conceded, that is, as "non-contractual elements of contract" — for example, enthusiasm, co-operation, flexibility, a willingness to adjust to change etc., are subsumed to the logic of exchange (Roche, 1987b). The result may be a further need for rules and standards to "substitute for" the social norms eroded through the routine conduct of collective bargaining.

The evolution of Irish industrial relations since about 1960 illustrates many of the lacunae and unintended effects of pluralism. When faced with an increasingly confident and strongly organised workforce, companies resorted to a model of "good industrial relations" which built upon the foundations of long-established traditions and practices. This model seems not to have reduced worker pressure on wages, contained industrial conflict or increased the leeway available to companies to organise work and direct work effort without provoking strong and well-organised employee resistance. What emerges in the Irish case, therefore, is hardly an instance of industrial relations conflict becoming little more than a "frictional" force in an otherwise smooth progression towards advanced industrial society. During the 1960s and 1970s, on the contrary, industrial relations conflict and union wage pressure appeared to government and employers to be intractable to existing industrial relations practices and prescriptions. The wage-price spiral came to be seen by the same parties as a chronic threat to competitiveness, and the trend in industrial conflict as a serious discouragement to foreign investment — the cornerstone of the State's strategy of industrialisation and economic development. In spite of the growing sophistication of industrial relations, the model of "good industrial relations" enshrining pluralist practices was brought increasingly into question and a growing sense of industrial relations "crisis" arose.

The major exponents of the "crisis" argument were employers and governments, but trade unions too sometimes questioned the viability of current practices (McCarthy, 1973). The immediate result of growing disillusionment in the 1970s was a progressive politicisation of wage bargaining — a trend at variance with one of the central predictions of liberal theory. On the side of employers, one of the longer-term consequences has been a new popularity of versions of "monistic" or "unitarist" industrial relations in which the role of trade unions is restricted. This is one of the most salient developments in Irish industrial relations during the late 1980s and 1990s. In common with their counterparts in other countries, Irish employers have shown growing interest in "human resource management" techniques, and other departures from established pluralist practice can also be identified. Thus, in many sectors of Irish business, employers have sought to promote "flexibility" by dismantling standardised conditions of employment and job security; and flexibility has also been pursued by hiving off parts of production, maintenance or amenities to subcontractors, by making greater use of part-time workers, and by increased resort to "atypical" forms of employment contract. Moreover, in some companies and sectors, the challenge to pluralism has been less sophisticated, involving growing resistance to union recognition, or the reassertion of traditional doctrines of managerial prerogative (Roche, 1992; McGovern, 1988).

In sum, the creation of a system of industrial citizenship based on the "joint regulation" of working conditions has proven not to be a panacea for the economic and social conflicts released by industrialisation and economic development. In the 1990s the very survival of major features of pluralist industrial relations at company and workplace levels is coming into question. "Unitarism" in various guises is back on the employers' agenda. The Federation of Irish Employers appears no longer to be disposed to encourage new companies to concede union recognition rather than explore other industrial relations strategies. Unions have also complained that the IDA has tacitly retreated from its traditional policy of encouraging incoming multinationals to adapt to local industrial relations practices (McGovern, 1988: 89–90). Unions are obviously very aware of recent revisions in the ideological and strategic positions of employers and the state. Thus far, they have not regarded the reappearance of unitarism as the most serious threat with which they are faced. But there is growing concern and debate within the union movement about the likely future impact on unionisation of the waning support for industrial relations on the pluralist model.

THE POLITICS OF INDUSTRIAL RELATIONS IN IRELAND

Liberal theory predicted the progressive depoliticisation of industrial relations. At face value, party politics in Ireland seems consistent with the liberal prediction. The political ideologies of the major parties with respect to industrial relations have not been distinctive, and thus the governments they have formed have not followed markedly different industrial relations strategies. Both Fianna Fáil and Fine Gael have sought and, to a greater or lesser degree, managed to maintain working-class support for their policies. The main parties' "catch-all" approach to political mobilisation has meant that conflicts arising from the sphere of industrial relations have not been politicised in a visibly class-partisan way. In contrast with the United Kingdom, industrial relations has never figured as a key issue in Irish elections. The policy of the Labour Party on industrial relations issues has traditionally been distinct from those of the two major parties in placing emphasis on the extension of industrial and economic democracy. But Labour policy on these issues has had little direct effect on Irish industrial relations, owing to the electoral weakness of the Labour Party until 1992 and, consequently, the Party's minority status in inter-party and coalition governments.

While the similarity of approach of the major parties is the most salient feature of party politics in industrial relations, important differences of emphasis and "political style" can nonetheless be identified. Fianna Fáil governments have favoured active involvement in industrial relations and collective bargaining rather less equivocally than inter-party governments or Fine Gael–Labour coalitions. The political ideology of Fianna Fáil, which views the party as a "national" party or party of "national consensus", places few ideological constraints on intervention in industrial relations, if this is seen to be warranted by circumstances. Indeed, the promotion of "social partnership" between the state and the peak federations of unions and employers has come to be regarded as the direct expression in economic policy of the party's emphasis on fostering "national consensus". A broadly similar posture is evident in the stance adopted on unions and collective bargaining by the Fianna Fáil-Labour Coalition which took office in 1993. The surge in Labour Party electoral support in the 1992 General Election came from across the social-class spectrum. Thus in the early 1990s Labour, in effect, became more of a "catch-all" political party. This could conceivably temper aspects of Labour's traditional industrial relations policy and draw the Party closer to Fianna Fáil policy.

Fine Gael's ideology is permeated by political and economic liberalism of a character which reflects the party's original support-base among larger farmers, the propertied middle class and the professions. From the 1950s the party moved towards a more social-democratic politics, which found its clearest expression under Garret FitzGerald's leadership, and this facilitated the adoption of a more *dirigiste* approach to economic policy making. The liberalism still inherent in Fine Gael's political ideology, even under FitzGerald, resulted in a higher level of equivocation on union involvement in public policy-making than was characteristic of Fianna Fáil. Nonetheless, Fine Gael's liberalism stopped short of distaste for active state involvement in pay bargaining, and well short of that expressed in the "free market" policies of the Thatcher Conservative governments in the United Kingdom. In any case, the party's stance was tempered in government during the 1970s and early 1980s through its being in coalition with Labour.

What bears emphasis is that the absence of clear class-based party politics in Irish industrial relations cannot be understood in terms of forces unleashed by industrialisation. The character of Irish party politics with respect to industrial relations must be traced, rather, to the circumstances in which the Irish party system emerged. In this sense, much of the politics of industrial relations in Ireland has to be understood in terms of the "pre-history" of modern industrial relations, considered earlier in the chapter. Nor should the broadly similar positions of the main political parties on industrial relations be viewed as unchangeable. In the mid-1980s a new party, the Progressive Democrats (PDs), emerged on the liberal right of Irish politics. In spite of its origins as a breakaway from Fianna Fáil, the PD Party espoused a neoliberal ideology which declared itself hostile to restrictive and monopolistic institutions and practices. The party polled impressively in the 1987 election. For a time, the PDs seemed set to coalesce in future elections, and possibly governments, with Fine Gael — itself experiencing realignment following the retirement of Party leader Garret FitzGerald. This raised the prospect of a more ideologically divided party-politics of industrial relations. It was a prospect that did not go unnoticed by trade union leaders when they entered talks on a national wage agreement with a Fianna Fáil government after the 1987 election. The fortunes of the PDs declined sharply in the general election of 1989, and the organisation opted to participate in coalition with Fianna Fáil. However, the realignment in party politics threatened by the appearance of the PDs indicates that political circumstances are still capable of recasting the politics of industrial relations in Ireland in a more class-partisan mould.

If considerable electoral and ideological scope has long existed for the adoption by government of an active, interventionist approach to industrial relations, up to the 1960s only the exceptional circumstances of wartime were seen to warrant a departure from a non-interventionist approach. For much of the State's history, a preference prevailed for keeping politics out of industrial relations (Roche, 1987a). However, in the 1960s, in response to growing trade union organisation and power, a rising level of industrial conflict and forceful trade union wage pressure, Irish governments began to adopt a more interventionist stance. In the following decade, pay determination became increasingly politicised, as unfettered collective bargaining fell from favour and governments sought to promote concertation with union and employer federations.

The limited success of national bargaining during the 1970s has been examined in a number of studies of the period (O'Brien, 1981; Roche, 1987a; Hardiman, 1988; and Roche, this volume). In attempting to explain the weakness of centralised wage bargaining in Ireland, Hardiman concludes (1988: 151) that the involvement of unions in concertation during the 1970s tended to "take a pluralist, pressure-group form rather than one characteristic of (neo-corporatist) political exchange". While the limited success of concertation during the 1970s cannot be denied, what bears emphasis in the present context is the degree to which pluralist interest representation was modified at the political level during the decade, as successive governments sought to avoid the damaging effects attributed to "free", or politically unfettered, collective bargaining. The politicisation of industrial relations between 1970 and 1981, though heavily compromised by practices and structures built up for long before, represented a significant departure from the politics of industrial relations as projected by liberal theories of industrialism.

In liberal theory, industrial relations are supposed to become "insulated from the political process". In neo-corporatist concertation, this obviously is not the case; indeed, the objectives of the "social partners", and of unions in particular, come to be shaped in important respects by the opportunities opened up by access to public policy. Specifically, wage pressure in the labour market is traded off, in the main, against economic and social policy measures which benefit employees in general, irrespective of their occupational situation or status. In consequence, politicised wage bargaining tends to stand opposed to pressures towards sectionalism in the trade union movement (see Goldthorpe, 1984: 326; Regini, 1984: 124–5).

Nor has the experiment in tripartism of the 1970s and early 1980s proven to be an aberration — in the face of international economic upheaval — from a secular trend towards depoliticisation. Between 1987 and 1990, unions, employer associations and government again entered a central, tripartite agreement, the Programme for National Recovery (PNR), after five years of decentralised bargaining. Considerable controversy remains regarding the achievements of the PNR — as distinct from the benign effects on the Irish economy of the international economic recovery with which the agreement coincided in the late 1980s. The parties to the PNR were critical of its limited achievements; the unions, in particular, felt that little progress had been made in tackling unemployment. Yet in a manner unprecedented in the history of tripartism in Ireland, all parties to the agreement pointed to areas or issues with respect to which they considered themselves "winners". The success attributed to the PNR was a major factor in the background to the negotiation of the Programme for Economic and Social Progress (PESP) in early 1991 and the negotiation of the Programme for Competitiveness and Work (PCW) in 1994. A second cycle of politicised wage bargaining has thus lasted for seven years and is scheduled to last for ten. This raises the question of the factors responsible for the emergence of a more stable tripartism, and the related question of whether secular trends in Irish industrial relations may lead to the *institutionalisation* of political exchange as a more or less permanent feature.

The economic and political conjuncture in which the PNR was negotiated and implemented was very different from that obtaining during the informal and formal experiments in tripartism of the 1970s and early 1980s. In 1987 the Irish economy was almost universally seen to have reached its nadir. The public finances had run virtually out of control; the level of unemployment was unprecedented in the State's history; emigration had risen sharply, and union membership had declined dramatically over the preceding seven years. In such a context, market forces began to impinge decisively on free-for-all bargaining, progressively widening pay differentials hitherto fixed by institutional forces. More generally, as discussed earlier, the pluralist model of industrial relations was coming under threat from employers. In addition, the realignment of Irish politics attending the emergence of the PDs held out the prospect of growing support for neoliberal policies and politics. Faced by these circumstances, Irish trade unions thought it advisable to take stock and opt for politics — as much as anything else to find shelter from the storm. In the event, a slow economic recovery set in during the life of the PNR and the party political base for neoliberal policies seemed to disappear in the general election of 1989.

Against the background of such extreme contingencies, "political exchange" proved to be more stable than before and unions and employer associations more inclined, or better able, to "deliver" the consent of their respective constituencies. The terms of the PESP provided for slightly higher pay rises than those of the PNR, but allowed more scope for local bargaining in the private sector and relaxed restrictions on "special" relativity claims in the public services. The viability of PESP commitments by the government on pay and social policies was seen to depend, at the time of negotiation, on optimistic assumptions regarding economic growth. By mid-1991 these assumptions were confounded by the worsening international economic situation. The Minister for Finance responded in the Autumn of 1991 by calling for the renegotiation of the PESP. A torrent of protest came from the unions, especially those in the public services. Yet the PESP survived and was replaced by the PCW (see Roche, this volume).

It may be that the economic and political contingencies of the late 1980s and early 1990s are of critical importance in underpinning tripartite wage bargaining. They may also appear, with hindsight, to have been highly unusual. Specifically, the PNR and the two succeeding centralised agreements may come to be viewed as agreements negotiated, as it were, "out of the last ditch" — providing an Irish parallel to the successful and, never again to be repeated, British incomes policy of the late 1940s and early 1950s.

What, also bears consideration in the context of the theory of liberal pluralism, however, is the possibility — one cannot, it has to be said, speak of the probability — of an alternative scenario. The pronouncements of a number of senior trade union officials in recent years regarding future strategies give rise to the possibility that the ICTU may attempt to institutionalise "political exchange" in the context of a ten-year programme of trade union policies. These policies include collective goods and services of a distinctly class-related character — employment, social policies, union rights etc. (see ICTU, 1990). Such an approach could indicate the operation of a "learning curve" on the part of union leaders concerning the constraints and opportunities of centralised, tripartite bargaining. It might also point to deepening pessimism regarding the likely future achievements and consequences of free-for-all bargaining, given the changes in employer strategies now in train. In short, influential sections of the Irish trade union movement have perhaps made a strategic decision to "opt for politics" in a potentially more far-reaching way than in the recent past. Such a strategy will, of course, have to be contingent on the results of tripartism. The alternative now faced by unions is to revert to decentralised bargaining in a changing system of industrial relations, and attempt to engage in "pressure-group" politics to counter any trends not tractable to collective bargaining alone.

More than sixty years on from the beginnings of industrialisation in the independent Irish State, the choice between politicised industrial relations and the "autonomous" industrial relations envisaged by liberal theory remains open to trade unions, employers and the State. It is a choice of major significance for the political economy of Irish society. It has not been precluded — nor will its outcome be determined — by social forces associated with industrialisation or economic development. The electoral viability of an interventionist stance on industrial relations derives from the catch-all nature of

Irish party politics. In the Irish case, politicised industrial relations and catch-all party politics "coexist", albeit in an unstable amalgam and in a manner which limits the effectiveness of tripartite concertation (see Hardiman, 1988). Politics and national governance currently turn in important respects on the government's success in managing tripartism. The future is open. Political realignment to the liberal right could undermine tripartism, as, in the short term, could economic circumstances. Alternatively, underlying trends in industrial relations could lead to the institutionalisation and stabilisation of political exchange.

CONCLUSION

This chapter has presented a review of the development of Irish industrial relations in the context of the liberal theory of industrialism. It has been found necessary to question the overall validity in the Irish case of the successive claims made by the theory. The peaking of worker militancy in the period 1907–20 was shown to have no meaningful link with the pace or character of industrialisation. Its roots were to be found, rather, in the contagion of British ideas and institutions, cyclical economic developments and the abnormal economic, political and social conditions of the First World War and Anglo-Irish War. While attempts to promote or engage in concerted action by Irish unions have always been compromised by union multiplicity and organisational fragmentation, no clearly defined trend towards "exclusive unionism" can be identified. Some of the forces unleashed by industrialism were shown to "constrain" union fragmentation and to encourage more "inclusive" forms of organisation, increasing the capacity for concerted action by trade unions. The evolution of practices and management techniques consistent with a pluralist understanding of "good industrial relations" failed to bring about a secular decline in strike activity. Thus far, at least, industrial conflict has proven to be "durable". The growing conviction of Irish governments that collective bargaining needed to be harnessed more directly to business performance and macroeconomic management led to the growing politicisation of industrial relations during the 1960s and 1970s. In the recession of the 1980s employers also showed renewed interest in essentially unitary models of industrial relations, and these are now subject to significant experimentation. The new vogue in unitarism and the reassertion of managerial prerogative at company level have been paralleled by the re-emergence since 1987 of politicised industrial relations at national level. Both trends run directly counter to the predictions of liberal theory. Options as between different sets of social and political arrangements for the conduct of industrial relations are still available to unions, employers and governments. These options, furthermore, have strikingly different economic and social consequences. Ultimately, this is the most telling evidence against the supposed logic of industrialism on which the liberal theory relies.

Footnotes

* This chapter is an abridged and slightly amended version of "The Liberal Theory of Industrialism and the Development of Industrial Relations in Ireland" in J. H. Goldthorpe and C. T. Whelan (eds.), *The Development of Industrial Society in Ireland*, Oxford: Oxford University Press for the British Academy (1992).

[1] For a somewhat different version of this approach see Gallie's discussion and critique of the "Mann-Giddens" thesis (Gallie, 1983: ch. 11).

[2] Clearly the liberal representation of the maturation of labour movements over the course of industrialisation carries strong undertones of the "end of labour history". Regulated or institutionalised industrial relations is presented as the really momentous social invention of industrialism. "Constitutional" decision-making in industry — involving professional managers and workers organised independently in unions — halts the political and social momentum of industrial conflict. The study no less than the practice of industrial relations becomes properly concerned with the complex "web of rules" through which the pragmatic day-to-day compromises between managers and workers receive expression (Dunlop, 1958).

[3] The most detailed accounts of union militancy during the period can be found in O'Connor (1988) and Lysaght (1982).

[4] The only specification of a tillage acreage variable that produced statistically notable results was where tillage acreage was expressed as a ratio of numbers working in agriculture (including farmers and "relatives assisting"). Such a variable might be regarded as a very rough indicator of county-level differences in the balance of demand and supply of agricultural labour. When this variable was entered it produced a statistically significant coefficient. The coefficient was negatively signed, however, contrary to theoretical expectation, and would suggest that where the balance of demand over supply favoured workers, there was a lower propensity to organise. The result is thus probably a statistical accident and can be ignored.

[5] In interpreting relative shares for that year it has to be borne in mind that 1985 was the trough of a deep labour market recession. This would have affected the membership share of the more "exposed" general unions more than other union types, and would, thus, have led to a short-run cyclical drag on the relative performance of open unions.

[6] They were not, however, to enjoy the same strike immunities as private sector workers until the 1980s.

[7] A review of industrial relations in multinationals in the early 1980s concluded that they were not materially different from home-based companies. (Kelly and Brannick, 1985).

References

Attley, W. (1986): *Address at the National College of Industrial Relations*, Dublin: National College of Industrial Relations.

Booth, C. (1902): "The Economic Distribution of Population in Ireland", in W.P. Coyne (ed.), *Ireland: Industrial and Agricultural*, Dublin: Brown and Nolan.

Census of Population: *General Reports for Ireland, (1891); (1909); (1911)*, London: HMSO.

Clarkson, J.D. (1926): *Labour and Nationalism in Ireland*, New York: AMS Press.

Committee of Inquiry on Industrial Relations (1981): *Report of the Committee of Inquiry on Industrial Relations*, Dublin: Government Publications.

Commons, J. (1932): "Labour Movements", *Encyclopaedia of the Social Sciences*, Vol. 8, New York: Macmillan.

Coyne, W.P. (ed.) (1902): *Ireland: Industrial and Agricultural*, Dublin: Brown and Nolan.

Cronin, J. (1979): *Industrial Conflict in Modern Britain*, London: Croom Helm.

Cullen, L.M. (1972): *An Economic History of Ireland Since 1660*, London: Batsford.

Dahrendorf, R. (1959): *Class and Class Conflict in Industrial Society*, London: Routledge and Kegan Paul.

Dunlop, J.T. (1958): *Industrial Relations Systems*, New York: Holt.

Fitzpatrick, J.D. (1977): *Politics and Irish Life*, Dublin: Gill and Macmillan.

Fitzpatrick, J.D. (1980): "Strikes in Ireland, 1914–1921", Saothar, 6: 26–39.

Flanders, A. (1970): *Management and Unions: The Theory and Reform of Industrial Relations*, London: Faber.

Flora, P., Krause, F. and Pfenning, W. (1983): *State, Economy and Society in Western Europe, 1815–1975: A Data Handbook*, Vol. 1, London: Campus Macmillan.

Foster, R. (1988): *Modern Ireland 1600–1972*, London: Penguin.

Fox, A. (1966): "Industrial Sociology and Industrial Relations", Royal Commission on Trade Unions and Employer Associations, 3, London: HMSO.

Gallie, D. (1983): *Social Inequality and Class Radicalism in France and Britain*, Cambridge: Cambridge University Press.

Gershuny, J.H. (1983): *Social Innovation and the Division of Labour*, Oxford: Oxford University Press.

Goldthorpe, J.H. (1984): "The End of Convergence: Corporatist and Dualist Tendencies in Modern Western Societies" in J.H. Goldthorpe (ed.), *Order and Conflict in Contemporary Capitalism*, Oxford: Clarendon Press.

Gorman, L., Handy, C., Moynihan, T. and Murphy, T. (1974): *Managers in Ireland*, Dublin: Irish Management Institute.

Gorman, L., Hynes, G., McConnell, J. and Moynihan, T. (1975): *Irish Industry: How It's Managed*, Dublin: Irish Management Institute.

Greaves, D. (1982): *The Irish Transport and General Workers Union: The Formative Years*, Dublin: Gill and Macmillan.

Gunnigle, P. and Shivanath, G. (1988): "Role and Status of Personnel Practitioners — A Positive Picture", *Irish Journal of Business and Administrative Research*, 9: 1–9.

Hardiman, N. (1988): *Pay, Politics and Economic Performance in Ireland 1970–87*, Oxford: Clarendon Press.

Institute of Public Administration (1982): *Personnel and Industrial Relations Directory*, Dublin: Institute of Public Administration.

Irish Trade Union Congress (and Labour Party): *Annual Reports*, various years, Dublin: ICTU.

Irish Trade Union Congress (1990): *Ireland 1990–2000: A Decade of Development, Reform and Growth*, Dublin: ICTU.

Kahn-Freund, O. (1972): *Labour and the Law*, London: Stevens.

Keating, M. (1987): "Personnel Management in Ireland", in T. Murphy (ed.).

Kelly, A. and Brannick, T. (1985): "Industrial Relations Practices in Multi-National Companies in Ireland", *Journal of Irish Business and Administrative Research*, 7: 98–111.

Kendall, W. (1975): *The Labour Movement in Europe*, London: Allen Lane.

Kennedy, K., Giblin, T. and McHugh, D. (1988): *The Economic Development of Ireland in the Twentieth Century*, London: Routledge and Kegan Paul.

Kenny, B. (1985): *The Spatial Dimensions of Trade Union Organisation in Ireland: A Case Study*, (unpublished) MA thesis, St. Patrick's College, Maynooth.

Keogh, D. (1982): *The Rise of the Irish Working Class*, Belfast: Appletree Press.

Kerr, C. (1955): "Industrial Relations and the Liberal Pluralist" in *Labour and Management in Industrial Society*, New York: Doubleday, 1964.

Kerr, C., Dunlop, J., Harbison, F., and Mayers, C. (1960/1973): *Industrialism and Industrial Man: The Problems of Labour and The Management of Economic Growth*, London: Penguin Edition.

Korpi, W. (1978): *The Working Class in Welfare Capitalism*, London: Routledge and Kegan Paul.

Laffan, M. (1985): ""Labour Must Wait": Ireland's Conservative Revolution" in P.J. Corish (ed.), *Radicals, Rebels and Establishments*, Belfast: Appletree Press.

Lester, M. (1958): *As Unions Mature*, Princeton, New Jersey: Princeton University Press.

Lipset, S.M. (1969): *Revolution and Counter-Revolution*, London: Heinemann.

Lorwin, V. (1954): *The French Labour Movement*, Boston, Mass.: Harvard University Press.

Lysaght-O'Connor, D.R. (1982): *Class Struggle in the Irish War of Independence and Civil War*, (unpublished) MA thesis, University College Dublin.

McCarthy, C. (1973): *The Decade of Upheaval: Irish Trade Unions in the Nineteen Sixties*, Dublin: Institute of Public Administration.

McCarthy, C. (1982): "Productivity Agreements: The Problem of the Spurious", *Journal of Irish Business and Administrative Research*, 4: 99–107.

McGovern, P. (1988): *Recent Developments in Antiunionism in Ireland: An Exploratory Study*, (unpublished) M.B.S. dissertation, University College Dublin.

Mitchell, A. (1974): *Labour in Irish Politics*, Dublin: Irish University Press.

Moore, M. (1988): *A Study of Alternative Industrial Action in the Eighties*, (unpublished) M.B.S. dissertation, University College Dublin.

Murphy, T. (ed.) (1987/1989): *Industrial Relations in Ireland: Contemporary Issues and Developments*, Dublin: Department of Industrial Relations, University College Dublin.

Murray, S. (1984): *Survey of Employee Industrial Relations in Irish Private-Sector Manufacturing Industries*, Dublin: Industrial Development Authority.

O'Brien, J.F. (1981): *A Study of National Wage Agreements in Ireland*, Dublin: Economic and Social Research Institute.

O'Brien, J.F. (1987/1989): "Pay Determination in Ireland: Retrospect and Prospects" in T. Murphy (ed.).

O'Connor, E. (1980): "Agrarian Unrest and the Labour Movement in County Waterford 1917–1923", *Soathar*, 6: 40–58.

O'Connor, E. (1988): *Syndicalism in Ireland: 1917–1923*, Cork: Cork University Press.

Regini, M. (1984): "The Conditions for Political Exchange: How Concertation Emerged and Collapsed in Italy and Great Britain", in J.H. Goldthorpe (ed.).

Riordan, E.J. (1920): *Modern Irish Trade and Industry*, London: Methuen.

Roche, W.K. (1981): "Convention and Change in Irish Industrial Relations: Comparisons and Differentials", in W.K. Roche. and F. Quinn, *Trends in Irish Industrial Relations*, Dublin: National College of Industrial Relations.

Roche, W.K. (1987a): "State Strategies and the Politics of Industrial Relations in Ireland since 1945", in T. Murphy (ed.).

Roche, W.K. (1987b): *Social Integration and Strategic Power: The Development of Militancy Among Electricity Generating Station*

Workers in the Republic of Ireland, 1950–1982, (unpublished) D.Phil. thesis, University of Oxford.

Roche, W.K. (forthcoming): "Organisational Dynamics and the Business Cycle: Aspects of the Growth and Performance of British Trade Unions in the Republic of Ireland", *British Journal of Industrial Relations*.

Roche, W.K. (1992): "The Liberal Theory of Industrialism and the Development of Industrial Relations in Ireland", in J.H. Goldthorpe and C.T. Whelan (eds.), *The Development of Industrial Society in Ireland*, Oxford: Oxford University Press for the British Academy.

Roche, W.K. (1992): "Modelling Trade Union Growth and Decline in the Republic of Ireland", *Irish Journal of Business and Administrative Research*, 13: 86–102.

Roche, W.K. and Larragy, J. (1987/1989): "The Trend of Unionisation in the Irish Republic", in T. Murphy (ed.).

Roche, W.K. and Larragy, J. (1990): "Cyclical and Institutional Determinants of Annual Trade Union Growth in the Republic of Ireland: Evidence from the DUES Data Series", *European Sociological Review*, 6: 49–72.

Ross, A.M. and Hartmen, P.T. (1960): *Changing Patterns of Industrial Conflict*, New York: Wiley & Sons.

Rumpf, E. and Hepburn, A.C. (1977): *Nationalism and Socialism in Twentieth- century Ireland*, Liverpool: Liverpool University Press.

Ryan, W.P. (1991): *The Irish Labour Movement from the Twenties to Our Own Day*, Dublin: Talbot Press.

Slichter, S.H., Healy, J.J. and Livermash, E.R. (1960): *The Impact of Collective Bargaining on Management*, Washington, DC: Brookings Institution.

Strauss, G. (1951): *Irish Nationalism and British Democracy*, London: Batsford.

Sturmthal, A. (1951): "Comments on Selig Perlman", *Industrial and Labour Relations Review*, 14: 483–96.

Tomlin, B. (1966): *The Management of Irish Industry*, Dublin: Irish Management Institute.

Wallace, J. (1981): *Industrial Relations in Limerick City and Environs*, Limerick: National Institute for Higher Education.

Wallace, J. and O'Shea, F. (1987): A Study of Unofficial Strikes in Ireland: Final Report, Dublin: Stationery Office.

CHAPTER 2

THE TREND OF UNIONISATION

William K. Roche

The 1980s proved to be a particularly difficult decade for trade unions
in Ireland. Between 1980 and 1987 Irish unions lost some 70,000
members, declining from 55 per cent to 44 per cent of the civilian
employee workforce and from 62 per cent to 57 per cent of total employees at work. This represents the most serious, sustained loss of
membership since the recession of the 1920s. Fully comparable data
are not yet available for the period since 1987. Judging from membership data for unions affiliated to the Irish Congress of Trade Unions,
however, it appears that the rate of decline decreased after 1987; and
there may even have been a very modest net rise in membership
during the early 1990s. Still, by 1987 the membership gains achieved
by Irish unions since the early 1970s had been wiped out.

This chapter explores the factors which have influenced the trend
of unionisation in Ireland over a period of 60 years. The chapter begins with a theoretical analysis of the forces which influence whether
people choose to join and remain members of trade unions. It then
presents a detailed examination of the manner in which these forces
have affected the growth and decline of unionisation in Ireland during a number of phases over the period from 1930 to 1990.

THE GENERAL THEORY OF TRADE UNION GROWTH AND DECLINE

The trend of unionisation is conventionally studied in either of two
ways: by explaining the trend in the annual percentage rate of change
in total trade union membership, or by explaining the trend in annual
levels of union membership as a percentage of potential trade union
membership. The latter ratio is known as "trade union density" and
can be expressed in different ways depending on how "potential trade
union membership" is defined.

Irrespective of the precise manner in which the trend of unionisation is defined in concrete terms, essentially the same explanatory questions are posed: how can we account for people's decision to join or not to join unions? And how can we account for the decision of people who are already unionised to remain union members or to leave their unions? Changes in overall trade union membership or density levels represent the net result of both sets of decisions.

Three distinct sets of factors influence the decisions employees make concerning whether to join a trade union or to remain a member, if they have already joined. They can be described as *cyclical*, *institutional* and *structural* factors. Each set of factors will be examined in turn.

Cyclical Influences

Cyclical influences emanate from the business cycle and affect both the inclination and opportunity of people to join trade unions. For example, it is expected, other things being equal, that the greater the rate of increase in wage levels, the greater the inclination of people to join trade unions, or to remain trade union members. This is attributed to the operation of a "credit effect": the sharper the rate of increase in wage levels, the more unions tend — correctly, or otherwise — to be "credited" with the capacity to deliver wage rises in collective bargaining.

In a similar way, the inclination of people to join, or remain within, trade unions is expected to be positively associated, other things being equal, with the rate of inflation. Inflation may influence unionisation through a so-called "threat effect": the higher the rate of inflation, the more likely it becomes that people will turn to trade unions for protection from a threatened squeeze on their living standards. Over long periods of time in Europe and other developed economies, inflation has tended to reflect excess demand and business buoyancy. If this is the case, unionisation should also increase with the rate of inflation because of the positive general impact of business prosperity on people's willingness to join unions, on the ease with which unions gain recognition, and on the perceived strength and effectiveness of unions. (Obviously, wage and price trends can interact in various ways to influence unionisation; see Bain and Elsheikh, 1976: 62–5). As will be discussed below, contrary to expectations, inflation appears *not* to have directly encouraged unionisation in Ireland. The reasons for this will be traced to the general condition of the Irish labour market during periods of high inflation, as well as to the features of the Irish system of wage bargaining.

The degree of "tightness", or conversely "slackness", in the labour market is another cyclical variable that affects unionisation. The tighter the labour market becomes — whether measured in terms of the rate of unemployment or changes in the level of employment — the greater, on balance, the probability that unions will gain members. A tight labour market reduces the risk of retaliation by employers in the event of employees opting to unionise, and thus reduces the cost of unionisation to employees. Labour market buoyancy might also enhance the bargaining confidence and power of unions, and hence their attractiveness to members and potential members. The degree of labour market tightness also affects the opportunity to unionise in a rather obvious way. With more employees in the workforce, unions find themselves with an increased pool of potential members. When people lose their jobs in a slackening labour market they may lose their incentive, or even their right, to remain trade union members.

Other similar cyclical influences may also affect aggregate trade union membership, for example, the rate of change in labour productivity, or the rate of change in money or real profit levels, but these are likely, at best, to be of secondary importance relative to the effects of more immediate labour market forces (see Roche and Larragy, 1990).

Institutional Influences
Institutional influences arise from the manner in which the institutions regulating the labour market and industrial relations are structured. Of primary importance here are such things as employment and industrial relations legislation, state policies and employer strategies. Laws may be passed which either help or hinder the efforts of trade unions to recruit, organise and represent members. An example of the former is the 1946 Industrial Relations Act which established the Irish Labour Court, and of the latter is the series of revisions to trade union and industrial relations laws introduced during the Thatcher era in the United Kingdom (see Roche and Larragy, 1990; Freeman and Pelletier, 1990). A less direct influence is the general stance adopted by governments towards trade unions. If governments view unions as an inevitable, or even desirable, feature of economic and business life, they may pursue policies which support unionisation. For example, the broadly positive approach to unions adopted by successive Irish governments from about the late 1940s resulted in very tangible benefits. The ease with which unions could organise in the public sector is one such benefit; the policy of state

agencies such as the IDA of encouraging multinationals to recognise trade unions is another.

In like manner, the ideologies and strategies of employers may exert an important influence on unionisation. Such strategies may influence employer reactions to the short-run changes in labour market conditions, discussed above. But employer strategies are not shaped solely, or, even in the main, by short-term considerations, but by longer-term ideologies, fashions and projections regarding the "best" way to manage employees. Views on the advisability of accepting and supporting a union presence in the company represents a critical variable in employer strategies. Where "doing business with unions" is believed by employers to be the best means — or the only viable means — of managing employees, unions face an easier task in gaining recognition and membership than where they face outright hostility, or more subtle opposition. In contrast with cyclical influences, which may lead to short-run fluctuations in trade union membership, institutional influences more usually shift the rate of growth over longer periods. The scale of such shifts and whether their effect is positive or negative depends of course on the precise character of the influences in question.

Two further institutional influences should also be noted. The political composition of governments may influence trade union growth. Governments of left-wing and social democratic political parties might be expected to adopt a more benign approach to trade unions and their activities than governments of a right-wing or liberal political stripe. The same logic might hold in the case of the political composition of coalition governments. Coalitions in which left-wing, labour or social democratic parties participate are more likely to pursue policies supportive of trade union growth than coalitions in which they are excluded, or play a very marginal role. Where party politics does not divide at all clearly in terms of a left-right split, and where industrial relations issues are not emphatically "politicised", the political complexion of governments may have no influence on the trend of unionisation. Ireland emerges as such a case, as will be discussed below.

Finally, the level at which collective bargaining, especially wage bargaining, is conducted might affect unionisation. It could be argued that the greater the degree to which bargaining is conducted at the level of individual companies or workplaces, the greater the likelihood that unions will routinely bring pressure to bear on employees to join the union, or, if already in membership, not to drop out through apathy or a belief that it is possible to "free ride" on other people's support and contributions. Again the structure and practice of wage bargaining in Ireland turns out to have had broadly neutral implications for unionisation due to the particular manner in which centralised and decentralised "wage rounds" occurred in the Irish case. This will be discussed below.

Structural Influences
The third major series of influences on unionisation arises from the changing structure of the workforce and changes in the wider social and political structure of societies. It is well established that unions find it easier to penetrate some industrial sectors than others. The traditional heartlands of trade union movements have been in working-class communities in such industries as mining, dockworking, manufacturing, utilities and transport. Unions internationally have also generally found it easier to recruit and retain members in the public sector than in private business. Blue-collar workers have shown a higher inclination to unionise than white-collar workers. Gender and occupational differences in propensity and opportunity to unionise have also been revealed by research. Men usually appear more inclined to unionise than women, or they may simply have more opportunities to join unions. Part-time workers and other workers on "untypical" employment contracts have tended to be characterised by lower rates of unionisation than workers on conventional full-time, permanent contracts. The scale of the enterprises in which people work has also been shown to be an important influence on the probability that they will be a union member. Higher levels of unionisation are more likely in large-scale enterprises than in small.

The significance for the trend in union growth of these and other structural differences in the inclination and opportunity of employees to join unions, should be immediately apparent. As the distribution of the workforce changes over time across sectors, occupations, genders, types of employment contract (full-time, part-time, permanent, non-permanent etc.) and enterprise sizes, the trend of unionisation either accelerates or decelerates — depending on the manner in which these structural effects aggregate or combine. Over a very long time, net structural effects probably first lead to accelerated trade union growth, as male, blue-collar manufacturing employment grows proportionately in the workforce. Gradually, net structural effects lead to a deceleration of the growth trend, as white-collar, female and tertiary sector employment grows.

Analytically distinct from these structural influences is a further structural effect, usually termed the "saturation effect". As union density rises, progressively fewer workers remain outside unions and a point is reached beyond which the inclination or opportunity to join unions of those who remain non-members increases significantly. In simple terms, the "membership market" becomes saturated.

Many structural differences in inclination or opportunity to unionise are not, however, invariant over time, introducing a further complication into the theory of union growth. Institutional changes can also affect structural differences in levels of unionisation. For example, unions in the Irish public service were denied a formal role in the determination of pay and conditions until 1950 or later. Following the introduction of the conciliation and arbitration systems for different categories of public servants, unions in the public service assumed a more effective and visible role in determining pay and conditions. This change in State policy towards its own employees probably contributed to an improvement in the density of public sector unionism relative to the private sector. A further institutional change that affected existing gender differences in unionisation was the abolition of the marriage bar in the public service in the early 1970s and the subsequent "normalisation" of at least this aspect of employment for married women across Irish industry.

Changes in the wider social and political structures of societies also change structural differences in propensities to unionise. Over a long period, such dimensions of wider social outlooks as views on women's employment and attitudes to the "propriety" of white-collar and professional workers joining trade unions undergo change. Such changes in social outlooks interact back upon structural differences in probabilities of unionisation, altering their scale.

In a broader sense, too, the value placed on collective association and collective action by people may change, with significant implications for trade unions. One such aspect of long-run sociological change is the progressive erosion of the value placed on solidarity in the cultures of working-class communities (see Goldthorpe et al., 1971). An example of a much discussed trend in contemporary culture which may further affect unions is the alleged growth of "post materialism" or "post modernism", supposedly leading to impatience with bureaucracy, rules, standardisation and autocratic forms of control and representation (see Inglehart, 1990: 340; Rose, 1988).

Closely related to changing social structure and culture is the influence exerted on union growth of changing political structure and culture. Public attitudes to the value and role of trade unions are subject to long-run change, and the changes which occur can influence the general popularity of unions. Unions in virtually all Western nations, albeit to varying degrees, had to struggle to gain the status of lawful organisations. A measure of social acceptability, or even respectability, was gradually gained once the taint of criminality was removed. Following the resistance mounted to Fascism by union leaders in Europe during the 1930s and the destruction of Europe in the Second World War, unions in Western Europe came to be viewed as bulwarks of democracy and partners in post-war economic and political reconstruction. A generally benign view of the role of unions in economic and political affairs came to dominate public attitudes. And so it remained up to the 1970s or beyond. The ascendancy of liberal political attitudes in many European countries during the 1980s brought into question this positive view of trade unions. Sometimes, as in Great Britain, the reappraisal of unions resulted in their being portrayed as obstructionist, outmoded and economically malign.

Structural influences on union growth tend, in the main, to change very slowly over a long period of time. As such, their primary impact is on the underlying trend in unionisation.

They can, however, exert a more abrupt or medium-term effect on unionisation, as, for example, when a recession leads to a dramatic change in the structure of the workforce and economic activity, or when a social cataclysm, like war, leads to abrupt change in the prevailing climate of popular opinion.

Cyclical influences lead to short-run fluctuations around the trend dictated by structural change, while institutional influences increase or reduce the level of growth over the periods of time in which the influences in question remain in force.

Figure 2.1 summarises this theoretical framework for comprehending the sources of trade union growth and decline. It is now well established that the influences outlined above prove to be of varying empirical importance across different nations and, possibly, across different periods of time within nations. Thus, for example, the Wagner Act introduced in the United States in 1937 to aid union recruitment and organisation, appears to have permanently intensified the degree to which cyclical and structural variables influence union growth (Stepina and Fiorito, 1986).

FIGURE 2.1: INFLUENCES ON TRADE UNION GROWTH AND DECLINE

Type of Influence	Examples	Manner in which Effect on Union Growth is Exerted
Cyclical Influences	Rate of change in: wages, prices employees at work, unemployment, profits & productivity	Effects reflected in *short-run* changes
Institutional Influences	Legislative initiatives; changes in bargaining levels; political composition of governments; employer ideologies/strategies	Development may accelerate or re-tard growth during *particular periods*, or on a long-term basis
Structural Influences	Changing sectoral/occupational/gender composition of workforce level of employment concentration general social attitudes to trade unionism	Usually structural changes occur in-crementally and their impact is re-flected in *long-run* trends in union growth

International differences, and differences over time in the influence of cyclical and other factors on unionisation, point to the importance of detailed empirical research in each national case, informed by comparisons drawn from research on other countries. Only in this way is it possible to unravel the ways in which the various influences outlined above come together to shape the trend of unionisation.

Research on the growth and decline of unionisation often makes use of techniques of statistical modelling which attempt to isolate the discrete effects of the different influences on unionisation. These techniques may pose their own technical problems. A discussion of the application of statistical time-series modelling to data on unionisation in Ireland is beyond the scope of this chapter. However, the analysis to follow takes account of the findings of such research. (For a detailed discussion of Irish research findings based on time-series modelling, see Roche and Larragy, 1990; Roche 1992a).

TRENDS IN TRADE UNION MEMBERSHIP AND DENSITY IN IRELAND

As outlined above, one of the most obvious direct influences on the trend in trade union membership is the trend in potential membership or in the unionisable workforce. In examining trends in unionisation over long periods of time it is often convenient to allow for this direct influence on membership levels by analysing the trend in union density. Two indicators of union density are conventionally used. The first, sometimes known as "workforce density", defines union density as the unionised proportion of the total civilian employee workforce, comprising employees at work plus the unemployed. The second indicator, sometimes described as "employment density", is the unionised proportion of civilian employees in employment. No one of these indicators is intrinsically better than the other. Clearly, employment density is the better indicator of variations in union success in organising those at work. Workforce density, on the other hand, provides an indicator of the degree to which unions organise the total employee workforce. Irish trade unions have not by tradition — or, in any event, have not until recent years — pursued an active policy of retaining unemployed members. As such, it might be thought that the trend in employment density represents the most interesting issue to address in an analysis of unionisation in Ireland. In the following sections of the chapter trends in each type of union density are considered, in addition to the simple trend in union membership.

Between 1930 and 1987 trade union membership in the Irish Republic increased from under 100,000 to 457,000. Workforce density rose from about 17 per cent in the early 1930s to about 43 per cent in 1990, while employment density rose from 28 per cent to 55 per cent over the same period. These long-run trends indicate the major strides made since independence by Irish unions in extending their organisational base and increasing their influence over the determination of pay and conditions.

TABLE 2.1: LEVELS OF UNIONISATION IN IRELAND, 1930–90(A)

	Membership	Annual Rate of Change (b) %	Employment Density (c) %	Workforce Density (d) %
1930	99,500		20.0	16.8(f)
1935	130,000		22.6	18.6
1940	151,600		26.2	22.9
1945	172,300		27.7	25.4
1955	305,600		45.7	41.6
1965	358,000		52.4	48.8
1975	448,800		59.3	52.3
1980	527,200	1.99	61.8	55.2
1981	524,400	-0.54	61.5	53.5
1982	519,900	-0.53	60.3	51.4
1983	513,000	-1.24	61.1	49.7
1984	500,200	-2.50	60.7	48.2
1985	483,300	-3.38	59.9	46.6
1986	471,000	-2.54	58.0	45.0
1987	457,300	-2.93	56.2	43.1
1988(e)		(2.92)	(57.1)	(44.2)
1989		(-2.54)	(55.6)	(43.4)
1990		(0.82)	(54.6)	(43.2)

Notes: (A) Series presented here differ, usually slightly, from previously published estimates due to data revision.

(b) In calculating annual rates of change in trade union membership, estimates of annual levels of membership were adjusted to improve the validity or reliability of the rates of change series. The rationale for adjusting the series and the methodology adopted are outlined in Roche and Larragy (1989; 1990).

(c) $\dfrac{\text{Employment}}{\text{Density}} = \dfrac{\text{trade union membership}}{\text{civilian employees at work}} \text{ X } 100$

As union records and Registrar of Friendly Societies returns used to compile the series do not consistently distinguish between employed and unemployed union members, levels of employment density may be inflated.

(d) $\dfrac{\text{Workforce}}{\text{Density}} = \dfrac{\text{trade union membership}}{\text{civilian employees workforce}} \text{ X } 100$

(e) Estimates in parentheses from 1988–1990 were derived for the annual affiliated membership of unions affiliated to the Irish Congress of Trade Unions. These estimates were adjusted in a manner analogous to the adjustments made to the earlier membership series (see note (A) and the sources cited therein).

(f) Value for 1931.

Sources: DUES Data Series on Trade Union in Ireland (Department of Industrial Relations, University College, Dublin and University of Mannheim Centre for European Social Research, Germany); Irish Congress of Trade Unions, *Annual Reports*.

Table 2.1 and Figures 2.2–2.4 illustrate the long-run trend and short-term, or year-to-year, changes in membership and density over the period since 1930. It is clear that the trends are characterised by phases during which membership and density grew rapidly, indeed sometimes dramatically, and phases during which these indicators of unionisation rose or declined more gradually. It is also clear that the years since 1981 witnessed the most sustained and sharp reduction in union membership and density of the period as a whole. Figures 2.4a to 2.4c indicate that considerable short-run or year-to-year fluctuations are evident in the trend in membership and density. The Figures again underline the sharp reverse in trade union fortunes which occurred during the 1980s.

The trend in either workforce or employment union density since 1930 can be divided into *six* broad phases. The contours of these phases are evident in Figures 2.2–2.6, though several caveats should be borne in mind. First, the identification of phases, and of time-points delimiting phases, is inevitably somewhat arbitrary. Second, the trends in membership and in workforce and employment density are by no means wholly concurrent. These caveats aside, it seems reasonable to delineate and discuss the following broad phases during the period 1930–90.

1. A phase of significant growth in unionisation during the 1930s.

2. A phase of highly variable union growth during the Second World War.

3. A phase of dramatic acceleration in unionisation between 1945 and the early 1950s.

4. A phase during which unionisation rose more gradually, but still significantly, from the mid-1950s to about 1970.

5. A phase during much of the 1970s in which the growth of unionisation proceeded slowly.

6. A phase of generally declining unionisation during the 1980s.

Each phase is discussed in turn, applying the framework outlined earlier and summarised in Figure 2.1.

FIGURE 2.2: TRADE UNION MEMBERSHIP AND POTENTIAL TRADE UNION
MEMBERSHIP IN IRELAND 1930–90

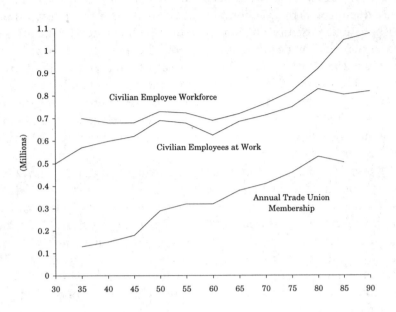

FIGURE 2.3: TRADE UNION DENSITY IN IRELAND 1930–90

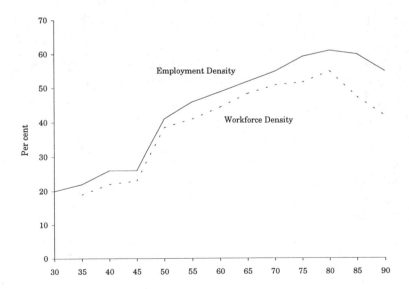

FIGURE 2.4: (A) ANNUAL RATE OF CHANGE IN TRADE UNION MEMBERSHIP

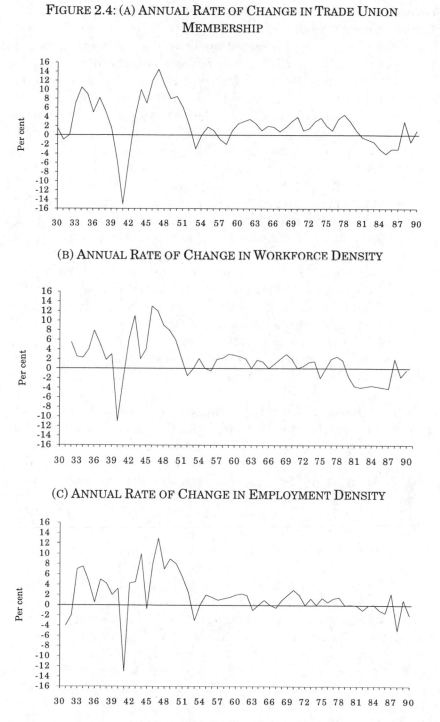

(B) ANNUAL RATE OF CHANGE IN WORKFORCE DENSITY

(C) ANNUAL RATE OF CHANGE IN EMPLOYMENT DENSITY

Industrial Recovery and Labour Market Buoyancy:
Unionisation 1930–39
The level of membership reached by 1945 was just about similar to
that recorded when the Irish Free State was founded in 1922. The
closing years of the First World War witnessed the first phase of rapid
mass union membership growth in Ireland: the membership of unions
affiliated to the Irish Trade Union Congress and Labour Party rising
from 110,000 in 1914 to 250,000 in 1920 (Roche & Larragy, 1986).
From 1922 union membership fell in the wake of declining money
wages and falling employment. The trend stabilised in the early
1930s and membership began to rise again from 1934 in the wake of
the industrialisation programme launched by the first Fianna Fáil
Government. Money wage levels revived during the 1930s, though
real wages effectively stagnated. Industrial employment expanded
rapidly. It is clear, therefore, that in the period between the Wars the
trend of unionisation in the Irish Free State followed the general
course of the economic or business cycle. The proportionate rise during the decade in numbers employed in the industrial heartlands of
trade unionism, especially manufacturing, also represented a *struc-*
tural spur to the union membership revival of the 1930s. Little significant change occurred however in the institutional context of unionisation.

War-Time Labour Market Regulation and Unionisation
Trade union membership fluctuated sharply during the greater part
of the "Emergency" period. Between 1940 and 1943 membership fell
from 148,000 to 139,000. However, density appears to have risen from
1942 to 1944, having fallen spectacularly in 1941. It has to be emphasised that considerable caution is necessary in interpreting the
pattern for these years owing to the difficulty of developing reliable
estimates of potential membership and to the effects of the Trade
Union Act 1941 on the numbers of trade unions registering and thus
entering the statistics for the first time. Such caution aside, the decline in membership and density of the early War years reflected
above all a cyclical down-turn in employment, as war-time shortages
of industrial raw materials began to bite. The haemorrhage of membership in 1941 reflects an acceleration in job losses through 1940
and 1941 but also the impact of two concurrent institutional changes
in the circumstances of unions. The first of these was the imposition
of a wage freeze in spring of 1941. This measure, soon modified by the
creation of "wage tribunals" to control pay rises, threatened to render
unions virtually redundant in respect of their most vital function: the

determination of pay and conditions. The second institutional influ-ence was the enactment of the Trade Union Act, 1941. This legisla-tion, designed to rationalise trade union structures and to reduce un-ion multiplicity, required unions to lodge a deposit with the High Court as a condition for qualifying for a licence to engage lawfully in collective bargaining. As a result, some small unions, unable to afford the minimum license deposit, appear to have disbanded. The wage rises permitted by the wage tribunals and the recovery of employ-ment levels towards the end of the War account for the recovery in union membership and density from 1942.

Cyclical Recovery and Institutional Innovation: Unionisation from 1946 to the Early 1950s

The most rapid advances in union membership and density since the foundation of the State were recorded in the years following the Sec-ond World War or "Emergency". A sharp recovery in membership and density appears to have set in during 1944 and 1945, as first money wages and then real wages rose — real living standards rising for the first time since 1939 (Roche and Larragy, 1986). The sharp squeeze which the period of the Emergency imposed on wages was to contrib-ute to a sharp rise in union membership and density during the sec-ond half of the 1940s. When war-time wage controls were removed in 1946, trade union membership and density accelerated sharply. Dur-ing the years which immediately followed, trade unions expanded as employees looked to them to restore and improve their living stan-dards. The institutional and economic conditions of the Emergency also increased the "transparency" of unions' role in wage negotiations by sparking off the first widespread "pay rounds" to occur in the Irish economy. The sharp fall in working-class living standards, which re-sulted from general rises in the price level, built up wage pressure across different sectors of the Irish labour market. With the removal of wage controls in 1946, unions representing employees throughout the economy came to the "starting line" together, as it were, for the purposes of negotiating improvements in pay and conditions of em-ployment. This was the first time that such a degree of "synchronisation" had occurred in the timing of wage claims across a wide industrial front. The involvement of unions in the statutory wage control machinery which replaced the wages "standstill" or freeze from 1942 may also have accustomed union officials and mem-bers to the notion of a general "norm" or a "going rate" of pay rises. This idea may have been further reinforced by the widely reported deliberations of the Labour Court, which had been established in

1946 to control the melee of pay rises anticipated after the ending of wage control.

So by participating in the early post-war pay rounds, which had been triggered by the circumstances of the Emergency and the return to peace-time conditions, Irish unions directed strong wage pressure into large pay rises and benefited from the process in terms of membership growth. This again shows the influence that changes in the institutions of industrial relations and collective bargaining may have on trends in union membership and density. Here, a new means of determining pay rises, the "pay round", favoured unions by giving their wage-bargaining efforts greater prominence. Moreover, the setting up of the Labour Court in 1946 symbolised the advent of a more tolerant or supportive approach to trade unions on the part of the Irish State. A similar change in State strategy was responsible for the granting of recognition to public service unions and the establishment of the civil service conciliation and arbitration schemes between 1946 and the early 1950s. The Labour Court actively sought to encourage union recognition in sectors where it had hitherto been opposed by employers — adding further institutional support to the expansion of trade union membership.

The economic revival which set in during the late 1940s also afforded a relatively buoyant context for pay bargaining and unionisation. Employment expanded rapidly, increasing the pool of potential union members. The wage rounds delivered sharp rises in money and real wages. Cyclical influences thus underscored the benign institutional influences of the period. The concurrence of both sets of influences in the immediate aftermath of the cyclical and institutional contortions of war-time led to the sharpest and most sustained spurt of unionisation in the history of the State.

The Labour Party first entered coalition government in 1948. A radical new left-wing republican party, Clann na Poblachta, also participated in the inter-party government. The participation of parties of the left in government, during this period of dramatic growth in union membership and density, raises the question of whether, during this phase and more generally, a party-political influence on unionisation might be evident in Ireland. Specifically, the issue is whether, other things being equal, Labour Party participation in coalition governments fostered a rise in the level of unionisation. In fact, the statistical evidence points against the occurrence of a general and consistent party-political effect on unionisation over the period since 1930 (see Roche and Larragy, 1990: 65–7).

The reasons for the contrasting record of Ireland and countries like Germany and the United Kingdom, where party politics has impacted significantly on unionisation, are not difficult to identify (for a discussion of the impact of party politics in (West) Germany, see Armingeon, 1988; and see Carruth and Disney, 1988, for a discussion of party politics and unionisation in the UK).

The major Irish political parties were formed around the "national question" rather than along direct social-class lines. Both Fianna Fáil and Cumann na Gaedheal/Fine Gael, albeit to different degrees, have adopted a "catch-all" approach to mobilising electoral support — seeking to appeal to voters across the social-class spectrum. As a result, industrial relations have seldom assumed political importance in the competition between the parties for votes and support. What is distinctive about the policies of the major Irish parties, rather, is that they have not diverged sharply on issues relevant to unionisation: for example, union power, industrial disputes and employee rights. The policy of the Labour Party has differed from those of the other parties in giving greater emphasis to issues like employee rights and industrial democracy. But given the "centrist" positions of the other parties on issues relevant to unionisation, the differences between them and Labour have not been as marked as differences between left-wing/social democratic parties and conservative, liberal or Christian democratic parties in the rest of Europe. Moreover, because Labour has entered coalitions as a junior partner, the Party has not decisively shifted the centre of gravity of its partners' policies on industrial relations. Until 1992 Labour participated in coalitions dominated by Fine Gael, succeeding, at most, in shielding unions from the Party's liberal instincts in economic policy — instincts that *might* otherwise have found expression in curbs on union power. Paradoxically, therefore, Labour in government has tended to underscore the centrist tendencies of Irish politics on the subjects of unions and industrial relations. As a result, and in contrast with experiences of countries like the UK and former West Germany, the course of unionisation in Ireland has not been materially affected by the parties or coalitions of parties holding power during different periods.

In the United Kingdom, the policies of the Conservative and Labour parties have diverged sharply on industrial relations and trade unions. Elections have indeed been fought primarily on such issues. In 1974 Edward Heath fought a general election, during a national strike by miners, under the slogan "Who Governs Britain?". The 1979 election, won by Margaret Thatcher, occurred in the wake of the so-called "Winter of Discontent", the winter of 1978–79, during which the Labour Government's incomes policy broke down in the most serious wave of industrial conflict in many years. The election ushered in Margaret Thatcher's radical programme of reform of industrial relations and trade union law. More than a decade of Conservative law reform has seriously debilitated British trade unions and contributed to a decline in union membership and density (Carruth and Disney, 1988).

That the political composition of Irish governments has not affected unionisation in the past does not mean that party politics in Ireland need remain forever inert where unions are concerned. Changes in both the policies and the electoral fortunes of parties might alter the pattern of the past 60 or 70 years. In 1987, for example, the prospect emerged of a realignment of Irish politics to the right, with the emergence of the Progressive Democrats (PDs) and the departure of Garret FitzGerald from the leadership of Fine Gael. In the event, the PDs failed to retain their early electoral momentum; and the new leader of Fine Gael, Alan Dukes, sought, like FitzGerald, to steer an independent social democratic course for the Party. Under Dukes' successor, John Bruton, the policy stance of Fine Gael on issues relevant to industrial relations and trade unions has moved ostensibly closer to that of the PDs. Fine Gael, however, has also declined electorally, leading to renewed calls from within the Party for an alliance with the PDs. The potential remains then for a Fine Gael-PD alliance which might be disposed to adopt a stance on trade unions significantly to the right of the stances adopted by Fianna Fáil and the Labour Party. Also yet unknown is the impact on the fortunes of unions during the 1990s of a Labour Party with more influence in Cabinet than at any time since the foundation of the State.

The Gradual Growth of Unionisation during the 1950s and 1960s

Though union membership virtually stagnated during the 1950s, union density increased, albeit very much more gradually than during the second half of the 1940s. Dips occurred around the trend in 1953 and in 1956. These dips reflected the twin recessions of the early and mid-1950s, during which employment fell significantly. In the first of the decade's recessions workforce density fell as union members lost their jobs and dropped out of their unions. Employment density also declined. This was probably a reflection of a general decline in the actual and perceived effectiveness of trade unions, particularly as the dramatic progress in wages of the late 1940s was arrested. In the second recession of the 1950s workforce density again declined simultaneously with the trend in membership, but this time employment density held up.

The general pace of growth in membership and density evident during most of the 1950s was maintained during the 1960s. It might be surprising that unions during the 1960s failed to increase the pace of growth above that of the 1950s. The 1960s, after all, was a decade of economic buoyancy, rising inflation, significant employment growth and low unemployment. The sharp escalation of industrial conflict might also be interpreted as an indicator of increased determination by employees and their unions to improve pay and conditions. As wage rounds occurred more frequently and resulted in larger settlements, the underlying trend in money wage rises also rose above the level of the previous decade.

The statistical evidence suggests that the positive effects on unionisation of the institutional innovations of the second half of the 1940s had worn off by the early 1950s; and so too had the spur provided by the labour-market and institutional contortions of the Emergency period. The rising frequency of wage rounds during the 1960s thus provided little further institutional impetus to unionisation beyond the credit effect associated with wage gains *per se*. The statistical evidence on industrial conflict also suggests that strikes, on balance, have a neutral effect on unionisation in Ireland. Those employees who may be galvanised into joining unions by industrial disputes appear to be balanced by those who lose their appetite for unionisation because of negative experience of striking. Again it has to be pointed out that disentangling the discrete effects of industrial action on unionisation poses technical difficulties (see Roche and Larragy, 1990: 67). However, from the evidence available, the industrial relations "upheaval" associated with the sharp rise in industrial conflict during the "decade of upheaval" seems not to have affected union membership or density levels one way or another.

Nor is it likely that changes in the structural composition of potential union membership exerted a significant drag on the trend in density during the 1960s as compared with preceding decades. If, as seems reasonable, we view agriculture, forestry and fishing, commerce and private services as examples of sectors in which density was relatively low, structural change should on balance have accelerated the trend in density during the 1960s. Between the 1951 and 1961 censuses the proportion of employees at work accounted for by agriculture fell from 12.7 per cent to 9.2 per cent. The fall accelerated during the next decade, with the result that by the 1971 census only 4.8 per cent of employees at work were occupied in farming. Between

1961 and 1971 the proportion of employees at work accounted for by commerce and private services appears to have fallen slightly from about 26.5 to 25 per cent. During the previous decade it had in fact risen from under 24 per cent. A similar pattern emerges when we look at trends in the gender composition of employees at work in the 1960s as compared with the 1950s. During the ten years between 1951 and 1961 the level of female participation in the workforce rose on aggregate by an average annual level of 0.16 percentage points. This compares with an apparent slight fall in the level of female participation among employees at work during the next ten years. Compared with the 1961 census figure of just over 33 per cent, the 1971 census returns a female participation rate of 32.3 per cent. On the other hand, the flow of employees into manufacturing industry slowed somewhat during the 1960s. In 1951 just under 22 per cent of employees at work were occupied in manufacturing, compared with 25.5 per cent in 1961 and 27.7 per cent in 1971 (Flora et al., 1983: tables on Ireland). The rate of increase in the proportion of the workforce employed in white-collar occupations was also fairly uniform during the 1950s and 1960s. Over the entire period 1930–90, this one dimension of structural change may have retarded union growth to some modest degree.

The Deceleration of Unionisation and the Effects of Recession: The 1970s

The 1970s present a more complicated picture with regard to the course of union membership and density. However, well-defined cyclical and other effects are nonetheless apparent. One major feature of the decade overall is that the rates of growth of both workforce and employment density were significantly lower than during the previous decade. In short, the pace of unionisation, however it is measured, slowed down significantly.

During the early 1970s union membership grew moderately but workforce density virtually stagnated. A significant dip occurred in workforce density in the wake of the first oil crisis. Both membership and density recovered strongly in the late 1970s. This recovery reflected the fillip to economic activity delivered, in the short-term, by the economic programme of the Fianna Fáil administration which entered office in 1977. The expansionary programme, financed in large measure by current budget deficits and foreign borrowing, laid strong emphasis on job creation in the public sector. The fragile economic recovery had a number of benign consequences for trade unions. First, numbers at work rose sharply and the labour market tightened significantly. Second, employment growth was concentrated in the public sector, in semi-state companies, the public service, education and the health services, where levels of union organisation were particularly high and where union membership, in many instances, was almost an automatic result of taking up a post. Third, economic buoyancy and a tighter labour market provided a positive context for the wage negotiating activities of trade unions, enabling the "credit effect" to benefit unionisation.

In 1979 trade unions in Ireland recorded their highest ever level of workforce density, when they organised nearly 56 per cent of the workforce. The recovery of the late 1970s was halted by the second oil crisis and the resulting recession. That year was to be a watershed. For the next seven years unionisation in Ireland was to go into steep decline.

The trend in employment density was again less impressive than during the previous decade. Employment density was also less cyclically volatile than the trend in workforce density. This is understandable in that workforce density is directly affected by job losses and gains. As net employment falls union members lose their jobs and their ability or inclination to remain union members is reduced. As net employment rises more people come into contact with existing union members and activists at the workplace. Unions can also more effectively represent them in a tighter labour market. In each of these ways unionisation is encouraged by employment growth. The direct impact of job losses on workforce density is apparent in the dip in the trend after the first oil crisis, when modest gains in membership were offset by job losses. The direct impact of net employment gains is apparent in the recovery of workforce density after 1977.

Employment density is not affected directly by changes in the level of employment, as by definition this indicator of unionisation seeks to measure the level of unionisation among those at work. The series is thus less cyclically volatile. However, indirect effects of variations in labour market conditions, and of trends in wages, are nonetheless apparent: for example, in the slackening pace of employment density after the first and second oil crises and in the recovery of the post 1977 period.

Inflation, another cyclical influence identified in the theory of unionisation, rose exceptionally sharply during the 1970s, posing the question of whether the "threat effect", or any other effects of inflation, encouraged employees to unionise during the decade. Inflation appears in fact not to have consistently benefited unions in Ireland — either during the 1970s or any other period — in the manner evident in a number of countries. The two inflationary peaks of the 1970s occurred in the wake of the two oil shocks. In this respect they are part of a more general tendency for inflation in Ireland to peak in periods during which the labour market slackens sharply. In short, inflation has posed the most serious threat to Irish employees' living standards during times when their capacity and that of their unions to defend real wages has been at its weakest.

This phenomenon of "stagflation" has probably meant that any positive impact inflation may have had on people's propensity to unionise has tended to be countervailed by the negative effects of a very slack labour market. The negative association between inflation and labour market buoyancy in Ireland also undermines the second reason why inflation is expected theoretically to encourage unionisation. Contrary to an important premise of the theory, inflation in Ireland was not usually an indicator of general business buoyancy. As such, Irish employers were not any more inclined to adopt a soft stance towards unionisation in periods of high inflation. Any industrial disruption resulting from employer resistance to unionisation during such periods would not have been more costly, in terms of profits foregone, than at other times — on the face of it, the opposite was, in fact, the case.

There may also be other reasons for the lack of direct association between inflation and unionisation in the Irish case. In their seminal study of union growth and the business cycle in the United Kingdom, Sweden, Australia and the United States, Bain and Elsheikh (1976) confirm the operation of a threat effect in all cases except Australia. They explain the Australian exception in terms of the operation of that country's arbitration system, which tended to tie wage adjustments to movements in the retail price index, effectively neutralising the threat posed by inflation to workers' living standards (Bain and Elsheikh, 1967: 94–6). The salience of the cost of living principle in wage round and national pay bargaining in Ireland may have had a similar effect (see O'Mahony, 1965; McCarthy et al., 1975; O'Brien, 1981). As it became seemingly automatic for wage levels generally to rise in line with retail prices, Irish employees may not have been as strongly predisposed to unionise as workers in countries where no such quasi-automatic link was built into the wage bargaining system. There remains, finally, the impact that the almost endemic high inflation of most of the post-war period up to the mid-1980s may have had in "inuring" Irish employees to rising prices — reducing their confidence in unionisation as an effective protective measure.

If we can therefore discount inflation as a significant direct contributor to unionisation in Ireland, we are still left with the question of why the exceptional wage rises of the 1970s did not contribute to higher levels of union density than those recorded. Money wages rose exceptionally sharply during the 1970s; and during the overall period since 1940 a "credit effect" can be confirmed statistically in the impact of wage trends on Irish unionisation (see Roche 1992a).

A promising answer to this puzzle is that the centralisation of wage determination during the decade retarded the operation of the credit effect. No less than nine national wage agreements or national "understandings" (as the agreements of 1979 and 1980 were known) were negotiated during the decade and not a single decentralised round or "free-for-all" occurred. It has been suggested that employees during the 1970s tended to believe that national pay awards came from "Dublin or from Heaven" and that neither unions nor employers received any credit for them. Bain and Elsheikh (1976: 109) have deployed a similar argument to account for the weakness of the credit effect in Sweden, when compared with other countries.

Whatever validity the Bain-Elsheikh hypothesis may have in accounting for differences between countries in the scale of credit effects, it does not, in fact, square with the statistical data on the effects over time of levels of wage bargaining in Ireland. What the data indicate is that central agreements — whether during the 1970s or over the period 1930–90 as a whole — did not, in fact, retard unionisation in Ireland (Roche, 1992a). But the reasons why the level of collective bargaining appears not to have influenced the pace or level of unionisation in Ireland, as compared with other countries, may nevertheless be revealing.

Central wage agreements in Ireland during the 1970s permitted considerable scope for supplementary wage bargaining at sectoral and company levels. From the evidence available, these local bargaining opportunities were seized assiduously by unions (see O'Brien, 1981; Fogarty et al., 1981; Hardiman, 1988). Unions then had ample opportunity to demonstrate their effectiveness at levels closer to members and potential members than national-level bargaining. Moreover, until the 1980s, decentralised wage rounds resulted primarily from negotiations at industry level and involved little real bargaining at the level of the workplace, other than what was required to confirm the application of the "going rate". Thus free-for-alls during the greater part of the period since 1930, were still rather remote from employees and required little more than passive trade union involvement at the level of the enterprise or workplace. Given the overall institutional features of wage bargaining in Ireland, then, there can be little surprise that whether national or decentralised rounds were in operation had little impact on the course of unionisation.

Change in the structural composition of the workforce was another factor that probably had little negative effect on unionisation during the 1970s. Judging from OECD data on numbers of employees at work in distribution, private services and financial services, in 1970 just over 21 per cent of all employees were occupied in these mainly low density sectors, compared with 22 per cent in 1978. The level of employment in manufacturing barely changed over the decade. A rise in the level of employment in the public sector, from 29 per cent to 34 per cent, represented a structural change that was conducive to unionisation. No significant change occurred in the female activity rate during the 1970s (see Blackwell, 1986: Table 3.4). The only ongoing trend in the composition of the workforce that might have exerted a drag on unionisation was a rise in the proportion of white-collar employees from about 47 per cent of the employee workforce in 1970 to about 53 per cent in 1980. It has to be borne in mind, however, that a significant part of this growth in white-collar employment was accounted for by the expanding public sector — which was anything but hostile to unionisation.

Of some possible impact on unionisation during the 1970s was the high level of *employment turnover* in union strongholds within manufacturing industry. The 1970s witnessed a considerable transformation of manufacturing employment. Many long-established businesses, and even whole sectors of manufacturing, suffered decline. Particularly strongly affected by both trends were industries like textiles, engineering and clothing. In their traditional manufacturing heartland, unions were faced with building up a new membership base in new establishments to offset the loss of membership in the old establishments which were disappearing. Even allowing that IDA policy favoured unionisation in new multi-national plants during the decade, unions had to come to terms with the recruitment and retention of members in "greenfield" companies, often located in rural areas with little tradition of trade unionism. In expanding sectors of manufacturing, like electronics, they also often had to contend with sophisticated policies developed to resist unionisation.

In addition to industrial restructuring, a difficult labour market, and the apparent non-operation of a threat effect, we must look to the so-called "saturation effect" to account for the slackening pace of unionisation in Ireland during the 1970s. The saturation effect is con-

firmed in research as one of the near constants affecting unionisation
in a number of countries (see Bain and Elsheikh, 1976); and so it
proves in Ireland (Roche, 1992a). Quite what precise interpretation to
put on the strong statistical association between union growth and
the existing level of union density is, however, debated (compare, for
example, Carruth and Disney, 1988 and Visser, 1990). As discussed
earlier, the saturation effect describes the tendency for recruitment to
grow more difficult as fewer people are left to unionise. Saturation
arises both because union recruitment efforts come up against pockets of employees with little inclination or opportunity to unionise and
because unions themselves become progressively more disinclined to
incur costs and expend effort organising the remaining hard core of
non-members.

There may be no simple direct relationship, however, between the
level of union density and the ease or eagerness with which recruitment takes place. This is because the saturation effect may be outweighed at lower levels of density by a so-called "enforcement effect".
Where unions have gained a critical mass of representation in companies, they may be able to win employer co-operation in extending
their membership base further; they may also prove capable of enforcing closed shop arrangements and other supports to organisation,
like the automatic deduction of union dues from wage and salary
payments (Bain and Elsheikh, 1976: 67–70). So as density rises from
a low level unions may enjoy a growing capacity to "enforce" supports
to organisation. As density rises to progressively higher levels, however, the saturation effect tends to dominate recruitment and suppress union growth. The impact of the saturation effect on recruitment helps account for the slow-down of unionisation in Ireland during the 1970s, but the processes involved probably began to take effect earlier than this.

If the saturation effect retards union growth at high levels of density, through its effect on recruitment, the enforcement effect may
also counter union decline by buttressing union organisation at the
workplace. As the two effects interact at high levels of union density,
the saturation effect may retard union growth in the upswing of the
business cycle and the enforcement effect may retard union decline in
the downswing. Thus at high pre-existing levels of union density,
unions may find it both progressively harder to recruit additional
members and progressively easier to retain them once recruited. In
this way we can account for one of the most salient features of the
trend of union membership and density over long periods of time. As
is apparent in Figures 2.4a to 2.4c, membership and density levels

fluctuated sharply in Ireland during the early years of the period 1930–90, when density levels were low, but fluctuated much more moderately during more recent decades when density levels were appreciably higher. The same essential pattern is apparent in long-run trends in unionisation in many countries (see Bain and Elsheikh, 1976: 2; Visser, 1990).

Evidence from other countries also suggests that at high levels of union density the saturation and enforcement effects may weaken the influence of wage and price trends on unionisation. It appears that at high levels of density the contribution of wage rises to unionisation is reduced (see Bain and Elsheikh, 1976: 109). Such an occurrence in Ireland would have further weakened the credit effect of the exceptionally large wage rises of the 1970s.

The operation of the saturation effect, both as a discrete influence and, possibly, as a force suppressing the positive influence of wage rises, is consistent with the deceleration of membership and density growth during the 1970s. The operation of an enforcement effect is also consistent with relatively moderate membership losses during the recessions of the 1970s, as compared with the downswings of previous decades.

Unionisation in Decline: The 1980s

During most of the 1980s union membership declined, as also did workforce and employment density. Unions report that membership stabilised towards the end of the 1980s and began to recover during the early 1990s. Data comparable to those in Table 2.1 are not yet available for the early 1990s to examine trends after 1990.

The decline in membership and workforce density during the 1980s was critically influenced by the scale of unemployment. As growth in the workforce significantly outpaced job creation, progressively larger numbers of trade union members and potential members found themselves without jobs and saw little need for union membership. However, of particular significance is the decline which occurred during the decade in employment density. Even measured in terms of unions' success in organising employees at work, the level of unionisation declined significantly during the 1980s. As unemployment can have no direct impact on unions' ability to retain their membership base among those in jobs, the trend in employment density during the decade again points to the complex of factors influencing unionisation.

The saturation effect would have continued to constrain union recruitment during the 1980s. The further worsening of job losses after

the second oil crisis is a major factor accounting for the falling trend
in workforce density during the 1980s. The number of employees at
work fell sharply in the early to mid-1980s and recovered only marginally during the remainder of the decade. While pay bargaining
reverted to decentralised rounds in 1982, the sharp reduction in the
pace of wage rises during the rest of the decade probably reduced the
credit effect unions gain through wage bargaining.

The recession, growing international competition, more volatile
product markets and changing management ideology also encouraged
a change in management attitudes to unions during the 1980s. As
outlined earlier, the stance of employers and managers towards unions can have an impact on unionisation. Managers may support or
resist union recognition; they may encourage or discourage employees
to join recognised unions; and they may try either to reinforce or undermine the representative role of trade unions, as expressed through
collective bargaining and its associated supports and procedures.
From about the mid-1940s to the 1980s growing numbers of employers and managers in Ireland seemed satisfied to accept that strong
independent trade unions and adversarial collective bargaining were
immutable features of the fabric of industrial relations practice. No
doubt many employers accepted trade unions simply because they
believed that doing business with them was unavoidable in the Irish
context. Such a view would have been reinforced by the supportive
policies of successive Irish governments and by the progressively
more helpful policies of the IDA and the Shannon Free Airport Development Company (SFADCO). By the 1970s, these development
agencies actively sought to encourage incoming multinationals to
grant "pre-entry" closed shops, known as "pre-production agreements", to the major Irish unions. The growing employer acceptance
of unionisation was reinforced also by a wider European tendency to
regard unions as a major and unmoveable feature of modern industrial relations. The dominant post-war model of industrial relations
practice, known in the academic literature as the "pluralist model",
envisaged "good industrial relations" as involving strong unions and
professional managers regulating employment through elaborate
collective agreements. The parties to these agreements were admon-
ished to support them by developing detailed procedures governing
the handling of negotiations, disputes, grievances and discipline (see
Roche, 1992b).

Beginning in the early to mid-1980s, the claims of this model to
point the way to the achievement of "good industrial relations" began
earnestly to be questioned. New management theories, especially the

influential, if heterodox, theory of "human resource management", made it respectable, even indeed fashionable, to challenge the prevailing orthodoxy. At their conferences and in their training programmes managers began to imagine a different kind of industrial relations — an industrial relations in which unions and collective bargaining would play a greatly reduced role, or no role at all. It became *de rigueur* to question the wisdom of the pillars of the pluralist model, including the advisability of recognising unions and encouraging unionisation. Also on the rise was resistance to unionisation spurred less by new currents of thinking than by the reassertion of old-fashioned anti-unionism based on traditional doctrines of management "prerogative". Anti-unionism of this kind had waxed and waned over the post-war period — especially among small employers. Not surprisingly, it tended to peak during periods of high unemployment.

The decline of union membership and density during the 1980s appeared to reinforce the ideological or theoretical attraction of human resource principles for some managers and the more straightforward attraction of traditional anti-unionism for others. From evidence available on the incidence of strikes and disputes over union recognition, there are indications that both alternatives to pluralist practice gained strength during the 1980s (McGovern, 1989; Roche, 1992a). Data on the incidence of union avoidance in "greenfield" manufacturing and service companies, both Irish and foreign-owned, are consistent with these indicators of a toughening of employers' attitudes to unionisation (Gunnigle, 1992).

The discrete effects on unionisation of such institutional influences as management policy and strategy are intrinsically hard to separate out in statistical studies. Nevertheless, using the incidence of disputes over union recognition as a broad indicator of management stance, the tentative statistical evidence suggests that unionisation has been retarded during periods in which employers have resisted recognition relatively strongly (Roche, 1992a). The 1980s is certainly one such period. The statistical evidence on the specific impact of human resource management policies on unionisation during the 1980s is less clearcut (see Roche and Turner, 1994). Moreover, the recent policy decision of the ICTU to advise its affiliated unions to co-operate with HRM policies, provided that guarantees of union security and involvement are forthcoming, may become an important catalyst in forging a style of human resource management which includes unions. Thus both HRM policies and the union response to them are in their infancy in many Irish organisations, and their joint effects are likely to take some time to become evident. What can nevertheless be concluded with some confidence on the basis of the empirical evidence available is that the management climate facing Irish trade unions turned significantly colder during the 1980s — colder than at virtually any other time since the Second World War. This has made it harder for unions to gain recognition, to recruit members and, possibly, to retain them once recruited.

Even more difficult to test is the effect of popular opinion on unionisation. Again during the 1980s there were indications — not least in the debates and initiatives of unions themselves — that Irish unions came to be perceived in public opinion as outmoded and out of step with the sweep of change in modern society. In part, such perceptions were influenced by declining trade union membership and power. A more general popular unease with bureaucracy, male-biased institutions, autocratic styles of decision making, standardisation and inflexibility also seemed to rub off on popular attitudes to trade unionism. The Irish Congress of Trade Unions itself recognised by the end of the decade that unions would have to ensure that they were perceived to be more in step with wider aspects of social change in modern Ireland (ICTU, 1989). Unions were mindful also of the threat that they might lose ground in the process of public policy-making. Union leaders opted to enter tripartite national pay bargaining in 1987 in part because they feared growing marginalisation on economic, political and social levels (Roche, 1992b). While statistical evidence cannot be adduced to demonstrate the impact on unionisation of the "climate of public opinion", it is reasonable to suggest that public attitudes to unions were less favourable during the 1980s than for most of the post-war period and that this may also have depressed the trend in unionisation.

Recessionary conditions during much of the 1980s compounded the organisational problems of unions by accelerating structural change in the workforce. Adopting *Labour Force Survey* (LFS) definitions of sectors, and again making assumptions regarding those sectors with relatively high and low levels of union density, we find evidence for the 1980s of a pattern of change in the composition of potential membership which posed new difficulties for unions.

First, the share of production industries in the employee workforce declined from 30 per cent in 1979 to 27 per cent in 1990. This is the first indication of a significant fall in this sector, and it represents a reversal of a structural trend which had favoured unionisation since the 1930s. Combining the LFS sectors "commerce, insurance, finance and business" with "professional services" (excluding the public serv-

ices, health and education), a sharp acceleration of employment is
evident in "private" or "traded services" during the 1980s. LFS data
indicate that between 1979 and 1990 the proportion of employees at
work accounted for by these sectors increased from 34 per cent to 41
per cent. It must be borne in mind that this domain includes highly
unionised areas, like banking and insurance, as well as poorly unionised sectors, like the non-associated banks, professional services, contract cleaning and restaurant and catering services of all kinds. However, over this period the major growth in service employment occurred outside the relatively highly unionised commercial sector.
Moreover, it is unlikely that the growth which did occur within the
commercial sector was concentrated in the relatively well unionised
banking and insurance industries.

So in the private sector, employment has been growing since the
1980s in areas where the obstacles to unionisation are considerable.
Among these obstacles are the difficulties attending the recruitment
and retention of members in small-scale enterprises, the deterrent
effect on employees of employer hostility to unionisation and the difficulty of organising employees on casual or part-time contracts. The
embargo on recruitment in the public service, which began to have an
impact on employment levels from around the mid-1980s, has also
eroded this traditional union stronghold. Between 1980 and 1990
employment in the public sector overall declined from 34 per cent to
31 per cent of the employee workforce.

Uniquely during the 1980s, virtually all aspects of structural
change in the composition of the workforce compounded the problems
of trade unions. Employment fell proportionately in the public sector;
the level of female and white-collar employment continued to rise,
and employment declined in the traditional trade union heartlands of
manufacturing, utilities and transport. Prior to the 1980s dimensions
of structural change which disadvantaged unions were more than
counter-balanced by favourable dimensions of structural change.
Overall, then, structural change from the 1930s to the 1970s probably
favoured unions and certainly did not greatly retard unionisation.
Beginning in the 1980s virtually all aspects of structural change
worked to the disadvantage of unionisation. These structural trends
will continue in the 1990s, when they will be one of the most serious
obstacles facing Irish trade unions.

CONCLUSION

This chapter has examined the general or aggregate trend of unionisation in Ireland in the context of the theory of trade union growth and decline. It has shown how cyclical, institutional and structural forces influence unionisation. The analysis of unionisation presented in the chapter has taken account of some of the special features of the Irish labour market and has identified the reasons why some influences shown to have an impact on trends in unionisation in other countries, particularly politics and the system of wage bargaining, have not affected unionisation in Ireland. The chapter implies that any attempt to project the future course of unionisation must consider the likely impact of the three types of influences identified and must also recognise the possibility that their discrete or joint effects may change over time. Finally, it should be emphasised that despite the sharp decline in membership and density during the 1980s, the level of unionisation in Ireland in the early 1990s remains in the middle of the range for European countries. Notwithstanding the changes underway in the workplace and in the structure of the workforce, unions in Ireland retain a major role in the conduct of relations between employers and their staff — recent rumours of their imminent demise are greatly exaggerated.

References

Armingeon, K. (1988): "Trade Unions Under Changing Conditions: The West German Experience", *European Sociological Review*, 5: 1–23.

Bain, G.S. and Elsheikh, F. (1976): *Trade Union Growth and the Business Cycle*, Oxford: Basil Blackwell.

Blackwell, J. (1986): *Women in the Labour Force*, Dublin: Employment Equality Agency.

Carruth, A. and Disney, R. (1988): "Where Have Two Million Trade Union Members Gone?", *Economica*, 55: 1–19.

Flora, P., Pfenning, W. and Krause, F. (1983): *State, Economy and Society in Western Europe 1815–1975: A Data Handbook*, Vol. 2, London: Campus Macmillan.

Fogarty, M., Egan. D., Ryan, L. (1981): *Pay Policy in the 1980s*, Dublin: Federated Union of Employers.

Freeman, R. and Pelletier, G. (1990): "The Impact of Industrial Relations Legislation on British Union Density", *British Journal of Industrial Relations*, 28: 141–64.

Goldthorpe, J.H., Lockwood, D., Bechhofer, F. and Platt, J. (1971): *The Affluent Worker in the Class Structure*, Cambridge: Cambridge University Press.

Gunnigle, P. (1992): "Management Approaches to Employee Relations in Greenfield Sites", *Journal of Irish Business and Administrative Research*, 13: 20–36.

Hardiman, N. (1988): *Pay, Politics and Economic Performance in Ireland 1970–87*, Oxford: Oxford Clarendon Press.

Inglehart, R. (1990): *Culture Shift in Advanced Industrial Societies*, New Jersey: Princeton University Press.

McCarthy, W.E.J., O'Brien, J.F. and O'Dowd V. (1975): *Wage Inflation and Wage Leadership*, Dublin: Economic and Social Research Institute.

McGovern, P. (1989): *Union Recognition and Union Avoidance* in T. Murphy (ed.), *Industrial Relations in Ireland: Contemporary Issues and Developments*, Dublin: Department of Industrial Relations, University College Dublin.

O'Brien, J.F. (1981): *A Study of National Wage Agreements in Ireland*, Dublin: Economic and Social Research Institute.

O'Mahony, D. (1965): *Economic Aspects of Industrial Relations*, Dublin: Economic and Social Research Institute.

Roche, W.K. and Larragy, J. (1986): *The Formation of the Irish Trade Union Movement and Organisational Developments Since 1945*, Working Paper, Dublin: Department of Industrial Relations, University College Dublin.

Roche, W.K. and Larragy, J. (1989): "The Determinants of the Annual Rate of Trade Union Growth and Decline in Ireland: Evidence from the DUES Data Series", *DUES Working Papers*, Dublin: University College Dublin and University of Mannheim.

Roche, W.K. and Larragy, J. (1990): "Cyclical and Institutional Determinants of Annual Trade Union Growth in the Republic of Ireland: Evidence From the DUES Data Series", *European Sociological Review*, 6: 49–72.

Roche, W.K. (1992a): "Modelling Trade Union Growth and Decline in the Republic of Ireland", *Journal of Irish Business and Administrative Research*, 13: 87–103.

Roche, W.K. (1992b): "The Liberal Theory of Industrialism and the Development of Industrial Relations in Ireland" in J.H. Goldthorpe and C.T. Whelan (eds.), *The Development of Industrial Society in Ireland*, Oxford: Oxford University Press for the British Academy.

Roche, W.K. and Turner, T. (forthcoming, 1994): "Testing Alternative Models of Human Resource Policy Effects on Trade Union Recognition in the Republic of Ireland", *International Journal of Human Resource Management*.

Rose, M. (1988): "Attachment to Work and Social Values" in D. Gallie (ed.), *Employment in Modern Britain*, Oxford: Blackwell.

Stepina, L.P. and Fiorito, J. (1986): "Towards a Comprehensive Theory of Union Growth and Decline", *Industrial Relations*, 25: 248–64.

Visser, J. (1990): "In Search of Inclusive Unionism", *Bulletin of Comparative Labour Relations*, 18.

CHAPTER 3

THE DEVELOPMENT OF TRADE UNION ORGANISATION

Brendan MacPartlin

The trade union movement is a long-established social institution which has roots that run deep. It came into being as a necessary counterpoint to the power of capital in industrial society and has flourished on a difficult terrain. The pattern of trade unionism as it is today is the outcome of a long history of struggle and to comprehend it this article will look at its historical development as well as at its present structure and context. It gives an account of the trade union as an organisation as well as of the structure of the whole movement. As the movement is made up of an amalgam of autonomous organisations it has made many attempts to reform its structures and these will be given special attention in the latter part of the chapter. For purposes of clarity, the structure of the trade union movement in the Republic of Ireland only will be addressed, leaving the dynamics of its overlap with the Northern Ireland structure for another time.

TRADE UNION DEVELOPMENT

Trade unionism has its origins in the asymmetry of the relationship between capital and labour. Capital and labour are dependent on each other, sharing common goals, but at the same time having conflicting interests. Capital is in the stronger position but its advantage is countered by labour's ability to enhance its power through collective action. Collective action uses the threat of withdrawal of labour to compel the managers of capital to negotiate on the terms of co-operation. Capital is willing to make concessions in order to contain conflict and establish order and predictability. The balance of the relationship has changed over the course of history and, correspondingly, so also has the character of trade unionism. Figure 3.1 provides a model of various configurations of the relationship between capital and labour. One aspect of the relationship is obtained by locating it at different points on a continuum which connects the polarities of co-operation and conflict. A second aspect is obtained by locating it on a continuum between the poles of equality and inequality of power. This yields a model of four ideal-type relationships, namely, Combination, Classical Trade Unionism, Intermediary Trade Unionism and Partnership.

FIGURE 3.1: THE CAPITAL LABOUR RELATIONSHIP

Equal Power	Partnership	Intermediary Trade Unionism
Unequal Power	Combination	Classical Trade Unionism
	Co-operation	Conflict

Combination

One of the features of the early part of the industrial revolution was the emergence of movements of solidarity such as friendly societies, trade clubs and combinations. Because the contract of employment was not an even-handed relationship between two equal parties, workers learned to combine together to change the conditions of the contract and improve their situation. They discovered that unity is strength. A long-standing tradition of Combination Acts culminating in those of 1799 and 1800 made such combinations illegal. Informal combinations developed nevertheless which were more in the nature of small local trade clubs than of formal trade unions. Their limited activities were confined to a very small fraction of workers and only slightly affected employers' control. Because of the inequality of power between employer and labour, the only viable posture for individual workers was to co-operate with the interests of employers. They are represented in Figure 3.1 at the conjuncture of unequal power and co-operation.

Classical Trade Unionism

The belief gained ground that social conflict would decline if organisation were permitted, and led to the repeal of the Combination Acts in 1824. Social policy became less unfavourable to trade unionism over the course of the nineteenth century, and trade union organisation progressed unevenly across occupations and industries. It was the craft workers who, from 1851 onwards, established a form of trade union organisation that persists to this day. The amalgamated craft unions had full-time officers, central administration, regular subscriptions, financial reserves, a formal rule book and a democratic system of policy determination. Their way of working in the best interests of their members was by the enforcement of the "common rule" of the trade. Besides the use of mutual insurance and parliamentary statute, they also began the practice of collective bargaining. They co-ordinated themselves as a movement by assembling annually as a congress of trade unions. They won public acceptance and got legal recognition of trade unions through the Trade Union Act, 1871. In 1889 the semi-skilled workers succeeded in organising general unions. Freedom to strike with immunity from the law was finally fully conceded in 1906 by the Trade Disputes Act which stood as a charter for trade union activity.

The amalgamated craft unions formed the basis of Irish trade unionism in the second half of the nineteenth century. The foundation of the Irish Trade Union Congress (ITUC) in 1894, the Irish Transport and General Workers' Union (ITGWU) in 1909 and the Labour Party in 1912 added to its distinctiveness. The great confrontation of the 1913–14 lockout and the subsequent growth of trade union membership confirmed the separate existence of the Irish movement. The recessionary years of the 1920s saw a decline in trade unionism following the decline in the effectiveness of classical economics.

Intermediary Trade Unionism
A policy of state intervention in the economy in the 1930s promoted industrialisation and along with it an extension in the practice of collective bargaining. The political and industrial aspects of the working class movement were separated when the Labour Party split from the Irish Trade Union Congress so that each could pursue its own appropriate objectives. The passing of the Industrial Relations Act, 1946, further established collective bargaining as the mechanism for regulating industrial conflict. As collective bargaining elaborated patterns of wage rounds at local, industry or national levels, trade unionism developed its role of mediating between capital and workers. It had achieved recognition by public opinion, employers and the law; and it achieved organisational stability in the face of economic uncertainties. It took on the role of a quasi-public body as it began to take on public functions and responsibilities in a growing number of tripartite bodies. The Keynesian approach to state intervention in the economy and the long boom in economic expansion after the Second World War supported the growth of intermediary trade unionism. Membership grew continually from the mid-1930s until 1980 with only a small interruption during the war. White-collar trade unionism

grew rapidly during this time, largely because of the expansion in white-collar occupations.

The Keynesian approach to the economy faltered during the 1970s and appears to have been abandoned in the deep recession of 1981. The weakening of trade union power in the 1980s and the challenging conditions of a globalised and deregulated market called for a new strategy from trade unions.

Social Partnership

It came to be appreciated that trade union organisation affected the economy to the extent that its own interests required that it take responsibility for the consequences of its achievements. The trade unions therefore, after a period of marginalisation and crisis entered on a strategy of Social Partnership with government and other interest groups. It moved from an adversarial stance on industrial relations to a co-operative one. The scope of collective bargaining was broadened and wage increases were foregone in return for progress on social and political issues. The unions had been accused of being dominated by short-term concerns, sectional interests and short-sighted relativities. Now it was challenged by this new context to develop its capacity for longer term strategy. Major restructuring ensued and today the trade union movement is stronger and more coherent than at any time in its past.

TRADE UNION FUNCTION

A trade union is in the first place a means of maximising the power of workers through organisation and co-ordination. It seeks the empowerment of workers through collective action — "united we stand" — in order to redress the inequalities of the individual contract of employment. Perhaps the most authoritative definition of a trade union is that given by the Webbs (1920: 1), namely, "a continuous association of wage earners for the purpose of maintaining or improving the conditions of their working lives". A more recent expression of trade union purpose which coincides with the Webbs' definition and broadens its focus claims that "the *raison d'être* of every union is to exert influence on the terms and conditions operating in the labour market" (Mueller-Jentsch, 1981).

Three aspects of trade union function might be considered: firstly, the economic aspect which addresses wages and conditions; secondly, the aspect of control and the regulation of work; and finally, the determination of wider social and political values.

Substantive Economic Goods

The negotiation of wages and other terms of employment such as hours and holidays is considered by most trade union members to be the major function of trade unions. Individual workers seek to maximise their earnings to the extent that it does not interfere with their notion of an acceptable standard of living. The union will seek to maximise real wages to the extent that they do not have the effect of disemploying others. Defensive goals come to the fore when gains are threatened. The slogan of the General Strike of 1926 in Britain captures the tenacity of trade unionism in such circumstances: "Not a penny off the pay, not a second on the day". If a trade union is big enough to affect the economy significantly, its concern for maximising real wages and employment levels raises the question as to how the system is to cope with its demands. Trade unions then acquire a role in relation to productivity and the wider economy if they wish to make gains in real wages. At this point it is no longer particular economic goods that are targeted but the system which is the basis of the recurrent delivery of those goods.

Job Regulation and Procedural Goals

A further aspect of the union's function is to protect its members in the employment relationship. In the interests of capital, management is constrained by the exigencies of the marketplace to exercise control over decision making in the workplace. Employees attempt to ameliorate the impact of such decision making on their own job interests by organising to make their voices heard. They want not just desirable substantive goals but control over the means of securing desirable goals. They want control over their work as well as over the returns from work. They want to establish rights, set up joint procedures and elaborate fair rules; in short, they want a social order which will recurrently produce satisfactory outcomes rather than once off substantive rewards. Collective bargaining and a system of wage rounds constituted a social order which regularly adjusted to pressures, resolved conflicts and recurrently produced substantive goods in a broadly satisfactory manner. Procedural agreements and codes of practice set up an order that could satisfy expectations of fairness on many of the issues that arise at work. Joint regulation resolves the tensions between management prerogative and worker control. It is a reasoned way of managing the ongoing struggle over this frontier of control. When business is good there is scope for unions to gain ground. In times of recession or severe competition they are constrained to make concessions.

Social Change
The failure of the trade-off between wages and employment has led to
a questioning of the collective bargaining system and led the unions
in Ireland to engage in political exchange. Wage increases were sacri-
ficed in return for consideration in a range of social issues such as
education, healthcare, taxation and employment creation. This type of
exchange has continued for the period of social partnership when the
trade union movement has come to understand itself as an integral
part of Irish society and intends to influence changes in that society.
Unions have always held as an objective the achievement of change in
society at large. Trade unionism was intimately linked with the development of the democratic ideal and especially with rights such as
the freedom of association and freedom of speech from which are derived the right to strike and the right of collective bargaining. When
the division between capital and labour was more marked, trade unions often held revolutionary and socialist goals. During the Keynesian period of the mid-twentieth century they aspired to the social
democratic objective of equal distribution of primary social goods.
Under the conditions of global competition characteristic of the 1980s
the world economy has thrown up a wide range of problems — unemployment, the debt crisis, the dominance of multinationals,
changes in work organisation — all of which present a threat to organised labour worldwide and call for a response of international
solidarity. Ratzinger (1986) has pointed out that the trade union
movement "is a reasoned struggle for justice and for social solidarity"
and that "the serious socioeconomic problems which occur today cannot be solved unless new fronts of solidarity are created" (Ratzinger,
1986). Trade union leaders themselves see the issues in a similar
light:

> The concept of working people standing together as a form of activity,
> as a means of asserting their rights as human beings, and of demand-
> ing a say in how their lives are shaped has developed a great many of
> our concepts about how democracy should work in a democratic soci-
> ety. The values of trade unions are the values of working people, and
> can simply be set out as follows: justice; freedom; equality; the crea-
> tion of a just society (Attley, 1986).

THE TRADE UNION AS AN ORGANISATION

To examine the trade union as an organisation is to treat as permanent and institutionalised what is essentially a movement or process

of social interaction. The type of organisation precipitated in time and space by the trade union movement is more in the nature of a mutual benefit association than of a business organisation. It is a voluntary association with voluntary membership, objectives of mutual benefit, non-profit goals, democratic procedures and moral commitment on the part of its members. It is a democratic system for prioritising and representing the interests of its members. On the other hand, it is like any other organisation in that it aims to survive and to achieve its goals efficiently. To this end it has developed an administrative aspect which, like other organisations, co-ordinates by authority, has specialist functions and relies on a complex communicative network. It is the balance between this latter administrative rationality and the former representative rationality that determines the effectiveness of the union.

Trade Union Organisation
The institutions and processes whereby trade unions arrange their internal administrative, representative and authority systems are complex and have evolved over time with a view to effectiveness. Figure 3.2 gives a model of the organisation of a trade union.

FIGURE 3.2: MODEL OF A TRADE UNION

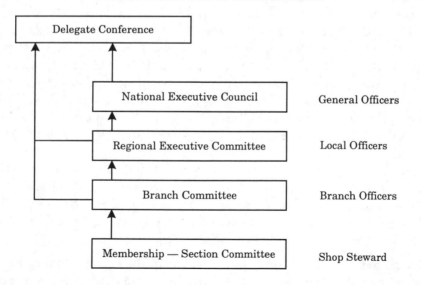

The Branch. The branch is the basic unit of trade union organisation. It may be geographically-based and made up of people who work in different industries in a particular area. It may be industry-based and made up of people who work in different companies in the same business. Or it may be plant-based as when all the members of a branch work in one large enterprise. The branch plays a pivotal role in internal union affairs, as a channel of communication, disseminating policy and instructions downward and the views of the membership upwards. Branch policy on terms and conditions of employment and other matters is determined at ordinary general meetings as well as at its Annual General Meeting (AGM). The Branch Committee is elected at the AGM as are the delegates who are sent to the union Delegate Conference. The branch has problems of apathy and low attendance at meetings. The branch secretary who is sometimes a full-time official looks after the administration and the negotiating business of the branch.

Policy-Making Level. When unions were small, their policies were made at meetings of the entire membership by simple democracy. As unions grew in size, methods of representational democracy were developed. The "Delegate Conference" is the top policy-making body of the union. The function of the Conference is to debate motions put by the members through their branches or put by the National Executive Council. If the motions are adopted they are called resolutions and become the policy of the union. A second function of the Conference is to act as a controlling body to which the NEC and the general officers of the union are accountable. The Delegate Conference represents the lay membership of the union and assembles not more frequently than annually and sometimes biennially. It elects a "National Executive Council" (NEC) to carry out its policies and to administer and control the union between Delegate Conferences, meeting regularly throughout the year. The majority of NEC members are lay members of the union branch and carry on their day jobs. The "General Officers" of the union, on the other hand, are usually full-time employees of the union and may be appointed or elected to their positions. These officers are the General Secretary, the General President and the Vice President. They are agents of the NEC and the Delegate Conference and implement their policies and decisions in the daily management of union affairs.

Regional Organisation. This is an increasingly important feature of Irish trade unionism. It is primarily an administrative convenience in an effort to bring service to members in all parts of the country. Regions may also have seats on the NEC and thereby add to the scope of representative democracy.

Workplace Organisation. Trade unionism as a movement lends itself to collective action outside the sphere of established institutions which is then formalised as permanent organisation. The role of workplace representatives came into being as an informal movement when collective bargaining and job regulation developed in the workplace. The shop steward emerged strongly in the UK after the Second World War and in Ireland in the 1960s. The role is now formalised in the rule book of many unions. The shop steward is an employee who is accepted by management and by the union as a lay representative of the union and its members with responsibility to act on their behalf at workplace level.

The "Section Committee" is a more recent phenomenon. It attends to the union business of a section of employment within a branch. It provides a forum for developing positions on the issues of particular workplaces — a function which the branch cannot perform as precisely. The Section Committee and the shop steward are vital to the development of sustained support for trade unionism among the membership.

We have seen that the union operates at a strategic level in the formulation of policy, at industry level through the branch and at shopfloor level through the shop steward. It implements its policies principally by engaging in collective bargaining which may be carried out at national level, at industry level or at enterprise level. It may be that the development of the union at these various levels reflects collective bargaining activities. The strength of the union as an organisation lies in the solidarity of the members and the way in which their interaction generates organisational patterns.

Trade Union Governance

The modern union is a complex organisation in which representative and directive functions are exercised in both an upward and downward direction. The interaction of the members is facilitated by democratic methods and the securing of their goals is ensured by efficient organisation. Democratic method is the "government of the people, by the people, for the people". In a union the members direct policy deliberation and goal formation. They do it through a process of representing and articulating their own interests. The policy-making committees at all levels are elected from lay members as well as from full-time officials.

Full-time officers, many of whom have come up through the ranks of the membership, are employed to reduce the burden on the members of implementing union business and to ensure the efficiency of the organisation in achieving its objectives. If the administrative and bureaucratic aspects of trade union organisation are overemphasised, the drive for efficiency gets out of balance. It has been argued that under these circumstances voluntary democratic organisations tend towards an oligarchical style of government and create a hierarchy with power and influence concentrated in the formal office holders, particularly at the apex of the organisation. The goals and decisions of the organisation then reflect the leadership's views more than those of the membership. The measure of effectiveness of a union, however, is neither its efficiency nor its democracy, but its capacity to countervail the power of capital and make gains for its members. In developing capacity for effectiveness, unions in different situations have had varying balances between democracy and efficiency. Small craft unions tend to have a high level of participation by members in the management of the union and a relatively small number of full-time officers who are drawn from the ranks and are closely identified with the craft. Turner (1965) called this type of government "executive democracy". General unions, by contrast, recruit across a range of occupations. The rank-and-file show a low level of participation and their interests are looked after by professional full-time officers. The groups are held together by the top officers of the union among whom the general secretary takes a leading role. Turner refers to this form of government as "Popular Bossdom".

The challenge for trade union government is to get the right balance between efficiency in collective bargaining and democracy in internal governance, and it is the appropriateness of this balance which determines the effectiveness of the union. A key to effectiveness is the quality and extent of membership participation. If the active members influence policy formulation and goal selection, they will guide full-time officers in their aspirations.

THE STRUCTURE OF THE TRADE UNION MOVEMENT

The present structure of the trade union movement is the outcome of a long history of action based on the perceived interests of different groups of workers. If it appears confusing, it is because the growth of employing organisations is uneven and it is they who are the first organisers of labour. Combination, as we have seen, was based on the need of employees in particular job territories to unite around their workplace interests. Such patterns of interaction across industrial society amounted to a movement within which trade unions were precipitated as organisational forms. A tendency towards wider unity has been expressed in movements towards the form of the "One Big Union" as in the mushrooming and collapse of the Grand National Consolidated Trade Union of 1834. It is an example of enthusiastic movement without adequate organisation. On the other hand, the success of the Amalgamated Craft Unions from 1851 onwards demonstrates the effectiveness of tight organisation based on sectional interest when operating in a hostile terrain. The success of the general unions may be attributed to a balance between movement and organisation which was appropriate to the conditions of the labour market served by those unions. It may be that the talents of Jim Larkin provided the inspiration and movement needed for Irish Labour and that the organisational skills of William O'Brien consolidated and built on the base of movement. Trade unions emerge as autonomous organisations for the purpose of representing their sectional interests. But they emerge from a common background of shared experience and shared interpretation which gives rise to consensus on strategy. Trade Union structure has developed through "the dialectic between the drive for sectional representation and organisational autonomy and the need for broader unity and concerted action" (Hyman, 1975). The tendency towards concerted action has manifested itself in the founding of a co-ordinating body in congresses of trade unions and in the tendency towards amalgamations between unions. A congress is the coming together of autonomous unions to represent the collective will and purpose of the whole movement. The Irish Trade Union Congress (ITUC) was founded 100 years ago in 1894 as an Irish differentiation from the Kingdom-wide Trade Union Congress (TUC) founded in 1868. At that time, the British amalgamated craft unions were the dominant bodies in the trade union movement along with the Belfast and Dublin Trades Councils. The first two decades of the twentieth century saw spectacular growth in general unions. This was accompanied by a growth in Irish unions of a craft, general and white-collar nature. The unwieldy structure gave rise to attempts at rationalisation.

The One Big Union, 1919
The first major restructuring of the trade union movement in Britain was brought about by a merger wave which followed in the wake of the Trade Union (Amalgamation) Act, 1917. The Act had eased the conditions under which mergers were permitted. At the same time William O'Brien, as acting secretary of the ITGWU, was giving thought to the Irish trade union movement which was made up of about 70 unions representing 250,000 workers. Many of the unions

were weak local societies with overlapping job territories. At the 1919 Annual Delegate Conference of the Irish Trade Union Congress (ITUC), a subcommittee of which he was a member produced a "Memorandum Respecting Amalgamation" which proposed as an ultimate objective the formation of a single all-inclusive Irish workers' union. The idea of the One Big Union (OBU) for all workers which would eventually take over control of industry through political and industrial activities occurred in the syndicalist ideology which was current at that time. O'Brien proposed that the trade union movement be organised into ten industrial sections, namely, transport, construction, distribution, food and drink, engineering, clothing and textiles, printing and paper, public services, extractive industries and miscellaneous. Each section would operate at local and national level. The council of local industrial sections would act like a trades council. The council of sections at national level would be the governing body of the whole union. The debate which followed the proposal favoured the OBU as a long-term objective but the British-based amalgamated unions were anxious to retain their British and Kingdom-wide character and preferred to rationalise structure in a step-by-step process of encouraging mergers among unions in similar job territories. The Conference voted in favour of the motion but there was no decision to take any immediate steps to implement it and the idea gradually petered out.

The Trade Union Commission, 1936–39

Trade union organisation expanded with industrialisation in the 1930s. It was a time of inter-union rivalry and disputes especially between the ITGWU, the Workers' Union of Ireland (WUI) and the amalgamated unions. In 1936, Seán Lemass, the Minister for Industry and Commerce, advised Congress that the government would intervene unless something was done about inter-union conflict. Congress set up a Commission of Inquiry on Trade Union Organisation. The amalgamation of unions in the same industry was but one of five areas for inquiry. O'Brien quickly presented a plan for re-organisation which was an adaptation of his 1919 plan. In it he analysed the fragmented nature of the movement and proposed ten industrial groupings. He was aware that relations had deteriorated since 1919 and avoided being obvious about attempting to establish the dominance of the ITGWU through the plan. When the Commission reported to the Annual Delegate Conference of Congress in 1939, O'Brien's report was rejected in favour of one put forward by Sam Kyle of the amalgamated craft unions which did not recommend reorganisation. Two camps emerged in Congress among the supporters of these two reports, reflecting a crystallisation of ideological and national patterns. The dilemma of accommodating British and Irish institutions was a central issue.

Some European countries had by this time achieved significant rationalisation of their trade union structures. For example, Norway had experienced growing industrialisation from 1905 onwards, accompanied by a parallel growth in unionisation. It had attempted in 1920 to rationalise its union structures without success and had subsequently used enabling legislation. By 1937 it had reduced the number of unions in its system to 39 of which 34 were affiliated to the Trade Union Centre.

Ireland attempted to regulate and rationalise the trade unions by means of the Trade Union Act, 1941. Two measures were prescribed by the Act. The first was the licensing of the function of negotiation. The second was to establish a tribunal whose function it was to decide between competing unions which of them had the rights to the organisation of any particular job territory. The purpose of the tribunal was to reduce the number of unions operating in the country. In effect it would exclude British-based unions who could not under the Act make application for sole negotiating rights. The Tribunal was established in 1943 and worked well until it was appealed to the Supreme Court by the National Union of Railwaymen and was found to be repugnant to Article 40 of the Constitution. The Tribunal went out of use and the Act had failed to reduce the multiplicity of unions working in the State.

All attempts at rationalising the trade union movement had not only failed but the tensions generated came to a head in the fissuring of its structure in 1945. A group of unions broke away to form a new Congress, the Congress of Irish Unions (CIU) leaving the ITUC with the mainly British-based unions.

The Irish Congress of Trade Unions and Restructuring

The way back towards healing the schism between ITUC and CIU began in 1954 in the context of modern Ireland when Lemass once again threatened government action unless the unions rationalised their structure. They set up a joint committee which reported to the conferences of both Congresses in April 1954. During the wage round of 1955 the unions experienced the lack of a unified centre as the negotiations process turned into a disorganised free-for-all. One outcome of this experience was that the Unity Committee worked to set up the Provisional United Organisation in January 1956. This body proved its usefulness in the working out of the 1957 wage round and continued to act as an umbrella body for both Congresses. Eventually in

February 1959, through the statesmanship of leaders like John Conroy, a merger of ITUC and CIU was brought about and was named The Irish Congress of Trade Unions (ICTU). The ICTU has since then been the central co-ordinating authority for the trade union movement for the whole of Ireland.

The Structure of the Movement

Firstly, we will outline the normal structure of Congress. Its governing authority is the Delegate and Special Conferences. Trade unions and Trades Councils are entitled to send delegates with voting rights to these Conferences, in proportion to the size of their memberships. The Executive Committee (about 29 people) is elected at the Conference and is responsible for implementing the decisions of Conferences and for the conduct of the general business of Congress. A General Purposes Committee deals with urgent matters between executive council meetings. A system of subcommittees is used to further special issues.

The function of such a co-ordinating body is "to represent the collective will and purpose of the Trade Union Movement". Trade unions are autonomous bodies in their own right and affiliate to Congress in a voluntary capacity. Therefore the authority of Congress is based on voluntary mutual obligation. In a structure of multiple unions with overlapping jurisdictions, the role of co-ordination, even on specific issues, is complex. Table 3.1 gives some idea of the changing complexity of trade union structure from 1940–83 (Roche and Larragy, 1988).

The proportion of trade union membership affiliated to the Congresses was in the region of 90 per cent during the period covered by this table. During the time of two Congresses, from 1945 to 1959, total affiliation reached a peak of approximately 93 per cent. There were significant shifts in the proportion of members affiliated to different categories of unions. The general unions increased their share of membership from about 45 per cent to 50 per cent in the mid-1950s, reducing gradually to 48 per cent in the 1980s. Craft union membership fell from 17 per cent in 1940 to under 12 per cent in 1983. The membership of white-collar unions fell from 28 per cent in 1945 to 20 percent in 1960 and then rose steadily to 35 per cent in 1983. The decline in "other manual unions" arises out of the decline of single-industry and occupational unions which have tended to be absorbed by general unions. These trends arise out of changes in job territories which reflect structural factors in a changing environment. The impact of such changing conditions on the number of unions can be seen in Table 3.2 which shows a gradual decrease in the number of unions.

Such gradual reduction in the number of unions did not meet the requirements of a Congress charged with the responsibility "to endeavour to reconcile the views and relationships of unions organising similar classes of workers and by the encouragement of amalgamation to reduce the number of such unions" (ICTU Constitution).

TABLE 3.1: PERCENTAGE OF MEMBERSHIP BY TYPE OF UNION
AFFILIATED TO CONGRESS

Year	General Unions	White Collar	Craft Unions	Other Manual	British Unions
1940	45.5	24.1	16.9	13.5	22.4
1945	44.3	28.6	15.8	11.3	21.4
1950	55.3	21.5	14.1	9.2	18.0
1955	57.1	20.7	13.4	8.8	14.2
1960	57.2	20.9	13.2	8.7	13.0
1965	55.8	22.2	13.6	8.7	14.0
1970	52.9	24.9	13.7	8.5	14.3
1975	48.6	31.3	11.5	8.6	15.3
1980	49.4	33.7	11.8	5.1	14.1
1981	49.8	33.5	11.4	5.3	14.2
1982	49.9	33.5	11.4	5.2	13.9
1983	47.6	35.4	11.7	5.3	13.9

Source: W.K. Roche and J. Larragy (1987/89: 24).

TABLE 3.2: NUMBER OF TRADE UNIONS FOR SELECTED YEARS 1940–93

Decade / Year of Decade	1940s	1950s	1960s	1970s	1980s	1990s
1st	120				90	84	59
2nd			123			82	58
3rd						83	57
4th		115				80	55
5th						75	
6th						72	
7th			97	89	71	
8th						71	
9th						62	
10th				85	60	

Sources: Irish Congress of Trade Unions, W.K. Roche and J. Larragy (1986).

Moreover, the problems that arose out of such a multiplicity of over-lapping unions had to be dealt with. In order to fulfil its function of reconciling the relationship between unions, ICTU set up the Constitution Committee. This in turn produced a series of subcommittees in the 1960s to deal with the various problems of trade union structure. Most important among these were the Committee on Trade Union Organisation, the Disputes Committee, the Appeals Board, the Demarcation Tribunal, and the Industrial Relations Committee.

The Committee on Trade Union Organisation, 1962–67

The 1962 Annual Conference of Congress set up a Committee on Trade Union Organisation to make an analysis on the structure of the movement and to recommend policy for future developments. It set out to "encourage unions catering for similar categories of workers to consider amalgamation" (Annual Report, 1963: 40). A Special Conference was held in Greystones in October 1964 at which delegates formed groups based on nine separate industries and discussed the feasibility of amalgamations. A general desire for amalgamations was expressed "as long as the others were willing to join my union". Nobody was ready to put the identity of their own union on the line in the interests of the wider group. Craft unions were notably strong about maintaining their identity, especially those which had members in both Northern Ireland and the Republic of Ireland. A further barrier to change was the belief that the attitude of the general membership was against amalgamations. Working parties of union leaders in the various sectors continued to meet, but at the Annual Conference of 1966 it was reported that no progress had been made. The Committee was discontinued after the 1967 Conference. It began to appear by this time that the best hope for progress lay with Jim Larkin (Jr) of the WUI and John Conroy of ITGWU, who were discussing the possibility of finding the way forward through the healing of the ancient schism between their two unions. Both men died, however, within a short time of each other towards the end of the decade, and thereby brought the talks to an end. Other events of that time, especially the difficulties encountered in the Maintenance Workers' strike of 1969 convinced trade unionists that their movement stood in urgent need of rationalisation.

Disputes Committee. The task of the Disputes Committee is to investigate disputes between unions and enable the people involved to reach agreement. The members of the committee are drawn from the Disputes Committee Panel which is maintained by Congress. If agreement is not reached, the Disputes Committee submits a report and recommendations to the Executive Council. The Executive Committee will then make their recommendation to the unions with a request that it be implemented. Nineteen such reports were reported for the period 1991–93 (ICTU, Report of Executive Council, 1991–93). Most of the disputes which are dealt with concern jurisdiction over members. This is an area which had been particularly troublesome and on which the Trade Union Act, 1941, had attempted to regulate. The constitution of ICTU, particularly Rule 47, provides regulation for the "transfer of members" as follows:

> For the purpose of developing and maintaining co-operative and friendly relations between organisations, the following provisions shall be observed by affiliated organisations in respect of transfer of members.
>
> (a) Each union should include in its membership form, questions on the applicant's past and present membership of another union or unions.
>
> (b) No member or ex-member of another union should be accepted until that union has been consulted.
>
> (c) No member of another union should be accepted when under discipline, engaged in a trade dispute or in arrears with contributions, except with the consent of the other union.
>
> (d) Where any grade, group or category of workers, or the workers in any establishment, form a negotiating unit and their wages or conditions of work are determined by negotiations conducted by a single union of which the majority, or a substantial proportion of the workers concerned are members, no other union shall organise or enrol as members any workers within that negotiating unit (that is, workers within that grade, group, category or establishment) save only with the consent of the union concerned, except that such consent shall not be withheld where there is evidence that 80 per cent or more of the workers in the grade, group, category or establishment wish to transfer in the case of a firm where representation rights have been established more than two years before the date of application to transfer.
>
> (e) Congress further urges unions to consider the possibility of joint working arrangements relating to sphere of influence, recognition of cards, machinery for resolving differences and conditions for the transfer of members. Unions organising similar classes of

workers, or organising different classes of workers within the same industry, should as far as possible make joint working agreements.

The Constitution also provides that unions, in addition to observing the above provisions, should consider the possibility of joint working agreements relating to spheres of influence, recognition of cards, machinery for resolving differences and conditions for transfer of members. Unions organising similar classes of workers, or organising different classes of workers within the same industry, should, as far as possible, make joint working agreements. A number of unions have joint working agreements. While such groups appear to have been a rationalisation of activity by the unions and have functioned usefully over the years, they have not necessarily had any bearing on the merging of unions in their areas.

Demarcation Tribunal. The Demarcation Tribunal was established in 1963 to deal with disputes between unions on matters relating to the demarcation of work. Such disputes usually concern the content of jobs such as a dispute between a general workers' union and a crafts union as to which of its members should perform certain kinds of tasks. The tribunal investigates and determines such disputes either on its own initiative or at the request of either party. It may summon member organisations before it and its decision is final and binding on the parties. The 1993 Report of the Executive Council shows the committee to be made up of six senior officials.

The Appeals Board. The Appeals Board was set up in 1963 following the setting up of the Committee on Trade Union Organisation which was concerned with promoting amalgamations. It had been anticipated that, following the merger of a smaller union with a larger one, members of the smaller union might feel that they were not getting adequate service from the merged union. The Appeals Board would provide a means of redress. Moreover, there had been some breakaway unions formed by groups of members who did not feel that their interests were being met by larger unions — for example, the National Busman's Union seceded from the Irish Transport and General Workers' Union in 1962. The Appeals Board heard cases of groups of union members or of individual members who could appeal on grounds of "lack of service" when a union failed to do what was reasonable in the circumstances. If the Appeals Board failed to gain agreement to and implementation of recommendations from the union, the members were then free to leave and join another union.

Industrial Relations Committee and the All Out Strike. The solidarity of the practice of not passing the picket had been misused during the 1960s to the extent that the Conference of 1970 resolved that Congress should become the recognised body to authorise pickets in respect of any trade dispute where a picket is placed with the object of securing a stoppage of work by all trade unionists employed in a particular firm. The right of an individual union to undertake a strike and place a picket with its own members is not affected. Other workers, in that case, may continue to work but will not undertake any work which is proper to the striking members. Regulation by Congress has brought more order into industrial relations. The procedure for "all out" strike pickets is that the union or unions in question apply to the Industrial Relations Committee of Congress which meets with (a) the striking union; (b) consenting union or unions; (c) objecting union or unions; and (d) any union which establishes that it has the right to be consulted, on the grounds that it has members directly involved. The object of these meetings is obviously to secure agreement between the unions involved.

The Schregle Report, 1975
Centralised wage bargaining came with the decade of the 1970s and constituted a new context for trade union action. The method of bargaining constrained the unions to co-ordinate their processes of interest representation and to deliver on their national agreements. It is not surprising then that the question of rationalisation arose yet again. This time Congress appointed an outside consultant to analyse the structure of the movement and to make recommendations. Johannes Schregle of the International Labour Organisation (ILO) reported to the 1974 Annual Conference of Congress and submitted a memorandum in 1975 on the "Restructuring of the Irish Trade Union Movement". He proposed that:

> The solution to the problem of rationalising the Irish trade union movement lies in the adoption of a structure based on industrial unionism with, at the top, a national centre, the powers of which should be stronger than those of the present Congress. The crucial problem is how to attain this objective (Schregle, 1975: 32).

A central recommendation was that the two leading general unions — the FWUI and the ITGWU — should amalgamate and thus open the way for further movement. Congress organised a seminar based on group deliberation with a view to promoting discussion and implementation. Government passed the Trade Union (Amalgamations)

Act, 1975, in order to facilitate and encourage amalgamations but it did not have the effect which was hoped for. The Commission of Inquiry (1981: 64) turned its attention to the fact that "the representation of a relatively small workforce by such a large number of unions gives rise to many serious problems" and that "trade union structures ... stand in obvious need of reform and rationalisation". Trade unionists themselves wanted to restructure the trade union movement to make it more rational and effective but the General Secretary of Congress lamented in 1987 that:

> The gap between, on the one hand, the expression of a general desire for change and, on the other hand an apparent inability to translate this desire into practice, is still the major issue facing trade unions in the area of trade union organisation (Cassells, 1987: 19).

It is only after 1987 that radical change in the structure was achieved through mergers.

The Cardiff Committee, 1983–87
In 1983 the President of Congress, Paddy Cardiff, introduced the topic of rationalisation as of the utmost urgency if trade unionism were to remain relevant in a changing environment. The economic and institutional context had changed to one in which trade unionism had been weakened by unemployment and loss of membership. In 1983 there were 80 unions representing 478,840 members. Sixty-two of these unions had a membership of less that 5,000 and represented 18.1 per cent of the workforce. Eighteen unions with memberships above 5,000 represented 81.9 per cent of the workforce. Twenty-five mergers had taken place since 1959 of which at least half originated in mergers of their British parent unions. Cardiff believed that former attempts at promoting rationalisation had failed because of "bureaucratic procedure" and because "there was no connection between the reports and the individual unions". It required "somebody on the ground to go after it" (Cardiff, 1993)[1]. He volunteered his services and when the Working Party on Trade Union Organisation was set up in 1984 he was nominated chairperson. His approach was to put little on paper and to avoid blueprints. He approached groups such as the building trades, the teachers' unions and the post and telecommunications unions. In 1988 the building unions announced the Building and Allied Trades Union (BATU) merger and in 1989 the post and telecommunications unions announced the Communication Workers' Union (CWU) merger. A Review Group was set up in early 1989 to address the issue of general change in the 1990s, and appears

to have superseded the Cardiff Committee. The intention to merge the FWUI and the ITGWU was announced at the same time and was accomplished in the foundation of SIPTU in 1990.

A Key Merger and Transformation

The SIPTU merger was the key to a wave of mergers which has transformed trade union structure since 1985. Figure 3.3 gives a time series of Merger Intensity magnified by 100 and serves to justify the claim that a wave of mergers transformed trade union structure since 1985. Column A gives the number of Irish unions involved in mergers. Column B gives the number of Irish- and English-based unions involved in mergers in the Republic of Ireland. Column C gives the total number of unions in the Republic. Merger intensity is the number of unions involved in mergers as a proportion of the total number of unions in the system. Column D gives Merger Intensity multiplied by 100. It can readily be seen from Figure 3.3 that the frequency of union mergers rises 100 per cent above any previous level in the 1985–89 period and even higher again in the 1990–93 period. Table 3.3 shows that the absolute number of mergers increased substantially from 1985 onwards. The smaller rise in the frequency of mergers in the 1965–69 period is associated with an increase in merger frequency in the United Kingdom which began in 1966 (Buchanan, 1974; 1981). More than half of the mergers recorded in the five-year period 1965–69 were of UK origin.

In 1993 there were 52 trade unions affiliated to Congress in the Republic, representing 463,647 members. Eighty per cent of the members are in eleven unions with over 10,000 members. Four per cent of the membership is in 26 unions with less than 2,000 members each. The classification of selected large trade unions in Figure 3.3 suggests that the contours of trade union structure are beginning to emerge in stronger power blocs, some of which are aligned with industrial sectors. What was formerly a fragmented set of overlapping organisations has now taken on a simpler and clearer outline. Figure 3.4, although simplifying by focusing on key features, nevertheless suggests that Irish trade unionism is no longer the fragmented and conflicted movement that has so often been criticised in the past.

TABLE 3.3: FIVE-YEAR MOVING AVERAGE OF MERGER INTENSITY

Five-Year Periods	Number of Unions in Mergers		Total Number of Unions	B/C x 100
	(A)	*(B)*	*(C)*	*(D)*
	Irish	*Irish/English*		
1940-44	0	0	120	0
1945-49	1	2	120	1.6
1950-54	4	3	115	2.6
1955-59	1	2	115	1.7
1960-64	0	4	123	3.3
1965-69	7	12	97	12.4
1970-74	2	6	93	6.5
1975-79	7	9	88	10.2
1980-84	6	8	83	9.6
1985-89	12	15	67	22.4
1990-93	12	15	58	25.9

Source: Number of unions involved in mergers 1940–84: Roche and Larragy (1986). Other figures derived from documentary research and observation.

FIGURE 3.3: MERGER INTENSITY FOR FIVE-YEAR INTERVALS, 1940–93

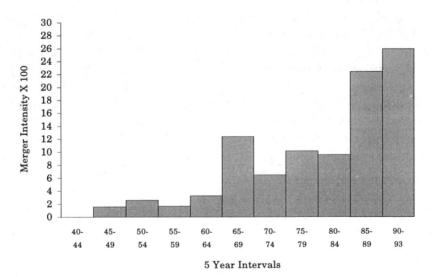

FIGURE 3.4: CLASSIFICATION OF SELECTED LARGE TRADE UNIONS, 1994

Industry Sector	Trade Unions	Membership
General	SIPTU	190,500
	ATGWU	19,500
Education	ASTI, INTO, TUI	40,100
Public Service	IMPACT, CPSU, PSEU	45,000
Engineering & Electrical	TEEU	22,000
Distribution	MANDATE	27,000
Construction	BATU, UCATT	15,000
Telecommunications	CWU	19,600
Other Professionals	MSF	21,000

Further rationalisations will almost certainly occur. Some of the large British unions such as ATGWU and UCATT are engaged in merger talks in Britain and these will have implications for the Irish structure. Some of the smaller Irish unions are likely to transfer engagements to larger unions. Moreover, the exclusion from this discussion of the unions of Northern Ireland is a further simplification of the notion of an Irish structure which avoids the overlap of British and Irish institutions in that territory. Figure 3.4 also obscures the complications of the internal arrangements of new unions such as SIPTU, IMPACT and MSF. Time is needed for the "bedding down" of these mergers and for the growth of cultures which can withstand the centrifugal tendencies of "breakaways" which were a feature of the past. More importantly, time is needed for organisational development which will facilitate the effectiveness of internal democracy and the service of the members.

Cassells (1987) does not appear to have expected such a transformation of trade union structure which raises the question as to why change took place at this point in time. The answer may lie in the interaction between conducive contextual conditions and the decision of trade union leaders to "go for it".

The political economy appears to have made a major transition which was signalled by the oil crisis of 1979 and the recession of 1981–83. Wage-fixing institutions changed during this period with collective bargaining moving from national to enterprise level. Margaret Thatcher's accession to power and Ronald Reagan's sacking of the Air Traffic Controllers are potent symbols of a new attitude to efficiency in the economy. In this context, two factors were especially worrying in Ireland throughout the 1980s: the ever-increasing unemployment and national debt levels. There were two further worries for trade unions, namely, their membership losses and the climate of hostility towards their interests. The perception of the trade unions was not only of economic and political crisis in the country, but of a crisis for trade unionism itself. It responded strategically to its perception of a crisis situation: "If organised labour is to remain a force for social change in these conditions then it cannot leave events to chance. It must take steps, including devising strategies, to achieve change" (ICTU, Annual Conference, 1986). It called on government to change its approach and to take a long-term view on measures to combat unemployment, and it was willing itself to change. The opportunity came with the change of government in 1987 when the Tallaght Strategy of parliamentary consensus and the collective bargaining strategy of Social Partnership were undertaken. Involvement in Social Partnership constrained the trade union movement to develop its capacity for strategy. It was well rehearsed on what needed to be done about its own structures. The crisis of 1986 had threatened it to the extent that it was ready to change. The success of Social Partnership in 1987 gave it the motivation to seize the opportunity for change.

CONCLUSION: TRADE UNION CAPACITY FOR STRATEGY

Writers on neo-corporatism identify the unity and centralisation of the trade union movement and especially the capacity for centralised strategic action as essential facilitating conditions for political exchange. Writers such as Hardiman (1988) suggest that the absence of a capacity for strategy was an important factor in the failure of the centralised agreements of the 1970s to achieve wage restraint in return for concessions on social issues. Breen et al. (1990: 180) propose that:

> The factor most likely to undermine future neo-corporatist initiatives is the continued inability of trade union and employer federations to sustain a strategy which transcends sectional interests.

Participation in Social Partnership appears to have had the effect of constraining the unions to make the choice for restructuring to the extent that it has been able to project a ten-year strategy of social and economic programmes. With such an improved capacity for strategy, the trade union movement is better equipped to exchange economic restraint for wider social justice measures. At the same time it has the capability of returning to adversarial methods if that is what is called for.

If the proposal that structure is a function of strategy (Chandler, 1962) holds for trade unions as well as business organisations, then we should expect new strategic initiatives from the unions. ICTU (1989) has committed itself to change with a view to shaping the future. It has faced up to the issue of the developing European Union with its policy to "Make Europe Work for Us" (1990). It has faced the challenge of international solidarity and believes that "there is a distinctive trade union response, based on the nature, history and traditions of the movement, to the struggle for justice and equality worldwide" (Keyes and Regan, 1992). It has taken a stance on technological and organisational change in its policy documents *New Forms of Work Organisation* (1993) and *Managing Change* (1995). And it has made a joint statement with IBEC on its policy towards participation in the workplace. It has abandoned its adversarial style in favour of a co-operative one.

> Traditionally trade unions have confined themselves to negotiating about pay and other conditions of employment. We should concern ourselves with all the factors that make a company competitive and workers' jobs secure — product development, marketing, investment, efficiencies. We believe in public enterprise that is efficient, dynamic and growing and we should work to make State companies "centres of excellence" (ICTU, 1993).

Trade unionism appears to have entered on a new phase of strategy in its commitment to Social Partnership. Its ability to reform its own structures would suggest that, rather than going into decline as an anachronism, it will continue to play a role as the guarantor of fairness in the relationship between labour and capital.

Footnote

[1] Interview with P. Cardiff, former General Secretary of the Federated Workers' Union of Ireland, 1993.

References

Attley, W. (1986): *Address to the National College of Industrial Relations*, Dublin: National College of Industrial Relations.

Buchanan, R.T. (1974): "Merger Waves in British Trade Unionism", *Industrial Relations Journal*, 5: 37–44.

Buchanan, R.T. (1981): "Mergers in British Trade Unions, 1949–79", *Industrial Relations Journal*, 12: 40–9.

Cassells, P. (1987/1989): "The Organisation of Trade Unions" in T. Murphy (ed.), *Industrial Relations in Ireland: Contemporary Issues and Developments*, Dublin: Department of Industrial Relations, University College Dublin.

Chandler, A.D. Jr. (1962): *Strategy and Structure: Chapters in the History of the American Industrial Enterprise*, Cambridge, Mass.: MIT Press.

Committee of Inquiry on Industrial Relations (1981): Report of the Committee of Inquiry on Industrial Relations, Dublin: Government Publications.

Hardiman, N. (1988): *Pay, Politics and Economic Performance, 1970–87*, Oxford: Clarendon Press.

Hillery, B. (1987/1989): "The Irish Congress of Trade Unions" in T. Murphy (ed.), *Industrial Relations in Ireland: Contemporary Issues and Developments*, Dublin: Department of Industrial Relations, University College Dublin.

Hyman, R. (1975): *Industrial Relations: A Marxist Introduction*, London: Macmillan.

Irish Congress of Trade Unions (1963): *Annual Report*, Dublin: ICTU.

Irish Congress of Trade Unions (1989): *Trade Unions and Change: Shaping the Future*, Dublin: Irish Congress of Trade Unions.

Irish Congress of Trade Unions (1990): *Ireland 1990–2000: A Decade of Development, Reform and Growth*, Dublin: Irish Congress of Trade Unions.

Irish Congress of Trade Unions (1990): *Make Europe Work for Us*, Dublin: Irish Congress of Trade Unions.

Irish Congress of Trade Unions (1993): *New Forms of Work Organisation: Options for Unions*, Dublin: Irish Congress of Trade Unions.

Irish Congress of Trade Unions (1995): *Managing Change: Review of Union Involvement in Company Restructuring*, Dublin: Irish Congress of Trade Unions.

Keyes, D. and Regan C. (1992): *Forging Links and Trading Places*, Dublin: Irish Congress of Trade Unions/Trocaire.

Mueller-Jentsch, W. (1981): *Trade Unions as Intermediary Organisations*, Frankfurt am Main: Institut fur Sozialforschung.

O'Mahony, D. (1964): *Industrial Relations in Ireland*, Dublin: Economic and Social Research Institute.

Ratzinger, C. (1986): *Christian Freedom and Liberation*, London: Catholic Truth Society.

Roche, W.K. and Larragy, J. (1986): "Pattern of Merger and Dissolution of Trade Unions in Ireland Since 1940", *Industrial Relations News*, 38: 15–22.

Roche, W.K. and Larragy, J. (1987/1989): "The Trend of Unionisation in the Irish Republic" in T. Murphy (ed.), *Industrial Relations in Ireland: Contemporary Issues and Developments*, Dublin: Department of Industrial Relations, University College Dublin.

Schregle, J. (1975): *The Restructuring of the Irish Trade Union Movement*, Geneva: International Labour Organisation.

Turner, H.A. (1965): *Trade Union Growth, Structure and Policy*, London: Allen & Unwin.

Webb, S. and Webb, B. (1920): *The History of Trade Unionism*, London: Longman.

CHAPTER 4

MANAGING INDUSTRIAL RELATIONS AT ENTERPRISE LEVEL

Thomas Turner and *Michael Morley*

The study of industrial relations is predominantly seen as being concerned with the organisation of labour and the institutions of collective bargaining devised to manage areas of conflict between management and labour, but underlying these concerns is the fundamental managerial task of eliciting productivity from labour (Brown and Nolan, 1988). Thus management are concerned with industrial relations only to the extent that they facilitate the firm's goals. Consequently, the task of management in the production process is to arrange workplace relations in a manner which is most efficient in achieving higher productivity, lower unit costs and improved profitability (Turnbull, 1991). This chapter begins by setting the task of labour management in the context of economic trends, product markets and organisational features while the latter section of the chapter assesses the evidence for a shift towards a resource approach to labour management in Irish firms.

ECONOMIC TRENDS AND INDUSTRIAL RELATIONS

Three sets of economic influence have exerted pressure on industrial relations in the developed industrial countries from the 1970s. Firstly, macroeconomic forces that determine domestic wage and price changes are increasingly affected by expanding global competition in product markets; secondly, the structure of financial markets, the market for corporate control and access to capital is increasingly emphasising short-term returns to capital over long-term development, particularly in the United States and the United Kingdom; finally, technological change, primarily production function influences, has altered the optimum scale and nature of production (Mitchell and Zaidi, 1991). In particular, the inter-relationship between technological developments and increased competition is viewed by some academic commentators as rendering traditional mass production systems and its supporting institutions redundant (Piore and Sabel, 1984; Marshall, 1992). Although changes in technology, such as the development of information technology and robotics, generally provided the possibility of new ways of working, Marshall (1992) argues that it was competition which made new working arrangements essential for the economic survival of firms. Along with the twin forces of competition and technology (and partly as a result), consumer demand for high quality customised products increased, fragmenting the traditional mass markets of standardised products. While the standardised mass production system was production-driven the competitive environment of the 1990s is largely consumer-driven. The altered economic conditions of the 1980s and 1990s, Marshall claims, do not just change the "magnitude" of the requirements for economic success, but also alter the necessary structures and policies. These new structures and policies centre on developing three key factors at firm level; product quality, productivity and labour flexibility.

According to Piore and Sabel (1984), these developments herald a new industrial revolution and a major restructuring of capitalism. The economic viability of firms depends on their ability to restructure and withstand increased global competition and the fragmentation of mass markets. In the 1970s and 1980s both firms and national economies that were capable of offering more diverse and customised products fared better than more traditional producers of standardised mass products (Streeck, 1992). Firms that are flexible enough to engage in small-batch or customised production can command higher profit margins and are less vulnerable in their market position. Alternatively, traditional producers of standardised mass products faced greater competition from low-cost economies in developing countries, particularly in the area of labour costs. Labour-intensive industries such as textiles are especially vulnerable to this type of competition. In general, Piore and Sabel (1984) argue, firms who compete in standardised mass markets must be able to reduce wages and operation costs in order to survive; whereas firms involved in producing for discrete or specialised market segments are able to give employees significant benefits in the form of enhanced employment security and high wage levels (Tailby and Whitson, 1989).

Consequently, firms require new systems of work organisation, employment contracts and working time arrangements to provide the flexibility necessary to adjust to the recessionary conditions of the 1980s (Rubery and Wilkinson, 1994) and to the fragmentation of mass markets. Cost leadership firms set out to become competitive through low-cost production methods and low operational costs, while firms pursuing an alternative differentiation strategy seek to be unique along some dimension such as product range, quality and design (Porter, 1985). With either strategy labour flexibility is essential, albeit in different forms. In the former case, firms adjust to changes in product demand through their capacity to rapidly adjust the number employed and the level of wages, for example, through the increased use of casual and part-time employees. Firms in this scenario serve mass markets with standardised products. Alternatively, firms may treat their human resources as a potentially creative resource for adding value in the production process and adjust to changes in product demand by re-deploying employees within the firm to production areas where demand is greatest. More importantly, the emphasis on the customised nature of the products produced and the importance of quality and service allows the firm to respond in a more strategic and creative manner to fluctuations in product markets.

BUSINESS AND LABOUR STRATEGY LINKAGES

These generic business strategies are closely associated with two distinct human resource strategies which can be defined in terms of whether employees are considered mainly as a factor to be controlled or as a potential source of competitive advantage. Storey's (1989) distinction between a "hard" and "soft" approach to the management of human resources appropriately captures the essence of these strategies. While the "soft" version views employees as a resource to be developed, motivated and integrated into the firm, the "hard" version is more selective in its treatment of employees, emphasising the need to use employees in a flexible and cost-effective manner. Friedman (1977) makes a similar distinction between a strategy of direct control and responsible autonomy for the management of labour. In the direct control strategy management attempt to control workers through close supervision, detailed rules for doing tasks and detailed time schedules. Alternatively, with a strategy of responsible autonomy, workers are encouraged to take responsibility for their work, supervision is kept to a minimum and company policy is aimed at encouraging employee commitment and loyalty to the company. In practice, most firms tend to be located somewhere between these two strategies. Table 4.1 outlines the type of employment practices associated with each strategy. These practices can be grouped into four generic areas: employment and recruitment practices; employee investment policies; employee autonomy and discretion; and patterns of industrial relations. Although presented in an integrated manner in Table 4.1, the choice of a particular employment practice in one area does not necessarily influence choice in other areas. For example, stable long-term employment relationships can be accompanied for many employees by low levels of training, poor relations between management and labour, and close monitoring and control of employees. However, the logic of a strategy of differentiation and a resource approach to human resources (usually referred to as flexible specialisation, that is, the combination of product innovation, technology and functional labour flexibility), with its emphasis on product innovation, a high level of employee skills and increased employee involvement, requires an integrated approach to a firm's employment practices. However, a move to flexible specialisation on the production side cannot be automatically associated with the development of high trust relations on the employment side (Rubery, 1994). Furthermore, technical innovations and work reorganisation in the 1980s has not always been beneficial for employees (see for example, the case studies in Tailby and Whitson, 1989). This tends to undermine any facile linkage between a firm's human resource strategy and its business strategy. In any case, many firms in practice attempt to compete on price and product innovation at the same time (Marchington and Parker, 1990).[1] Given the increase in market pressure, technological developments and fragmentation of mass markets outlined earlier, firms are faced with a number of uncertainties and dilemmas. In markets where product design, quality and service are more important determinants of success than simple price levels, management require not merely employee compliance but the commitment and willingness of employees to co-operate in the production process. Conversely, in the cost/utility approach, management attempt to reduce their dependence on employees through the use of atypical employment forms, close control of the production process, and simple repetitive-type jobs. As Streeck (1992: 259) observes:

> micro-electronics circuitry can be used for cutting costs by eliminating skills and human intervention, as well as for increasing product quality and variety by enriching the productive capacities of well-trained workers.

TABLE 4.1: HUMAN RESOURCE STRATEGIES AND EMPLOYMENT
PRACTICES

	Employees as a Cost / Utility	*Employees as a Resource*
Employment Practices	Core-periphery strategy seeking numerical flexibility of labour	Emphasis on functional flexibility of labour inside the firm — long term relationship with employees
Employee Autonomy and Discretion	Direct monitoring and tight control of employees	Stress on employee involvement and autonomy
Employee Investment Policies	Negligible training ensuring replaceable and disposable employees	Extensive training and development of employees
Climate of Industrial Relations	Relations between management and employees are adversarial and conflictual	Relations between management and labour are based on mutual interest and co-operation

Thus firms can pursue a strategy aimed at controlling labour through new forms of employment contracts and computerised work systems. In the resource approach the problem for management is to find the most appropriate policies to release employees' creative and innovative potential. Firms pursuing a utility approach are mostly concerned with external labour market rigidities which hamper the rapid adjustment of labour supply to market demand, while firms pursuing a resource strategy are mainly concerned with distortions to the employer–employee relationship, particularly that introduced by collective bargaining and its interference with the development of appropriate individualised contracts and arrangements (Rubery and Wilkinson, 1994).

ORGANISATIONAL INFLUENCES AND CONSTRAINTS AFFECTING THE FIRM'S LABOUR STRATEGY

A number of external and internal factors affect the choice of a firm's labour strategy. In particular, the firm's product market, national/regional levels of unemployment, management's capacity to implement a particular labour strategy, the presence of a trade union, and the national prevailing institutions of industrial relations are all significant factors. There are a number of theoretical frameworks which relate a firm's market position in terms of market share and product demand with an appropriate managerial strategy for managing labour (e.g. Schuler, 1988; Thomason, 1984; Marchington and Parker, 1990). Marchington and Parker (1990) argue that in order to understand the extent of managerial choice in handling employee relations, the extent of market pressure must be taken into account. The opportunity for choice is related to senior management's perception of market pressures. From the evidence of four case study companies, it appeared that where these were extreme, management saw its primary task as engineering the best fit with external market contingencies which appeared beyond their control. In such circumstances management perceived little room for manoeuvre in how to conduct employee relations (Marchington and Parker, 1990). As a consequence, management in the company experiencing the highest pressure from the market adopted an adversarial stance towards labour. This appeared to supervisors and line managers in this company to be the appropriate approach to employee relations given the unpredictability of the market. In contrast, another case study company with a favourable market environment had the opportunity to introduce a range of polices which enhanced the status and security of employment and create a climate for a more co-operative style of industrial relations. While these four case studies support a close relationship between product markets and management strategies, it would be erroneous to conclude (or generalise) that management have no choice but must conform to the dictates of the market.[2] The most notable feature of employment practices and industrial relations in general is their extensive heterogeneity rather than their homogeneity even across firms in similar industries and producing similar products. Decisions concerning a firm's employment policies can originate from inside the firm and not from market pressures. Such decisions, in the case of multi-national subsidiaries are often decided at corporate headquarters and not individual subsidiaries in multi-national companies (Geary, 1992).

A second factor influencing managerial strategy is the ease of availability of employees. Firms are more likely to resort to the use of atypical forms of employment when the labour market is relatively slack (Rubery, 1994). Indeed, the evidence from two national surveys in the UK in 1987 indicated that few employers had a conscious core–periphery manpower strategy (Hakim, 1990). An increased use of peripheral workers was due primarily to traditional and opportunistic approaches by firms in a labour market characterised by increased unemployment.

Even where firms are not responding in an opportunistic manner a familiar argument is that the use of sophisticated human resource policies, the resource approach to labour, reflects a wider strategic capability on the part of human resource management departments and general management (cf. Guest, 1987; Purcell, 1989). Indeed, the results of a survey of more than 200 Irish companies supports this relationship, with firms having a high capacity for strategy (as measured by the participation of the personnel manager at board level, in corporate strategy, in the formalisation of a human resource strategy and its implementation) strongly and consistently associated with all of the sophisticated human resource practices measured in the survey (see Roche and Turner, 1995).

A fourth significant area of constraint on managerial strategies is the presence of a trade union in the firm and the prevailing national system of industrial relations. Roche and Turner (1995) examined the factors influencing the implementation of sophisticated human resource policies across 200 Irish organisations and concluded that the most plausible explanation of the results observed lay in the influence of the wider institutional system of industrial relations and that this accounted for the low usage of performance-related pay systems and job flexibility arrangements in the establishments surveyed. Established industrial relations practices inside the firm (such as union preferences for standard pay rates) were viewed as inimical to the acceptance of performance-based pay systems and attempts to increase the flexibility of jobs as impinging on the effort reward bargain, an area which is closely monitored by employees. Moreover, the ability of management to adjust both its labour supply externally or labour usage internally is constrained and open to challenge where employees are organised collectively. As we have noted, the nature of the employment relationship contains both conflicting and mutual interests. Unionisation is an expression of this difference and employees through the collective power of the trade union seek to adjust the effort-reward bargain in their favour and implement employment arrangements which reflect their material interests in terms of wages, working conditions, security of employment and due process concerns for fair grievance and disciplinary procedures. Not surprisingly management strategies in industrial relations often tend to be pragmatic and short term in focus, relying on an effort-reward bargain and employment system which has emerged over time in response to product market exigencies and the balance of power between management and trade unions (see Hakim, 1990; Rubery, 1994). What this highlights is the different sets of interests inside the firm between owners, managers and employees. These sets of interests can provide the basis for co-operation between the various parties but they can also be in conflict. The nature and source of these interests arise from the separate goals which management and labour seek from the firm and the employment relationship.

THE EMPLOYMENT RELATIONSHIP: AN ARENA FOR CONFLICT AND CO-OPERATION

The need to manage and control labour stems from the nature of the firm's goals and the nature of the employment relationship. Labour is a derived demand, that is, it is a factor of production which is employed in order to realise the firm's goals which in a market economy can be defined as profit maximisation. The realisation of profits are affected by a number of inputs into the production process which include the quality of raw materials, the efficient use of technology, the design of products, marketing strategies, and investment and financial strategies. However, the labour input differs in critical ways from these other inputs which arise from the peculiar nature of the employment relationship as a mode of economic exchange (see Blyton and Turnbull, 1994; Brown and Nolan, 1988; Edwards, 1986; Leibenstein, 1987). Firstly, labour is more than just a commodity and is not as freely exchanged in the market as are other non-human goods. Secondly, the employment relationship is a continuous and on-going relationship between the employer and employee — it is not a once-off exchange. While numerous reasons can be advanced to explain the existence of stable and long-term employment relationships in firms, it is chiefly a result of: trade union struggle;[3] employer interests in retaining employees due to investments sunk in recruitment; and training and employee costs in leaving their employment because of the firm-specific nature of their skills and the general material and emotional costs of moving jobs. Thirdly, the employment contract is incomplete and open-ended. Wages are specified in advance but many aspects of the work and working conditions are not specified. The amount and type of effort required from employees, and even the times it is to be expended in,[4] is a variable open to interpretation by both management and employees. As Brown and Nolan (1988: 341) observe "the act of hiring is a necessary but not sufficient condition for the completion of the task required". Effort is a variable which is always open to some degree of discretionary choice by individual employees (Leibenstein, 1987). Because of the open-ended nature of the effort bargain and its relationship to prevailing wage levels, there is a conflict of interests between employees and management at the point of production. The goals of the firm require management to extract the maximum labour power from employees at the lowest possible costs, at the same time employees in return for their labour seek to maximise their wages and conditions of employment. Conflict, therefore, arises out of the clash between workers seeking high pay and job security and the employer's pursuit of profit (Katz and Kochan, 1992). Equally, however, both parties have a mutual interest in the continuing economic viability of the firm which provides a basis for co-operation. Employers require at least a minimum of compliance from employees if the firm is to operate and employees need a job in order to exchange their labour for a wage. This provides a set of common interests between management and labour but is not in itself a sufficient basis for avoiding conflict over both the distribution of profits in terms of the proportion of rents going to employees and the intensity of effort required from employees.

STRATEGIC CHOICE AND UNCERTAINTY

Because of the inherent conflict of interests in the employment relationship and the indeterminate nature of labour effort, management need to exert control over the labour process in the interests of the firm's owners. At the very least, the employer has to do better than to simply hire workers and let them work as they please (Bowles, 1985). However, the attainment of management goals such as high productivity, low unit costs and improved profitability present difficult choices and dilemmas for the management of labour. Firstly, the extraction of labour effort from employees is not a costless process for the employer. Bowles (1985) argues that the amount of work done per hour is a function of the cost of inputs used to elicit work from workers. These inputs refer to the costs of incentive schemes, employee monitoring (both technical and supervisory), the extent of fringe benefits, performance appraisal schemes, internal promotion schemes and the level of wages paid. Secondly, mere employee compliance is insufficient in most organisations as a basis for producing goods and services. In most cases employers also need to secure active employee consent and co-operation in the production process in order to enhance economic performance (Blyton and Turnbull, 1994).[5] Thirdly, employees may resist or subvert managerial attempts to extract labour effort. Even in non-union firms employees can withdraw active consent and offer only passive compliance causing the firm to deploy more costly surveillance methods to monitor effort levels. In unionised firms the possibility of resistance to managerial strategies is obviously greater. Furthermore, given the nature of the employment relationship, different sets of problems arise with the utility and resource approaches to managing labour. As Friedman (1977) points out, there are contradictions which constrain and limit a comprehensive application of the direct control or responsible autonomy strategies. Employees subject to tight supervision are likely to resist being treated like machines in ways which are detrimental to organisational effectiveness. Besides, employees working under a direct control regime are unlikely to suddenly assume a creative and committed approach to the firm's goals when management require it. Alternatively, it is unlikely for employees to continuously identify their interests with those of top management. While such an identity of interests may be possible in the short term, adjustments to market changes, downturns in the business cycle and changes in technology and consumer demand can end in redundancy for even the most committed employees. Labour management strategies emerge from the interplay of these tensions and, along with issues such as the cost of eliciting employee effort, the need to go beyond mere employee compliance and the possibility of employee resistance are often in practice ad hoc in nature rather than coherent and intentional outcomes. For some firms the cost factors, for example, of winning employee consent and co-operation may be prohibitive or a firm's intended labour strategy may fail because of employee resistance.

To summarise this section, long-term shifts in global competition, technological developments and mass markets have rearranged the context in which the firm operates, though it is the firm's immediate external environment combined with internal factors which exerts a strong influence on a firm's labour strategy. Changes in mass markets, competitive pressures and technology have engendered greater product market uncertainty which, while increasing the range of options available to management, provides no certainty concerning the best way to manage labour. In a market economy firms seek the most effective and least costly strategy to optimise the returns from human resources, but they must contend with employee resistance to those changes which are perceived as inimical to employee interests, that is, with the constraints inherent in the employment relationship. Figure 4.1 summarises the relationships discussed between the management of labour and the economic, product market and organisational contexts.

FIGURE 4.1: FACTORS INFLUENCING LABOUR MANAGEMENT STRATEGIES

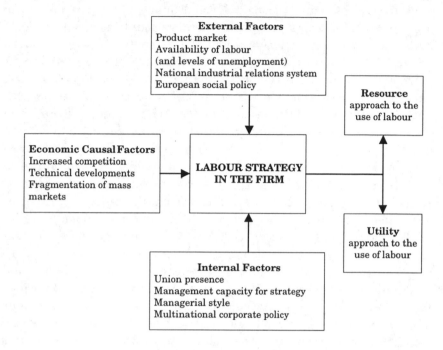

LABOUR FLEXIBILITY: THE EMPLOYERS RESPONSE

A key response of firms to the pressures of the market is the search for labour flexibility. Firms emphasising workforce flexibility through core–periphery strategies are most concerned with rigidities in the external labour market, while firms adopting a resource approach to human resources are more concerned with internal labour rigidities inside the firm. External rigidities include: (a) labour costs flexibility — the degree to which the price of labour can be adjusted to demand and supply shocks originating in the market, (b) fixed labour costs — this refers to taxes of all kinds on labour; (c) social protection systems — the effect of levels of welfare income on the incentive to take up employment; and (d) employment legislation — the legislative obstacles (and costs) to the rapid adjustment of labour.[6] Labour market flexibility is a critical feature of the current debate on competitiveness in the European Union. The European Commission's (1994a) White Paper on growth and employment in Europe emphasised the need for a "more efficient labour market" and also the need for a "new solidarity" and argued for a "thoroughgoing reform of the labour market" through greater flexibility in the organisation of work (both numerical and functional flexibility), reduced labour costs, higher levels of skills, and proactive labour policies. Equally, the report noted the high degree of convergence among member countries on the need to maintain social protection systems. The Commission's subsequent White Paper (1994b) outlining its approach to social policy and labour market issues for the period 1995 to 1999, attempted to balance the need for reform of the labour market to encourage economic growth and employment with the preference for social consensus in tackling these problems rather than relying solely on market mechanisms. In practice, this compromise takes the form of consolidating the body of current employment and related legislation while freezing any new initiatives for the present. The Commission's policies of balancing labour flexibility and social protection reflects the different pressures and orientations of employer organisations and trade unions.

A central objective of the Irish Business and Employers' Confederation[7] (IBEC) is the creation of a business environment which enables and encourages employers to be competitive in national and international markets (e.g. *IBEC News*, September 1994 and various recent Annual Reports). As such, external rigidities in the labour market are of significant concern to IBEC, and in this context, its role as a lobby force articulating the general interests of its members has become, we would argue, its most critical function. These concerns include overall wage costs, the level of taxes on labour, levels of unemployment benefit and employment legislation. Firms, according to IBEC, should be able to exercise maximum flexibility and discretion in their own particular markets in setting wage levels and non-wage benefits (see *IRN Report*, 1995, 16: 9). The existence of "high" legal minimum wages are seen as contributing to the high cost structure in Europe and reducing European competitiveness (IBEC, 1993). Not surprisingly, the success of recent national wage agreements is essentially due to the modest wage increases negotiated (Roche, this volume). A large proportion of wage costs in Ireland are due to taxes on labour, and IBEC, along with the Irish Congress of Trade Unions (ICTU), have advocated reductions in this area. Unlike ICTU, however, IBEC perceive the high level of labour costs as being caused "above all" by the expensive social security systems prevailing in Europe and Ireland which discourages the unemployed from rejoining the workforce because the size of benefits are too large relative to wage levels in employment (IBEC, 1993). Since the passing of the Single European Act in 1987, the European dimension of IBEC's role has expanded considerably. The act involved the establishment of a formal mechanism for "social dialogue" between the social partners:

labour, employers and government in the formulation of policy in the European Union. In this role, IBEC through UNICE, the European employer representative body, has vigorously opposed many of the directives emerging from the Social Action Programme (agreed in 1990) which were designed to implement the principles of the Social Charter. The Social Action Programme consists of 49 legally binding directives and recommendations aimed at "levelling up" employment rights in the European Union (Hourihan, this volume). The proliferation of legislation "on top of an already over-regulated market" was considered by IBEC to be unacceptable because of its impact on labour costs and work organisation practices (see IBEC, 1994a; IBEC, 1994b; *IRN Report*, 1995, 16: 9; *IRN Report*, 1995, 5: 16). However, IBEC's formal stance may be an exaggeration of the impact of the Social Action Programme on its members. In a survey of Irish firms in 1992 only a small number envisaged having to make major changes with the full implementation of the Social Charter.

TABLE 4.2: EMPLOYMENT PRACTICES AND THE SOCIAL CHARTER*

Employment Practice	Major change	Minor change	No change	Don't know
	%	%	%	%
Working hours/shifts	21.7	31.2	34.1	10.9
Use of part-time, temporary, fixed term contracts	3.6	23.9	48.6	17.4
Health and safety	15.2	40.6	29.7	10.9
Equal treatment of men/women	2.2	10.1	72.5	10.1
Procedures for consultation and participation of employees	19.6	27.5	32.6	17.4

N=269

* The question asked was: "Would the full implementation of the EC Social Charter require a change in your personnel policies in any of the areas below?"

Source: Price Waterhouse Cranfield Project, Department of Personnel and Employment Relations, University of Limerick.

The two frequently reported areas requiring major changes were working hours and employee participation and these accounted for only 20 per cent in both cases of companies surveyed. Despite the seeming difference of emphasis between members and the association, the role of IBEC in articulating members' interests at national and European level is likely to grow. In particular, the European dimension will become more important as the rules governing the use of labour and the rights of labour are increasingly harmonised in the European Union. IBEC's concern in the debate on harmonisation is chiefly one of reducing external rigidities in the external labour market. Deregulation of the labour market is, though, somewhat counter-balanced by a strong commitment to training and development of employees within companies which would be directed through em-ployer associations (IBEC, 1993). In the following sections we assess firm-level approaches to the management of labour. Our analysis of management strategy is guided by the framework in Table 4.1 which included: employment practices; investment in training; employee autonomy; and the evidence of change in firm-level industrial rela-tions.

EMPLOYMENT PRACTICES AT FIRM LEVEL

The core–periphery model of employment involves the breaking up of the existing hierarchical structure of the firm so that radically differ-ent employment policies can be pursued for different groups of work-ers. Within this scenario, the "core" is composed of full-time staff, en-joying relatively secure challenging jobs with good pay and employ-ment conditions, while the "periphery" is composed of an amalgam of temporary, part-time and contract groups with less favourable pay and employment conditions and less job security or training and pro-motion opportunities. To evaluate the extent to which Irish firms use a core–periphery employment strategy we draw on the national fig-ures detailing the incidence of atypical employment and a number of firm-level surveys. Labour force figures for the Irish labour market indicate an increased use of atypical forms of employment since 1980. Atypical employment is defined as any form of employment which deviates from full-time, permanent contracts of employment. It in-cludes; part-time workers, temporary and casual employment, fixed-term contracts, home-based work, government training schemes and sub-contracting. Both the incidence of part-time work and temporary employment have increased since 1979 (Dineen, 1992). Between 1983 and 1989 the proportion of the employed workforce (excluding the self-employed) on such contracts increased from 9.3 per cent to 12.7 per cent, representing an overall increase in the use of these forms of employment of 33 per cent, while the numbers employed in *regular* part-time work increased by 80 per cent. The increase in the use of atypical employment indicates that many firms are using these em-ployment forms as a mechanism to adjust labour supply to immediate changes in product demand. However, it should be noted that despite these increases, the majority of employees, 87 per cent, remained in standard employment in 1989. Table 4.3 reports the results of a survey of 269 public and private sector companies carried out in 1992.[8]

TABLE 4.3: PROPORTION OF WORK-FORCE ON NON-STANDARD CONTRACTS

	< 1%	1–10%	11–20%	> 20%	No. of Firms Responding
Cranfield Survey	%	%	%	%	
Part-time	49	37	7	7	216
Temp/Casual	31	52	11	6	225
Fixed Term	49	27	6	17	206
Home Work	97	2	1	-	127
Greenfield Site Survey[9]					
Temp/Casual	32	28	13	27	53

Source: Gunnigle, McMahon and Fitzgerald, 1994.

The more frequently used forms of employment, part-time work, temporary casual work and fixed-term contracts are still only a small proportion of total employment in the majority of companies. In only 14 per cent of the companies surveyed did part-time workers account for more than 10 per cent of employees, with the figure rising to 17 per cent for temporary employees and 23 per cent for fixed term contracts. A survey of 200 companies by Wickham (1993) confirms this relatively low usage of atypical employment forms. The study concluded that Ireland had a relatively low incidence of part-time and fixed-term contract work compared with the major European countries (see also Drew, 1990). Yet the survey also indicated that there had been a recent rise in the importance and use of non-standard employment but that this was confined to companies in which non-standard work was already well established. However, there is some evidence that non-standard employment is on the increase in the manufacturing sector which is traditionally associated with standard forms of employment. New medium/large companies setting up in Ireland between 1987 and 1992 appear to be using temporary/casual labour to a greater extent than established companies. It has been argued that greenfield sites offered firms unique opportunities in the 1980s to pursue a flexible employment strategy given slack labour markets and economic recession (Gunnigle, 1995). Indeed, this appears to be the case in relation to the use of temporary/casual workers with 40 per cent of new companies reporting that such workers accounted for more than 10 per cent of employees and in 27 per cent of companies for more than 20 per cent of all employees (Table 4.4). The Cranfield survey also indicates an increase in the use of part-time work, temporary work and fixed term contracts (Table 4.3).

Public sector establishments reported a greater increase in the use of all forms of atypical employment, except home-based work, than private sector establishments (Morley and Gunnigle, 1994).

TABLE 4.4: TRENDS IN ATYPICAL EMPLOYMENT ARRANGEMENTS

	Increased	Same	Decreased	Not Used	Missing
	%	%	%	%	%
Part-time Work	31.2	23.8	6.3	27.5	11.2
Temp/Casual Work	34.6	33.5	13.8	8.9	9.3
Fixed-Term Contract	30.9	26.0	3.3	27.9	11.9
Home-based Work	3.0	7.4	—	68.8	20.8
Sub-contracting	29.7	27.1	4.5	27.9	10.7

N=269

Source: Adapted from Morley and Gunnigle, 1994.

An examination of the employment strategy in three US electronics firms established in Ireland underlines the difficulties associated with the use of a core–periphery strategy (Geary, 1992). At two of the firms the proportion of temporary employees was kept at or below 10 per cent while in the third firm up to 70 per cent of production operatives were on temporary employment contracts. In the latter case the dependence on temporary labour generated tension and conflict between temporary and permanent employees. Management's preferred strategy in each firm was to "minimise" its dependence on temporary employees where possible. The high proportion of temporary employees in one company was not just a response to a volatile market situation, but was due to recruitment restrictions imposed by corporate headquarters in the United States. All three firms advanced similar reasons for limiting the number of temporary employees: the difficulty of training temporary workers, the potential of temporary labour to jeopardise management's efforts to maintain the commitment of the primary workforce and the difficulty of terminating temporary workers contracts once they have been employed (Geary, 1992). In general, peripheral employees tend to have lower levels of productivity, require closer supervision, have higher turnover rates and a lower commitment to the firm than core employees (Suttle, 1988; Flood, 1990). Keenan and Thom (1988) also highlight a number of practical problems associated with a core–periphery strategy. Firstly, they suggest that efforts to develop and implement the model can create more problems than the model actually solves, particularly where sub-contracted labour is being used as redundancies are occurring. Secondly, by having such a distinction in the work-force, the insecurity of employment and the lack of career prospects may stimulate resentment and frustration among peripheral workers. Furthermore, in terms of a societal cost, a two-tier work-force creates unhealthy distinctions. Moreover, such a distinction may lead to a further widening of the skills gap and future skill shortages, thus inhibiting national ability to compete with other industrialised nations.

Internal Functional Flexibility

Given the relatively low use of atypical employment forms and the associated difficulties and problems for firms, a strategy aimed at developing greater labour flexibility inside the firm would appear to offer substantially greater benefits. Cappelli and McKersie (1987) argue that for firms pursuing a "value-added" or "productivity-enhancing" approach (i.e. a strategy of reducing labour costs for firms experiencing increasing market pressure through the reform of existing work systems) the most important option available is to alter work rules through job redesign. While many firms automatically resort to cutting wages and benefits, this can have a quick and negative effect on morale which in turn affects productivity through a number of mechanisms such as absenteeism and turnover. In contrast, work rule changes are easier to implement than wage and benefit cuts, tend to become permanent (unlike wage cuts) and can be a key source of comparative cost advantage because they cannot be easily identified and copied by competitors (Cappelli and McKersie, 1987).[10] Such work rule changes can be viewed as a strategy to increase functional flexibility inside the firm.

Functional flexibility can be defined as the expansion of skills within a workforce, or the ability of firms to reorganise the competencies associated with jobs so that the job holder is willing and able to deploy such competencies across a broader range of tasks (Morley and Gunnigle, 1994). This process may result in employees moving into higher or lower skill areas, or a combination of both and is often referred to as multi-skilling. The extent of research in Ireland on changes in work rules and functional flexibility generally is rather meagre. This may be due to the difficulties of measuring changes in work rules and the complex web of work rules which are unique to each firm. From the Cranfield survey it is possible to address the broad trends in functional flexibility. A sizeable proportion of respondents reported that jobs in their companies had become more flexible especially in managerial and clerical occupations (Table 4.5).

TABLE 4.5: CHANGE IN THE SPECIFICATION OF JOBS*

	Management	Professional / Technical	Clerical	Manual
	%	%	%	%
More Specific	25	15	13	9
No Change	38	44	50	45
More Flexible	35	27	33	24
Don't Know/ missing	2	14	4	22

* Respondents were asked whether there had been a major change in the specification of jobs in their organisation in the last three years.

Source: Adapted from Morley and Gunnigle, 1994.

Despite the increases, it is notable that the majority of jobs are either unchanged or have become narrower.

In a study of 13 medium/large unionised manufacturing firms the personnel manager in ten of the companies believed that working practices had been made less restrictive in recent years, particularly in the area of work organisation (Turner and Morley, 1995). However, only six believed that they had achieved the optimum degree of flexibility from employees.

The most frequently cited areas in which greater flexibility occurred were less restrictions on the introduction of new technology, greater transferability between sections/departments/shifts, greater amounts of teamwork (usually as a result of reorganisation) and wider responsibility for quality. As one personnel manager put it:

> In recent years the views of management and unions have tended to converge somewhat more than in the past. This is occurring on the basis that change is necessary for survival. Shop stewards, more than

ever before, are beginning to understand the wider issues of company performance and competitiveness.

The area in which most organisations are finding it difficult to gain agreement appears to be multi-skilling. A majority of personnel managers interviewed maintained that the union limits management's freedom in this area, and in those organisations where negotiations on multi-skilling have taken place, almost invariably they have been long and protracted. As a result, a number of respondents emphasised the cost constraints of multi-skilling and relatedly the organisation's reluctance to upgrade employees. A majority also highlighted the lack of resources allocated to training and development as an additional factor limiting action in this area.

The evidence to date on this form of flexibility is relatively rare and is largely confined to manufacturing industry (Suttle, 1988). Some larger organisations have taken a number of initiatives in the area of multi-skilling, such as the ESB and TEAM Aer Lingus in the semi-state sector and Krups Engineering and Aughinish Alumina in the private sector. It has been argued (Gunnigle and Daly, 1992) that "add-skilling" or "extra-skilling" may be more appropriate descriptions of these developments than multi-skilling. This argument is based on the evidence that functional flexibility among skilled workers largely involves those categories receiving training in and agreeing to undertake other prescribed tasks in addition to their traditional trade, for example fitters undertaking electrical/instrumentation work. There is, of course, evidence of organisations claiming to have total functional flexibility in their operations. However, as Gunnigle and Daly (1992) note, such functional flexibility would appear to pertain only in unskilled assembly-type work where there is a minimal training requirement and it is thus relatively easy to deploy workers across a large range of tasks as required.

From the admittedly sparse data on functional flexibility reviewed here it is possible to advance two observations. Firstly, a significant proportion of firms in the private sector indicate that work rules are changing and becoming less restrictive and more flexible. Secondly, that these changes do not appear to involve any dramatic shifts such as in-depth multi-skilling of employees.

To summarise managerial approaches to labour flexibility: there is no evidence to support the extensive use of a core–periphery employment strategy in Irish firms. Neither, on the other hand, is there any compelling evidence that firms are achieving a high level of internal functional flexibility in terms of a radical restructuring of work rules such as the dismantling of traditional occupational boundaries. However, we would argue that on balance managerial strategies reflect in this area (whether voluntarily or not) a trend towards the resource approach to the management of labour rather than the utility approach.

EMPLOYEE AUTONOMY AND DISCRETION

Employee autonomy is a central feature of the resource model of labour management. Employee involvement and autonomy can be defined at two levels. Firstly, participation and discretion by the individual in the organisation and execution of the work (usually referred to as direct participation). The second level involves employees or their representatives having a formal input into the management of the enterprise (defined as indirect participation). Indirect participation, in the Irish context, is legislated for in the Worker Participation (State Enterprises) Acts of 1977 and 1988, which provide for both employee representation on the boards of the largest state-controlled companies and sub-board structures (see Kelly and Hourihan, this volume). There are no such provisions for direct participation though a resource model of labour management in the European context would likely include both direct and indirect participation.

Conditions must be right for increased employee discretion or direct participation to operate successfully. Indeed, in the foreword to *New Forms of Work Organisation* (ICTU, 1993), the General Secretary of ICTU, Peter Cassells, argued that:

> . . . the introduction of these new forms of work organisation requires a different style of management than normally practised in Ireland . . . work organisation and production methods that depend on training, motivation, flexibility and continuous improvement can only be developed and sustained by open participative management.

In many organisations, employee autonomy has become a virtual buzzword, but what it means in practice is often unclear. Dobbs (1993) suggests that while there is often agreement about the way an empowered employee should behave, there is little concern on which conditions are necessary for fostering enough involvement and restructuring a traditionally hierarchical organisation. Both the introduction of new forms of work practices such as quality circles and teamwork which are associated with increasing employee autonomy and discretion and the actual impact on employee jobs are poorly researched in Irish organisations.

A study carried out by the Irish Congress of Trade Unions revealed that most of the new forms of work had been introduced in the mid to late 1980s principally to increase productivity, reduce unit costs, to guarantee quality to customers and to have more flexible and adaptable operations (ICTU 1993: 28). Among the range of initiatives relating to employee autonomy and discretion introduced in the twelve companies studied were: employee involvement programmes designed to encourage employees to make suggestions and generally take a greater interest in and ownership of their work; communication and information–sharing programmes; individualising initiatives relating to individual appraisals; investment in training; reward system modification including increases for co-operation with on-going change, knowledge–based pay, and share ownership schemes; and a range of manufacturing initiatives relating to total quality management and world class manufacturing. The introduction of the new forms of work was initiated by management to improve efficiency and productivity for competitive reasons. Unions and workplace representatives found themselves largely responding to management proposals for change. The involvement of unions and representatives arose either in relation to formal agreements relating to structural matters and house agreements on co-operation with on-going change, or in relation to information and consultation on the implementation of initiatives (ICTU, 1993). The researchers identified a number of factors which determine the extent to which the initiatives have been successfully implemented. The key factors were competitive circumstances, degree of management understanding and commitment to the initiatives, parent company and customer pressures and the relationship between management, employees and workplace representatives. In relation to the latter the research identified three types of trust relationships in the companies sampled. Three of the companies had low trust/traditional adversarial relationships, four had more positive relationships but there continued to be a significant degree of mutual suspicion and the remaining had co-operative relationships. The evidence collected in the study pointed to a positive relationship between the sophistication and depth of the initiative and the degree of trust evident in the relationship.

A more detailed analysis of changes in work structures is available from Turner and Morley (1995). In a survey of 400 employees across nine companies respondents were asked to assess whether their jobs had improved along four dimensions: (a) that work had become more interesting; (b) is less tightly supervised than before; (c) gives more freedom to decide how to do work; and (d) is more enjoyable to do. As

Table 4.6 indicates a large proportion of employees on each dimension believed that their job had changed in recent years.

TABLE 4.6: CHANGES IN WORK STRUCTURE

Dimensions	White Collar		Blue Collar	
	Yes	No	Yes	No
	%		%	
1. Job more interesting	81.2	18.8	53.3	46.7
2. Less tightly supervised	48.5	51.5	39.4	60.6
3. More freedom in work	60.0	40.0	45.9	54.1
4. More enjoyable to do	52.9	47.1	44.2	55.8

Source: Turner and Morley, (1995)

These results do not differ significantly according to age or gender. The four dimensions were subsequently grouped together as one factor (alpha = 0.68) measuring the extent of improvement in respondents' jobs. Is this indicative of a resource or a utility perspective on the management of labour? The limited evidence available here appears to indicate some evidence of the former. However, more research is necessary to confirm this.

EMPLOYEE INVESTMENT POLICIES

A strong emphasis on training and development as a means of securing competitive advantage is a central feature of the resource approach to the management of labour. Over the past three decades, Ireland has been the focus of much debate concerning the lack of competitiveness of indigenous firms in the traded area, and the consequences of this problem for economic growth, employment and the balance of payments (Dineen 1992; Heraty 1992). However, apart from such apparent problems as the lack of indigenous raw materials and peripheral location to markets, factors internal to the firm which are also perceived as weaknesses included poorly trained managers and an inadequate investment in human resources (Galvin, 1988; Roche and Tansey, 1992). Specifically, the Culliton Report (1992) argued that the low profitability of private industry during the prolonged recession of the 1980s led to a skills gap in many industries and an overall lack of investment in human capital.

Aside from a weak economic performance, Irish companies (unlike some of their counterparts in other European Countries), are not required to invest a minimum proportion of annual turnover, or its equivalent, on updating the skills and knowledge of their employees. Nor are they obliged to make known the amount they spend annually on the training and development function. In this respect it is difficult to establish any definitive statistics on training and development since organisations have differing perceptions of what constitutes training. Also, many companies tend to rely on informal training strategies and mechanisms, further compounding the problem of quantifying training expenditure.

Expenditure on Training and Development

Heraty's (1992) exploratory survey of training and development indicated that expenditure (the proportion of their company's annual salaries and wages budget spent on training and development activities) varies widely with organisational size and sector, with the highest frequency (27 per cent) being recorded in the 0.51–1.00 per cent budget bracket. Expenditure ranged from less than £30,000 in smaller organisations to as high as £1 million in larger concerns. Smaller organisations are obviously spending less on training and development than their larger counterparts. Clearly, these figures must be treated with some caution, both for the reasons alluded to above, and also because respondents were asked to indicate expenditure levels within given budget brackets. More significantly the expenditure on training and development appears to be increasing over the last three years (Gunnigle et al. 1994).

Training expenditure increased across all categories of employees, with slightly higher increases recorded for managerial and professional/technical employees (Figure 4.2). This trend is broadly similar for both public and private sector respondents, union and non-union establishments and indigenous and foreign-owned companies. Again, larger organisations reported higher increases than did their smaller counterparts, particularly for managerial/professional employees. Medium-sized organisations employing between 300 and 500 employees reported the greatest increases which may indicate that, while organisation size is important, other factors such as the external environment, may also account for increased spending on employee development.

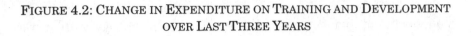

FIGURE 4.2: CHANGE IN EXPENDITURE ON TRAINING AND DEVELOPMENT OVER LAST THREE YEARS

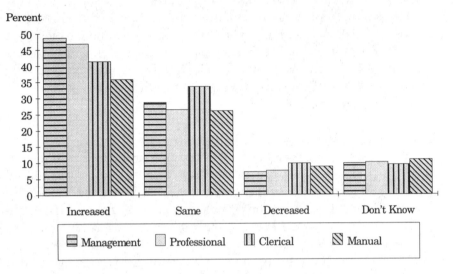

N= 269

Source: Adapted from Gunnigle, Flood, Morley and Turner, 1994.

The distribution of expenditure in terms of the number of days' training received by categories of employee tends to decrease as one moves down the organisation hierarchy. Managerial employees tend to receive between 3–5 days (36 per cent) and 5–10 days (32 per cent) of training per year. When cross-tabulated with organisation sector, the results reveal that managerial employees in the private sector are more likely to receive at least 5 days training than are employees in the public sector (29.4 per cent as against 17.2 per cent). This trend is broadly similar across organisation sizes except in the case of managerial employees in companies employing less than 100 employees — here they receive between 1 and 3 days formal training, significantly less than managerial employees in larger firms who averaged 5–10 days. Results from Heraty's (1992) survey are broadly similar, with over half of the companies surveyed (54 per cent) indicating that managerial employees receive at least 8 days formal training per year, and that all other categories of employees receive at least 1–3 days training. Management development was undertaken by 76 per cent of respondents.

From the evidence available it appears that investment in employee training and development has increased reflecting a trend towards the resource approach to the management of labour. The expenditure on training at firm level has increased across all categories of employees, with slightly higher increases recorded for managerial and professional/technical employees. More general macro-level trends in the numbers entering higher education in the OECD countries would appear to support the emergence of a knowledge-based work-force. For example, the proportion of eligible school leavers in Ireland entering full-time third level education increased from 10 per cent in 1965 to 35 per cent in 1991 (see HEA, 1995). The evidence is that the trend in the proportion of eligible school leavers entering higher education is likely to continue in all the OECD countries.

CHANGES IN EMPLOYEE ATTITUDES AND INDUSTRIAL RELATIONS

The resource approach to the management of labour is associated with the development of a skilled, flexible and motivated work-force (see Walton, 1985; Beer et al., 1984). Since a favourable working climate is viewed as an essential prerequisite for labour flexibility inside the firm (see Dastmalchian et al., 1991) it implies union management relations based on trust and co-operation. Conversely, industrial relations in the utility approach to labour are prone to be adversarial with low levels of trust between the parties (Fox, 1974). The trends, noted earlier, in product markets, global competition and technological developments, it is argued, has created both the basis and necessity for a new order of industrial relations (Kochan et al., 1986; Piore and Sabel, 1984; for a more critical appraisal see Hyman, 1989; Terry, 1989; Basset, 1986; Dunn, 1990). This new order of industrial relations is characterised at the collective level by union and management co-operation and a "new realism" among employees of the impact of product markets on wages and job security. The conflict of interest inherent in the employment relationship is transposed to a conflict which originates in the market place and not inside the firm. Thus employees are not in conflict with their employer but with his competitors. A new order in industrial relations implies both a shift in employee attitudes and a change in industrial relations patterns away from the traditional adversarial style identified by the report of the commission of inquiry on industrial relations in 1981. To assess the evidence for change in Irish relations we draw on a study of 13 medium/large unionised manufacturing companies which included a survey of employees in nine of the companies (Turner and Morley, 1995). There were significant economic and industrial relations changes in Irish manufacturing from 1980. Productivity per worker almost doubled between 1980 and 1989, the number employed in manufacturing declined during this decade and the number of strikes dwindled to negligible levels after 1990 (Turner and Morley, 1995; Foley and McAleese, 1991; Brannick and Doyle, this volume). However, it remains to be shown whether this industrial peace has shifted industrial relations away from the traditional adversarial approach towards more co-operative labour–management relations.

EMPLOYEE PERCEPTIONS OF MANAGEMENT

Relations between management and labour are commonly gauged by the extent of a "them-and-us" attitude among employees and management, that is, whether management and employees are on opposite sides or the same side.[11] It is possible to compare the results of a recent survey (Turner and Morley, 1995) with a previous survey carried out in 1979 (Whelan, 1982) measuring this question. Whelan (1982) concluded that Irish workers displayed extremely high levels of distrust in management generally. Overall only 38.5 per cent of workers surveyed believed that workers and management were on the same side. This compared quite unfavourably with survey findings in Britain. In Goldthorpe et al.'s (1968) study of affluent care workers in Luton, the majority of workers (73 per cent) believed they were on the same side as management. Similarly, Wedderburn and Crampton (1972) reported 80 per cent of the sampled workers agreeing with the statement and Cotgrove and Vampley (1972) in their survey of process workers in high technology areas such as chemicals and oil processing plants, recorded a positive response of 70 per cent. Turner and Morley's (1995) survey indicates little change in the levels of trust between workers and management between 1979 and 1993.

Indeed, an even smaller proportion of employees, 30 per cent compared to 38.5 per cent, believed that management and workers are on the same side. More surprisingly, the percentage of white collar workers agreeing with the statement declined from 41 per cent in 1979 to 24.5 per cent in the 1993 survey. A majority of employees, excluding professional workers, apparently perceived a conflict of interests in the employment relationship. However, a majority of employees (56 per cent) also believed that full teamwork was possible in their company (Turner and Morley, 1995). A large number of employees would appear to have made a distinction between the conflict of interest inherent in the employment relationship and the possibility of co-operation with management. While approximately 57 per cent of manual workers believed that management and workers were not on the same side, 39 per cent of this group of workers, nevertheless, believed that full teamwork was possible. A majority of respondents also believe that management in their companies behaved fairly towards employees. It is particularly notable that almost 54 per cent of unskilled manual workers agreed with this statement. Finally, 60 per cent of all respondents agreed with the statement that employees and management co-operate in their company in order to compete against companies with similar products. Only 22 per cent disagreed with the statement.

Some of the evidence from Turner and Morley's (1995) study lends support to the view that a new realism has emerged in these companies. A large proportion of employees across all occupations believed that they were working harder now than in pervious years. The majority of employees indicated that full teamwork was possible and also that employees and management co-operated in order to compete against other companies. However, there was no evidence of an ideological crisis for unions. Excluding professional workers, a majority of employees believe that a conflict of interest existed between management and workers. Although a majority of employees indicated that they were working harder, there was no clear relationship between increased work effort and market awareness and, more significantly, a comparison of employee attitudes towards management between 1979 and 1994 revealed little change in employee perceptions of a "them-and-us" divide.

CHANGES IN INDUSTRIAL RELATIONS PATTERNS

In order to evaluate the changes in the pattern of industrial relations over time, companies were measured in terms of a range of processes and styles using Purcell's (1981) four ideal typical patterns of industrial relations. Two patterns are associated with antagonistic relations between management and labour: uninhibited antagonism and antagonistic constitutionalism; and two patterns with co-operative relations: co-operative constitutionalism and adaptive co-operation. According to Purcell (1981) these four patterns are ideal typical styles and unlikely to completely correspond to real situations but are a useful heuristic device allowing comparison between companies and also within a company over time. In the *uninhibited antagonism* pattern, industrial relations are conducted in an ad-hoc, conflict-based manner, with bargaining advantages frequently exploited by either side when circumstances permit. The relationship is marked by mutual suspicion and distrust. *Antagonistic constitutionalism* prevails where the agreed procedures and institutions are used as a means of expressing the distrust and aggression which exists between both parties. Management tends to adopt an inflexible and formal plant-wide industrial relations procedures and see this as their best defence against the unions whom they distrust but are forced to deal with. *Co-operative constitutionalism* is characterised by high trust and co-operation between the parties which takes place within the framework of comprehensive agreements. Procedure agreements are seen more as a flexible arrangement than a rigid framework. The union is accepted as a necessary partner in the plant by most managers, and conversely the union officers see the company and its management as generally trustworthy.

The dominant characteristic in the *adaptive co-operation* pattern is high trust and co-operation between negotiators, which extends to institutional trust but is embodied in the personal relationship between a few key people on either side, supported by their advisers. There are few, if any, formal written agreements, especially of a procedural nature, or if there are, they are largely ignored, being replaced by the informal, adaptive relationship between the negotiators.

To assess whether a new industrial relations was emerging in the companies studied, that is, a shift to more co-operative labour management relations, a number of industrial relations processes were measured: the bargaining arrangements in each company; the extent of formalisation in union-management relationships; the manner in which issues are regulated; and lastly, union-related processes (see Purcell, 1981).[12] Companies were measured both in terms of their present pattern of industrial relations and the pattern prevailing approximately ten years previously. There was a distinctive shift from extreme antagonistic relations towards less antagonistic and more co-operative-style relations. Six companies had a co-operative constitutional pattern of industrial relations compared to three in the past. More significantly only one company still had an extremely antagonistic pattern of relations. Five companies experienced a *substantial* positive shift in their industrial relations pattern during the 1980s. Three of these companies changed from antagonistic to co-operative relations, one company experienced increased co-operative relations and the remaining company changed from inhibited to constitutional antagonism (for a discussion of the causes of these shifts, see Turner and Morley, 1995: chap. 4–5). Despite such shifts, six companies remained in the category of antagonistic relations, albeit of a lower intensity. There was least change in managerial perceptions of union presence in the firm. Personnel managers were asked to indicate the nature of the relationship between management and unions under three categories: (a) avoidance or marginalisation of the union; (b) acceptance of unions but unions need to be kept under control and at arm's length; and (c) acceptance of the union as a legitimate and trusted bargaining partner. Unions in nine companies were perceived as organisations which needed to be kept at arm's length while the union was regarded as a trusted bargaining partner in four companies. This represented a significant shift from the prevailing pattern in the past when only one company regarded the union as a trusted bargaining partner. Compared to other industrial relations areas, union processes appear to have changed least during the 1980s. In this vein it is notable that only two of the companies had initiated any forms of union-management representative structures of any type.

While the direction of change in employee effort levels, employee attitudes and patterns of industrial relations in the companies studied is indicative of some shift towards the kind of labour–management relations associated with a resource approach to managing labour, the extent of change appears to be relatively modest. Whether this represents a long term evolution in Irish industrial relations — a pattern evident, according to Schuster (1990), in the advanced industrial societies — or a cyclical process, as Purcell (1981) argues, in which the conflict of interest inherent in the employment relationship will come to be reasserted, remains unclear.

CONCLUSION

Long-term shifts in global competition, industrial technologies and product markets have created a business environment which, despite the increased market pressure on firms, has increased the range of business and human resource strategies available to management. In terms of the firm's labour strategy, the task of management is to arrange workplace relations and personnel practices in the most efficient manner for achieving company goals such as profit maximisation. However, there are both mutual and conflicting interests in the relationship between employer and employee which influences management's approach to the use of labour. Management's need to control labour in the production process arises because of the basic conflict of interests inherent in the employment relationship and the indeterminate nature of labour effort. Essentially, management face a dilemma between ensuring the most profitable organisation of work and gaining the commitment and co-operation of employees. As we have argued, labour strategies can be distinguished in terms of the different emphases given to a variety of employment practices used to secure an efficient work organisation and the commitment and co-operation of employees. A utility approach to the management of labour seeks to use employees in a flexible and cost-effective manner reacting to market fluctuations by a rapid adjustment of employment numbers. Commitment to the firm is sought only from a core of permanent employees and the organisation of production and use of technology is arranged to ensure that jobs are routine and low-skill and employees are easily disposed of and replaced as required. Alternatively, the resource approach is premised on the assumption that the efficient organisation of work is achieved *through* the active commitment and co-operation of labour and the emphasis is on investing in employees as a potentially rewarding resource for the firm.

Overall, the evidence presented in this chapter supports some shift towards a resource approach to the management of labour. Where information is available there is some consistency in the findings. There is no evidence to support any comprehensive emergence of the flexible firm scenario as prescribed in the core–periphery employment model, while there is some evidence of an increase in internal functional flexibility. Employee autonomy and discretion in the form of direct participation would also appear to be increasing, albeit at a relatively slow pace. Investment in employees also appears to have increased. This trend is broadly similar for both the public and private sectors, union and non-union, foreign and indigenously owned establishments. Predictably, the number of days' training is highest for managerial employees and lowest for manual categories. Finally, in relation to firm-level industrial relations, the direction of change in the case study evidence presented here is consistent with the kind of labour–management relations associated with a resource approach to managing labour.

A critical question concerns the social consequences of the utility and resource approaches to the management of labour both for the individual employee and the general welfare. Salaman (1993) argues that particular employment arrangements can have implications for societal divisions through the distribution of many of the psychological experiences and the material resources which constitute the determinants of class. Choices about skill levels, supervisory control techniques, employee autonomy and monetary rewards determine the employee's experience of work which either reinforces existing class structures *or* restructures work and work relations in a manner which reduces existing social divisions. The utility approach is more likely to reproduce existing social divisions in the workplace as management respond opportunistically to a slack labour market and/or a disorganised workforce to implement strategies which are most effective in the short term in maximising profitability. Alternatively, the resource approach has the potential to restructure work relations in ways which do not reproduce expected class experiences through the redesign of work to increase skill levels, greater employee autonomy and responsibility for their job, the dismantling of traditional hierarchical and bureaucratic organisational structures and a reduction of income differentials within the firm. However, for this potential to be realised some form of joint regulation is required which involves employees and their representatives having an input into decisions in personnel areas such as training and development, long term manpower policy and manpower deployment; and in financial and production areas such as investment policy, product design and productivity issues. A jointly regulated resource strategy also has positive social and economic outcomes at the societal level. By increasing the stock of skills available in the economy and reducing social divisions in the workplace the resource approach has the potential to improve the long-term efficiency and productivity of the labour force and achieve a high level of social cohesion at the firm level.

APPENDIX

Employer associations are organisations which represent employer interests and play a valuable role in both national and company-level industrial relations. In 1995, Department of Enterprise and Employment records indicated that there were 11 employer associations holding negotiation licences representing a total of 9,419 employer members. The largest employer association is the Irish Business and Employers' Confederation (IBEC). Representing the interests of 3,234 employer members' it was formed in 1 January 1993 following the merger of the Federation of Irish Employers (FIE) and the Confederation of Irish Industry (CII). From an industrial relations perspective IBEC performs two central functions for its members: it provides an advisory/information service and it represents and articulates members interests at local, national and European level.

The organisational structure of IBEC is presented in Figure 4.A1. The role of the general membership of affiliated organisations is to elect the General Council comprising 250 representatives from the Confederation's regions, sectors, and industry consultative groupings.

FIGURE 4.A1: ORGANISATIONAL STRUCTURE OF IBEC

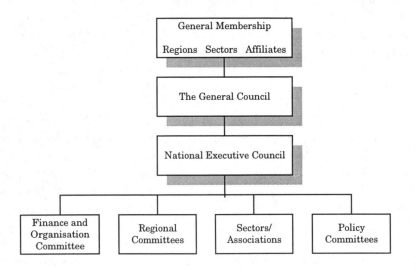

Source: Daly, 1994.

The General Council determines overall policy and appoints the National Executive Council. The National Executive Council is primarily responsible for formulating policy within the overall objectives of the Confederation and appointing the key specialist committees and the permanent secretariat in connection with the director-general and federation secretary. The director-general and the full-time staff are responsible for carrying out the primary activities and services of the association (Gunnigle et al., 1995).

IBEC provide a comprehensive range of services to its members in the following areas (Daly, 1994):

- **Employee and Industrial Relations** — Advice is provided on employee-related issues

- **Legal Support** — Provides assistance on employment law problems

- **Research and Information Service** — Administers information and advice on all aspects of employment legislation, personnel policies and procedures, pay and conditions of employment and international affairs

- **Economic Affairs Division** — Monitors and assesses the economic climate and responds to economic developments as they arise

- **Occupational Health and Safety Service** — Provides advice and information on all aspects of safety and conducts safety audits

- **Training and Management Development Service** — Specialist training and development services are designed to meet the needs of individual members

- **Employee Relations Service** — Suggests practical and innovative approaches to personnel management issues

- **Equality Service** — Members are advised on the legal requirements to be met under equality legislation and given assistance on dealing with discrimination claims.

These services are perceived by members as the most useful function of the association (for a review of the structure and objectives of employer associations, including IBEC, see Gunnigle et al., 1995). The representative role of IBEC occurs at three levels, local, national and European. At the local level, representation takes the form of involvement and support for members in third-party processes of mediation, arbitration and local negotiations. However, as Table 4A.1 indicates, between 1983 and 1993 the demand for local representation declined in all third-party situations.

TABLE 4.A1: IBEC INVOLVEMENT IN THIRD-PARTY PROCESSES

Activity	No. of Cases per Year		
	1983	*1993*	*1983-93 % change*
Labour court investigations	460	219	- 52
Labour court conciliations	1,062	765	- 28
Employment Appeals Tribunal	265	235	- 11
Rights Commissioner	439*	289	- 34
Consultation with members	7,095	4,737	- 33
Trade union negotiations	3,414	1,220	- 64

* 1984 figures.

Source: IBEC annual reports for 1983 and 1993.

The decline in activity in support of local negotiations in member firms was probably a result of the resumption of national wage agreements after 1987. Centralised wage agreements serve to increase the representative role of employer associations at national level, allowing them a substantial input into the formulation of government social and economic policy (see Roche, this volume).

Footnotes

[1] An example of this is provided by a German company, Bayer Diagnostics, located in Dublin (*IRN Report*, 1995, 11:14–5). Formerly Technicon, the plant was bought by Bayer in 1990. Severe market pressure threatened to close the company unless major changes were implemented. The measures taken were: voluntary redundancies of 120 supervisors; a pay cut up to £70 per week; annual leave reduced by five days; attendance bonus scrapped; and a new reduced grading structure. Altogether costs were cut by 32 per cent. At the same time the company emphasised the development of employees, investing 5 per cent of payroll costs in training and encouraging further education for employees.

[2] Take, for example, the Danish cleaning group International Service System (ISS), who are now the second-largest company in the contract cleaning business in Ireland. In an industrial sector which is traditionally associated with low wages, non-standard employment contracts and poor working conditions, ISS run extensive training courses (mainly funded from EU grants) for its staff and customers and seeks a co-operative relationship with trade unions (Gerald Flynn: *Sunday Tribune* Business Section, 9 April 1995: 3). This resource approach to employees is a result of ISS's business strategy which targets its services at organisations which require specialist expertise such as hi-tech manufacturing plants and hospitals.

[3] As Edwards (1979) and Jacoby (1984) have shown the development of internal labour markets (secure employment, career ladders, standard payment systems and fringe benefits) in the United States reflect the outcome of worker struggle, political pressures and union bargaining as much as any efficiency considerations and were not a managerial innovation but were imposed from below. Empirical research also indicates that the presence and strength of trade unions in firms compared to non-union firms affects the existence and extent of internal labour markets across similar industries and controlling for structural features such as size and workforce skills (Pfeffry and Cohen, 1984; Sibert and Addison, 1991; Turner, 1994).

[4] Although the number of actual working hours are detailed in the employment contract there are many occasions when management expect employ-

ees to increase their effort levels particularly in service industries where business may fluctuate during the day. Also for many white-collar workers in private sector organisations (notably white-collar professional and administrative employees) the hours stipulated in the employment contract merely sets the base hours to be worked. In practice these employees are "expected" to work many extra unpaid hours in order to fit in with the prevailing organisational culture and qualify for promotion in the future.

[5] As Blyton and Turnbull (1994) observe the employer is interested in the actual performance of work in terms of the physical, mental and emotional labour expended at work. In service-type industries where direct customer contact is a central feature of company business emotional labour can be deemed to be integral to business success. Hochshild (1983:7) defines emotional labour as "the management of feeling to create a publicly observable facial and body display". It is a resource used not in pursuit of fulfilment as in everyday life but to make money and requires employees to induce or suppress feelings in order to sustain "the outward countenance that produces the proper state of mind" in the customer.

[6] Among the developed industrial countries the labour market in the United States is perceived to approximate most closely to a deregulated and flexible labour market. Pay bargaining is decentralised and in a majority of cases pay is agreed individually between employer and employee rather than collectively; employment legislation is minimal — for example, no restrictions on dismissals and no provision for severance — as a result geographical mobility and rates of job turnover are higher in the US than other OECD countries (OECD, 1986).

[7] IBEC represents approximately 4,000 employers, employing 300,000 employees. Given the position of IBEC as the central employer's association, our subsequent discussion focuses on its role in Irish industrial relations (see also appendix).

[8] This survey was part of the Price Waterhouse Cranfield Project which covered 15 European countries. The research centre is based at the Cranfield School of Management in the UK. The Irish survey was co-ordinated through the University of Limerick and directed by Patrick Gunnigle.

[9] The data reported here comes from a survey of all companies employing more than 100 employees (53 in total) which were established in Ireland in the years 1987–1992 carried out by P. Gunnigle, Dept. of Personnel and Employment Relations, University of Limerick.

[10] Cappelli and McKersie (1987) group work rules into rules relating to *deployment* (e.g. hiring, promotion, transfers, layoffs and scheduling), *production standards* (manning levels, effort levels and work pace) and *compensation systems* (wage rates, incentives, wage structures).

[11] Often referred to as the "football team" test question and regularly used in employee surveys (for comprehensive reviews see Ramsay, 1975 and Ramsay et al., 1990). Whelan's (1982) survey of 1,000 workers in the Dublin region in 1979 used a team analogy question to measure employee attitudes towards management. The question used to measure them-and-us attitudes in Whelan's survey were phrased in a slightly different manner in Turner and Morley's survey (see Chap. 3: 71).

[12] Case material on these areas was obtained through interviews with the personnel manager in each company, with shop stewards and line manager interviews providing a supportive source of information. Personnel managers were provided with a four-point scale for each industrial relations area and asked to indicate the appropriate position of their company. Each position corresponded to one of the four industrial relations patterns, though this was not disclosed to the interviewee.

References

Basset, P. (1986): *Strike Free*, London: MacMillan.

Beer, M., Spector, B., Lawrence, P.R., Mills, D.Q. and Walton, R.E. (1984): *Managing Human Assets*, New York: Collier MacMillan.

Blyton, P. and Turnbull, P. (1994): *The Dynamics of Employee Relations*, London: MacMillan.

Bowles, S. (1985): "The Production Process in a Competitive Economy: Walrasian, Neo-Hollesian and Marxian Models, *American Economic Review*, 75 (1): 16–36.

Brown, W. and Nolan, P. (1988): "Wages and Labour Productivity: The Contribution of Industrial Relations Research to the Understanding of Pay Determination", *British Journal of Industrial Relations*, 26 (3): 339–61.

Cappelli, P. and McKersie, R. (1987): "Management Strategy and the Redesign of Workrules", *Journal of Management Studies*, 24: 441–62.

Cotgrove, S. and Vampley, C. (1972): "Technology, Class and Politics: The Case of Process Workers", *Sociology*, (VI).

Culliton, T. (1992): *A Time For Change: Industrial Policies for the 1990s*, Report of the Industrial Policy Review Group, Dublin: Government Stationery Office.

Daly, A. (1994): "Representing Employers: The Irish Business and Employers Confederation" in T. V. Murphy and W. K. Roche (eds.) *Irish Industrial Relations in Practice*, Dublin: Oak Tree Press.

Dastmalchian, A., Blyton, P. and Adamson, R. (1991): *The Climate of Workplace Relations*, London: Routledge.

Dineen, D. (1992): "Atypical Work Patterns in Ireland: Short-Term Adjustments or Fundamental Changes?", *Administration*, 40 (3): 248–74.

Dobbs, J. (1993): "The Empowerment Environment", *Training and Development*, February: 55–7.

Drew, E. (1990): *Who Needs Flexibility? Part-time Working: The Irish Experience*, Dublin: Employment Equality Agency.

Dunn, S. (1990): "Root Metaphor in the Old and New Industrial Relations", *British Journal of Industrial Relations*, 28: 1–31.

Edwards, P. (1979): *Contested Terrain*, New York: Basic Books.

Edwards, P.K. (1986): *Conflict at Work: A Materialist Analysis of Workplace Relations*, London: Blackwell.

European Commission (1994a): "Growth, Competitiveness, Employment: The Challenges and Ways Forward into the 21st Century", *White Paper*, Luxembourg: Office for Official Publications of the European Communities.

European Commission (1994b): "European Social Policy — A Way Forward for the Union", *White Paper*, Luxembourg: Office for Official Publications of the European Communities.

Flood, P. (1990): "Atypical Employment: Core–Periphery Manpower Strategies — The Implications for Corporate Culture", *Industrial Relations News:* 9–10.

Foley, A. and McAleese, D. (1991): *Overseas Industry in Ireland*, Dublin: Gill and MacMillan.

Fox, A. (1974): *Beyond Contract: Work, Power and Trust Relations*, London: Faber and Faber.

Friedman, A. (1977): *Industry and Labour*, London: MacMillan.

Galvin, P. (1988): *Managers for Ireland: The Case for the Development of Irish Managers,* Report of the Advisory Committee on Management Training and Development, Dublin: Government Stationery Office.

Geary, J. (1992): "Employment Flexibility and Human Resource Management: The Case of Three American Electronic Plants", *Work, Employment and Society*, 6 (2): 251–70.

Goldthorpe, J., Lockwood, P., Beckhoffer, F. and Platt, J. (1968): *The Affluent Worker: Industrial Attitudes and Behaviour*, Cambridge: Cambridge University Press.

Guest, D. (1987): "Human Resource Management and Industrial Relations", *Journal of Management Studies*, 24 (5): 503–21.

Gunnigle, P. (1995): "Collectivism and the Management of Industrial Relations in Greenfield Sites", *Human Resource Management Journal*, 5: (3) 24–40.

Gunnigle, P., Flood, P., Morley, M. and Turner, T. (1994): *Continuity and Change in Irish Employee Relations,* Dublin: Oak Tree Press.

Gunnigle, P., McMahon, G. and Fitzgerald, G. (1995): *Industrial Relations in Ireland: Theory and Practice*, Dublin: Gill and MacMillan.

Gunnigle, P. and Daly, A. (1992): "Craft Integration and Flexible Working Practices", *Industrial and Commercial Training*, 24 (10) 10–17.

Hakim, C. (1990): "Core and Periphery in Employer's Workforce Strategies: Evidence from the 1987 ELUS Survey", *Work, Employment and Society*, 4 (2): 157–88.

HEA (1995): *Interim Report of the Steering Committee's Technical Working Report, Steering Committee on the Future of Higher Education*, Dublin: Higher Education Authority.

Heraty, N. (1992): "Training and Development: A Study of Practices in Irish Based Companies", mimeo, University of Limerick.

Hochshild, A. (1983): *The Managed Heart: Commercialisation of Human Feeling*, Berkeley: University of California Press.

Hyman, R. (1989): "Dualism and Division in Labour Strategies" in R. Hyman (ed.), *The Political Economy of Industrial Relations*, London: MacMillan.

IBEC (1993): "European Social Policy — Options for the Union: IBEC's Preliminary Response", December, Dublin: Irish Business and Employers Confederation.

IBEC News (1994A): "Policy Contradictions", September, Dublin: Irish Business and Employers Confederation.

IBEC (1994B): *EU Social Policy: A Guide for Employers*, December, Dublin: Irish Business and Employers Confederation.

ICTU (1993): *New Forms of Work Organisation: Options for Unions*, Dublin: Irish Congress of Trade Unions.

Industrial Relations News Report (1988–1995): *IRN Report*.

Jacoby, S. (1984): "The Development of Internal Labour Markets in American Manufacturing Firms" in P. Osterman (ed.), *Internal Labour Markets*, Cambridge, Mass.: MIT Press.

Katz, H. and Kochon, T. (1992): *An Introduction to Collective Bargaining and Industrial Relations*, New York: McGraw-Hill.

Keenan, J. and Thom, A. (1988): "The Future through the Keyhole: Some Thoughts on Employment Patterns", *Personnel Review*, 17 (1): 20–4.

Kochan, T., Katz, H. and McKersie, R. (1986): *The Transformation of American Industrial Relations*, New York: Basic Books.

Leibenstein, H. (1987): *Inside the Firm: The Inefficiencies of Hierarchy*, Cambridge, Mass: Harvard University Press.

Marchington, M. and Parker, P. (1990): *Changing Patterns of Employee Relations*, Hemel Hempstead: Harvester Wheatsheaf.

Marshall, R. (1992): "Work Organisation, Unions and Economic Performance" in L. Mishel and P. Voos (eds.), *Unions and Economic Competitiveness*, New York: M.E. Sharpe Inc.

Mitchell, J. and Zaidi, M. (1991): "International Pressures on Industrial Relations: Macroeconomics and Social Concertation" in T. Treu (ed.), *Participation in Public Policy Making: The Role of Trade Unions and Employer Associations*, Berlin and New York: W. De Gruyter.

Morley, M. and Gunnigle, P. (1994): "Trends in Flexible Working Patterns" in P. Gunnigle, P. Flood, M. Morley and T. Turner, *Continuity and Change in Irish Employee Relations*, Dublin: Oak Tree Press.

OECD, (1986): *Flexibility in the Labour Market: The Current Debate*, Paris: Organisation for Economic Co-operation and Development.

Pfeffry, J. and Cohen, Y. (1984): "Determinants of Internal Labour Markets in Organisations", *Administrative Science Quarterly*, 29: 55–72.

Piore, M. and Sabel, C. (1984): *The Second Industrial Divide: Prospects for Prosperity*, New York: Basic Books.

Porter, M. (1985): *Competitive Advantage: Creating and Sustaining Superior Performance*, New York: Free Press.

Purcell, J. (1981): *Good Industrial Relations: Theory and Practice*, London: MacMillan.

Purcell, J. (1989): "The Impact of Corporate Strategy on Human Resource Management", in J. Storey (ed.), *New Perspectives on Human Resource Management*, London: Routledge.

Ramsay, H, (1975): "Firms and Football Teams", *British Journal of Industrial Relations*, 13 (3): 396–400.

Ramsay, H. (1990): "Options for Workers: Owner or Employee?", in G. Jenkins and M. Poole (eds.), *New Forms of Ownership*, London: Routledge.

Roche, F. and Tansey, P. (1992): *Industrial Training in Ireland*, Dublin: Government Stationery Office.

Roche, W. and Turner, T. (1995): "The Human Resource Policy Sophistication of Organisations in Ireland: Markets and Internal Influences", Working Paper No: IRHR 95/1 Dublin: Business Research Programme, Graduate School of Business, University College Dublin.

Rubery, J. and Wilkinson, F. (1994): "Introduction" in J. Rubery and F. Wilkinson (eds.), *Employer Strategy and the Labour Market*, Oxford: Oxford University Press.

Rubery, J. (1994): "Internal and External Labour Markets: Towards an Integrated Analysis", in J. Rubery and F. Wilkinson (eds.), *Employer Strategy and the Labour Market*, Oxford: Oxford University Press.

Salaman, G. (1993): "Work Design and Corporate Structures" in J. Allen, P. Braham and P. Lewis (eds.), *Political and Economic Forms of Modernity*, Cambridge: Polity Press.

Schuler, R. (1988): "Organisational Strategy and Organisational Level as Determinants of Human Resource Management Practices", *Human Resource Planning*, 10 (3): 125–41.

Schuster, M. (1990): "Union Management Co-operation" in J. Fossum (ed.), *Employee and Labour Relations*, Washington: Bureau of National Affairs Series.

Sibert, W. and Addison, J. (1991): "Internal Labour Markets: Causes and Consequences", *Oxford Review of Economic Policy*, 7 (1): 76–92.

Storey, J. (1989): "Introduction" in D. Storey (ed.), *New Perspectives on Human Resource Management*, London: Routledge.

Streeck, W. (1992): "Training and the New Industrial Relations: A Strategic Role for Unions?" in Marino Regini (ed.): *The Future of Labour Movements*, London: Sage.

Suttle, S. (1988): "Labour Market Flexibility", *Industrial Relations News*, No. 38.

Tailby, S. and Whitson, C. (1989): "Industrial Relations and Restructuring" in S. Tailby and C. Whitson (eds.), *Manufacturing Change: IR and Restructuring*, Oxford: Blackwell.

Terry, M. (1989): "Recontextualising Shopfloor Industrial Relations" in S. Tailby and C. Whitson. (eds.), Manufacturing Change IR and Restructuring, Oxford: Blackwell.

Thomason, G. (1984): *A Textbook of Industrial Relations*, London: Institute of Personnel Management.

Turnbull, P. (1991): "Trade Unions and Productivity: Opening the Harvard 'BlackBones'", *Journal of Labour Research;* 12 (2): 135–50.

Turner, T. (1994): "Internal Labour Markets and Employment Systems", *International Journal of Manpower*, 15 (1): 15–26.

Turner, T. and Morley, M. (1995): *Industrial Relations and the New Order: Case Studies in Conflict and Co-operation*, Dublin: Oak Tree Press.

Walton, R.E. (1985): "Towards a Strategy of Eliciting Employee Commitment based on Policies of Mutuality" in R.E. Walton and P. Lawrence (eds.), *Human Resource Management: Trends and Challenges*, Boston MA: Harvard Business School Press.

Wedderburn, D. and Crampton, R. (1972): *Workers Attitudes and Technology*, Cambridge: Cambridge University Press.

Whelan, C. (1982): *Worker Priorities, Trust in Management and Prospects for Workers Participation*, Paper No. 111, Dublin: Economic and Social Research Institute.

Wickham, J. (1993): *New Forms of Work in Ireland: An Analysis of the "New Forms of Work Activity"*, Working Paper No: WP/93/31/EN Dublin: European Foundation for the Improvement of Living and Working Conditions.

CHAPTER 5

PAY DETERMINATION, THE STATE AND THE POLITICS OF INDUSTRIAL RELATIONS

William K. Roche

This chapter examines pay determination in Irish industrial relations in the context of attempts by the State to influence the conduct of collective bargaining. It is scarcely possible to describe or analyse pay determination in Ireland without considering the role of the State in industrial relations. At various times since independence in 1922, governments have intervened directly in the process of pay determination: for example from 1941 to 1946, when pay was subject to statutory control; from 1970 to 1980, when governments gradually became a "social partner" with unions and employers in national pay agreements; and from 1987 to date, when the state was a direct party to three separate national tripartite agreements on pay and a range of economic and social policy issues. During periods in which governments have opted to remain outside the direct process of negotiating or controlling wage rises, it is still possible to identify an underlying logic in their stance towards collective bargaining. While differences in the priority accorded to industrial relations matters by governments are apparent, at no stage in Irish economic history has collective bargaining over pay and conditions ever been ignored by the State. This is hardly surprising considering the influence which collective bargaining may have — or is commonly perceived to have — on such critical issues as inflation, unemployment, competitiveness, foreign investment, industrial conflict, social and political order and stability.

In tracing the course of pay determination since the foundation of the State in the context of changes in governments' stances towards collective bargaining, we are essentially involved in identifying the changing boundaries between politics and industrial relations in Ireland. The shaping and reshaping of the boundaries between the realms of politics and industrial relations is one of the major themes in writings on industrial relations, and specifically on pay determination, in Europe during the past two decades. It is thus necessary to examine the Irish experience against the background of what is known about the politics of industrial relations and pay determination in Europe. The first section of this chapter presents a review of the major themes and conclusions of writing and research in this area. Subsequent sections of the chapter apply this framework to analyse the course of pay determination in Ireland.

I

STATE STRATEGY, COLLECTIVE BARGAINING AND PAY DETERMINATION

It is possible to outline three broad ways in which the state can seek to influence pay determination and the wider conduct of industrial relations. These theoretical models of state strategy have been useful in understanding major changes in the role of governments in industrial relations in European countries, as well as in making comparisons between the contrasting roles of government in European countries. The three models can be described as the strategy of the *auxiliary state*, the *neo-corporatist* strategy and the strategy of *market control*. The strategies differ in terms of the central measures adopted by the state in seeking to influence or regulate the activities of unions and employers. They are outlined in turn and then used to comprehend the role of governments in Irish industrial relations.

(i) Pay Determination and the Auxiliary State

The idea of an *auxiliary* and essentially *residual* role for the state was central to the British tradition of "free collective bargaining" established in the nineteenth and early twentieth centuries as the trade union movement developed into a mass economic and social force. Within this tradition, the parties to industrial relations, and in particular the unions, insisted on settling their affairs without direct state interference. Not alone were state attempts to intervene in pay determination regarded as invalid, but, in addition, legislative initiatives to reform union structure or control industrial action were vehemently opposed. The role envisaged for the state was that of acting, and possibly of legislating, in an auxiliary capacity by providing unions and employers with public facilities and institutions, like labour courts and conciliation services of various kinds, to which they might resort when in dispute. It was also consistent with this broad approach that the state might provide unions and employers with inducements to reform and consolidate their own organisations. The state might also seek to influence the conduct of industrial relations generally, and the conduct of wage bargaining, in particular, through moral suasion: that is, through appeals to the parties to modify current activities in the light of their longer-term interests, or in the interest of the "common good".

But the logic of this model was to regard activities of these kinds as marking out the limits of legitimate political action in industrial relations. To go beyond these limits, it was held, was both unnecessary and counter productive. Political stability and economic and social peace were best fostered by encouraging "industrial self-government" or "free collective bargaining" to the maximum degree. In practice this approach both to public policy-making and to collective bargaining over pay and conditions characterised Irish industrial relations from the late nineteenth century to the 1960s — leaving aside the exceptional circumstances of the "Emergency" (1939–45), which led the government of the day to control pay determination. Under free collective bargaining, thus understood, wage determination was dominated by the immediate economic and social forces bearing on employers and unions. Political forces and designs were of little direct significance.

(ii) Pay Determination under Neo-Corporatism

Views of the proper role of government in some other European countries differed sharply from those associated with the notion of unfettered collective bargaining and the auxiliary state. The so-called "neo-corporatist" model was one alternative of long vintage in some European countries. From the 1970s writers on industrial relations, as well as political scientists and historians, began to use this model to comprehend what they saw as the major direction of change, during the 1960s and 1970s, in the role of governments in industrial relations in the countries of Western Europe (Schmitter, 1979; Maier, 1984). It was pointed out that the practice of pay determination and the role of governments comprehended by the neo-corporatist model in Western Europe bore strong similarities to what had long been familiar in Scandinavian countries (Korpi, 1978; 1983). (Scandinavian social scientists, however, were uneasy with the use of the neo-corporatist label to portray wage-bargaining practices in their countries). The neo-corporatist model was applied with equal vigour to the changing role of the state in industrial relations in countries like the United Kingdom, which, by international comparisons, seemed long to have favoured a residual and largely auxiliary role for governments (Currie, 1979; Middlemas, 1979). The model was deemed also to be relevant to developments in Ireland from the 1960s (Roche, 1982).

In a neo-corporatist system of pay determination, bargaining over pay and conditions is no longer conducted by autonomous unions and employers or employers' associations, who guard their mutual dealings against encroachment by the state. Rather the spheres of politics and industrial relations overlap: collective bargaining over pay and conditions becomes directly tied to government decision-making, especially in the areas of economic and social policy. Unions and employers admit the government as a negotiating partner in what becomes an essentially tripartite process of bargaining. The government and the various agencies of the state gain direct influence over pay determination in the economy. In return, unions and employers gain direct influence over public policy in areas of critical concern to their respective constituencies: in particular, taxation, employment creation and social programmes. The direct influences on pay determination broaden out to encompass government macro-economic and social policy. These essentially longer-run concerns are accorded higher priority than direct economic forces emanating from labour markets or social forces like comparisons or relativities.

In return for gaining direct influence in the making of public policy, union and employer leaders are expected to co-operate with the state by "delivering" their constituencies' support for jointly agreed policies, including the pay norms specified in pay agreements (Panitch, 1980; Goldthorpe, 1984). In a neo-corporatist model of industrial relations the state effectively "co-opts" the federations or "peak associations" of unions and employers into the process of governance. To further and support the practice of promoting "social partnership" or "social contracts" with the peak associations of labour and capital, legislative and policy measures may be promoted to encourage the centralisation of authority in union and employer federations and to reduce union multiplicity and fragmentation in representation among employers (Schmitter, 1979).

It is generally held that the strongest examples of neo-corporatist pay determination and industrial relations in Europe are to be found in Scandinavian countries and in the small democracies of the European continent, especially Denmark, Austria and Switzerland (see the contributions to Goldthorpe, 1984; and see Korpi, 1978; 1983). The model has also been applied to postwar state strategy in West Germany although some doubt its direct applicability to the German case (see Thelan, 1991). Writers on neo-corporatism use the prefix "neo-" to distinguish between the corporatism they believe to be evident in liberal democracies during the postwar period and the corporatism of countries like Germany and Italy under the Nazi and Fascist regimes of the 1930s.

(iii) Pay Determination and Neo-Liberalism

The third strategy of *neo-liberalism* will not play a major part in the analysis of change in industrial relations in Ireland. However, it is discussed here briefly both because of its intrinsic interest as an alternative to the auxiliary state and neo-corporatism and because it represents the approach of Conservative administrations to the conduct of industrial relations during the 1980s and 1990s in Great Britain and Northern Ireland. This approach also captures the broad thrust of Federal Government policy on industrial relations in the United States during the Reagan-Bush era (Kochan et al., 1984; Kaufman, 1993) and provides the rationale for the restructuring of industrial relations in New Zealand since the 1980s.

The major defining feature of neo-liberalism or, as it is also sometimes known, *"neo-laissez-faire"*, is an insistence by government that the free operation of labour markets, rather than supportive state policies or dialogue with interest groups, should be relied upon to ensure that conduct of pay bargaining and industrial relations results in outcomes that are macro-economically benign.

Neo-liberalism as a context for pay determination involves the systematic targeting by government of factors believed to impede the "free" operation of the labour market. In industrial relations the emphasis of public policy is on curbing trade union organisation and power through legislative reforms in such areas as industrial action and the rights of employees and employers to resist unionisation. In the labour market the emphasis is on "deregulation", especially through the removal of minimum wage standards and the dilution of rights in respect of employment security. Dialogue at national level with trade unions is dispensed with and incomes policy is disavowed in favour of reconstituting "competitive" labour markets. Quasi-market devices of various kinds are introduced into the public sector to "proxi" the market disciplines faced by managers and unions in the private sector. For example, "cash limits", which amount to limits on the wage funds available to finance wage rises, are imposed by government to confront managers and unions negotiating pay with a trade-off between pay rises and the retention of employment levels. Collective bargaining is decentralised to allow managers to adjust rates of pay to take account of market conditions for different categories of staff and in different regions. Core groups of senior managers and public servants may have their pay removed from the ambit of collective bargaining altogether by the expediency of individual pay agreements, frequently incorporating performance-based pay. Pay and conditions for groups of public service workers involved in the provision of ancillary services are "put back into competition" with the private sector. This is achieved through "compulsory competitive tendering": a procedure in which contracts for ancillary and professional services are awarded by public authorities on the basis of cost competition between current public providers of those services and the private sector (see Farnham and Horton, 1993). The degree to which industrial relations in the United Kingdom have been reshaped along such lines is apparent from a recent comprehensive survey of workplace industrial relations (Millward, 1994). The scale and depth of the changes wrought in the context of pay bargaining and industrial relations in the United States is also the subject of a series of recent noted works (see Kochan et al., 1984; Kaufman, 1993).

ASSESSING THE ALTERNATIVE MODELS

The international literature on the politics of industrial relations and pay determination over the past two decades has been concerned mainly with three interrelated issues. First, how can the origins or development of neo-corporatism in many European countries — and in some cases its subsequent demise — in the postwar period be understood? Second, are certain industrial relations conditions necessary for neo-corporatism to take root and survive as a central feature of pay determination which is judged to enhance economic performance. Third, which model or models of state strategy allow economies best to adjust to international economic pressures and trends, and with what particular set of outcomes in terms of wage levels, industrial conflict and competitiveness? These three questions are interrelated, as will be shown.

(i) The Emergence and Sometimes Demise of Neo-Corporatism

The reasons for the rise of the neo-corporatist model or, as some writers prefer to put it, the neo-corporatist system, of industrial relations can most readily be identified. Neo-corporatism gained ground in Western Europe during the 1960s and 1970s in response to attempts by governments to address problems of inflation, flagging economic performance and escalating industrial conflict (see Crouch and Pizzorno, 1978). Within a macro-economic policy context dominated by

Keynesian measures, the economic perils of the 1960s and 1970s seemed best handled by building on the existing dialogue between unions, employers and government by bringing wage bargaining directly into discussion. Unions had by then attained significant levels of density and representation in most West European countries. As such, their influence over pay determination could not be ignored. Nor, it appeared, could they realistically be marginalised. Such an option never really arose, in any case, in countries where socialist or social democratic governments were in power. If unions were deemed to be sufficiently strong to determine a key economic variable such as inflation, and if they could not be marginalised, then attention turned to ways of involving them, along with employers, in macro-economic policy making. The general tendency across a number of countries was to invite unions to play a role in economic management, in return for assurances on their part that they would refrain from exploiting their labour market power to the fullest extent in pursuit of sectional wage rises. The option of wage rises agreed on the basis of a consensus between employers, unions and the state as to what was macro-economically sustainable was deemed by advocates of neo-corporatist arrangements to be more successful for the trade union constituency in the long run. The alternative for unions was to win wage concessions in the short run through free collective bargaining, which, it has argued, would inevitably result in a wage-price spiral: wage rises outstripping productivity growth and generating inflation and a higher level of unemployment. In the process, industrial conflict would lead to a further worsening of economic performance and undermine investor confidence. The option of negotiating centrally with employers and the government in tripartite talks held out the prospect of being able to achieve, by direct political means, long-cherished objectives of the labour movement like social policy improvements, tax reform, a role in industrial policy and influence over economic policy itself.

Different national historical experiences, institutional frameworks and prevailing economic conditions influenced the ways in which neo-corporatism developed and the ways in which it was given expression in European countries (see esp. Maier, 1984).

The late 1970s represented the high tide of neo-corporatism in many European countries. During the 1980s, government policy in many countries continued to emphasise the control of inflation and improvement of competitiveness. To these aims was added the additional major concern of controlling public expenditure. During the 1970s governments generally had resorted to increased public borrowing to institute a series of policies to cope with recessions sparked off by the two oil crises of 1974 and 1979. Neo-corporatist deals, involving new and better social policies, price subsidies and job creation often contributed to increased public spending, financed in major part by rising public debt. By the early to mid-1980s levels of public borrowing in a number of countries were no longer sustainable. Simultaneously, liberal and conservative parties gained election victories in countries like the United Kingdom, the Netherlands and Germany. The deep recession of the 1980s and structural change in the composition of the workforce also resulted in falling or stagnating levels of union density in many countries. These factors, in combination with varying degrees of disillusionment with 1970s experiments in neo-corporatism, led to a shift in some countries towards a greater reliance on markets to control wage bargaining and industrial relations. The strongest instance of such a shift was the new Conservative government strategy in the United Kingdom. However, while neo-corporatist practices and institutions still defined the main parameters of government, union and employer policy in countries like Germany, Sweden and the Netherlands, principles associated with the market control strategy also gained some considerable ground: for example, the decentralisation of collective bargaining, the deregulating of labour markets, and the dismantling of tripartite structures (see Baglioni and Crouch, 1990). While neo-corporatism was reigned back nearly everywhere — with the exception of Ireland from 1987 to 1990 — only in the United Kingdom, in the United States during the Reagan-Bush era and in New Zealand during the second half of the 1980s, did neo-liberalism dominate state strategy in industrial relations.

(ii) The Conditions for Stable Neo-Corporatism

A series of structural conditions facilitate the development and stability of neo-corporatism. Of primary importance is the degree to which trade union and employer federations are capable of developing policy on behalf of their respective constituencies and of "delivering" the support of those constituencies when tripartite deals are agreed. Trade union movements, like those of Germany, Sweden and Austria, based on small numbers of centralised industrial unions, co-ordinated by powerful trade union federations, are significantly more capable of negotiating central agreements and of making them stick than are fragmented union movements, like those in Ireland and the United Kingdom, comprised of relatively large numbers of craft, general and occupational unions. Also important in underscoring neo-corporatism is the state's capacity for consistent policy-making; the credibility of its policy commitments in the eyes of employer and union federations; and the degree to which unions, in particular, can trust government to deliver on policy commitments favourable to organised labour. The role of social democratic governments in underscoring neo-corporatism in a number of countries has been emphasised by a series of writers (see Goldthorpe, 1984). Unions share a higher degree of ideological affinity with Labour and social democratic parties and may indeed be affiliated to them. As social democratic parties and unions seek to appeal to the same core constituency, unions can have greater confidence of the eventual gains from neo-corporatist deals. It has also been observed that "catch all" political parties, like the main Irish parties, make poor bargaining partners for both unions and employers (see Hardiman, 1988: ch. 7). This is because such parties aim to be "all things to all men" and will be driven by the logic of this political stance to eschew consistent long-term economic strategies in favour of buying off short-term pressure from their various constituencies. Policies dictated by considerations of short-term political advantage are unlikely to be optimal in economic terms and may be highly damaging through their effects on inflation, debt, investment confidence and general credibility.

A number of writers have criticised the emphasis in the main body of the neo-corporatist literature on *structural prerequisites* for stable tripartite exchange between unions, employers and the state. It has been argued that structural conditions may be less important for the emergence and stability of neo-corporatist arrangements than the strategic calculations of unions, employers and governments regarding the costs and benefits of centralised as compared with decentralised bargaining (Armingeon, 1986; Regini, 1984). Obviously, these calculations will sooner or later have to contend with the organisational capacity of the parties themselves and of their bargaining partners to develop policies on behalf of their members and to deliver their members' support. In the short term, however, such things as deep crisis in the economy, or a serious threat to the security of any, or all, of the parties to industrial relations, might tilt the balance in favour of neo-corporatism — even where structural conditions are unfavourable. Thus, Regini (1984: 132) calls attention to such factors as possible "functional equivalents" to centralisation in union and employer federations and the dominance of government by social democratic parties. In a similar sense, it has been observed that a focus on centralisation in union and employer organisations and on the centralisation of bargaining underestimates the degree of neo-corporatism in countries like Germany and Switzerland, where sector- and plant-level bargaining is co-ordinated by powerful employer organisations (see Henly and Tsakalotos, 1992: 570).

(iii) The Effectiveness of Alternative Models

One of the reasons for the interest aroused by the neo-corporatist literature in the 1970s and 1980s was the argument often advanced that corporatism led to superior outcomes in macro-economic terms and in terms of workers' standards of living than alternative models of state strategy and collective bargaining. A series of writers have advanced the counter-intuitive argument that the higher the degree to which industrial conflict in Western societies was contained by neo-corporatist deals and arrangements, the greater has been the capacity of unions to deliver significant and sustainable improvements in living standards and job security for their members. In short, it has been argued that union quiescence or moderation in the labour market was consistent with, and indeed a prerequisite for, significant union progress in the "political market" instituted by neo-corporatist arrangements for collective bargaining (Pizzorno, 1978; Korpi, 1978; 1983; Cameron, 1984). It has also been argued that neo-corporatist arrangements allowed some countries to absorb better the economic shocks associated with the oil crises of the 1970s and the international economic recessions of the 1980s. Specifically, the responsiveness of real wage levels to increases in the rate of unemployment was found to be higher in corporatist economies (see Henly and Tsakalotos, 1992). The more favourable overall economic performance of Germany, Switzerland, Austria and the Scandinavian countries in the aftermath of the oil shocks, was also attributed to those countries' neo-corporatist arrangements for wage determination and economic policy-making. More generally, it has been argued that neo-corporatism increases the overall "governability" of advanced industrial societies (Schmitter, 1981).

More recently, the argument that there was a direct linear relationship between levels of neo-corporatism in wage bargaining and economic performance has been qualified by researchers. Attention has focused on the possibility that there may be a "hump-shaped" relationship between the degree of neo-corporatism and levels of economic performance rather than the simple linear relationship assumed in earlier studies. The hump-shaped or U-shaped relationship implies that highly centralised and stable neo-corporatist arrangements are conducive to economic success, as are highly decentralised systems, such as that of the United States, where collective bargaining is neither extensive nor strong, markets are deregulated and the neo-liberal policies of government seek to underscore labour-market flexibility. The poor performers in economic terms, it is argued, are those countries burdened with intermediate levels of centralisation or moderate degrees of corporatism (Calmfors and Driffill, 1988). If this proposition is valid it suggests that strong neo-corporatist, or alternatively strong neo-liberal, systems of collective bargaining may suit current international economic conditions, whereas the auxiliary state allied with a high degree of autonomy in wage bargaining, or weak neo-corporatism, may prove equally unsuited. This still leaves open, of course, the social and political viability of alternative arrangements in different national cases. Irrespective of whatever intrinsic merits they may have, neo-liberal arrangements might prove viable in the social and political circumstances of the USA or UK in the 1990s and completely unviable in Ireland. But taking up the argument of those claiming that the extremes of the wage-bargaining spectrum are better in economic terms than intermediate arrangements, we may ask in what different ways are the polar extremes of strong and weak labour market regulation held to be conducive to economic performance? And what are the consequences of either set of arrangements for the parties to industrial relations?

In theory, neo-corporatist bargaining arrangements allow unions and employers to take account of the macro-economic and long-run implications of their wage bargaining activities in a way which is not possible under free-collective bargaining backed by strong union power in the labour market. In neo-corporatist deals union and employer *federations* bargain on behalf of their respective constituencies and they, unlike the many interests of which they are composed, cannot ignore the effect of their decisions on macro-economic performance. They are, in effect, involved in wage setting for the national economy and the implications for price levels and unemployment are immediately apparent. In return for agreement by unions and employers on sustainable wage rises, the state commits itself to general policy measures which promote economic performance, as well as addressing other specific objectives of unions and employers, such as tax reform, social policy improvements and economic development. Consensual centralised policy-making of this kind should allow wage determination to adjust more easily to international economic trends and shocks. At the other extreme, when the state promotes a high degree of labour-market flexibility and collective bargaining and trade union power are curtailed, market forces may bring about real wage flexibility in the face of economic shocks and rising unemployment. In intermediate cases, where union power is considerable and collective bargaining occurs on a fragmented and sectional basis, neither of these mechanisms operate (Henly and Tsakalotos, 1992: 575–78). Corporatist deals and arrangements may be too weak to ensure that wages are adjusted centrally in the light of macro-economic forces. At the same time, labour markets and industrial relations may be insufficiently flexible to permit wage determination to adjust at a decentralised level to unemployment and international economic pressures.

Even assuming that neo-corporatist and neo-liberal models of pay determination may be equally effective in terms of keeping unemployment at relatively low levels, it must be recognised that they are likely to lead to sharply different outcomes in other important respects. A major criticism of neo-liberal wage-fixing arrangements, as radically exemplified by the United States, is that economic adjustment is focused to such a degree on real wage flexibility that sustained productivity growth and real-wage growth are impaired. Firms find it so easy to adjust real wage levels to market forces that the role of product and process innovation in competition is lost sight of. Training and human resource development are neglected and domestic and international competitive postures come to be based primarily on cost-cutting. In industrial relations terms, real wage levels fall or stagnate over long periods; employers resort to an increasing degree to short-term, part-time and other "flexible" employment contracts; and employee involvement in decision making and innovation takes a back seat to managerial direction. Such a neo-liberal scenario has met with criticism from North American advocates of "human resource management" or the "new industrial relations" (Kochan et al., 1993), from critics of Conservative government strategy in British industrial relations (Nolan, 1989; Millward, 1994) and from advocates of neo-corporatism in the Single European Market (Henly and Tsakalotos, 1992). The other side of the coin of deregulated labour markets and downwardly flexible real wages may be extensive poverty, social exclusion and the marginalization of racial and other minorities (Galbraith, 1992).

Strong neo-corporatist bargaining arrangements, on the other hand, have been associated with more equalitarian economic and social outcomes, higher incentives for competing through innovation in processes or products, higher levels of employee involvement in management decision-making and lower levels of social exclusion (Henly and Tsakalotos, 1992). At the same time, the centralisation of wage bargaining has also been associated with high levels of personal taxation, high levels of state determination of consumption patterns and strong central controls on economic behaviour.

Thus it is apparent that important economic, social and political themes inform the debate on alternative arrangements for wage bargaining and public policy. It will also be apparent that assessments of alternative arrangements raise difficult issues concerning appropriate criteria of success and failure; in the choice of criteria it is hardly surprising that socio-political ideology plays no small part, however tacitly it may be brought to bear. Finally, the debate on the effects of alternative arrangements for pay determination is also complicated by the problems that inevitably arise in unravelling the chain of causation linking wage-bargaining practices and structures to key economic variables like unemployment and competitiveness.

Notwithstanding these concerns, no examination of the course of pay bargaining in Irish industrial relations can ignore the major themes that arise in the international research literature on wage determination and state strategy. In remaining sections of the chapter, the themes of this literature will inform our review and interpretation of developments in Ireland.

II

IRELAND FROM 1922–1958: FREE COLLECTIVE BARGAINING AND THE CONTAINMENT OF LIBERAL AND CORPORATIST TENDENCIES IN STATE POLICY

The industrial relations system inherited by the Independent Irish State in 1922 inevitably bore the stamp of British practices and traditions, as these had evolved since the second half of the nineteenth century. From the 1870s to the early twentieth century, unions gradually achieved lawful status as the conduct of industrial relations and the resolution of industrial disputes were wrested free from the grip of the criminal and civil legal codes. As unions in both islands had gained considerable power in the labour market before they became organised politically and before the advent of universal adult suffrage, they came to rely primarily on their power in collective bargaining with employers to defend and improve pay and conditions. Gradually the State sought to facilitate collective bargaining by enacting statutes to regulate the affairs of trade unions and to remove trade disputes from the ambit of the law. In addition, public conciliation and arbitration facilities were placed at the disposal of parties to industrial disputes to encourage dispute resolution and contain industrial conflict. In recognition of the growing legitimacy of industrial relations based on collective bargaining, a Labour Department was established in the British Board of Trade; the Department was replaced during the First World War by a Ministry of Labour. The Ministry opened an Irish department in 1919. Also in 1919 the Industrial Courts Act provided a statutory basis for public conciliation and arbitration facilities. This Act effectively remained the legal basis of Irish disputes resolution and industrial relations machinery until the establishment of the Labour Court in 1946.

However, the First Dáil set up its own Department of Labour in 1919 and sought to undermine the British disputes resolution system by setting up conciliation boards and commissions of inquiry into industrial relations in a number of industries (O'Connor, 1988: 105). This semi-underground conciliation system intervened in a significant number of industrial disputes. A parallel system of land courts and a wider judicial system were established to the same end of subverting British civil administration. The wider system of Republican Courts played a key role in suppressing agrarian radicalism in the period from 1919. This manifested itself in cattle drives and land seizures. Agricultural co-operatives and soviets also sprang up on occupied lands and properties (Strauss, 1951; O'Connor, 1988; Kotsonouris, 1994). Initially, Irish Republican Army (IRA) insurgents had participated in cattle drives and land seizures. The Republican leadership, fearful that class struggle might disrupt the national revolution, issued edicts against Republican military assistance to agrarian militancy. Gradually the IRA became a police force to the Republican judicial system and its role changed to one of supporting the institutions of private property and ensuring compliance with the decisions of the Republican Government and its judicial system. With the establishment of the Provisional Government following ratification of the Treaty, the Free State army and sections of the police force were used to protect property and preserve civil order in a series of bitter industrial disputes, particularly on the land. During the final phase of the spate of factory occupations, the Free State army was instrumental in evicting striking workers (Younger, 1979). O'Connor (1988: 157–64) has catalogued the strong current of repression in the State's actions in industrial disputes during 1922–23, as the Civil War threatened the fledgling Saorstat administration and industrial conflict came to be regarded as potentially highly subversive. With the subsequent abolition of the Department of Labour in the new administration of the Irish Free State, the conciliation service became a responsibility of the Department of Industry and Commerce. This Department operated on the basis of the legal code and administrative practices established under British rule.

Union reliance on collective bargaining, coupled with a largely auxiliary but otherwise non-interventionist tradition of public policy-making, represented the two pillars of the dominant model of industrial relations in Ireland during the first two decades of independence. Within the broad parameters of this model, there were notable differences of emphasis in the stances of governments during the 1920s and 1930s.

The Cumann na Gaedheal Government and Industrial Relations

The Cumann na Gaedheal Government of W.T. Cosgrave showed relatively little interest in the problems of industry or industrial relations; and no significant institutional or public policy innovation in industrial relations occurred during the 1920s. The primacy in Cumann na Gaedheal policy of a competitive agricultural sector and the party's strong emphasis on fiscal orthodoxy in the management of the public finances influenced the stance adopted towards unions and the labour market. The Government of the Free State looked on as employers across a broad front pressed through with wage cuts following the postwar collapse of prices, sharply rising unemployment and the deep recession of the 1920s (O'Connor, 1988: chs. 5–6). As an employer, the Government participated in the general trend of wage cutting. The salaries of public service workers and teachers were reduced in order to economise on public spending. It was indeed a canon of Cumann na Gaedheal economic policy that wage and profit levels were too high and had to be reduced (Mitchell, 1974: 194–202). This stance led to a serious clash between the Government and the Labour Party opposition over the building of the Shannon hydro-electric power station in 1925–26. The Shannon scheme was the largest industrial project undertaken by the Free State. The project's main contractor set a wage rate for unskilled workers which the unions and the Labour Party claimed could not be considered a "living wage". The Government refused to enforce a "fair wages" clause in regulations for the granting of public contracts, claiming that it was not the function of the state to intervene in industrial relations and that wages should be settled by market forces. Attempts by the unions to boycott the scheme and organise unskilled workers ended in failure. As an employer, the Government also stridently refused to concede arbitration machinery in the public service. This was resisted on grounds of the imperative to control public spending and because of Cosgrove's insistence on the constitutional principle of ministers retaining direct responsibility for determining civil service salaries (see McGinley, this volume). While the Cumann na Gaedheal Government's involvement in industrial relations and pay determination was limited, the State's posture during the 1920s was influenced by the economic liberalism underscoring its general economic policy. Such a posture, however, stopped well short of the radical imposition of liberal economic principles on industrial relations — a stance which in recent decades has become familiar as "neo-liberalism".

Pay Determination in the Inter-War Period

Little statistical data are available on the general trend in pay during the 1920s. What data are available, as well as secondary sources for the period point to a downward trend in wage and salary levels generally. This trend set in during 1920–21, following the ending of the boom in prices and wages during the First World War. In conditions of economic buoyancy and relatively strong labour demand from 1917, unions in Ireland launched a wages offensive or movement, spearheaded by the rapidly growing Irish Transport and General Workers' Union (Greaves, 1982: chs. 10–14; O'Connor, 1988). This general wages movement was the closest Irish unions were to come to precipitating a general "wage round" until the years immediately following the Second World War or "Emergency". Throughout the 1920s, union efforts focused on fighting wage cuts imposed by employers in line with conditions in different sectors of the economy. In some sectors, including the civil service, salary levels were linked to the cost of living index and fell almost automatically as price levels declined (Sweeney, 1990: 52–64).

In the run-up to the 1932 election the Cumann na Gaedheal Minister for Finance, Ernest Blythe, announced further intended cuts in the pay of teachers and gardai in order to effect economies in public spending (Coogan, 1993: 429). The Fianna Fáil administration which came to power in 1932, with Labour Party support, adopted a significantly more supportive stance towards unions and industrial relations during the remainder of the 1930s. Fianna Fáil embarked on a programme of social legislation, which included measures on industrial relations. Additional machinery for wage-fixing and conciliation was established and an Agricultural Wages Board was re-appointed (O'Connor, 1992: ch. 6). The programme of industrialisation and import substitution launched by Fianna Fáil had a profound effect on employment growth, the revival of union membership and the recovery of wage levels during the 1930s. As industrial employment grew dramatically in increasingly protected markets, unions were able to impose upward pressure on wage levels for the first time since the closing years of the First World War. The Fianna Fáil Minister of Industry and Commerce, Sean Lemass, whose department was responsible for industrial relations matters, was to play a leading role in industrial relations for the greater part of the next four decades. During the 1930s Lemass's stance exemplified the tradition of an auxiliary role for government in industrial relations. However, this stance was by no means unequivocal and it was to change radically during the 1940s. Against a background of rising levels of industrial conflict and bitter inter-union disputes during the 1930s, Lemass set himself the task of encouraging trade union rationalisation. This subject had animated debate within the Irish Trade Union Congress for some time, but had become bogged down in the vested interests of unions and tensions between Irish and British-based organisations. Adopting as his blueprint the strongly nationalist principles of the General Secretary of the ITGWU, William O'Brien, Lemass introduced the Trade Union Act, 1941. The Act made it more difficult to establish a trade union, regulated the right to negotiate pay and conditions by instituting a system of "negotiating licenses" and sought to arrive at a position in which unions might be awarded sole negotiating rights in a bargaining unit. The latter section of the Act was subsequently declared unconstitutional, with the result that in future the State would rely primarily on voluntary incentives for union mergers as a means of promoting trade union rationalisation. In the public services, the State as employer was still slow to grant arbitration machinery on terms acceptable to public service unions. Despite an electoral pledge in 1932 that arbitration would be conceded, Fianna Fáil was defeated on a motion on this issue in the Dáil in 1938; the principle had now been conceded but Government and unions could not agree on the institutional machinery for the joint determination of pay in the public domain.

Fianna Fáil, Industrialisation and Industrial Relations

During the 1930s Fianna Fáil's economic and industrial policies harboured coporatist tendencies, but curiously these were not developed into fully-blown corporatism, nor were they brought to bear in the field of industrial relations. The industrialisation strategy involved a high level of intervention in business. The economic policy of Fianna Fáil, in particular, the Government's critique of liberal market economics, its economic nationalism and welfarist social policy, had much in common with lines of policy in contemporary Fascist states (Daly,

1992: ch. 4). During the decade, as a result of protectionism and State-fostered industrial development, a strong web of informal contacts grew up between civil servants and leaders of interest groups, particularly representing sections of business. These channels were sometimes used to "sound out" opinion before public policy proposals were finalised (Daly, 1992: 118). Moreover, Daly (1992: chs. 4–6) has pointed to the centralising and authoritarian features of Lemass's administrative style, as his Department of Industry and Commerce gradually assumed a high degree of control over economic affairs.

Corporatist propensities such as these failed to develop during the 1930s into ideological commitment to classical corporatist doctrine, or into more pragmatic corporatist modes of intervention into industry and industrial relations. Collective bargaining proceeded unfettered by state controls; the state continued to adopt a largely auxiliary posture towards the conduct of collective bargaining and industrial relations. No centralised agreements, tripartite councils or committees emerged to control collective bargaining or to harness industrial relations to the State's economic and industrial policies.

The corporatist tendencies in Government policies during the 1930s were tempered by aspects of the economic and political structure of the period. While corporatist doctrine — refracted in Ireland through the theory of "vocationalism" associated with Catholic social teaching — was influential during the 1930s, it received strongest support from elements within Fine Gael (Manning, 1970). Vocationalism became the social and political blueprint of the quasi-Fascist Blue Shirt movement, built mainly on the disaffection of large farmers suffering the effects of the economic war with Britain and disgruntled elements within the police and army. The urban working class and the native business class benefited from the economic and social policies of Fianna Fáil and found little attraction in vocationalism or blueshirtism. The adoption of vocationalism by Fine Gael was in itself one reason for Fianna Fáil's avoidance of corporatism, in spite of its resonance with key elements of Fianna Fáil's programme. While vocationalism had become the ideological banner in public affairs of the Catholic social movement during the 1930s, Whyte (1980: ch. 3) has emphasised the newness and weakness of that movement in Ireland in comparison with continental European countries. This limited the popular and political appeal of vocationalism (see Daly, 1992: 116–8).

When Fianna Fáil, in response to an opposition motion, agreed to establish a Commission on Vocational Organisation, the strong adherence of ministers and senior civil servants to the tenets of British liberal constitutional theory also became apparent. Senior civil servants appearing before the Commission generally resisted the central corporatist principle of devolving policy to interest groups on grounds of its incompatibility with ministers' responsibility to parliament for decisions within their areas of responsibility. Essentially the same position was adopted by various ministers in reaction to the publication of the Commission's report in 1944 (Whyte, 1980: ch. 4). Lemass was to become involved in a wrangle with the Commission's chairman, Bishop Michael Browne of Galway. The controversy arose over the report's pointed criticism of Lemass's Department of Industry and Commerce for its failure to consult interest groups when devising policy. However, as Farrell has argued (1983: 71–2), the incident also highlights Lemass's characteristic rejection of doctrine or ideology and his preference for pragmatism in addressing economic issues. Much the same stance was revealed in de Valera's comment that vocationalism "will have to a natural growth" and should "come from below and not be superimposed from the top" (quoted in Whyte, 1980: 109).

Structural factors also constrained the programmatic or practical development of corporatism during the inter-war period. Daly (1992: 131–2) has pointed to the divisions within Irish capital during the period, especially between the business elite based on large export-oriented companies, which had benefited from the free trade policies of Cumann na Gaedheal, and the new capitalist class fostered by the protectionism of Fianna Fáil. Within the trade union movement there were bitter divisions between rival unions and their leaders and between British and Irish-based groups of unions. Corporatism was also held in check by the weakness of union power and organisation and the underdeveloped nature of collective bargaining. The rising level of industrial conflict during the 1930s was put down primarily to inter-union conflict and evoked a legislative response in proposals to promote trade union rationalisation. While the industrialisation strategy of Fianna Fáil allowed union membership and density to recover from the haemorrhage of the 1920s, the level of union density and organisation remained modest during the 1930s. Protectionism also allowed unions to win real wage gains in collective bargaining for the first time since the foundation of the State. It took time, however, for the view to develop that free collective bargaining, within protected markets, might exert unsustainable upward pressure on prices, or that protected industries might have little incentive to operate efficiently in respect of management practices generally or labour practices specifically.

Lemass's Corporatist Blueprint

Gradually, such problems became a central concern of Sean Lemass as Minister for Industry and Commerce. By the mid-1940s, Lemass's critique of the shortcomings of protectionism was to lead him to propose a remarkable programme for the restructuring of Irish collective bargaining and industrial relations along corporatist lines. Other factors were also at work in his adoption of a much stronger interventionist stance on economic affairs and industrial relations. The level of control over economic life attained by his two wartime departments of Supplies and Industry and Commerce was one factor; the debate on economic reconstruction and the adoption of Keynesianism in the UK was another (Girvin, 1989). When war broke out in 1939, a series of measures was planned to control Ireland's economy. In 1941 wages were pegged at their existing levels by the Wage Standstill Order. In response to protest from the unions, Lemass was instrumental in softening the impact of pay control. The wage standstill was soon modified into a system of wage tribunals which permitted increases on cost-of-living grounds. However, wages lagged prices to a considerable degree and working-class living standards fell sharply.

In a cabinet committee charged with planning for economic reconstruction in postwar Ireland, Lemass formulated radical proposals on the reconstruction of collective bargaining and industrial relations. In essence, he now proposed that a Ministry of Labour be established to "control and direct" all aspects of labour policy. He also argued that the economic controls established during the Emergency should be maintained (Girvin, 1989: 138). Controls were envisaged over wages, industrial relations and the right to organise and negotiate. It was also proposed that labour should be directed into different industries. Equally radical proposals for direct intervention in the micro-economy of business were also developed. As Girvin concluded (1989: 138; 155), these proposals represented an overtly corporatist mode of directing the economy and they would have taken Ireland closer to Mediterranean dictatorships than to her liberal democratic West European neighbours. Lemass continued to advocate a radically corporatist approach to economic organisation and industrial relations until the late 1940s. It was his intention that the Labour Court, established under the Industrial Relations Act 1946, would become the cornerstone of a new approach to wage determination. Free collective bargaining would be replaced by a system which would regulate wage levels in accordance with national economic imperatives (Girvin, 1989: 165). Other proposals were put forward to control prices and promote industrial efficiency. The proposals on industrial efficiency included provisions for the establishment of "development councils" in industries, consisting of representatives of workers, industrialists and third parties. The agenda to be addressed by these councils was broad, encompassing product and market research, methods of production and labour utilisation and technical training (see Lee, 1989: 292). This amounted to a remarkable programme of institutional change, which would have instituted what we might now describe as "micro-corporatism" at industry level. Lemass's proposals for the promotion of industrial efficiency sought to complement the macro-corporatist proposals for the control of business and labour in accordance with the perceived imperatives of national economic development.

The fate of the Lemass reform proposals remains to be fully documented. However, the major reasons for the failure of the programme are apparent. Trade unions, without opposition from employers, insisted on the Labour Court operating solely as an honest broker in disputes. The principle of the Court regulating wage determination in accordance with the dictates of national economic policy or performance was flatly resisted (see McCarthy, 1978: 6–7). The Court thus became the cornerstone of voluntarist free collective bargaining and exemplified the tradition of an auxiliary role for the state in industrial relations. Lemass's broader policy proposals on directing labour policy and on promoting efficiency in industry were watered down in the face of resistance from within the government and the public service, especially from the Department of Finance. Even the watered-down proposals met with dogged resistance from business. Lemass's Industrial Efficiency Bill lapsed when the Dáil was dissolved in 1947. The first Inter-Party Government, which came into office in 1948, did not proceed with the legislation.

The Containment of Liberal and Corporatist Tendencies

The Lemass proposals of the period 1942–47 showed the extent to which some members of the political establishment — though rejecting corporatist/vocationalist ideology and blueprints — were prepared to move away from traditions of public policy in industrial relations and economic affairs inherited from Britain and to adopt a strongly corporatist approach. The episode also indicates the degree of resistance such a posture faced from unions and employers with strong vested interests in the prevailing system. The political acceptability of voluntarism during the 1920s and 1930s and the subsequent attractions of corporatist solutions to economic problems can be understood in terms of the changing features of industrial relations and economic activity over the period.

During the 1920s the Cumann na Gaedheal Government could all but ignore trade unions and industrial relations. The primary focus was on promoting agricultural development within a policy framework based on free trade. The problems of industry or the issue of industrial development were very much of subsidiary concern. Trade unionism in agriculture had virtually collapsed by the mid 1920s and needed little response from employers or the State. In industry and the public services wage cutting was extensive and went with the grain of the Government's concern to lower production costs and public expenditure. Trade union membership and density plummeted from about 1921. During the 1920s the level of organisation among those at work was probably below 20 per cent. In such circumstances the liberal tendencies in state policy hardly needed to be brought to bear on industrial relations in any rigorous way. During much of the 1930s circumstances also favoured the *status quo* in industrial relations. While union membership and organisation recovered from the early 1930s, the level of union density among those at work had reached only about 25 per cent by 1939. Wage levels also revived during the decade but no economy-wide, co-ordinated wage bargaining, such as would emerge after 1946 in "pay rounds", was yet known. Wage determination was fragmented over company, local, district and sometimes industry-level bargaining units. Union weakness and the "balkanisation" of wage bargaining meant that wage rates had not yet become a critical variable in macro-economic management; and besides, the State's conception of macro-economic policy was still largely restricted to promoting industrialisation behind tariff and quota barriers. The rise in industrial conflict during the decade was put down not to excessive and damaging wage militancy, but to inter-union conflict. As a result, the major legislative initiative rooted in the experience of the 1930s was the Industrial Relations Act, 1941 which sought to rationalise trade union organisation. Gradually, however, Lemass became concerned about the ability of unions to push wages up in protected markets and about union and employer collusion in inefficient labour and production practices. Protectionism had to be made efficient and this might require curbs on wages and government inspection and control of industry.

The Emergency acted as a catalyst for these views. Wage control was successfully enforced. A high level of control was also attained over the operation of business and economic activity. In consequence, the State had attained the capacity for a strongly interventionist role in economic organisation. The prospect of the return to peacetime and normal economic activity provided an opportunity to innovate in legislative and institutional terms; to accelerate the pace of industrial and economic development and to address the latent problems associated with protectionism in an unregulated labour market.

The problems of adjusting to peacetime economic conditions, particularly the prospect of a return to unfettered collective bargaining after a period in which real pay had fallen sharply, provided further impetus towards change. So too did the new interventionist policies being pursued in the UK. The failure of the Lemass reform programme and the successful defence of the *status quo* by business and trade unions pointed to a number of major features of prevailing economic and political arrangements. The strength of union commitment to unfettered collective bargaining had its counterpart in the resolve of business elites to avoid state-imposed programmes of economic efficiency or reform. The preservation of the *status quo* was underscored by the weakness at popular, party or interest-group levels of alternative ideologies of political and economic organisation, like corporatism or vocationalism. Perhaps, after all, de Valera had been correct in suggesting that if corporatism in Irish circumstances was to gain ground, it would do so only "organically" from the ground up, rather than imperatively, on the basis of far-reaching legislative proposals imposed by the State. Something akin to this concept of "organic" corporatism was soon to become apparent in Irish industrial relations. When it did become apparent it was to bear the traces of some of the abortive proposals for the radical restructuring of Irish industrial relations put forward during the 1940s.

III

FREE TRADE, ECONOMIC ADJUSTMENT AND THE GRADUAL DEVELOPMENT OF NEO-CORPORATIST STRUCTURES AND PRACTICES, 1958–80

The bedding down of the Labour Court into the adversarial system of industrial relations, based on unfettered collective bargaining over pay and conditions, represented the high water mark of the auxiliary state tradition and free collective bargaining in Irish industrial relations. From the second half of the 1940s to 1970, "pay rounds", based almost exclusively on bipartite pay bargaining between unions and employers, became a core feature of Irish industrial relations. Though the State tried — through general economic policies and postures, and sometimes through direct threats to legislate — to influence the conduct of collective bargaining over pay, it refrained from direct intervention in pay determination. The Labour Court, the State's main industrial relations institution, was prevented from adopting anything other than an auxiliary role in resolving industrial disputes over pay and conditions.

Pay Determination and the Advent of Pay Rounds

The origins of the round system can be traced to the circumstances of Irish industrial relations between 1939–46. After the outbreak of the war in 1939 the Irish economy was seriously affected by shortages of raw materials and the industrial revival of the 1930s was halted. Wages stagnated and then, from May 1941, were controlled by the Wage Standstill Order. This gave way in April 1942 to wage adjustments regulated by statutory wage tribunals. However, as price levels soared ahead of wage rises, real living standards fell sharply. In consequence, strong wage pressure built up across the economy and was released when wartime wage controls were lifted. The ending of legislative wage control in September 1945 brought all bargaining groups to the "starting line", as it were, at one point in time, synchronising pay bargaining to a degree never before witnessed. The operation of wage tribunals may also have accustomed trade union officials to the idea of a "wage norm" or going rate of increase, which was to be an important feature of rounds. The synchronisation of wage adjustments, and the idea of a going rate of increase, may also have been reinforced by the widely publicised deliberations of the new and unfamiliar Labour Court. From 1946 to 1970 the pay round phenomenon, characterised by "open seasons", or periods of intense bargaining activity, followed by "closed seasons", or periods of inactivity, became a central feature of Irish industrial relations.

During the 1940s and 1950s, rounds acquired a number of well-defined features (see O'Mahony, 1965). First, changes in the cost of living played a central role in triggering rounds and influenced the level of wage rises negotiated. Other principles, such as relating wage rises to increases in national production and profitability were also avowed by the unions. However, these principles were of secondary importance in the earlier rounds. The claim by unions that wages in some employments or applying to particular groups were low — or had fallen out of line — in comparison with other comparable employments or groups also became an important feature of the dynamic of wage rounds. Rounds also became part of the social psychology of wage determination. Though union and employer opinion was confused as to precisely what a "pay round" was (McCarthy et al., 1975), the parties to collective bargaining assigned numbers to rounds; once a round was underway, unions expected to participate, and union comparisons drawing attention to what "comparable" groups of workers were gaining under the pay rounds became coercive on employers. With the exception of the ninth round, also known as the 1964 National Pay Agreement, wage round increases took the form of cash rather than percentage rises in basic rates and salary levels. Up to the 1960s there appears to have been a significant degree of dispersion or variation in the pay rises gained by different groups of workers in the same rounds. While O'Mahony (1965), writing primarily about rounds in the 1940s and 1950s, could not identify any bargaining groups which consistently acted as "pace-setters" in rounds, wage agreements in certain bargaining units, in particular, among building and construction workers and among clerical workers in the ESB, strongly influenced the general course of bargaining. Up to the ninth round/1964 National Pay Agreement, wage round agreements were generally open-ended or contained no termination dates (although several national agreements contained procedures for terminating agreements). Neither national pay agreements, nor pay agreements in decentralised pay rounds, made provision for sanctions to ensure union or employer acceptance or set down procedures to regulate industrial disputes.

A precise profile of wage determination during the 1960s is possible, thanks to a detailed study of the six wage rounds spanning the period from late 1959 (the seventh round) to 1970 (the twelfth round) (McCarthy et al., 1975). This study was based on statistical data collected from 202 bargaining groups, covering approximately 50 per cent of the employee workforce during the decade. Wage rounds over the period involved "short, active periods" of intense bargaining activity, lasting anywhere from 3 to 12 months. Where rounds occurred following national pay bargaining during the 1960s, they took less time to move to completion than decentralised rounds or "free-for-alls". Rounds during the decade recurred at intervals of from 12 to 15 months. While the data available cannot provide a global indicator of the inclusiveness of the rounds, in terms of their level of penetration of the workforce, the 202 bargaining groups included in the survey point to a high level of penetration. In fact, only three of the groups surveyed missed out on one of the six rounds studied by McCarthy et al. (1975). It must be borne in mind, however, that some industrial sectors and occupational groups during the decade did not adjust pay on the basis of round bargaining, possibly because of a low level of unionisation or employer resistance to trade union recognition. For example, workers in the insurance industry were not directly covered by wage-round bargaining, although the discretionary wage rises conceded by employers in individual salary reviews probably "shadowed" wage round rises to a significant degree. The same would have been true of unorganised white-collar workers in companies and industries in which blue-collar workers engaged in wage-round bargaining. McCarthy et al.'s (1975) data indicate that there was considerable variation in the levels of settlements under each of the rounds. But they stress that variation between bargaining groups over the complete series of rounds was considerably lower, indicating that over the course of the six rounds studied, wage increases of the same general order of magnitude were achieved by virtually all of the bargaining groups surveyed. Although wage rounds appear over a period of years to have dictated a minimum level of increase below which employers could not easily hold wage levels, they do, not seem to have put a "ceiling" on wage rises or rates as decisively as they put a "floor" under wages. Some bargaining groups surpassed the average level of increase over the series of rounds. This was due to such things as labour scarcity, union militancy or "pushfulness", employers' capacity to pass wage rises on in prices without losing markets and the profitability of companies in the bargaining unit. It was also found that over the course of the 1960s rounds, a tendency emerged for entry patterns of different bargaining groups into rounds to become more consistent. This suggests that the bargaining groups had evolved a kind of informal "queuing system" over the course of the rounds, whereby most groups of workers joined rounds after a wage reference group had negotiated a settlement, while other groups had come to adopt a "pace setting" or wage-leadership role across successive rounds.

During the 1960s, then, and in contrast to the 1950s, it is possible to identify "wage leaders" and "wage followers" in pay rounds. McCarthy et al. (1975) claim that skilled craftsmen in the construction industry and allied industries (electrical contracting) and maintenance craftsmen employed in virtually all industries — but organised nationally for collective bargaining — were the major "wage leaders" during the decade. They became wage leaders by striking "key wage bargains" with employers which initiated general wage rounds by providing influential pay targets for other bargaining groups.

The dynamics of wage determination among wage leaders were strongly shaped by the institutional features of the bargaining units involved, and the economic characteristics of the sectors in which they were located. McCarthy et al. (1975) claim that the extreme volatility of the multi-union bargaining coalitions in construction, electrical contracting and the maintenance crafts sectors exerted a direct influence on union wage policy and pay determination. Wage targets tended to emerge from a process of inter- and even intra-union competition for influence and membership. The underlying insecurity of some of the crafts involved added further to the competitive nature of the process of setting wage targets among unions and strengthened the resolve of the multi-union coalitions to pursue wage claims militantly. For example, inter-union relations in the construction industry were complicated by the demarcation tensions and general union insecurity which arose from the advent of off-site prefabrication.

Also important in the dynamics of wage determination among wage leaders were perceived inequities or anomalies in the wage rates of the groups involved in comparison with other bargaining groups. McCarthy et al. (1975) stress that micro-economic and macro-economic factors played, at most, a residual role in shaping the wage policies of unions. In comparison with the fundamental role of "institutional" factors (inter-union and intra-union conflict, "fair comparisons", the maintenance of relativities etc.), economic conditions appear only to have been important in allowing unions to make ambitious wage targets stick in negotiations with employers. Among the wage followers, bargaining conditions were less volatile. Here, "fair comparisons" and other social influences on wage targeting again appear to have been considerably more influential than most economic variables.

A further trend in wage-round bargaining during the 1960s was the tendency for settlements to rise over the course of rounds, with the result that the "early starters" frequently came back seeking supplementary wage rises on grounds of comparability. A two-tiered bargaining system had thus evolved, comprising wage-round rises and supplementary rises. Most such "supplementary wage bargaining" occurred during the course of rounds. Between rounds bargaining activity did not however altogether cease.

The 11th and 12th pay rounds, which occurred between 1967 and 1970, saw the advent of fixed-term agreements in decentralised rounds. This new trend followed on from the 1964 National Pay Agreement — the first round based on a fixed-term agreement. Unlike the 1964 round, however, the fixed-term agreements which emerged in the 11th and 12th rounds were not of a standard duration. As many agreements extended to two or more years, increases tended to be paid in several phases. The notion of fixed-term and standard duration wage agreements was to emerge in the series of nine national pay agreements negotiated between 1970 and 1980. The termination dates of 12th round wage agreements, concluded during 1969–70, were scattered over a period of nearly two years. This occurred because over successive rounds a number of bargaining groups had concluded longer agreements in return for higher wage rises than those prevailing under the rounds. The cumulative effect of this development was that wage agreement termination dates underwent significant dispersal, posing a major problem for those negotiating national wage agreements during the early 1970s. As a consequence of the growing dispersal of wage-round agreement termination dates, national wage rises, then under negotiation, would not have been applied to the basic rates of a significant number of prominent bargaining groups for up to two years after the agreements were concluded. This threatened to undermine national bargaining as the rises involved would have appeared so distant to some bargaining groups as to be scarcely worth contemplating. Such groups might then have mobilised against the acceptance of the terms of national wage agreements. In a remarkable piece of "institutional engineering", employers and unions agreed to compress the round pattern through a complex series of "substitution payments". By the mid-1970s, the span of entry dates of bargaining groups into new round agreements had thus been reduced to about three months and the task of negotiating national wage agreements had been rendered less hazardous.

It is clear that wage determination over the period from 1946 was much more strongly influenced by unions and collective bargaining than during the inter-war period. During the 1950s and 1960s union density expanded significantly, reaching a level of 57 per cent by 1970. White-collar workers gradually became more highly organised, with the result that their salaries were increasingly adjusted through collective bargaining. Civil servants and other public service workers now participated in pay round bargaining through the various schemes for conciliation and arbitration in the public services. Public service workers tended to be among the "wage followers" in rounds. Adopting a policy of entering rounds when they were well underway meant that the state avoided setting wage targets for the private sector. A further advantage of this policy was that by the time public service pay rises were due, the State could avail of the added tax buoyancy arising from pay-round rises outside the public service (O'Brien, 1987).

X

The localised and highly fragmented bargaining structure of the inter-war period had given way to a bargaining structure dominated by multi-union and multi-employer bargaining units of wide scope or coverage. These bargaining units were organised on the basis of industrial sectors, regionally differentiated industrial sectors, districts, crafts and, in the case of large industrial concerns, on a company basis. The pay rises negotiated in this bargaining structure were highly visible and the various bargaining units were tied together, as we have seen, through the pay comparisons which animated pay rounds. In consequence, pay determination was now becoming of critical macro-economic significance. Any earnest attempt by the state to engage in macro-economic policy or management could no longer ignore the wage-fixing system and its economic consequences. The significance of pay determination for macro-economic management and adjustment was gradually to become one of the major themes of public policy; and the priority accorded to pay determination on the public policy agenda was to be one of the factors encouraging the development of neo-corporatism. The drift to neo-corporatism in Irish industrial relations was first apparent, however, in the growth of consultative structures loosely linked with economic planning and adjustment.

The Drift to Neo-Corporatism: Consultative Bodies
By the late 1950s the State had resolved to shift economic policy away from protectionism and to embrace export-led industrialisation. Foreign direct investment was now to be relied upon to be the engine of job creation and economic growth. The task of adjusting protected Irish industries to competition was to lead public policy again into the realms of labour practices, industrial relations and pay bargaining.

The drift from the model of the auxiliary state towards neo-corporatism in Ireland can be divided into two phases. During the first phase, which roughly covers the 1960s, trade union representatives joined a number of primarily consultative bodies established in association with the drive towards industrial development in the context of economic planning. Throughout this first period, however, collective bargaining as such remained inviolate. When political intervention in pay determination was occasionally considered by government, the trade union movement used the threat of withdrawal from collaborative relationships in consultative bodies to repulse state intervention.

During this period of significant experimentation in consultation with union and employer organisations, the institutional basis for further state intervention into industrial relations was established. In the second phase of the drift towards neo-corporatism, covering the repeated negotiation of national pay agreements and the two tripartite national understandings of the period from 1970 to 1980, the State intervened in industrial relations to a degree scarcely conceivable a couple of decades earlier. With active State involvement in industrial relations came direct trade union involvement in the process of public policy-making.

With the move towards the liberalisation of trade and economic planning from the late 1950s, Sean Lemass was instrumental in the creation of consultative bodies involving unions, employers and sometimes the leaders of other social interest groups, such as the farming bodies. The early documents drafted to guide economic planning, such as *Economic Development* (1958), pleaded for more joint consultation between the state, unions and employers. A number of consultative bodies were soon established. These were regarded as a response to essentially *technical* problems, from the resolution of which all parties could benefit. The parties to the various consultative bodies were enjoined to co-operate in economic adjustment and expansion. This was deemed to be possible without confronting fundamental questions of income distribution. To confront such issues as the proper distribution of national income as between pay and profits, or the relative incomes of employers, the self-employed and different categories of employees would inevitably be politically highly contentious and would mean straying into the terrain of collective bargaining. Joint consultation was represented as being "of extreme importance for steady economic development" and was understood to emphasise "common interests rather than differences" (NIEC, 1966).

It was on the basis of this working premise that the unions appointed representatives to the Irish National Productivity Committee (INPC), the Committee on Industrial Organisation (CIO) and the National Industrial and Economic Council (NIEC). These tripartite bodies were established on the initiative of Lemass. Much in the same spirit and in the belief that a "new era" was dawning in industrial relations, unions and employers also established the bipartite National Employer-Labour Conference (ELC), a body which was later to become central to corporate control (see ICTU, 1962). This was a remarkable growth of consultative tripartite and bipartite institutions in the space of three years.

The INPC was established in 1959 as a joint consultative body charged with improving productivity throughout Irish industry. The CIO (1961) was set up to conduct detailed surveys of some 22 indigenous industrial sectors likely to experience the first competitive effects of economic liberalisation. The Committee issued detailed recommendations for the adaptation of these industries to the rigours of foreign competition (see O'Neill, 1964).

The NIEC was to be the main consultative body in the field of economic planning. The Council had been given a very wide brief, but was responsible, in particular, for monitoring pay and price trends (ICTU, 1964). Even before NIEC had begun its work in earnest, the limited effectiveness of relying on a web of collaborative bodies to oversee economic adjustment, while collective bargaining remained unregulated, had become clear. In 1963 the Government issued a White Paper, entitled *Closing the Gap*, which discussed pay controls and implied that the Employer-Labour Conference might become a vehicle of incomes policy. In protest, unions withdrew from the ELC and threatened to pull out of all the other collaborative institutions. Free or unfettered collective bargaining was still sacrosanct to the unions. In the event, Lemass's threat to impose pay controls secured a national pay agreement in 1964 and the NIEC set about the task of examining a range of issues with a bearing on economic development.

The Council acknowledged quite early that pay restraint was central to economic expansion. It stressed that an incomes policy which sought to match pay rises to economic output would pose not merely technical problems — for example, how pay and price controls might be administered or how ignorance of the pay-price spiral might be dispelled — but also, and more critically, would have to confront problems of justifying the relative pay rises due on grounds of fairness to wage and salary earners and earners of profits, dividends, professional fees etc. (NIEC, 1965). The operation of an incomes policy would inevitably involve a new form of "orderly" collective bargaining. The NIEC had thus forged the intellectual and policy links between economic planning and the reform of collective bargaining. While these themes were developed in subsequent reports (NIEC, 1967) it was not until the end of the decade that NIEC developed firm proposals for a body which would administer pay adjustments in accordance with rationally defensible criteria (NIEC, 1970). The Council collapsed in the face of the very tensions its policy papers sought to address and because it appears to have threatened the policy-making role of the core civil service (see Jacobsen, 1994: 92). Its influence had in any event been very limited.

By the late 1960s, unions, employers and the State, collaborating in tripartite consultative bodies, were prepared to countenance, at least in principle, proposals which would involve a departure from unfettered collective bargaining to a new form of "orderly collective bargaining". But free collective bargaining and the established pay round system were also coming under pressure on other fronts. As early as the late 1940s, the State had shown itself prepared, in difficult economic circumstances, to press for "more orderly" pay determination. In 1947 and in 1963 governments had threatened legislation to force unions and employers to fall into line by accepting pay rises deemed to be economically sustainable. What were increasingly viewed as fundamental problems with the operation of the wage round system and unfettered collective bargaining also hardened the resolve of the state to reform pay determination.

The Drift towards Neo-Corporatism: Centralised Pay Determination

As discussed, the Government had intended that the Labour Court would form part of an integrated voluntary incomes policy, and in 1947 detailed proposals for a prices and incomes policy were outlined. These proposals also carried a threat from the Taoiseach, de Valera, that if pay restraint was not forthcoming a statutory pay norm might be imposed. This threat was enough to secure the negotiation of a national agreement through the Labour Court in 1948. In fact, until the 1970s, this simple "threat-response" pattern of state influence over collective bargaining was to be a characteristic feature of state-union relations. Lemass complemented this stance by acting as a facilitator in the negotiation of two national pay agreements.

During the 1950s the unions came to accept the role of the Labour Court as "honest broker" in pay disputes but strongly objected to Labour Court declarations on the level of pay appropriate "in the public interest". The first chairman of the Labour Court sought to modify the "honest broker" traditions on which the Court was based by seeking to base pay rises on centrally determined pay standards (see McCarthy, 1978). This move in the direction of neo-corporatism was firmly repulsed by the unions. Otherwise, the parameters of the system of conflict resolution provided by the Labour Court remained unchanged until the 1970s.

Unprecedented rises in real pay were achieved through the round system. The Government continued during the 1950s and 1960s to avow its commitment to the auxiliary state tradition of public policy-making and to free collective bargaining (see *Third Programme*, 1969). The State also continued to extend its influence through moral suasion and threats to legislate, in an attempt to centralise pay determination. The Irish Congress of Trade Unions, for its part, made a guarded affirmation that the objectives of trade unionism might require action in the political and legislative spheres (ICTU, 1966); and the leadership attempted to gain support for a concerted pay policy. There was a clear drift towards centralism on both sides. The Federated Union of Employers (subsequently the Federation of Irish Employers and now the Irish Business and Employers' Confederation) was gaining increased membership and stature and strongly favoured centralised pay bargaining.

Increasingly during the 1960s, a series of economic and industrial relations difficulties were attributed to the wage round system and to free collective bargaining. First, a persistent rise in the inflation rate was attributed to the wage leadership phenomenon central to the dynamics of wage rounds. Second, wage costs now came to be seen as a key factor in competitiveness in the exposed sector of the Irish economy and such costs were ratcheting upwards as a result of the round system. Third, the level of industrial conflict rose dramatically over the decade. Fourth, the attempts of the industrial development agencies to attract multi-national companies to Ireland were seen to be jeopardised by perceptions of poor industrial relations in the country.

These factors, in conjunction with the reassessment of collective bargaining by the NIEC, and by the state and union and employer federations, represent the *mediate* influences on the centralisation of collective bargaining during the 1970s. The *proximate* influence or trigger to centralisation, however, was the cataclysmic maintenance craftsmen's dispute of 1969 (see McCarthy, 1973: ch. 5). This long-running strike had a devastating effect on economic activity across a broad industrial and commercial front. The stoppage provoked bitter conflict between craft and general unions and demonstrated that employer disunity in the face of strong union wage pressure could turn out to have very serious consequences for wage costs. The 30 per cent pay-round increases sparked off by the strike settlement were quite without precedent in wage bargaining. The strike and its consequences were seen as portents of continuing industrial strife and economically unsustainable wage rises.

The NIEC's 1970 *Report on Incomes and Prices Policy* now viewed it as axiomatic that economic growth and unregulated collective bargaining were incompatible. Yet again, however, it was a state initiative which led to centralised pay adjustment. When in 1970 negotiations on a national agreement in the reconstituted Employer-Labour Conference broke down, the Government introduced a hastily drafted Prices and Incomes Bill. Statutory control of pay was threatened in the event of a national norm failing to emerge through "voluntary" negotiations. Despite bitter opposition by the ICTU, based once more on an avowal of the principle of free collective bargaining, the threat led to the successful negotiation of the first national agreement for six years. This agreement was a watershed. It represented the beginning of a prolonged suspension of decentralised collective bargaining, and heralded a significant change in the politics of pay determination.

Between 1970 and 1980, eight further central agreements followed; four of these emerged from bipartite negotiations (1972–76), and the other four (1977–80) were products of tripartite negotiations. In reality, the distinction between bipartite and tripartite negotiation cannot be sharply drawn during the decade.

Governments exerted considerable influence, albeit not in direct formal talks, on the negotiating process leading to the first four agreements. In particular, meetings between unions and government were now becoming commonplace.

By 1974 a number of features of the new form of centralised collective bargaining were clear. First, as inflation pushed progressively larger numbers of employees into higher tax bands, tax concessions (and later tax reform) had become a major focus of dialogue between unions and government. Government attempts to encourage unions to agree moderate pay rises in the context of national pay agreements revolved mainly around policy concessions on taxation and social security benefits.

Second, and related, the consequence of union-government dialogue on these issues was that budgetary policy — the most important economic policy instrument in the hands of the State — had now become linked into the process of national pay determination. The "carrot" of budgetary concessions had replaced the stick of threats to impose statutory pay controls in dealings between Government and the unions. In 1975 a supplementary budget was introduced to soften the impact of sharp price rises in the wake of the first oil crisis. In return, the unions agreed to adjust downward the price-indexation provisions contained in the 1975 national pay agreement (O'Brien, 1981). Reflecting on the linkage now apparent between Government budgetary policy and national pay agreements between unions and employers, O'Brien (1981: 144) commented that this: "may eventually be seen in retrospect as the most profound change in the nature, functions and prerogatives of democratic government in the history of the State". But the incorporation of budgetary policy into an increasingly tripartite bargaining relationship between unions, employers and the State was only the beginning of a process that was to lead to union and employer inputs into specific areas of economic and social policy.

The third feature of the new regime of pay determination evident by the mid-1970s concerned the pattern of support for and opposition to national pay bargaining within delegate conferences of the Irish Congress of Trade Unions. Craft unions tended to oppose national pay agreements because they explicitly sought to squeeze their jealously guarded pay differentials over general workers and constrained their industrial muscle. These features of national agreements made them attractive to general workers, especially as the agreements set minimum wage increases which employers would find it difficult to withhold, however weakly organised groups of employees might be. However, British general unions, like the Amalgamated Transport and General Workers' Union (ATGWU) opposed national pay agreements on ideological grounds, consistent with the stance on collective bargaining and incomes policy of the union's British parent organisation. White-collar unions also frequently opposed national pay agreements for reasons similar to those of craft unions. Sometimes, as in the case of the British Association of Scientific and Managerial Staffs (ASTMS), this posture was overlain by ideological opposition derived from head-office thinking on pay determination. Public service unions tended to support national pay agreements, though their support could swing to opposition on occasions when they faced specific difficulties in category negotiations with public service management. Facing a difficult and not entirely stable or predictable balance of support and opposition, the ICTU leadership also had to contend with rising expectations on the part of affiliated unions and their members regarding the concessions that should be sought in return for entering "social partnership" with employers and the State.

Before examining the further development and effects of neo-corporatist tripartism during the second half of the 1970s, it is important to portray the main features of the national pay agreements themselves.

Pay Determination under Centralised Agreements in the 1970s

Centralised pay agreements had, of course, been concluded at various points in the late 1940s, the 1950s and the 1960s. But it is important to distinguish between these and the centralised deals of the period 1970–80. During the period from 1946 to 1970 most central pay deals were little more than broad agreements on the increases permissible under evolving rounds. These agreements allowed centralised rounds during the 1960s to run their course in considerably less time than decentralised rounds, but the agreements themselves were rudimentary. The agreements of the 1970s were considerably more sophisticated and had three basic elements: (a) provisions for basic pay rises, (b) provisions for "above the norm" (ATN) and (from 1972) "below the norm" (BTN) rises and (c) provisions for conflict avoidance. Basic pay rises tended to be framed with a view to compressing the pay structure or reducing the earnings gap between high and low paid groups, on grounds of promoting equity or fairness. This involved formulating basic pay rises in such a way that they contained minimum and maximum cash increases (pay floors and pay ceilings) and tapering percentage increases within these cash limits. In agreements towards the end of the decade there was a shift away from the reduction of differentials towards their preservation. Such a shift of priority reflected pressure from craft workers and highly paid groups of administrative and technical workers. The basic pay norm provisions of national agreements also allowed for partial or full pay indexation against inflation.

Provisions for ATN increases allowed unions and employers to conclude agreements for additional pay rises on grounds of added productivity or on grounds of serious pay anomalies coming to light. The productivity criterion was intended to encourage the revision of work practices to bring about higher levels of efficiency and improve competitiveness. The anomalies criterion provided a safety valve in circumstances where the operation of wage bargaining resulted in groups of employees falling behind other groups with whom they had a historic pay relativity. The anomalies provision of national pay agreements represented a response to the highly interrelated character of wage-bargaining units in Irish industrial relations and the strong sentiments of fairness or unfairness aroused by "coercive comparisons" between different groups of employees. In the words of one prominent commentator on national pay bargaining during the 1970s, the ATN provisions of successive wage deals were designed to "allow the parties room to breathe". Curiously, by the end of the decade, the anomalies provision was being successfully used by better-paid groups of workers to win back more favourable differentials with lower-paid groups which had been eroded through the compressive effects on pay of the basic provisions of successive national pay agreements. The employers' side in national negotiations sought to restrict the scope for ATN increases, while unions, understandably, sought to increase it. BTN provisions in national agreements allowed scope for employers to plead "inability to pay" basic wage increases.

The final basic element in national agreements involved arrangements for conflict resolution. All nine agreements set down procedures designed to minimise industrial conflict. Industrial action was ruled out in all agreements unless an employer refused, without reason, to pay the basic national pay rise or refused to comply with a Labour Court recommendation regarding ATN or BTN claims. Disputes arising under the agreements were to be resolved by direct negotiations and if the parties failed to agree at that level disputes were to be referred to the Labour Court. The agreements remained voluntary. No sanctions could be used against unions or employers failing to comply with the terms of the agreements, other than the threat of expulsion from Congress or employers' associations. The provisions for conflict avoidance led to a very sharp rise in the number of cases going to the Labour Court (see Murphy, this volume).

The series of national agreements from 1970 reveal a growing attempt by employers, including the government as employer, to impose tighter control on second-tier pay adjustments allowable under "anomaly" and "productivity" clauses. The government imposed an embargo on "special claims" in the public services in 1976. On two occasions special legislation was devised to prevent the associated banks — represented by a union not affiliated to the ICTU — from settling with their staffs above national pay norms.

Observers of established industrial relations institutions recognised a change in their mode of operation under national pay bargaining. McCarthy (1978) examined the development of the Employer-Labour Conference and contrasted the operation of the Labour Court prior to and under centralised bargaining. In discharging the new monitoring functions assigned to them under the national agreements, sub-committees of the Employer-Labour Conference sought to proceed on the basis of "non-adversary inquiry" (McCarthy, 1978). This non-adversarial approach to industrial relations was analysed earlier in relation to the bipartite and tripartite consultative initiatives adopted during the 1960s. Now such an approach was being brought to bear on aspects of pay determination. The national agreements also changed the practice of the Labour Court. For the first time in its history, the Court felt obliged to follow precedent and have concern for consistency in its decisions (McCarthy, 1978: 12 and see *Annual Report of the Labour Court*, 1977; 1979).

Thus, in significant respects pivotal institutions of Irish industrial relations were adjusting to a new role that involved them in the administration of the central pay agreements. These agreements were still, in formal terms, bipartite, though from the early 1970s they had effectively emerged from a trilateral negotiating process. Soon the bridge was to be crossed to tripartism and more elaborate agreements involving formal commitments by the State on economic and social policy.

"Social Partnership" and the Emergence of National Understandings

From about the mid 1970s, the terms "social partnership" and the "social partners" were increasingly used to describe the new process of centralised negotiations between the leaders of unions and employer federations and senior civil servants and government ministers.

In order to analyse the development and consolidation of social partnership during the second half of the 1970s, we will concentrate in greater detail on the two national agreements negotiated in 1977 and 1978 and on the "national understandings" negotiated in 1979 and 1980. The 1976 national pay agreement had attempted to ensure the continuance and institutionalisation of tripartite wage agreements by providing for a series of tripartite discussions over the period 1977–78, which were to cover a wide range of public policy issues (see *Budget, 1977*). At the 1977 tripartite conferences, the Government outlined its preparedness to concede 50 million pounds in tax concessions, provided that a moderate national pay agreement was achieved. Further inducements to the unions, as outlined in a Green Paper, *Economic and Social Development 1976–1980*, were also debated in the conference. In fact the ICTU complained that government representation in the tripartite meetings was inadequate, and even demanded that the Taoiseach should chair the talks. A pay agreement finally emerged from this tripartite process, and tax concessions were integral to its acceptance. At the Special Delegate Conference held by Congress to ratify the agreement, new definitions of state-trade union relations were forthcoming. John Carroll of the ITGWU told delegates: "Whether we like it or not, we are now at an evolution (sic) on our economic scene. We cannot divorce political action and industrial action" (ICTU, 1977), while Matt Merrigan of the ATGWU also acknowledged the changed situation, recognising that "national agreements (were) political acts" (ICTU, 1977).

With the return of Fianna Fáil to government in the same year, a new institution was added to the corporate matrix: the Department of Economic Planning and Development, under Martin O'Donoghue. The new department further formalised the process of tripartite negotiation. Again, the budget was used to provide tax inducement to pay restraint, and to deliver a veiled threat of alternative controls if these inducements failed. Again a central agreement was reached, but it was accepted only by a narrow margin after very difficult negotiations. This general sequence was repeated in 1979, but now with an even more elaborate structure of bipartite and tripartite "working parties" under the control of O'Donoghue's new department. The working parties covered taxation, health, education, employment and worker participation. The new concept of a "national understanding", encompassing commitments on these wide-ranging issues, figured in a White Paper, *Programme for National Development 1978–1981*.

In spite of these developments, a Special Delegate Conference of Congress rejected a motion favouring the opening of talks on a national agreement. Although the Congress Executive now had no mandate to enter negotiations, talks moved into the grey area of the working parties. Ostensibly these were confined to discussions of the White Paper, the implications of Ireland's entry into the European Monetary System and the forthcoming budget (ICTU, 1979). The Executive Council of Congress, well aware of not having a mandate to negotiate along traditional lines, explained that they were simply engaged in talks on "Trade Union Policy Proposals" with the Government. While Congress kept its constituent unions informed, the communications were general enough to leave them room to press ahead. This they did in a manner which both avoided deadlock on the mandate question and warned of the consequences of a return to decentralised collective bargaining (ICTU, 1979).

At a Special Delegate Conference in March, the growing momentum of a protest by pay as you earn (PAYE) taxpayers, involving the largest popular demonstrations against Government policy in the history of the State, posed further problems for Congress. The PAYE movement threatened to disrupt the corporate working arrangements with the State. ICTU General Secretary, Ruaidhri Roberts, decried populist agitation, based on demonstrations against the Government. Although somewhat confused at the request for a new mandate to negotiation on the "Trade Union Policy Proposals", delegates assented and talks continued within the working-party structure. In April, Congress leaders appeared with the Government before the press and television cameras to announce their "National Understanding" — a novel deal which involved concessions on a wide range of economic and social policy issues, and included the establishment of a National Development Corporation to expand state enterprise. The latter provision satisfied a long-held goal of the unions. Nonetheless, a Special Delegate Conference of Congress rejected the new agreement. The State now threatened to impose a coercive sanction in the form of a 7 per cent pay limit in order to back up what it had secured in the voluntary tripartite process. This strategy was successful: the national understanding re-emerged with only minor revisions after new negotiations. Employers and Congress delegates, fearing the alternative, accepted it. Yet again, therefore, the threat of legislative intervention had secured a national agreement.

In the next round of negotiations the sequence of events was not dissimilar to 1979. The "courtship stage" of the negotiations began with a pre-budget submission by Congress and a reply by the Government in the budget speech. Yet there was one significant difference: the neo-corporatist dialogue was now endangered by the reluctance of the Federated Union of Employers (FUE) — up to now a strong supporter of central bargaining — to settle on terms agreeable to the other two parties. This time Congress received an enthusiastic mandate and talks spiralled out on a bipartite and tripartite basis for six months. At the final stages in September, the talks collapsed twice in ten days, leading to what amounted to crisis intervention by the Government. Taoiseach Charles Haughey addressed the FUE national executive and managed to press them into resuming negotiations by pledging guarantees on aspects of the 1981 budget. The second national understanding was successfully concluded but the FUE were openly resentful of the "undue political pressure" brought to bear on them, and responded by commissioning three experts to review national bargaining since 1970.

The Limits of Neo-Corporatism and the Collapse of Social Partnership

It is clear that Irish industrial relations during the 1970s reached levels of centralisation never before known in peacetime. It is also clear that in significant respects the conduct of industrial relations, especially with regard to the central concern of pay determination, moved towards the neo-corporatist model outlined in section I of this chapter. The State sought actively to promote central wage deals between unions and employers. The federations of unions and employers became major actors in industrial relations, at least circumscribing the activities of unions or companies in direct negotiations over pay and conditions. The Labour Court moved from acting purely and simply as an "honest broker" in industrial disputes to a new role which involved the implementation, and to a degree the "policing", of the terms of national agreements. As the decade wore on, talks on pay became increasingly tripartite in character. Working parties, involving public servants and union and employer representatives, became a feature of public policy-making. Periodic meetings between ministers and representatives of the "social partners" became commonplace. At the close of the decade formal tripartite agreements were concluded. From the early 1970s, budgetary policy had been used by governments to underwrite national pay deals. By the close of the decade, a wide range of public policy issues had been placed on the negotiating table. The issues discussed and bargained over in the national agreements and understandings were the stock issues of neo-corporatist systems in European countries: pay rises and pledges on industrial peace were traded by the unions for commitments by employers to create jobs and undertakings by the State to promote job creation, control inflation, improve tax equity and implement social policies favourable to employees.

Thus, during the 1970s, what had been a decentralised system of pay determination and industrial relations, underpinned by an auxiliary tradition of State policy, had been recast in important ways in a neo-corporatist mould. But it is important to stress also the ways in which Irish arrangements for centralised tripartite pay agreements during the 1970s differed, both in terms of their features and their consequences, from those of classic neo-corporatist nations like Austria, Denmark or Sweden. This can best be done by considering the objectives and achievements of the parties to "social partnership" during the 1970s and the factors that help explain the short-fall between objectives and achievements.

In assessing the agreements it is helpful to follow Hardiman (1988: ch. 4) in distinguishing between issues of primary concern to the unions and issues to which employers and the Government assigned priority. It must also be recognised that whether tripartism and centralised pay agreements can decisively influence some of these issues in the Irish case is strongly doubted by some commentators. To the degree that bargaining arrangements could have made a difference to macro-economic and other relevant outcomes during the decade, the gap between objectives and outcomes appears wide indeed on many issues.

Unions repeatedly entered national agreements to protect real earnings and the basic features of national pay agreements (price indexation and wage floors) were designed to further this objective. By and large, real earnings rose over the decade at rates of between 3 and about 6.5 per cent, with rises of about half of 1 per cent or less occurring in 1974, 1976 and 1980. In spite of negotiating nominal wage rises in high double figures throughout the decade, unions only managed to achieve modest improvements in real pay. But even these improvements were further reduced or reversed by the rising burden of taxation on PAYE taxpayers during the decade (Murphy, 1986). In spite of the fact that tax concessions were integral to national pay agreements over much of the decade, the tax-take from employees rose precipitously; workers in virtually all PAYE categories were affected (Murphy, 1986).

It was a repeated refrain of employers and government that pay restraint was necessary if competitiveness was to be maintained and employment levels were to be protected and increased. While numbers at work rose over much of the decade, so too did the rate of unemployment. This climbed precipitously from under 5 per cent in 1970 to close on 9 per cent in 1980. In the eyes of unions the agreements failed to convert pay restraint into job retention or creation to anything like the degree that was necessary in the light of the growth in labour supply. Unions also used the agreements to improve social policy provisions of various kinds. While major improvements indeed occurred, Hardiman (1988: 106–7) has emphasised research findings showing that state policies made no significant inroads into social inequality and disadvantage. In spite of progress in extending social benefits, unions came away from the national understandings, in particular, with a conviction that the social policy commitments pledged had not been secured.

If unions could readily find grounds for doubting the effectiveness of the agreements, or the seriousness of the resolve of the other social partners to deliver on their commitments, employers and the state could equally readily point to major gaps between objectives and achievement in areas of particular concern to them. Employers and the state looked to the national agreements to deliver pay restraint in order to preserve competitiveness and foster economic growth. This objective was seriously compromised by the virtual institutionalisation of bargaining over ATN claims. So extensive and significant was bargaining below national level that in effect a second-tier of pay determination developed during the 1970s (Fogarty et al., 1981). An indication of the extent and significance of "secondary" bargaining in the public service is provided by the fact that by 1979–80 "special" pay awards cost more than the standard national pay adjustments themselves (*Budget, 1981*). Bargaining activity at this second tier, often though not always focused on anomalies and productivity, neutralised the "solidaristic" objective of national bargaining to promote social justice by reducing differentials between relatively well-paid and poorly-paid groups. The agreements contained elaborate procedures for minimising industrial conflict and the volume of business dealt with by the various services of the Labour Court indeed rose under national pay bargaining. Yet the level of industrial conflict recorded during the 1970s was higher than in any other decade in the history of the State (see Brannick, Doyle and Kelly, this volume).

Trends in competitiveness during the 1970s pointed on aggregate to reasonably good progress. In the early to mid-1970s Ireland's unit labour costs declined relative to her main trading partners (Hardiman, 1988: 84–7). But such highly aggregated trends are the outcome of many factors and disguise the fact that the ability of companies and businesses in Ireland to compete differed markedly from sector to sector. The capital intensive, export-oriented, multinational sector was little troubled by wage cost pressures, while indigenous companies in exposed traditional sectors (textiles, furniture, engineering etc.) were often forced to fight for survival on the very margin of viability. National wage agreements sought to impose similar basic wage norms on all sectors. The result was that across significant areas of Irish business they were viewed as undermining competitiveness. Finally, the level of public spending and the level of public debt ratcheted upwards during the 1970s. This reflected, in part, the cost of the commitments entered into by the state under the national agreements — not least commitments on public service pay. The use of public sector job creation to "prime" the economy in the years from 1977, under Martin O'Donoghue's version of extended social partnership, proved particularly costly in this respect.

All in all, therefore, none of the parties to national agreements could point to solid and persistent evidence that their objectives were being realised in centralised bargaining. Notwithstanding the fact that they still chose to negotiate nine agreements in a row, the objective facts regarding the areas addressed by the deals compounded the difficulties of renegotiation. Creeping disillusionment was also apparent, for example in the decision of the Federated Union of Employers to review the operation of the agreements.

The intractability of the main economic problems which national bargaining was supposed to tackle, the yawning gap between objectives and achievements and the cost, especially to the State, of brokering national pay deals, eventually led to the collapse of national pay bargaining in 1981. In the words of a prominent FUE figure, the system eventually "collapsed under its own weight". No overriding forces in the immediate circumstances of 1981 can account for the demise of national agreements during that year (Redmond, 1985). The seeds of the collapse of national bargaining had been sown over a number of years of unrealised expectations and undelivered commitments.

The poor track record of the pay agreements can be traced in some degree to structural and ideological features of the underlying system of industrial relations in Ireland. While the experiment in social partnership between 1970 and 1980 led to considerable institutional innovation, and widened significantly the agenda of collective bargaining at national level, the social partners stopped short of developing any permanent institution or forum for tripartite discussions and negotiations, such as occurred in some other countries with centralised bargaining. It is also noteworthy that while by the mid-1970s national agreements had effectively become tripartite deals, negotiations nevertheless remained for all intents and purposes bilateral: unions and employers negotiating together and each party holding separate talks with government. A more serious weakness of social partnership, however, arose from the problems each of the parties had to confront in attempting to negotiate agreements and to deliver on their commitments when deals were concluded. As outlined in Section I of the chapter, the literature on neo-corporatism suggests that centralised systems of trade union and employer organisation, or a high level of consensus between the parties regarding the most effective means of tackling economic problems, are preconditions for stable and effective neo-corporatism. Centralised trade union and employer organisations make it easier for leaders to develop policies for all sections of membership and to deliver their members' compliance with the terms of agreements. The highly fragmented character of the Irish trade union system meant that the ICTU had few sanctions to apply to bring recalcitrant affiliates into line. The ultimate sanction of expulsion from Congress was of limited value when it came to strengthening trade union discipline under the national pay agreements, and, in effect, the only line of influence open was the use of moral persuasion over union leaders. The FUE similarly had limited authority over members and could do little more than warn recalcitrant member companies of the adverse consequences for employers of failing to stand firm against union pressure on national pay norms. The co-existence within ICTU of general, craft, white-collar and quasi-industrial unions also meant that pressure for the adoption of different policy priorities arose directly out of the basic underlying structure of the trade union system. Craft unions, for example, sought the preservation of pay differentials, while general unions attempted to bring about their reduction. Conflicting union priorities compounded the difficulty of concluding coherent policy positions; it also made it likely that any grouping of unions which felt that their immediate priorities were being undermined would simply ignore or counter the terms of the pay deals. So, for example, craft unions persistently sought to maintain or restore differentials in contravention of ICTU policy on wage compression. Important white-collar unions, like the Association of Scientific and Managerial Staffs, opposed to the principle of centralised pay bargaining, tended simply to ignore the agreements in practice. As Hardiman (1988: ch. 6) has shown, similar problems arising from the diversity of employers' situations and interests compounded policy development and weakened the control of members in the case of the main employers' associations, especially FUE.

The State's ability to act consistently and with credibility in national pay bargaining was limited by both policy and political factors. Among the central objectives and assurances of successive governments under national pay agreements were commitments to reduce inflation and unemployment and to reform taxation. The problem with the first two objectives was that the success with which Irish economic difficulties might be tackled depended in major respects on international economic trends which were beyond the control of domestic economic policy. In the area of tax reform the room for manoeuvre was curtailed by the pressure on public revenue which arose from the terms of the agreements themselves. It was narrowed further, and more seriously, by the policy of promoting economic development through a fiscal regime based on tax holidays and breaks on foreign investment. The political veto power of organisations representing farmers also closed off another potential source of tax revenue. Hardiman (1988: ch. 7) stresses that the "catch-all" Irish political party system also imposed strong pressure on governments to buy off short-term pressure from lobby and interest groups through *ad hoc* policy concessions. Government short-termism and capitulation to lobby pressure worked against the consistent and long-term deals and alliances between the State and economic interest groups evident in classic European cases of neo-corporatism.

But constraints such as these, serious as they undoubtedly were, might not have proved debilitating for social partnership had the parties to the process shared similar views on the policies necessary for tackling economic problems. Employers argued that excessive wage rises fuelled inflation and accelerated unemployment, a theory which governments were disposed to accept but which was entirely rejected by the unions. The unions' position was that unemployment reflected more than anything else deficient demand, a state of affairs which had to be tackled by expansionary fiscal and demand policies. Unions sought improved social policy provision and favoured public sector job creation, while employers resisted increased public spending on the grounds that it resulted in the "crowding out" of private investment and precluded the creation of "productive" employment in the private sector. Such differences of approach to economic problems greatly complicated the process of concluding national pay agreements and rendered the deals reached more fragile than they might otherwise have been. A further important aspect of the ideological or theoretical dissension which weakened the Irish experiment in social partnership was the absence of any close ideological affinity between the trade unions and the Government. It was observed in Section I that stable central agreements or neo-corporatist arrangements are typically underpinned by close agreement or co-operation between politically-committed unions and governing parties of a socialist or social-democratic stripe. Where such co-operation exists unions are more likely to agree to under-exploit their power in the labour market in return for guarantees that their objectives will be more effectively pursued in the political arena, through legislative, economic and social policy measures. Little such co-operation was possible in the Irish case, however, given the weak electoral strength of the left and the ambivalence that has always characterised the relationship between the unions and the Labour Party in coalition. Irish unions had developed strong labour market organisation before they developed political organisation, with the result that their policies were focused primarily on collective bargaining rather than political exchange with governments. This policy stance was further reinforced by the development of a party system based, at least initially, on the "national question". The nationalist parties, especially Fianna Fáil, captured the major share of the working-class vote in the first decades after independence. The early disadvantage faced by the Labour Party was to be compounded during the 1960s and 1970s, as the major parties, Fianna Fáil and Fine Gael, shifted their profiles and policies in response to social changes among the electorate. Thus the Labour Party in the 1970s had been unable to gain sufficient electoral strength to overcome the strong tradition of independent wage bargaining among its trade union "allies". On the other hand, the major parties of Government fell well short of developing social democratic policies which could have had sufficient appeal to unions to persuade them to suspend the use of their market power in return for assurances regarding social and economic policies.

"Social partnership" during the 1970s can, then, be regarded as a weak form of neo-corporatism. While it certainly changed the focus of union and employer policies with respect to pay determination and industrial relations, it failed to re-orient union and employer behaviour decisively from the postures associated with decentralised collective bargaining. Compromised by structural features of the Irish system of industrial relations, by the absence of consensus between unions, employers and the state on how best to tackle economic problems, by the short-termism of governing political parties and by the extreme economic turbulence of the two oil crises and their aftermath, social partnership proved incapable of setting in train the "virtuous circle" of classic neo-corporatist systems. Instead of a virtuous circle in which pay restraint contributed to positive economic outcomes, which in turn provided further support for tripartite bargaining, a vicious circle was set in train. Trends in disposable pay and trends in unemployment both worsened; employers in many sectors faced intensifying competitive pressures and increasingly uncertain trading conditions; the state was forced simultaneously to raise tax levels on employees and to resort to borrowing to fund spending commitments. The cumulative effects of these trends undermined centralised pay bargaining in 1981.

IV

THE RETREAT FROM TRIPARTISM 1981–87: PAY DETERMINATION, THE DRIFT TO COMPANY-LEVEL BARGAINING AND THE UNRAVELLING OF PAY ROUNDS

Attempts in 1981 to negotiate a further national pay agreement to follow the Second National Understanding of 1980 failed and for the first time in over a decade the parties to industrial relations faced a return to decentralised pay determination. It appears that a major proximate factor which contributed to the breakdown of the national pay system in 1981 was a hardening of the negotiating stances of employers and the State. This had come about in part because of a reappraisal of the benefits and effects of national pay bargaining. The unions, for their part, saw little merit in moderating their demands further in the face of stiffer resistance from the other parties. The problems they and their members faced in 1981 — high levels of taxation, rising unemployment, inflation etc. — were essentially those they had faced during the preceding decade. A further factor complicating the negotiations was the changed political climate within government following the advent of a Fine Gael-Labour Coalition in June 1981. The Coalition, led by Garret FitzGerald, laid particular emphasis on controlling the runaway public finances and was determined that public service pay rises would be contained much more tightly than under previous agreements (see FitzGerald, 1991: 453). There were also indications that some of the Fine Gael ministers were less than convinced of the merits of national tripartite agreements (Redmond, 1985). This probably reflected the advent to senior ministerial office of Fine Gael politicians of neo-liberal leanings, in particular, John Bruton and (then at least) Alan Dukes.

Deepening Recession, Ad Hoc Measures and the Auxiliary State

For the next six years pay was again determined by decentralised collective bargaining. During this period the state reverted to a broadly non-interventionist approach to the overall conduct of industrial relations. Gone were some of the attempts to foster consultation common throughout the 1960s. Many institutions established in the heyday of consultationism still survived. One of these, the National Economic and Social Council, the successor to the NIEC, was later to play a pivotal role in setting the scene for the return to centralised bargaining. The optimism associated with the first flush of consultation, however, had long disappeared. The State's posture during most of the 1980s involved keeping unions at arms length from the public-policy process, while, at the same time, respecting, whenever possible, the long-established tradition of supporting collective bargaining and its associated institutions. However, the kind of *ad hoc* attempts to influence pay bargaining that had been common over much of the post-war period up to 1970 were back again in the 1980: Government declarations on the need for pay moderation, indications of tougher measures if circumstances warranted, and stop-gap measures adopted in the hope of setting a voluntary ceiling to pay and other cost increases, such as the decision in 1981 to establish a "Committee on Costs and Competitiveness" to provide advice on sustainable pay rises.

As an employer the State now sought to attenuate direct pay comparability between the private sector and the public service by putting greater emphasis on the principle of the exchequer's "ability" to pay. While various attempts were made to impose zero or very low increases in the public services, these were usually abandoned or revised at the first signs of militancy by public service unions. An important exception was the decision to set aside a sizeable arbitration award won by teachers in 1986. This measure was an exceptional — though not unprecedented — departure from the tradition of government acceptance of the outcomes of the public service conciliation and arbitration schemes. Nevertheless, no attempt was made to reform public service pay determination in any way. The State as employer effectively resorted to more *ad hoc* measures such as tighter controls on "special" pay claims, pay pauses and phasing arrangements for public service pay increases. Given the Government's stress on controlling the public finances it was inevitable that public service pay would remain a very thorny issue in relations between the State and unions. Persistent turbulence over public service pay, and the Government's disinclination to return to tripartism, made for difficult relations with the trade union movement in general. Reflecting on Government-union relations over the period 1984–87, Garret FitzGerald (1991: 454) was to recall that "meetings between us and the ICTU were formal, often tense, and on the whole unproductive throughout our term".

The State's approach to private sector pay determination was largely "hortatory" in character. In the first round following the collapse of national pay bargaining, the Government sought to establish a low pay norm in the public sector early in the round, hoping that this might moderate wage settlements in the private sector. This manoeuvre provoked the ire of the FUE. The Federation was concerned that the non-trading sector might now set inflationary and competitively unsustainable rises for the exposed sector. According to FitzGerald (1991: 453), this policy was nevertheless repeated by the government in subsequent years. Soon, however, public service settlements lagged behind those in the private sector and the public service reverted to being a wage follower. The waning of Government enthusiasm for social partnership, in the wake of mounting crisis in the public finances, was bolstered by the new popularity of decentralised bargaining on the part of employers. In the deep recessionary conditions prevailing after 1980, employers were confident that certain of the objectives of national pay agreements were now more attainable in decentralised pay determination. Thus inflation began to edge downwards after 1983, the level of industrial conflict declined and employers appeared to be gaining a tighter grip over working practices.

Pay Determination: Company-Level Bargaining and the Unravelling of Pay Rounds

The return to "free-for-all" bargaining in 1981 heralded seven years of decentralised pay determination. Between 1981 and the return of national tripartite bargaining in 1987, five "rounds" of pay increases occurred. However, the round system underwent significant change. The features of pay determination between 1981 and 1987 bore no direct comparison with rounds over the period from 1946 to 1970. Indeed by the mid-1980s, some commentators were calling attention to the disappearance or "death" of the pay round phenomenon as it had been known since 1946. The main features of pay determination over the period can be sketched in outline, though it should be noted that no detailed study of pay determination in the 1980s, comparable in scope to that of McCarthy et al.'s (1975) study of the period 1959–70, was conducted over the period.

The first notable feature of pay determination during the 1980s was that, with the exception of the 22nd round of 1981–82, levels of wage rises *within* individual pay rounds varied significantly from bargaining group to bargaining group and from company to company. Moreover, no pattern of cross-compensation across series of rounds, such as that highlighted by McCarthy et al. in the case of the rounds during the 1960s, emerged. On the contrary, firms and sectors tended to do consistently well or badly across the series of rounds during the 1980s. In consequence, wage levels underwent significant dispersion and long-established relativities could no longer be maintained by unions. The "winners" and "losers" in the new pay regime were evident enough. Foreign-owned, export-oriented high technology firms tended to do relatively well, with manufacturing generally doing well relative to distribution and services. The public sector gradually fell well behind the rest of the field. By the 24th round of 1984–85, the Labour Court appeared to have formed the view that the concept of a pay norm was no longer relevant to the practice of pay determination now that pay rises varied widely from employment to employment (Grafton et al., 1984: 9). The second notable feature of rounds in the 1980s was the growing dispersal of termination dates of round agreements. Between 1982 and 1985 termination dates for round agreements had widened out from 3 months to 21 months; "early starters" were now clearly very far ahead of "late entrants" in pay rounds (O'Brien, 1987: 111). With growing dispersion in termination dates, decentralised pay rounds of the type familiar during the 1950s and 1960s were unravelling. During these decades rounds comprised "separately identifiable, non-concurrent cohorts of wage agreements", clustered into short active periods (O'Brien, 1987). Rounds now began to overlap to a significant degree and the pattern familiar during the 1950s and 1960s of short active bargaining periods followed by lulls in pay bargaining activity was disappearing. Thus, by 1986, a small number of companies had already entered a 26th round, while others had yet to conclude the 25th round. The public sector brought up the rear, entering the 25th round in May 1986, with an agreement that was to run until the end of 1988. In addition to the tendency for termination dates in the private sector to grow more dispersed, the public sector was now effectively settling pay on a different cycle to the rest of the economy. Public sector "rounds" lagged well behind pay adjustments in the private sector — a reflection of more protracted negotiations and relatively long agreements. Moreover, public service pay settlements tended to be modest relative to private sector trends in a number of industries. The last series of pay rises negotiated in many areas of the private sector before the return to centralised collective bargaining in late 1987 was numbered the 27th round. In the public sector, the last sequence of rises negotiated at a sectoral level before the return to centralised pay bargaining was numbered the 25th round (see McGinley, this volume). The parties to industrial relations still spoke in terms of "rounds" when referring to pay rises. But now the term tended increasingly to describe little more than the disposition of a particular pay deal in a sequence of pay adjustments which by convention had been assigned numbers: the 22nd, 23rd, 24th pay rounds etc. The term was otherwise losing analytical meaning in the face of changes in the empirical features of pay determination (see von Prondzynski, 1985).

Dispersion in levels of wage rises and in termination or wage-settlement dates were bound up with a third major feature of pay determination during the 1980s: the growing influence of the business and competitive circumstances of individual companies on pay determination and the declining importance of comparability, wage relativities and simple cost-of-living criteria. It will be recalled that the dynamics of pay rounds during the 1960s were anchored primarily in these "institutional" forces and that research suggested that their significance was considerably greater than micro-economic factors. In the competitive and labour market conditions of the 1980s, unions were unable to deploy comparisons across companies and sectors with the coercive force apparent during earlier decades. Employers now insisted that wage adjustments and pay structures should reflect such things as profitability, competitiveness and productivity at company level. Concessions were now more frequently sought by employers as a condition for agreeing basic pay-round increases; issues like changes in labour practices to improve productivity were no longer tackled in secondary pay bargaining, but instead became a feature of negotiations over basic pay-round awards.

Closely related to the growing importance of "market" or (in the public service) fiscal and competitive criteria in pay determination was the decentralisation of bargaining units during the 1980s to the level of the enterprise or firm. In the 1950s and 1960s, pay was determined for large numbers of employees in multi-employer (and frequently multi-union) bargaining units, based on industrial sectors or districts within various sectors. Only in the case of larger employers had there been a tradition of company-level bargaining. Again, frequently company-level bargaining was conducted in multiple bargaining units covering separately craft, white-collar and general workers. With the advent of increasing numbers of multi-national companies during the 1960s and 1970s, company-level bargaining grew further in importance. In the 1980s, a series of large multi-employer bargaining units across a range of indigenous industries collapsed, or were allowed to fall into disuse, and the enterprise became a major focus for collective bargaining for the first time in Irish industrial relations. Multi-employer bargaining units disappeared in sectors like maintenance crafts, dairy co-operatives, bakeries, bacon curing, engineering contracting, hotels and oil distribution. This trend reflects changes in the competitive circumstances of the industries affected. Horgan (1987: 171) has attributed the breakdown of industry-level bargaining units in part to the great number of firm-level pay increases concluded under supplementary or second-tier bargaining during the 1970s. As wage structures diversified among firms in bargaining units, the wage-setting machinery which they provided simply became irrelevant when centralised collective bargaining came to an end.

Further pressures for shift of pay bargaining to company level arose from trends such as the growth of concentration in some industries (e.g. dairy co-operatives) and a stronger emphasis by employers on company-level competitive strategy. The growth of international competition also favoured the decentralisation of bargaining structure. Conditions favour multi-employer bargaining particularly strongly where many firms compete strongly in product markets. In such circumstances, firms coming together for the purpose of wage-fixing may succeed in "taking wages out of competition". With the growing internationalisation and liberalisation of trade during the 1980s, increasing numbers of Irish companies faced international competitors in their domestic or foreign markets. In such competitive circumstances it was no longer possible to take wages or labour costs out of competition by combining with domestic competitors alone and perhaps conceding pay rises in line with domestic inflation. Bargaining units could no longer be made coterminous with product markets. It now became more important to control labour costs directly and to use company-level bargaining to obtain pay settlements in line with international trends in the product markets in which companies sought to compete. These factors spurred growing numbers of businesses to engage in company-level collective bargaining. The trends in question also meant that the wage guidelines issued to member companies during the 1980s by the FUE were no more influential in practice than those issued by the ICTU or the Government (Grafton et al., 1983).

A final issue bearing comment is the issue of wage leadership during the 1980s. Again the pattern differed from the 1960s, when highly volatile multi-employer and multi-union bargaining units covering craftsmen in construction and allied industries repeatedly set in train a competitive dynamic which sparked off "key wage bargaining" and initiated rounds. In the 22nd round of 1981–82, the public service set the pace for the round. In subsequent rounds, no consistent "pace setters" were identifiable, in part a reflection of the unravelling of rounds referred to above. Influential pay headlines tended nevertheless to be set by foreign-owned firms settling early in rounds; employees in these firms enjoyed the highest pay settlements over the course of the 1980s.

V

ECONOMIC CRISIS, RECOVERY AND THE RETURN OF NEO-CORPORATIST AGREEMENTS, 1987–94

Notwithstanding the ease with which the parties to industrial relations reverted to decentralised collective bargaining during the 1980s, the prospect of centralised bargaining had not altogether lost appeal. For the unions, the new pattern of pay determination posed a number of serious problems. While pay rises during the 1980s generally outstripped price rises, the effects of the income tax system resulted in serious reductions in real disposable income for union members. Low-paid members were now unprotected by the wage floors which national agreements had imposed and wage levels had undergone a significant degree of dispersion. The widening out of pay differentials under decentralised rounds and the fragmentation of collective bargaining threatened progressively to undermine the cohesion and solidarity of the trade union movement. The hazards attending such a trend were not lost on the leaders of the major unions. Unemployment continued to rise, sapping the labour market power of unions, though not to the degree that real or nominal pay levels were under serious threat.

Public sector unions, meanwhile, representing about half of total trade union membership, were falling behind the private sector and practically falling out of what remained of the round system. Embargoes on recruitment, early retirement schemes and career break schemes, imposed to cut public spending by reducing public service numbers, led to increased work loads and declining morale. The option of continuing to engage in sectoral-level bargaining with governments beset by chronic fiscal problems was looking less and less attractive to public service unions. But virtually all sections of the trade union movement were suffering, albeit to varying degrees, from the most sustained and serious losses in trade union membership recorded since the 1920s. Between 1980 and 1987, unions suffered a net loss of some 50,000 members. For many unions losses of such a scale meant serious financial difficulties. Membership attrition and financial strain were particularly serious in the larger general unions owing to their direct exposure to the effects of the business cycle, their relatively elaborate branch networks and reasonably good levels of service. With such serious setbacks occurring in membership and organisation, union leaders began to fear that what was happening to unions in Britain — under the neo-liberal regime of Margaret Thatcher's Conservative government — might also occur in Ireland. Given all the trends apparent in union membership, collective bargaining and the labour market, the prospect of marginalisation was no longer fanciful. The emergence of the Progressive Democrats in Irish politics in 1984 also raised the possibility that an Irish political party might embrace a strong neo-liberal policy on labour markets and trade unions.

For employers decentralised bargaining had gone hand in hand with a rise in industrial peace. During the decade, as the recession deepened, levels of strike activity had fallen. While wage trends had moderated considerably, when compared with the 1970s, pay rises still outstripped inflation and were seen by employers as a continuing threat to competitiveness (see Hardiman, 1988; 1992).

In fact, from 1980 to 1986 hourly earnings increased at a higher rate in Ireland than in European Monetary System (EMS) countries, in spite of rising unemployment and declining trade union power (see NESC, 1990: 384).

The failure of the State to reform PAYE taxation, indeed the rising burden of taxation on PAYE workers during the 1980s, imposed added pressures on employers. The growing tax wedge, associated with rising levels of tax and social security contributions, became a major concern of employers. The failure of the state to reform income tax and social security was also seen to imperil competitiveness and discourage job creation. The government had still not succeeded in curbing borrowing decisively — a recurring employer concern. It has also been suggested that the FUE was disappointed with employers' progress in restructuring labour practices under decentralised bargaining (see Hardiman, 1992), especially as recession and rising unemployment gave them the whip-hand more decisively than at any time since 1946. Thus decentralised bargaining had been a success for employers, but not an unqualified success. The rate of increase in earnings relative to Ireland's main competitors remained a concern; a number of other employer concerns, in particular taxation and borrowing, were not being addressed radically under the new pay and public-policy regime. National agreements had held out the prospect, at least, of linking progress in these areas with pay bargaining and pay restraint.

The Coalition government struggled with chronic fiscal problems, until eventually, in 1987, disagreement over expenditure cuts led to the resignation of Labour ministers from the government. A general election followed. The Labour ministers had struggled in cabinet with some success to maintain or improve the value of social benefits (see NESC, 1990: ch. 7). This stance had imposed considerable strain on the Coalition (FitzGerald, 1991: ch. 14; Collins, 1993: 103–21). But yet the Labour ministers' stand had not made their relationship with the unions any easier (Collins, 1993: 128–9).

During its time in opposition, Fianna Fáil had witnessed the mounting friction between the public service unions and the Government. The fiscal crisis and the need to control public spending and government borrowing were now viewed by all the major parties as imperatives of public policy. While Fianna Fáil put up dogged opposition to the Coalition's expenditure cuts, the Party accepted the logic of the Government's policy. Fianna Fáil had not accepted, however, the wisdom of seeking to govern and impose fiscal disciplines through arms length dealings with trade unions and other interest groups. During its period in opposition Fianna Fáil were aware that the unions were growing disillusioned with the government and especially with the Labour Party. Spotting an opportunity, the Party embarked on a strategy of wooing the trade unions. The immediate purpose of the Fianna Fáil overtures to union leaders seems to have been to explore whether a number of major unions might be persuaded to disaffiliate from Labour and affiliate instead to Fianna Fáil. The Fianna Fáil emissary to the unions was Bertie Ahern, a future Minister for Labour and Finance, who was to become a key player in pay talks between Fianna Fáil and the unions. In the 1987 general election, Fianna Fáil campaigned on a platform of opposition to cuts in social spending and supported a return to centralised pay agreements. The Party returned to power in a minority administration and set about implementing the fiscal policy of the Coalition, but with a degree of rigour that astonished many commentators. Given the scale of the task the Government set itself and the hugely deflationary implications of bringing the public finances under control, the Fianna Fáil government was concerned to avoid confrontation with unions, especially unions in the public service.

The broad thrust of the Government's strategy for pay bargaining was based on a document published by the NESC in 1986. The document, *A Strategy for Development, 1986–1990*, set out a policy framework for controlling public spending and promoting economic recovery. In the manner of NESC reports, the 1986 report met with the support of the main economic interest groups, particularly the unions and employers.

The new Government now promoted talks on a national pay agreement in accordance with the principles laid down in the NESC report. The unions were predisposed to return to centralised pay bargaining for the reasons already outlined (and see Roche, "Industrialisation and the Development of Industrial Relations", this volume). Employers were less convinced that a central pay agreement would prove better than the continuation of decentralised bargaining. However, the prospect of agreement on a very moderate pay rise, combined with tight control over second-tier bargaining, drew them into a national agreement. The Programme for National Recovery (PNR), a three-year agreement on pay and economic and social policy measures, was concluded in 1987. The PNR was similar in scope to the two national understandings of 1979 and 1980, but much more modest with respect to pay and spending commitments on social policy. The agreement also set down a broadly consensual position on tackling the economic crisis. Targets were also agreed for stabilising the debt/GNP ratio. Shortly after concluding the PNR, the Government published its estimates for the following year. The planned spending programme made provision for massive cuts of £485 million (see Collins, 1992: 128–30). Yet Taoiseach Charles Haughey managed to survive trade union protest with the deal intact. The Government's strategy was further bolstered when Alan Dukes, who had succeeded Garret FitzGerald after the general election as leader of Fine Gael, embarked on his so-called "Tallaght strategy". This bound the main opposition party into supporting the economic programme of the Government, provided that decisive action continued to be taken to bring the public finances under control (Collins, 1992: ch. 11).

The control of public expenditure and the gradual reduction of the debt/GNP ratio became central pillars of the PNR and the two succeeding national tripartite agreements. This ratio fell from 131 per cent in 1987 to 120 per cent in 1989 and to 105 per cent in 1994 (having risen in 1993, following the devaluation of the Irish pound in the EMS). As European integration gained momentum in the late 1980s, Irish macro-economic policy was increasingly oriented towards adjusting the domestic economy to European economic integration. This further bolstered the policy of reducing the debt/GNP ratio. Ireland joined the European Monetary System in 1979 and became committed by the mid-1980s to a policy of maintaining the value of the Irish pound within the narrow band of the European Exchange Rate Mechanism (ERM). The stable currency regime thereby achieved — until late 1992 — had allowed Irish interest rates to converge on German rates, bringing down both domestic interest rates and inflation. Irish inflation and interest rates were thereby decoupled from Britain and declined below British levels.

The adoption of a macroeconomic policy centred on the EMS narrowed the scope for tackling economic problems through domestic fiscal policy, especially as exchange controls were gradually phased out. Irish interest rates, and the inward and outward capital flows on which they depended, now became very sensitive to changes in domestic policy measures. In a review of economic performance and prospects conducted by the NESC, in preparation for negotiations to follow the ending of the PNR, the macroeconomic policy centred on the ERM was explicitly endorsed as providing the best available policy context, within which economic policy and pay determination should be conducted. While the report prepared in the run up to the original PNR (NESC, 1986) had eschewed proposals on pay policy, the second major report of its kind sought to link macroeconomic policy centred on the EMS with proposals on the centrality of "negotiated consensus over incomes" (NESC, 1990: ch. 14). NESC was now effectively promoting centralised bargaining — if not in so many words.

The PNR and the two tripartite deals that followed presented the NESC proposals on stabilizing the debt/GNP ratio and promoting an exchange rate policy linked to the EMS as the agreed position of the social partners. In the PNR no target was set down for debt stabilisation. In the two subsequent agreements explicit targets were agreed; the debt/ GNP ratio was to be reduced to 100 per cent up to 1993 (*Programme for Economic and Social Progress*, 1991: 11), and to 95 per cent by 1996 (*Programme for Competitiveness and Work*, 1994: 51).

Such a degree of consensus and consistency with regard to the fiscal and macroeconomic parameters of centralised bargaining and pay determination had not been forthcoming during the 1970s. National pay agreements and understandings had been characterised by sharply divergent views on economic management and on the role of pay, competitiveness and public spending in economic growth. The agreed fiscal and monetary targets of tripartism during the 1980s, being more concrete, could also impose serious pressure on the consensus between the social partners, as events were to prove.

Given Britain's initial refusal to join the EMS, the Irish policy of pegging the value of the punt to the Deutschmark exposed the Irish currency to the hazard of periodic sharp rises in value against sterling whenever sterling weakened internationally. Because Britain remained Ireland's single most important trading partner, this spelled a serious decline in export competitiveness. Twice, in response to such pressures, Ireland devalued the punt in the EMS: in 1983 and in 1986. Britain's decision to enter the EMS — albeit within the wide band of the ERM — appeared to reduce the dangers attendant on the Irish policy of shadowing the DM. In 1992, however, the value of sterling collapsed and Britain tumbled out of the EMS. This time, Ireland accorded priority to preserving the value of the punt in the ERM. As the punt came under intense speculative pressure, its value rose sharply and unprecedentedly against sterling, leading to a sharp drop in the competitiveness of Irish exports to Britain. The currency crisis of late 1992 and early 1993 tested to the limit the consensus between the social partners on the EMS-focused macroeconomic strategy, which was now the cornerstone of the second tripartite programme of the 1980s, the PESP. In the face of mounting job losses and threats of a catastrophic rise in unemployment, the ICTU supported the government's dogged refusal to devalue. This stance was adopted in the teeth of fierce criticism from opponents to the policy from within the trade union movement and outside. Eventually, when it became clear that support from other Community countries, especially Germany, was not forthcoming, the government bowed to the speculative pressure and accepted a forced devaluation of the Irish pound. The decision of the ICTU — taken in the face of mounting job losses and sharply rising interest and mortgage rates — to stick with the macroeconomic policy endorsed by the PESP suggested a degree of consensus on economic policy during the 1990s not apparent in the earlier phase of sustained tripartism during the 1970s.

Also central to the PNR and the succeeding agreements were government commitments to reduce the burden of taxation on PAYE tax payers, to improve social policy provisions, to enact employment legislation, to promote industrial development, to increase employment and to encourage partnership and employee involvement at industry and enterprise level (the 1994–97 agreement). In the PNR and the succeeding agreements, most policies in these areas, excluding employment creation, were set out as broad principles or aspirations rather than in terms of specific quantitative targets.

The PNR was judged a major success by unions, employers and the state. On its expiry in 1990, they negotiated a further programme along the same lines. The Programme for Economic and Social Progress, like the PNR, was a three year agreement on pay, economic and social policy, covering the period 1991 to 1993. The PESP survived greater turbulence than the PNR. In addition to the currency crisis of late 1992, the parties to the PESP were faced with four major problems. The first of these was a move by the government to postpone "special" pay rises in the public sector in 1991 owing to a serious budgetary overrun. The second flash point arose out of differences in union and employer postures regarding a PESP clause permitting local bargaining up to a ceiling of 3 per cent. The PESP local bargaining clause sparked conflict and controversy in 1993 in the run up to negotiations on a new national programme. The third flash point arose from cuts in social welfare payments, which became known as the "dirty dozen" social welfare cuts, imposed by the Fianna Fáil-Progressive Democrats Coalition. For the unions, the changes in social welfare payments were in breach of the PESP. The fourth point of conflict, which arose in the final year of the PESP, and so perhaps imperilled talks on a new national programme more than the PESP itself, was a decision by the Coalition government in the 1993 budget to impose a 1 per cent income levy on income tax payers.

The PESP survived these controversies and was succeeded by a further three-year tripartite deal in 1994, the Programme for Competitiveness and Work (PCW). National tripartite agreements had thus survived for seven years in circumstances of deep economic crisis and gradual economic recovery. The PCW is due to run until the end of 1996. Tripartism had also survived two changes of government: the first involving a Coalition of Fianna Fáil and the Progressive Democrats in 1989 and the second a Fianna Fáil-Labour Party Coalition, which took office in 1992.

Before considering the nature and basis of the seemingly more consensual and stable tripartism in the period since 1987, the basic features of pay determination under the recent generation of central agreements will be examined.

Pay Determination under the Tripartite Programmes

Under tripartism from 1987, generally applicable pay norms were again agreed by unions and employers. The PNR contained separate private sector and public service agreements. Both agreements set down basic pay increases of 3 per cent per annum on the first £120 of basic weekly pay and 2 per cent on any amount over £120. A minimum cash increase of £4 per week was to be paid in instances where the percentage increase fell below this sum. No further cost-increasing claims were to be lodged in the private sector during the currency of the agreement. The pay terms of the PNR were to apply to wage and salary levels from the termination dates of agreements then current, unless otherwise agreed at local level. That no uniform implementation date was set down was inevitable given the spread of termination dates of the then-current pay agreements. In October 1987, some 27th round claims had already been settled in decentralised bargaining — frequently on the basis of rises in excess of PNR increases — while some 26th round agreements had yet to be concluded. Agreements negotiated in the months following the ratification of the PNR tended to follow PNR norms. The Labour Court sought to incorporate the pay terms of the PNR in recommendations. Thus the PNR terms came to exert considerable influence over 27th round claims settled from late 1987 and on 28th round settlements, in instances where these were being negotiated. The clause in the PNR pay agreement enabling the parties to vary the terms of the deal by agreement at local level allowed unions and employers to bring new agreements into line with both the timescale and the levels of pay increase set down in the Programme. For example, a three-year agreement concluded in a manufacturing company in early 1988 provided for a first-phase payment of £1 extra on the first phase of the PNR and the PNR terms thereafter. The first phase adjustment was in lieu of a 27th round increase and took workers in the company into the PNR as a 28th round agreement (see *IRN Report*, 1988, 5: 2). In many other instances, "interim" deals were concluded to cover the period from the expiry of 26th round increases to the coming into force of the PNR. While many companies sought to adjust PNR terms locally to converge on the timescale set down in the agreement (i.e. from late 1987 to 1990), others simply agreed to apply the PNR on termination of 27th round agreements, with the result that PNR increases were still being applied to basic rates up to six months after the agreement was ratified nationally. A significant minority of agreements concluded in late 1987 or early 1988 differed from the terms of the PNR — many of these involved foreign companies. The dominant pattern in the private sector involved using local adjustments and interim deals to bring about a convergence of starting dates for PNR agreements. The great majority of PNR starting dates fell into the period late 1987 to February 1988 (see *IRN Report*, 1988, 10: 4–5). The spread of termination dates of pay settlements in the 27th round had been as wide as about 21 months. Local negotiations under the PNR significantly narrowed this range, streamlining this aspect of the pay round system. It is remarkable that local negotiations under the PNR had pulled in the spread of termination dates in much the same way as the complex nationally-engineered "substitution agreements" of the early national pay agreements during the 1970s.

In the great majority of instances, the levels of pay increases agreed in local negotiations under the PNR conformed to the Programme's pay norms. Profitable sectors, such as chemicals and pharmaceuticals, and successful export-oriented companies conformed to PNR norms, with little apparent wage drift. These sectors and companies had diverged sharply from traditional sectors and indigenous companies under decentralized collective bargaining over the period 1981–87. The main employers' federation, FUE, had embarked on a concerted campaign to persuade member companies, especially those located in buoyant sectors, to hold the line against any attempts by unions to win further concessions on pay (see *IRN Report*, 1988, 17: 13). A review of private sector pay settlements over the 12-month period from October 1987 to October 1988 concluded that less than 7 per cent of pay agreements fell outside the terms of the PNR and over 80 per cent covered the full three-year period stipulated in the Programme. Public sector bargaining units implemented the PNR without exception (*IRN Report*, 1988, 43: 14). Pay costs were being contained in the public service through voluntary redundancies, early retirements and a policy of replacing only one in ten of those leaving.

In the public service, the PNR pay agreement was for three and a half years, with effect from the expiry dates of 25th round agreements then current. A six-month pay pause was to precede the payment of PNR increases. The public service agreement also sought to regulate the payment of "special" pay rises. These remained permissible under the conciliation and arbitration systems. However, where special pay rises were won by groups of public service workers, the increases were to be applied on a phased basis, in accordance with an agreed formula and timetable. Separate arrangements were agreed for the commercial semi-state bodies to permit PNR increases to be meshed with increases agreed or recommended by the Labour Court and other adjudication bodies prior to the negotiation of the Programme.

Both private and public sector pay agreements ruled out industrial action in support of improvements in pay in excess of those laid down in the agreements. The PNR also laid down a timetable for talks at national level on a "framework agreement" to regulate the reduction of normal weekly working hours in instances where the normal working week was 40 hours or more.

Immediately following ratification of the PNR by employer associations and the ICTU, the Labour Court welcomed the agreement and stated that it intended to pursue a policy of supporting the implementation of the pay agreement. PNR pay increases were applied at local level over the period 1987–90 with little conflict or friction. Given the spread of termination/settlement dates in agreements current in late 1987, actual annual increases in earnings during this period were not greatly in excess of PNR norms. The second-tier bargaining activity common under national pay agreements was not apparent under the PNR. Given the low rate of job creation and high and rising level of unemployment during most of this period, the absence of wage drift is hardly surprising. Yet PNR wage norms continued to "stick" towards the close of the period, when unemployment fell, job creation recovered and significant economic growth was recorded (see NESC, 1990: 418). The framework agreement on working hours also led to a round of reductions in working time in the closing year of the Programme. By 1990 the 39-hour working week had become the standard for manual workers. The hours round had cut normal working hours with remarkably little industrial conflict (see Roche and Redmond, 1994).

The PESP made provision for increases of 4 per cent during the first year of the agreement, 3 per cent during the second year and 3.75 per cent during the third year. Minimum cash floors were again agreed: £5 per week during the first year of the PESP, £4.25 per week during the second year and £5.75 per week during the third year. These increases were to be applied on termination of existing agreements in each particular employment or industry.

In contrast with the PNR, PESP permitted local negotiations for a further 3 per cent in the second year of the Programme. Such locally-negotiated increases were to arise, as the text put it, "exceptionally". Separate guidelines on the 3 per cent clause were agreed for the public service and the construction industry. In the public service, negotiations on the 3 per cent were to focus on the restructuring of grades and greater flexibility. Alternatively, not more than one "special" claim could be processed up to a ceiling of 3 per cent; any balance payable would be subject to discussions and reference to a third party.

Like the PNR, the PESP enjoined unions and employers to promote industrial harmony and to avail of the Labour Relations Commission/ Labour Court, or other agreed machinery, in the event of a dispute occurring. Strikes or other forms of industrial action were to be set aside on issues covered by the agreement, provided that a union or employer was acting in accordance with the agreement.

In general, PESP increases were applied smoothly on the expiry of PNR agreements. A survey of 550 settlements, involving 100,000 workers, concluded in the private sector up to late 1991, indicated that the great majority complied with PESP norms (*IRN Report*, 1991, 42: 2). A "compliance rate" of 90 per cent was recorded and many agreements settling above PESP norms had been concluded, or had been under negotiation, prior to the completion of PESP talks.

The major difficulties faced by the PESP arose over a clash between the Government and public service unions, following a serious budgetary overrun in 1991, and over differences of posture between unions and employers regarding the 3 per cent payable in local negotiations in 1992–93. The PNR had phased and deferred the payment of "special" awards in the public service, giving rise to serious budgetary difficulties in 1991 and threatening further difficulties in 1992. The Government responded by insisting on the renegotiation of PESP in the public service. Following a period of months during which the PESP seemed to be heading towards collapse, agreement was reached to "cap" the basic PESP increase (3 per cent in 1992) at £5 per week and to defer special awards due in 1992 until 1993, with full retro-

spection. The debacle added to the resolve of public service management that the system of pay determination in the public service was
in need of major change.

Local negotiations over the 3 per cent clause were conducted in the
context of a campaign by the Federation of Irish Employers (as the
FUE had been renamed) to persuade employers to insist on concessions in return for paying the 3 per cent. The unions sought to win
the 3 per cent without concession. The PESP was not explicit on this
question, except insofar as it envisaged that the 3 per cent would be
paid "exceptionally". A review of local bargaining during the second
year of the PESP revealed that 31 per cent of PESP pay agreements
(concluded up to September 1992) implemented the local bargaining
clause in some form (see *IRN Report*, 1992, 36: 14–15). A review of
local bargaining agreements revealed that almost half involved significant concessions by employees; a further quarter involved minor
changes and 14 per cent seemed to involve no trade-offs (see *IRN Report*, 1992, 37). In all, 76 per cent of the local agreements contained
concessions which the research classified as ranging from "minor" to
"radical". Local bargaining activity over the 3 per cent continued beyond the second phase of the PESP in many instances; companies
settling early tended to be located in relatively buoyant sectors like
pharmaceuticals, engineering and food, drink and tobacco. Local bargaining activity also resulted in a significant volume of cases being
referred to the Labour Relations Commission and the Labour Court.
In the great majority of these instances, concessions were also agreed
for the 3 per cent. While the PESP pay agreement had envisaged negotiations over the 3 per cent occurring "exceptionally", local bargaining clearly occurred on a widespread basis. At the same time, the
PESP had not explicitly tied the 3 per cent to trade-offs on productivity, but this is what transpired in practice in the great majority of
cases — though by no means in all. The degree of rigour with which
agreed productivity concessions were delivered cannot be established.
It remains the case that local or second-tier bargaining in the private
sector under the PESP was generally contained within the 3 per cent
ceiling and involved productivity-linked trade-offs at company level.
This represented a sharp contrast with second-tier pay bargaining
under national pay agreements and understandings. Over the course
of these latter agreements, wage pressure typically focused on pay
relativities, or resulted in productivity deals of dubious value.

In the public service, the management side entered negotiations
with the unions over the 3 per cent clause by issuing a detailed programme of changes to public service grading structures, contracts and

procedures for pay determination. Taken together the proposals envisaged the most radical change in public service industrial relations since the establishment of the conciliation and arbitration systems. Hardly surprisingly, the proposals aroused considerable controversy among public service unions; the unions were divided on the merits of the changes proposed. Given the scope of the changes under discussion, the 3 per cent negotiations in the public service were carried forward into the PCW. Under the terms of the PCW, the 3 per cent award can be applied in the public service provided that changes agreed result in "savings and an improved quality of public service" (*Programme for Competitiveness and Work*, 1994: 80).

Alternatively, a single "special" claim can be processed by any bargaining group for an amount not exceeding 3 per cent. Negotiations on the "special" must take account of the "need for efficiency, flexibility and change"; and a timetable is set down for the phasing — in four instalments — of any rises agreed.

The situation regarding expiry dates of pay agreements at the close of the PESP merits consideration. The flexibility permitted under the PNR resulted in a narrowing of the range of expiry dates, reversing the trend that had set in under decentralised pay bargaining during the 1980s. Company and sectoral pay agreements under the PESP broadly confirmed this state of affairs. Notwithstanding the reduced spread of expiry dates under the PNR and PESP, the time interval between early starters and late followers remains significant. Data available on expiry dates of PESP agreements involving Service, Industrial and Professional Trade Union (SIPTU) members, throw light on the current situation regarding the timing of pay adjustment (SIPTU Research Department, 1994). Given the size of SIPTU's membership, and the union's industrial and occupational diversity, data on SIPTU agreements provide a reasonably good indication of the general pattern regarding agreement expiry dates. More than 400 PESP pay agreements, involving over 78,000 employees organised by SIPTU expired between September and December 1993. This group included major public sector bargaining units like local authority and health workers and several semi-state companies; in the private sector, the early starters included a number of pharmaceutical companies and oil companies; the largest groups of workers settling in the private sector were covered by national sectoral agreements emanating from joint labour committees. Most remaining agreements expired throughout 1994. During that year agreements involving over 124,000 members expired in some 500 bargaining units. A small number of PESP agreements, covering about 1,000 members continued into 1995, expiring at various intervals throughout that year. So even if the small number of "laggards" with expiry dates during 1995 are excluded, judging by the SIPTU data, the spread of expiry dates in pay agreements still span an interval of some 15 months.

The bargaining structure on the basis of which PESP and PCW agreements were negotiated remains diverse. The trend towards decentralisation in bargaining units that became evident with the return to decentralised pay bargaining in the 1980s may largely have worked itself through. In many areas of the private sector company-level bargaining units are now firmly established. Multi-employer industrial and sectoral bargaining units continue to survive in sectors characterised by the existence of many small to medium sized businesses operating in competitive product or service markets. Examples of such industries are contract printing, public houses and hotels, garages and the construction industry. Also relevant here are the labour-intensive and low-pay industries regulated at national industrial level by joint labour committees. In the public sector, the semistate companies negotiate at company level, while in the public service the bargaining units framed by the various conciliation and arbitration schemes continue to negotiate pay and conditions.

Conforming to the now familiar pattern, the PCW set down pay increases over the three years of the agreement: 2 per cent over the first twelve months of the agreement; 2.5 per cent over the next twelve months, 2.5 per cent for the first six months of the third year of the agreement and 1 per cent for the remaining six months. Again minimum cash floors were set down and the standard stipulations on the observance of industrial peace were contained in the text of the agreement. Unusually, the PCW agreement on pay and conditions enjoins employers and unions to co-operate in the provision of training and in the promotion of employee involvement at company and workplace levels. This latter non-pay clause arose as a compromise in the face of pressure from the ICTU to introduce provisions for employee involvement and participation in Ireland.

Neo-Corporatism since 1987 in Economic and Institutional Context

Evidently, the tripartite agreements of the period since 1987 have proved more stable than those of the 1970s and may prove more durable. The agreements have also been linked by some commentators with positive economic and social trends during the period. The tripartite deals have, of course, met with considerable criticism as well, especially from liberal economists who view all forms of centralised agreements as aberrations from flexible labour markets which, in theory, permit wages to vary from sector to sector and occupation to occupation in response to supply and demand.

Given the problems that inevitably arise in disentangling the effects of the agreements *per se* on economic, social and industrial relations trends from the effects of the wider economic environment, there remains much scope for controversy over the merits of the new tripartism. The remainder of this chapter will review economic and other trends since 1987 in the context of the objectives of the tripartite programmes. The chapter will conclude by examining contrasting assessments of the new tripartism and its effects.

As before, when considering national pay agreements during the period 1970–80, it is helpful to assess performance against objectives in the case of unions, employers and the state.

National bargaining was embraced by the unions from 1987 as a means of more effectively protecting and improving real disposable pay. Real pay had fallen under free collective bargaining during the 1980s in response to the interaction of modest pay rises, inflation and rising personal taxation. It has been estimated that the scale of the decline in living standards over the period 1980–87 was from between 7 to 11 per cent (NESC, 1990: 36). Since 1987 real disposable pay has risen. It has been estimated that from 1987 to 1992 the real take home pay of single workers rose by some 5 per cent and that of married workers by over 3 per cent. In part these improvements in real disposable pay reflect changes in PAYE taxation agreed in the PNR and PESP. Over the period from 1987 the standard rate of tax was reduced, as was the highest tax rate; the standard rate band was also widened. However, tax relief was also removed from life assurance premia. Some short-term tax changes, such as the imposition of the 1 per cent income levy, were successfully challenged by the unions. Overall, in contrast with the 1970s, changes in taxation modestly reduced the tax burden on the PAYE sector. The share of personal taxation in total tax revenue has stabilised — albeit at a high level (32 per cent) relative to EU countries (26 per cent on average) — while that of corporate taxation has risen.

The record on employment and unemployment has proven to be very disappointing. During the period 1987–90 net employment grew by more than 15,000 per annum and the level of unemployment fell sharply. From 1991 to the end of 1993 the level of employment remained stable (NESC, 1993: 21). A slow-down in the level of emigration was an important contributor to rising and stable unemployment levels. Emigration to Britain in particular fell significantly after the ending of the "Lawson boom" of the late 1980s. In the first six months of 1994 the level of unemployment again declined, but overall the record since 1987 has been dismal.

Unions also sought to protect and improve social programmes in tripartite bargaining. Since about 1990 the real value of social welfare payments to most categories of recipients has risen significantly, having stagnated over the period 1987–89; the standard of living of social welfare recipients relative to those at work has varied depending on benefit categories, but the general trend has been upward (see NESC, 1993: 425–6). Spending on health underwent serious retrenchment during the 1980s, the falling trend extending into the period of the PNR, generating protests from unions which threatened initially to undermine the Programme. From 1990 the real value of health spending rose again, and by the end of 1991 Ireland was close to the OECD average for exchequer spending on health provision (NESC, 1993: ch. 17). Unions also obtained commitments in the Programmes on improvements in statutory protection for various groups of workers. These have led to a series of revisions to employment legislation, most notably the extension of various entitlements to "permanent part-time workers" and the tightening up of unfair dismissals legislation. Finally, unions entered tripartite bargaining in 1987 to a significant degree to avoid marginalisation and in a bid to halt the serious setbacks to membership and organisation suffered during the period from 1980.

The sharp decline in union membership and density experienced during the 1980s appears to have bottomed out in 1987; since then membership has revived modestly and organisation has been maintained. Unions continue to face serious challenges to recognition at company level, coming both from Irish employers adopting a traditional anti-union stance and from foreign multinationals pursuing more sophisticated "union substitution" strategies (see Roche, this volume). An attempt to introduce a provision on union recognition in the PCW failed in the face of employer resistance. Nationally, unions have secured an input into public policy-making through the Programmes themselves and through consolidating their position as a key constituency with rights of representation on state boards, committees and policy forums. The feared marginalisation of the late 1980s has been avoided under the tripartite programmes.

Employers re-entered tripartism to some degree out of disillusionment with the trend in pay under free collective bargaining. Pay rises under decentralised bargaining had been higher than anticipated in the context of declining inflation, sharply rising unemployment and increased managerial power. The pay norms agreed under the PNR and PESP met with a surprising degree of acceptance considering the extensive second-tier pay bargaining that had developed under national pay agreements during the 1970s. As outlined above, the increases negotiated centrally in the PNR and PESP were applied locally in the great majority of instances, even in relatively profitable and buoyant sectors. Local variations in excess of national norms were by no means unknown, but never amounted to wholesale free-riding on the terms of the pay deals. Given the historical record, the 3 per cent clause of the PESP might reasonably have been expected to trigger second-tier pay rises without accompanying concessions on labour productivity. Even remaining sceptical regarding the depth of the recorded productivity concessions, the general pattern under local bargaining in 1993 was for employers to demand, and for unions to agree, changes in labour practices in return for pay rises. Overall, in sharp contrast to the 1970s, locally-negotiated pay drift has not emerged as a significant feature of pay determination in the period since 1987. "Special" pay rises continued to pose serious difficulties in the public service, and public service workers have insisted on maintaining relativities with workers in the private sector. Progress on changing the system of public service pay determination has been considerably slower than governments and private sector employers would have wished. However, the reform of public service pay and the grading system on which public service pay determination is based is now seriously on the agenda. Meanwhile, public management have continued the long-familiar practice of conceding special pay rises but deferring and phasing the resulting increases to lessen their budgetary impact.

The imperative to maintain competitiveness has been a fixed concern of employers throughout the history of collective pay determination in Ireland. The period since 1987 presents a mixed record on pay and cost competitiveness. The trend in the earnings of Irish workers in manufacturing relative to Ireland's trading partners — when corrected for exchange rate variations, the most straightforward index of cost competitiveness — improved from 1987 to 1989. From 1990 Ireland's competitive position weakened somewhat, due mainly to declining differential wage rises relative to the UK, declining inflation in the UK and the depreciation of Sterling (NESC, 1993: 42–4). Trends in unit wage costs, which take account of changes in productivity as well as in wages, provide a better measure of competitiveness. However, in practical terms this measure is perilous in the Irish case due to the impact on changes in unit labour costs of the high productivity multinational sector and sharp divergences in productivity between sectors. What the measure nevertheless reveals for Ireland during the 1980s is a significant fall in unit labour costs and improved competitiveness on this measure (see Teague, 1994). Thus, overall, competitiveness improved over most if not all of the period of tripartism since 1987 and it remains unclear whether the setbacks of the period from 1990, reflected in relative wage trends, indicate a new trend or a temporary setback.

The national wage agreements of the 1970s had failed to deliver industrial peace. During the period of free collective bargaining between 1981 and 1987 the incidence of strikes and the number of working-days lost fell significantly, although the number of workers involved remained high (see Brannick, Doyle and Kelly, this volume). Under tripartite bargaining all indicators of industrial conflict show a sharp reduction. The relative incidence and seriousness of strikes over pay has also declined significantly. These declines are of particular significance given the economic recovery experienced after 1987. It also bears emphasis that many of the most serious and protracted incidents of industrial conflict during the period of tripartitism arose not over straightforward wage militancy but in response to attempts by companies to restructure labour practices radically in the face of serious commercial difficulties. Disputes in banking and in a series of semi-state companies, notably RTE, Aer Lingus, TEAM, Irish Steel and CIE, can best be understood as defensive struggles by unions to preserve pay and conditions in the face of management insistence on radical change. Other protracted disputes have arisen over union recognition, most notably at Pat the Baker and Nolan Transport.

Government and employers have lauded the contribution of tripartism to the maintenance of competitiveness and industrial peace. The role of tripartism in bringing the public finances back under control has already been discussed. Each of the programmes explicitly endorsed the prevailing macro-economic strategy based on maintaining the value of the punt within the EMS narrow band and progressively reducing the debt/GNP ratio. Progress on these fronts has been evident. The forced devaluation of the punt in 1993 led to a once-off rise in the debt/GNP ratio. The currency crisis also revealed the competitive hazards attending an exchange-rate policy which took no direct cognisance of trends in the value of the punt relative to the currency of Ireland's main trading partner. Employers, the government and many commentators regard public sector pay as a major financial problem which has not been adequately addressed by the Programmes. Employers claim that trends in public sector pay should reflect to a greater degree what the exchequer can afford and also take account of the relative employment security of public servants. Governments have shown greatest concern with the budgetary implications of special pay rises, and increased impatience is evident with "stop-start" mechanisms which allow for the deferral and phasing of special awards.

Overall, with the exception of the record on employment and the level of unemployment, developments since 1987 are in closer harmony with the objectives of tripartism than was the case in the previous period of sustained tripartism during the 1970s. Moreover, economic and industrial relations trends since 1987 show significant improvements over those recorded during the return to decentralised bargaining in the 1980s.

How these trends are to be understood, and what they reflect with respect to the character and consequences of tripartism during the late 1980s and early 1990s, remains a matter of considerable controversy. One point is, however, uncontroversial. The return to centralised bargaining in 1987 was the outcome of profound crisis affecting the labour market, public finances and business performance and confidence. The Irish case of a return to tripartism provides a pointed illustration of the argument of a number of writers, reviewed in Section I, that conditions other than centralised organisation on the part of unions and employers, or social democratic dominance of governments, can lead to neo-corporatism. But while profound crisis may have led to the re-emergence of neo-corporatism, the features and longer-term stability and durability of crisis-induced neo-corporatism pose a series of questions. In the Irish instance these questions have met with different answers; and the developments at issue may in truth be too recent to allow sufficient perspective for arriving at a reliable set of conclusions. Current interpretations of tripartism since 1987 will be considered and assessed in conclusion.

One line of interpretation views developments since 1987 as little more than the state using corporatism as a vehicle for the imposition of macro-economic adjustment on powerless workers. By locking unions into agreements with strong deflationary consequences, and which ran in parallel with programmes of cost cutting in the public sector, some argue that the Programmes neutralised what would otherwise have been intense union resistance to Government policy (see von Prondzynski, 1992). A number of objections can be raised against this view. Doubtless, Governments' continuing concern to engage in concertation with unions reflected a belief that economic management and adjustment could be accomplished with less disruption, and at lower political risk, than proceeding unilaterally in the teeth of union opposition. Nor can it be doubted that the economic problems and circumstances of the period from 1987 left little room for major union gains. But unions also retained the capacity to adopt a strategic posture, even in the parlous circumstances of the late 1980s. Their return to tripartism was based on an assessment that the net effects of centralised bargaining were more beneficial than relying on free collective bargaining in circumstances of labour market and fiscal crisis. The unions have sought to trade wage moderation and economic peace for a role in macro-economic policy-making and state commitments on areas such as taxation, the maintenance of social programmes and the regulation of the labour market. Von Prondzynski's (1992) verdict on tripartism, which amounts to portraying it in terms of neo-liberal policy measures within a corporatist shell, takes insufficient account of the alternatives facing unions in 1987; their assessment of the longer-term strategic opportunities of tripartism and the real, if modest, achievements of the Programmes in the areas of taxation, social programmes and employment legislation.

Teague (1994) adopts a similar line of argument and feels the need to distinguish between corporatism Irish-style since 1980, which he terms "developmental corporatism", and the "social corporatism" of European states like Austria, Denmark and Sweden. The Irish experience with corporatism since 1987, he argues, amounts to little more than unions agreeing to a programme of severe measures to adjust the Irish economy first to fiscal crisis and then to European integration. In this exercise the social goals central to European corporatism were all but ignored and the positive consequences of tripartite consensus on pay and income distribution failed to materialise. Teague is particularly critical of union assent to the strong currency policy and views union enthusiasm for the Programmes as the product above all of a concern to appear "good Europeans" (Teague, 1994: 14). Developmental corporatism portrays circumstances in which economic and political elites engage in a "national development strategy" geared towards economic modernisation. This type of corporatism ignores many of the social and labour market objectives of social corporatism. In Ireland, Teague (1994: 27) claims, it was driven by elites, including groups of union leaders, "imbued with a vision of a modern Ireland in a new Europe".

That Irish corporatism differs substantially from classic European cases, with respect to the economic context in which it has operated, as well as with respect to certain of its features and consequences, is uncontroversial (see Roche, 1987; Hardiman, 1988; 1992). What can be contested is Teague's insistence on the need to recognise a new species of corporatism, "developmental corporatism", to portray the Irish experience.

Even allowing that Irish tripartism has been introduced in circumstances of extreme economic difficulty, which inevitably have limited its impact on economic performance, Teague's case for developing a new concept of corporatism, so-called "developmental corporatism", to portray the Irish experience with tripartism since the late 1980s, rests on a series of questionable premises. The internal dynamics of developmental corporatism are not outlined in any detail by Teague, but those details that are sketched — the trade union elite sanctioning drastic policies in order to join a modernising drive and to look like "good Europeans" — appear implausible and unhelpful in comprehending the dynamics of tripartism in Ireland. Those dynamics, though heavily constrained by major economic difficulties, compounded by demographic trends and structural problems, and constrained also by features of the industrial relations and political system, are better comprehended in terms of the generally familiar logic of neo-corporatist exchange between economic interest groups. That neo-corporatism might arise in last-ditch circumstances of economic crisis, and might be oriented heavily to addressing crisis conditions, is familiar from the general literature on corporatism; that economic and fiscal circumstances might limit the objectives and achievements of neo-corporatism is also well understood (see Sharpf, 1991; Mjoset, 1992: Part V); that structural conditions might also impose limits to neo-corporatist initiatives is finally well understood. These issues have been considered by writers on centralised pay bargaining in Ireland (see Roche, 1987; Hardiman, 1988; 1992). Finally Teague's argument that tripartism in Ireland since 1987 has ignored "social objectives" is flatly contradicted by the trend in social and health spending and progress on employment legislation. His claim (1994: 24) that tripartism has not adopted an equalitarian stance on pay dispersion is based on data on public service pay differentials alone. Given the apparent success of the Programmes in binding workers in well-paid industries and occupations to the general pay norms, it can reasonably be argued that the Programmes have at least constrained market forces which would otherwise have resulted in a higher level of wage inequality generally.

Teague's contention (1994: 40) that industrial relations and pay determination in Ireland sit poised between the "adversarial employee relations practices of the past" and more effective (social) corporatist arrangements is less contentious and poses perhaps the most important question concerning tripartism since 1987. That is, to what degree can developments since 1987 be viewed as heralding a move towards more stable and effective neo-corporatist arrangements than proved possible in the circumstances of the period 1970–81?

This is a question considered by Hardiman (1992) in her review of the PNR and the PESP. Hardiman emphasises the effects on the tripartite agreements of the extremely serious economic circumstances in which they were concluded. In contrast to Teague, she suggests that the very limited room for manoeuvre available to all parties to the deals may be the key to the apparently greater stability and effectiveness of tripartism in the 1980s as compared with the 1970s. Given the magnitude of the problems which faced the social partners, individually and collectively, there was little room for the wage drift, back-sliding and auction politics which had debilitated national bargaining during the 1970s and early 1980s. The international economic recovery which set in from 1987 also contributed to a general perception that tripartism in the 1980s and early 1990s had been successful.

Hardiman (1992: 351–6) appears to suggest, however, that the underlying features of the industrial relations and political systems, which had limited the effectiveness of tripartism during the 1970–81 period, remain essentially unchanged. The diversity of interests within the trade union movement continued to pose problems for the ICTU leadership, now, it appeared, more firmly committed to a central strategy of engaging in tripartism as a means of copying small open European economies like Austria, Finland and Denmark. For Hardiman the conditional nature of support for tripartite programmes and the patterns of support and opposition apparent during the 1970s continue to be evident in the internal politics of the trade union movement.

The impact of the major trade union merger wave of the 1980s and early 1990s, and the consequent growth in trade union concentration on such organisational tensions, will take some time to determine. The current major trend appears to be for the traditional polarities between British and Irish unions and between craft and other unions to decline in favour of a new line of potential conflict between public service and private sector unions and employees. Also of potential significance for the prospects of tripartism is the succession to union leadership in the late 1980s of a number of figures with a distinctly more European outlook on trade union policy and strategy. The new generation of leaders like Peter Cassels, Bill Attley, Philip Flynn and John O'Dowd, appear significantly more concerned to learn lessons from

European countries, especially the small European economies, than their predecessors. In this respect, they seem less inclined to want to be seen as "good Europeans", or "modernisers", in the sense proposed by Teague (1994), than to move the trade union movement along a path that holds out the prospect of a "social market economy", involving sustained wage growth, high-skill industries, regulated labour markets and extensive social programmes.

The fiscal crisis of the late 1980s and early 1990s limited the scope for governments to engage in auction politics and engendered a greater degree of consistency in economic policy. Whether greater revenue buoyancy might trigger a return to the short-termism of the 1970s remains an open question. The underlying shape of the party system remains unchanged, in spite of major shifts in electoral support for the main political parties in recent years. What may be significant in this respect, considering the importance in expenditure terms of the public service pay bill, are the attempts being made by public service management to reform the public service grading system and, at least, to open debate on public service pay determination. These initiatives may fail and lead to a return to stop-go waves of special claims, or they may succeed and provide a new degree of predictability and order in public service pay.

Making a point also emphasised by Teague (1994), Hardiman (1992: 356) notes that effective mechanisms linking pay restraint to employment generation continue to prove as elusive in the late 1980s and early 1990s as during the 1970s.

Thus, the sustainability and effectiveness of neo-corporatist programmes remain matters of debate. While the programmes have proved more stable than those of the 1970s, and have been associated with economic and social gains on all sides, many of the underlying features of Irish industrial relations and politics, which eventually undermined tripartism during the 1970s, remain unchanged. Others, for example consensus on economic policy, union concentration and the outlooks of influential sections of union leadership, appear to have changed. How significant those changes may prove to be remains to be determined.

CONCLUSION

This chapter has examined the course of pay determination over a period of some 70 years in the context of the changing contours of state policy towards the conduct of industrial relations and pay bargaining. The chapter charted the increasing economic and political significance of collective bargaining, as a growing proportion of the workforce were unionised and bargaining arrangements came to exert a major influence on macroeconomic policies and outcomes. The changing postures of governments towards collective bargaining were influenced directly by such developments and by the priority accorded to industrial development in national policy and politics and the particular strategies of industrial development pursued. A corporatist strategy towards industrial relations had first been urged by Sean Lemass in the circumstances of postwar economic readjustment. This had failed in the face of the commitment of unions and employers to the status quo. The eventual move towards some form of neo-corporatist accommodation with unions and employers was influenced initially by the policy of industrialisation in the context of an open economy. The operation and effects of the pay round system of pay determination during the 1960s added further impetus to attempts to control and centralise collective bargaining. The economic turbulence of the 1970s was met with a series of nine national pay agreements. By the close of the decade all the parties to tripartism found reasons to doubt the effectiveness of centralised bargaining. But the return to decentralised collective bargaining over the period 1981–87 proved no panacea for any of the parties to industrial relations. Wages grew more sharply than employers anticipated; trends in competitiveness were unimpressive and the pace of wage increases seemed unaffected by rising unemployment. Unions feared marginalisation, and lost large numbers of members; their remaining members suffered declining disposable incomes. The state faced a mounting fiscal crisis which appeared intractable — at least at sustainable political cost — to existing policies. The result was a return to tripartism from 1987, encouraged first by profound economic crisis and then by a growing consensus that such a course appeared to be succeeding. Different assessments have been made of tripartism since 1987 and of the prospects of centralised bargaining. The critical test of tripartism will surely come with economic recovery. Then, either recent achievements will be reinforced by a "virtuous circle" in which success will feed commitment to centralised bargaining, in anticipation of further success, or the constraining forces which eventually debilitated national bargaining during the 1970s will again find expression and undermine centralised bargaining.

References

(a) Government Publications

(All published by the Government Publications Office, Dublin)

1957. *Economic Development.*
1963. *Closing the Gap.*
1969. *Third Programme for Economic and Social
        Development 1969–.*
1976   *Economic and Social Development, 1976–1980*
1977. *Budget, 1977.*
1979. *Programme for National Development, 1978–81.*
1981. *Budget, 1981.*
1987. *Programme for National Recovery.*
1991. *Programme for Economic and Social Progress.*
1994. *Programme for Competitiveness and Work.*

(b) Books and Articles

Armingeon K. (1986): "Formation and Stability of Neo-Corporatist Income Policies: A Comparative Analysis", *European Sociological Review*, 2: 138–47.

Baglioni, G. and Crouch, C. (1990): *European Industrial Relations: The Challenge of Flexibility*, London: Sage.

Cameron, D. (1984): "Social Democracy, Corporatism, Labour Quiescence and the Representation of Economic Interest in Advanced Capitalist Society" in J.H. Goldthorpe (ed.).

Calmfors, L. and Driffill, J. (1988), "Bargaining Structure, Corporatism and Macroeconomic Performance", *Economic Policy: A European Forum*, 6: 13–61.

Collins, S. (1992): *The Haughey File: The Unprecedented Career and Last Years of the Boss*, Dublin: O'Brien Press.

Collins, S. (1993): *Spring and the Labour Story*, Dublin: O'Brien Press.

Coogan, T.P. (1993): *De Valera: Long Fellow Long Shadow*, London: Hutchinson.

Crouch, C. and Pizzorno, A. (eds.) (1978): *The Resurgence of Class Conflict in Western Europe Since 1968*, 2 vols., London: Macmillan.

Currie, J. (1979): *Industrial Politics*, Oxford: Oxford University Press.

Daly, M. (1992): *Industrial Development and Irish National Identity, 1922–1939*, Dublin: Gill and Macmillan.

Farnham, D. and Horton, S. (1993): *Managing the New Public Services*, London: Macmillan.

Farrell, B. (1983): *Sean Lemass*, Dublin: Gill and Macmillan.

FitzGerald, G. (1991): *All in a Life: An Autobiography*, Dublin: Gill and Macmillan.

Fogarty, M., Egan, D. and Ryan, W.J.L. (1981): *Pay Policy for the 1980s*, Dublin: Federated Union of Employers.

Galbraith, J.K. (1992): *The Culture of Contentment*, London: Sinclair-Stevenson.

Girvin, B. (1989): *Between Two Worlds: Politics and Economy in Independent Ireland*, Dublin: Gill and Macmillan.

Goldthorpe, J.H. (1984): *Order and Conflict in Contemporary Capitalism: Studies in the Political Economy of Western European Nations*, Oxford: Clarendon Press.

Grafton, D., Sheehan B. and Murphy, Y. (1983): "The Twenty-Third Wage Round: An Industrial and Economic Analysis of Pay Settlements During 1983/84", *Industrial Relations News Report*, September 1983 (supplement).

Grafton, D., Murphy, Y. and McDermott, V. (1984): "The Twenty-Fourth Wage Round: An Industrial and Economic Analysis of Pay Settlements During 1984/85", *Industrial Relations News Report*, November 1984 (supplement).

Greaves, D. (1982): *The Irish Transport and General Workers' Union: The Formative Years*, Dublin: Gill and Macmillan.

Hardiman, N. (1988): *Pay, Politics and Economic Performance in Ireland, 1970–87*, Oxford: Clarendon Press.

Hardiman, N., (1992): "The State and Economic Interests: Ireland in Comparative Perspective" in J.H. Goldthorpe and C.T. Whelan (eds.), *The Development of Industrial Society in Ireland*, Oxford: Oxford University Press for the British Academy.

Henley, A. and Tsakalotos, E. (1992): "Corporatism and the European Labour Market after 1992", *British Journal of Industrial Relations*, 30: 567–86.

Horgan, J. (1987): "The Future of Collective Bargaining" in T. Murphy (ed.).

Industrial Relations News Report (1979–94): *IRN Report*.

Irish Congress of Trade Unions: *Annual Reports* (for years cited in text), Dublin: ICTU.

Jacobsen, J.K. (1994): *Chasing Progress in the Irish Republic*, Cambridge: Cambridge University Press.

Kaufman, B. (1993): *The Origins and Evolution of the Field of Industrial Relations in the United States*, New York: ILR Press.

Kochan, T.A., Katz, H. and McKersie R.B. (1984): *The Transformation of American Industrial Relations*, New York: Basic Books.

Kochan, T.A. (1993): "Managing Transformational Change: The Role of the Human Resource Professional", *International Journal of Human Resource Management*, 4: 569–90.

Korpi. W. (1978): *The Working Class in Welfare Capitalism*, London: Routledge and Kegan Paul.

Korpi, W. (1983): *The Democratic Class Struggle*, London: Routledge and Kegan Paul.

Kotsonouris, M. (1994): *Retreat From Revolution: The Dail Courts, 1920–24*, Dublin: Irish Academic Press.

Labour Court: *Annual Reports* (years cited in text), Dublin: The Labour Court.

Lee, J.J. (1989): *Ireland 1912–1985: Politics and Society*, Cambridge: Cambridge University Press.

McCarthy, C. (1973): *The Decade of Upheaval: Irish Trade Unions in the Nineteen Sixties*, Dublin: Institute of Public Administration.

McCarthy, C. (1978): *Problems in the Field of Dispute Resolution*, Third Countess Markievicz Memorial Lecture, Dublin: Irish Association for Industrial Relations.

McCarthy, W.E.J., O'Brien, J.F. and O'Dowd, V.G. (1975): *Wage Inflation and Wage Leadership*, Dublin: Economic and Social Research Institute.

Manning, M. (1970): *The Blueshirts*, Dublin: Gill and Macmillan.

Maier, C.S. (1984): "Preconditions for Corporatism" in J.H. Goldthorpe (ed.).

Middlemass, K. (1979): *Politics in Industrial Society: The Experience of the British System Since 1911*, London: Andre Deutsch.

Millward, N. (1994): *The New Industrial Relations?*, London: Policy Studies Institute.

Mitchell, A. (1974): *Labour in Irish Politics 1890–1930*, Dublin: Irish University Press.

Mjoset, L. (1992): *The Irish Economy in a Comparative Institutional Perspective*, Dublin: National Economic and Social Council.

Murphy, T. (1986): "Take-Home Pay: An Examination of Trends in Wages, Wage Taxes and Inflation", *Industrial Relations News Report*, 17.

Murphy, T. (1987/89) *Industrial Relations in Ireland: Contemporary Issues and Developments*, Dublin: Department of Industrial Relations, University College Dublin.

National Economic and Social Council (NESC) (1986): No. 83. *A Strategy for Development*, 1986–1990, Dublin: NESC.

National Economic and Social Council (NESC) (1990): No. 89. *A Strategy for the Nineties*, Dublin: NESC.

National Economic and Social Council (NESC) (1993): No. 96. *A Strategy for Competitiveness, Growth and Employment* Dublin: NESC.

National, Industrial and Economic Council (NIEC) (1965): No. 11. *Report on the Economic Situation*, Dublin: NIEC.

National, Industrial and Economic Council (NIEC) (1966): No. 15. *Arrangement for Planning at Industry Level*, Dublin: NIEC.

National, Industrial and Economic Council (NIEC) (1967): No. 18. *Report on Full Employment*, Dublin: NIEC.

National, Industrial and Economic Council (NIEC) (1970): No. 27. *Report on Incomes and Prices Policy*, Dublin, NIEC.

Nolan, P. (1989): "Walking on Water? Performance and Industrial Relations Under Thatcher", *Industrial Relations Journal*, 20: 81–92.

O'Brien, J.F. (1981): *A Study of National Wage Agreements in Ireland*, Dublin: Economic and Social Research Institute.

O'Brien, J.F. (1987): "Pay Determination" in T. Murphy (ed.).

O'Connor, E. (1988): *Syndicalism in Ireland, 1917–1923*, Cork: Cork University Press.

O'Connor, E. (1992): *Labour History of Ireland 1824–1960)*, Dublin: Gill and Macmillan.

O'Mahony, D. (1965): *Economic Aspects of Industrial Relations*, Dublin: Economic and Social Research Institute.

O'Neill, E. (1964): "Re-Organisation and Adaptation of Industry", *Administration*, 12: 48–54.

Panitch, L. (1980): "Recent Theorisations of Corporatism: Reflections on a Growth Industry", *British Journal of Sociology*, 31: 159–85.

Pizzorno, A. (1978): "Political Exchange and Collective Identity in Industrial Conflict" in C. Crouch and A. Pizzorno (eds.) Vol. 2.

Regini, M. (1984): "The Conditions for Political Exchange: How Concertation Emerged and Collapsed in Italy and Great Britain" in J.H. Goldthorpe (ed.).

Redmond, V. (1985): *An Analysis of the breakdown of National Agreements and Understandings*, unpublished MBS thesis, Dublin: University College Dublin.

Roche, W.K. (1982): "Social Partnership and Political Control: State Strategy and Industrial Relations in Ireland" in M. Kelly, L. O'Dowd and J. Wickham (eds.), *Power, Conflict and Inequality*, Dublin: Turoe Press.

Roche, W.K. (1987): "State Strategies and the Politics of Industrial Relations in Ireland since 1945" in T. Murphy (ed.).

Roche, W.K. and Redmond, M. (1994): "Legislation, Collective Bargaining and the Regulation of Working Time in Irish Industrial Relations" in R. Blanpain, J. Rojot, and E. Kohler (eds.), *Legal and Contractual Limitations to Working Time in European Union Member States*, Leuven: Peters.

Schmitter, P. (1979): "Still the Century of Corporatism?" in P.C. Schmitter and G. Lehmbruch (eds.), *Trends Towards Corporatist Intermediation*, London and Beverley Hills: Sage.

Schmitter, P. (1981): "Interest Intermediation and Regime Governability" in S. Berger (ed.), *Organizing Interests in Western Europe*, Cambridge: Cambridge University Press.

Services, Industrial and Professional Trade Union (SIPTU)(1994): *Report on Programme for Economic and Social Progress: Expiry Dates*, unpublished report prepared by the SIPTU research department.

Sharpf, F.W. (1991): *Crisis and Choice in European Social Democracy*, Ithica, New York and London: Cornell University Press.

Strauss, G. (1951): *Irish Nationalism and British Democracy*, London. Batsford.

Sweeney, G. (1990): *In Public Service: A History of the Public Service Executive Union 1890–1990*, Dublin: Public Service Executive Union with the Institute of Public Administration.

Teague, P. (1994): *"Pay Determination in Southern Ireland: Towards Social Corporatism?"*, unpublished working paper, Jordanstown: Department of Applied Economics and Human Resource Management, University of Ulster.

Thelan, K.A. (1991): *Union of Parts: Labor Politics in Post-War Germany*, London: Cornell University Press.

von Prondzynski, F. (1985): "The Death of the Pay Round", *Industrial Relations News Report*, 24: 16–20.

von Prondzynski, F. (1992): "Ireland: Between Centralism and the Market" in R. Hyman and A. Ferner (eds.), *Industrial Relations in the New Europe*, Oxford: Blackwell.

Whyte, J.H. (1980): *Church and State in Modern Ireland 1923–1979*, Dublin: Gill and Macmillan.

Younger, C. (1979): *Ireland's Civil War*, London: Fontana.

CHAPTER 6

INDUSTRIAL RELATIONS IN THE PUBLIC SECTOR

Michael McGinley

This chapter considers industrial relations in the public sector under
five main headings: the contexts of public sector industrial relations;
an overview of the public sector; the negotiation systems; industrial
relations outcomes and the future.

THE CONTEXTS OF PUBLIC SECTOR INDUSTRIAL RELATIONS

The Role of Government

Ireland's public sector employs some 277,000 workers (1996) — 21 per
cent of the total number employed in the economy. The 1996 pay bill
for public service workers whose pay is met from the annual current
budget is just over £4.8 billion or 38 per cent of the total current expenditure, £12.5 billion net. Figure 6.1 shows these key figures in a
slightly wider context. The public sector's growth and cost will be ex-
plored later.

The size of the public sector depends largely on the role of the
state in society. Kennedy (1985) in a review of the role of the state in
economic affairs identifies three categories of state intervention:

- income redistribution

- stabilisation of employment and prices, and

- development of the nation's economic potential.

In any economy, the aims of economic policy may be mutually inconsistent. In Ireland's small open economy there is the further problem that
the government has little control over many of the key issues which are
believed to contribute to economic success. Kennedy (1985) asserted that
"the desire to accomplish a radical diminution in the economic role of
government represents a retreat from reality and a reluctance to confront

FIGURE 6.1: GOVERNMENT EXPENDITURE

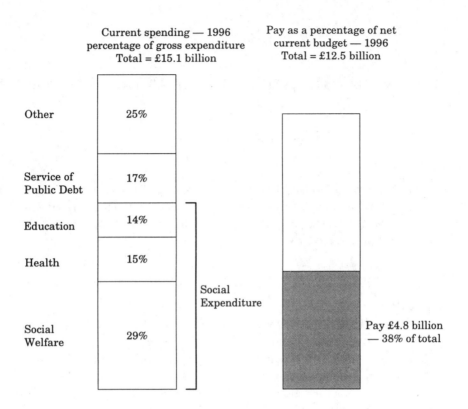

Current spending — 1996
percentage of gross expenditure
Total = £15.1 billion

Pay as a percentage of net
current budget — 1996
Total = £12.5 billion

Other — 25%

Service of Public Debt — 17%

Education — 14%

Health — 15%

Social Welfare — 29%

Social Expenditure

Pay £4.8 billion — 38% of total

Source: Administration Yearbook and Diary, 1997

the serious economic and social problems facing an evolving world". Even if this were valid in 1985 many Western economies are continuing to reduce the economic role of government.

Attitudes to state involvement in the economy have special relevance for industrial relations in the public sector. The government may be confronted all at once with demands bearing on its role as manager of the economy and also on its perceived responsibility to provide fair settlement systems (the level playing pitch idea). It may, at the same time, be asked to respond to pay demands from its own workforce. In essence, the government is asked to be manager, referee and player — a combination of roles which makes a winning performance difficult.

The attitude of government to the public sector in Britain is described by Beaumont (1992) as follows:

> . . . the generally hostile position of the government (for economic, ideological, and industrial relations reasons) towards the public sector has essentially remained constant . . .

This contrasts with the Irish mixture of ambivalent benevolence to the public sector, our pragmatic reaction to events and a tendency for governments to give priority to what will carry us through to the next election — in other words, just muddling through.

The International Setting

Beaumont (1992) found that, despite vast international differences, "many of the contemporary issues and developments in public sector industrial relations . . . appear to transcend individual systems . . .". Among the current trends he mentions are:

1. Since the late 1980s privatisation has become an international phenomenon, for example Germany (Volkswagen), Canada (North Canada Power Commission), France (four major industrial enterprises — GCE, St Gobain, CGCT, Matra).

2. Many programmes supported by the International Monetary Fund in developing countries involved public expenditure cuts and public sector wage restraint.

3. A 1993 OECD study found that the share of public sector employment (excluding public enterprises) in OECD countries increased from 11.6 per cent in 1960 to 17.7 per cent in 1977. In the early 1980s public sector employment as a percentage of non-agricultural employment was 39 per cent in Sweden, 36 per cent in France, 32 per cent in Britain, 28 per cent in Italy, 27 per cent in West Germany and 19 per cent in the USA. In the years 1951–81, public sector employment doubled in most western countries except the USA.

4. There were wide differences in the proportion of women in public sector employment in an eight-country study, 1965–77, ranging from 70 per cent in Sweden to one third in Japan and Australia. The public sector is becoming more female intensive over time.

5. Public sector workers tend to be more highly educated than those in the private sector. They also tend to be older.

6. Many advanced countries, for example Sweden, Germany, Japan and Italy, have specific legislation covering various aspects of public sector industrial relations, such as the extent of unionisation, the means for determining conditions, the right to strike and the resolution of disputes. Britain is, however, an exception.

7. The public sector is highly unionised in many countries, for example Sweden, Germany, UK, and Japan. The USA and, to a lesser extent Italy, are exceptions.

Irish controversies are clearly not unique.

The National Setting

Economic conditions have major implications for industrial relations generally. Public sector industrial relations affect the national economy directly and in turn are affected by the economic and political fortunes and misfortunes of the country. Irish economic issues are conveniently discussed by Leddin and Walsh (1995) and in Reports Nos. 96 and 99 of the NESC. The *Quarterly Bulletin* of the Central Bank and the *Quarterly Economic Commentary* of the Economic and Social Research Institute comment on current trends, highlighting movements in GNP, unemployment and inflation and scrutinising the public finances. All of these issues are of great economic significance as well as being topics of intense debate both in industrial relations and in politics.

The public finances have a direct bearing on industrial relations generally, not least because of the impact of income tax on take-home pay. In public sector industrial relations public finance is a central theme. Figure 6.1 showed that 38 per cent of the current budget is spent on public service pay and also that 17 per cent of expenditure goes on service of the public debt. In 1995 public debt at about £31 billion was equivalent to 91 per cent of GNP (Central Bank, *Quarterly Bulletin*, Winter 1996). The new EU measure of public borrowing expresses the "General Government Deficit" as 76 per cent of GDP in 1996 (NESC, Report No. 99). This debt was built up since 1974 mainly by borrowing to meet day-to-day expenditure including, of course, the pay bill.

The size of the public service pay bill depends on the numbers employed and on pay levels. Table 6.1 gives an overview of the share of the net current budget spent on pay since 1970.

TABLE 6.1: PAY IN THE CURRENT BUDGET 1970–96

Year	Current Budget £ million	Public Service Pay in Budget £ million	Pay as % of Total
1970/71	491	134	27%
1971/72	571	163	29%
1972/73	663	200	30%
1973/74	798	253	32%
1974/75	1,037	314	30%
Break in Series			
1975	1,331	479	36%
1976	1,664	584	35%
1977	1,994	667	34%
1978	2,391	801	34%
1979	2,893	997	35%
Break in Series			
1980	3,439	1,392	40%
1981	4,419	1,729	39%
1982	5,537	1,982	36%
1983	6,309	2,175	35%
1984	6,950	2,335	34%
1985	7,642	2,500	33%
1986	8,125	2,625	32%
1987	8,323	2,759	33%
1988	7,989	2,845	36%
1990	8,437	3,160	37%
1991	9,034	3,422	38%
1992 (revised)	9,816	3,750	38%
1993 (revised)	10,523	4,087	39%
1994	11,165	4,356	39%
1995	12,029	4,564	37%
1996 (est.)	12,516	4,813	38%

Source: McGinley 1991, (updated).

OVERVIEW OF THE PUBLIC SECTOR

Definitions

Defining the Irish public sector is relatively simple, despite some confusion over the two key terms, the public service and the public sector. The public sector, defined as all those employed by or under the State, consists of eight main groups shown in Table 6.2.

TABLE 6.2: COMPOSITION OF THE PUBLIC SECTOR

Group	Numbers Employed 1996 (thousands)
Health	65
Education	58
Civil Service	31
Local Authorities	27
Defence	14
Garda (Police)	11
Non-commercial State Bodies	8
Public Service	216
Commercial State Bodies	62
Public Sector	277

Source: Administration Yearbook and Diary, 1996. (*Note:* Totals affected by rounding to nearest thousand.)

The non-commercial state bodies do not, in general, sell services to customers. They provide "free" services to the public — examples are FÁS (Foras Áiseanna Saothair — The Training and Employment Authority), the Industrial Development Agency and Bord Fáilte (the Irish Tourist Board).

Public service employees are defined in this chapter as all those whose pay is met each year entirely or almost entirely from the current budget. The public sector is defined as the public service with the addition of the workers in the commercial state bodies who are paid by the companies themselves. There has not been consistency in the use of the terms even in the two major works on public sector numbers — Humphreys (1983) uses the term public service to describe all groups, while Ross (1986) introduces the new term "public domain" for the public sector. Over the years the statistics for public sector numbers have improved but they are still not entirely reliable. Indeed, the Institute of Public Administration's Yearbook and Diary warns that some of the figures they present "are estimates (especially in the cases of local authorities, education sector and health services) and while they may be taken to show a trend, they should be treated with caution".

Expansion of the Public Sector
Table 6.3 charts expansion in five major public service groups over 20 years.

TABLE 6.3: PUBLIC SERVICE GROWTH 1970–90

Category	1970	1980	1990	per cent change	
		Thousands (part-timers converted to full-time equivalents)		1970–80	1970–90
Civil Service (excluding Posts and Telegraphs)	20.1	34.1	28.6	+70 %	+42 %
Gardaí	6.5	9.6	10.9	+48 %	+68 %
Defence Forces	9.8	15.5	14.4	+58 %	+47 %
Health Services	38.8 (1971)	59.5	58.4	+53 %	+51 %
Education	33.1	49.1	51.0	+48 %	+54 %
TOTAL	108.3	167.8	163.3	+55 %	+51 %

Source: McGinley, 1991

The modest fall of 4,500 between 1980 and 1990 has been more than reversed since then. In 1996, the numbers employed in these areas reached 180,400, up 67 per cent on 1970. The main structural changes affecting these figures since 1970 have been the establishment of the health boards in 1971, taking health functions mainly from county councils; the halving of the civil service with the setting up of Telecom Éireann and An Post in 1984; the transfer of about 2,000 forestry service civil servants to the newly established commercial state body, Coillte, in 1989 and the transfer of some 600 staff to the newly formed commercial state body, the Irish Aviation Authority in 1994. Non-commercial state bodies and local authorities whose pay has fallen almost entirely on the budget only since domestic rates were abolished are not included in the table above.

Privatisation
The numbers in the Irish public sector have not, so far, been greatly affected by one of the trends of our time — privatisation. The services to be provided by government in any society depends to some degree on ideology. The mood elsewhere, especially in the UK and USA, is for small government with strong pressure to let the private sector take over functions heretofore discharged by government. So far Irish privatisation has been confined largely to the commercial state bodies,

although there is an increasing move right across the public sector to contract out work such as security, catering and cleaning. Irish Life and the Irish Sugar Company, employing about 4,000 between them, have already been privatised and others may be in the pipeline. It is not so much ideology which underlies these moves as an effort to bail out an exchequer weighed down by massive burdens of welfare and debt and, of course, an annual pay bill of almost £5 billion.

Special Industrial Relations Features
Significant features of the Irish public sector which may have special industrial relations relevance are summarised below.

1. The public sector is distinguished by blocks of employees which are large by Irish standards. Part-time working has not yet made a great impact. EU trends suggest that a big increase in part-timers is likely.

2. The commercial state bodies are the only part of the public sector to decline in numbers since 1970 but the decline has not been as great as the decline in this area in Britain.

3. In the public service, there are three groups with a relatively small number of separate grades — education, defence and garda (police). The other four have varied work-forces but note one big group in the health authorities — some 26,000 nurses.

4. About half the public sector has a negotiation system peculiar to itself — conciliation and arbitration — while the other half has access to the Labour Court/Labour Relations Commission system which also covers the private sector. The Department of Finance attempts to keep tight control over all aspects of the public service industrial relations system, especially pay settlement.

5. Trade union density is high in the public sector — about 80 per cent compared with less than 40 per cent in the private sector. An ICTU committee co-ordinates union activity in the public service. About 52 per cent of ICTU affiliated members in the Republic of Ireland are in the public sector.

6. Public service pay at £4.8 billion in 1996 accounts for 38 per cent of the Government's current budget.

7. Many public sector groups provide essential services, for example workers in electricity, some health areas, police and prison staffs and air traffic controllers.

8. Two of the smaller public service groups are predominantly male — the garda and the defence forces.

9. Strikes patterns are notable for the recurrence of long strikes involving thousands of workers, especially in commercial state bodies.

THE NEGOTIATION SYSTEMS IN THE PUBLIC SECTOR

This section looks first at the background to the institutional arrangements for industrial relations in the public sector and then examines how they operate at present. The negotiation arrangements in the public sector in 1986 are summed up in a reply to a Dáil question reproduced in Table 6.4.

There are two negotiation systems in the public sector. About half the workers use the Labour Court/Labour Relations Commission system to which private sector workers have access. The other half have a system of conciliation and arbitration. The background to this separate negotiation system must be examined as it is sometimes alleged that the system itself gives unduly favourable treatment to those covered by it, a view which may exaggerate the influence of institutions and systems on the outcome of pay negotiations.

Background

Negotiation arrangements for the civil service were the subject of much political dispute right from the establishment of the Irish Free State in 1922 (Advisory Conciliation and Arbitration Service, 1980; McGinley, 1976; 1986; 1991; Official Reports Dáil Éireann, 7 (45), 1924). In 1917 a Conciliation and Arbitration Board was set up to deal with pay claims by government employees in the UK, including Ireland. It had three members, a High Court judge as chairman, a representative of "the employing class" and one of workers. Its decisions had to be unanimous and the parties had to agree in advance to accept and implement decisions. Arbitration was abolished in 1920 on the recommendation of the House of Commons' Geddes Committee, set up to recommend more efficient methods. Geddes argued that arbitration was not consistent with the newly introduced Whitley arrangements for joint consultation. Arbitration was not reintroduced in the British civil service until 1925 (O'Connell, 1968).

TABLE 6.4: PUBLIC SECTOR ADJUDICATION

Access to adjudication bodies for the main employee groups in the public sector.

	Arbitration Boards		Labour Court	
	Category	*Numbers (approx.)*	*Category*	*Numbers (approx.)*
Civil Service non-industrial	Grades up to Assistant Secretary	30,800	—	—
industrial	—	—	All categories	8,000
Gardaí	All ranks excluding Commissioners	11,400	—	—
Teacher (1st + 2nd level and RTCs)	All categories	43,000	—	
Other education groups	VEC clerical etc. staff	1,000	Other categories	8,000
Health Boards (a)	Officer grades (includes general nurses)	23,500	Manual and craft grades; psychiatric nurses	16,000
Voluntary hospitals (a)	—	—	All categories	16,000
Local authorities	Officer grades	10,000	Servants	25,500
Non-commercial State Bodies	—	—	All categories	9,000
Commercial State Bodies ESB	—	—	All categories; in theory, seldom used (b)	12,000
An Post and Telecom Éireann	Temporary voluntary C & A schemes for most grades; civil service arbitrator	8,500 / 18,000	Legal entitlement to go to Court waived temporarily	
Others	—	—	All categories	49,200
		146,200		143,700

(a) In the health area, officer grades viz. General nurses, paramedical and clerical grades employed directly by the Health Boards have access only to arbitration. Similar grades in voluntary hospitals have access only to the Labour Court.

(b) ESB have their own Industrial Council.

Source: Reply to Dáil Question by Mr. Vincent Brady, 6 March 1986.

Before arbitration was abolished in 1920, the UK civil service grading system for general grades was formalised by a reorganisation committee of the National Whitley Council in 1920 and in May 1920 the basis on which civil service pay was fixed was revised at arbitration (Duncan and Ryan, 1946).

The Irish National Teachers' Organisation, set up in 1868, formally registered as a trade union in 1918 and affiliated to the Irish Trade Union Congress and Labour Party. In 1918, they brought a pay claim to arbitration despite Treasury objections which buckled after a one-day strike. In 1920 the teachers were again at arbitration and got a sizeable increase just before arbitration was abolished.

Before 1922 an Irish Civil Service Joint Council had been set up to advise the National Whitley Council in London on Irish matters. Immediately after the new Irish Government took over in 1922 General Michael Collins, Minister for Finance, and W.T. Cosgrave, President of the Executive Council (equivalent to Taoiseach now), met a staff deputation pressing for the creation of a National Whitley Council on British lines. The civil war and the death of Collins took place before a final decision was taken. In 1924, President Cosgrave made it clear that Whitley Councils would not be accepted: "But it is not right that Ministers should divest themselves of their powers and responsibilities by leaving it to such bodies to say what salaries will be payable in the civil service or not" (Official Reports, Dáil Éireann, 7, (45), 1924). Some such body as the Police Representative Council which provided the police "with a definite mouthpiece for putting forward their views on questions affecting conditions of service" was what the government had in mind. Negotiation was not envisaged.

In 1926 an advisory Civil Service Representative Council had its first meeting. It was boycotted by several civil service unions, notably the big Post Office Workers' Union, led by Bill Norton, a Labour deputy in 1926 and 1932–65, and leader of the Labour Party 1932–60. The Institution of Professional Civil Servants and the Civil Service Clerical Association also stayed away to show their displeasure.

While the denial of effective negotiation machinery and arbitration was seen as a major source of grievance, it should be recalled that two major groups — national teachers and the civil service — had had important reviews of their pay and conditions just before independence. In the 15 years after 1922 prices fell and pay was linked indirectly to price levels.

During the 1932 election campaign, Fianna Fáil promised to introduce arbitration in the civil service if elected. A commission on the civil service was set up in June 1932, chaired by the conservative ex-

Secretary of the Department of Finance, Joseph Brennan (Commission of Inquiry into the Civil Service, 1932–35). It was asked to submit an interim report on "the application of the principle of arbitration already accepted by the Government". Its interim report of February 1934 recommended that arbitration should "take place only on specific issues to be agreed on each occasion between the Minister for Finance and the body of Civil Servants concerned". This formula was rejected by the unions with Norton to the fore. Arbitration now became a political issue. Norton pressed hard for arbitration and the issue was raised on the floor of the Dáil several times. But the Government did not yield.

There was great turmoil in Irish politics after Fianna Fáil's accession to power in 1932 — the land annuities were withheld, agricultural prices collapsed, the Blueshirts appeared and the IRA revived. Ireland's economic woes were a reflection of the worldwide depression but from the mid-thirties on there were signs of recovery. The government's policy of developing infant industries behind high tariffs began to bear fruit. The adoption of a new constitution in 1937 and a new trade agreement with Britain promised stability. But in the industrial relations arena all was not well. Nineteen thirty-seven was a year of great industrial disruption and still holds the record for days lost in strikes in Ireland in one year — 1.75 million days. The trade union movement was driven by discord especially over the issue of British based unions. Inter-union disputes in the workplace were common. ITUC tried to solve the problem under pressure from Sean Lemass, Minister for Industry and Commerce, but their efforts ended in 1940 in procedural farce (McCarthy, 1974; Lyons, 1973).

In 1938, Labour, generally Fianna Fáil's ally in the 1930s, voted with Fine Gael on a motion demanding arbitration. The Government was defeated and de Valera, recently successful in the economic talks with Britain, went to the country and got an overall majority. A Fianna Fáil government steeling itself for neutrality in the war against fascism had no intention of bringing in arrangements which would reduce its control over a major part of its budget.

Public sector industrial relations in the 1930s and 1940s were much influenced by two public service trade union leaders who were also TDs — Bill Norton and T.J. O'Connell. O'Connell was General Secretary of the Irish National Teachers' Organisation from 1916–48 and was a Labour deputy from 1922–32 and Labour leader from 1927–32 when he was replaced by Norton. From 1924–57 Norton was General Secretary of the Post Office Workers' Union — the biggest civil service union — and also played a leading role in the Labour

Party. He was Tánaiste and Minister for Social Welfare in the 1948–51 inter-party government and Minister for Industry and Commerce in the 1954–57 government. His accession to ministerial power was to play a crucial part in the evolution of the present public sector negotiation system.

After the war, a great flood of pay claims was expected and Lemass moved to modernise the state conciliation system which was still based on the Conciliation Act, 1896. His Industrial Relations Act, 1946 was passed at a time when the Labour movement was split over allegations of communism, the British-Irish issue in unions and the ever-present Larkin-O'Brien rancour. To this background, the Act denied access to the new Labour Court to a major part of the public service. There were genuine fears that access to the Court would draw civil service associations closer to the trade union movement and inevitably embroil them in the politics of the "fruitless squabbling of bitter men". The reservations voiced by Cosgrave in 1924 about the government losing its sovereignty were also in the background. There were fears too that the reduction in real incomes in the war years might give the public service a strong case for massive pay rises which would receive sympathy from an adjudicating body not amenable to government influence and with no responsibility for raising the money to foot the pay bill. In the debate on Lemass' Industrial Relations Bill, Norton moved an amendment to allow the public service access to the Labour Court but it was defeated. Within two years, Norton was Tánaiste and Minister for Social Welfare in the inter-party government of 1948–51. Jim Larkin had died in 1947 and O'Brien had retired from the ITGWU in 1946.

The long awaited desire for arbitration was now to be fulfilled. A scheme of conciliation and arbitration for civil service was introduced in 1950 and made permanent in 1955. Similar schemes were introduced for other public service groups — teachers (1954, 1955), gardaí (1962), local authorities (1963).

The Conciliation and Arbitration Schemes
Before looking at the operation of the public service conciliation and arbitration schemes in detail, a comment on government/ministerial control and the co-ordination of trade union activities in the public sector is called for.

In public service conciliation and arbitration the government may be compared to the board of a holding company operating close control over the day-to-day operations of its subsidiaries. In government the Minister for Finance has the prime responsibility for all cost-increasing activities. The Minister's sanction is required for all expenditure, including expenditure arising from industrial relations activities. Department of Finance officials monitor closely all on-going negotiations and all offers of any significance must have Finance approval in advance. The method of control varies from area to area but the main objective remains the same — to keep operating costs to a minimum.

Control is tightest in the civil service. The main negotiation is done at the General Council which is chaired by a Department of Finance official at Secretary level. Depending on the issues at stake, the Minister may be consulted personally on proposed offers and in major cases the Minister may consult the government. The government lays down policy on major issues, for example the line to be followed on general pay claims. Officials negotiate within the policy guidelines keeping the Minister and, if necessary, the government informed of progress. Occasionally Ministers may meet the unions to try to break a logjam in major negotiations.

Each department has a Departmental Council for issues affecting its own staff. Senior departmental officials — "the official side" — negotiate on claims but offers have to have the prior approval of the Department of Finance. It can happen that Finance officials disagree with their colleagues at departmental level on the merits of a claim, and if they cannot reach a common position ministers and even the government may become involved.

In the conciliation and arbitration arrangements for teachers, gardaí and the Army, Finance officials work closely with officials from the Departments of Education, Justice and Defence. The personal involvement of ministers in these sensitive areas is not unusual, either to sort out differences at official level or on rare occasions to negotiate directly on claims.

The position is different in the local authorities and health boards. The management here are County Managers and Chief Executives of Health Boards and two Boards (The Local Government Management Services Board and the Health Service Employers Agency) coordinate negotiations. The Department of Finance, however, monitors offers through the officials of the Departments of the Environment and Health, quelling the independence of local negotiators. The arrangements for arbitration in this area are unusual in that either side may reject a finding within six weeks, but such rejection is rare.

In the state bodies, the government seeks to monitor and influence significant negotiations. Close control is exercised over the non-commercial bodies. The commercial state bodies are also closely watched, especially as some of them supply essential services.

The Department of Finance's job of controlling pay is a difficult operation, not least because unions are often critical of the Finance role. Non-pay conditions are also controlled closely — many of them with major cost implications, for example pensions.

Finance control cannot be directly exercised at arbitration. Here, the management side make their presentations in rebuttal of union submissions and both sides await the finding of the arbitrator. The findings often set headlines which, in effect, predetermine conciliation offers on many other claims. The ability of officials (predominantly from the Department of Finance) and trade union leaders in convincing the arbitrator is central.

Ministers are especially sensitive about any threatened strikes in the public service, especially if they threaten sensitive services, for example air traffic, prisons, welfare payment, school examinations, security. Ministerial monitoring of official negotiators is intense in such situations.

In 1995 there were 14 ICTU unions in the Republic of Ireland catering solely for the public sector, with a total membership of about 140,000. Most of these unions confine themselves to one area in the public sector. Workers in most state sponsored bodies and in some public service areas are represented by general unions rather than by unions confining themselves to the public sector. The proportion of workers in unions is much greater in the public sector than in the private sector. Indeed, 52 per cent of ICTU members in the Republic of Ireland are in the public sector.

Two principal mechanisms co-ordinate the public service unions. Within individual conciliation and arbitration schemes staff panels are set up as a forum for unions to formulate claims. These panels are akin to groups of unions in the private sector and through them managements avoid simultaneous negotiations with different unions on similar claims. At national level, the Public Services Committee of ICTU provides a forum for joint action on major issues. The public service unions play an influential role in ICTU. The high density of union membership in the public service contributes to this. The quality of several union general secretaries from the public service has also enhanced the status of the public service in ICTU. Charles McCarthy (Teachers' Union of Ireland), Maurice Cosgrave (Post Office Workers' Union) and Dan Murphy (Public Service Executive Union) are three examples of public service trade union officials who have held the presidency of ICTU with distinction.

The following extract from McGinley (1976) gives a brief description of the operation of the nine separate conciliation and arbitration schemes in operation at that time. Since then the Minister for Finance has replaced the Minister for the Public Service and the Civil Service has been halved with the setting up of An Post and Telecom in 1984. While the Industrial Relations Act, 1990 made some changes in the Labour Court system, no fundamental changes have been made in the conciliation and arbitration system since its introduction over 40 years ago. In the Programme for Competitiveness and Work (1994) the Government and ICTU agreed that discussions on public service pay determination and industrial relations machinery would be completed by 31 March 1994. This deadline was not met. Some important changes were agreed in the civil service in October 1994. These are described later.

Operation of the Conciliation and Arbitration Schemes

The main features of the nine C & A schemes are best summarised under seven headings: (a) grades covered, (b) recognition of unions, (c) conciliation procedures, (d) items for discussion at conciliation, (e) arbitration procedures, (f) items for arbitration, and (g) treatment of arbitration reports.

Grades Covered

The scope of the schemes is very wide. The civil service scheme covers all grades up to and including Higher Executive Officer level (Assistant Principal level for professional grades). Of the 49,700 civil servants, about 2,000 are above this level. The 47,700 workers, under the scheme, are organised in about 800 grades. Officers above the rank of Chief Superintendent are not covered by the C & A scheme for police. County Managers, Assistant County Managers and Chief Executives of Health Boards do not come within the scope of the local authority scheme. There is no upper limit in the other schemes — those for teachers, Vocational Education Committee and County Committee of Agriculture staffs, Postmasters and Branch Managers of employment exchanges. The pay of workers above the level of the schemes has been considered by the Review Body on Higher Remuneration in the Public Sector, appointed in May 1969 under the chairmanship of Dr. Liam St John Devlin. The Review Body is also concerned with the pay of members of parliament (including government members), judges and chief executives of state-sponsored bodies.

Recognition

All the schemes have rules about recognition of unions or staff associations. The usual provision is that associations/unions wishing to be recognised for purposes of the schemes will seek recognition from management — most schemes specify the Minister for the Public Service as the recognising authority. Civil service associations must not be affiliated to any political organisation — an exception is made for associations which had such an affiliation before 1 April 1949 (notably, the Post Office Workers' Union). There is provision for consultation with the staff before recognition is given to new associations. Most schemes provide for staff panels which represent all the recognised unions. Some 50 unions/associations have been recognised under the civil service scheme. The main ones are the Civil and Public Services Staff Association, representing (among others) the big grades of clerical assistant, clerical officer and staff officer, the Post Office Workers' Union, the Irish Post Office Engineering Union, the Institute of Professional Civil Servants, the Civil Service Executive Union and the Federation of Government Employees. Many of the smaller associations are affiliated to the Civil Service Alliance. All of the civil service unions are composed solely of civil servants. Three teachers' unions — the Irish National Teachers' Organisation, the Association of Secondary Teachers in Ireland and the Teachers' Union of Ireland — represent teachers. Representative bodies, set up under statute, represent the gardaí. Professional staffs of County Committees of Agriculture are organised in one union — the Irish Agricultural Advisors' Organisation. Postmasters and branch managers of employment exchanges have their own organisations. Some 15 unions are represented on the staff panel for the local authority scheme with the Local Government and Public Services Union, the Irish Nurses' Organisation and the Irish Medical Union being especially important. General unions have recognition for some of the local authority officers. Most of the big public service unions are affiliated to the Irish Congress of Trade Unions (ICTU) and play an active part in it.

Conciliation Procedures

Most of the schemes have one conciliation council where management (typically termed the "official side") and unions (the "staff" side) negotiate under a chairman — usually the chief official side representative. The civil service scheme provides for a general council for matters of service-wide concern and departmental coun-

cils for discussions of local interest. There is provision in some schemes for a mediator appointed by the then Minister for Labour to act as chairman under certain circumstances. The official side is composed of a specified number of officials representing the department to which the group involved is attached and, under some schemes, the Department of the Public Service. Representatives of the Local Government Staff Negotiations Board form the official side under the local authority scheme. The staff side is usually appointed by a panel of staff representatives set up in accordance with the terms of the schemes. Each side has a secretary. Reports are prepared of discussions on claims and agreed by both sides. The reports may record agreement or disagreement. The recommendations in the reports are submitted to the appropriate minister(s) — usually the Minister for the Public Service. Save on very rare occasions agreed recommendations are accepted.

Conciliation Discussions

A wide range of items may be discussed at conciliation. There are some variations between the schemes but the tendency has been for the range of items for discussion to be widened. The main items specified for discussion are:

- Pay
- Allowances (including subsistence, travelling and disturbance allowances)
- Overtime rates
- Hours
- Grading
- Principles governing recruitment, promotion, discipline, superannuation and annual sick leave.

Matters not specified may be discussed by agreement of both sides.

Arbitration Procedures

Each of the schemes provides for an arbitration board with an independent chairman, appointed in most cases by the government in agreement with the staff side. All boards have representatives of the official side and the staff side and, under a recently agreed arrangement, two Labour Court members when requested by either side for a particular claim. Other interests are represented on some *boards, for example managers of schools on the Teachers' Board. A statement of case and counter statement are prepared by the union and official side on each claim. Claims are considered by the board in private, save on the rare occasion when one side requests a public hearing. Offers or counter-offers made at conciliation are not disclosed at arbitration. The chairman reports on each claim with his finding usually to the Minister for Public Service. [The chairmen have usually been eminent senior counsels, for example Mr. T.K. Liston, SC, Mr. R.N. Cooke, SC, Mr. Sean Gannon, SC, (now Mr. Justice Gannon), Mr. J.A. D'Arcy, SC (now Judge D'Arcy), Mr. Sean D. O'Hanrahan, SC].*

Items for Arbitration

The schemes specify what matters may go to arbitration. A typical list of arbitration items includes claims for, or in regard to, the rates or the amount of:

- *pay and allowances in the nature of pay*

- *overtime*

- *total weekly hours of work*

- *annual and sick leave*

- *subsistence allowances*

- *travelling, lodging and disturbance allowances.*

Claims coming for arbitration must have been discussed at conciliation and have been disagreed there. Agreed recommendations from conciliation on arbitrable items which are not accepted by the Minister for the Public Services are also arbitrable — this type of claim rarely arises. Disputes on arbitrability of claims are settled by the Arbitration Board.

Treatment of Arbitration Board Reports

The typical arrangement is that reports of the board are sent by the chairman to the Minister for the Public Service, who presents it to Dáil Éireann within one month of receipt. Within three months the finding must be accepted or a motion for rejection or modification moved in Dáil Éireann. The local authority scheme is unusual in that findings of its Arbitration Board go to both sides, either of which may reject them within six weeks.

A few points in relation to the Conciliation and Arbitration Schemes are particularly noteworthy:

1. The procedures for union recognition accept that all groups covered by a particular scheme are entitled to have a union to represent them. They are not, however, free to be represented by whichever union they care to choose. The Minister for Finance has the crucial role on recognition matters since there is an unwritten rule that in the civil service that only unions composed solely of civil servants will be recognised. There has been a slight relaxation in this policy recently when IMPACT — an amalgamation of a local government and a civil service union — retained civil service recognition even though it is not now composed solely of civil servants. When large numbers of civil servants were transferred to An Post and Telecom Éireann in 1984, some of them, especially those in the clerical/executive area, continued to be represented by civil service unions though they were no longer civil servants. Non civil service unions have on occasion sought to organise civil servants but have been resisted by both the Minister and the unions. Indeed the local authorities and the health boards are the only major groups in the conciliation and arbitration system in which this exclusivity does not apply.

2. At the conciliation or direct negotiation stage the unions form a staff panel through which all claims are filtered thus reducing the likelihood of mutually inconsistent claims. The staff panels negotiate with management on claims with the sponsoring union in the lead role.

3. In effect, almost any issue may be discussed at conciliation but only a narrow range of items may be taken to arbitration. An arbitration claim is brought by the sponsoring union and not by the staff panel except in the rare case where the staff panel itself promotes a claim affecting everyone, for example a general pay claim.

The essential difference from the private sector is that disagreed pay claims go to an arbitration board for a finding rather than to the Labour Court for a recommendation. While Labour Court recommendations have been rejected by both unions and, less frequently, by managements, it is extremely rare for a public service arbitration board finding to be rejected or even modified. The government is not obliged to accept Arbitration Board findings but under most of the schemes — the local authority scheme is an exception — it is required to move a motion in the Dáil if it wants to vary a finding. The first such motion arose following the fourth report of the Civil Service Arbitration Board in 1952 on a claim for a general increase in pay — the 4th Round. Sean MacEntee was Minister for Finance in a Fianna Fáil government with five seats short of a majority. MacEntee, "fully imbued with the financial orthodoxy of the establishment" (Browne, 1981), moved a motion to modify the arbitration finding. The strong union protests with public meetings and marches played a part in the defeat of Fianna Fáil in the general election of May 1954. The new Fine Gael-led coalition paid the arbitration award in full. With a few exceptions governments have accepted arbitration findings since then. A government decision in 1986 not to pay the full arrears of a pay increase recommended at arbitration for teachers caused great controversy including a series of short strikes by teachers.

Another difference from Labour Court practice is that the arbitrator is not told of any offers made at the conciliation stage, a fact which makes for long arbitration hearings compared with the Labour Court.

The chairmen of Arbitration Boards are appointed with the agreement of the unions, usually for a year. The procedure is for management, with the agreement of the appropriate minister or the government, to suggest one or more names to the staff side for consideration. If the staff side does not agree with any of the suggested names they may ask for others. Stalemate rarely arises. On occasion, the government has been criticised by the unions for delay in appointing or reappointing an arbitrator. Delay caused much protest in the mid-1980s and again in 1993 as the unions felt that the delay was a tactic to make them more amenable or simply an effort to delay the processing of arbitration claims. Up to the 1970s, the various schemes had different arbitrators but the current practice is to have the same chairman for all boards. The arbitrator has immense personal power. Decisions by him (there has never been a woman) can cost the Exchequer huge sums on a continuing basis. Most arbitrators have been eminent lawyers and some have later become High Court judges.

In the 1960s different arbitrators were involved in what become known as the public service "status round". The tone was set by an increase of 23 per cent agreed at conciliation level for the then pivotal grade of Clerical Officer in the civil service. At a time when inflation rarely exceeded 5 per cent a wave of special increases averaging 20 per cent emerged from the conciliation and arbitration system. This was on top of the 9th round general pay rise of 12 per cent in 1964. There was great alarm and solutions to the problem were sought by worried ministers. The pay system itself was a prime object of attack.

The feeling was that a system separate from the Labour Court was no longer warranted. But the public service unions would not agree and the government lacked the will or the inclination to proceed without agreement.

Paddy Hillery, Minister for Labour, produced a compromise solution in his Industrial Relations Act, 1969. He took power to appoint two Labour Court members to each Arbitration Board but undertook not to do so until he got the unions to agree. Agreement was not forthcoming, except for the teachers who voluntarily accepted the Labour Court members on their boards. Following protracted negotiations, all the schemes were amended in the 1970s to allow for the addition of Labour Court members at the request of either side for individual arbitration claims. An element of farce now entered. Labour Court members were introduced at arbitration on a number of occasions but they made no real contribution to the proceedings. The chairman had at the end of the day to decide each case. Hillery's provision, as adapted, was allowed to lapse.

Another change which failed to make an impact was a provision introduced in the 1970s whereby a mediator appointed by the Minister for Labour could be introduced to help with stalled conciliation discussions. This idea was borrowed from the private sector where industrial relations officers have had great success as conciliators. In the public service, management had been used to making their final offers in direct discussions and the attempted reform effectively lapsed when management could not be persuaded to improve offers when the mediator entered the scene.

The report of the Commission on Industrial Relations 1978–81, chaired by Séamus Ó Conaill (1981) gave much space to the public service. It recommended that the arbitration boards in the public service should be replaced by a separate division of a proposed Labour Tribunal which would replace the Labour Court and would also cover workers generally. They hoped this would be done by negotiation with staff interests and recommended a two-year limit for the change-over. By this time, the public service unions had achieved a high degree of influence and were a key group in ICTU. They opposed the idea, and despite growing criticism of the outcome of public service pay negotiations, neither Ministers Quinn of the Labour party nor Ahern of Fianna Fáil grasped the nettle in their proposals for legislation which eventually reached the statute book as the modest Industrial Relations Act, 1990. Recent efforts to reform the public sector systems will be discussed at the end of this chapter. It may well be that improved performance in public sector industrial relations is affected only marginally by institutions and that the key to success has more to do with government leadership in difficult times and the abilities of negotiators.

Groups Not Covered by Conciliation and Arbitration

The conciliation and arbitration schemes cover grades up to quite senior levels — Principal in the Civil Service. This left the highest grades without any appeal forum for pay settlements. A feature of general pay rises down the years has been tapering which narrows differentials leaving the higher paid relatively worse off. The widening tax wedge exacerbates this trend (OECD, 1987). Pressure from top grades for independent review of pay met with success in 1969 with the setting up of the Review Body on Higher Remuneration in the Public Sector with a mandate to review, at the request of the Minister for Finance, the pay of civil servants and local authority officers outside the scope of conciliation and arbitration, chief executives of state bodies, members of the Houses of the Oireachtas (parliament), including ministers, and the judiciary and other top groups which might be referred to it by the minister. The minister's initiative is crucial — groups may not put a claim before the Review Body but their views are fully heard when the Review Body is considering ministerial requests for review. In 1984 the senior civil service grades of Assistant Principal and Principal were removed from the Review Body's ambit and given their own conciliation and arbitration scheme.

In 1984 virtually all the staff of the Department of Posts and Telegraphs — 28,000 (about half the civil service) — were removed to form two major commercial state bodies, An Post and Telecom Éireann. These were no longer in the public service and now had access to the Labour Court. It was agreed, however, with ministerial approval that the new bodies would retain access to the arbitration board "for a temporary period". This is in contrast with the other state bodies — with one major exception, the Electricity Supply Board (ESB) — where the final stage in negotiation is normally accepted to be the Labour Court. Negotiation arrangements in all but three of the state bodies follow the private sector pattern described elsewhere in this book (see Chapter 5).

Three major commercial state bodies do not use the Labour Court system. As well as An Post and Telecom Éireann, the Electricity Supply Board has its own arrangements. Any group of workers in the economy with the co-operation of management can agree on a private adjudication system for disputes. But it is surprising that three major state companies employing between them about half the total in all state bodies opt not to use the state-provided Labour Court system which has been widely accepted. The reason why An Post and Telecom still use public service arbitration may be understood, if not explained, by the fact that both management and unions have been using it since 1950. Indeed, the Post Office Workers' Union played a lead role in the genesis and operation of the scheme. The ESB's experience is different.

The ESB, employing over 10,000 workers, is one of Ireland's most important companies. Apart from its economic significance as a supplier of a basic commodity to industry, its industrial relations impact is central. It is undoubtedly a supplier of an essential service. Its pay and other conditions may become a target in other parts of the public sector as well as in employment generally. Canning (1981) gives a useful account of ESB industrial relations following the changes recommended in the Fogarty Report (1969). On the issue of finality in dispute settlement Canning summarises the position as follows:

> For many years previously (before 1969), there was provision for arbitration in ESB industrial relations through the medium of the ESB Tribunals which were statutory bodies under a chairman appointed by the Minister. Claims not resolved in direct negotiation were normally submitted to the relevant tribunal, which heard evidence and issued its decision. In theory this should have been the end of the matter and indeed the ESB habitually accepted the tribunal findings, but in practice the unions felt free to reject decisions and by the late sixties they were doing so with growing frequency. Moreover, awards made by the tribunals in key ESB disputes were causing concern elsewhere and there was an increasing clamour for their abolition and the use of the Labour Court instead.

Fogarty recommended the abolition of the tribunal system and the Industrial Relations Act, 1969 removed their statutory basis. The unions objected and a campaign of action by them succeeded in getting the Minister for Labour and the ESB management to agree to the continuation of the tribunals in a non-statutory form. A new ESB Joint Industrial Council was set up in 1970. The Council has five members — a chairman and a permanent representative of both management and staff with two added members for each hearing, one from each side. It hears evidence, takes written submissions and makes a recommendation, which is non-binding unless agreed otherwise in advance. The Council handled an average of 100 cases a year in the 1970s. The failure of the ESB and the government to change the system illustrates the old industrial relation adage about giving the lion's share to the lion.

Six very diverse groups in public service with access to the Labour Court/Labour Relations Commission system are listed in Table 6.5.

TABLE 6.5: PUBLIC SERVICE CATEGORIES WITH ACCESS TO THE LABOUR COURT/LABOUR RELATIONS COMMISSION

Category	Number (1986)
Civil Service Industrials	8,000
Education area	8,000
Health Boards	16,000
Voluntary Hospitals	16,000
Local Authorities "Servants"	25,500
Non-commercial State Bodies	9,000
Total	82,500

Source: Dáil Debates, 1986

Apart from some of the workers in the health area and in the non-commercial state bodies, most of these workers are not highly paid, being engaged in semi-skilled or skilled manual work. Their rates of pay do not often come to public notice as a result of strike action. Indeed their pay may be linked to conciliation and arbitration categories who make the running. Apart from the period 1982–87, national level bargaining has operated in Ireland since 1972 for basic pay rises. Civil service industrials have a Joint Industrial Council chaired by an Industrial Relations Officer of the Labour Relations Commission (Cox and Hughes, 1989). If agreement is not reached a claim may be referred to the Labour Court. Other groups have less formal arrangements, with the Labour Court being the final fall-back. It would be a mistake to assume that the work of these categories is not of high importance. The distress caused when streets are not cleaned or when sewers back up are witness to the contrary. A peculiar anomaly arises for nurses. Health board nurses have access to the local authority conciliation and arbitration scheme while nurses in the voluntary hospitals come under the Labour Court/Labour Relations Commission as do health board psychiatric nurses. The potential for co-ordinated operations in both theatres has not been ignored by nursing unions.

INDUSTRIAL RELATIONS OUTCOMES

The outcomes of the industrial relations system in the public sector are, in effect, the conditions applying to some 277,000 workers which have been negotiated between management and unions within this system. Three issues will be examined here: (a) the criteria for pay settlement, (b) the outcome of pay bargaining and (c) some non-pay conditions. Beaumont (1982) makes the point that "in Britain, the performance of public sector industrial relations tends to be overwhelmingly seen in terms of wage outcomes (together with the associated issue of strike activity)" and adds that this is very much the situation internationally.

Criteria for Pay Settlement

It is well to distinguish between two important elements in the pay scene — existing pay patterns and changes in these patterns from time to time. Most commentators place great emphasis on pay changes at a particular time and take as given the broad pattern of pay relationships which have emerged down the years. But the pattern of pay relationships reflects hundreds of value judgements made over time on the worth of particular jobs. There is no necessary logic or equity in the pay patterns of today. They are the outcome of past power struggles, changes in technology, shifts in consumer tastes and, let it be admitted, the accumulation of the mistakes of generations of negotiators. Changes in pay in a particular pay round are relatively minor adjustments of the existing pattern. The industrial relations system is not geared to take an overview of the system so as to produce a more logical and more equitable matrix of pay relationships. The system is rather like a steeplechase with much jockeying for position and not a little bumping and boring. Income tax, a major mechanism for income redistribution, has direct relevance to take home pay but it does not normally enter the negotiation picture. Occasional attempts have been made to adjust relativities overall as, for instance, in the early national pay agreements of the 1970s which deliberately gave relatively more to the lower paid.

Two early reports show how difficult it is to arrive at usable criteria for fixing pay in the public sector. In 1937 the Minister for Finance set up a Committee of Inquiry into Ministerial and Other Salaries with John Shanley, MD as Chairman (1937). In January 1923 the Dáil had accepted the recommendations of a parliamentary Select Committee that ministers should be paid £1,700 a year and the President of the Executive Council (equivalent to the Taoiseach) £2,500 a year with £360 of this free of tax. In 1929 a Joint Committee of both Houses recommended that the salaries of ministers remain unchanged. When Fianna Fáil came to power in 1932 salaries were reduced to £1,500 a year for the President and £1,000 for ministers by voluntary acceptance of the persons concerned. The new figures were to be entirely free of tax. The Shanley Committee decided that the rates being paid in 1937 — the same as those in 1932 — were too low. They felt that rates in British Commonwealth countries and in some small European countries were no guide, nor was the £10,000 a year paid to the British Prime Minister. One line urged in evidence was that ministers' pay should bear some relation to the income of "those holding the leading positions in the professions, business and other skilled and specialised occupations". The committee concluded that ministers' pay should be good enough to attract some of the best minds in the nation. They examined incomes in other occupations, compared ministers with "other members of the community" and took particular note of the salary of the Chief Justice (£4,000 a year) and of Supreme Court judges (£3,000 a year). They decided that a substantial increase was warranted but considered that the service of the State should, in some degree, remain "idealised" and that financial rewards should be on a very moderate scale and take account of the cost to the public purse. They recommended £3,000 a year for the President (Taoiseach) and £2,250 for ministers, all salaries to be fully subject to taxation. A new system of ministerial pensions was also recommended.

Duncan and Ryan (1946) had even greater difficulty. Duncan, Professor of Political Economy at Trinity College Dublin, and Ryan, a TCD Scholar, were retained by the Association of Higher Civil Servants to report on the pay of higher civil service grades. (Ryan played a distinguished part later on in Irish academic and public life as Professor W.J.L. Ryan, price theory expert, and chairman of the National Industrial Economic Council in the 1960s). In 1946 Duncan and Ryan set out to compare the pay of higher civil servants in 1914 with pay in 1945/46, to compare higher pay levels in the civil services of Ireland and the UK, to assess the share of the higher civil service in the national income and to investigate the relationship between the remuneration of the higher civil service and "the level in commerce and industry and in outside employment generally". They summarised the principles recommended by various commissions for settling civil service pay (see Table 6.6).

Duncan and Ryan reported that the greatest difficulty was "experienced in finding an adequate number of 'administrative' posts

TABLE 6.6: PAY PRINCIPLES FOR THE OFFICIAL CIVIL SERVICE

Reports 1914-35	Recommended Principles
1914 Royal Commission on the Civil Service (Macdonnell Commission)	The Government should be a model employer.
1923 Anderson Committee	The employer should pay what is necessary to recruit and retain an efficient staff.
1927 The Industrial Court — Award No 1325 on Post Office servants	The maintenance of a fair relativity as between their wages and those in outside industries as a whole.
1931 Tomlin Commission	Civil Service pay should reflect a long term trend both in wage levels and in the economic conditions of the country. The "Model Employer" principle was not useful. The higher grades did not compare favourably with outside rates for comparable work and should get an increase when the economic situation allowed.
1935 Brennan Commission on the Irish Civil Service	Pay should be sufficient to recruit and retain efficient staff. Pay should bear some relationship to that in comparable outside employment without "undesirable lack of harmony".

Source: Duncan and Ryan, 1946.

in Irish commerce and industry". Comparisons could not be made with banks where managers had no definite scales. Some comparisons with secondary teachers were made. They wrote to 15 of the largest industrial and commercial companies and had interviews with 11 of them. They could not identify a "typical" commercial executive. There was little evidence of grading of commercial staff and they said it was "not unnatural" that no information was disclosed about salaries at the top levels. The main views they got in the private sector were about the short hours of higher civil servants, the unpressurised jobs, the security, the automatic promotion and pensions. Businessmen, they found, regarded the civil service as "probably too well paid" but refused to divulge the factual bases for this conclusion. Despite this lack of enthusiasm in the business sector — most unwelcome to the union that had commissioned the report — Duncan and Ryan reported that "the incomes of higher civil servants are not keeping pace with the rest of the community", that the higher civil service as a class were losing ground in relation to other classes and occupations and that the situation could be remedied only by an upward revision of basic salary scales. The union had to wait for five years before getting any out-of-line or special increases for senior civil servants and the special increase then given was designed merely to compensate for cost-of-living increases denied to them before 1946.

Pay negotiators, arbitrators and committees have over the years attempted to lay down criteria for settling relative levels of pay. The Report of the British Royal Commission on the Civil Service 1953–55 chaired by Raymond Priestley (1955) set out principles for settling civil service pay. These were tremendously influential in Ireland. Two criteria were highlighted: (a) comparison with the pay of outside workers doing similar work and (b) where such comparisons were lacking — internal relativities.

In Britain an elaborate Pay Research Unit was set up following the Priestley Report to provide a sound basis for comparisons. In Ireland the comparison principle was indeed applied but internal relativities assumed great importance from an early stage. Certain key grades were identified early on, for example Clerical Officer and Engineer Grade III (Civ'l). Once these key grades had been fixed the second Priestley principle, internal relativities, was used to settle the pay of a wide range of workers on jobs with no real counterparts outside the public service. The reliance on internal relativities has become a marked feature of Irish public service pay negotiation leading to the paradox that special increases spread so widely that the description "special" is almost meaningless.

In Britain the Megaw Committee on Civil Service Pay (1982) diluted somewhat the Priestley principle of fair comparison. They said that comparative data must be viewed in their proper perspective "to ensure greater public confidence in the system, and to ensure that it is cost effective". In this enigmatic statement Megaw was asserting that the government's ability to pay must be taken into account. Gretton and Harrison (1982) reviewed Megaw in depth in "How Much Are Public Servants Worth?".

The Review Body on Higher Remuneration in the Public Sector, chaired by Liam St John Devlin (1972), discussed six possible criteria for settling pay in its second report:

1. Comparison with the pay movements or comparison with current rates in other employments and the related question of supply/demand;

2. Cost-of-living changes;

3. Changes in national productivity, past or projected;

4. The performance of the employees concerned;

5. Internal relativities within the employment concerned; and

6. The national interest.

The Review Body decided that the criteria they should follow were comparisons with current rates (not with pay movements unless duties had remained the same over time), internal relativities and the national interest. They said that comparisons with current rates were a reliable and inevitable criterion. They also accepted the national interest as a valid criterion but in terms so vague as to be almost meaningless, for example they would not recommend unjustifiable increases which could lead to demands elsewhere. The Review Body, in effect, adopted the Priestley principles. Indeed, they went a bit further in asserting that comparisons were a "reliable criterion". Reliability depends essentially on the care with which comparisons are applied over time in the messy business of fixing pay.

In its 1987 general report the Review Body, now chaired by Dermot Gleeson, adhered to the 1972 criteria adding on the public finances that they had taken "account of the need to establish an appropriate relationship between remuneration levels in the public and private sectors and of the current critical state of the public finances" — a somewhat obscure statement on a matter of crucial importance but echoing the sentiment as well as the vagueness of Megaw.

The degree to which Irish arbitrators should take account of the government's ability to pay has been controversial. The chairmen of the main Arbitration Boards are appointed by the government with the agreement of the unions. Peter D. Maguire SC had an unusually short stint as civil service arbitrator in 1982. In a report on a claim by inspectors in the Department of Education the question of the state of the public finances arose. The management representatives "adverted to the current state of the public finances and the urgent need to reduce the current budget deficit . . ." The arbitrator rejected the pay claim but dismissed the submission on the public finances as follows:

> No regard is being taken of the economic argument submitted by management which is considered wholly irrelevant to procedure at arbitration . . . It is regrettable that management continues to introduce this submission at arbitration level, having regard to its obvious irrelevancy and also having regard to the fact that in this instance as in others although given full opportunity to do so no serious effort was made to put what would be the appropriate facts and figures before the Board . . . it is not understood how the Board or the Chairman could . . . adopt what was requested in this case . . . a "conservative approach" to an award. It is not understood how such an approach could be accurately quantified in money terms . . .

The dilemma of an arbitrator in allowing for inability to pay on the part of the state is clearly expressed.

Hugh Geoghegan SC was, for nine years, chairman of the main public service arbitration boards before being appointed to the High Court. The issue of the state's ability to pay and the general principles of pay settlement were addressed with great clarity by Geoghegan in 1985 on two pay claims. He accepted that outside comparisons should constitute the primary basis for determining equivalent civil service pay claims and that "outside comparisons constituted independent objective criteria on which the Board could rely". But he also accepted that for the board to disregard the economic and financial position of the state would be a wholly unreal position and if this stance were taken, "the continued existence of the scheme would be threatened". He asserted that "there could be no justification for treating the Government any differently from any other employer" and stated that "it has been the practice of the Labour Court and other arbitration bodies to take the financial circumstances of an employer into account". However, the degree to which his findings on the claims were affected by the state's financial troubles was not quantified reflecting, perhaps, the dilemma expressed by the previous chairman three years before.

In October 1994 extended discussions on the amendment of the civil service Conciliation and Arbitration scheme were successfully concluded. The following provisions on criteria for negotiations were inserted in the scheme:

CRITERIA:

88. At each stage of the procedure under the scheme for dealing with claims i.e. conciliation, discussions under the Facilitator, consideration by the Adjudicator or the Arbitration Board, the following factors (in addition to any other considerations adduced by either side in any particular case) will be taken into account:-

- *the necessity to ensure that the State as employer can continue to recruit, retain and motivate staff of the calibre required.*

- *the necessity to take account of the prevailing position in relation to any national policy on pay which may be agreed between the Irish Congress of Trade Unions and the Government as employer from time to time.*

- *the necessity to take account of the state of the public finances, including the consequences of the Treaty of European Union, and the general economic and employment situation.*

- *the necessity to take account of the extent to which working conditions, the organisation of work, pay, perquisites, conditions of employment and other relevant benefits of civil service grades differ from those of employees in other employments doing similar jobs or jobs of the same level of responsibility.*

- *the necessity to ensure that the civil service can continue to adapt to necessary changes, to achieve greater efficiency and effectiveness and to match increases in productivity in the remainder of the economy.*

Principles and criteria are less than half the story in the ambiguous business of pay negotiation. The abilities of trade unionists, management negotiators and adjudicators in turning principles into pay rates in the negotiation process are central. The key management group in the public sector is the government itself which comes under tremendous pressure to avoid strikes, especially in sensitive areas. It is easy to have industrial peace and the high regard of your workers if the commonest word in your negotiating vocabulary is "yes". In the next section, the record of pay negotiation in the public sector will be scrutinised.

The Outcome of Pay Bargaining
Public sector pay bargaining has become the focus of much public debate in recent years, largely because about 40 per cent of the government's current budget is spent on public service pay. Much of the

publicity is taken up by negotiating parties trying to influence the expectations of the other side in the hope of doing a good deal when they come to the bargaining table. Expectations are, of course, crucial to outcomes in industrial relations. Salamon (1992) places great emphasis on the role of the media in conveying information and moulding opinion in negotiation generally.

There is not much detailed analysis of Irish public sector pay trends. In the early 1960s, the Economic and Social Research Institute published some papers on Irish industrial relations generally (Nevin, 1963; O'Mahony, 1964 and 1965). Since then, apart from references in general texts the main sources have been articles, for example McGinley (1976, 1986, 1991) and Gaffney (1979), short feature articles in *Industrial Relations News* and, of course, newspaper articles. In the public service, the researcher at least has the advantage that pay rates are published. By contrast, in the private sector there is little information available on either pay movements or pay levels although *Industrial Relations News* has been a useful source of detailed information on many pay deals negotiated with unions in recent years. There is almost nothing publicly known about pay settlements for non-unionised workers even though this area is becoming increasingly important — less than 50 per cent of Irish workers are now in unions. Official statistics on pay in the economy as a whole are meagre. OECD publishes an index showing pay comparisons for the "government sector" as a percentage of industrial earnings. In 1996 the Central Statistics Office introduced a Public Sector Average Earnings Index starting in 1988.

Appendix I to this chapter gives details of all the pay increases given to two important civil service grades between 1945 and 1996. Secretaries and Clerical Officers, grades at the top and near the bottom of the clerical-administrative structure, have been chosen to illustrate important issues. The civil service retains the title "Secretary" for the heads or chief executives of civil service departments.

The main points emerging from this analysis are:

1. There is a crucial distinction between general increases which apply to all workers and "special increases" for particular grades. Since 1945 both grades got general increases under the 28 general pay rounds. Some of these general increases deliberately gave a higher percentage to the lower paid, often by way of a guaranteed minimum increase. There are further details in Appendix III.

2. When national agreements operate, for example 1964, 1970–81, 1987 to date, the general rounds in the public service are close to those in the private sector. When national agreements are not in operation the public service tends to have fairly uniform general increases reflecting the fact that there is effectively just one employer — the government. The private sector, on the other hand, quickly develops very disparate increases as individual employments make separate settlements which often remain confidential. As a result of the lack of information public-private sector comparisons in times of decentralised bargaining are somewhat speculative.

3. There has been a strong tendency for lower paid grades to narrow their differentials with higher paid workers as a result of general pay rounds. In the public service this trend is clearly shown in the two grades examined in Appendix I. There is, however, a tendency for higher grades to get higher special increases than lower grades, offsetting the narrowing of differentials in the general rounds. Indeed, special increases have had the effect of widening the differentials between Secretaries and Clerical Officers. Income tax has, of course, the effect of narrowing the gap between the take-home pay of workers at different pay levels.

4. Inflation affects the timing and amount of general increases. This was particularly noticeable in the 1970s when inflation reached record levels.

5. There has been a speeding up in the frequency of special increases since 1970. This may reflect the efficiency of public sector unions in pursuing claims or it may be an indication of a failure of public sector pay to keep pace with that in the private sector, necessitating frequent "topping up".

It is not necessary here to look very closely at the general increases obtained under the 28 rounds since 1945. It is noteworthy that public service unions have tended to favour national-level as against decentralised bargaining. The Public Services Committee of ICTU was a strong, cohesive and respected force in ICTU and their stance on any proposed national pay agreement can be critical. Following discussion in the ICTU Public Services Committee, the public service unions usually act in concert on major issues but they are not required to do so and independent action is not unknown. It will be recalled that many public service workers, especially those not covered by conciliation and arbitration, are members of general unions, notably SIPTU.

"Special increases" for public service workers in Ireland are often heavily criticised by the government, private sector employers and commentators. These increases are additional to the 28 general pay rounds since 1945. Prior to the national pay agreements of the 1970s, most public service grades had three special reviews — the first in the 1950s following the introduction of conciliation and arbitration. These increases were generally low, matching the prevailing depressed economic conditions. The next series of special increases, generally dating from 1 January 1964, were very high even allowing for the economic euphoria of the 1960s. It became known at the time as the "status round", presumably as it was perceived to change the status of public servants in the pay stakes. The conventional wisdom was that private sector pay had forged ahead in the early 1960s, leaving the public service with a lot of catching up to do. The going increase which emerged at maxima of scales in the status round was about 20 per cent, with some groups getting over 30 per cent. The ninth general round of 12 per cent applied from 1 February 1964 resulting in a public service pay increase of about 34 per cent in one month at a time when inflation was not high. From then on the public service pay bill was to be of central significance to the annual budget. Just before the national pay agreements began in 1972, there was a third series of special increases in which most grades got a 10 per cent rise in two phases (1 October 1970 and 1 April 1971).

There was an effort to use the national pay agreements of the 1970s to cut back on special increases by laying down increasingly tight criteria for them. Ironically, this misfired and, spurred on by unprecedented inflation, unions and especially public service unions became masters of the new legalistic type of bargaining which the criteria demanded. Furthermore, the new type of bargaining copperfastened pay relationships which had previously been less compelling. The criteria laid down for special increases in the national pay agreements/understandings 1970–81 are summarised in Table 6.7.

The public service emerged from the 1970s with a system of pay linkages clarified and reinforced. In addition, public service numbers had increased by 55 per cent in the decade. The government was severely criticised by FUE (now IBEC) for its inability to contain special increases as well as other failures and in 1981 national pay bargaining collapsed. Fogarty et al (1981), reporting for the FUE, referred to the public service as having "a spiral of leapfrogging pay comparisons of its own, sometimes accompanied by over-manning, and largely independent of what is happening in the competitive sector of the economy".

TABLE 6.7: CRITERIA FOR SPECIAL INCREASES 1970–81

National Agreement		Criterion
1st	1970	To remove genuine anomalies in pay where rates of pay had in the past been related
2nd	1972	(a) Claims based on a specific relationship
3rd	1974	(b) Claims based on falling or being out of line with the general level of pay for similar work
4th	1974	Claims based on alleged serious inequity — increases over 1.5 per cent to go to the Labour Court or Arbitration
5th	1975	
6th	1977	Only claims in before 1 November 1976 to be processed
7th	1978	Claims based on serious inequity or claims based on being out of line with the general level of pay for similar work, increases over 2 per cent to go the Labour Court or Arbitration
1st National Understanding 1979		Claims bases on previously well established relationships — increases in two phases the first not before 1 July 1979
2nd National Understanding 1980		Claims bases on previously well established relationships. Claims based on being out of line with generally established standards to go to the Labour Court/Arbitration, earliest date 1 April 1981.

Source: McGinley, 1991

The effort to contain special increases in the 1980s concentrated on deferred implementation rather than on the criteria to be met, no doubt with the aim of lessening the impact of any pay rises on the next budget whatever about the long term effect. Table 6.8 shows the phasing regimes which applied 1981–96.

TABLE 6.8: PHASING OF PUBLIC SERVICE SPECIAL INCREASES 1981–96

Agreement / Statement	*Action on Special Increases*
Bruton's Budget of 21 July 1981	Public Sector to plead inability to pay (2nd National Understanding)
22nd Round — 1st Public Service Pay Agreement of 1 December 1981	Moratorium on special increases until 1 January 1983
Budget of 30 July 1982	No special increases in 1982 or 1983
Agreement between unions and management	Increases deferred to 1 October 1983. 40 per cent of any increases to be paid then
23rd and 24th Round — 2nd Public Pay Agreement and Arbitration findings (1 September 1983 and 1 January 1985)	40 per cent of special increases Service to be paid from 1 October 1983, a further 2.5 per cent from 1 December 1984, balance 1 September 1985
25th Round 1 May 1986 — based on agreement in the civil service	One third from 1 December 1987 One third from 1 December 1988 One third from 1 July 1989
26th Round — the PNR 1988–90	40 per cent 1 July 1989, 30 per cent 1 April 1990, 30 per cent 1 October 1990 for those who had not got a special increase since 1986. Otherwise 40 per cent 1 May 1991, 30 per cent 1 March and 1 September
27th Round — the PESP 1991–93	Generally, a 3 per cent ceiling, starting 1993. Discussions to be held regarding costs over 3% in later years.
28th Round — the PCW 1994–96	Groups which had not completed negotiations under the PESP to process either (A) claims based on restructuring/productivity or (B) increases not over 3 per cent on a phased basis (April '94 - June '97)

Source: McGinley, 1991 (updated).

Special Increases 1991–96
The formula for special increases in the PESP and the PCW needs
some explanation. On 13 December 1991 the Minister for Finance,
Bertie Ahern, announced that the remaining basic increases due under the PESP could not be paid as envisaged in the public service.
Similarly some special increases being phased in would have to be
deferred. The unions saw this as a repudiation of the PESP and a national strike in the public sector was threatened for 28 January 1992,
the day before the Budget. Urgent discussions were held and before
the strike was due a compromise was worked out for the basic increases in the public service. They would be paid in full but on a
slower timetable than originally agreed. A full review of the pay settling system in the public service, effectively the C & A schemes, was
also agreed which led eventually to the rather modest changes in the
civil service scheme described elsewhere in this chapter (see pages
268 and 269).

    Given the row over basic increases it is not surprising that nego-
tiations on special increases were rarely successful. No important
special increases were agreed under the PESP in the public service.
The PCW provision on special increases repeated the PESP cap of 3%
but held out the prospect of more for claims based on restructur-
ing/productivity. Such claims were to be settled by negotiation. Reference to arbitration was not envisaged. Several groups sought special
increases under the restructuring /productivity formula so as to avoid
the cap of 3%. Negotiations on all major claims were most protracted.
The only large public service groups to have settled by the end of
1996 were prison officers, army officers and the crucial civil service
grades of Executive Officer and Higher Executive Office (EO/HEO).
Over the years the 4,500 EO/HEOs have become pivotal pay grades
for many public service categories vastly larger than themselves, e.g.
teachers, nurses and local authority grades — see McGinley (1991).
Following extended and difficult negotiations the EO/HEOs reached
agreement on a restructuring/productivity deal in mid-1996. The
terms of the agreement which are quite complicated are summarised
in Table 6.9.

TABLE 6.9: THE EO/HEO SPECIAL INCREASES UNDER THE PCW AT SCALE MAXIMA

Maxima at 1 June 1994	Revised Maxima Maxima phased in from 1 October 1994 (7/12ths), 1 June 1996 (3/12ths) and 1 June 1997 (2/12ths)	
EO £18,404	£19,655 — increase of 6.8%. This figure to apply after six years on the normal maximum. An increase of 3.4% applied to those on the normal maximum and of 2.5% to those just below the maximum.	£20,428 — increase of 11%. This is the maximum of an enhanced scale to which 25% of EOs are to advance.
HEO £22,258	£23,906 — increase of 7.4%. This figure to apply after six years on the normal maximum. An increase of 3.7% applied to those on the normal maximum and of 2.6% to those just below the maximum.	£24,706 — increase of 11%. This is the maximum of an enhanced scale to which 30% of HEOs are to advance.

In addition new entrants to the EO grade will be on a reduced minimum of £9,100 — 5.1% below the old minimum of £9,586. New entrants will not get the long service maxima of £19,655 and £23,906 to be enjoyed by serving staff over six years on the maximum. Instead they will have the maxima appropriate to serving staff with three years on the maxima i.e. £19,009 (EO) and £23,053 (HEO). The net result of these somewhat Byzantine calculations is that after the application of the PCW basic increases the scales with effect from 1 January 1997 are EO: £9,658 x 14 increments — £20,087 and HEO: £19,942 x 7 increments — £25,081. In both cases there is a three year wait for the final increment. The maxima of the higher scales for EO and HEO are £21,323 and £25,788. However, these scales are not final as they do not contain the final phase of the special increase (2/12ths) due on 1 June 1997. The agreement on the special increase had twelve Productivity/Flexibility clauses. It remains to be seen if these clauses will result in measurable gains for management.

It is difficult to estimate how much the complicated EO/HEO deal is worth to the staff involved. It is distinctly more favourable to long service people. When the deal is fully operational after 1 June 1997, depending on the assumptions made on length of service within the grades, the deal could cost 5–6% of EO/HEO payroll. In the early years the cost would be much less due to the phasing in arrangements.

The special increase for EOs and HEOs continues to set standards for other grades traditionally linked to them for pay purposes. The grades below them and above them in the civil service hierarchy are seeking special increase under the PCW in protracted negotiations. Negotiations with teachers and nurses have been very difficult. The claim for special increases for 26,000 nurses was originally lodged in 1993 under the PESP. It was not until November that a draft deal was put out to ballot in the four unions concerned. The Irish Nurses' Organisation with 15,000 members (mainly general nurses) rejected the deal 60/40. IMPACT members rejected it also but by a narrow majority. SIPTU and the Psychiatric Nurses' Association voted narrowly in favour. The rejected deal resembles the EO/HEO agreement in that those with long service do best. The draft agreement for some 40,000 teachers also ran into difficulties when only one of the three teachers' unions — the INTO — accepted what was on offer. As in the EO/HEO deal the teachers' offer gave more to some groups than to others, thus creating problems for the unions.

It is clear from the figures in Appendix I that efforts to contain special increases in the public service have not been very successful. The theory of public service pay settlement would suggest that this must be because pay in the private sector is setting expensive headlines. At the highest level this may seem credible — after all the Secretary of the Department of Finance who has had huge special increases in recent years still earns less than half of what the top men in the large banks get. But this anecdotal evidence is not enough. As long as pay rates generally remain unreported, it is impossible to say if the public service pay escalation of recent years is following or leading the private sector.

Three issues affecting negotiations on public service pay increases are of special importance: the institutions for settling pay; the principles underlying pay settlement and any criteria derived from them; and the abilities of pay negotiators and the attitudes of arbitrators. It is probable that the abilities of pay negotiators and the attitudes of arbitrators are the key factor. It is easy to make the mistake of concentrating too much on institutions. Able negotiators can work effectively in a range of institutional settings and it is they who put the flesh on principles and criteria.

Non-Pay Conditions

The extent to which non-pay conditions are subject to negotiation depends largely on management. In the public sector, management prerogative has narrowed over the years. In the main conciliation and arbitration schemes a wide range of issues were specified as discussible at conciliation from the outset. In practice, almost any issue affecting groups of staff can be discussed. Detailed procedures have been agreed for the handling of issues which do not lend themselves to negotiation in the usual manner, notably grievance procedures which can be activated in disciplinary cases and procedures for pursuing allegations of sexual harassment. The subjects dealt with at the civil service General Council illustrate the major non-pay issues discussed at conciliation level. They include promotion, grading, equality, health and safety and travelling and subsistence.

There is not a great emphasis on productivity bargaining in the public sector outside the commercial state bodies. The recent efforts to introduce productivity elements into bargaining from special pay increases under the PESP/PCW have yet to prove that they can produce results.

THE FUTURE

Recent discussions on the reform of industrial relations in the public service has focused largely on the conciliation and arbitration schemes. The criticism of these schemes is that they are separate from the system that applies to other workers in the economy. Why should over 700,000 employees come under the Labour Court/Labour Relations Commission system while many public servants and the staffs of three major commercial state bodies have special arrangements of their own? This question is somewhat ironic when it is recalled that the public service had a real sense of grievance when Seán Lemass' Industrial Relations Act, 1946 excluded the public service from the Labour Court. Conciliation and arbitration was, to a degree, a second best option developed after 1950. Institutions, however, develop attractions over the years. By the time the Commission on Industrial Relations argued strongly for the abolition of the public service system in 1981, the public service had become wedded to arbitration and resisted all efforts to have the Labour Court take over. The public service unions are broadly happy with the arbitration system. While occasional arbitration findings upset the unions or the government, there was a feeling that the system was giving a fair deal all round. Indeed, one eminent arbitrator, T.K. Liston SC, felt he was doing well if he "kept both sides equally unhappy".

But the suspicion lingers. Is the public service doing too well in the pay stakes? Is the arbitration system too "cosy" and inward-looking? If arbitration is not a privilege, why do three major state-sponsored companies with access to the Labour Court continue to use it (An Post, Telecom) or something very close to it (the ESB)? The growing burden of public service pay has made answers to these questions a matter of urgent public concern.

Early in 1992 the Department of Finance tabled detailed proposals for the reform of the system of pay determination in the civil service and almost three years later — in October 1994 — discussions on the proposals concluded with an amended Conciliation and Arbitration Scheme. Bertie Ahern, then Minister for Finance, regarded the launch of the amended scheme as "an historic occasion" and expressed the hope that there would now be a "more transparent and realistic system". He also said that the amended civil service scheme would provide a model for schemes in the local authorities, education, the Gardai and the Defence Forces. The main changes in the amended scheme are as follows:

1. The replacement of the mediator at conciliation level by a "facilitator". The mediator was introduced in the 1970s and was to be appointed by the Minister for Labour but the system was quietly abandoned. The new facilitator is to be agreed by both sides for each claim.

2. There will be two forms of arbitration in future: an Arbitration Board for pay claims and other claims "involving significant extra expenditure" and an Adjudicator for other claims.

3. The Arbitration Board would consist of a Chairperson appointed by the Government in agreement with the staff side, a member nominated by union representatives and a member nominated by the government. The government would fix the length of the term of appointment of Board members.

4. Grading claims become arbitrable for the first time by the Adjudicator.

5. Civil service grades could seek a review of their pay every four years. An independent unit in the Labour Relations Commission

would be asked to confirm that the factual information assembled by both sides to a claim constituted "an adequate and representative information base as an input to negotiations". The unit could add additional factual information.

6. Five criteria to be taken into account in handling claims were agreed. They are reproduced above at page 258.

Only time will tell whether these changes are really "historic". The Fianna Fail/Labour government was replaced in December 1994 by a coalition in which Ruairi Quinn of the Labour Party become Minister for Finance. It was only in September 1995 that the staff and official sides reached agreement on a person to be appointed chairperson of the new Arbitration Board (barrister Gerard Durcan). The government's nominee on the Board is Derek Hunter formerly Chief Executive of the Local Government Staff Negotiations Board, and the staff side nominee is Kevin Duffy, ICTU. The new Board had not heard any cases by the end of 1996. One non-pay case had been heard by the new Adjudicator (barrister Gerard Kelly).

Government tardiness in implementing the changes may, perhaps, reflect the fact the changes are, on balance, more favourable to the unions than to management. The agreement to make grading arbitrable is a major concession which could be costly in the medium term. The introduction of the Adjudicator will speed up the processing of non-pay claims. The proposed unit in the LRC has some resemblance to the UK Civil Service Pay Research Unit which played an important role in UK negotiations until it was dropped by the Thatcher government. Some trade unionists see such a unit as helping the unions to establish their claims. The four year term for pay claims cuts both ways. It introduces some order into the special claims minefield but it also creates expectations of a special rise every four years. The criteria agreed for all negotiations may be valuable to management but public service unions showed in the 1970s how adept they could be in using written criteria to their own advantage.

Some years may elapse before all the elements in the public service revise their negotiation systems on civil service lines. However, until the continuation of separate arbitration for the public service is seriously addressed any changes are likely to be more procedural than substantive.

NESC Report No 96, *A Strategy for Competitiveness, Growth and Employment*, discusses trends in public service pay in a section on

Incomes Policy and Competitiveness. They make the interesting observation:

> Taking 1975 as a starting point, government sector pay has increased at an annual rate fractionally higher than average earnings. This suggests that in the long-run, wage determination mechanisms produce broadly comparable pay movements across public and private sector employments.

Even allowing for the dearth of valid statistics on pay movements this is a remarkable statement. It may call in question much of the conventional wisdom on the dangers of a separate public service pay settlement system. It certainly raises issues about the whole debate on pay settlement where conclusions are frequently based on assumptions rather than on solid facts.

NESC Report No 99, *Strategy into the 21st Century* (November 1996), devotes a full chapter to wage bargaining. A discussion on public sector wage developments concentrates heavily on comparisons between the public and private sectors since 1987. The only figures for trends in private sector pay are the statistics on pay in industry which employs only about 20 per cent of those at work. The NESC analysis is accordingly, flawed. Valid comparisons cannot be made between the public and private sectors until comparable figures are available, possibly by enlarging the Labour Force Survey to cover pay.

A new three and a quarter year Programme, Partnership 2000, was agreed in February 1997. The public sector basic pay increases are the same as for the private sector with slightly worse phasing in arrangements, 2 per cent is provided for local bargaining so that the deal is very similar to PESP.

Public sector pay problems are not likely to be solved by the new deal. Two key questions remain — the growth in the size of the public service and pay levels. There is no evidence of a will to contain numbers. Nor is there anything on the agenda to bring about real change in the pay settling machinery. So Irish society seems to be happy to settle for a pragmatic reaction to events in this area — or just muddling through.

APPENDIX I

INCREASES UNDER GENERAL PAY ROUNDS APPLIED TO THE MAXMIMUM
PAY OF THE GRADES OF SECRETARY AND CLERICAL OFFICER 1945–97

Round No	Effective Date	Secretary of Department	Clerical Officer
		per cent increases at max	
1st	1 Nov 1946	13.8	11.4
2nd	1 Nov 1948	5.9	6.8
3rd	15 Jan 1951	9.1	12.1
4th	1 Nov 1952	4.0	7.4
5th	1 Nov 1955	7.2	8.6
6th	1 Apr 1958	2.2	4.0
7th	15 Dec 1959	6.7	6.7
8th	1 Nov 1961	12.5	14.0
9th	1 Feb 1964	12.0	12.0
10th	1 June 1966	1.1	4.6
11th	1 June 1968	9.0	9.1
	1 June 1969	3.3	5.1
12th	1 Apr 1970	7.0	7.0
	1 Jan 1970	9.3	9.2
Cumulative increase in Rounds 1-12:		168.0%	209.0%
13th	1 Jan 1972–1 Jan 1973	6.0	12.0
14th	1 June/July 1973 (part only,	5.4	9.2
15th	1 June 1974–1 Mar 1975	23.1	29.9
16th	1 June 1975–1 June 1976	19.7	21.1
17th	1 August 1976	2.1	6.1
18th	1 Apr 1977–1 Nov 1977	3.4	8.0
19th	1 Mar 1978–1 Mar 1979	10.2	10.2
20th	1 June 1979–1 Mar 1990	17.3	19.3
21st	1 Oct 1980–1 June 1981	15.8	16.4
22nd	1 Dec 1981–1 Jan 1983	13.5	14.4
23rd	1 Sept 1983–1 Feb 1984	8.2	8.2
24th	1 Jan–1 July 1985	6.1	6.1
25th	1 May 1986–1 May 1987	7.2	7.2
26th (PNR)	1 Jan 1988–1 Jan 1990	6.6	8.0
27th (PESP)	1 Jan 1991–1 Dec 1993	11.1	11.1
28th (PCW)	1 April 1994–1 Jan 1997	8.3	8.3
Cumulative increase in Rounds 13-28:		357.4%	509.0%
Cumulative increase in General Rounds 1–28 (1945–97)		1,139%	1,799%

APPENDIX II

SPECIAL INCREASES IN MAXIMUM PAY OF THE CIVIL SERVICE GRADES OF
SECRETARY AND CLERICAL OFFICER 1945–97

Effective Date	Secretary of Department	Clerical Officer
	per cent increases	
15 January 1951 *	13.3	—
12 September 1955	—	4.6
1 April 1960	6.2	—
1 January 1964	16.4	22.9
1 April 1965	8.0	—
1 April 1970	—	9.7
1 Oct 1970	5.0	—
1 April 1971	4.7	2.4
1 April 1974	5.0	—
1 June 1974	3.6	—
21 June 1978	8.5 (Review Body)	—
1 July 1978	—	4.3
1 January 1979	—	4.1
26 June 1979	14.1 (Review Body)	—
26 June 1980	12.3 (Review Body)	—
1 September 1980	—	14.5
1 January 1983	—	(at maximum only) 5.5
1 July 1988	15.0 (Review Body)	—
1 July 1989	7.3 (Review Body)	2.4
1 April 1990	5.1 (Review Body)	1.7
1 October 1990	4.8 (Review Body)	1.7
1 April 1994	8.6 (Review Body)	1.0
1 May 1995	7.9 (Review Body)	—
Cumulative special increases 1945–96	283.6%	102.0%

* The Secretary's increase of 13.3 per cent from 15 January 1951 represented the removal of the "supercut" which was applied prior to 1946. Under the "supercut" higher paid grades got less compensation for cost of living increases than lower paid colleagues.

APPENDIX III

MAXIMA OF SECRETARY AND CLERICAL OFFICER COMPARED 1946, 1971, 1981, 1997

Summary	*Secretary*	*Clerical Officer*	*Clerical Officer's maximum as per cent of Secretary's*
Effective Date	*maximum pay*		*maximum*
	£	£	%
1 Nov 1946	1,775	440	24.8
1 April 1971 (before National Agreements/ Understandings)	6,960	1,766	25.4
1 June 1981 (after National Agreements/ Understandings)	27,403	7,406	27.0
1 Jan 1997 (after PNR/ PESP/PCW)	78,089	15,239	19.5
Cumulative Pay Increases 1945–97	*Secretary* 4880%	*Clerical Officer* 3750%	

References

(a) Government Publications

1924. *Official Reports of Dáil Éireann, 17(45).*
1935. *Report of the Commission of Inquiry into the Civil Service, 1932–35.*
1937. *Report of the Committee of Inquiry into Ministerial and Other Salaries etc.*
1969. *Final Report of the Committee on Industrial Relations in the Electricity Supply Board.*
1972. *Report of the Review Body on Higher Remuneration in the Public Sector.*

1981.   *Report of the Commission of Inquiry on Industrial Relations.*
1987.   *Report of the Review Body on Higher Remuneration in the Public Sector.*

(b) Books and Articles

Advisory, Conciliation and Arbitration Service (1980): *Industrial Relations Handbook*, London: HMSO.

Beaumont, P.B. (1992): *Public Sector Industrial Relations*, London: Routledge.

Browne, V. (ed.) (1981): *The Magill Book of Irish Politics*, Dublin: Magill.

Canning, L.S. (1981): "Public Sector Industrial Relations: The Case of the Electricity Supply Board" in H. Pollock (ed.), *Industrial Relations in Practice*, Dublin: O'Brien Press.

Central Bank of Ireland (1993): *Annual Report, 1992*, Dublin: Central Bank of Ireland.

Central Bank of Ireland (1993): *Quarterly Bulletin*, Autumn, Dublin: Central Bank of Ireland.

Committee of Inquiry into Civil Service Pay (1982): *Report of Committee of Inquiry into Civil Service Pay*, London: HMSO.

Cox, B. and Hughes, J. (1987/1989): "Industrial Relations in the Public Sector" in T. Murphy (ed.), *Industrial Relations in Ireland: Contemporary Issues and Developments*, Dublin: Department of Industrial Relations, University College Dublin.

Duncan, G.A. and Ryan, W.J.L. (1946): *Report of an Inquiry into the Present Remuneration of the Higher Grades of the Civil Service*, Dublin: Association of Higher Civil Servants.

Fogarty, M.P., Egan, D., and Ryan, W.J.L. (1981): *Pay Policy For The 1980s*, Dublin: Federated Union of Employers.

Gaffney, S. (1979): "Industrial Relations in the Public Sector", *Administration*, 27: 322–9.

Gretton, J. and Harrison, A. (1982): *How Much Are Public Servants Worth?*, Oxford: Blackwell.

Humphreys, P.C. (1983): *Public Service Employment*, Dublin: Institute of Public Administration.

Industrial Relations News (1992–96): Numerous articles and news items.

Institute of Public Administration (1996): *Administration Yearbook and Diary, 1996*, Dublin: Institute of Public Administration.

Kennedy, K.A. (1985): "The Role of the State in Economic Affairs", *Studies*, 74: 130–44.

Leddin, A.J. and Walsh, B.M. (1995): *The Macro-Economy of Ireland*, Dublin: Gill & Macmillan.

Lyons, F.S.L. (1973): *Ireland Since the Famine*, London: Fontana.

McCarthy, C. (1974): "From Division to Dissension: Irish Trade Unions in the Nineteen Thirties", *The Economic and Social Review*, 5: 469–90.

McGinley, M. (1976): "Pay Negotiation in the Public Service", *Administration*, 24: 76–95.

McGinley, M. (1986): "Pay Negotiation in the Public Service 1976–86", *Administration*, 34: 470–504.

McGinley, M. (1991): "Pay 1970–1991 — The Issue of Specials", *Industrial Relations News*, 34: 17–22.

National Economic and Social Council (1993): *A Strategy for Competitiveness, Growth and Employment*, Dublin: NESC Report No 96.

National Economic and Social Council (1996): *Strategy into the 21st Century*, Dublin: NESC Report No 99.

Nevin, E. (1963): *Wages in Ireland 1946–62*, 12, Dublin: Economic and Social Research Institute.

O'Connell, T.J. (1968): *100 Years of Progress: The Story of the Irish National Teachers' Organisation 1868–1968*, Dublin: Irish National Teachers' Organisation.

OECD (1987): *Economic Surveys, Ireland*, Paris: OECD.

O'Mahony, D. (1964): *Industrial Relations in Ireland: The Background*, 19, Dublin: Economic and Social Research Institute.

O'Mahony, D. (1965): *Economic Aspects of Industrial Relations*, 19, Dublin: Economic and Social Research Institute.

Ross, M. (1986): *Employment in the Public Domain in Recent Decades*, 127, Dublin: Economic and Social Research Institute.

Royal Commission on the Civil Service (1955): *Report of the Royal Commission on the Civil Service 1953–55*, London: HMSO.

Salamon, M. (1987/1992): *Industrial Relations*, London: Prentice Hall.

CHAPTER 7

MULTINATIONALS AND INDUSTRIAL RELATIONS PRACTICES

William K. Roche and *John F. Geary*

The impact of multinational companies on Irish industrial relations practice has long been the focus of scholarship and debate. The orientating question has generally been which effect has had the greater influence: the so-called "country-of-operation" effect or "country-of-origin" effect? The general view among Irish industrial relations scholars has been that the former effect has exerted a greater influence. In this chapter, we examine the relationship between these two effects and argue that the host-country effect, once thought to be the predominant effect or pattern, has increasingly been overridden by country-of-origin effects.

The chapter begins by examining the growth of foreign investment in Ireland and details the type of production facilities that are located here. The relevant industrial relations literature is then reviewed, concentrating initially on what we term the orthodox view, wherein it is argued that MNCs coming to Ireland have conformed to "local" industrial relations practice and traditions. In the remainder of the chapter this view is problematised by examining a number of issues, such as union recognition, industrial relations practices and out comes, collective bargaining and incomes policies, industrial conflict, and human resource policies.

MULTINATIONAL COMPANIES IN IRELAND

Overseas multinationals have formed the backbone of industrial policy in Ireland since the 1960s. From the early 1930s to the 1950s Ireland had implemented an "inward-looking" strategy of industrialisation based on import substitution. Foreign companies had attained a significant foothold in a number of industries during the 1920s: particularly, in the food sector, car manufacturing (Ford) and insurance.

With the imposition of protectionist measures during the 1930s, indigenous manufacturing companies had become the engine of industrialisation and employment growth. By the 1950s this policy had run out of steam: the scope for further industrial expansion through import substitution was limited; and the level of manufacturing employment virtually stagnated during the decade.

During the 1960s, new foreign investment was confined largely to "mature", labour-intensive industries like clothing, footwear, plastics and light engineering. From the late 1960s, the pattern of foreign investment shifted towards more technologically advanced, capital-intensive industries like electronics, computer hardware and software, machinery, pharmaceuticals and medical equipment. The new technologically advanced industries contributed very significantly to industrial growth. By the early 1990s, foreign-owned firms accounted for 45 per cent of total manufacturing employment, 55 per cent of manufacturing output and 76 per cent of manufactured exports (O'Malley, 1996). Most foreign-owned investment has been undertaken by US-owned multinationals. Ireland was chosen as a convenient location from which to produce for European markets; Irish industrial policy also provided very favourable incentives and tax holidays for foreign firms locating in the country. Presently, profits in manufacturing and internationally traded services are taxed at 10 per cent. In addition, Irish labour costs continue to remain low in comparison to most other European economies.

Typically foreign multinationals have located only the more routine fabrication stages of their production in Ireland. In consequence, large proportions of their work-forces have performed tasks with low skill-content (Murray, 1984; Enderwick, 1986; Jackson, 1987). Multinational work-forces also tend on aggregate to have higher levels of female employment and younger age-profiles (Toner, 1987). Overall assessments of the job characteristics of multinational compared with indigenous manufacturing enterprises have concluded that the latter are more likely to be associated with industrial processes requiring skilled work and judgement (Murray, 1984: 42). Foreign multinationals have also been characterised by a low level of linkages with the local economy (O'Malley, 1992). Multinationals frequently located outside Dublin or other major urban centres. This reflected the availability of higher levels of grants and incentives for industries willing to locate in less-developed regions. It also reflected the low priority accorded to place of location *within* Ireland by multinational enterprises that had chosen Ireland for reasons other than immediate proximity to the services and infrastructure of large urban centres.

The early 1980s witnessed a slowing-down in new foreign investment in Ireland. Industrial policy also again shifted direction to provide greater incentives to indigenous enterprises possessing, or capable of attaining, sufficient scale to compete successfully in export markets. Much attention has also been given to the development of "clusters" of enterprises in sectors where Ireland is seen to possess the capacity to build successful export industries. The 1980s and early 1990s have also witnessed large-scale employment losses in foreign multinationals in product markets characterised by major international shake-outs. The flagship industry of the 1970s, computing, was particularly badly affected, with companies like Digital, Amdahl and Wang closing down entirely, or laying off large sections of their Irish work-forces. Nevertheless, attracting foreign investment to Ireland remains a key element of industrial policy. The most recent *Operational Programme* (1994), for instance, sees in foreign investment the opportunity to increase employment; transfer technology and management skills to Irish industry; and foster the development of the indigenous sub-supplier base (O'Malley, 1996).

This dual emphasis on attracting foreign-owned companies and developing indigenous industry has attained considerable success. Grant-aided Irish-owned enterprises have recently been accredited with having over-taken grant-aided foreign firms in creating employment (O'Malley et al., 1992). Further, and notwithstanding the job losses in the computer industry at the end of the 1980s and early 1990s, foreign-owned industry — in particular with the recent arrival and expansion of companies like Intel, IBM, Hewlett Packard, Oracle and other firms in the computer software and tele-marketing industries — continues to contribute substantially to employment growth.

INDUSTRIAL RELATIONS IN FOREIGN MULTINATIONALS: THE ORTHODOX VIEW

The dominant position in Irish industrial relations commentary and scholarship during the 1970s and 1980s has been that foreign MNCs have conformed to "local" industrial relations traditions and practices. The role of the main development agencies, the Industrial Development Authority (IDA) and the Shannon Free Airport Development Authority (SFADCO), in encouraging incoming MNCs to recognise trade unions and adapt to local traditions of industrial relations, was frequently emphasised in this regard. A dramatic dispute which occurred over union recognition in the late 1960s in a US company, EI Shannon (a subsidiary of GEC), was often viewed as both an illustra-

tion of the futility of attempting to impose an "alien" industrial relations tradition on Irish work-forces and as an exceptional — though
by no means unique — lapse from a more general tendency to adapt
to local industrial relations practice.

The most detailed elaboration of this view can be found in a paper
by Kelly and Brannick (1985), which examined the industrial relations features of a sample of 27 MNCs in Ireland, based on interviews
conducted with personnel and industrial relations managers and
trade union officials. The sample was stratified to be broadly representative of the sectoral spread, size-range, location and technology
characteristics of the population of MNCs. MNCs widely regarded as
having "good" and "poor" industrial relations were also included in
the sample.

Concentrating on the issues of job security, information disclosure,
consultation and trade union recognition practices, Kelly and Brannick (1985: 109) came to the conclusion that no evidence could be
found to "support the contention that MNCs were materially different
(in industrial relations terms) from home-based companies". As they
put it (1985: 109):

> In general MNCs are regarded as no different than Irish firms and the
> trend seems to be one of conformity with the host country's institu-
> tions, values and practices.

Fears for job security were confirmed among managers and union officials in MNCs, a reflection of the mobility of foreign capital. However, union officials did not necessarily see indigenous firms as offering higher levels of job security (Kelly and Brannick, 1985: 101–3).
Regarding the disclosure of information on the performance of MNCs'
Irish subsidiaries, trade union officials interviewed felt that the existing practice was largely comparable with known developments in indigenous companies. This was also the case with consultation practices (Kelly and Brannick, 1985: 107).

In the area of union recognition, Kelly and Brannick (1985: 107–
8), suggested that recognition disputes like that which had occurred
at EI Shannon, were isolated incidents: the "general picture was one
of a widespread acceptance of the union's role".

Kelly and Brannick's interpretation of their research data was
heavily influenced by an international literature pointing to the
dominance of "host-country effects" in MNCs' postures towards the
countries in which their subsidiaries were located. Their research in
turn fed into, and reinforced, mainstream commentary on industrial

relations in MNCs in Ireland. Enderwick (1986), for example, while specifying a series of *a priori* reasons for expecting industrial relations in MNCs to be different (scale effects, corporate strategy effects, capital-intensity effects etc.), accepts the "evidence" that these factors were outweighed by host-country effects in the Irish case. For Enderwick, MNC conformance with host-country industrial relations traditions in Ireland can be explained in terms of a number of features of the kinds of MNCs locating there. Convergence, he suggests, is a rational course in instances where investors are unfamiliar with the Irish labour market; where development agencies favour, or expect, conformance and are willing to become catalysts for change in areas of particular concern for MNCs (for example, multiple unionism); and where lack of vertical integration within MNC production systems reduces the vulnerability of the international corporation to union power and industrial stoppages in subsidiaries (Enderwick, 1986: 6–8). Finally, Enderwick suggests that the branch-plant nature of many MNCs in Ireland, with limited linkage activity to the local economy, has limited the diffusion of novel management practices to subsidiaries (1986: 9).

Both Kelly and Brannick and Enderwick show an awareness of differences between MNCs and indigenous companies with respect to industrial relations. These differences, however, tend to be presented as mere matters of nuance; as indicative of little more than isolated deviations from the general pattern, or as being of limited significance. Following the lead of Kelly and Brannick and Enderwick, a number of commentators on industrial relations in MNCs during the 1980s emphasised conformance and adaptation to local practice (McMahon et al., 1988; McCann, 1988).

THE ORTHODOXY UNRAVELS

Even during the period addressed directly by Kelly and Brannick and by Enderwick (roughly the 1960s to the mid-1980s), differences were apparent between MNCs and indigenous companies which were of no little significance for the conduct of industrial relations and collective bargaining. These can be divided up into the following areas.

Trade Union Recognition

It is true that MNCs were typically willing to recognise trade unions in their Irish subsidiaries over much of the period up to the 1980s. But recognition increasingly took on the familiar form of so-called "pre-employment agreements". These involved the effective establishment of "pre-entry closed shops" through company agreement to recognise a single trade union for all manual workers. Development agencies like IDA and SFADCO acted as brokers in the process of concluding pre-employment agreements.

The beneficiaries of such deals were usually large general unions. Single-union deals such as these frequently gave way to slightly more complex bargaining arrangements, involving, perhaps, a craft union representing skilled workers. But the bargaining arrangements involved were simpler to operate than the multiple union arrangements frequently encountered in larger indigenous companies. For example, a study comparing foreign MNCs and Irish companies in the early 1980s, indicated that employees in 39 per cent of the latter were represented by three or more unions, compared with 29 per cent of foreign MNCs. Surprisingly, the same study indicated that single-union representation was prevalent in 34 per cent of Irish companies compared with 38 per cent of foreign MNCs — a considerably lower relative incidence of single union representation in the MNCs than might be expected. This can perhaps be accounted for by the age profile of the "stock" of MNCs included in the sample; a comparison of MNCs established during the 1970s, when single-union pre-employment agreements appear to have become standard, would likely have revealed a different picture. The study found that multiple unionism was associated with higher levels of strikes and other forms of industrial action, particularly where the number of unions in an enterprise exceeded two (Murray, 1984: 9).

More recent research on union recognition in "greenfield" sites established over the period 1987–1991 points to the clear preference for single-union recognition agreements among foreign MNCs willing to recognise unions (Gunnigle, 1993).

The Rising Incidence of Non-union MNCs

While the available evidence for the early 1990s would indicate that there is little difference between levels of union recognition in Irish and foreign-owned companies — 76.2 per cent of indigenous companies and 79 per cent of MNCs (Cranfield Price Waterhouse survey) — it should be pointed out that, since the 1980s, unions have found it increasingly difficult to gain recognition.

As outlined above, commentators during the 1970s and 1980s tended to view the union recognition debacle at EI Shannon in 1967 as an aberration from the main pattern on industrial relations in foreign MNCs. By the mid 1980s a different posture was evident, at least among some commentators. EI Shannon now came to be seen as the first indication of a growing insistence by new US multinationals to remain non-union. Throughout the 1970s and into the 1980s, multinationals in the electronics sector, many of them of US origin, sought to avoid union recognition. Many were now proving to be more successful than earlier proponents of the non-union strategy in practising "union substitution". Toner (1987) argued that the rise of non-union foreign MNCs reflected a specific country-of-origin effect: namely, the anti-union ideology of the US parents of Irish subsidiaries. This view now became something of an orthodoxy in itself. Based on multivariate analysis of data collected in 1992, Roche and Turner (1994), have argued, in contrast, that the rise of the non-union phenomenon can better be understood as a sector-specific phenomenon arising out of the competitive and technological exigencies of the high-technology electronics sector. What bears emphasis in the present context, however, is that such a sectoral effect outweighed host-country effects, permitting an employee relations culture to grow up in a key sector which was strikingly different to that familiar in indigenous companies. In the research on greenfield companies established during the period 1987–1991, Gunnigle (1993) provided further evidence of the prevalence of non-union strategies among firms in high technology sectors. Again many of these companies were of US origin. Gunnigle stresses that the decision to opt for non-union employee relations was usually taken in the corporate headquarters of foreign MNCs.

The viability of a sector-specific industrial relations culture, based on foreign MNCs, was aided by a change in policy on the part of the main Irish development agencies. During the 1980s IDA and SFADCO appear to have relaxed considerably, or even to have abandoned, their earlier policy of encouraging foreign MNCs to grant union recognition and adapt to local traditions of industrial relations. In parallel with this trend, the main employers' federation in the field of industrial relations, the Federation of Irish Employers (now the Irish Business and Employers' Confederation), also established a new unit to assist and service member companies which opted to remain non-union.

Recent research has revealed a more general growth of resistance to trade union recognition in Ireland during the 1980s and 1990s (Gunnigle, 1993; McGovern, 1988). This is evident from a number of indicators: the volume of recognition disputes being referred to third-party institutions (the Labour Relations Commission and Labour Court) rose dramatically in the 1980s and the number of strikes related to union recognition have also increased significantly over recent decades. In the 1960s, for example, there were 21 strikes, 24 in the 1970s, 24 again in the 1980s and 8 for the first four years of the 1990s. The average length of these strikes and the number of working days lost, too, show a striking increase over recent years, indicating a hardening in managerial resistance to union recognition. It should also be emphasised that this increase in the number of strikes related to union recognition is made more remarkable by the overall decline in strike activity in Ireland since the early 1980s.

One of the most striking features of the data is the predominance of Irish firms. Roughly 80 per cent of recognition disputes took place in indigenous companies, with the vast majority taking place in companies of fifty employees or less. Also of note is that of the last 13 recognition strikes which occurred between 1986 and 1993 not one includes a foreign-owned company.

Thus, the manner in which employers have tried to resist unionisation would seem to differ significantly between multinational companies and indigenous companies. With the latter, many of whom are small and medium-sized employers, management have resorted primarily to old-fashioned techniques in union avoidance and suppression, reflecting the resurgence — in circumstances of intensified market competition and high unemployment — of traditional unitarist anti-unionism. This has given rise, in cases like Finneglas Teo, Lett & Co. Ltd., River Valley Products, Pat the Baker, Nolan Transport and Dunnes Stores, to bitter and protracted disputes. Only in the case of foreign MNCs is there any evidence of well-formulated union substitution strategies. Here the main obstacle is represented by the adoption of human resource management techniques, where the use of new forms of work organisation, employee involvement and innovative payment systems is designed, in part at least, to render union organisation irrelevant and unnecessary.

When we look at the overall picture for trade union membership, the differences in levels of union density between foreign-owned and indigenous companies is quite small. Table 7.1 reveals something approximating to a curvilinear relationship, where indigenous companies are more likely to have no members or a lower trade union density than multinational companies, but at the other end of the table, it is clear that a greater proportion of Irish-owned firms have a higher trade union density than multinationals.

TABLE 7.1: PROPORTION OF STAFF IN TRADE UNIONS

	Indigenous	*MNC*
	%	%
No members	22.2	16.2
1–25%	6.3	3.8
26–50%	7.9	19.0
51–75%	19.0	24.0
76–100%	41.3	33.3

Industrial Relations Practices and Outcomes

In 1984, the IDA commissioned a study of industrial relations practices in foreign MNCs and Irish companies in manufacturing (Murray,
1984). This survey of a sample of 151 enterprises pointed to significant differences in industrial relations policies, practices and outcomes. The survey also pointed to a number of "country-of-origin effects". US companies, for example, were more likely to lay claim to
distinctive human resource policies than either other foreign companies or Irish companies. International companies generally placed
greater emphasis on direct communication of policies to staff. Foreign
companies also possessed better resourced personnel/industrial relations function than Irish firms. Again American companies were distinctive in terms of levels of resourcing and a higher tendency to hold
first-line supervisors accountable for good employee relations
(Murray, 1984: 33–52).

Nearly all US and other foreign companies also insisted on con-
ducting negotiations at enterprise level, compared with 60 per cent of
Irish companies. Foreign companies were also much more likely to
claim that they adopted a strategic posture on collective bargaining
and industrial relations issues (Murray, 1984: 47). With respect to
policies on pay determination, Irish companies emphasised external
comparisons and relativities, whereas foreign MNCs were more likely
to emphasise competitive criteria in wage-fixing. Foreign MNCs were
also considerably more likely to state a preference for "individualistic"
strategies of employee relations over "collectivist" strategies based on
the dominance of dealings with union representatives (Murray, 1984:
49). Information disclosure was also much more highly developed in
foreign MNCs. Industrial relations outcomes over the period 1981–4
(the imposition of non-strike sanctions, flexible labour deployment,
resort to third-party mechanisms for dispute resolution) also favoured
foreign MNCs to a significant degree, although the incidence of

strikes over the period differed little between foreign MNCs and indigenous companies.

Employer Representation

The available evidence would indicate that the vast majority of MNCs have joined the main employers' federation, IBEC (previously FUE/FIE). They are to some extent at least a distinct grouping within this organisation. As is outlined in more detail below, foreign-owned companies have tended to confine their use of its services to seeking information, often to issues pertaining to labour law and have preferred, in the main, to settle their wage rates as individual companies and not as part of any group. In contrast to many Irish companies, MNCs do not have the same need for IBEC participation in negotiations as their personnel departments are better resourced for this function.

Collective Bargaining and Incomes Policy

Differences between foreign MNCs and indigenous companies with respect to union recognition, procedural arrangements and wage policies (the degree of emphasis placed on institutional versus competitive forces etc.) have already been alluded to. Other differences with respect to collective bargaining and wage policies were also apparent from the 1970s. In the nature of these areas, it is often difficult to obtain precise data for the purpose of comparison. Nonetheless, it is possible to provide some indication, for example, of the relative willingness of foreign MNCs to abide by pay norms determined in centralised collective bargaining.

Murray (1984) established that US MNCs made greater use of merit/performance-based payment systems for salaried staff. US companies appeared less likely than either Irish or other foreign MNCs to utilise incentive/bonus plans for manual workers. This finding conflicts somewhat with the findings of a 1980 survey of wage payment systems in manufacturing. This survey by Mooney (1980), also found that US MNCs tended to favour flat-rate payment systems for manual workers, but revealed that proportionately more British and continental European establishments than Irish establishments operated individual and plant-wide bonus schemes in the case of manual workers (Mooney, 1980: Ch. 3).

In determining pay rises, foreign MNCs also emerged in the study by Murray as placing more emphasis on competitive considerations than comparisons and relativities. A study of foreign MNC members conducted by FUE in 1980 reported that virtually all claimed to base their Irish pay policies on conditions prevailing in Ireland rather than in their parent companies (FUE, 1980: 45).

The emphasis on competitive considerations and the greater scope in MNCs for enterprise-, plant- or individual-level payments (for salaried employees in the case of US MNCs and for manual workers in the case of MNCs of other national origins) raises the important question of the wage-bargaining behaviour of foreign MNCs, especially under the centralised pay agreements which operated in Ireland from 1970 to 1980 (9 national pay agreements) and since 1987 (3 tripartite programmes). The first issue of relevance here is the membership status of foreign MNCs in IBEC. Given foreign MNCs firm preference to conduct pay negotiations at company level, it is not surprising that they have tended to use the general advisory and information services of IBEC rather than seek IBEC representation in negotiations (cf. Murray, 1984; Hardiman, 1988, Ch. 6). This finding is consistent with Gunnigle's data on greenfield operations established in the period 1987–91. It indicates that foreign MNCs have enjoyed greater autonomy with respect to wage bargaining than was typical of Irish companies. How have they chosen to exercise this autonomy?

Hardiman's study (1988) of national wage agreements in Ireland over the period 1970–80 implies that MNCs added significantly to the problems of FUE in securing members' compliance with national pay norms. The relatively high capital intensity of MNCs in a number of sectors, their relative profitability and their export orientation, distinguished them from many areas of indigenous industry and provided them with much greater leeway to improve on national pay norms. A review of national pay bargaining conducted by FUE itself, made explicit reference to the problem posed for the Federation by "many firms in manufacturing (which) are offshoots of transnational companies with limited commitment to the Irish economy" (Fogarty et al., 1981: 29). This was an unusually pointed reference to problems with a section of membership — especially in a report which was clearly pulling punches. Little direct evidence has been adduced, however, of above-average wage drift among MNCs during the decade, or of direct wage spillover from MNCs to indigenous companies. A study of industrial relations in the mid-west region, centring on Limerick, where many multinationals had located during the 1970s, did find that 71 per cent of multinationals had paid increases above national pay norms during the 1970s, compared with 52 per cent of Irish firms (Wallace, 1982: 189).

More generally, MNCs during the 1970s were deemed by commentators to have both the capacity and the resolve to adopt wage policies which took little cognisance of national pay norms or consideration of domestic incomes policy. MNCs themselves informed FUE, in a survey, that national pay agreements had either had little effect on their "industrial relations climate" (16 per cent) or had "proved helpful" (67 per cent) (FUE, 1980: 47).

With the return to decentralised pay determination over the period 1981–7, foreign MNCs tended consistently to agree relatively high pay settlements). Murray (1984: 12) found that foreign MNCs were more likely to conclude above-average pay settlements with shopfloor employees over the course of the 22nd to the 24th rounds (1982–4). Foreign MNCs also paid significantly higher salary increases to their managerial employees and slightly higher levels of additional payments to shopfloor employees over the period 1982–4. They appear also to have been more concentrated among "early starters" or "middle-term" settlements over the course of these rounds. The deals concluded by foreign MNCs with the major general unions early in the course of rounds tended to set headlines for other bargaining groups during the course of decentralised pay bargaining.

The return to centralised negotiations in 1987 witnessed a significant change in the wage bargaining behaviour of MNCs. In contrast to previous years when foreign companies acted as wage leaders and set their wages with a higher degree of autonomy from national wage rounds and wage norms, the vast majority of foreign companies appear to have abided by wage agreements struck at national level. With the Programme for National Recovery (PNR), 1987–1990, for instance, it is estimated that 95 per cent of all settlements recorded by the IRN were in accordance with the terms of the national wage agreements. This high compliance rate was also matched by a reduction in wage drift between foreign owned firms and domestic companies. Significantly, too, the level of compliance was particularly marked amongst MNCs in the chemical and pharmaceutical sector. A similar level of compliance was found with the Programme for Economic and Social Progress (PESP), 1991–1993. Many of the agreements which did breach the terms of the PESP were in the process of being negotiated before PESP came into force and many contained a so-called self-financing element where changes in work organisation, the introduction of new technology, team working, TQM and co-operation with ongoing change were agreed to by employees and their representatives.

It is worth pointing out that, if there was a threat posed to the PESP at this time — that is where wage increases exceeded the terms of the agreement — it came from within the commercial semi-state sector — the Electricity Supply Board — and not from foreign-owned companies. There have been, however, a small number of foreign-owned companies which have not acted in accordance with the terms of national wage agreements. These include such companies as Cadbury's, De Beers and Apple Computers. These companies, all of whom are unionised, have usually paid well above going rates. A small number of other foreign companies, for example Boxmore Plastics, attempting to introduce flexible working did not comply with PESP rates.

There is another partial exception to this picture of general uniformity in wage settlements. Recent research by Sheehan (1996) has led to the identification of "pockets" of companies most notably in the pharmaceutical and chemical sector in the Cork region which have paid wage increases above the terms of the most recent national agreement, the PCW. Sheehan's tracking of pay agreements among a number of companies which would have traditionally paid higher wage increases during the decentralised bargaining period found, with one exception, that all companies continued to maintain their independence from national wage norms. Examples here include companies such as Pfizer Pharmaceuticals, Cara Partners and Abott Ireland. Interestingly, as well as being able to exceed national wage norms, some of these companies have also chosen to conform to wage norms at various points. This suggests first, that both management and unions in these organisations did, and can, act independently of national wage agreements; second, that when these companies chose to abide by national agreements, the unions did not possess the means to extract further concessions from management; and finally, this "bargaining independence" is perhaps better thought of as a pragmatic response to the benefits of abiding by, or diverging from, national wage norms and does not, in itself, reflect a principled commitment or opposition to centralised bargaining (Geary and Lalor, 1996).

It is important to note, though, that these "above the norm" (ATN) increases have been confined to a small number of companies and that they have not had significant knock-on implications in other foreign-owned or indigenous organisations either because unions have been unwilling or unable to exploit the opportunity afforded by such ATN wage increases. Furthermore, Sheehan's research shows that most companies which could have afforded to pay ATN increases did not do so. Thus, the majority of foreign- and Irish-owned companies continue to adhere to recent wage agreements negotiated at a national level.

This preference for conforming to national wage agreements is also revealed in evidence from two further sources: Sexton (1996) and the Price Waterhouse Survey (1992). First, Sexton's analysis of real earnings trends reveals that, although there were significant variations in wage movements within manufacturing in the 1970s and through much of the 1980s, there was a significant change from 1987 with the reintroduction of national wage agreements. In the former period, above-average wage increases had been particularly evident in the drink and tobacco industry and also in the chemical industry, which is dominated by MNCs. Since 1987 the evidence would suggest there has been considerable convergence in real earnings increases across all manufacturing sectors, with the partial exception of the drink and tobacco industry. It would seem that the moderation and compliance demonstrated by foreign-owned companies in comparison to that which characterised this sector in the 1970s and early 1980s is a reflection, inter alia, of the severity of inter-subsidiary competition within multinationals. In such circumstances of cross-plant comparisons, the "need" to be "good citizens" in adhering to the terms of national wage agreements can provide management with a convenient excuse to concede moderate wage increases (Geary and Lalor, 1996).

The data in Table 7.2 also illustrate, particularly in relation to the pay of manual and clerical employees, employers' conformance to national pay agreements. Establishment-level bargaining, as one might have expected, is rare amongst indigenous companies for all categories of employees, but amongst foreign companies, it is far more prominent with about a fifth of organisations settling pay at this level for all employees. The data reveal that individual mechanisms of pay are not widely used for manual employees, but there would seem to be a clear preference by both multinational companies and Irish companies to settle pay for managerial, professional and technical staff and, to a lesser extent, clerical employees at the level of the individual.

In sum, while national wage agreements are the predominant means for settling pay in both foreign-owned companies and indigenous companies, in those instances where companies seek to supplement nationally agreed wage increases, or perhaps where they act autonomously from national wage agreements, establishment- and company-level bargaining are the most often used.

TABLE 7.2: LEVEL AT WHICH PAY IS DETERMINED

	Managerial	*Prof/Tech*	*Clerical*	*Manual*
	%	%	%	%
A. Multinational Companies				
National/industry-wide collective bargaining	12.3	21.0	35.2	66.7
Regional collective bargaining	—	1.9	6.7	9.5
Company/Division	38.1	32.4	32.4	22.9
Establishment level	20.0	22.9	21.9	21.0
Individual	56.2	42.9	29.5	10.5
B. Indigenous Companies				
National/industry-wide collective bargaining	20.6	31.7	50.8	58.7
Regional collective bargaining	—	1.6	6.3	6.3
Company/Division	28.6	28.4	28.6	19.0
Establishment level	12.7	17.5	9.5	6.3
Individual	54.0	39.7	19.0	7.9

Source: Price Waterhouse Survey

A second issue here is whether foreign-owned companies act as wage leaders or followers when it comes to wage levels. The available evidence would suggest that multinational companies tend to pay higher wages than Irish companies. A survey of wage levels in the manufacturing sector found that the average wage for workers in Irish-owned companies in 1990 was £11,585, compared to £13,844 of employees in foreign companies (Hourihan, 1993). While the difference here is quite striking, some caution is required in interpreting such aggregate figures. We do know, for example, that wage levels vary significantly between different sectors of the economy. In the electronics industry, for instance, where multinational companies recruit a predominantly unskilled and semi-skilled young, green, female workforce, wages are often at or below the average. In other sectors, like pharmaceuticals, chemicals and drink, where a greater proportion of the workforce are occupied in skilled and professional categories, wages levels are often higher (cf. Sexton, 1996). As well as the industrial sector and structure of employment, another key element is the nature of the labour market: for unskilled and semi-skilled employees there is little competition for labour, and, as a consequence, there is not the same pressure to pay above going rates. As one rises, however, through the skill categories, the labour market tightens considerably. With engineering graduates, for instance, indigenous and foreign-owned companies face considerable competition from German-, English- and Dutch-based companies. In this instance, multinational companies are often forced to act as wage-level leaders in order to recruit and retain the skills they require.

Finally, and here the evidence is scant, findings from a number of case study investigations (e.g. Geary, 1991; O'Hehir and Keating, 1992) would suggest that, in the case of US-owned enterprises, corporate headquarters exercise considerable control over pay administration.

Strike Performance

While Murray (1984) found that indigenous companies had a higher incidence of the use of non-strike sanctions in industrial disputes, foreign MNCs emerge as having higher levels of strike activity over the period from 1960 to the end of the 1980s. However, the contributions of MNCs of different nationalities to the overall strike record differed significantly over the period. US MNCs figured prominently in the aggregate strike record during the 1960s when US investment was concentrated in strike-prone "mature" industrial sectors like the car assembly industry. During the 1970s the relative strike record of US firms declined and the decline continued into the 1980s. This reflected the sectoral shift of US investment during this period into electronics, chemicals and pharmaceuticals. It also reflected the rising incidence of non-union US companies. Kelly and Brannick (1991) also claim that new human resource policies played a role in reducing the strike record of US MNCs. The improvement in the strike record of US multinationals during the 1970s and 1980s was paralleled by a deterioration in the record of British companies. This reflected the intensified competitive pressures experienced by British MNCs. A wave of British MNCs had entered Ireland during the 1930s, when state policy sought to industrialise through import substitution. A second wave had entered from the late 1950s in response to capital incentives. Both waves of British investment were concentrated in mature product sectors like food, drink, tobacco and textiles. With the growing liberalisation of trade from the mid-1960s, and Ireland's entry to the EEC in 1973, these enterprises came under more intense competition. This resulted in major restructuring and rationalisation programmes which provoked a sharp rise in industrial conflict.

Thus, overall foreign MNCs displayed higher levels of industrial conflict over the period as a whole from the 1960s. This aggregate relative strike record, as well as changes in the strike profile of different sectors of foreign capital, reflected the sectoral distribution of overseas investment and competitive pressures bearing on the product markets serviced by MNCs.

Third Party Involvement in Disputes

The available evidence here would indicate that we can make a clear distinction between multinational companies that are unionised and those that are non-unionised. The former companies have been as likely to use the Labour Relations Commission's (LRC) dispute resolution and conciliation services as indigenous companies. However, non-union multinationals rarely, if ever, seek to use such services. This would seem to hold true for both large non-union foreign companies like DEC and IBM and smaller companies like Raychem. Many non-union multinational companies tend, however, to inform the LRC of plans they have for major organisational change or restructuring. (Such companies may have employees who are union members and, in anticipation of their making contact with an LRC official, management often think it sensible to tell the LRC of its plans.)

As yet, it is too early to draw any firm conclusions on the extent to which foreign companies use the Commission's advisory services. This service was established in 1991. In sum, it would seem that there are few differences here between foreign and Irish-owned companies, save for non-union multinational companies who do tend not to avail of the services of the LRC in the resolution of disputes.

Transnational Collective Bargaining

There is little evidence that transnational collective bargaining or solidarity in dispute situations developed in the wake of the dramatic expansion of MNC activity in Ireland. Kelly and Brannick (1985: 104–6) discounted even the relevance of seeking management and union views on information disclosure concerning the corporate functioning of MNCs on the grounds that Irish unions are unlikely to have had any success in obtaining such information. Murray (1984: 50) provides an indication that US companies may have been more willing than others to provide corporate financial information to employees, but the validity of the finding is rendered suspect due by the low response rate to questions probing information disclosure practices.

While the Irish Congress of Trade Unions is affiliated to the ETUC and many unions are affiliated to international union groupings and federations in specific sectors, there is little evidence of solid activity on co-ordinated collective bargaining or international collective bargaining. Unions with headquarters in the UK comprise about 14 per cent of Irish trade union membership. This membership is divided nearly evenly across British craft, general and white-collar unions. British unions have traditionally provided their Irish offices with information on UK parent companies in industries where they have negotiated with those companies on both sides of the Irish Sea. A significant example is provided by the insurance industry. Such activity has tended to be the limit to which bargaining information and activity has been co-ordinated. The primary stance traditionally taken by unions in the UK to their Irish membership in various sectors has been to ensure that rates of pay in Ireland did not significantly undercut those prevailing in the UK and divert investment to Irish operations. Other aspects of international co-operation have largely amounted to symbolic gestures, for example, Irish contributions to strike funds in the case of protracted British disputes, like the British mining strike of 1984.

The recent EU Works Council Directive, however, is likely to have significant implications for the conduct of collective bargaining within MNCs. Organisations which come under the remit of the Directive will have to establish a European Works Council (EWC) to inform employees on company issues which are of a transnational nature. The legislation to provide for this came into force in September, 1996. While reaction to the Directive has varied, most commentators are agreed that it does represent a significant development in Irish industrial relations. For the first time, apart from the Worker Participation (State Enterprises) Acts of 1977 and 1988, employers will be legally accountable to an employee representative body. But, perhaps more importantly, the exchange of information between representatives from different branch plants, which the EWCs will undoubtedly facilitate, may lead, if not to the development of formal collective bargaining at European level within companies, then at least to informal bargaining of an indirect or "arm's length" kind.

New Employer Policies
It was noted above that research by Murray (1984) found that US MNCs in Ireland were more likely to claim to have adopted a distinc-

tive and sophisticated approach to human resource management than other organisations. More recent evidence would suggest that multinational companies have been more successful in introducing new employee involvement initiatives and new work structures than their Irish counterparts. Evidence for the Price Waterhouse survey, for instance, reveals that MNCs were more likely than Irish companies to inform professional/technical, clerical and manual staff of the company's financial performance and its business strategy. Quality circles, suggestion schemes, attitude surveys were also more widely used in foreign-owned companies. Interestingly, though, nearly two-thirds of Irish companies and MNCs communicated with their employees through trade union structures.

With regard to work organisation, it was found that Irish-owned firms had, for all categories of employees, made jobs more specific. Multinational companies were far more likely to depart from Tayloristic work structures and adopt wider job profiles with more flexibility between work tasks.

In all, then, it would seem that management in MNCs have progressively given added emphasis to developing a direct and "individualistic" relationship with their employees and less to their dealings with trade unions. Accompanying the implementation of these new policies is often an employer expectation that unions relinquish traditional bargaining agendas and adversarial tactics for a relationship which relies more on "partnership" and "co-operation" with management and a sharing in the "responsibility" for the achievement of business objectives. Clearly, it is difficult to know how well-formulated and coherent these initiatives have been, but we can be sure that management are experimenting with new approaches to industrial relations and that unions are being forced to respond to new labour management practices.

CONCLUSION

This chapter has reviewed the impact of foreign-owned companies on Irish industrial relations. In particular, it has questioned the "orthodox" view within Irish industrial relations scholarship that MNCs' industrial relations practices have, in the main, conformed to traditional Irish practice. While it is conceivable that host-country effects may have overridden country-of-origin effects in the early years of Irish industrialisation, specific differences between the industrial relations practices of Irish-owned companies and MNCs did begin to emerge during the second wave of inward investment in the

1960s, if not before. These differences have in part reflected differences of scale, differences in sectoral composition, differences in market and competitive positions and differences originating in the role of Irish subsidiaries in the international companies.

These differences have probably become more pronounced during the 1970s and 1980s and, perhaps even more so, with the third wave of international investment as the sectoral and product markets of MNCs changed more sharply from those of indigenous companies. The change in the positions of development agencies like the IDA and SFADCO have also contributed to allowing country-of-origin effects to gain ground on host-country effects. This is most strikingly evident in the electronics sector where a distinctive industrial culture has grown up.

This growing influence of country-of-origin effects has in turn been paralleled by a practice and institutional "spill-over effect" *into* Irish industrial relations. This is evidenced not only by Irish employers' experimentation with new human resource management policies and a preference for single-union and pre-production agreements, but also by Irish unions' willingness to co-operate with new employer strategies and see them attain a wider diffusion. In particular, the Irish Congress of Trade Unions' publication of two recent reports ("New Forms of Work Organisation" and "Managing Change") is a clear indication of its willingness to work with the new industrial relations, as long as certain safeguards for trade unions are met. In summary, then, it would seem that the industrial relations practices of MNCs operating in Ireland are acting as a catalyst for change and that convergence is from "host-country practices" towards "foreign companies' practices" and not vice versa as per the orthodoxy.

Footnote

[1] The Price Waterhouse Cranfield Project on Strategic Human Resource Management was established in 1989 and is designed to analyse the nature of HRM practices at enterprise level in Europe. The Irish node of the study which collected the data reported in this paper was located at the University of Limerick and was co-ordinated by Patrick Gunnigle, Michael Morley and Thomas Turner.

References

Enderwick, P. (1986): "Multinationals and Labour Relations: The Case of Ireland", *Journal of Irish Business and Administrative Research*, 8: 1–11.

Federated Union of Employers, (1980): *Employment Conditions and Industrial Relations Practices in International Companies in Ireland*, Dublin: Federated Union of Employers, Report No. 50.

Fogarty, M., Egan, D. and Ryan, W.J.L. (1981): *Pay Policy for the 1980s*, Dublin: Federated Union of Employers.

Geary, J.F (1991): *Human Resource Management in Practice: Labour Management in Irish Electronics Plants*, University of Oxford, unpublished D.Phil. dissertation.

Geary, J.F and Lalor, T. (1996): "Industrial Relations: Collective Wage Negotiations", in J. Sexton and P. O'Connell (eds.), *Labour Market Studies — Ireland*, Commission of the European Union, DGV, Employment, Industrial Relations and Social Affairs: Luxembourg.

Gunnigle, P. (1993): "Exploring Patterns of Industrial Relations Management in Greenfield Sites: Evidence From the Republic of Ireland", Mimeo, University of Limerick.

Hardiman, N. (1988): *Pay, Politics and Economic Performance in Ireland: 1970-1987*, Oxford: Clarendon Press.

ICTU (1993): *New Forms of Work Organisation,* Dublin: Irish Congress of Trade Unions.

ICTU (1995): *Managing Change: Review of Union Involvement in Company Restructuring,* Irish Congress of Trade Unions, Dublin: ICTU.

Jackson, P. (1987): *The Position of Women Workers in Overseas Manufacturing Plants in Ireland — A Social Study*, Dublin: University College Dublin, unpublished D.Phil. dissertation.

Kelly, A. and Brannick, T. (1985): "Industrial Relations Practices in Multinational Companies in Ireland", *Journal of Irish Business and Administrative Research*, 7: 98–111.

Kelly, A. and Brannick, T. (1991): "The Impact of New Human Resource Management Policies on US MNC Strike Patterns: The Case of Ireland", *Midwest Review of International Business Research*, Ohio: 51–4.

MacMahon, G., Neary, C. and O'Connor, K. (1988): "Multinationals in Ireland — Three Decades On", *Industrial Relations News Report*, 6: 15-7.

McCann, J. (1988): "The 'New' Industrial Relations Arena of Human Resource Management: Union–Non-Union", *Industrial Relations News Report*, 28: 14–9.

McGovern, P. (1988): "Increasing Opposition to Unionisation in the 1980s", *Industrial Relations News Report*, 45: 15–18.

Mooney, P. (1980): *An Inquiry into Wage Payment Systems in Ireland*, Dublin: Economic and Social Research Institute.

Murray, S. (1984): *Survey of Employee/Industrial Relations in Irish Private Sector Manufacturing Industry Carried Out for the Industrial Development Authority*, Dublin: IDA.

O'Hehir, S. and Keating, M. (1992): "Pay as a Strategic Lever for Change: The Experience of Multinationals in Ireland", *Industrial Relations News Report*, 46: 15–19.

O'Malley, E. (1992): "Problems of Industrialisation in Ireland", in J.H. Goldthorpe and C.T. Whelan (eds.), *The Development of Industrial Society in Ireland*, Oxford: Oxford University Press for the British Academy.

O'Malley, E. (1996): "Industrial Policies", in J. Sexton and P. O'Connell (eds.), *Labour Market Studies — Ireland*, Commission of the European Union, DGV, Employment, Industrial Relations and Social Affairs: Luxembourg.

O'Malley, E., Kennedy, K.A. and O'Donnell, R. (1992): *The Impact of the Industrial Development Agencies*, Report to the Industrial Policy Review Group, Dublin: Stationery Office.

Operational Programme for Industrial Development 1994–1999 (1994): Dublin: Stationery Office.

Roche, W.K. and Turner, T. (1994): "Testing Alternative Models of Human Resource Policy Effects on Trade Union Recognition in the Republic of Ireland", *International Journal of Human Resource Management*, 5: 721–53.

Sexton, J. (1996): "Wage and Salary Trends", in J. Sexton and P. O'Connell (eds.), *Labour Market Studies — Ireland*, Commission of the European Union, DGV, Employment, Industrial Relations and Social Affairs: Luxembourg.

Sheehan, B. (1996): Forthcoming M.Comm. Thesis, Graduate School of Business, University College Dublin.

Toner, W.P. (1987): *Union or Non-Union? — Contemporary Employee Relations Strategies in the Republic of Ireland*, London School of Economics: unpublished D.Phil. dissertation.

Wallace, J. (1982): *Industrial Relations in the City of Limerick and Environs: Final Report*, College of Business, University of Limerick.

CHAPTER 8

INDUSTRIAL CONFLICT

Teresa Brannick, Linda Doyle and *Aidan Kelly*

Industrial relations conflict is a commonplace characteristic of Western industrial societies. In many countries, including Ireland, the strike pattern is frequently the subject of public and political debate. Data on strikes are used as one of the primary indicators of the climate of an industrial relations system, or of the collective bargaining relationship. In this paper, we present and consider various dimensions of industrial conflict in Ireland.

THE STUDY OF CONFLICT

According to Clark Kerr (1964: 171), there are a variety of manifestations of industrial conflict:

> Its means of expression are as unlimited as the ingenuity of man. The strike is the most common and most visible expression. But conflict with the employer may also take the form of peaceful bargaining and grievance handling, of boycotts, of political action, of restrictions of output, of sabotage, of absenteeism, or of personnel turnover. Several of these forms, such as sabotage, restriction of output, absenteeism, and turnover, may take place on an individual as well as on an organized basis and constitute alternatives to collective action. Even the strike is of many varieties. It may involve all the workers or only key men (sic). It may take the form of refusal to work overtime or to perform a certain process. It may even involve such rigid adherence to the rules that output is stifled.

The study of conflict, and in particular the study of strikes, has been an active pursuit of many researchers over past decades. This chapter presents only a brief outline of the major theories of strike activity. Many different theories have been developed to consider the causes and patterns of strike activity. One obvious approach is the study of the industrial relations system (institutional factors), which is dealt with elsewhere in this text. We examine below the issues associated with theories based on economic factors, sociological forces as well as those based on the political perspective.

The Economist's Perspective

Economic models have tended to dominate the study of industrial conflict. These models have concentrated on the relationship over time between economic conditions, as represented by the business cycle, and the level of strike activity (often strike frequency). Many economists hold that there is an overall positive relationship between the business cycle and strike activity. In other words, they believe that improvements in economic prosperity will lead to increases in the level of strike activity — that strikes increase at peaks in the business cycle and decrease during a downturn in business activity (see Edwards, 1978; Sapsford, 1975). A positive association between economic prosperity and strike activity is believed to exist for two main reasons. Firstly, if the strike is a form of protest it is in the union's interest to protest when conditions are not at their worst. Hoffer (1951: 27–28) notes:

> Discontent is likely to be highest when misery is bearable; when conditions have so improved that an ideal state seems almost within reach. A grievance is most poignant when almost redressed . . . It is not actual suffering but the taste of better things which excites people to revolt.

The second view is that the strike may be a "strategic weapon" (Snyder, 1975) which unions use to maximise their gains from employers. Obviously, unions are most likely to maximise their gains when business conditions are favourable.

Hibbs (1976) states that the key economic variables which influence strike frequency are the demand for labour, as represented by the unemployment rate, the movement in real wages and finally changes in the profit ratio of the organisation. Edwards (1992) notes that unemployment is the most useful measure of business conditions and that the level of unemployment has an inverse relationship with strike frequency. Mulvey (1968) examined this relationship using Irish data for the period 1941 to 1966 and found that there was, in fact, an inverse relationship between the level of unemployment and the level of strike activity. In relation to the second economic variable, an increase in prices will have an impact on the purchasing power of workers and is likely to lead to a trade union demand for a cost of living increase. Thus, movement in real wages is also believed to have an inverse relationship with strike levels, that is, as real wages decrease, the level of strike activity increases. Finally, the profit ratio of the enterprise is believed to have a positive relationship with strike frequency.

It should be noted, however, that there is little consistent agreement as to the economic variables that influence strike activity across countries. In fact, the research results that do exist arise from tests of statistical models of the business cycle effects and these results often show different variables as being important in different countries. They also show differences in the relative importance of the variables over time (see, for example, Snyder, 1975; Cronin, 1980). One can, therefore, suggest that the results of the economic models have been inconclusive thus far.

Sociological Perspective

The sociological approach tends to see the strike as an expression of class conflict and as a natural outcome of changes in the social forces of society. The industrial or macro-sociological perspective stems from the belief that the actions of workers are driven by the situation in which they find themselves and that economic factors are only important in so far as they provide the initial impetus leading to a change in the social system.

Hyman (1977) notes that there had been a strong belief that the institutionalisation of industrial conflict which began during the 1950s and 1960s would lead to a decrease in strike activity over the long run. This perspective was later abandoned as the hypothesis was not borne out in practice, particularly when one considered the increase in strike activity that emerged during the 1970s. Hyman proposes that there have been two main approaches adopted by sociologists in relation to the study of industrial conflict. Firstly, some sociologists examine cross-sectional variations in strike-proneness. Hyman notes that such theories of strikes involve considering the differences between work groups, companies, industries and even countries. Several theories have been developed in this way. For instance, some authors (Kerr and Siegel, 1954) found that certain industries appeared to be consistently strike-prone, even across national boundaries. They note that miners, dockers and seamen exhibited the highest propensity to strike. This situation would also appear to be true in Ireland, as will be shown later. Other sociologists have identified the technology employed by the organisation as the factor which has the greatest influence on propensity to strike. All of the above theories focus on the structural determinants of industrial relations but it is unlikely that any one of these separate theories can fully explain the total strike activity in an organisation.

Edwards (1992) notes that a second sociological approach involves a consideration of the different causes over time of strikes. One of the best-known models is that of "strike waves". The belief is that the capitalist system progresses through long waves of activity and that the pattern of strike activity can be associated with this wave-like motion. It is recognised that there are short term fluctuations due to the business cycle but it is held that there is an overall trend of growth and decline. These wave like motions, known as "Kondratieff waves", are said to exert an influence on the amount and the timing of class conflict, with a major explosion of conflict arising at the wave peak and followed by declining levels of conflict during the downward movement of the wave. Edwards (1992), however, cites several problems associated with this theory, particularly the lack of reliable strike data prior to the turn of this century. He states that this lack of data has limited the study to only two Kondratieff waves, as each cycle is estimated to be 50 years long. A further problem alluded to by Edwards is the influence of the two world wars on the wave motion. Recent research has concluded that the relationship between the waves and the level of strike activity was not as direct as had been earlier suggested. Yet, Edwards holds that the theory itself may be of use in explaining the decline in strike activity experienced throughout the developed countries during the 1980s and 1990s. He notes that if, as is suggested, there was a peak of the wave toward the end of the 1960s, which was accompanied by massive industrial disruption, particularly on the continent, then developed countries are currently experiencing a downward movement of the wave and should also be experiencing a decline in strike activity. This will be seen to be the case in Ireland.

The Political Science Approach

The political science approach to the study of conflict emerged during the 1970s. The founding principle of the approach was a belief that the level of strike activity was determined by the power of organised labour. Hibbs (1978), a well-known proponent of this view, argues that conflict is driven by changes in the "political economy of distribution" rather than by sociological, economic or other factors and that this is reflected in the power that labour/social democratic parties have over the final distribution of income in society. Hibbs' view is that strikes emerge as one manifestation of the conflict between different social classes over the distribution of resources and, in particular, over the distribution of national income and that strike levels tend to be lowest in countries where the unions were engaged in political activity. The hypothesis offered by Hibbs is that long-run change in the level of conflict is driven by the changes in power that emerge during the struggle over distribution. In other words, conflict is seen as the outcome of a struggle for control of power at the centre and is believed to be most common where one group loses power. Korpi and Shalev (1979) developed this thesis to explain international variations in levels of industrial conflict. For Korpi and Shalev, levels of strike activity are *negatively* associated with levels of working-class political mobilisation and organisation in different countries. In countries like Sweden, where a strong social democratic political party has been successful in gaining a high level of electoral support over long periods of time, conflict over the distribution of income takes place primarily in the political arena. Trade unions focus their attention on agreements with government and trade off industrial peace in the labour market for advances in the "political market": i.e. in social and economic programmes designed to protect employees and to maintain a low level of unemployment. In countries where working-class political identity and political mobilisation are weak, for example Canada and the United States, unions must rely primarily on their power in the labour market to protect and improve their members' conditions. The result is a relatively high level of strike activity and a high placing in international leagues of strike activity. Korpi and Shalev (1979) writing about Ireland's relative strike record up to the 1970s, view the Irish case as one in which relatively weak working-class political mobilisation results in a relatively high level of industrial conflict.

Edwards (1992) cites several authors who have expressed concern about the use of such a model. In particular, he points to Franzosi who argues that if strikes are assumed to be a response to a crisis/change at the national level then why do strikes occur in different countries at the same time. Furthermore, in taking the case of Italy, Franzosi has shown that strikes often lead to crisis at the national level rather than the other way around. Thus, Franzosi's findings would appear to contradict the theory on several levels.

THE DEFINITION OF INDUSTRIAL CONFLICT AND MEASUREMENT PROBLEMS

As stated above, this chapter is concerned only with overt conflict, that is to say, conflict which is represented by some form of work stoppage arising from a dispute between employers and employees; it may be related to a central collective bargaining issue such as pay or working conditions; it may also be sympathetic in character, where employees refuse to work as a mark of support for a conflict which exists between other groups of employers and employees, or of a secondary nature where employees are prevented from working due to lack of basic materials which in itself follows from a primary conflict. Hyman (1977: 17) notes that strikes are normally associated with some form of collective organisation, usually a trade union, and he defines a strike as "a temporary stoppage of work by a group of employees in order to express a grievance or enforce a demand." Clearly, there is also much latent conflict between employers and employees which may not be manifested in strike action, but such conflict is not considered in the present analysis.

The first set of official statistics relating to strikes in the Republic were published in 1922. The method of compilation has hardly changed since then. The following extract from the Irish Trade Journal of 1925 shows how strike statistics were to be compiled and reported:

> Reports of a dispute involving a stoppage of work are received in the first instance from several sources, including the local employment exchange, trade unions, employees and the press. Thereupon the manager of the local employment exchange is requested to ascertain from the disputants: 1. the trade or occupation affected; 2. the names of the parties; 3. the approximate number of work people involved; 4. the date on which work has ceased; 5. the cause of dispute; 6. the date on which work was resumed; 7. the terms of settlement.

In addition, this information was to be collected only where the strike lasted at least one day and involved, in total, ten or more work-days. The Irish Trade Journal of 1963 contains a broadly similar statement as that of 1925 in relation to the collation of dispute data:

> Only those disputes which involved a stoppage of work and which were reported to the Department of Social Welfare are covered in this survey. Reports are received from several sources including local employment office, trade unions, employee associations and the press. When a dispute is reported the manager of the local employment offices obtains certain information on a prescribed form and the present statistics are based on the results of these enquiries. Disputes which lasted less than one day or which involved an aggregate loss of less than ten working days are excluded.

The firm is the basic reporting unit for compilation purposes. All types of disputes are covered, but political strikes have not been recorded in Ireland. Workers included in the statistics are those actively involved in the stoppage and those laid off because normal operations are impossible due to supply difficulties or picketing. "Work-days lost" in a period, which is the basic measure employed, is calculated by reference to the numbers involved and the duration of the strike. Prior to 1963 Sundays and public holidays were excluded from the calculation and with the introduction of the five-day week in that year Saturdays are now excluded except where Saturday work is relevant to the employment contract. The criteria underlying the compilation of Irish strike statistics are in accordance with the recommendations of the International Labour Organisation, which, in summary, state that disputes should be classified by cause, industrial grouping, duration, number of workers involved, results and settlements (International Labour Organisation, 1926).

This is the format for the way that strikes are supposed to be reported and presented. However, in practice there is some question as to the validity of the final figures as representing the precise picture in relation to strikes. It is unclear how strike statistics *have* actually been compiled over the last 60 years as distinct from how they *should* have been compiled. From our own enquiries it would appear that the principal source of information is the network of employment exchanges, of which there are about 40 scattered throughout the country and some 90 sub-exchanges. Newspapers are the main source of information regarding disputes; and where they are reported, the exchanges forward the appropriate forms to the disputants; in practice, exchange managers often find the parties reluctant to provide the necessary information and the accuracy of that supplied might also be open to question. Once the exchange sends the forms to the disputing parties it regards its function in the collection system as terminated. The parties to the dispute are then expected to forward a completed record to one of several agencies. The aggregation of this data then becomes the source document for the official strike statistics and is presented monthly and annually.

Other sources of strike statistics include the records maintained by the Monitoring Unit in the Department of Labour and the industrial relations officers attached to the Labour Relations Commission. Also the Labour Court, when investigating a case, may discover previous stoppages of work which had not been reported. In this way some of the smaller stoppages manage to find their way into the overall strike records. On balance, the strike record as a whole is very likely to be an underestimate of the actual level of strike activity (Goodman, 1967). There are similar difficulties in other countries, and while various methods are employed in the collection of data, all systems seem to experience some difficulties (Fisher, 1973). In the Irish case, the main problem concerns the strike frequency index; many small strikes, which meet the official criteria, may not be reported as they may be regarded as insignificant or remain undetected. However, this situation has little impact on the other two strike indices: workers involved and work-days lost (Brannick and Kelly, 1983).

STRIKE INDICES

The principal indices which feature in the majority of studies on strikes internationally, and which are usually employed in the analysis of available Irish data, include the frequency of stoppages, the breadth of such stoppages (their duration), and the number of workdays lost. Stern (1978) notes a consensus among researchers with regard to these indices. However, he goes on to point out that there is a multiplicity of methodologies utilised with each dimension. For example, of the 22 studies examining strike frequency, 12 used a raw count measure, 5 used both raw counts and standardised measure, while the remainder used standardised measures only. A similar variety of measures had been used in examining strike breadth and duration. Thus, interpretation and attempts at comparison are obviously difficult. Nonetheless, the three indices continue to be central to the analysis of strike activity and it is important that each index is properly understood.

Frequency of Strikes

The frequency of strikes is the measure of the number of stoppages over a specified time period. It is frequently forwarded as a valid index of strike activity because of the suggested impact which numerous small strikes are said to have. The Donovan Commission (1968) underlined the importance of paying sufficient attention to the number of strikes and not just to the aggregate number of work-days lost, particularly in view of the effect which they had on management where general confidence was at risk.

　　Turner (1969) takes issue with this proposition, arguing that small strikes generally have less than proportionate economic effects compared with big ones. As a consequence he views the number of workdays lost as a superior index to strike activity. In an earlier study,

Knowles (1952) detected some strength in the "frequency" index. A study of strike activity in Britain between 1911 and 1947 showed the number of strikes to be most sensitive to trade cycle fluctuations of the period and Forchheimer (1948) also wrote of its lasting quality across a number of national studies:

> Only frequency follows fairly distinctly the cyclical pattern. This reaction is strongest in Great Britain, Germany and Canada, but there is a trace of it in the graphs for all countries. This makes for a kind of international agreement in the short run changes of the frequency of disputes.

Galambos and Evans (1977) point to a further deficiency in this index. They note that on the one hand strike data may show a fall in the number of stoppages between one year and another, but a substantial increase in the total work-days lost for the same time period. They further point out that the impact of the number of strikes will vary between industries, depending upon how essential it is to achieve continuous operation, how costly it may be to stop and restart processes and the extent to which capital costs are relatively heavier than labour costs.

Breadth of Strikes

The breadth of strikes refers to a measure of the number of workers who participate in the work stoppages. As with frequency it has some limitations. For example, it is possible for the number of workers involved in disputes to drop for a time, thus implying some improvement, while at the same time experience an escalation of the total work-days lost. Silver (1977) suggests four reasons why the number of workers involved in strikes is not a very sensitive indicator: (1) the occurrence and not the degree of involvement is indicated in the statistic and when a rise takes place it could be the result of a change in the form of strike activity rather than an escalation of industrial strife; (2) the statistic also counts employees put out of work because of strikes, but who are not strikers themselves; (3) there may be some workers in the more strike-prone sectors of the economy who will be counted more than once because of their frequency of striking; (4) no account is taken of changes in the labour force or in the degree of unionisation, both of which clearly set limits on the number of potential strikes. Some of these difficulties have been in evidence in analyses of Irish strike patterns (Kelly and Brannick, 1985).

Duration of Strikes

This index refers to the length of strikes, usually in terms of days of work lost. On its own this index is not very informative; when it is associated with the aggregate number of strikers it leads to a working days lost index (duration of the strike in days multiplied by the number of strikers involved in the action) which is widely used in assessing trends both within and between countries. When comparing stoppages in different countries the duration of the disputes is often cited. Yet, the typical situation in some countries may be that strikes only last for a number of days, while in other states stoppages may be of several weeks duration. Thus, in judging the strike position of a country or one of its sectors it is probably safest to utilise all available indices. It is doubtful if any one of the indices would lead to an accurate expression of the status of strikes.

IRISH STRIKE TRENDS

Figure 8.1 contains a record of work stoppages for the period 1922–95; it indicates for each year the total number of work-days lost, the number of workers involved, and the number of disputes which began in each year. The total number of work-days lost reached a peak in 1979 when the one million mark was exceeded for the third time. The aggregate figures fluctuated substantially during this period with certain years, such as 1923, 1937, 1947, 1951, 1952, 1961, 1964, 1965, 1966, 1968, 1969, 1970, 1974, 1976, 1978 and 1979 experiencing comparatively high aggregate days lost. A cursory examination of the date in Table 8.1 shows a peaking in strike activity during the 1960s on the total work-days lost index; the early 1970s saw a downturn with a return to higher rates during the late 1970s and early 1980s. For the 1992–95 period all three strike measurements were much reduced and the number of strikes was the lowest ever recorded. Care should be taken when interpreting these trends as the period 1982–86 recorded the highest ever number of workers involved.

The Report of the Commission of Inquiry on Industrial Relations (1981) in its references to strikes, contains the following observations: "the average yearly number of work-days lost has been rising continuously since the 1940s; since the 1950s, the average number of work-days lost has almost trebled and the average number of workers involved in disputes has more than trebled." However, on their own, strike statistics are not very informative; in viewing these trends one must also take account of changes that may have taken place in the

TABLE 8.1: FIVE-YEARLY STATEMENTS OF NUMBERS OF STRIKES,
WORKERS INVOLVED AND WORK-DAYS LOST, 1922–95

Year	Number of Strikes	Workers Involved	Work-days Lost
1922–26	471	79,128	2,594,218
1927–31	301	17,876	607,325
1932–36	463	41,250	869,058
1937–41	541	59,750	2,299,418
1942–46	426	35,112	609,196
1947–51	786	91,993	1,742,393
1952–56	401	46,550	962,282
1957–61	299	58,709	800,275
1962–66	418	141,664	2,219,011
1967–71	606	194,100	2,805,715
1972–76	817	168,899	2,038,178
1977–81	712	174,968	3,424,294
1982–86	686	306,388	1,951,079
1987–91	272	68,415	766,519
1992–95	146	48,290	407,725

Source: Strike series in all tables derived from Strikes Data file, Department
of Industrial Relations, University College Dublin.

TABLE 8.2: ANNUAL AVERAGE STRIKE FREQUENCY, BREADTH AND
WORK-DAYS LOST CONTROLLED FOR EMPLOYMENT 1922–95

Year	Frequency	Breadth	Days Lost
1922–26	165.5	27.0	n/d
1927–31	101.0	6.0	0.2
1932–36	148.8	13.3	0.3
1937–41	169.7	18.7	0.7
1942–46	130.5	10.8	0.2
1947–51	217.2	25.4	0.5
1952–56	111.6	13.0	0.3
1957–61	88.7	17.4	0.2
1962–66	114.1	38.7	0.6
1967–71	155.0	49.7	0.7
1972–76	199.2	44.2	0.5
1977–81	148.1	36.4	0.7
1982–86	144.5	64.6	0.4
1987–91	49.3	12.4	0.1
1992–95	31.0	11.7	0.09

levels of employment. The proportion of the workforce engaged in non-agricultural activities and the proportion of the workforce represented by trade unions (which are obviously important in the general explanation of strike activity) both increased substantially over the period as a whole and, particularly, in recent decades (see Roche, this volume). Table 8.2 shows strike trends when the data is controlled for employment levels. From this table we can see that the number of strikes in relation to employment levels has fluctuated considerably since the foundation of the state. However, since the mid-1970s strike frequency has been on the decline and the lowest rate ever was recorded in the 1992–95 period. It is also evident from Table 8.2 that between the early 1960s and the mid-1980s the annual average number of strike-days per employee was consistently high, ranging from 0.4 to 0.7, but dropped dramatically to 0.09 in the 1992–95 period. Edwards (1992: 361) suggests that the recent fall off in industrial disputes may, in part, be due to the fundamental shift in industrial relations away from the traditional adversarial approach and toward approaches based on the "generation of commitment". A further impact in Ireland has been the introduction of centralised bargaining in the form of the national agreements since 1987 and their contribution in promoting industrial peace.

THE PATTERN OF STRIKE ACTIVITY

The data contained in Tables 8.1 and 8.2 and Figure 8.1 provide a general picture of the Irish strike pattern over the past 74 years and indicate the changes which have taken place in strike frequency, level of worker involvement and volume of work-days lost due to strikes. It can be seen that all three indices are broadly pro-cyclical with respect to economic changes. For example, if one examines the annual trend in the number of strikes since 1922 one can identify such a cyclical trend. For instance, the decline in strike activity experienced in the 1920s is associated with recession and stagnation in the economic environment during that decade. This was followed by an increase in strike levels during the 1930s corresponding to a period of industrialisation and so on for the subsequent decades (see Roche, this volume). What is also of interest is that there is no compelling evidence of the withering away of industrial action.

In order to gain a better understanding of Irish strike activity we need to consider the data at a more disaggregated level. For example, it would be useful to know whether strike rates are different in the

FIGURE 8.1A: ANNUAL TREND IN NUMBER OF STRIKES

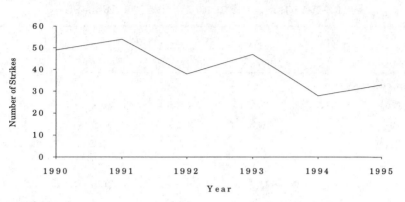

FIGURE 8.1B: ANNUAL TREND IN NUMBER OF WORKERS INVOLVED

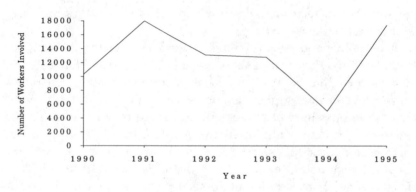

FIGURE 8.1C: ANNUAL TREND IN NUMBER OF WORK-DAYS LOST

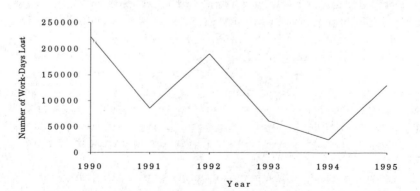

TABLE 8.3: PERCENTAGE SHARE OF STRIKES, WORKERS INVOLVED AND
WORK-DAYS LOST BY PRINCIPAL SECTOR, 1960–95

| | Period | | | |
Sector	1960–69	1970–79	1980–89	1990–95
Public/Semi-state				
No.	17.9	18.3	29.1	47
WI	36.3	32.5	68.9	61
WDL	23.3	37.8	37.7	27
Private				
No.	82.2	81.7	70.9	53
WI	63.7	67.5	31.1	39
WDL	76.7	60.2	62.3	73

public and private sectors and also which industrial sectors have the
worst and best strike records.

Data on public and private sector strike levels for the 36-year period 1960–95 are shown in Tables 8.3 and 8.4. The public sector is
defined as including central and local government, state-controlled
enterprise and various support agencies. Over the period, the private
sector has seen its share of strikes fall dramatically. The public sector
now accounts for almost half of all strikes, up from 20 per cent in the
late 1970s. In addition its share of workers involved in strike activity
has doubled from about one-third to two-thirds in recent years. This
would seem to suggest that public sector has become more strike
prone than in the past. For a number of reasons it is perhaps not surprising that the public sector's share of strikes should have increased
over recent decades. Firstly, it was not until 1982 that public servants
were included under the immunity provisions of the 1906 Trade Disputes Act. Secondly, the government has recently adopted a tighter
stance on public sector spending. This has resulted in downsizing
within the public sector in general and the introduction of a commercial ethos in public sector companies. This "commercialisation" of the
public sector has caused several productivity disputes (RTE and CIE
being recent examples). Finally, the issue of "specials" under national
agreements since 1987 has also led to widespread unrest in the public
sector.

The strike pattern in the private sector is quite different. Here, although the frequency remains relatively high, the proportion of

TABLE 8.4: AVERAGE ANNUAL STRIKE RATES FOR THE PRIVATE AND
PUBLIC SECTORS CONTROLLED FOR NUMBERS EMPLOYED

| | | Sectors | |
Strike Index	*Period*	*Private**	*Public*
Strike Frequency	1960–69	14	8
(per 100,000 employees)	1970–79	22	11
	1980–89	13	10
	1990–95	2	7
Workers Involved	1960–69	36	57
(per 100 employees)	1970–79	40	41
	1980–89	21	89
	1990–95	5	27
Work-days Lost	1960–69	60	53
(per 100 employees)	1970–79	65	85
	1980–89	34	40
	1990–95	12	12
Average Strike Duration	1960–69	11.7	9.2
(days)	1970–79	14.6	10.8
	1980–89	21.4	11.5
	1990–95	20.9	6.5

* Non-agricultural workforce

strikers has halved from 63.7 to 32.9, but the strikes themselves tend
to be of a much longer duration. However, we need to take account of
the employment base in order to establish whether there truly are
differences in strike activity between the public and private sectors.
Table 8.4 contains the relevant date for the years 1960–92. For both
the private and public sectors all three strike indices declined in the
1990s. Of particular note is the extent of the decrease in the strike
frequency for the private sector as compared to the decrease experienced in the public sector. The decline in average strike duration continued for the public sector but the private sector continued a trend
evident over recent decades for the duration of strikes to remain at a
high level. Prior to the 1990s the strike frequency rate was considerably lower in the public sector but in the 1990s public sector workers were three times as likely to strike than their counterparts in the
private sector. It may be seen clearly that throughout the 1960s,
1970s and 1980s in terms of both worker involvement and work-days,
public sector employees were much more prone to engage in strike

activity. The public sector continued to experience higher levels of workers involvement into the 1990s. However the average strike duration was only one-third that of the private sector. These different characteristics balance each other out resulting in both sectors having similar work-days lost rates. In fact, the greater level of worker involvement in public sector strikes is the root cause of the sector's overall adverse performance as measured by the worker involvement and work-days lost indices (Kelly and Brannick, 1983).

The data in Tables 8.5 and 8.6 provide an indication of the strike-proneness of the various industrial sectors in the economy. Within the private sector there have been considerable variations in strike activity between the different sub-sectors and within the same sub-sectors over time. Since 1922 the mining and turf production sector has produced more strikes and work-days lost per employee than any other sector, but strike rates have declined by approximately 300 per cent over the 70 year period. Several international studies on inter-industry strike patterns have also identified the mining sector as being particularly strike prone, and while many explanations have been offered at various times, such factors as the nature of the work, the homogeneity of the workforce and technology seem to be of particular importance (see, for example, Kerr and Siegel, 1954; McCarthy, 1970; Smith et al., 1978; Durcan et al., 1983).

Apart from the agriculture, forestry and fishing sector, which rarely experiences strike activity, there has been a remarkable evenness in the strike frequency rates of most other sectors, although the inter-sectoral pattern has been characterised by considerable variation in the rate of work-days lost per employee. Two sectors with extensive public ownership, transport and communication, and electricity, gas and water, have featured consistently in the strike record, while the building and construction sector has experienced a considerable decline in both strike frequency and work-days lost per employee. Kelly and Brannick (1988) have proposed several reasons for the obvious decline in strike activity in the building and construction sector. They note that the sector has experienced massive expansion and sharp declines over the period under examination. Between 1961 and 1971 the number of people employed in the sector expanded by 42 per cent but then decreased by 30 per cent between 1981 and 1986. Table 8.5 shows that there is a definite association between the levels of strike activity and the levels of employment in this sector. The authors stated that this sector suffered from high levels of unofficial strike activity and that this level of activity was caused primarily by

TABLE 8.5: AVERAGE ANNUAL STRIKE, FREQUENCY PER EMPLOYEE BY
SECTOR, 1922–81

	Average Annual Strike Frequency per 100,000 Employees			
	1922–41	1942–61	1962–81	1982–92
Manufacturing	21	21	28	17
Agriculture, Forestry & Fishery	n/d	1	0.3	0.6
Building & Construction	52	30	16	3
Transport & Communications	22	18	25	2
Electricity, Gas & Water	26	24	33	29
Mining, Turf etc.	163	98	54	30

TABLE 8.6: AVERAGE ANNUAL WORK-DAYS LOST PER EMPLOYEE BY
SECTOR, 1922–81

Sector	Average Annual Work-days Lost per 100,000 Employees			
	1922–41	1942–61	1962–81	1982–92
Manufacturing	517	435	708	458
Agriculture, Forestry & Fishing	n/d	4	2	9
Building & Construction	2,467	173	533	78
Transport & Communications	1,583	434	2,029	485
Electricity, Gas & Water	381	952	503	1,033
Mining, Turf etc.	3,381	2,296	3,270	503

the unique work environment of the sector. Kelly and Brannick state
that the physical conditions of work are quite difficult and that many
workers are employed on a casual and contract basis. The authors
note that the sector does not exhibit inter-group solidarity and that
the workers themselves are only concerned with maximising their
short term personal gains. The authors conclude that the unofficial
nature of many of the disputes in this sector and the small number of
employees involved in each dispute is, therefore, not surprising. The
most heterogeneous sector, in terms of the range of industrial activities undertaken, is the manufacturing sector, and here one may also
observe a marked decline in strike performance.

The further disaggregation of this sector's data, contained in Table
8.7a and 8.7b, provides an indication of varying strike trends within
manufacturing since the foundation of the State in 1922. Kelly and
Brannick (1988) state that many of the variations in the individual

sub-sectors were due to the effects of economic and industrial policy developments. Data for the printing and paper, metal, engineering and chemical products sectors display a continuous deterioration in their respective strike performances. In the printing and paper sector, while there has been a remarkable uniformity in the strike frequency over time (also the least strike-prone), the average days lost per employee climbed steadily until the early 1980s, but dropped dramatically in the 1982–92 period. There are also contrary trends on the two indices for the food, drink, tobacco and textile sectors, all of which illustrate the various shapes by which strikes may be distinguished. Some sectors have few strikes, but experience large losses in work-days: such strikes are either long drawn-out events, or may involve large numbers of workers, or a combination of both factors. Sectors with many strikes but low losses in work-days, such as the textile sector, obviously involve strikes of short duration or involve small numbers of strikers. The different strike patterns partly reflect the influence of the unique technological, organisational and economic conditions found across the different industrial environments of the individual sub-sectors.

LARGE STRIKES, UNOFFICIAL STRIKES AND STRIKE ISSUES

Three further features of the Irish strike pattern need to be considered. These are the extraordinary impact which large strikes have on the overall strike record, the extent of unofficial strike action and the nature of the issue in dispute. A few summary statistics provide a clear picture of the impact of large strikes. In a study which defined a large strike as one resulting in the loss of 30,000 or more work-days, it was found that 57 per cent of all days lost (5.7 million days) during the period 1960–79 were due to 43 large strikes (Kelly and Brannick, 1983). This represented only 2 per cent of the total number of strikes for this period but had an obvious impact on the strike measures. During the 1980s the proportion of work-days lost resulting from large strikes fell back to 32 per cent but rose dramatically to 65 per cent for the early 1990s. The effect of large strikes on the overall record, therefore, continues to be considerable. On several occasions (such as the bank strikes of 1966, 1970 and 1976 and the Post Office strike of 1979, the Dunnes Store strike of 1995, the Waterford Crystal strike of 1990) single national strikes have been responsible for a majority of days lost during particular years and greatly affect Ireland's position in the international strike league table.

TABLE 8.7A: AVERAGE ANNUAL STRIKE FREQUENCY PER 100,000
EMPLOYEES BY MANUFACTURING SUB-SECTOR, 1922–92

	Year			
Manufacturing	*1922–41*	*1942–61*	*1962–81*	*1982–92*
Food, Drink, Tobacco	25	21	26	26
Textiles	29	22	22	28
Clothing, Footwear	13	11	16	9
Furniture, Woodwork	28	35	23	18
Printing, Paper	11	13	13	13
Chemical Products	28	20	28	51
Metal, Engineering	24	40	41	29
Clay Products, Glass, Cement	—	—	42	8

TABLE 8.7B: AVERAGE ANNUAL WORK-DAYS LOST PER 1,000 EMPLOYEES

	Year			
Manufacturing	*1922–41*	*1942–61*	*1962–81*	*1982–92*
Food, Drink, Tobacco	679	338	683	717
Textiles	941	251	443	391
Clothing, Footwear	326	161	144	152
Furniture, Woodwork	527	686	151	166
Printing, Paper	433	1,201	1,641	410
Chemical Products	1,321	791	809	847
Metal, Engineering	324	575	881	769
Clay, Products, Glass, Cement	—	—	960	770

The significance of unofficial strike action is illustrated in Table 8.8
and Figure 8.2 (1967 was selected as the starting point as there was
insufficient quantitative data on unofficial strikes prior to this). This
form of conflict, representing the absence of the imprimatur or official
endorsement of the trade union concerned, had become more prevalent in the 1970s and was identified by the Commission of Inquiry on
Industrial Relations (1981) as a particularly worrying feature of Irish
strike activity.

The frequency of unofficial strike action was particularly high during
the 1970s, a decade which saw an unbroken series of nine national
pay agreements. By way of contrast, during the period 1987–95, when
a national centralised bargaining structure was in place the level of
unofficial conflict was very low. In these bargaining circumstances

TABLE 8.8: AVERAGE ANNUAL STATEMENTS OF UNOFFICIAL STRIKES,
WORKERS INVOLVED AND WORK-DAYS LOST 1967–92

Year	% of Unofficial Strikes	% of Workers Involved	% of Work-days Lost
1967–71	60	35	10
1972–76	70	62	33
1977–81	64	56	27
1982–86	41	13	17
1987–92	36	18	11
1993–95	20	8	10

FIGURE 8.2: ANNUAL STATEMENTS OF THE PERCENTAGE OF UNOFFICIAL
STRIKES, WORKERS INVOLVED AND WORK-DAYS LOST

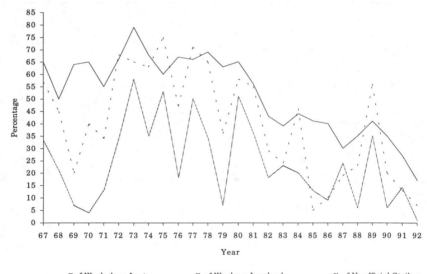

no-strike pledges are normally given by trade unions and if overt
conflict does occur it is invariably classified as unofficial. The precise
causes of unofficial action remain unclear. An explanatory study by
Brannick and Kelly (1984) attempted to examine the phenomenon of
unofficial action in Ireland. The study involved gathering information
from 32 senior trade union officials, who represented almost 82 per

TABLE 8.9: STRIKES BY MAJOR ISSUE 1960–92

Period	Strike Index	Strike Issue (percentage)				
		Pay	Pay-Related Issue	Dismissal / Suspension	Working Conditions	Redundancy / Lay-Off
1960–64	No.	31.1	16.6	20.0	9.7	1.6
	WI	26.1	32.9	11.8	18.3	0.9
	WDL	26.3	46.1	5.2	26.0	0.3
1965–69	No.	24.0	20.7	21.0	12.7	4.6
	WI	53.5	24.2	7.5	23.5	1.1
	WDL	54.1	35.1	3.8	16.7	0.8
1970–75	No.	18.1	21.1	21.1	9.6	6.7
	WI	19.9	20.2	15.4	12.0	5.2
	WDL	49.7	13.8	8.3	5.8	5.7
1975–79	No.	17.9	29.1	16.6	8.2	8.2
	WI	21.7	34.5	11.6	7.0	12.1
	WDL	47.0	23.3	5.8	3.2	7.0
1980–85	No.	22.1	24.6	15.5	5.6	10.6
	WI	26.4	21.3	8.8	4.6	5.7
	WDL	33.9	26.5	9.7	4.6	5.5
1985–89	No.	10.9	9.1	14.2	4.6	10.9
	WI	15.4	3.2	1.8	19.5	2.3
	WDL	12.3	9.8	2.9	1.9	11.7
*1990–92	No.	12.8	11.3	22.7	10.6	12.8
	WI	36.5	18.0	8.7	4.5	5.0
	WDL	13.8	37.8	5.0	2.5	3.6

* Three-year period

cent of the union membership in this country at the time. They found that union officials themselves differed in their views as to whether unofficial action should be made official, with almost 50 per cent of the officials surveyed stating that they would not give explicit support to unofficial action. Yet, even though officials were divided on the issue of whether to give official support, 70 per cent of the respondents said that they would favour some form of union intervention in trying to resolve the dispute. In trying to provide an explanation for unofficial action, Brannick and Kelly concluded that the actual practices and procedures used by both the employers and trade unions may provide a partial explanation for the occurrence of unofficial strike action. When asked the reasons for unofficial action, almost 40 per cent of the respondents (12 unions) stated that unofficial action was an expression of their members dissatisfaction with the official procedures applied by the trade union. Other reasons cited by the respondents included sympathetic action with staff dismissals and the personal characteristics of those involved in the dispute. The authors found that 78 per cent of the union officials believed that unofficial action has a damaging affect on trade unions. Over 70 per cent of the respondents saw ways of reducing the levels of unofficial action. The most widely cited solution was improved trade union procedures for dealing with their members' grievances, which should remove the potential for unofficial action to arise in the first instance.

Finally, strike issues analysed over a 32-year time period are presented in Table 8.9. It is evident from this table that there have been major shifts in the proportion of strikes attributed to the different issues. Pay had traditionally been an important issue but declined in importance in the 1980s since the introduction of the Programme for National Recovery (1987) and its successors. The high level of workers involved in the 1990–92 period can be explained by a small number of pay disputes in the public sector, which involved large numbers of workers but were of short duration. Although the issues of dismissal and suspension had steadily declined in importance during the earlier decades, the percentage of strikes caused by the dismissal/suspension issue has reached an all time high in the 1990s. There has also been a rise in the importance of redundancy/lay-off as a strike issue in recent years.

CONCLUSION

The data presented here shows that there is a broad cyclical trend associated with all three indices (frequency, breadth and duration) and that the number of strikes exhibits an overall upward trend for the period to 1987 with a sizeable decline since then. We have also noted the marked contrast in trends between the public and private sectors. The public sector now experiences greater strike frequency with significantly greater numbers of workers involved, but the strikes themselves are of a relatively shorter duration. The private sector, on the other hand, exhibits a much reduced level of strike activity, with a lower number of workers involved and strikes of longer duration. Within the private sector itself we have seen that there are large differences in the strike-proneness of sectors with some displaying considerable change over time. Mining and turf production is a particularly clear example of this: over the 71-year period the strike rate per 100,000 employees dropped from 163 to 30 for the sector, representing a reduction of 300 per cent over the period. This compares with other sectors exhibiting traditionally high levels of strike activity such as building & construction and transport & communications. In contrast, the electricity, gas & water sector is one which has experienced a large increase in the number of work-days lost. The experience of individual sub-sectors within manufacturing were also examined. Of particular interest is the case of unofficial strikes. These show a dramatic downward trend since the mid-1970s but still represent a sizeable one-third of all strikes occurring. Finally, at a time when strike activity has been at its lowest for many decades this brief examination of the historical picture may serve a useful purpose in reminding us of the strong cyclical tendencies in levels of industrial conflict.

References

Brannick, T. and Kelly, A. (1983): "The Reliability and Validity of Irish Strike Data and Statistics", *Economic and Social Review*, 14: 249–58.

Brannick, T. and Kelly, A. (1984): "Voluntarism and Order in Trade Unions: Union Officials' Attitudes to Unofficial Strikes", *Journal of Irish Business and Administrative Research*, 6: 70–80.

Committee of Inquiry on Industrial Relations (1981): Report of the Committee of Inquiry on Industrial Relations, Dublin: Government Publications.

Conservative Political Centre (1968): *Fair Deal at Work: The Conservative Approach to Modern Industrial Relations*, London: Conservative Political Centre.

Cronin, J.E. (1980): "Strikes, Cycles and Insurgencies: The Economics of Unrest" in T.K. Hopkins and I. Wallerstein (eds.), *Process of the World-System*, Beverley Hills: Sage.

Durcan, J.W., McCarthy, W.E. and Redman, G.P. (1983): *Strikes in Post-War Britain*, London: George Allen and Unwin.

Edwards, P. (1978): "Time Series Regression Models of Strike Activity: A Reconsideration with American Data", *British Journal of Industrial Relations*, 16: 320–34.

Edwards, P. (1992): "Industrial Conflict: Themes and Issues in Recent Research", *British Journal of Industrial Relations*, 30: 361–404.

Fisher, M. (1973): *Measurement of Labour Disputes and their Economic Effects*, Paris: OECD.

Forchheimer, K. (1948): *Some International Aspects of the Strike Movement*, Oxford University Institute of Statistics Bulletin, 16–7.

Galambos, P. and Evans, E.W. (1977): "Work Stoppages in the United Kingdom, 1965–70: A Quantitative Study" in E. W. Evans and S.W. Greigh (eds), *Industrial Conflict in Britain*, London: Frank Cass.

Goodman, J.F. (1967): "Strikes in the United Kingdom: Recent Statistics and Trends", *International Labour Review*.

Hibbs, D.A. (1967): "Industrial Conflict in Advanced Industrial Societies", *American Political Science Review*, 70: 1033–58.

Hibbs, D.A. (1978): "On the Political Economy of Long-Run Trends in Strike Activity", *British Journal of Political Science*, 8: 153–75.

Hoffer, E. (1951): *The True Believer*, New York: Harper.

Hyman, R. (1977): *Strikes*, Glasgow: Fontana/Collins.

International Labour Organisation (ILO) (1926): *Methods of Compiling Statistics of Industrial Disputes, Studies and Reports*, 10, Geneva: ILO.

Kelly, A. and Brannick, T. (1983): "The Pattern of Strike Activity in Ireland 1960–1979: Some Preliminary Observations", *Journal of Irish Business and Administrative Research*, 5: 65–77.

Kelly, A. and Brannick, T. (1985): "The Strike-Proneness of Public Sector Organisations", *Economic and Social Review*, 16: 251–71.

Kelly, A. and Brannick, T. (1986): "The Changing Contours of Irish Strike Patterns: 1960–1984", *Journal of Irish Business and Administrative Research*, 8: 77–88.

Kelly, A. and Brannick, T. (1988): "Strike Trends in the Irish Private Sector", *Journal of Irish Business and Administrative Research*, 9: 87–98.

Kerr, C. (1964): *Labour and Management in Industrial Society*, New York: Doubleday.

Kerr, C. and Siegel, A. (1954): "The Inter-Industry Propensity to Strike: An International Comparison" in A. Kornhause, R. Dubin and A.M. Ross (eds), *Industrial Conflict*, New York: McGraw Hill.

Knowles, K.G. (1952): *Strikes — A Study in Industrial Conflict*, Oxford: Basil Blackwell.

Korpi, W. and Shalev, M. (1979): "Strikes, Industrial Relations and Class Conflict in Capitalist Societies", *British Journal of Sociology*, 30: 164–87.

McCarthy, W.E. (1970): "The Nature of Britain's Strike Problem", *British Journal of Industrial Relations*, 8(2).

Mulvey, K. (1968): "Unemployment and the Incidence of Strikes in the Republic of Ireland 1942–1966", *Journal of Economic Studies*, 3: 73–84.

Royal Commission on Trade Unions and Employers' Associations (1968): *Report of the Royal Commission on Trade Unions and Employers' Associations, 1965–1968*, London: HMSO.

Sapsford, D. (1975): "A Time Series Analysis of UK Industrial Disputes", *Industrial Relations*, 14: 242–49.

Silver, M. (1977): "Recent British Strike Trends: A Factual Analysis" in E.W. Evans and S.W. Greigh (eds), *Industrial Conflict in Britain*, London: Frank Cass.

Smith, C.T., Clifton, R., Makeham, P., Creigh, S.W. and Burn, R.V. (1978): *Strikes in Britain*, London: Department of Employment.

Snyder, D. (1975): "Institutional Setting and Industrial Conflict: Comparative Analysis of France, Italy and the United States", *American Sociological Review*, 30: 259–78.

Stern, R.M. (1978): "Methodological Issues in Quantitative Strike Analysis", *Industrial Relations*, 17: 32–42.

Turner, H.A. (1969): *Is Britain Really Strike-Prone? A Review of the Incidence, Character and Costs of Industrial Conflict*, Cambridge: University Press.

CHAPTER 9

THE RESOLUTION OF INDUSTRIAL DISPUTES

Thomas V. Murphy

It is almost 50 years since present mechanisms for the resolution of
industrial disputes were first put in place with the establishment of
the Labour Court under the Industrial Relations Act, 1946. Over the
years many changes and developments were introduced culminating
in the first major overhaul of the system through the Industrial Relations Act, 1990. This chapter examines two aspects of dispute resolution, procedures and the role of third parties. Procedures are analysed
in terms of their basic construction as well as the principles underlying
the approaches of employers and trade unions to their design. Third
parties are examined in three parts: (a) the development of the system of third-party intervention in industrial disputes is traced from
the Industrial Relations Act, 1946, and before; (b) the nature of *good*
industrial relations is considered in view of the specific responsibility
for the promotion of good industrial relations which was assigned to
the Labour Relations Commission under the Industrial Relations Act,
1990; and (c) activity trends and developments in conciliations and
Labour Court investigations are analysed over the period 1947–93.

INDUSTRIAL RELATIONS PROCEDURES

The rules which regulate the relationship between employer and workers
may be either substantive or procedural in content. Substantive rules
are those which establish norms or intentions in the form of specific
conditions of work, such as pay, staffing, work arrangements and rules
of attendance and non-attendance. Procedural rules deal with method
rather than substance; they describe the arrangements by which the
parties negotiate the substantive rules and also the machinery through
which differences between the parties will be resolved. These differences may emerge during the negotiation of the rules or in their administration, that is, their application, interpretation, and enforcement
by management. The most important of the procedural arrangements in

company level industrial relations are examined below in terms of their content, objectives and underlying principles.

Functions of Industrial Relations Procedures

In any work community there is a need for orderly, consistent and known methods for dealing with the working relationships between employer and employee and, in particular, there is a need to resolve the differences which arise from those relationships. Procedures are, therefore, of central importance in industrial relations. To derive a more specific meaning of procedure, however, we must examine the objective or purpose of a specific procedure, for example, a procedure for dealing with complaints or grievances, or the areas where procedures have acquired a special significance. Jointly agreed procedures have evolved to cover issues which previously would have been regarded as the prerogative or responsibility of management. However, with the increased influence of trade unions in workplace affairs, jointly agreed procedures provide a structural device for reconciling differences which arise, free of disruption. Under jointly agreed procedures there is a crucial fluidity in the authority that decides on procedural arrangements and for supporting their operation. It ceases to be solely a management responsibility and becomes shared with representatives of employees. For both sides procedures establish a *modus vivendi* reflecting the interests and strengths of the parties. They represent an acceptance by both sides of the need for voluntary restraint in the use of unilateral power. For management this raises the fundamental issue of control because it implies a compromised right to manage resulting in a weakening of their ability to direct, supervise, reward and discipline workers. For trade unions it means the acceptance of limitations on their right to engage in industrial action and the added difficulties which this raises in persuading their members that "going through procedure" is as much in their interests as it is in management's.

Role of Third Parties in Procedures

Most procedures contain two distinct phases; the first covers direct dealings between the parties aimed at a negotiated settlement, and the second follows on from the failure of direct negotiations and involves the processing of the problem issue through some form of conciliatory arrangement. This usually entails the engagement of a third party, that is, a party or agency sharing no interest in the issue with the parties and, which is, therefore, independent as between them.

The state is clearly the most powerful third party in industrial relations and in many countries the state imposes legal constraints on the conduct of the principal parties to collective bargaining, particularly in the area of dispute settlement and in the use of force. In Ireland the state chooses not to exert direct influence on the settlement of disputes. It prefers instead to leave the parties free to pursue their differences in a voluntary fashion. Although the manner in which disputes are to be settled is not stipulated, the state does facilitate their peaceful settlement by providing extensive third party services which, in keeping with Ireland's voluntarist tradition, the parties are free to use or not to use; and should they choose to use them they are free to accept or reject recommendations which might emanate from the third party. The principal role of the third party is to assist the parties in dispute to reach a settlement. There are four basic forms of third-party intervention: conciliation, adjudication, formal arbitration and investigation.

Conciliation (Mediation). The terms conciliation and mediation are sometimes used interchangeably. The role of the conciliator has been described as follows:

> The role of the conciliator is to assist the parties in dispute to reach agreement. He provides a channel of communication when direct negotiation has broken down or become ineffective, he canvasses possible new approaches, he defines common ground and remaining points of difference, he provides the parties with assessments of the situation, he does everything in his power to promote agreement, but he is the midwife and not the parent of any agreement eventually reached (Commission on Industrial Relations, 1975).

Anthony (1977) has described mediation as a "more purposeful and less tentative" process in which the mediator searches for possible solutions which the parties then negotiate upon in the expectation of reaching an agreement. The Royal Commission, quoted above, sees the mediator performing a service similar to that of the conciliator, but in addition the mediator "will be prepared if necessary to propose his own solution in a final bid to provide a basis for the ultimately necessary agreement." Conciliation is one of the principal forms of third-party intervention used by employers and trade unions in Ireland. It is administered, since 1990, by Industrial Relations Officers of the Labour Relations Commission, having previously operated under the Labour Court since 1946 and within the Department of Industry and Commerce previous to that. That such a seemingly benign form of intervention should be so successful at settling disputes is a matter of puzzlement to some. About three out of four cases are settled at conciliation here; in the UK the rate is about two out of three. (Lowry, 1990: 22) Despite a wide literature on the subject, conciliation remains a poorly understood process (McNally, 1991). In fact there is no theory of conciliation. Stevens (1967) explains that this is because investigators have tended to focus solely on the process itself while ignoring the wider collective bargaining process of which it is an integral part. He suggests (1967: 272) that

> unless an investigator has some theories about the agreement process — about why and in what ways the parties do or do not reach agreement in their own negotiations — it is difficult to see how he can analyze the contribution of the mediator to the settlement of their conflict.

Kerr (1954) provides a penetrating insight into the mediation process and the contribution the mediator can make to the resolution of the conflict which the parties cannot provide for themselves. He describes a number of major potential contributions as follows:

Reduction of irrationality. A more rational climate for negotiations can be created by the mediator by giving the individuals an opportunity to vent their feelings to him or her; by keeping personal recriminations out of joint discussions, and by reminding the parties of the objective issues in dispute and the consequences of coercive confrontation.

Removal of nonrationality. Mediation can assist the parties in reaching an appreciation of reality by clarifying the intentions of the parties towards each other, the issues in dispute, and leading them to accurate assessments of the costs of aggression and the prospective outcomes of such conflict.

Exploration of solutions. In addition to helping the parties explore solutions which have occurred to them independently, the mediator can generate new solutions for their consideration. Several means to the same end will often exist in collective bargaining and a mediator can assist by formulating solutions in which a certain gain for one party can be secured at minimum cost to the other.

Assistance in graceful retreat. Most collective bargaining involves some retreat by both parties from their original positions and indeed much of the fascination of collective bargaining is in the tactics of retreat. The mediator can assist the retreat in a number of ways. Acting as a go-between he or she can speed up the pace of retreat for both sides by making offers that are more revocable. The more revocable a concession the easier it is to make. The mediator can also help "save face". Defeat or partial defeat at the hands of a third party is more palatable than a similar surrender to the opposing party. Much of the assistance which the conciliator/mediator can provide to the disputants stems from the basic technique of separating the parties. This enables a more informal atmosphere to develop (ILO, 1973: 67). More importantly, however, it gives the mediator control of the communication structure and generally facilitates persuasion. Separate caucuses provide forums where the mediator may receive confidential and privileged information from each party. Also, in connection with the generation of alternate solutions, the technique gives the mediator the opportunity to get each party to adopt the solution as his or her own, thus avoiding the danger, inherent in making the suggestion to those parties simultaneously, that one party might embrace it and the other feel impelled to oppose it (Stevens, 1967: 285–6).

Adjudication. Adjudication takes place in the context of disputes over rights and obligations of a legal kind. Adjudication is usually carried out by special courts, and results in the determination of issues through the application of prescribed legal principles to the specific circumstances of each case. Decisions are legally enforceable. This role is adopted by the Employment Appeals Tribunal in Ireland in respect of disputes concerning the Redundancy Payments Acts, 1967–91; the Minimum Notice and Terms of Employment Acts, 1973–91; The Unfair Dismissals Acts, 1977 and 1992; the Maternity Protection of Employees Acts, 1981–91; the Protection of Employees (Employers' Insolvency) Acts, 1984–91; and the Worker Protection (Regular Part-Time Employees) Act, 1991. The Tribunal disposes of approximately 5,000 cases each year, the bulk of these under the redundancy, terms of notice, and dismissal acts. The Labour Court also adopts an adjudicative role in relation to the Anti-Discrimination (Pay) Act, 1974, and the Employment Equality Act, 1977. These acts provide statutory entitlement to equal pay and conditions of employment respectively for men and women.

Arbitration. Third party intervention in a dispute may be in the form of arbitration, in which case the arbitrator will proceed to make an award which disposes of the issue. Outside of the special case of the public sector, arbitration is a relatively rare occurrence in Irish industrial relations and is confined to the less major issues. Indeed, this is also the position internationally. Seemingly when the issue is of importance to the parties they rarely risk leaving the decision to an outsider, however impartial he or she might be. The Labour Court does, on occasion, act as arbitrator in disputes but these are usually confined to less serious industrial relations issues. Examples are where one or both of the parties wish to dispose of a non-major issue; where guiding principles exist, such as a collective agreement, which the arbitrator can interpret and apply to a given situation; or, in the case of a serious dispute where the major items have been resolved through negotiation and some lesser items remain to be disposed of. Therefore, despite its appearance as an eminently civilised way of behaving, the process of arbitration seems to have little appeal for the parties. Lockwood (1955: 335–45) deals, comprehensively, with the limitations of arbitration as a means of industrial peace insofar as the more major industrial relations issues are concerned, and concludes that

> arbitration is limited to special circumstances where there is a calculable advantage in its use: by weakly organised groups of employers and employees; by parties who fear absolute defeat in the event of a struggle; in conditions of favourable trade and employment when the arbitrator and the union both realize that the employer will sooner give increases than battle.

Nevertheless, the finality of the process of arbitration has strong appeal and has led to an interesting adaptation of the conventional model, first developed in North America and particularly in Canada, and more recently in Britain. The new process is given various names but is most commonly referred to as *pendulum* arbitration. The process is examined in a later section.

Formal Investigation or Fact-Finding. Formal investigation or fact-finding is the final form of third party intervention whereby the third party establishes the facts relevant to the dispute and issues a recommendation to the parties. Although there is an element of fact-finding in other forms of third party intervention, the process of formal investigation represents a specific development in a number of countries, including Ireland, in the post-war period. The basis of the Labour Court's involvement in dispute settlement is of this type, and usually follows where a dispute has not been resolved through conciliation. The first Chairman of the Labour Court, R.J. P. Mortished, described the Court's approach to investigations as follows:

The Court does not function as a Court of Law does, finding facts and, when it has found them, applying to them a set code of rules, exercising its discretion, if at all, only in accordance with precedent. It has to deal, not with legal rights but with human interests, emotions, and prejudices, at work in circumstances that vary from case to case and from time to time. The Court does not enforce existing law; rather by a process of inquiry and conciliation, it helps to create a kind of voluntary law or common rule (Mortished, 1947: 679).

GRIEVANCE PROCEDURES

The handling and resolution of employees' grievances is a significant task of management and trade unions alike. Whereas the more important issues of pay and conditions come up for negotiation only periodically, and usually no more than once a year or so, the task of dealing with grievances and complaints of workers requires the constant and sometimes daily attention of supervisors, managers, and worker representatives. The issues involved may concern an individual worker or a group of workers; the issue may be small or may be of great significance, with serious and far-reaching consequences. Whatever the scale of the problem, however, all grievances bear a single dominating characteristic: they possess the potential to cause industrial relations disruption. A small issue may start as such and may affect only a single worker. Left unattended, however, or carelessly handled, it can become no less harmful than an issue more widespread and seemingly more important to employees' collective interests.

A grievance may be defined as a complaint by a worker or a group of workers against the way in which an agreement or understanding between management and union has been implemented and thereby interpreted. Grievances can occur concerning the parties' rights under an agreement, arising out of the application of the terms of the agreement to a specific case. A rights issue of this kind may be distinguished from an interest issue which arises at the stage of negotiating the actual terms of the agreement. For example, under an agreement on promotion in a company the policy of selection for promotion may be specified in detail. The agreement may stipulate that appointments to promotional positions be regarded as the exclusive right of existing staff; that service in the company be a primary criterion for selection and so forth. The terms of the agreement, therefore, define each party's rights. When a dispute arises over a particular case of selection for promotion, or over the application of the agreed policy in a particular case, we speak of dealing with a rights issue, arising, perhaps, out of difference in interpretation of the terms of the agreement. When the policy and terms of the promotion agreement are being negotiated in the first instance, then we speak of the interests of each side being reconciled, and a dispute at this stage would concern a matter of interest between the parties. The practice of distinguishing between disputes of interest and disputes of rights is formally followed in a number of countries, including the US, Canada, Germany and New Zealand.

In the context of industrial relations in Ireland, however, there is a thin line separating disputes of interest and right, so that the difference is rather academic. Employment rules and standards in most Irish work situations stem from a variety of sources apart from the written agreement. These include regulations and policies unilaterally introduced by management, unwritten agreements and understandings — whether between management and union, or local management and shop stewards — as well as established custom and practice of the workplace. In practice it can be difficult to distinguish between a challenge to the way in which a rule has been interpreted by management in its application to a particular case and an effort by the challenger to impose a more favourable version of the rule. This difficulty in distinguishing between interest and rights issues is reflected in the fact that none of our dispute settling agencies operate under the distinction. The area of statutory rights is, however, one in which rights may be identified. Laws on equality, dismissal, redundancy etc., define minimum rights and standards of behaviour. They also provide facilities to resolve disputes over their application and interpretation. To summarise, therefore, a grievance, in the Irish context, covers all manner of complaints, whether involving an individual or a group of workers, including those complaints concerned with the way in which an employment rule or standard has been applied, whether the source of the rule or standard is a regulation or policy unilaterally introduced by management, a written or unwritten agreement or understanding between management and worker representatives, a custom and practice of the workplace, or legislation.

Form and Substance of Grievance Procedures

The grievance procedure or local disputes procedure is now a common feature of Irish workplaces. This was not always so. A study in the early 1960s found them in use in very large organisations only (O'Mahony, 1964). Studies during the 1970s and the 1980s indicated that they were by then widely in use (Gorman et al., 1975; Murray,

1984). The benefits which the parties derive from joint procedures are considerable. The obvious benefit is the avoidance of costly disruption by providing an orderly way of dealing with day-to-day disputes. Implicitly, a procedure entails restraint in the use of force over an issue until successive stages of discussions have been exhausted in a continuing effort to find an agreed solution. Constraining union power in this way is clearly attractive to management. But why, one might ask, would a trade union agree so readily to have its hands tied in negotiations in this way? From the point of view of the union side there has to be some solid reason for them to accept such a constraint on that most cherished of all principles of trade union action, the right to strike. Apart from what it gains through the avoidance of costly disruptions, the trade union organisation profits from the arrangement because of the enhancement to its status within the workplace. Jointly agreed procedures acknowledge the union's right to represent its members' interests before management and legitimises the day to day policing role of shop stewards and local trade union structures (Murphy, 1989). Finally, procedures have an obvious educational role in workplace affairs and play an important part in strengthening the authority of personnel departments and trade union officials in their respective organisations. By clarifying methods for the handling of problem issues at shop-floor level, and by providing a framework with set roles defined for supervisors, managers and local union representatives, they make a significant contribution to the professionalisation and stability of collective bargaining relationships.

Typically, there are four stages to a grievance procedure (see Figure 9.1). In the first stage of the process the complaint is examined at successive levels of management. The complaint is referred by the worker(s) concerned to the appropriate supervisor and if a satisfactory result is not found then it may be taken to the next management level, and so on. Although workers will be encouraged by management to fully utilise this stage in the process, it is sometimes "bypassed" by workers. Failure to resolve the matter at this first stage may lead to it being referred to a shop steward or local representative of the worker concerned. Having investigated the circumstances surrounding the issue he or she may decide to raise the matter with the appropriate manager. The accessibility of management to workplace representatives varies from workplace to workplace. In some it may be very extensive, while in others accessibility may be limited to certain union officials only. Should these discussions fail to produce a settlement of the matter, the steward may decide to take

the issue in dispute to the appropriate trade union official. At this
stage the dispute enters a more formal stage. The "external" union
becomes involved and the local official takes up the case on behalf of
the worker(s) concerned. Discussions are arranged with the appropriate company representative(s), the personnel manager, plant/office
manager and/or an official of an employers' association. It is usual for
solutions to most complaints and grievances to be found at one or
other of these three initial stages of the grievance process. Occasionally, though, this may not be the case and the assistance of an
outside third party may be sought.

FIGURE 9.1: STAGES OF A TYPICAL GRIEVANCE PROCEDURE

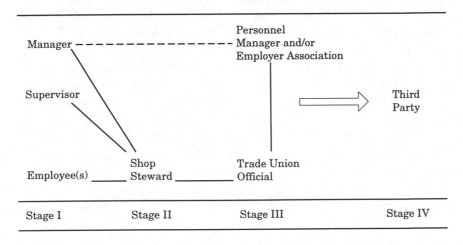

Although no single procedural format exists which would suit every
employment situation, most procedures contain these four component
parts. Other features which may be observed in practice include:
time-limits for the execution of the different stages; a requirement to
have the grievance submitted in writing; the stipulation that work
continue without interruption while the grievance is being discussed
in procedure; and, more recently, the "no-strike" clause. The first two
features, although not widely practised in Ireland, are sometimes evident in multinational companies whose practices at "home" contain a
high degree of formality. The last two features involve issues of fundamental importance to each side in the collective bargaining relationship and both need to be examined closely if one is to fully appre-
ciate the difficulties involved in making procedures work in practice,
and to understand the depths of feelings and opposition which they

can generate when threatened. The first of these concerns management's right to manage; the other concerns the right to strike.

The Right to Manage

The right to manage raises the very practical question of the status of the issue or the basis on which work continues while the dispute is being processed through procedure. Should management prerogative prevail, that is, the right of management to decide and implement a specific decision and for that decision to stand until such time as a different decision is agreed through the grievance process; or, should the status quo prevail, on the basis that no change be implemented until jointly agreed through negotiation? These are fundamental questions which are of considerable practical importance to the efficient operation of collective bargaining at local level. Whichever prevails in practice tells a lot about the power balance between the two sides. Although seldom written into grievance procedures, the concept of the "status quo" can sometimes constitute the de facto position in a workplace where trade union leadership manages to exercise strong influence over work issues. Although this is not a common characteristic of industrial relations practice in the economic climate of the 1990s, it was a problem which complicated management in many workplaces in earlier decades. Hugh MacNeill, one of the most prominent and respected personnel practitioners of the period, captured the frustration of many managers when he said:

> Management today is essentially by consent; unions know the effect of withholding consent — the power of their veto — and will use it. This is probably the single most significant characteristic of industrial relations at the end of the 1970s; a virtually uncontested right to bargain on any matter affecting people at work; to regulate what they will do, how they will do it, and what they will get for doing it. Only the strategic decisions are still excluded from the process (MacNeill, 1980: 58).

Practice over recent years has undergone much change in this area. Management prerogative clauses are now incorporated more widely into collective agreements and especially in organisations experiencing severe competitive pressures. Sometimes, however, an agreement is strangely "silent" on this seemingly indispensable aspect of procedural practice. (The suggested form of grievance procedure recommended by joint union-management sub-committees of the National Employer/Labour Conference in 1962 and again in 1972 were also "silent" on the matter.) There are several possible reasons for such exclusions; it may be due to poor drafting by the negotiators of the procedure; or it may represent a pragmatic decision not to acknowledge formally what may be the actual situation on the "ground"; or it may reflect the difficulty of reaching a mutually satisfactory expression of the respective positions of the parties on such a potentially explosive issue; or (and perhaps more usually of late) the reason may be the clear dominance of the bargaining power of the company. In the latter case, the situation may be one where total flexibility is a recognised imperative of the work regime and the risk of company pull-out a real consideration. However, this is a position of dominance which, discretion at least would suggest, should not be exercised in a heavy-handed way, and where conflict may best be avoided through detailed planning of change and its careful implementation.

The ESB represents a case where these two competing principles — the "status quo" versus management's "right to manage" — had to be reconciled if there was to be a realistic prospect of the procedures operating smoothly. It arose in the context of the ESB comprehensive agreements first negotiated during the 1970s and concerned the attempt to resolve disputes over demarcation, a particularly serious matter in the case of the ESB (see Comprehensive Agreement, 1977: Appendix 1). In a remarkable piece of procedural construction the unions' preference for the "status quo", and management's right to manage were both acknowledged and provided for. The relevant section of the Agreement reads:

> The status quo will be maintained during the utilisation of the procedures and relevant provisions of category agreement(s) on division of work will be observed.
>
> 1. Whenever a demarcation dispute arises where, LIFE, PLANT or SUPPLY, including supply to individual consumers, is in immediate jeopardy, management will decide how the work is to be done, and the decision will be implemented. The dispute will then be processed (through procedure).

So, in a matter of a few lines both parties' positions were respected, the unions' right to be consulted prior to the introduction of change, and management's right to manage in circumstances of their greatest priority, that is, when life, plant or supply is threatened.

New-Style Agreements
Interest has been growing in recent years in a variety of new procedural mechanisms designed to reduce the likelihood of coercive acts

in industrial disputes, and generally to make the bargaining process between employers and trade unions more efficient. Although most of these initiatives are directed at bringing finality into the bargaining procedures, one should not ignore the consequences of these procedural changes for the bargaining behaviour of the parties in their direct dealings. The United States has been the source of most of these new ideas. So far, the extent of the innovation on this side of the Atlantic, and particularly in Ireland, is small and, for the most part, confined to greenfield sites, and often in the context of a single-union agreement. Two features of this emerging trend will be examined: the no-strike clause; and pendulum arbitration, sometimes referred to as "final-offer" or "flip-flop" arbitration.

The No-Strike Clause. It is clear from the discussion earlier that a grievance procedure, or a disputes procedure, represents a form of "no-strike" agreement insofar as it involves an undertaking to refrain from coercive acts while an issue is "in procedure". This is an undertaking which expires once the procedure has been exhausted. Any attempt to extend the restraint on industrial action beyond the final stage of the procedure is certain to meet with strong resistance from trade unions because it is seen by them as a threat to the right to strike. As a consequence the very suggestion of compulsory arbitration as a final stage of procedure can produce hostile reactions. Nevertheless, Ireland has witnessed the introduction of "no-strike" agreements in a number of companies over recent years. Because of their reliance on compulsory arbitration as a final procedural stage they can be more accurately described as "dispute procedures with built-in resolution" (Wickens, 1987). It is important not to exaggerate the prevalence of these procedures as, for the most part, they appear to be confined to situations where special circumstances apply.

The example of their introduction into Packard Electric and their eventual replacement by a less restrictive clause proposed by the unions concerned is instructive. In 1987, following a prolonged strike, the workers accepted settlement terms which included the adoption of a comprehensive labour agreement which contained a no-strike industrial peace clause or a guarantee of supply clause. In return, the company gave a guarantee that there would be no forced redundancies during the life of the agreement and built in additional stages to the grievance and disciplinary procedures. The agreement expired in 1989. When the new agreement was being negotiated the company sought the inclusion of the following clause in the section of the agreement dealing with industrial peace:

In the context of the implementation of the Agreement the right of the Unions to take industrial action is reaffirmed, but the Unions and the employees agree that for the period of this Agreement they will not implement any form of industrial action. All disputes will be dealt with and finalised through procedures.

Equally, the right of the Company to implement Compulsory Redundancies due to business reasons is reaffirmed but the Company agree that for the period of this Agreement it will not implement forced redundancies.

Where an issue or dispute has been to the Labour Court, Employment Appeals Tribunal, or other third party, as provided for in this Agreement, the decision or recommendation of the third party will be accepted by all parties to this agreement.

As might be expected, the unions, objected strongly to these clauses and instead proposed one which offered a wide range of safeguards against industrial disruption, short of a no-strike provision. The dispute was referred to the Labour Court which found in favour of the company's proposal, saying that it was its "opinion that it is essential for its commercial dealings that the binding undertaking required by them should be conceded to the Company for the duration of the Agreement . . ." (LCR 12466: 6). In its recommendation, the Court also noted that the company had indicated that, when negotiating the next agreement in 1991, it would be prepared to accept at that time the form of agreement proposed by the Unions. This was duly done when the agreement was renegotiated in 1991.

Pendulum Arbitration. Pendulum arbitration restricts the role of the arbitrator to the choice between the final positions of the parties and expressly forbids any compromise between the final claim of the union and the final offer of the employer (Burchill, 1989: 13–4). The mechanism was developed in the US and was a response to two of the most common criticisms levelled against conventional arbitration: that it transferred the power of decision making to an outsider, and that arbitrators tended to "split the difference" between the positions of the parties, or at least gave the claimant a "bit more" than he or she was last offered (Wood, 1985: 417). Last offer arbitration also promised to overcome two other defects of the conventional approach, namely, the "chilling effect" and the "narcotic effect". The first stems from the assumption that the arbitrator will "split the difference", so that when arbitration seems a likely prospect, the parties take up more extreme positions. The "narcotic effect" applies to the case where the parties become excessively reliant on the services of the arbitrator and make minimal efforts to resolve their differences through direct negotiations. For these many reasons, therefore, the mechanism of final offer arbitration seemed to offer "promising and constructive reform" (Wood, 1985: 418). It is a mechanism, however, which is not without its own problems. The rigidity of the final offer choice can place the arbitrator in a difficult position. Disputes often involve complicated issues and the arbitrator can be faced with two complicated packages, both of which may be unsatisfactory (Wood, 1985: 419–20). The evidence so far available from its limited use in the UK is far from impressive and suggests that pendulum arbitration does not operate in the way the theory suggests it should and does not appear to be completely successful in deterring disputes. Part of the problem seems to stem from the fact that collective bargaining does not always operate in the economically rational or logical way sometimes suggested by textbooks (Medcalf et al., 1992: 42–3).

Codes of Practice

The Code of Practice on Dispute Procedures drawn up recently by the Labour Relations Commission represents an attempt to promote procedural innovation in Irish industrial relations, especially in the case of essential services. It was the first code of practice prepared by the Labour Relations Commission, and promulgated by the Minister for Enterprise and Employment, under the provisions of the Industrial Relations Act, 1990, and it covers dispute procedures, including procedures in essential services. In some countries workers in essential services are not allowed to strike under any circumstances. In others the legality of a strike may depend on the observance of particular procedures, such as an agreement that designated workers will remain at work to maintain a limited service (Labour Relations Commission, 1993: 21). The Commission of Inquiry on Industrial Relations in Ireland considered the case for the regulation of disputes in essential services and, in particular, a number of specific suggestions which included compulsory arbitration, and the granting of statutory powers to the appropriate government minister to require those organising or threatening industrial action in an essential service to defer such action for a maximum period of, for example, 60 days. The Commission doubted the likely effectiveness of the proposals and concluded that "the prohibition of industrial action in essential services is not something which could realistically be carried out by fiat" (Commission of Inquiry, 1981: 95–9). In February 1991, the then Minister for Labour wrote to the LRC indicating his wish, that having consulted with the FIE (now IBEC) and the ICTU, the Commission would consider drafting code(s) of practice on a number of issues, including a dispute procedure and the levels of cover to be provided in the case of disputes in essential services. Against a background of both actual and threatened industrial action in a number of public utilities during 1991, the Commission decided to give priority to these particular items. Following extensive consultations a draft code was submitted to the Minister in November of the same year. The Minister launched the Code in January 1992, and made an Order (S.I. No.1 of 1992) declaring the Code a code of practice for the purposes of the Industrial Relations Act, 1990 (LRC, 1991: 22). Under that Act, the terms of a code of practice are not legally binding. However, courts of law and industrial relations bodies may take account of any provisions of a code of practice which they deem to be relevant in determining any proceedings before them (Department of Labour, 1992a: 10).

The procedures in the Code provide a framework for the peaceful resolution of disputes between employers and trade unions, and gives practical guidance on how to operate them effectively. It covers both collective and individual issues. Although it advises that "dispute procedures should be as comprehensive as possible", and that "the actions required of the parties at each stage of the procedure should be clearly indicated", it does not deal directly with the difficult question, referred to earlier, of the status of an issue while it is in the course of being negotiated through procedure (Department of Labour, 1992b: 4). Section III of the Code urges employers and trade unions to have in place agreed contingency plans and other arrangements to deal with any emergency which might arise during an industrial dispute. In the particular case of employments providing essential services, the parties are encouraged to co-operate with each other in making arrangements concerning:

(a) the maintenance of plant and equipment;

(b) all matters concerning health, safety and security;

(c) special operational problems which exist in continuous process industries;

(d) the provision of urgent medical services and supplies;

(e) the provision of emergency services required on humanitarian grounds.

Section V of the Code deals with the need for additional procedures and safeguards for the peaceful resolution of disputes in the case of essential services. These services include those whose cessation or interruption could endanger life, or cause major damage to the national economy, or widespread hardship to the Community, particularly health services, energy supplies, including gas and electricity, water and sewage services, fire, ambulance and rescue services and certain elements of public transport. The list is indicative rather than comprehensive. Where procedures and safeguards which would ensure the continuity of essential supplies and services had not been introduced, then, according to the Code, agreements negotiated on a voluntary basis should include one of the following provisions:

(a) acceptance by the parties of decisions which result from the final stage of the dispute procedure; or

(b) an undertaking, that if either party finds the decision resulting from the final stage of the procedure to be unsatisfactory, they would agree on the means of resolving the issue without resort to industrial action, and the agreement to include provision for a review of the case after twelve months; or

(c) that the parties would accept decisions resulting from the final stage of procedure on the basis that an independent review would be undertaken at three-yearly intervals to examine whether employees had been placed at any disadvantage, and, if so, to advise on the changes necessary to redress the position.

The first of these provisions represents binding arbitration. From our earlier discussion of the subject, it is the least likely of the three provisions to be introduced by employers and trade unions in procedural agreements. The other two provisions introduce the notion of an interim settlement with the safeguard of review after a period of time. Although these may not suit the specific circumstances of each case, they do provide direction to employers and trade unions as to some of the ways of avoiding the costs and hardship involved in interruptions to essential services and supplies in the Community. Finally, in the case where the parties in an essential service have not concluded an agreement incorporating one of the above provisions, and a threat to essential services exists, the Code stipulates that the Labour Relations Commission will consult with the ICTU and the IBEC about the situation, with the aim of securing their assistance in the resolution of the dispute, including, where appropriate, arrangements for a continuation of normal working for a period not exceeding six months, while efforts are being made to secure a full settlement.

Limitations of Procedures

Procedures in industrial relations are far more than an arid formulation of agreed rules. They embody a common understanding of the appropriate way of dealing with matters in which both sides have an acknowledged interest. For both parties a breach of procedure can be far more serious than the dispute over a particular substantive issue for it may signify a breakdown in their mutually agreed relationship. For management and trade unions, therefore, the maintenance of procedure may be a policy in its own right. But procedural agreements are not always successful in preventing conflict. Breaches do occur and commitments to industrial peace are, sometimes, not honoured; unofficial strikes, although on the decline, have been a problem over many decades (Wallace et al., 1987), and are unlikely to disappear altogether from the industrial relations scene. One of the weaknesses attributed to procedures is that they are unenforceable under our voluntarist industrial relations culture. This is clearly a factor, but legal enforceability of itself is no guarantee against breaches of procedural agreements; several European countries where collective agreements are legally enforceable experience similar problems (Commission of the EC, 1984). Other, and more likely, causes for procedural breakdown include reasons of an "accidental" character — such as, poor design, mistakes and misjudgements by the parties, and organisational weakness — and acts of deliberate breach based on calculable bargaining advantage. Before leaving the topic it should be emphasised that orderly industrial relations may have more to do with the quality of the collective bargaining relationship between the parties than the procedural mechanisms in force. This issue is examined further below.

DEVELOPMENT OF SYSTEM OF THIRD-PARTY INTERVENTION

The implications of Ireland's voluntarist approach to industrial relations are clearly evident in its arrangements for the settlement of disputes and grievances between workers and employers. The state provides few ground rules for the parties to follow preferring, instead, to promote harmony in industrial relations not by directly regulating the process but by making available a system of services to assist the principals settle their differences. Except in certain well-defined circumstances, use of the state services does not imply a commitment to abide by findings or recommendations issued. The Industrial Relations Act, 1990 involved the first substantial change in state-provided dispute settlement mechanisms since these were first set in place by the Industrial Relations Act, 1946. The earlier Act established the Labour Court and gave it responsibility for a number of dispute settling activities. The later Act introduced the Labour Relations Commission with responsibility for some activities previously belonging to the Labour Court and added a new dimension of dispute prevention to its role. Prior to 1946 the Department of Industry and Commerce operated a system of conciliation, under the Conciliation Act, 1896, but it was a relatively undeveloped service with intervention, for the most part, taking place when a strike had already occurred or was threatened. It was, therefore, a service which could be characterised as crisis intervention.

There were two main reasons surrounding the decision to establish the Labour Court, of which the former Conciliation Section of the Department of Industry and Commerce was to be part (Quinn, 1952). One was the generally held view that the machinery for handling disputes was not satisfactory. The more important reason though was the fear that the resumption of free collective bargaining following the removal of wartime restrictions on wage increases would lead to widespread industrial disruption as workers and unions tried to recover losses in real wages. Under the 1946 Act, the Labour Court operated and developed two separate mechanisms of dispute settlement, conciliation and investigation. Reference in the 1946 Act to conciliation are few and brief. Section 16 of the Act empowered the Court to appoint officers to act as Conciliation Officers and Section 69 empowered the Chairman of the Court, before the Court undertakes the investigation of a trade dispute, to appoint a Conciliation Officer to act as mediator in the dispute for the purpose of effecting a permanent settlement or such temporary settlement as will ensure that no stoppage of work will occur pending the investigation of the dispute. Conciliation was to play a catalytic role in dispute settlement. Investigation, on the other hand, was established as a more formal intervention by the Court whereby the dispute would be investigated and a recommendation issued of the terms on which the dispute should be settled. In keeping with the tradition of voluntarism in industrial relations, the parties would neither be obliged to use the Court's services nor to abide by its recommendations. The Court comprises a chairman, a number of deputy chairmen and ordinary members. All of them are appointed by the Minister, and are paid out of public funds; but they are not civil servants and they do not act under instructions of the Minister. The ordinary members are nominated for appointment by employer and trade union organisations. They hold office for a term of five years, and can be removed only for stated reasons, and then only with the consent of the nominating organisation. The members of the Court are thus representative, reasonably secure in their tenure of office, and independent in the exercise of their functions. Their immunity from the possibility of pressure from outside is further guaranteed by the fact that their decisions are collective and not individual, and no differences of opinion among them may be revealed. The Court operates in divisions, with each division made up of a chairman (who may be one of the deputy chairmen) and two ordinary members, one of the latter being representative of workers and the other of employers (Mortished, 1946).

During the 1960s and 1970s a number of significant changes were made to the Labour Court system. The principal Act had required the Court to make a recommendation

> setting forth its opinion on the merits of the dispute and the terms on which, in the public interest and with a view to promoting industrial peace, it should be settled, due regard being had to the fairness of the said terms to the parties concerned and the prospects of the said terms being acceptable to them (Section 68).

Understandably, it was not easy for the Court to reconcile all four considerations, and under Section 19 of the 1969 Act the demands on the Court were simplified and since then the Court, in making a recommendation, is required to set forth its opinion on the merits of the dispute and the terms on which it should be settled. The new Act also established a new third-party service, the Rights Commissioner. The purpose of the new service was to remove from the more formal machinery of Labour Court hearings issues where only a single individual was involved or where the issue involved a group of workers but did not concern the more central matters of pay, holidays or hours of work. The intention was to lighten the workload of the Labour Court and provide a prompt mediation service for what might be regarded as the less major issues in industrial relations. Provision was also made for an appeal against a Rights Commissioner recommendation to the Labour Court but, interestingly, in such a case the parties are bound by the decision of the Court on the appeal (Section 8). The provision of the new service was a recognition of the volatility of many "small" issues in industrial relations whose potential to cause disruption was often no less than one seemingly more important to collective worker interests. A further new measure in the 1969 Act requires the Court to give priority to the investigation of disputes where the trade union or both parties agree in advance to accept the Court's recommendation, in other words, a form of arbitration (Section 20).

Two related pieces of legislation which were passed into law in the 1970s also made a significant impact on the Labour Court system: the Anti-Discrimination (Pay) Act, 1974 and the Employment Equality Act, 1977. Under these Acts disputes concerning equal pay entitlements and discrimination in employment on grounds of sex or marital status may be referred to an equality officer of the Labour Court for investigation and recommendation. Following a recommendation by an equality officer a party may appeal to the Labour Court against the recommendation or may appeal to the Court for a determination that the recommendation has not been implemented. The Court's determination in such circumstances is binding on both parties. The addition of an adjudicative function to the Court's activities was to cause some ripples of concern within the Court, perhaps reflecting the "uneasiness when an adjudicative service and a conciliation service coexist in the same organisation" (McCarthy, 1978).

Institutional Reform
In 1978 the then Minister for Labour appointed the Commission of Inquiry on Industrial Relations which was comprised of employer and trade union nominees as well as independent members. Concern had been growing for some time about the state of industrial relations in the country, its effects on our image abroad and, in particular, its potential to damage our capacity as a nation to attract international investment. The appointment of the Commission was seen as a step towards the reform of the system of industrial relations. The Commission was requested to consider and report on industrial relations generally and make recommendations on

1. the practices of employers and their organisations and of workers and their organisations under the system of free collective bargaining,

2. the relevance of statute law to industrial relations, and

3. the operation of institutions, structures and procedures.

However, shortly after its first meeting the trade unions withdrew their nominees because of the failure of the government to extend the scope of the Trade Disputes Act, 1906 to public sector workers then excluded. The Commission continued its work without a direct trade union input. As a result, its Report, which was published in 1981, contained the formal assent of the employers' nominees and independent members only. Responses to the Report were divided and predictable. All in all, it made no significant impact and generated little debate.

The attempt to reform industrial relations continued throughout the 1980s on the basis of discussions between successive Ministers for Labour and employer and trade union representative bodies. Four sets of discussion documents were issued by the Department in 1983, 1985, 1986, and 1988 (see Bonner, 1987/89). The final document became the basis of the Industrial Relations Bill which was published in December 1989 and which was passed into law by the Oireachtas in 1990. In addition to the reform of third party institutions, the Industrial Relations Act, 1990 introduced changes to trade dispute, trade union and industrial relations law. It was expected that the institutional reform measures would prove as important as the various other measures in achieving improved industrial relations. The principal measure of institutional change was the transfer of the Conciliation Service of the Labour Court as the main component of a new Labour Relations Commission whose main object would be the promotion of good industrial relations.

The demand for the Labour Court's services (conciliation and investigation) has grown dramatically over the years with the volume of cases exceeding 2,000 conciliations and 1,000 investigations in 1983. In addition, and despite the establishment of the Rights Commissioner Service, many issues of a trivial character were still being referred to the Court. Although the causes of this explosion in the use of dispute settlement facilities were many and varied, there was plenty of support for the view that many of those involved in collective bargaining were "losing the art of compromise" (Horgan, 1987/89: 198) and were not making a sufficient effort to resolve their differences in direct negotiations. Bonner (1987/89) expressed the view that what was needed was a new approach which allowed the industrial relations institutions of the state to pursue policies which stressed the responsibility of the parties to negotiate sensibly and resolve their differences through their own resources with referral to third party facilities confined to cases where sound industrial relations reasons existed. For this strategy to succeed it became necessary to focus institutional resources as much towards dispute prevention as dispute resolution. A new agency was clearly necessary to take on and develop this initiative. As well as being more numerous, the occasions requiring the stabilising influence of outside intervention were becoming more complicated and difficult to resolve. Concession-trading between employers and trade unions — under conditions of organisational rationalisation, business crisis, or redundancy — were features of collective bargaining in most sectors. If third-party intervention was to continue to make a meaningful contribution to the needs of employers and trade unions it would have to adapt and provide a more sophisticated range of services.

Bonner (1987/89) described the changes introduced in dispute settlement arrangements as having the following objectives:

1. to institute and assign a new and specific responsibility for the promotion of good industrial relations;

2. to encourage and facilitate a more active approach to dispute prevention and resolution,

3. to restore the original purpose and status of the Labour Court as a court of last resort, and

4. to make provision for a number of new functions and services.

For several reasons, it was felt that this new role of actively promoting better industrial relations practice could best find expression and development in a new agency. In the first place, a body such as the Labour Court with responsibility for investigating disputes and issuing recommendations was, it was felt, constrained from adopting a forceful role in the promotion of good industrial relations. A former Chairman of the Labour Court had stated that from its earliest days the Court had been "extremely cautious in its pronouncements not because it did not have strong views but because it did not want anything which would impede in any way its acceptability in its primary role of solving disputes." He concluded that it was "difficult and indeed it may be impossible for a court which is imbued with this spirit and tradition to accept responsibility for the channelling of the direction of future industrial relations developments in the economy" (Horgan, 1987/89: 200).

The Act of 1990 established the Labour Relations Commission and transferred to it a number of the dispute settling activities which previously belonged to the Labour Court. The Act added a new dimension to the Commission's dispute settling function: in addition to the now well-established conciliation function, it was to actively involve itself as an agent- of-change in bringing about improved industrial relations. This was to be the central task of a new Industrial

Relations Advisory Service which would be available to employers and trade unions. The Service was established by the Commission in 1992. The remainder of this article is devoted to an examination of the Labour Relations Commission and the Labour Court. In the case of the Commission, an attempt is made to articulate the notion of good industrial relations and to provide a strategic framework for the Commission's advisory function. Finally, trends in business volume and performance are analysed in respect of conciliation and Labour Court investigation activities since 1946.

LABOUR RELATIONS COMMISSION

Promoting Good Industrial Relations

What constitutes *good* industrial relations is a notoriously difficult question to answer as it depends very much on the perspective of the assessor and the criteria on which performance is based. The most obvious tell-tale symptoms of the serious industrial relations problem are usually taken to involve disruptions to business operations/services on a regular basis due to confrontations between management and workers, often before jointly agreed procedures have been exhausted and, perhaps, with an excessive reliance on third-party mechanisms in dispute settlement. Such problems may be due to any one of a number of causes, including, structures and procedures which are underdeveloped or inadequate for the task, poor judgement and unrealistic expectations, lack of competence on the part of negotiators, organisational weakness such as inadequate authority delegation or insufficient control over the activities of junior officials. However, those with direct experience of collective bargaining will be quick to point out that the absence of strikes or indeed the presence of industrial relations structures and procedures do not, in themselves, guarantee *good* industrial relations. Purcell (1981: ch. 2) has pointed out that "emphasis on the structural components severely understates, if not ignores, the problems inherent in making the structures work". The implication is that structures depend for their success on "process" questions such as the behavioural and attitudinal components of the bargaining relationship, and especially on the will of the parties to make them work. Clearly then, special attention has to be given to the quality of relationships when assessing the effectiveness or the ineffectiveness of industrial relations in a given situation.

Collective bargaining is a dynamic process which, in addition to having its own internal environment, is also heavily influenced by external environmental factors, of which economic and market conditions, and developments in the wider industrial relations system are a few. As changes occur in these external contexts they generate demands within organisations to which managements and worker representatives are required to respond. Gradual movements and shifts in environmental forces go to make up the normal diet of collective bargaining exchanges between the parties. However, from time to time, environmental shifts may be so severe that they trigger initiatives of a radical kind, or the adoption of unusually tough positions by the parties which can have strategic implications for established relationship patterns and, therefore, for the future effectiveness of collective bargaining. Examples of this are the trade union which encounters serious "slippage" in the pay of its members *vis-à-vis* comparable categories of workers elsewhere, and the company, because of intense competition, forced to seek a new balance between pay and productivity. Two very different patterns of bargaining relationships are commonly found. In the first, collective bargaining is conducted in what can be described as the "adversarial mode". This mode is manifested by tactics which are essentially exploitative in motivation, a minimalist attitude to the bargaining agenda in which the parties vigorously defend their perceived rights, and weak commitment to agreed procedures. In the second case industrial relations are conducted in what can be described as the "accommodational mode". Although adversarialism continues to be the prevailing basis of relations in this mode, sufficient trust is established between the two sides to allow a strong working relationship to develop within a bureaucratised framework. Behaviour is manifested by tactics which concentrate on the orderly settlement of disputes, a high degree of work-rule formalisation, and strong commitment by both sides to agreed procedures. Despite appearances to the contrary, this pattern of industrial relations probably describes most trade union and management experience in the area. Over time the parties may move from one pattern of bargaining to the other. A shift from adversarial to accommodational mode might occur, for example, if the costs of conflict became too high as result of which the parties reach a "pact" and begin to work together to resolve their differences in a more orderly manner. Moves from accommodational to adversarial, on the other hand, can occur when, for example, "order" in industrial relations bears an unacceptably high price and leads to one of the parties seeking substantial improvements in the exchange between pay and work, in a manner regarded by the other side as constituting reneging on the previous mutuality pact. This may sometimes result in only a temporary shift to adversarial mode with a return to normal accommodational arrangements later, but with trust weakened between the parties.

Beyond Adversarialism. The strategic options available to management and trade unions in their dealings are not confined to the above two patterns of behaviour. Indeed, in the context of recessionary conditions worldwide, intense business competitiveness and technological advancement, the tendency in each of the models towards an introspective focus makes them seriously flawed. Adversarialism leads to a concentration of effort on internal "battles" which are judged very much on short-term achievements, whereas the ultimate test of success or failure in collective bargaining has to be in terms of the compatibility of negotiated settlements with environmental imperatives. The accommodational model may be equally inadequate for the circumstances of the organisation because the habit and effort involved in maintaining order may, for some time, cloud the fact that the "ship is sinking".

Many distinguished writers on industrial relations have in the past put forward alternative models of co-operative collective bargaining on the basis that "if unions and management do not progress beyond conjunctive bargaining they forego opportunities from which both might benefit" (Chamberlain and Kuhn, 1965: 427). Walton and McKersie's model of "integrative bargaining" allows for opportunities for co-operation in the bargaining relationship to be fully exploited to the benefit of both parties.

The pattern is characterised by the fact that the parties willingly extend mutual concerns far beyond the familiar matters of wages, hours and condition. Productive efficiency, the solvency of the firm, equality, elimination of waste, advance of technology, employment security, and so on are treated as matters of common interest. "In as much as each has found areas in which the other can be instrumental to its own objectives, it is likely to act in such a way as to strengthen the other organization or its leaders" (Walton and McKersie, 1965/91: 188).

This description of high-trust relations may appear to lack credibility if only because it is relatively rare (Purcell, 1981: 56). But, given the harshness of the environment in which most organisations operate today, it may be wise for management and workers to consider whether the formal structures of industrial relations as operated in the past are sufficient to guarantee business success and even survival in the longer term. The way forward may be to consider fundamental redesign of collective bargaining arrangements so that opportunities for interest harmonisation can be exploited, the agenda for debate widened to include business policy performance and related issues, and joint collaboration exercised through meaningful participative structures. In cases experiencing fundamental change in business circumstances, real and lasting success in industrial relations may be achievable only where it ceases to be treated as a zero-sum game.

This brief discussion of the nature of "good" industrial relations has an obvious relevance to the Labour Relations Commission's general responsibility under the Act for "promoting improvements in industrial relations" (Section 25). Since the Commission's Advisory Service was established in July 1992 it has handled, including those on-going, 20 cases. Two reports were issued in 1993. The types of problems which these exercises have addressed have been largely to do with the efficiency of collective bargaining arrangements; in other words, investigating systems of industrial relation where these were not working satisfactorily in reconciling issues where the interests of company and workforce were seen to diverge. A more challenging and potentially more rewarding question which management and trade unions might ask each other about their industrial relations strategies is the extent to which they allow the synergistic potential of meaningful co-operation to be exploited in matters where the interests of organisation and employees converge. Reason would suggest that, at least in organisations confronting fundamental change in business circumstances, adversarialism, whether in its raw or bureaucratised form, may no longer be capable of serving, fully, the interests of either management or employees.

CONCILIATION: TRENDS IN BUSINESS VOLUME AND PERFORMANCE

This review of the operation of the Conciliation Service is based on data reported in annual reports of the Labour Court (1946–90), the Labour Relations Commission (1991–92) and on records of the Commission for 1993. Because of its essentially quantitative nature, the data does not adequately reflect many shifts of a more qualitative kind which may have occurred in the operation of the Service. One such recent development which has been noticed is that more and more of the cases in which the Commission is asked to assist involve issues of a complex nature requiring extensive consultations about the organisational arrangements and procedures for company/trade union negotiations. Sometimes the problem may be due to the way collective bargaining is structured, e.g., where the issues have universal impact throughout the workforce and affect several bargaining units. Typically, these cases are in situations involving major rationalisation, business crisis, and redundancy and involve the Commission in interventions of a more long-term nature. Nevertheless, analysis of the data does uncover a number of interesting trends.

Volume of Cases Handled

The volume of disputes referred to conciliation as well as the numbers of workers involved roughly doubled in each of the last three decades (Table 9.1). The rate of growth was even stronger if one allows for the Rights Commissioner Service which handles many cases which would previously have gone to conciliation. This "explosion" in referrals has been a matter of increasing concern down the years, but it now seems to have halted, at least on the basis of figures for the decade so far. In the first four years of the current decade, referrals are only marginally up and the number of workers involved fractionally down on the corresponding period in the 1980s. It seems, therefore, that the steady and dramatic growth which occurred throughout the period since the Service's inception may now be levelling off.

While the halt in the growth of referrals is certainly a development which is to be welcomed, it must be said that, in a number of respects, the level of referrals is high and reflects poorly on the collective bargaining performances of many employers and trade unions. Two features, in particular, of the cases handled at conciliation will help to illustrate this criticism.

"Small" Cases. The volume of disputes involving individual workers or groups fewer than five workers is running at about 20 per cent of all disputes dealt with at conciliation. Whereas these represent one-in-five of cases, they account for less than 0.02 per cent of workers involved in conciliation cases. Many are not settled at conciliation and are referred onwards to the Labour Court. In 1993 they represented about a quarter of all cases referred to the Labour Court. It appears that many of these disputes could be handled by the Rights Commissioner Service.

TABLE 9.1: DISPUTES AT CONCILIATION AND WORKERS INVOLVED:
YEARLY AVERAGES FOR EACH DECADE

	Cases Average p.a.	*Workers Average p.a.* *(000)*
1950–59	179	21
1960–69	380	72
1970–79	965	143
1980–89	1,737	288
1990–93	1,803	282

Source: Labour Court and Labour Relations Commission.

High-Frequency Users. Over 1992–93 the highest frequency users
of the conciliation service were twelve organisations who took an average of 33.5 cases each to conciliation (see Table 9.2). Between them
they accounted for 402 disputes or 12 per cent of the total, which represents one-in-eight of all disputes handled at conciliation. Eight of
the twelve organisations were from the public sector. A further 24 organisations (1993 only) were moderately high-frequency users of
conciliation, with an average of seven cases each, and, together, they
accounted for a further 12 per cent of conciliation cases. This time 17
of the 24 organisations were from the public sector. It is a matter of
concern that over 1992–93 three dozen organisations, together, were responsible for about one-quarter of all disputes handled at conciliation.
This must not be taken in any way as a criticism of employer and
trade union users generally. Most cases which come before conciliation do so for reasons that make sound industrial relations sense,
where there are serious issues of cost or principle or both at stake
between the parties. It must be said, however, that many other cases
which are brought raise doubts about the seriousness of the efforts of
the parties concerned.

In terms of the cases settled at conciliation, settlement rates have
been relatively stable, at the two-thirds level, over the bulk of the
period since the inception of the Service (see Table 9.3). It did decline
somewhat below this level during the 1970s and 1980s, but it would
seem that the emergence of national pay agreements during this period was the primary influence at work. In each year since 1989 settlement rates at conciliation have reached or exceeded the 70 per cent
level. In the three years since the establishment of the LRC settlements at conciliation have averaged over 77 per cent. This level of per-

formance about equals the best three-year average ever previously achieved, back in 1968–70, although the volume of cases at that time was less than one-third the number of cases currently being handled.

TABLE 9.2: HIGH AND MODERATELY HIGH-FREQUENCY USERS OF CONCILIATION, PUBLIC AND PRIVATE SECTORS (1992–93)

	High Users			Moderately High Users			Combined Totals		
	Pub	Priv	Total	Pub	Priv	Total	Pub	Priv	Total
Number Orgs	8	4	12	17	7	24	25	11	36
Number Cases	290	112	402	129	40	169	419	152	571
Average Cases/Orgs	36.3	28	33.5	7.6	5.7	7	16.8	13.8	16

Source: Labour Relations Commission.

Notes: 1) High-users based on 1992–93 (to Sept) records.
          2) Moderately high-users based on 1993 (to Sept) records.

When the number of workers involved in conciliation cases are considered, we find further and dramatic improvement in the performance of conciliation in recent years. Having consistently declined over four decades from 57 per cent in the 1950s to 35 per cent in the 1980s, the rate for the first four years of the 1990s soared to a remarkable 88 per cent. On closer examination, however, it is clear that the improvement commenced earlier, and around 1988 (See Table 9.4). In some respects this is a rather crude measure of conciliation performance since it can be affected by many other factors, such as the volume of "small" cases already referred to above, the size of bargaining units, etc. Indeed the decline in multi-employer/sectoral bargaining since the 1960s is a likely significant factor in the earlier fall in the rate at which workers were leaving conciliation with their cases settled.

THE LABOUR COURT

This review of the operation of the Labour Court is based on data reported in annual reports of the Court (1946–90), and provisional data supplied by the Court in respect of the years 1991–92. It is necessary to point out that because of its quantitative nature, the analysis does

TABLE 9.3: CONCILIATION: RATE OF SETTLEMENT AND WORKERS
INVOLVED AVERAGES FOR EACH DECADE

	% Settled	% Workers in Settled Cases
1950–59	67%	57%
1960–69	71%	53%
1970–79	57%	40%
1980–89	60%	35%
1990–93	76%	88%

TABLE 9.4: CASES SETTLED AT CONCILIATION: WORKERS INVOLVED
THREE YEARLY AVERAGES, 1985–93

	All Cases (000)	Settled Cases (000)	% Workers in Settled Cases
1985–87	262	83	32%
1988–90	150	100	67%
1991–93	326	298	91%

Source: Labour Court and Labour Relations Commission.

not adequately reflect many shifts of a more qualitative kind which
may have occurred in the operation of the Court. The "explosion" in
the number of disputes coming before the Court over recent decades
has been referred to earlier. In the case of Court investigations the
speed of the growth was slower to materialise than in the case of
conciliations. Conciliations began to experience fast growth in the
early 1960s, whereas the steep incline in Court hearings was delayed
to the early part of the 1970s, coinciding with the commencement of
national pay agreements. Unlike conciliations, in which the number of
cases seems to be levelling-off over the past few years, Labour Court
hearings have fallen significantly in the current decade so far. The
"drop" is of the order of 40 per cent in respect of total activity and also
of workers involved in hearings (Table 9.5). When direct comparison
is made with the corresponding three years of the 1980s, total activity
shows a decline of 30 per cent with workers involved falling from a
yearly average of 235,000 to 105,000, a drop of 55 per cent. Because of
the variety of "decisions" incorporated in figures of Labour Court activity,
and especially over the past decade, a closer examination of the data is
necessary. This reveals important shifts in "business" volume over the
last decade between investigation work of a traditional industrial re-

lations nature ("core" activity) and work where some element of binding effect applies to Court decisions (non- "core" activity). The latter includes, principally: (a) appeals against rights commissioner recommendations; (b) Section 20 referrals; (c) determinations under the equality Acts; (d) orders and decisions in respect of Registered Employment Agreements and the equality Acts. Table 9.5 and Figure 9.2 show core investigation work of the Court taking a decreasing share of Court hearings. It has declined from 88 per cent in the 1970s (this was the first decade in which this work appeared to a significant degree) to 55 per cent in the 1990s to date. When direct comparison is made with the corresponding three years of the 1980s, core activity shows a drop of 53 per cent as against a rise of 76 per cent in non-core work. In the latest year available, core work has dropped below half of total Court activity to 48 per cent.

TABLE 9.5: LABOUR COURT ACTIVITY
YEARLY AVERAGES FOR EACH DECADE

	Total Activity	Core Investigations	Core as a % of Total	Total Workers (000)
1950–59	92	92	100	34
1960–69	121	121	100	48
1970–79	364	319	88	103
1980–89	852	646	76	182
1990–92	592	328	55	105

Source: Labour Court and Labour Relations Commission.

Referrals of disputes to the Labour Court occur in circumstances where the Commission is satisfied that no further efforts on its part will advance the settlement of the dispute. Since about 1985, the number of cases being referred for investigation has been declining steadily and now stands at roughly half the earlier level (Table 9.6). The rate of referrals, i.e., referrals as a per cent of total conciliations, has dropped from 30.7 per cent in the period 1985–89 to 16.7 per cent in the period 1990–93. This may be due in part to the more vigorous policy towards the settlement of disputes at the conciliation stage pursued over recent years and referred to in the first annual report of the Commission (1991: 7).

FIGURE 9.2: LABOUR COURT AND CONCILIATION ACTIVITY, 1947–92

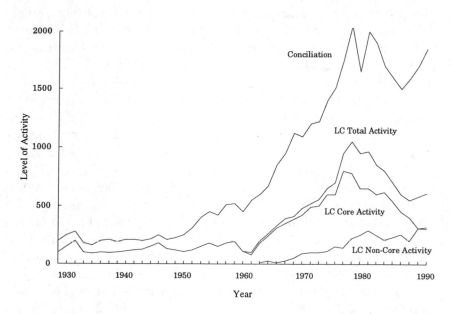

Sources: (i) Labour Court Reports 1947–90
(ii) Labour Court Data for 1991–92 (provisional) supplied by Court
(iii) LRC Reports 1991–92

TABLE 9.6: REFERRALS TO LABOUR COURT FROM CONCILIATIONS
REFERRED, TOTAL CONCILIATIONS AND REFERRAL RATES (1985–93)

	Referrals to Court	Total Conciliations	% Referrals
1985	629	2,021	31.1%
1986	617	1,892	32.6%
1987	55	1,787	31.1%
1988	464	1,571	29.5%
1989	409	1,450	28.2%
1990	368	1,552	23.7%
1991	184	1,880	9.8%
1992	307	1,935	15.9%
1993	346	1,844	18.8%

Source: Labour Court and Labour Relations Commission

CONCLUDING REMARKS

This article has examined two aspects of dispute resolution, procedures and third party intervention, and has identified a number of trends and developments in Irish practice over several decades. One of these developments relates to the use, which is now widespread throughout industry, of formalised arrangements for the settlement of disputes between management and workers. There is, however, occasional evidence only of restraint on industrial action being extended beyond the final stage of procedures in the shape of new-style agreements. Moreover, where this does occur special circumstances seem, for the most part, to exist. The Code of Practice on Dispute Procedures drawn up recently by the Labour Relations Commission represents an attempt to promote procedural innovation, especially in the case of essential services. The response of employers and trade unions will be an important determinant of the future stability of industrial relations here. A second development highlighted concerns the long-running "explosion" of referrals of disputes to conciliation and investigation services of the Labour Court the apparent halt in the growth of referrals of disputes to conciliation, and signs of significantly improved success at achieving settlements at the conciliation stage instead of being referred onwards to the Labour Court. Although the rate of referrals is still extremely high, there are indications that more and more of the responsibility to reach settlement is being shifted back on the parties themselves. Finally, the arrival of the Labour Relations Commission has introduced a new "reserve player" onto the industrial relations field, especially in relation to its advisory role. This seems destined to become an important service for management and employers, particularly in view of the difficult conditions surrounding most employments. The Commission will do well if it manages to emulate the success of the Labour Court over more than 40 years of industrial peace-making.

References

Anthony, P.D. (1977): *The Conduct of Industrial Relations*, London: Institute of Personnel Management.

Bonner, K. (1987/1989): "Industrial Relations Reform" in T. Murphy (ed.), *Industrial Relations in Ireland: Contemporary Issues and Developments*, Dublin: Department of Industrial Relations, University College Dublin.

Burchill, F. (1989): "Pendulum Arbitration: A Problem or a Solution?", *Industrial Relations News*, 29: 12–6.

Chamberlain, N. and Kuhn, J. (1965): *Collective Bargaining*, 2nd edition, New York: McGraw-Hill.

Commission of the European Communities (1984): *The Prevention and Settlement of Industrial Conflict in the Community Member States*, Luxembourg: Office for Official Publications of the European Communities.

Commission on Industrial Relations (1975): *Industrial Relations Procedures*, London: HMSO.

Committee of Inquiry on Industrial Relations (1981): *Report of the Committee of Inquiry on Industrial Relations*, Dublin: Government Publications.

Department of Labour (1992a): *A Guide to the Industrial Relations Act, 1990,* Dublin: Department of Labour.

Department of Labour (1992b): *Code of Practice on Disputes Procedures Including Procedures in Essential Services*, Dublin: Department of Labour.

Electricity Supply Board (1981): *Comprehensive Agreement between Electricity Supply Board and All Trade Unions Representing Employees in the ESB*, Dublin: ESB.

Gorman, L., Hynes, G., McConnell, J. and Moynihan, T. (1975): *Irish Industry: How It's Managed*, Dublin: Irish Management Institute.

Horgan, J. (1987/1989): "The Future of Collective Bargaining" in T. Murphy (ed.), *Industrial Relations in Ireland: Contemporary Issues and Developments*, Dublin: Department of Industrial Relations, University College Dublin.

International Labour Organisation (ILO) (1973): *Conciliation in Industrial Disputes: A Practical Guide*, Geneva: ILO.

International Labour Organisation (ILO) (1980): *Conciliation and Arbitration Procedures in Labour Disputes: A Comparative Study*, Geneva: ILO.

Kerr, C. (1954): "Industrial Conflict and Its Mediation", *American Journal of Sociology*, 60: 230–45.

Labour Court (1946–90): *Annual Reports*, Dublin: Stationery Office.

Labour Court (1989): *Dispute Concerning the Renewal of a Comprehensive Agreement, Recommendation No. 12466*, Dublin: Labour Court.

Labour Relations Commission (1991–92): *Annual Reports*, Dublin: Stationery Office.

Labour Relations Commission (1993): *The Resolution of Industrial Disputes, Report on International Conference Organised by the European Commission and the Irish Labour Relations Commission*, Dublin: Labour Relations Commission.

Lockwood, D. (1955): "Arbitration and Industrial Conflict", *British Journal of Sociology*, 6: 335–47.

Lowry, P. (1990): *Employment Disputes and the Third Party*, London: Macmillan.

McCarthy, C. (1978): *Problems in the Field of Dispute Resolution*, Third Countess Markievicz Memorial Lecture, Dublin: Irish Association for Industrial Relations.

MacNeill, H. (1980): "Management View" in D. Nevin (ed.), *Trade Unions and Change in Irish Society*, Dublin: Mercier Press.

McNally, N. (1991): *Conciliation in Ireland: An Exploratory Study*, (unpublished) M.B.S. dissertation, University College Dublin.

Medcalf, D. and Milner, S. (1992): "Risking all on a Two-Horse Race", *Personnel Management*, July: 40–3.

Mortished, R.J.P. (1947): "The Industrial Relations Act, 1946", *Journal of the Statistical and Social Inquiry Society of Ireland*, 18: 671–87.

Murphy, T. (1987/1989): "The Union Committee at the Workplace" in T. Murphy (ed.), *Industrial Relations in Ireland: Contemporary Issues and Developments*, Dublin: Department of Industrial Relations, University College Dublin.

Murray, S. (1984): *Survey of Employee Industrial Relations in Irish Private-Sector Manufacturing Industries*, Dublin: Industrial Development Authority.

National Employer/Labour Conference (1962*): Report of Sub-Committee on Grievance Procedures etc.*, Dublin: National Employer/Labour Conference.

National Employer/Labour Conference (1972*): Draft Report of Sub-Committee set up to consider Codes of Fair Employment and Dismissal Procedures*, Dublin: National Employer/Labour Conference.

O'Mahony, D. (1964): *Industrial Relations in Ireland: The Background, 19*, Dublin: Economic and Social Research Institute.

Purcell, J. (1981): *Good Industrial Relations: Theory and Practice*, London: Macmillan.

Quinn, K.P. (1952): *The Industrial Relations Act, 1946*, (unpublished), M.A. thesis, University College Dublin.

Stevens, C.M. (1967): "Mediation and the Role of the Neutral" in J. Dunlop and N.W. Chamberlain (eds), *Frontiers of Collective Bargaining*, New York: Harper and Row.

Wallace, J. and O'Shea, F. (1987): *A Study of Unofficial Strikes in Ireland*, Dublin: Stationery Office.

Walton, R.E. and McKersie, R.B. (1991): *A Behavioural Theory of Labour Negotiations: An Analysis of a Social Interaction System*, New York: ILR Press.

Wickens, P. (1987): *The Road to Nissan*, London: Macmillan.

Wood, Sir J. (1985): "Last Offer Arbitration", *British Journal of Industrial Relations*, 21: 3.

CHAPTER 10

COLLECTIVE LABOUR LAW

Anthony Kerr

INTRODUCTION

The Commission of Inquiry on Industrial Relations concluded, in its report published in July 1981, that voluntary means alone were incapable of importing the required degree of order to the collective relations between trade unions and employers, and that the many serious consequences of the failure of voluntary arrangements made it imperative that some alternative source of order be established. A majority of the Commission felt that the law could make an effective contribution towards curbing what the Commission saw as the undesirable consequences of Irish industrial relations. Principal amongst these was the strike rate. Research by Kelly and Brannick (1989) reveals that since the 1960s the average number of strike days per employee had steadily risen and in 1979 nearly one and a half million days were lost due to strikes, a large proportion of which were "unofficial".

The majority of the Commission, as well as recommending considerable institutional changes, made a number of specific recommendations concerning the law on industrial conflict, namely that workers would be required to comply with certain procedures, including a ballot, before taking industrial action and that certain limitations be placed on the type of issues over which industrial action could be taken. As Kelly and Roche (1983) have observed, the underlying philosophy of the majority was one which unambiguously sought a central role for legal regulation.

These recommendations, however, did not find much favour with successive governments and, despite the lack of any fundamental legislative change, the strike rate began to fall dramatically and there was also a considerable degree of trade union rationalisation. Nevertheless, the relatively healthy state of Irish industrial relations was not felt to justify complacency and the Programme for National Recovery, agreed in 1987, committed the Minister for Labour to holding discussions with the social partners about changes in the legislation which would provide "a better framework for collective bargaining and dispute settlement and help create conditions for employment-generating investment".

In February 1988 the Minister published a set of proposals which formed the basis for "prolonged and intensive" discussions which took place in 1988 and 1989 and which were described as a pragmatic package designed to oil the collective bargaining system with a view to minimising conflict and maximising co-operation (Ahern, 1989). In putting these proposals forward, the Minister said that he did not believe it was possible to achieve a complete consensus as to what the legislation should contain. What he would do would be to address the major issues which he felt were required to be tackled and to devise arrangements which would be workable and with which both sides could live. Consensus not compulsion would be the approach.

The prevailing policy amongst all political parties was that good industrial relations was primarily a matter for the parties involved and that the role of the law was merely to provide a framework within which collective bargaining could operate. Consequently, while there were sharp disagreements on certain details, both inside and outside the Oireachtas, the Industrial Relations Act 1990 received widespread support.

In enacting this important piece of legislation, the Oireachtas did not make the mistake of over-estimating the importance of law in industrial relations. The theme of the Act is not that the law has no place but that legislation on its own will not automatically lend to fewer strikes and an improved performance. Nevertheless, the Act undoubtedly increases rather than diminishes the role of the law in industrial relations (see, generally, Kerr, 1991a).

LEGISLATIVE BACKGROUND

Before the 1990 Act, the legislation fell into three broad categories. First, there was the legislation which had been inherited from the British — the Trade Union Acts 1871, 1876 and 1913; the Conspiracy and Protection of Property Act 1875 and the Trade Disputes Act, 1906 (as amended in 1982). Secondly, there were the Trade Union Acts 1941, 1971 and 1975 and thirdly there were the Industrial Relations Acts 1946, 1969 and 1976. (On all three categories, see Kerr and Whyte, 1985 and Kerr, 1991).

The first series of Acts was in clear response to a series of judicial decisions which ensured that, during their formative years, trade unions had to operate in a hostile legal climate. The civil status of trade unions, for example, was unlawful because their rules were considered to be in "restraint of trade". Organising a strike invariably involved the participants in civil liability in tort, especially liability for conspiracy and inducing breaches of contract. Picketing could be restrained on the ground that it constituted a nuisance. The legislation enacted between 1871 and 1913, however, as Wedderburn (1980) has observed, conferred no positive rights — neither a right to organise nor a right to strike. It provided "no more than a liberty to associate in trade unions and certain liberties of action by which trade unions can carry on industrial struggle". The technique employed was to confer statutory *immunities* for trade unions and their members against certain common law doctrines, such as restraint of trade. This legislation, however, did establish a framework within which collective bargaining could operate effectively and it abstained from any detailed interference in the internal affairs of trade unions except as regards the application of trade union funds for political purposes (a matter regulated by the 1913 Act). An important facet of this framework is the perception that collective agreements are not legally enforceable. Although the question of legal enforceability has yet to be definitively decided by the Irish courts, it should be noted that the Commission of Inquiry on Industrial Relations accepted that all trade unions and many employers would be opposed to any legislative step to give collective agreements the status of legally binding contracts and recommended against making such agreements legally binding by statute.

The aims of the 1941 Act, however, were much more dramatic than those of the earlier Acts. Whilst not interfering with the underlying philosophy of the earlier legislation, the Act attempted to drastically reduce the number of trade unions operating in Ireland. It provided for the licensing of bodies carrying on collective bargaining negotiations and it became a criminal offence for any body of persons to carry on negotiations for the fixing of wages or any other conditions of employment unless such body held a "negotiation licence" or was an "excepted body". Part III of the 1941 Act established a tribunal with the power to restrict the organisational activities of trade unions by granting determinations that a specified trade union alone should have the right to organise workers of a particular class. As can be seen below, this part of the Act did not survive a constitutional challenge. The 1971 Act made certain amendments to the licensing system, principally by requiring a minimum of 500 members and increasing the amount of the deposit that must be lodged with the High Court and the 1975 Act improved the procedure whereby two or more unions could merge. This last mentioned Act provides two distinct methods whereby trade unions can merge: first by amalgamation, where two trade unions merge to form a new union (as happened with the amalgamation in 1990 of the Irish Transport and General Workers' Union and the Federated Workers' Union of Ireland to form SIPTU) or, alternatively, by transfer of engagements, where one union officially transfers its obligations and assets to another union (as happened with the transfer of the Telecommunications Officials Union to the Communication Workers Union in 1991). A significant difference between effecting an amalgamation and effecting a transfer of engagement is that, in the latter case, a ballot only needs to be organised of the members of the transferring union whereas in the former case separate ballots of the members of both unions are required. In either case a simple majority of those voting is required.

The third series of Acts concerned institutional arrangements for the promotion of harmonious industrial relations and to this end the 1946 Act established machinery — the Labour Court — for the prevention and settlement of industrial disputes. The then Minister for Industry and Commerce — Sean Lemass, TD — believed strongly that trade unions should be given a significant place in the development of national policy and regarded the most important aspect of the legislation to be the public participation of the trade union movement in the consideration of methods to avoid industrial disputes. The 1946 Act virtually enshrined the principle of free collective bargaining and both the Act itself and the process by which it came to be enacted was actively supportive of the trade union movement.

The 1946 Act, in addition to establishing the Labour Court, also provided a system whereby collective agreements could be registered with the Labour Court which would apply to every worker of the class, type or group to which it is expressed to apply and his or her employer, notwithstanding that such worker or employer was not a party to the agreement. Despite the high hopes expressed by the Minister at the time of the Act's enactment, these hopes have largely remained unfulfilled (see Horgan, 1985). The 1946 Act also provided for the establishment of Joint Labour Committees whose function was to submit to the Labour Court proposals for regulating the conditions of employment and fixing the minimum rates of remuneration to be paid to the workers in relation to whom the committee operated. There are currently 16 such committees, the most recently established being that for Catering for Dublin and Dun Laoghaire which came into operation on November 27,1992.

The 1969 Act, in addition to making various amendments to the 1946 Act, also established the Rights Commissioner service to investigate trade disputes other than those connected with the rates of pay, hours or times of work, or annual holidays of a body of workers. The 1976 Act made various minor amendments to the 1946 Act but also provided for the establishment of a joint labour committee for agricultural workers.

The Constitution

Overshadowing all this legislation, however, is Article 40.6.1° (iii) of the 1937 Constitution in which the State guarantees liberty for the exercise, subject to public order and morality, of "the right of the citizens to form associations and unions". The importance of this provision became only too apparent in 1946 when the Supreme Court in *National Union of Railwaymen v Sullivan* [1947] I.R. 77 declared Part III of the Trade Union Act 1941 invalid having regard to the provisions of the Constitution as interfering with the right to associate. The Court took the view that a worker could not be said to enjoy the right to freedom of association if in reality the freedom of choice was non-existent.

Subsequently the Supreme Court interpreted Article 40.6.1° (iii) as guaranteeing, by necessary implication, the right of citizens not to join a trade union, if they did not so desire. This means that a trade union cannot mount a picket on an employer for the purpose of compelling non-union employees to join the trade union. It also means that an employer cannot lawfully dismiss an employee for refusing to join a trade union. While the full significance of this development remains to be teased out by the courts, it is clear that it has considerable implications for the legal status of "closed shop" agreements (see von Prondzynski, 1987). It would also appear that the courts are not prepared to accept that the constitutional guarantee of free association includes a right to have one's trade union recognised by one's employer for collective bargaining purposes and have held that there is no duty placed on an employer to negotiate with any particular body of citizens (see Casey, 1972 and Whyte, 1995). It should be noted, however, that some legislative provisions (such as section 16 of the Postal and Telecommunications Services Act 1983) do impose on particular employers (such as An Post and Bord Telecom Éireann) an obligation to set up machinery "in consultation with recognised trade unions" for the purpose of negotiations concerned with pay and conditions of service.

THE INDUSTRIAL RELATIONS ACT 1990

The Industrial Relations Act 1990 effected considerable changes in the law, both relating to trade unions and to industrial relations. Under the former there are provisions to reform trade dispute law, by introducing pre-strike ballots and restricting the use of injunctions, and to facilitate the further rationalisation of the trade union movement by further amendments to the 1971 and 1975 Trade Union Acts. Under the latter the major change provided for was the establishment of the Labour Relations Commission but the Act also contains provisions to amend and improve the procedures governing the establishment and operation of joint labour committees. The principal amendment to the Trade Union Act 1971 is to require a minimum membership of 1,000 before a trade union can apply for a negotiation licence.

The law in relation to trade disputes had become exceedingly complicated and the Trade Disputes Act 1906 (even as amended in 1982) increasingly failed to provide a clear indication as to the boundaries of what was or was not permissible in a trade dispute. The position of secondary picketing in particular was extremely unclear. Without the position ever having been definitively decided, the courts tended only to permit secondary picketing where there was a clearly discernible business connection between the premises picketed and the dispute. The legality of blacking an employer's goods or services was also doubtful, as being an unlawful interference in that employer's trade or business unprotected by any of the statutory immunities.

By repealing the 1906 Act in its entirety and reintroducing its provisions with amendments, the Minister hoped to resolve the problem of what was and was not permissible in a trade dispute. Section 10 re-enacts the immunities concerning criminal and civil conspiracy formerly provided for in section 3 of the Conspiracy and Protection of Property Act 1875 and section 1 of the Trade Disputes Act 1906 respectively. Section 12 re-enacts section 3 of the 1906 Act which provided an immunity concerning inducement of breach of a contract of employment, with the addition of a provision granting immunity to persons who threaten to induce a breach of a contract of employment or threaten to breach their own contracts of employment. The trade union itself is rendered immune from any actions in tort by section 13.

These immunities apply, however, only where the action in question is done "in contemplation or furtherance of a trade dispute" and "trade dispute" is defined in section 8 of the 1990 Act as "any dispute between employers and workers which is connected with the employment or non-employment, or the terms or conditions of or affecting the employment of, any person". The phrase "employment or non-employment" has been held to be wide enough to cover any dispute arising out of the employment or dismissal of any person and it does not matter whether the dismissal was fair or lawful. This definition of a trade dispute differs somewhat from that in the 1906 Act in that it is both broader and narrower. Although it removes disputes between workmen from its ambit, it now extends to all disputes connected with terms and conditions of or affecting employment, including recognition disputes.

An important change is to be found in section 9(2) which provides that none of the immunities will apply where the trade dispute concerns one individual worker and "agreed procedures availed of by custom or in practice in the employment concerned or provided for in a collective agreement for the resolution of individual grievances" have not been resorted to and exhausted. According to the Minister (Ahern, 1991), the reasoning behind this provision is to remove protection from individuals taking wildcat action, and from those supporting them, where there are agreed procedures available for the resolution of individual grievances.

Picketing

Section 11 effects major changes in the law on picketing. Subsections (1) and (2) respectively purport to regulate what are generally referred to as "primary" and "secondary" picketing. Unlike the position in the United Kingdom, however, picketers are not confined to their own place of work. They may lawfully picket any place where their employer works or carries on business. Where it is impracticable to picket the employer's place of business, such as where a dispute arises affecting one employer in a shopping centre or industrial estate, the picket may be placed at the "approaches to" the employer's place of business. Otherwise picketing an employer who is not a party to the trade dispute (that is, secondary picketing) is only permitted if it is reasonable for the picketers to believe at the commencement of their attendance and throughout the continuance of their attendance that that employer has directly assisted their employer, who is a party to the trade dispute, for the purpose of frustrating the strike or other industrial action. Subsection (3) expressly provides that any action taken by an employer in the health services to maintain life-preserving services during a strike or other industrial action shall not constitute such assistance. Subsection (4) further provides that a trade union official may accompany "any member of his union whom he represents" on a picket.

It is perhaps worth noting in this context the Irish Congress of Trade Union guidelines in respect of picketing at ports and industrial estates. Where picketing is directed against a premises located within a port or an industrial estate, the trade union engaged in the dispute should first seek permission from the Port Authority or the owner of the industrial estate for its members to attend outside the premises against which the picket is directed. In the event of permission being refused the picket will have to be maintained at the entrance to the port or industrial estate. In such an event the picket should clearly indicate the employment being picketed and every effort should be made to advise workers and their representatives at the port or industrial estate of the limit of the picket.

As under the 1906 Act, the purpose of the picket must be confined to "peacefully obtaining or communicating information, or of peacefully persuading any person to work or abstain from working". If the picket is placed for some other purpose, then the section cannot be relied upon. Consequently picketing a shop or a theatre with the object of persuading customers to boycott it is unlawful. Nor are the picketers entitled to disseminate false or inaccurate information.

Blacking

Although the legal status of picketing has been clarified by the 1990 Act, the status of blacking was not. Before the 1990 Act it was generally believed that if a trade union authorised the blacking of an employer's goods or services then it would be exposing itself to liability for unlawfully interfering with that employer's trade or business. The 1990 Act has done nothing to clarify the position and since section 12 does not confer any immunity for breach of an employment contract *simpliciter*, being confined to inducements of breach of contracts of employment and threats to break such contracts, the predominant view would appear to be that such action remains unlawful.

Secret Ballots

Undoubtedly the most significant changes in trade disputes law are those on secret ballots and injunctions. These provisions are very different to those currently pertaining in the United Kingdom. There, immunity for the organisers of industrial action from economic tort liability is conditional on the holding of a secret ballot of the workers concerned and the law is highly prescriptive as to what must appear on the ballot paper, such as the requirement that the following statement must, without being qualified or commented upon by anything else on the ballot paper, appear on every ballot paper: "If you take part in a strike or other industrial action, you may be in breach of your contract of employment". Moreover, in the United Kingdom, the ballot ceases to be effective at the end of a four week period beginning with the date of the ballot.

Section 14(2) of the 1990 Act stipulates that the rules of every trade union shall contain a provision that:

(a) the union shall not organise, participate in, sanction or support a strike or other industrial action without a secret ballot, entitlement to vote on which shall be accorded equally to all members whom it is reasonable to believe will be called upon to engage in the strike or other industrial action;

(b) the union shall take reasonable steps to ensure that every member entitled to vote in the ballot votes without interference from, or constraint imposed by, the union or any of its members, officials or employees and, so far as is reasonably possible, that such members shall be given a fair opportunity of voting;

(c) the committee of management or other controlling authority of a trade union shall have full discretion in relation to organising, participating in, sanctioning or supporting a strike or other industrial action notwithstanding that the majority of those voting in the ballot, including an aggregate ballot referred to in paragraph (d), favour such strike or other industrial action;

(d) the committee of management or other controlling authority of a trade union shall not organise, participate in, sanction or support a strike or other industrial action against the wishes of a majority of its members voting in a secret ballot, except where, in the case of ballots by more than one trade union, an aggregate majority of all the votes cast, favours such strike or other industrial action;

(e) where the outcome of a secret ballot conducted by a trade union which is affiliated to the Irish Congress of Trade Unions or, in the case of ballots by more than one such trade union, an aggregate majority of all the votes cast, is in favour of supporting a strike organised by another trade union, a decision to take such supportive action shall not be implemented unless the action has been sanctioned by the Irish Congress of Trade Unions;

(f) as soon as practicable after the conduct of a secret ballot the trade union shall take reasonable steps to make known to its members entitled to vote in the ballot:

    1. the number of ballot papers issued,

    2. the number of votes cast,

    3. the number of votes in favour of the proposal,

    4. the number of votes against the proposal, and,

    5. the number of spoilt votes.

Although the language is mandatory, the provisions are essentially permissive. The decision when and how to hold the ballot will be decided by the union's rules. The decision as to the question or questions that are to be asked is also that of the union. Nor is there any stated limit as to how long the mandate conferred by the ballot is to last.

Crucially, the Act does not outlaw "unofficial" action. What is outlawed by section 17 of the 1990 Act is action taken in disregard of or contrary to the outcome of a secret ballot. The immunities are still available to union members taking industrial action without holding a ballot. The consequence of taking such action, however, is that the restrictions contained in section 19 on the availability of interim and interlocutory injunctions will not apply.

Injunctions

These restrictions are designed to cut down the number of "labour injunctions". Much of the dissatisfaction and frustration which has manifested itself in the past in non-compliance with court orders and the consequent jailing of trade union members for contempt of court can be traced to the frequency with which injunctions were sought and granted in trade disputes.

An interim injunction may be sought *ex parte* by a plaintiff in a matter of urgency and there is no requirement that any steps be taken with a view to securing that notice of the application and an opportunity of being heard be given to the defendants. Such injunctions are usually for a 48–72 hour period, although they tend to last somewhat longer, often being continued pending the hearing of the interlocutory application. Applications for interlocutory injunctions, however, are heard on notice to the defendants and on the basis of affidavit evidence. If granted, the injunction continues to the full hearing of the action which could be as much as eighteen months away. The object of an interlocutory injunction is to prevent further injury to the plaintiff until the legality of the defendants' action has been finally pronounced upon.

Even with the clarifications effected by the 1990 Act, it would be relatively easy for employers to obtain interim and interlocutory injunctive relief. Once a conclusion is reached that the plaintiff has raised a fair question to be tried at the hearing of the action in which, if he succeeded, he would be entitled to a permanent injunction, the courts will not express any view on the strength of the contending submissions but will consider first whether the plaintiff can be adequately compensated by damages in the event of his being refused an injunction and succeeding in the action. Here the courts will ask whether damages will be an adequate remedy and whether there is a defendant liable to pay such damages who is able to do so. In all cases a plaintiff employer's loss will be purely financial and thus damages, in theory, would be an adequate remedy. However the combination of an inability to pay on the part of the individual trade union members and the immunity from liability on the part of their trade union makes it extremely improbable that plaintiffs will be able to obtain adequate compensation in the event of their establishing that the industrial action was unlawful. The court will therefore consider whether, in the event of the injunction being granted, the defendants can be adequately compensated for any loss they would suffer in the event of it being found that the action was lawful. Even though the courts will accept that part of the defendants' loss would not be financial the courts invariably hold that the balance of convenience favours granting an injunction.

Section 19 of the 1990 Act, however, has altered the approach of the courts to labour injunctions. Where a secret ballot has been held in accordance with section 14 and at least one week's notice of industrial action has been given, the employer will not be entitled to seek an injunction without giving notice to the union and the workers concerned. This provision thus prevents an employer seeking *ex parte* relief. The section further provides that an interlocutory injunction will not be granted restraining a strike or industrial action where, in addition to holding a secret ballot and giving due notice, the union establishes a fair case that it was acting in contemplation or furtherance of a trade dispute. The balance of convenience is thus irrelevant. This is well illustrated by the decision of Murphy J. in June 1993 in which he refused to grant an injunction to Bus Éireann restraining a one-day national strike organised by SIPTU (see *The Irish Times*, June 18, 1993).

Dispute Resolution Machinery

The 1990 Act also effects considerable changes in the institutional machinery for the prevention and resolution of disputes; changes which are likely to be more important than the trade dispute provisions in terms of the Act's impact on the handling of industrial relations conflict.

The principal feature of the Industrial Relations Act 1946 was the establishment of the Labour Court as an independent adjudicating body charged with the task of promoting harmonious industrial relations. The Labour Court fulfilled this function both by providing a conciliation service and by investigating trade disputes and making recommendations towards their settlement. Although it was intended that the reference of a dispute to the Court should be reserved for only the most serious and intractable disputes, a large number of essentially trivial disputes were being referred without the parties engaging in full negotiations at local level.

It was hoped that the establishment of the Labour Relations Commission would reverse this trend and restore the original purpose and status of the Labour Court; that of being the "final authoritative tribunal in industrial relations matters" whose recommendations would once again be documents "with great moral authority" (see Ahern, 1989). The Commission's main aim is to encourage a more pro-active approach to dispute resolution and prevention, with the main responsibility being shifted back to the parties themselves.

The 1990 Act provides that, except where there is specific provision for the direct reference of trade disputes to the Labour Court, trade disputes shall first be referred to the Commission. The Act goes on to provide that the Court will not normally investigate a dispute unless it receives a report from the Commission to the effect that the Commission is satisfied that no further efforts on its part will advance the resolution of the dispute and the parties have requested the Court to investigate. Section 38 of the Act empowers the Minister for Enterprise and Employment, where he is of the opinion that a trade dispute, actual or apprehended, affects the public interest or is of special importance, to refer the matter either to the Commission or the Court. This is contrary to the recommendations of the Commission of Inquiry on Industrial Relations who were of the view that the intervention of a body such as the Labour Court in disputes at the direct behest of the Minister might lead workers and employers to doubt the extent of its independence in other matters.

As well as taking over the Labour Court's conciliation service, the Commission is also empowered, amongst other things, to provide an industrial relations advisory service and to prepare codes of practice relevant to industrial relations. Three such codes of practice have been promulgated to date. The first was on *Disputes Procedures, including Disputes in Essential Services* (Statutory Instrument No. 1 of 1992), the second was on *The Duties and Responsibilities of Employee Representatives and the Protection and Facilities to be afforded them by their Employer* (Statutory Instrument No. 169 of 1993) and the third was on *Disciplinary Procedures* (Statutory Instrument No. 117 of 1996). Although section 42(5) of the 1990 Act provides that a failure on the part of any person to observe any provision of a code of practice shall not of itself render him liable to any proceedings, section 42(4) provides that a code of practice shall be "admissible in evidence" in any proceedings before a court, the Labour Court, the Labour Relations Commission, the Employment Appeals Tribunal, a Rights Commissioner or an equality officer, and the subsection goes on to provide that any provision of the code which appears to the court, body or officer concerned to be relevant to any question arising in the proceedings shall be taken into account in determining that question.

CONCLUSION

It has been argued that the changes enacted in the 1990 Act have a "restrictive rather than reformative effect on industrial relations law, to the detriment of trade unions" (Wilkinson, 1991) and considerable criticism has been expressed by some trade unions over some of the trade dispute provisions. Such concerns are, as yet, unfounded. There is little evidence to date for the proposition that the civil courts are interpreting the trade dispute provisions in a manner inimical to workers, although it must be conceded that, in the event of a dispute, a trade union official is now much more likely to seek legal advice before anything else. More importantly, however, the increased emphasis given to conciliation through the establishment of the Labour Relations Commission should ensure that more cases are settled at that level and fewer cases heard by the Labour Court. For, if the Commission is successful in providing a framework for the peaceful resolution of disputes and in convincing employers and trade unions that the primary responsibility for resolving disputes rests with them, then recourse to the law courts should not be necessary.

References

Ahern, B. (1989): *Industrial Relations in the 1990s: Consensus and Participation*, Fourteenth Countess Markievicz Memorial Lecture, Dublin: Irish Association of Industrial Relations.

Ahern, B. (1991): "The Industrial Relations Act, 1990, *Journal of the Irish Society for Labour Law*, 9: 25.

Casey, J. (1972): "Reform of Collective Bargaining Law", *Irish Jurist*, 17: 1.

Horgan, J. (1985): "The Failure of Legal Enforcement — A Review of the Registration of Agreements in the Labour Court", *Journal of the Irish Society for Labour Law*, 4: 28.

Kelly, A. and Brannick, T. (1989): "Strikes in Ireland: Measurement, Incidence and Trends" in T. Murphy (ed.), *Industrial Relations in Ireland: Contemporary Issues and Developments*, Dublin: Department of Industrial Relations, University College Dublin.

Kelly, A. and Roche, W.K. (1983): "Institutional Reform in Irish Industrial Relations", *Studies*, 72: 221.

Kerr, A. (1991a): *The Trade Union and Industrial Relations Acts of Ireland*, London: Sweet and Maxwell.

Kerr, A. (1991b): "Irish Industrial Relations Legislation: Consensus not Compulsion", *Industrial Law Journal*, 20: 240.

Kerr, A. and Whyte, G. (1985): *Irish Trade Union Law*, Abingdon: Professional Books.

von Prondzynski, F. (1987): *Freedom of Association and Industrial Relations*, London: Mansell Publishing.

Wedderburn, K. (1980): "Industrial Relations and the Courts", *Industrial Law Journal*, 9: 65.

Whyte, G. (1995): "The Constitutional of Labour Law", *Journal of the Irish Society for Labour Law*. 10:208

Wilkinson, B. (1991): "The Irish Industrial Relations Act 1990 — Corporatism and Conflict Control", *Industrial Law Journal*, 20: 21.

CHAPTER 11

STATUTORY EMPLOYMENT PROTECTION

Nuala Butler

INTRODUCTION

The nature of the employment relationship causes it to sit somewhat
uneasily within the general framework of our legal system. Traditionally, the collective relationship between an employer (or group of
employers) and his employees, through their trade union, has fallen
outside legal structures, a phenomenon known as "voluntarism". On
the other hand, the relationship between an individual employer and
his employee has developed from being dependant on the "status" of
the parties (that is, "master and servant") to being governed by the
laws of contract and, in disputes between the parties, the courts will
apply normal contractual principles. The contractual view of the employment relationship is based on the premise that both parties are
entering into the bargain and fixing the terms of the contract from an
equal position. This view is clearly at odds with the economic realities
of the employment situation, both in a general sense but particularly
in times of high unemployment. Over the last 25 years or so, the contractual model of the employment relationship has been profoundly
changed by a series of legislative provisions which take this inequality into account by granting to the employee a number of statutory
employment rights and imposing corollary obligations on the employer. These statutes do not alter the contractual basis of the relationship but do impose some contractual terms and regulate the
manner in which these terms themselves can be altered by the parties to the contract. This chapter examines the general nature of
statutory employment protection, the particular rights conferred on
employees by Irish statutes and the legal machinery provided for the
enforcement of these rights.

The earliest statutes regulating employment (as distinct from industrial relations) adopted the formula of imposing standards on the

employer and making the failure to comply with these standards a criminal offence (for example, The Factories Act, 1955). These Acts usually provided for the prosecution of these criminal offences by the Minister for Labour (now the Minister for Enterprise and Employment) but did not create rights as such for the individual employee. The enactment of the Redundancy Payments Act in 1967 marked a change and statutes regulating employment began to frame the legislation in a manner which provided specific rights for individual employees and an adjudicative machinery through which these rights could be enforced against individual employers. While some of the statutes relied on the ordinary courts to enforce these rights (for example, the Holidays (Employees) Act, 1973), it was recognised that the nature of employment litigation, coupled with the traditional attitude of the courts towards employment contracts and the unequal resources available to employers and employees to pursue litigation, required special adjudicative bodies. The bodies established or entrusted to deal with such statutory employment rights, namely the Employment Appeals Tribunal and the Labour Court, are designed to handle cases quickly and cheaply and to have expert knowledge of the specialised subject matter. However, the system has developed in an ad hoc manner and there is not one overall body to which all claims arising out of the employment relationship can be brought. In fact, an employee who is dismissed through sexual discrimination may find herself/himself suing her/his employer for arrears of wages and holiday pay in the District Court, for minimum notice in the Employment Appeals Tribunal (EAT) and for discriminatory dismissal in the Labour Court. Clearly, there is a case to be made for rationalising the system so that all statutory claims arising out of the one employment can be dealt with by one body at one sitting.

We have seen that the creation of statutory employment protection did not supplant the contractual basis of the employment relationship. Instead, legislation treats the contract of employment as a vehicle into which the State can imply statutory terms. The existence and termination of the relationship depends on agreement between the parties but the minimal substance of the relationship depends on statutory norms outside of the parties' individual freedom to contract. The law stipulates a minimum level of protection (also known as "threshold" or "floor" of rights) and prohibits the parties from contracting out of this minimum level. However, the parties are free to negotiate and agree on higher levels of protection — either individually or collectively — although any higher level agreed between the parties will not be enforceable through the statutory mechanism guaranteeing the threshold level. The advantage of fixing a minimum level of protection by statute is that all employees, whether or not they are working in industries that have organised trade unions, are guaranteed legal protection for that threshold level. The disadvantage is that where levels are fixed (especially financial compensation) the levels fixed are usually low and may of themselves act as a disincentive to employees to negotiate a higher level of protection.

Statutory employment rights, unlike for example, constitutional rights, are not absolute. So, while the Unfair Dismissals Act, 1977 is generally said to confer on an employee the right not to be unfairly dismissed from his or her job, in fact it does not prevent an employer from doing exactly that. Instead, the employees so-called "right" not to be unfairly dismissed becomes a right of action against the former employer and, usually, a claim for compensation. Similarly, the "right" under the Redundancy Payments Acts, 1967-91, is a right to claim compensation in the event of a redundancy; there is no right not to be made redundant and no right of employees to have input into managerial level decisions on redundancy. It is important to remember that, despite being termed "rights", the benefits conferred by statute on employers are not positive rights, but rather a right of action or remedy in the event of certain infringements taking place.

Finally, before turning to examine the contents of particular statutes, it is interesting to place the development of statutory employment protection in Ireland in the 1970s and 1980s in its legal and international context. Firstly, statutory regulation is not a feature exclusive to employment law. Since World War II, we have seen increasing legislative regulation of various aspects of modern life — for example, taxation, social welfare, planning, and road traffic legislation are all part of the same phenomenon. The creation of bodies outside the ordinary court system to resolve employment disputes arising under the legislation is mirrored in bodies like An Bord Pleanála and the elaborate appeals machinery within the Department of Social Welfare. Therefore, the statutory regulation of employment and the manner in which such regulation is effected is part of a wider trend of increased specialisation in the law. Secondly, many of the statutes dealt with in this article were enacted by the Oireachtas in response to international obligations which required the State to make certain protections available within our legal system. In particular, the Redundancy Payments Act, 1967, the Minimum Notice and Terms of Employment Act, 1973, and the Unfair Dismissals Act, 1977, were enacted to comply with International Labour Office Record Number 119 on the Termination of Employment at the Initiative of the Employer. The Anti-Discrimination (Pay) Act, 1974, and the Employment Equality Act, 1977, on the other hand, were enacted to fulfil specific European Community obligations arising under Directive 75/117 on equal pay and Directive 76/207 on equal treatment, themselves implementing the guarantee of equality between the sexes contained in Article 119 of the Treaty of Rome. It appears that successive Irish governments have been slow to take the initiative in enacting any employment legislation that does not have its basis in an international commitment.

EMPLOYMENT APPEALS TRIBUNAL

The Employment Appeals Tribunal (EAT), was established in 1967 under the Redundancy Payments Act. Originally called the Redundancy Appeals Tribunal, its sole jurisdiction was over disputes arising out of the Redundancy Payments Acts. However, as the scope of its jurisdiction was widened to include other employment matters, it was renamed the Employment Appeals Tribunal in 1977. The EAT belongs to a category of bodies known as "quasi-judicial bodies" or "administrative tribunals". These bodies exercise functions that fall between the pure judicial function exercised by the Courts and the administrative functions exercised by State Departments on behalf of the government. The role of the EAT contains a large element of independent adjudication together with an element of administration of statutory schemes. The latter, the administration of statutory schemes, is seen in the EAT's jurisdiction under the Redundancy Payments Acts, 1967-1991, and the Protection of Employees (Employers' Insolvency) Act, 1984, which is not limited to deciding on disputes between employees and employers but also covers disputes between employees or employers and the Minister for Enterprise and Employment concerning issues such as the payment of claims or rebates out of the Social Insurance Fund.

The Tribunal consists of a chairman, 17 vice-chairmen with legal qualifications and a panel of 40 lay members. The panel is composed of equal numbers of persons nominated by each "side" of industry. The ICTU nominates 20 members representative of employees' interests who bring to bear on Tribunal determinations their experience of working conditions and involvement in trade union activities at varying levels. Similarly, 20 members are nominated by employers' associations (such as IBEC, various professional bodies and farmers' associations) who represent the employers' view of industrial affairs and bring managerial experience to the EAT. The panel members are often spoken of as employee or employer representatives, but in fact they do not represent either management or unions in the cases that come before the Tribunal. They do not have to report back to and are not accountable to the bodies that appointed them. The chairman must be a practising barrister or solicitor with at least seven years experience. There is no requirement that the vice-chairmen be legally qualified, although to date, all vice-chairmen have been lawyers but not necessarily with seven years experience. The EAT sits in three-person divisions, each division consisting of a chairman (or vice-chairman) and two panel members, one from each "side" of industry. All three members of a division have an equal say in the outcome of a case. The composition of the EAT represents a balance between the practical experience of the panel members and the legal guidance of the chairman.

At present, the EAT hears cases arising under nine different statutes: redundancy cases under the Redundancy Payments Acts 1967-1991; claims for minimum notice under the Minimum Notice and Terms of Employment Act, 1973; unfair dismissals claims under the Unfair Dismissals Acts, 1977-1993 and The Maternity Protection Act, 1994, statutory claims against insolvent employers under the Protection of Employees (Employers' Insolvency Act), 1984; disputes as to the entitlements of part-time employers under the Worker Protection (Regular Part-time Employees) Act, 1991; appeals on the issue of deductions made by employers from employees' wages under the Payment of Wages Act, 1991; appeals on disputes arising from an employer's obligation to furnish a written statement of an employee's terms of employment under the Terms of Employment (Information) Act, 1994 and appeals on disputes as to an employee's entitlement to adoptive leave under the Adoptive Leave Act, 1995.

The number of claims referred to the Tribunal under each statute is vastly different. Some, such as the Minimum Notice and Terms of Employment Act, 1973, generate a very large number of relatively non-contentious minor claims; others, such as the Maternity Protection Act, 1994, almost by definition, will generate relatively few claims, but those that do reach the EAT involve substantial factual disputes and are usually quite contentious. The number of cases referred under each statute in 1994 (the last year for which official figures are available) is shown in Table 11.1. However, it is interesting to realise that this does not reflect the spread of Tribunal work as the bulk of time is spent in hearing unfair dismissals cases. On average, each division of the EAT is scheduled to hear two unfair dismissals cases each sitting day — one in the morning and one in the afternoon.

Along with these, a division is also allocated a number of shorter cases, usually either minimum notice or redundancy, to be heard in the morning session. Quite frequently, a large number of minimum notice or redundancy claims against the one employer will arise on the closure of a business and these claims are usually disposed of at one sitting since the circumstances giving rise to each claim will be virtually identical. On the other hand, unfair dismissals cases generally arise because of an employer's decision to dismiss one particular employee and often there will be serious conflict on the factual issues in dispute between the parties requiring evidence from a number of witnesses.

TABLE 11.1: SUMMARY OF APPEALS DEALT WITH BY THE EAT IN 1994

Act	Appeals referred	Appeals disposed of
Redundancy Payments	737	766
Minimum Notice and Terms of Employment	2772	2483
Unfair Dismissals	1133	1086
Maternity (Protection of Employees)	29	25
Protection of Employees (Employers Insolvency)	69	75
Worker Protection (Regular Part-time Employees)	38	26
Total Appeals	4778	4461

Source: EAT Annual Report 1994

Notes: 1. Not all appeals referred in 1994 were disposed of in 1994 and some appeals disposed of in 1994 were referred in 1993.
2. No figures were given in the 1994 Annual Report for claims under the Payment of Wages Act, 1991 and no claims were made under the Terms of Employment (Information) Act, 1991.
3. Maternity claims heard in 1994 were referred under the Maternity (Protection of Employees) Act, 1981.

The EAT was supposed to provide a speedy, informal and cheap forum for the determination of employment disputes, however, in recent years, it has been increasingly accused of "legalism" and concentrating on the legal and technical aspects of cases in a formal and inflexible manner. To some extent, "legalism" is an inevitable result of the adversarial nature of an EAT hearing where each side is under pressure to present its case to its best advantage. While parties are entitled to appear in person, it is more usual to be represented, either by a trade union or employer's association, by lawyers or, with the permission of the Tribunal, by some other person. Obviously, if both parties are represented by lawyers, the hearing will tend to become more formal and more akin to a court hearing. If either of the parties is unrepresented, there is an onus on the EAT itself to ensure that all of the facts are fully elicited and examined.

Whilst trade union representation is the most popular type of representation for employees, there is a marked difference in the level of trade union representation under the various statutes. Under the Redundancy and Minimum Notice Acts nearly 55 per cent of all employees who are represented are represented by a trade union official, which is not surprising when you consider the collective nature of those acts. On the other hand, less than 27 per cent of represented employees have trade union representation under the Unfair Dismissals and Maternity Acts, which is probably reflective of the weaker collective element to disputes under these statutes. (Interestingly, the balance of trade union representation has changed since the first edition of this book when the figures quoted for 1992 were 65 per cent and 15 per cent). Employers resort to representation by employers' associations in less than 20 per cent of all cases in which they are represented and the vast majority of employers choose to be represented by lawyers. In redundancy and minimum notice cases, a large number of employers either represent themselves or, in the event of their being insolvent, are represented by a liquidator or receiver. The figures for representation of parties before the EAT under all of the statutes during 1994 is set out in Table 11.2 and it can be seen that there is an overall disparity between the levels of legal representation of employers and employees except under the Unfair Dismissals and Maternity Protection Acts where the figures are remarkably even. Interestingly, the statutes under which employees have their highest level of trade union representation (the Redundancy and Minimum Notice Acts) are also those under which they have their highest levels of success.

Some of the nine statutes listed above confer substantive rights on employees — such as the right to a redundancy payment, the right not to be unfairly dismissed or the right to return to work after maternity leave. However, others are of a more procedural or administrative character. In particular, a statute such as the Worker Protection

TABLE 11.2: REPRESENTATION AT EAT HEARINGS DURING 1994

Statute	Employees			Employers		
	Trade Unions	Legal	Total	Employer Assoc.	Legal	Total
Redundancy Payments	215	158	373	50	181	231
Minimum Notice	394	443	837	85	487	572
Unfair Dismissals	231	630	861	132	654	786
Maternity (Protection of Employees)	2	16	18	0	14	14
Protection of Employees (Employees Insolvency)	9	10	19	0	0	0
Worker Protection (Part-time Employees	0	6	6	0	11	11
Payment of Wages	1	3	4	1	9	10

Source: EAT Annual Report, 1994.

Notes: 1. The low level of representation of employers under the Redundancy, Minimum Notice and Insolvency Acts is due to two factors: firstly, insolvent companies are represented by a receiver or liquidator and secondly, one employer frequently faces multiple claims under these Acts.
2. Maternity cases heard in 1994 were referred under the Maternity (Protection of Employees) Act, 1981.

(Regular Part-Time Employees) Act, 1991, does not create any new rights but changes the procedural rules under which existing substantive rights are applied, in this case, by reducing the number of hours per week (to eight) which an employee is required to work in order to qualify for protection under various employment statutes (most, but not all, of which themselves fall under the jurisdiction of the EAT). The Protection of Employees (Employers' Insolvency) Act, 1984, is essentially administrative in character in that it allows employees who have established a statutory claim for a sum of money from an insolvent employer to be paid by the Minister out of the Social Insurance Fund. Disputes between the Minister and a claimant can be referred to the EAT, but the vast bulk of claims under this statute are processed routinely by the Department of Enterprise and Employment. However, the EAT is frequently asked to determine claims which are in effect being conceded by the liquidator of an insolvent company in order that a claim may be made from the Fund.

A different procedural format appears in some of the more recent legislation such as the Terms of Employment (Information) Act, 1994, the Adoptive Leave Act, 1995 and the Payment of Wages Act, 1991. Under these statutes a dispute between the parties is initially referred to a rights commissioner from whose recommendation an appeal lies to the EAT. The rights commissioner service traditionally has had an industrial relations orientation and a rights commissioner will generally seek to resolve the dispute between the parties rather than adjudicate on each parties' rights. The hearings are informal and private with a high level of trade union participation. It is rare for lawyers to appear before a rights commissioner, even on behalf of an employer. This procedural change may represent a move towards a view of statutory employment rights as a collective, industrial matter rather than an individual, contractual matter. However, even if such a view is nascent it is still confined to a particular type of subject matter, generally of a more minor and technical nature. For example, disputes as to rights under the Maternity Protection Act, 1994, are referred to a rights commissioner, but dismissals under the same act are treated as unfair dismissals and are referred directly to the EAT unless both parties agree to the case being dealt with by a rights commissioner.

STATUTES CONFERRING SUBSTANTIVE RIGHTS

For the purposes of this chapter, it is intended to concentrate principally on those statutes which confer substantive rights, being the Redundancy Payments Acts, 1967-1991; the Minimum Notice and Terms of Employment Act, 1973; the Unfair Dismissals Acts, 1977-1993; and the Maternity Protection Act, 1994. The nature of the rights conferred by these statutes and their application and enforcement by the EAT will now be examined.

The Redundancy Payments Acts, 1967–91

The Redundancy Payments Acts set up a scheme whereby qualified employees can receive a lump sum payment (known as a "redundancy payment") on being made redundant by their employers and employers can recover a portion of the monies so paid by way of rebate from the Social Insurance Fund maintained in the Department of Enterprise and Employment. In order to qualify for a redundancy payment an employee must have worked for his employer for a minimum period of two years and must have been dismissed by reason of redundancy. A redundancy situation will clearly arise where a place of employment is totally or partially closed down so that the employee's job no longer exists. However, the circumstances may be less clear, for example, where an employer, due to a re-organisation of his business or modernisation of his work practices, has a decreased need for employees of a particular kind but the business itself is kept going. The general test is whether or not an employee is replaced — if he is then the probability is that a redundancy situation does not exist; if he is not then the probability is that a redundancy situation does exist. Other factors such as the turnover and/or profits of the employer's business may also be relevant. Finally, there are special provisions dealing with circumstances where employees are laid off or placed on short time.

An employee who is made redundant has a statutory right to a redundancy payment consisting of one week's pay plus half a week's pay for each year of employment between the ages of 16 and 41 years, plus a further week's pay for each year of employment over the age of 41. In the event of a redundancy situation arising, it is open to employees or their trade union to negotiate for higher levels of redundancy payments and this frequently happens in industries with strong union organisation. If an employer makes a statutory redundancy payment to a qualified employee, he can claim a rebate of up to 60 per cent from the Social Insurance Fund. In the event of an insolvent employer being unable to pay a redundancy payment, the payment can be made directly to the employee from the Fund. It is important to note that the employer's right to a rebate and the employee's right to a payment from the Fund in the event of insolvency only relate to the minimum statutory entitlements; higher levels of redundancy payment negotiated directly between the employer and his employees are not protected in this manner.

The redundancy scheme is administered by the Department of Enterprise and Employment and most claims, being non-contentious, do not involve the EAT. Claims come before the EAT where the employer disputes the employee's entitlement to a redundancy payment or, if the fact of entitlement is conceded, where the amount of the payment is disputed. Issues arising before the EAT include disputes over the length of time an employee was employed, whether or not he was offered "suitable alternative employment" and whether as a matter of fact an employee was laid off or placed on short time. Cases also arise where an employer or employee challenges the decision of the Minister or of a Deciding Officer with regard to contributions to the Fund or rebates from the Fund, or a Deciding Officer may refer a redundancy matter to the EAT for a decision. These latter provisions are only rarely invoked and most redundancy appeals deal directly with employee versus employer situations, usually with an employee claiming to be entitled to a payment which the employer has failed or refused to pay.

Minimum Notice and Terms of Employment Act, 1973

The Minimum Notice and Terms of Employment Act, 1973, grants employees the right to certain minimum notice of dismissal from their employers, or alternatively, payment in lieu of such notice. (The Act also grants employees the right to have the terms of their employment set out in writing — but the EAT does not deal with this part of the Act.) The amount of notice to which an employee is entitled will depend on the length of his service with the particular employer and increases proportionately with his service so that an employee who has worked between 13 weeks and 2 years is entitled to 1 week's notice whereas an employee who has worked more than 15 years is entitled to 8 weeks' notice and with increasing periods of notice due depending on the length of service between 13 weeks and 15 years.

In theory, the principal right conferred by the Act is the right to actual notice, but if the employer defaults in giving notice, the only remedy the EAT can award is payment in lieu. Unlike the right to a redundancy payment which arises automatically once an employee has been made redundant, the right to payment in lieu of notice only arises if the employee can prove actual loss. Therefore, an employee who is dismissed without notice but who immediately secures another job at the same or higher wage, so that he incurs no loss, will not be awarded a minimum notice payment.

The Act does not affect an employer's traditional right to dismiss an employee without notice for reasons of serious misconduct. Many of the contested cases under the 1973 Act deal with the factual issue of whether the employee's conduct was such that it entitled the employer to dismiss him without notice. However, the majority of minimum notice cases that come before the EAT arise in circumstances where the employer company is insolvent and the factual entitlement to notice payments is not disputed by the receiver or liquidator but where it is necessary to have a determination of the EAT in order for the employees to be paid directly from the Social Insurance Fund.

Unfair Dismissals Acts, 1977–93

The Unfair Dismissals Acts provide employees with a right to claim redress, including the possible remedy of re-employment, in the event of being unfairly dismissed by their employer. The Acts protect employees from unfair dismissal by laying down criteria by which a dismissal can be judged to be unfair and by implication setting the standards which must be complied with by the employer in carrying out a dismissal. Interestingly, the initial objective of the 1977 Act was to reduce the number of days lost to industrial action because of disputes over dismissals by providing employees with individual remedies that would obviate the need for collective action. The Acts apply to almost all employees who have one year's continuous service with an employer, unless the dismissal is due to pregnancy or trade union activity and certain other cases in which the one year qualifying period does not apply.

Under the Acts, a dismissal is presumed to be unfair unless the employer can establish grounds justifying the dismissal. This places the legal onus of proving the case on the employer, and usually he attempts to do this by establishing one of the statutory grounds that justify dismissal under the Act such as the employee's lack of capability, competency or qualifications; the employee's conduct; redundancy; the fact that the continued employment of the employee would contravene some other statutory requirement or some other substantial ground. Under the 1993 Act, the EAT can take account of the reasonableness of the employer's conduct leading to the decision to dismiss and also the failure of the employer to observe any agreed disciplinary procedures.

In the event of an employee being successful, the Tribunal can award either compensation or re-employment as a remedy. Compensation is by far the more common remedy awarded in roughly 75 per cent of successful cases, usually because of the practical difficulties in the implementation of an award of re-employment. There is a ceiling on the compensation that can be awarded of a maximum of 104 weeks' wages. In 1994, the average award was just under £5,000. Compensation is awarded in respect of an employee's actual loss so that if an employee secures alternative employment before the hearing, the EAT can only compensate him for actual periods of unemployment and for any difference in wages between the old and new jobs. Since the 1993 Act, there is a statutory exception to this principle in that a "basic award" of up to 4 weeks' pay may be awarded where the employee suffered no financial loss if it is "just and equitable in the circumstances", that is, if the conduct of the employer warrants some punishment. Prior to 1993, there was some disagreement as to whether social welfare payments and income tax rebates received by employees after dismissal should be taken into account and set off against loss of earnings when calculating the compensation to be awarded — the general practice was to make the deductions. The 1993 Act clarified the position by clearly providing that both such payments should be disregarded when calculating an employee's actual loss.

Re-employment as a remedy can take two different forms. Re-instatement involves the employee going back to the same job on the same terms and conditions he enjoyed immediately prior to his dismissal. Re-instatement takes effect retrospectively and preserves the employee's contract of employment and continuity of service so that the employee will be entitled to arrears of wages for the period between the dismissal and the determination. Re-engagement is more flexible in that the employee is returned to the same employer but not necessarily on the same terms or conditions. It allows the EAT to set out the terms on which the employee is to be re-employed to take account of, for example, the fact that he may by his conduct have contributed towards his own dismissal. The legal effect of re-engagement is to end one contract of employment and start another.

The Tribunal tends to examine the unfair dismissal cases that come before it from two different perspectives. Firstly, it looks to the substantive merits of the employer's decision to dismiss including the reasons put forward by the employer as justifying the dismissal, the reasonableness of both parties' behaviour, etc. However, even if a dismissal is substantively justified it may still be an unfair dismissal if the employer has not applied adequate procedures in carrying out his decision to dismiss. Over the past 15 years, through its case law the EAT has developed detailed guidelines for the correct procedures to be adopted in disciplinary and dismissal matters. These guidelines, although detailed, are not absolute and standards may vary, depending, for example, on the size of the employer's business, the number of employees employed and the employer's established practices. Generally speaking, an employee is entitled to warnings if his conduct or work performance is unsatisfactory; this is to allow him the opportunity to improve before the ultimate sanction of dismissal is imposed. If the employer is investigating specific complaints against an employee, the employee is entitled to notice of the allegations against him and an opportunity to put his side of the case before a final decision is taken. The employee is entitled to attend or be represented at any formal hearing to be held by the employer. The EAT may also have regard to any agreed disciplinary procedures that exist in the workplace.

Maternity Protection Act, 1994

A statutory right for female employees to take maternity leave from their employment was first introduced in Ireland by the Maternity (Protection of Employees) Act, 1981 — although many employers had operated maternity leave schemes on a private basis prior to that date. However, the statutory scheme introduced by the 1981 Act was beset by technical problems and imposed mandatory procedural requirement (of which many employees were unaware) before a woman could exercise all of her rights under the Act. The 1981 Act has since been replaced by the Maternity Protection Act, 1994, which relaxed these procedural requirements and also introduced a number of additional subsidiary rights.

The right to maternity leave is essentially two fold: firstly the right to paid leave for a period of up to 14 weeks with an optional 4 weeks unpaid leave and secondly, the right to return to work at the end of maternity leave. (The employee is not paid directly by her employer, but receives a pay related maternity allowance by way of social insurance). There are other minor rights such as the right to time off for ante- and post-natal care. An employers refusal to allow an employee to return to work after maternity leave constitutes an unfair dismissal under the Unfair Dismissals Acts, as does the dismissal of an employee for exercising any of the other legal rights conferred by the 1994 Act. On hearing a claim under the 1994 Act, the Tribunal has the same jurisdiction to award the same remedies as under the Unfair Dismissals Acts.

The 1994 Act also implemented European measures to protect the health and safety of pregnant and breastfeeding employees and employees who have recently given birth. If the employment poses a risk to such an employee and the employee cannot be moved to suitable alternative work on the expiry of protective leave as on the expiry of maternity leave. An employed father may be entitled to a period of leave if the mother of the child dies in or immediately after childbirth.

The Adoptive Leave Act, 1995, gives adoptive parents equivalent statutory rights as those given to natural parents under the 1994 Act. An employed adoptive mother or a sole male adopter will be entitled to a period of 10 weeks adoptive leave (with an optional additional 4 weeks unpaid leave) and will be entitled to return to work on the expiry of the adoptive leave.

Outcome of EAT Cases
There is a marked difference between the rates of successful claims under the various statutes. Under the Redundancy Payments Acts and the Minimum Notice and Terms of Employment Acts, where the EAT is not asked to evaluate the reasonableness of either sides behaviour but just to decide if all the requirements of a given legal situation exist, the success rate is high. At present, over 90 per cent of decided minimum notice claims and over 75 per cent of decided redundancy claims are successful and the success rate has increased steadily since both statutes were enacted. This is quite expected as the terms of both statutes are clear and it is a straight forward matter to advise a claimant if his claim should be pursued. Employees find it more difficult to bring a successful claim under either the Unfair Dismissals Acts or the Maternity legislation. Under these statutes, just over 50 per cent of the decided claims (excluding those settled or withdrawn) are decided in the employee's favour. Of the remaining cases where the employee loses, it appears that in roughly 10 per cent of cases the employee fails because he/she falls outside the scope of the statute so the Tribunal has no jurisdiction to hear the claim. In another 10 per cent of cases, the employee fails to establish as a fact that he was dismissed at all. In the remaining cases, the dismissal itself is found to be fair. While the success rate of unfair dismissal claims before the EAT is lower than under the other statutes, it is fair to assume that in the vast bulk of cases which are settled or withdrawn (nearly 61 per cent of cases in 1994 were settled or withdrawn prior to hearing) the employee is in fact paid some compensation. Table 11.3 shows the results of claims under these four statutes at intervals over a 14-year period.

Employment Equality
During the same period in the mid-1970s that saw the enactment of the bulk of the legislation discussed above, legislation was introduced, prompted by our European Union obligations, to give effect to the principle of sexual equality in employment. This legislation, consisting of two statutes, the Anti-Discrimination (Pay) Act, 1974, and the Employment Equality Act, 1977 (which under s. 56(2) of the 1977 Act are to be construed together), effectively forms the statutory basis of an "equality code". Much like the redundancy, minimum notice and unfair dismissals legislation, these statutes are framed in a manner which confers express statutory rights on individual employees and which provides the procedural structures for adjudicating individual

TABLE 11.3: OUTCOMES OF CASES HEARD BY THE EAT IN SELECTED
YEARS BETWEEN 1980 AND 1994

Year	Cases Referred	Decided	Allowed	Dismissed	Employees' % Success
Redundancy Payments Act					
1980	676	295	205	90	70%
1986	961	557	418	139	75%
1992	687	426	333	93	78%
1994	737	477	336	141	70%
Minimum Notice and Terms of Employment Act					
1980	1,048	574	382	192	67%
1986[1]	5,028	4604	4325	279	94%
1992	4,469	3429	3201	228	93%
1994	2,772	1951	1634	317	84%
Unfair Dismissals Act					
1980	754	300	115	185	38%
1986	938	473	199	274	42%
1992	1,027	424	229	195	54%
1994	1,133	426	234	192	55%
Maternity (Protection of Employees) Act					
1983[2]	19	14	5	9	36%
1986	26	5	2	3	40%
1992	37	17	10	7	58%
1994	29	12	—	12	0%

Notes:
1. Note the large increase in the number of minimum notice cases brought after the enactment of the Protection of Employees (Employers' Insolvency) Act, 1984, which allowed employees of insolvent employers to recover notice payments from the Social Insurance Fund. Note also the higher success rate post–1984.
2. No figures are available for 1980 as this statute was only enacted in 1981; 1983 is the first full year for which figures are available.
3. Maternity cases up to 1994 were heard under the Maternity (Protection of Employees) Act, 1981.

claims arising from these statutory rights. However, the procedural framework provided under the Equality Acts is not, as might have been expected, that of the EAT as under the other statutes. Instead, disputes arising under the Equality Acts are dealt with by the Labour

Court, a body whose primary functions concern industrial relations and not adjudication. Finally, it should be noted that not all statutes dealing with what generally be considered employment equality fell within the jurisdiction of the Labour Court — we have already seen that the Maternity (Protection of Employees) Act, 1981, creates rights which are enforceable through the EAT.

It has already been noted that much Irish legislative activity in the 1970s in the field of employment protection was prompted by external factors and, in particular, by the obligations assumed by Ireland's entry into the European Community in 1973. Article 119 of the Treaty of Rome lays down the principle that men and women must receive "equal pay for equal work". Although this principle is essentially an expression of social policy its roots are economic in that those member states which had legislative guarantees of equal pay (for example, France) feared that their industries would be disadvantaged if exposed to competition from other states where industries benefited from the cheaper labour costs of paying separate male and female rates. The obligation imposed by Article 119 was subsequently developed further by Directive 75/117 on equal pay and Directive 76/207 on equal treatment. Eventually, the European Community's equality policy went further than basic employment equality and extended to cover equality of treatment in a whole range of social welfare and social insurance matters. Because of the direct European roots of our Equality Acts, the decisions of the European Court of Justice on Directives 75/117 and 76/207 have been of fundamental importance in the development, implementation and understanding of the Equality Acts in Ireland. In fact, because the European Court of Justice has tended to take an expansive and policy-based approach to the Directives, its decisions are of more assistance in applying the legislative principles than those of the Irish High Court which tend to be narrowly-based and legalistic.

Despite the imposition of a legislative "equality code" between 1974 and 1977, the acceptance and implementation of the principle of equality in employment has been a slow process which is not yet complete. Legislation alone cannot and has not broken the traditional attitudes that encourage women to become nurses, teachers, shop assistants and clerk-typists while men become managers, tradesmen and farmers. A legislative policy which imposes contractual obligations on employers in respect of their female employees is only one method by which such attitudes can be changed and such legislation will work to best effect when accompanied by a programme of education and training. For example, when the Equality Acts were introduced it emerged that they faced a hostile reaction not only from employers but also from male employees and quite often from trade unions who feared that the provision of equal pay and equal opportunities for women would result in lower pay and less opportunities for men. The law must also recognise that not all discrimination suffered by women in the workplace is caused by the actions of their employers but may result from deep-seated attitudes that pervade employment structures in general. For example, it was not until the Worker Protection (Regular Part-Time Employees) Act, 1991, that the protection afforded by various employment statutes was extended to cover part-time employees, the vast majority of whom are women and a large number of whom are married women. To date, there is still no structure, legislative or otherwise, which provides safe, accessible and reasonably-priced child care facilities for working mothers — the absence of which is felt to be a major hurdle in the progress of women in the workplace.

The enforcement mechanisms provided under the Equality Acts are broadly similar but not identical. Both utilise the same bodies for the investigation and determination of claims — Equality Officers of the Labour Relations Commission and the Labour Court — but procedures by which an application is made under the two statutes are slightly different. Under Section 7 of the 1974 Act, an equal pay dispute is referred directly to an Equality Officer who investigates and decides the claim. The Equality Officer's recommendation may be appealed to the Labour Court. Under Section 19 of the 1977 Act, a dispute as to whether someone has been discriminated against is referred to the Labour Court which may refer it to an Equality Officer for investigation and recommendation. This provision also contains an option whereby the Labour Court can refer the dispute to conciliation by an Industrial Relations Officer for settlement — although this option is almost never exercised and, invariably, equality disputes are referred to an Equality Officer from whose recommendation there lies an appeal to the Labour Court.

There is an exception to the normal practice of disputes being dealt with firstly by an Equality Officer in respect of claims of discriminatory dismissal under sections 26 and 27 of the 1977 Act. These are dealt with directly by the Labour Court without reference to an Equality Officer. A discriminatory dismissal is, of course, also likely to be an unfair dismissal under the Unfair Dismissals Act, 1977, and an employee with sufficient service (there is a one year service requirement under the Unfair Dismissals Act, but not under the Employment Equality Act) may choose to bring her case under either statute. There is a procedural advantage to bringing an unfair dismissal claim in that a dismissal is presumed to be unfair so that the employer must justify his actions. Under the Employment Equality Act, 1977, the employee bears the onus of establishing that the dismissal was, in fact, discriminatory. As against this, any compensation awarded under the Unfair Dismissals Act, 1977, is loss-based so the employee can only be compensated in respect of loss actually suffered to a maximum of 104 weeks' pay. Under the Employment Equality Act, 1977, the Labour Court may award "such compensation as the Court thinks reasonable" subject to the same 104 weeks maximum. There is no requirement that the compensation relate to a loss actually suffered by the employee as a result of the dismissal and it may, in fact, represent damages for the employer's unreasonable behaviour.

Equality Officers are full-time officers of the Labour Relations Commission, usually drawn from the civil service staff of the Department of Enterprise and Employment. As the job is highly specialised dealing only with equal pay and discrimination disputes, they acquire considerable on-the-job experience. To date, no Equality Officer has been legally qualified and this is reflected in the nature of the proceedings before the Equality Officer which tend to be investigative, factually-based and informal. It is rare for parties to be represented by lawyers before an Equality Officer although representation by a trade union is quite frequent. The involvement of trade unions is reflected in the significant number of class or group claims that are presented where a trade union makes a claim on behalf of a large number of women in the same employment who are suffering from systematic employment or pay discrimination. It is also common for parties to represent themselves — and the investigative nature of the proceedings lends itself to such self-representation.

Once a dispute has been referred to an Equality Officer, he/she usually organises a preliminary hearing at which the parties attend for the purposes of clarifying the nature and the background to the dispute. The Equality Officer then conducts an investigation during which time the parties prepare and make written submissions. The investigation consists of workplace inspections, the examination of work-in-progress, interviews, the examination of documents and general information gathering. Work inspections are particularly important for the purpose of carrying out job evaluations in equal pay claims as the results will form the factual basis on which the claim of "like work" will be decided. Once the work inspection has been completed in equal pay cases, or the written submissions received in equality cases, the Equality Officer arranges the final hearing at which both parties are entitled to appear or be represented and to respond to each other's submissions.

If necessary, the hearing can be adjourned for further investigation or submission. The Equality Officer's investigation and hearing are conducted in private. The Equality Officer then issues a recommendation which may make such findings of fact as are necessary to determine the dispute. This recommendation is not of itself binding on the parties and in the event of the unsuccessful party refusing to comply, it will be necessary to appeal to the Labour Court for the purpose of enforcing the recommendation. In any event, if either party is dissatisfied with the recommendation they may appeal to the Labour Court within 40 days.

The Labour Court, like the EAT, is a body which sits in tripartite divisions consisting of a chairman and two ordinary members, one representing each side of industry. The Court itself consists of a chairman, two deputy chairmen and six ordinary members — three nominated by the ICTU and three by IBEC. There is no requirement in law or in practice that the chairman or his deputies be legally qualified. The Labour Court's principal functions arise under the Industrial Relations Act, 1946 (as amended) and concern the provision of an industrial relations disputes resolution service (see Chapter 9). Therefore, it was somewhat unexpected when jurisdiction over equal pay and equality claims was conferred on the Labour Court in 1974 and 1977 as these claims are essentially disputes over individual statutory employment rights, the type of subject matter more usually dealt with by the EAT. Whilst there was some initial hesitancy about the structures, and a feeling that this new adjudicative jurisdiction would sit uneasily with the Labour Court's traditional industrial relations role, as the Labour Court began to gain experience in dealing with equality issues and the Tribunal became increasingly criticised for its "legalism" and the involvement of lawyers in its proceedings, there appears to be a steady acceptance and satisfaction with the Labour Court's performance in the area.

The procedures before the Labour Court are not dissimilar to those before the Equality Officer. Since cases usually come before the Labour Court on appeal from an Equality Officer there is no need for a preliminary hearing as such. Instead, the Labour Court conducts an investigation, the parties are required to make written submissions of their arguments and then a hearing is organised which is held in private. The hearing itself is very informal with few procedural rules. Generally, the parties are invited to respond to each other's written submissions. Witnesses may be called and examined under oath. The Court itself may seek expert evidence or legal advice, but if it does so it must inform the parties of the nature of such evidence or advice and allow them to respond to it. In deciding the appeal, the Labour

Court does not limit itself to the technical merits of the Equality Officer's recommendation but must satisfy itself as to whether or not there was discrimination and make the appropriate determination without being limited by the terms of the Equality Officer's recommendation. The determination of the Labour Court is binding on the parties to the dispute and failure to comply with a direction of the Court is a criminal offence. There is a right of appeal on a question of law from the Labour Court to the High Court.

Employment Equality Agency
In the context of the Equality Acts, the Equality Officers and the Labour Court constitute the adjudicative structures provided by the Acts. However, the Employment Equality Act, 1977, goes further than the other employment statutes discussed in this chapter in that it also established an administrative body to provide the essential policy back up to the legislation. The Employment Equality Agency established under the 1977 Act consists of a chairperson who may be full- or part-time and, if necessary, a chief executive, who may be the same person as the chairperson, together with ten ordinary members, two appointed by employers' bodies and two by employees' bodies, three by the Council for the Status of Women and three by the Minister for Enterprise and Employment. It has a multifaceted role, principally of an investigative, overseeing nature expressed in the 1977 Act as working "towards the elimination of discrimination", promoting "equality of opportunity" and keeping "under review" the 1974 and 1977 Acts. To fulfil its role it has a wide range of powers including the power to issue codes of practice, to provide assistance for individual claimants in bringing their claims, to carry out formal investigations and to issue non-discrimination notices to persons in breach of the legislation and to undertake research and to disseminate information. The Agency enables the administrative enforcement of the legislation in circumstances where individual enforcement might be impossible or impractical. It has powers to directly enforce the legislation by bringing an application before the Labour Court under both Acts; it also has an exclusive right to initiate proceedings in respect of certain discriminatory acts, for example, discriminatory advertising. The existence and function of the Agency is a statutory acknowledgement of two factors that are not necessarily readily apparent from the framing of the Equality Acts in terms of individual employment rights. The first is the collective interest in equality issues and the second is the importance of developing on-going policy in the equality area in order to complement and support the statutory mechanisms.

The Anti-Discrimination (Pay) Act, 1974

The 1974 Act was enacted to give effect to the principle of "equal pay for equal work" and does so by providing in Section 2(1) that every contract under which a woman is employed shall have a clause to the effect that she is entitled to the same rate of remuneration as a man who is employed in the same place by the same or an associated employer if both are employed on "like work". Section 4 implies a term into every contract of employment giving effect to Section 2 so that every contract is automatically modified by virtue of the 1974 Act without the necessity of the parties taking any positive action. This implied term takes priority over any express term in the contract or any term in a collective agreement with which it is in conflict so that an employer cannot force an employee to contract out of her statutory entitlement to equal pay. Of course, it almost goes without saying that the contractual right to equal pay created by Section 2 and Section 4 applies equally to men as well as to women.

In order to establish an entitlement to equal pay a woman must bring herself within the terms of Section 2 of the 1974 Act by showing that she is engaged on "like work" with a male employed in the same place by the same employer. Firstly, she must identify the male with whom she wishes the comparison to be made — this male is referred to as a "comparator" — who must be an actual person. She cannot make a claim based on a comparison with what her employer would pay a hypothetical male although she can refer to a predecessor male who is no longer in her employer's employment. Both the claimant and the comparator must be employed under what is legally described as a "contract of service" to distinguish employees from independent contractors or freelance workers. The requirement that the claimant and the comparator be employed in the "same place" is usually satisfied by showing that they work in the same city, town or locality, but there may be occasions where employees of different branches of the one business located throughout the State are deemed to be employed in the same place if wages are set and determined centrally. "Associated employers" generally refers to associated companies and it seems to be accepted that individuals, even related individuals, cannot be associated employers.

Having identified an acceptable comparator the claimant must then show that they are engaged in "like work". Section 3 of the 1974 Act defines "like work" as work that is identical or interchangeable, work that is of similar nature with differences that are infrequent or unimportant or work that is "equal in value" in terms of the demands made on skill, the physical or mental effort involved, the responsibility of the work and the working conditions. Clearly the first two definitions are relatively straightforward and the early cases quickly established the equal pay entitlement where the work was identical or of similar nature. The notion of work that is "equal in value" has proved more complex and these cases have involved the Equality Officers and the Labour Court in lengthy, factually-based job evaluations in order to determine "equal value". Part of the difficulty in establishing "equal value" lies in inherent assumptions made about different types of work — usually to the effect that the work performed by men (for example, porters) is of more value and therefore merits more pay than that performed by women (for example, cleaners). When these types of job are evaluated they are frequently found to be of "equal value" thereby overriding the traditional attitudes towards "women's work".

There is a limitation to the general entitlement to equal pay if an employer can show under Section 2(3) that there are "grounds other than sex" which justify any difference in pay between male and female employees. These grounds refer to genuine, material differences other than the sex of the worker such as age, qualifications or experience but cannot be relied on by the employer to justify direct discrimination or as an excuse for indirect discrimination. The European Court of Justice has, over the past few years, developed a line of case law, which restricts the scope of the exception created by Section 2(3) by requiring that the "grounds other than sex" relied on to justify a disparity in pay must be objectively justifiable by reference to economic factors and must be necessary and appropriate to achieve that economic aim.

The Employment Equality Act, 1977

The Employment Equality Act, 1977, was enacted to combat discrimination based on sex or marital status and does so under Section 3 by outlawing discrimination in relation to access to employment, conditions of employment (except remuneration which is dealt with under the Anti-Discrimination (Pay) Act, 1974), training or experience, promotion, re-grading or the classification of posts in employment. The scope of the 1977 Act is very broad and it is intended to cover all forms of discrimination in relation to all aspects of employment from the recruitment stage through the job itself to career development. The interpretation of the 1977 Act, particularly in the light of the judgements of the European Court of Justice, has been both flexible and progressive. The prohibition of discrimination, not only on the grounds of sex but also on the grounds of marital status, counters not only the most blatant forms of discrimination but also traditional difficulties faced by married women, especially those with young children, in the workplace. This is seen in cases dealing with access to employment and recruitment and selection of employees where questions on application forms as to marital status or numbers of children, or questions at interview of a similar nature or relating to proposed child-care arrangements, have been held to be *prima facia* discriminatory. As it can be difficult in these cases to determine whether the outcome of the application or interview would have been different if the question had not been asked, it is usual to award a successful claimant compensation only in respect of the expenses incurred in making the application and in respect of the distress caused to her by the nature of the interview.

Section 4 of the 1977 Act provides for a technique similar to that contained in Section 4 of the 1974 Act whereby an "equality clause" is implied into every contract of employment which automatically modifies the contract to bring it into line with that of a person of the other sex doing work which is not materially different. There is also an exception in Section 4(3) akin to that contained in Section 2(3) of the 1974 Act under which the equality clause does not operate in respect of a variation between contracts which is genuinely due to a material difference other than the sex of the employees. Section 17 also allows discrimination where sex is a "genuine occupational qualification" for the employment in question.

One of the important features of the 1977 Act is the prohibition of indirect as well as direct discrimination. Because Section 56(2) of the 1977 Act provides that the 1977 and the 1974 Acts are to be construed together as one Act, the following observations also apply to equal pay. Direct discrimination is defined in Section 2 (a) and (b) as treating a person "less favourably" than a person of the opposite sex or marital status. Usually, it will be necessary to show that the employer, by his actions, intended to discriminate against persons of that sex or marital status. Indirect discrimination focuses not on the employer's intention but on the effect of his actions; if the effect is more onerous or burdensome on employees of one sex or marital status then it is likely that he is discriminating indirectly. Indirect discrimination is defined in Section 2(c) and the test of whether a requirement imposed by an employer is discriminatory is whether, assuming that the requirement is not essential for the employment in question, a substantially higher proportion of persons of the other sex or marital status is able to comply with the requirement.

Classic examples of indirect discrimination would include recruiting only newly qualified employees which is likely to exclude married women returning to the workforce after having taken time out to rear children. Imposing an upper age limit on eligibility for employment is likely to have the same effect. Imposing a requirement that an employee be able to accept a geographical transfer at short notice is likely to prejudice married employees of either gender who have children and other family responsibilities. However, there can be difficulties in proving indirect discrimination cases arising from the approach taken by the High and Supreme Court that a claimant must provide statistical proof of the disproportionate impact of the requirement on one sex or marital status in order to show the causal link between the requirement complained of and the alleged discrimination. In many instances this will be a burden that is impossible to discharge for an ordinary claimant who may not be backed by the research facilities of a trade union or the Employment Equality Agency.

Finally, when examining the 1977 Act, two specific issues have arisen which merit specific attention. One is the position of pregnant women, the other the issue of sexual harassment. In relation to pregnancy, there was an initial view that discrimination against pregnant women was not covered by the 1977 Act since there was no male equivalent with whom a pregnant woman could be compared. This view was rejected by the Labour Court which has held that the requirement of not being pregnant is one with which a substantially greater number of men (that is, 100 per cent) than women can comply and, therefore, discrimination against pregnant women is caught by Section 2 (c) of the 1977 Act. A more recent development has been the emerging attitude of the Labour Court to cases of alleged sexual harassment where it adopted the approach that employers are under a duty to ensure that employees enjoy working conditions that are free from sexual harassment. Requiring an employee to work in an abusive work environment constitutes less favourable treatment on the grounds of sex contrary to Section 2(a). Interestingly, it appears from the sexual harassment cases that an employer may be held liable under the 1977 Act for the acts of his employees (and possibly his customers) which constitute sexual harassment even if he personally took no part in the abusive behaviour.

The total number of cases decided each year by both the Equality Officers and the Labour Court under the 1974 and 1977 Acts is shown in Table 11.4.

TABLE 11.4: EQUALITY OFFICER RECOMMENDATIONS AND LABOUR
COURT DETERMINATION, 1976–92

Year	Equality Officer Recommendations			Labour Court Determination		
	1974 Act	1977 Act	Total	1974 Act	1977 Act	Total
1976	3	—	3	1	—	1
1977	17	—	17	7	—	7
1978	52	5	57	13	2	15
1979	52	14	66	23	1	24
1980	65	14	79	40	9	49
1981	55	20	75	17	7	24
1982	27	12	39	8	10	18
1983	28	22	50	11	7	18
1984	27	28	55	10	5	15
1985	17	18	35	9	9	18
1986	19	8	27	10	2	12
1987	14	11	25	7	2	9
1988	16	11	27	7	1	8
1989	10	12	22	4	4	8
1990	13	35	48	2	4	6
1991	8	23	31	8	6	14
1992	22	14	36	2	8	10
Totals	445	247	692	179	77	256

Notes:
1. It is interesting to note the steady rise in the number of claims peaking
between roughly 1978 and 1984 followed by a steady decline, presumably
reflecting the fact that as more of the central issues arising out of the legislation were decided, fewer claims needed to be initiated. It is also interesting
to note that the slight growth in claims before the Equality Officer from 1990
is not matched in a proportionate growth in appeals to the Labour Court.
2. These figures are based on the number of recommendations/determinations
issued and do not take account of claims withdrawn or discontinued for any
reason.

CONCLUDING REMARKS

The purpose of this chapter has been to provide an overview of the
range and structure of the statutory employment protection in force
in Ireland. In this regard, it was felt important to place the relevant
statutes in their legal and international context and to view such
statutory regulation as part of a broader process rather than as an
exclusive feature of employment law. The basic features of each of the

more important statutes have been outlined and examined with particular reference to the changes brought about by the Statute in the general employment law structure. It is worth noting that because of the, by now, large number of statutes dealing with employment rights we have a rather disparate and piecemeal legislative framework in which much cross referencing between the statutes may be necessary in order to ascertain the position under any of them. It would certainly provide for ease of reference and may even iron out various inconsistencies if the employment statutes were to be brought together and revised into one consolidating act equivalent to the Social Welfare (Consolidation) Act, 1981.

A lot of attention has also been paid to the institutional structures established under the various statutes in order to provide the necessary adjudicative framework for determining the rights and liabilities of individual employees and employers. In practical terms, the usefulness of any of the legislation will be enhanced or limited by the effectiveness of the institutions provided to operate the statutory schemes. The Employment Appeals Tribunal is interesting in this regard because it has been tailor-made by the legislation which it is required to enforce, unlike the Labour Court, which has had the equality jurisdiction added on to its more usual industrial relations function (although Equality Officers have exclusively equality functions). Despite this, there appears to be a more general level of satisfaction with the Labour Court's handling of equality cases than with the EAT's handling of its case-load which is seen as being somewhat inflexible and legalistic. The comparison may not be exactly fair, especially given the disparity in the workload of the Labour Court under the Equality Acts and that of the EAT under the statutes, the latter being much larger (compare the 1992 figures in Table 11.1 with those in Table 11.4). However, despite occasional criticisms there is a general level of satisfaction with the operation of both tribunals and there has been little serious agitation for major reform either of the legal structures or of the substantive content of the statutory rights themselves.

References

Curtin, D. (1989): *Irish Employment Equality Law*, Dublin: Round Hall Press.

Fennell, C. and Lynch, I. (1992): *Labour Law in Ireland*, Dublin: Gill and Macmillan.

Forde, M. (1992): *Employment Law*, Dublin: Round Hall Press.

Redmond, M. (1982): *Dismissal Law in the Republic of Ireland*, Dublin: Incorporated Law Society of Ireland.

von Prondzynski, F. (1989): *Employment Law*, London: Sweet and Maxwell.

CHAPTER 12

EMPLOYEE PARTICIPATION

Aidan Kelly and *Fintan Hourihan*

Aside from collective bargaining, Irish industry had not experienced any significant institutionalised form of employee participation until 1977. Ireland was unlike many westernised countries, which experienced work councils, productivity committees, profit-sharing arrangements, employees self-management, and employee involvement in day-to-day decision-making. The only opportunity to participate in Ireland was through the collective bargaining process. Collective bargaining here has been primarily concerned with the channelling of economic demands and the maintenance of job security (Hillery et al., 1975: 130–9).

Put simply, organisational democracy was not on the nation's agenda between 1922 and 1973, either for Irish politics or for the parties to the collective bargaining process. This is clearly reflected in the paucity of published material on the subject during this period. However, two significant acts of legislation have been introduced in recent times: the Worker Participation (State Enterprise) Acts of 1977 and 1988.

The 1977 Act provides for employee representation on the boards of seven of the largest state-controlled companies. It launched the notion of participation in industry into the forefront of industrial relations affairs. This experiment on employee participation seems to have established a firm foothold without overshadowing other industrial relations issues. Soon after the Department of Labour announced its intention to extend the system to a further six companies by the Autumn of 1984. This development provided evidence of commitment to the policy of creating participatory mechanisms in large organisations which are outside the framework of collective bargaining. And it represented a major departure in the practice of Irish industrial relations.

The 1988 Act allowed for the introduction of arrangements for sub-board structures; its purpose was to "underpin the development of worker involvement below the level of the board in the semi-state sector" according to the Minister for Labour, Bertie Ahern. Progress has been slower in the private sector and in spite of the continued efforts of the trade unions to seeing a greater drive towards participation, possibly through legislation, the intangible 1991 joint FIE/ICTU declaration on employee involvement has proven the most significant development. However, the recent enactment of the Transnational Information and Consultation Act, 1996 heralds a new era in employee participation.

In Ireland's first 50 years there was no ideological disagreement concerning strategic decision-making in industrial and commercial organisations. All such discussion and ultimate decision-making had always been the sole province of the controlling boards of directors and senior management. Although several state companies, such as CIE, have included labour nominees on the board, there is no evidence of any material union influence in the determination of major policy. The process of collective bargaining has been largely disjunctive, as no harmony of interests has been assumed (Poole, 1979). As a consequence of this overriding emphasis on trade union-based action, little effort was directed at achieving institutionalised participation.

In contrast, employee representation on boards rests theoretically in the realm of "the potential unity of different class interests" (Poole, 1979: 263). Such an innovation heralds the likelihood of considerable opposition from the prevailing collective bargaining interests. However, the experiment has survived and evidence suggests that it has been possible to achieve a satisfactory degree of integration between a co-determination type of participation and a collective bargaining system.

This chapter will assess the extent to which the new employee participation system has been able to function, and possibly achieve some legitimacy, alongside the traditional system of collective bargaining. Specifically, attention is directed at several important questions. To what extent has integration been possible? What forms of conflict, if any, have arisen between the two institutions? Are there any particular difficulties relating to substructures? What have been the experiences of the new employee directors? To what extent and in what circumstances have worker directors been able to exert influence? What role has the European Union to play in the development of employee participation? However, before discussing current and future issues of participation it is necessary to understand the historical and political environments which have shaped the Irish industrial relations system.

The British Legacy

Irish industrial relations developed in the context of wider traditions and experience in the United Kingdom. Ireland was a part of the United Kingdom before the establishment of the Irish Free State in 1922 (Report of Commission of Inquiry, 1981). Throughout the eighteenth and nineteenth centuries, workers formed trade clubs, associations, and friendly societies. These groups were involved in the often bitter struggle for organisational recognition and rights to bargain collectively. Their struggles became the foundation for the emerging philosophies and structures of industrial relations both in Britain and Ireland (Boyd, 1972). Trade unions developed during this period, observed George Daly, creating "a strong and usually justifiable sense of injustice which provided a rich and prolific seedbed for endemic hostility against not only employers but also against the establishment" (Daly, 1968: 70).

Events throughout the nineteenth century engendered in the emerging trade union movement a belief that the law favoured the owners and managers of capital rather than the worker. Therefore, apart from securing basic legislation recognising trade unions, any attempt to use the law to regulate industrial relations was perceived by the unions "as an act of open hostility to organised labour" (Roche, 1982: 4). A preference developed for the regulation of industrial relations through the process of free and voluntary collective bargaining between workers and employers, without the intervention of the state.

The Irish trade union organisation itself developed unevenly, with the early associations of tradesmen being confined to one particular occupation within a town or locality. Despite the size of the general unions at the beginning of this century the craft unions remained independent, with the result that Irish trade unionists continued to be organised mostly on an occupational basis rather than on industrial lines. Thus, prior to Independence there existed a large number of trade unions catering to a relatively small workforce.

The Nationalist Influence

The history of Irish trade unionism from 1923 to 1980 is one of structural fragmentation and internal dissension. These factors prevented any substantial reorganisation or rationalisation of the movement. During the first two decades of this century the growing spirit of nationalism began to penetrate Irish trade unionism. Between 1917 and 1923 many trade unionists departed from the mostly British-based trade unions and formed their own Irish-based unions (Boyd, 1972;

O'Hara, 1981). This led to an even greater fragmentation of the movement. Inter-union conflict along nationalist divisions culminated in the separation of the Irish Trade Union Congress, in 1944, into two separate congresses (McCarthy, 1977). The two organisations did not re-unite until 1959, when national allegiance began to decline as a significant trade union issue.

The emphasis on nationalism had debilitating effects on the trade union movement as a whole. This emphasis both increased the number of trade unions and prevented any attempts at a fundamental reorganisation of the movement. Thus, an enterprise in Ireland typically has a large number of unions, each independently representing its members and often negotiating separate agreements with the employer. This situation creates numerous problems in the conduct of collective bargaining. In addition, the multi-union structure hinders prospects for the introduction and implementation of employee participation.

Industrialisation and the Search for Consensus

Between 1922 and 1950 Irish industry remained virtually static. As Lee observed: "for over a century Ireland has been essentially a stagnant society" (Lee, 1980: 11). However, in the 1960s industrial growth became a political priority and foreign industries were enticed to locate subsidiaries in Ireland. National economic development was also a priority for the trade union movement. Improved economic development was seen as a means of preventing the loss of members through unemployment and emigration, as well as ameliorating the incomes and working conditions of its members.

The industrial strategy for growth was based largely on the principle of free enterprise, and caused no ideological disagreement. Although the trade union movement does not advocate social upheaval to achieve its objectives, it does aspire to reform capitalist society in the direction of greater social justice and equality (Peillon, 1982). The events of the 1960s and 1970s gradually led the trade unions into participation in government policy formulation in specific areas. At the same time, successive governments became more actively involved in the collective bargaining process. However, the relationship between the unions and government is an uneasy one. Although co-operation does occur, it is, as McCarthy notes, "more at arms length than hand-in-hand" (McCarthy, 1977).

During the 1960s joint consultative and co-operative bodies at the national level were developed. This formed the basis for an era of national wage agreements during the 1970s, and the effective transformation of the tradition of free collective bargaining. Although these agreements were entirely voluntary, in practice they assumed a quasi-legal status which was rarely challenged. Essentially, through a series of national wage agreements, the government traded off concessions in the areas of social and economic policy. In return they received a somewhat stable income policy and a period of comparative industrial peace. Thus, through the Irish Congress of Trade Unions (ICTU), the trade unions established a position of influence on a wide variety of government policies.

RECENT DEVELOPMENTS IN PARTICIPATION

Following the practice common in many studies (Heller, 1976: Dachler and Wilpert 1978; Dickson, 1981), this review will make a broad distinction between direct and indirect participation. Direct participation enables the employee to have some input or influence on the activities performed in the workplace, and involves the participation of the employee in his or her immediate task environment. Indirect participation applies to any situation where employees select representatives to influence or take part in the traditional managerial activities of the organisation. Employees are elected or appointed to such forums as consultative bodies, works councils, various works committees, and the governing board.

Direct Participation
On several occasions the ICTU emphasised the importance of involving employees in decisions which directly affect their work. A major criticism of the Worker Participation (State Enterprise) Act (1977) was that it failed to address this particular dimension. The ICTU's Annual Report of 1976 asserted:

> the demand for participation relates not simply to decision-making at the higher level of the enterprise but at all levels and not least at shop-floor level which is crucially important as it is here that the many questions relating to the quality of employment conditions and the work environment are determined and where there are the potential opportunities for employees to grow and develop as human beings (161–2).

A concern with involving employees at shop-floor level has also been expressed by managers and employers. Murphy and Walsh in their 1978 study interviewed managers on new forms of work organisation. Most of these managers felt that greater involvement of employees in decision-making generally was necessary and inevitable. However, in their survey of 21 companies they found little progress on direct participation (Murphy and Walsh, 1978: 131). While there were a few changes in work organisation, these were not always the result of conscious choice. Often the changes were required by technological developments. The disjunction between trade unions and employers, and between intentions and actions, is evidenced by the fact that neither the FUE nor the ICTU have developed explicit strategies to deal with direct participation (Murphy and Walsh, 1978: 31).

A discussion document on worker participation was published by the Department of Labour in 1981. This document indicated the government's positive attitude toward the notion of direct participation. However, the government believes that implementation should be negotiated through the collective bargaining process (Department of Labour, 1981: 45). It is unlikely that the trade unions or the employers would favour the use of statutory initiatives in this area. Some progress, albeit minimal, has occurred. In 1959 the Irish Productivity Centre was established to help improve and stimulate productivity in Irish firms. Another goal of the Centre (IPC) was to facilitate employee participation developments, through the design of systems to improve shop-floor involvement. But few enterprises have taken advantage of the system redesign service of the IPC. According to Murphy and Walsh (1978), there have been few developments in this area of participation because Irish employers and trade unions tend to think of participation in terms of representative structures.

Representative Participation

A study on joint consultation in Irish industry was undertaken by the IPC in 1976. This survey of 183 firms revealed that about one-third had some form of consultative procedure (including informal types) (Hanlon, 1976). The results of the survey showed that joint consultation in these firms had a negligible effect on absenteeism and discipline problems. Consultation mechanisms appeared to have little or no effect on productivity, the acceptance of new work methods, or the quality of work. Some advances in the area of employee amenities and in safety were reported.

While the trade unions have indicated a strong commitment to the principle of industrial democracy, it has not been a major issue in trade union/employer bargaining. In general, consultative structures are perceived by trade unionists as dealing with peripheral and trivial matters. In contrast, the collective bargaining process is considered to be the primary mechanism through which workers can influence decisions at the workplace. There are a few instances where joint consultation has had considerable impact on the management of the enterprise, but these are exceptional. Among the more prominent works councils in Ireland are those in Guinness and the B&I Line, both of which have long traditions of experimenting with participation mechanisms. As in Britain (McCarthy, 1967), Ireland has an influential cadre of shop stewards representing numerous trade unions at the local level. This structure makes the development of joint consultative machinery at the least difficult and most likely improbable.

The ICTU is far more enthusiastic than its affiliated unions in its commitment to the introduction of employee participation. At the Employer-Labour Conference (ELC) in 1970, trade union representatives proposed that a study be carried out on the feasibility of industrial democracy. A subcommittee of the ELC was established and subsequently examined the role and constitution of works councils. The subcommittee recommended that works councils should be established at all levels of industry. A non-statutory system was proposed, based on a collective agreement at the level of the ELC. This left to local negotiation the introduction of the works council within each enterprise. Representatives of the trade unions on the committee argued that a system with its basis in legislation would produce a rather mild version of what the trade union movement itself could devise (O'Sullivan, 1973). Ironically, the discussion document on this subject published in 1974 was a disappointingly bland document, which neither offended any party nor aroused any interest. Only two unions responded to the ICTU's request for comments on the document (ICTU Annual Report, 1975). Three years later the report of the committee had still not evoked any response. One senior trade union official concluded: "It cannot be denied that there is as yet very little demand in this country for formalised systems of industrial democracy — even collective bargaining and worker participation at board level — on the worker side" (O'Sullivan, 1973: 24).

State Initiative

We must look to the state to find the most substantial first step towards participation. As McCarthy pointed out: "In the Republic of Ireland the initiative (for employee participation) — in a practical and immediate sense — has come from the Government" (1975: 199).

While this observation may be a little unfair to the ICTU, it is clear that the ICTU's commitment to industrial democracy is not always evident in its affiliated unions. The origins of the state's concern with participation may be traced back to the late 1960s. Towards the end of that decade the trade union movement, employers, and the principal political interests began to express an interest in employee participation. This interest grew out of the increasing amount of information available on participation schemes in various European countries (Hillery, 1969). This information had become available due to Ireland's growing involvement in international economic institutions. The first concrete proposal for employee participation came in a resolution adopted at the 1967 Annual Delegate Conference of the ICTU (ICTU, 1968). This led to a conference in February, 1968 which was addressed by prominent international experts.

Around the same time employers became involved in the debate. In 1968 the Federated Union of Employers, together with the Federation of Irish Industries (both of which are now part of IBEC), formed a study group in order to formulate a policy on industrial democracy for employers (Goss, 1973). Members of the study group visited several European countries to study various employee participation practices. The group also commissioned an expert to report on the subject (Mulvey, 1972). The employer response to participation was typically to reject employee involvement at board level. Instead, employers sought to direct attention to the need for participation ideas to be developed at the workplace (Gray, 1969; Cuffe, 1969).

Within the political establishment interest in participation was mixed. The largest political party was Fianna Fáil, a largely conservative organisation which was then in government. Fianna Fáil favoured the development of participation on a voluntary basis within the prevailing collective bargaining arrangements, and preferably at the workplace level in the initial stages (Hillery, 1969; Goss, 1973).

Fine Gael was the principal opposition party and also a representative of traditional conservative interests. They advanced a slightly more radical policy. While supporting the development of participation through the collective bargaining system, Fine Gael also stated its intention to provide works committees within public enterprises (Goss, 1973). As with the government, it showed no inclination to introduce any new legislation for the private sector.

The Labour Party, predictably, offered the most dramatic alternative. Its 1969 Annual Conference adopted an explicit policy on employee democracy. This policy signalled the intention to seek participation in decision-making processes at all levels. The state enterprise sector was identified as the obvious starting point.

Thus, by the end of the 1960s, a fund of knowledge had been accumulated by employers and trade unions in anticipation of a possible initiative from government. From a tactical standpoint, both interest groups appreciated the need to be aware of contemporary developments in the field, in order to defend their respective traditions. The government, on the other hand, viewed participation as a means of reducing the risk of conflict between the social partners. However, there was little evidence of any intention to take a lead through the legislative process (Hillery, 1969).

It was a political impetus which eventually gave the idea of employee participation statutory force. This was the so-called 14-Point Programme, a party political manifesto published in 1973. When parliamentary elections were held in 1973, the ruling Fianna Fáil government had held power for four consecutive terms, spanning 16 years. In the election of 1973 the two main opposition parties were Fine Gael and the Labour Party. While ideological opposites, these parties decided to conduct the campaign on the basis of a joint program. The two parties reached agreement on 14 areas which they would address if elected to office, and one of these related to participation.

Specifically, the opposition explicitly agreed "to introduce employee participation in State enterprises and the election of employee representatives to State boards". Such an undertaking presented little difficulty for either party. It was already established very firmly in Labour Party policy. For Fine Gael the agreement was regarded as an inexpensive reform measure that could be accepted, particularly as it was to be confined to the public sector. The opposition parties together won a majority in the general election. The substance of their initiative on participation was the enactment in 1977 of the Worker Participation (State Enterprises) Act. This Act provided for the election of worker directors to the main boards of certain large state-controlled companies.

The Worker Participation Act, 1977

On assuming office, the new Minister for Labour established a Worker Participation Unit within the Department of Labour. Following preliminary research and discussions with various interested parties, the Minister issued proposals for the election of employees to the boards of certain state-controlled enterprises in July 1975.

Reactions to the proposed legislation among employers were muted (Murphy and Walsh, 1980b: 6). Neither the FUE nor any other employer commented publicly on the proposals. The trade unions were also slow to respond to the government's initiative. Only 11 unions bothered to make submissions to the ICTU following publication of the White Paper (ICTU Annual Report, 1976).

The ICTU, while extending general support to the proposed legislation, criticised several specific issues. Serious concern was expressed at the absence of any plans for the development of shop-floor participation. Congress was also critical of the power of executive management in large state-controlled organisations and therefore advocated a two-tier board system as defined in West German legislation. This system was preferred by the ICTU to the traditional unitary system of the Anglo-Irish tradition. Finally, the ICTU proposed that half of the board members should be elected by employees instead of the proposed one-third, and that voting rights should be restricted to the trade union membership in the respective enterprises. These proposed amendments were rejected by the Minister. The Worker Participation Act was eventually passed by the Dáil in 1977 with little change to the proposals originally outlined in the White Paper. In summary, the participation provisions created by the 1977 legislation are as follows:

1. The direct election of full-time employees to one-third of the seats on the board of directors, in seven state-controlled trading companies.

2. The franchise extends to all full-time employees.

3. Candidates for election may be nominated only by a trade union or other organisation (such as a staff association), which is recognised for collective bargaining purposes by the company concerned.

4. The term of office of the elected worker directors is three years.

5. The worker directors hold the same status as any other directors and are therefore entitled to the same rights and assume similar responsibilities.

6. Elections are conducted under the proportional representation system.

The seven companies named in the Act are major enterprises in the Irish economy and all are under the direct control of the state. Each of the companies has been established by particular statutes or under the Companies Act and is limited by guarantee. The activities of these companies include air transport (Aer Lingus); shipping, road and rail transport (B&I and CIE); peat production and processing (Bord na Mona); electricity generation and distribution (ESB); sugar beet and vegetable processing (Irish Sugar Company); and fertiliser manufacturing (Nitrigin Éireann). A provision was later introduced to extend the Act to include steel production (Irish Steel), gas distribution (Bord Gais), health insurance (VHI) and postal and telecommunications services (An Post and Bord Telecom). By 1994, ICTU estimated that the number of state companies with worker directors stood at 19.

The 1977 Act is mostly concerned with election procedures and does not influence the institution of collective bargaining. In addition there was no attempt to specify structural arrangements below the board, such as relationships among worker directors, the trade unions in the enterprise, and the employees as a whole. The government's position on the legislation was that it constituted an initial, but essential, step in the overall strategy for promoting employee participation. It was expected that providing for participation at the apex of the enterprise would become a catalyst for the formation of sub-board structures of participation.

It was becoming clear that few sub-board structures were being developed, and in 1980 the Department of Labour produced a discussion paper on the topic. The paper was critical of the lack of voluntary initiatives by employers and unions to establish structures for participation below the level of the board. In the discussion document, the Minister promised:

> to promote whatever legislation is required to provide the legal framework or administrative structure which may be necessary to make worker participation in Ireland a reality (Department of Labour, 1980: 6).

The frustration expressed by the Department of Labour was understandable when one considers the commitment of the social partners to the principle of participation. Up to then there had been two initiatives at the national level. First, there was the report of the Employer-Labour Conference on works councils, which had a negligible impact. The second initiative was the 1977 Act itself. At the time, this was taken by some as an indication that most trade unions would prefer an extension of the collective bargaining process as the most legitimate and adequate form of employee participation — similarly, most employers seemed to prefer collective bargaining as the primary means of regulating industrial behaviour. Other factors which explain this widespread reticence to developments in employee participation are examined later.

In 1986, the then Minister for Labour, Mr Ruairi Quinn, introduced a bill aimed at extending the scope of industrial democracy in state companies. This followed the report of the Advisory Committee on Worker Participation comprising representatives from the FUE and ICTU, nominees of the Minister for Labour. A majority of the Committee, which was chaired by Thomas Morrisey SJ, director of the College of Industrial Relations, favoured legislation. Otherwise, progress would be slow and "participation might become merely a peripheral item on the collective bargaining agenda, where the adversarial model is to the fore". But while the FUE came out in favour of participation in general, it believed voluntarism was essential as firms forced to introduce employee participation would feel "straight-jacketed." The Committee also estimated that there were only 50 works councils, or their equivalent, in the private sector. The 1986 Bill lapsed when a general election was called.

1988 Act — Sub-Board Participation

However, the 1987 Programme for National Recovery provided that legislation would be introduced enabling sub-board participation. The 1988 Act was broadly similar to the lapsed 1986 Bill. The Act provides that it is up to the management and employee representatives to devise mutually acceptable arrangements for employee involvement following a request from a majority of the employees. Though it provides for a direct initiative by employees within each workplace, it does not interfere with the freedom of management to develop its own proposals and to approach employee representatives about the development of sub-board participation. It is up to management and workers' representatives to work out arrangements best suited to the organisation. The whole range of options — from direct to representational forms of participation and from the highly structured to the relatively informal — are accommodated within the legislative framework. A total of 39 specified companies were included in the appendix as being suitable for the introduction of sub-board structures.

The Minister for Labour also outlined three basic requirements arising from the legislation: the exchange of views as well as the exchange of clear and reliable information between the enterprise and its employees; the communication in good time to employees of information likely to have a significant effect on their interests; and the distribution to all employees of views and information arising from the participative process.

The Act extended the worker director provisions to Aer Rianta and the National Rehabilitation Board. But the Minister noted that the original formula of reserving one-third of all board places was framed with commercial boards in mind. Greater flexibility was necessary in regard to non-commercial state companies. The level of employee representation in such companies would be dictated by the need to maintain the balance of representational interests and to ensure that the board remains an effective body. Each case would have to be considered on its own merits and the Act provided that the Minister for Labour could vary the number of worker directors below the one-third arrangement by order, subject to a minimum of two worker directors. The Act also provided that board level participation could be extended to additional enterprises without the need for further primary legislation — the 1977 Act confined its provisions to seven designated companies.

The 1988 Act also broadened the electorate covering nominations to the board to include employees of subsidiaries in certain circumstances. Their inclusion would be matters for the enterprise concerned, and proposals for their inclusion had to be sent to the Minister along with the views of the staff representatives. Before making an order the Minister for Labour had to consult the Minister for Finance and the Minister responsible for the state enterprise concerned.

The terms of office of worker directors was extended from three to four years and it was also provided that worker directors who cease to be employees of the state enterprise concerned must give up their board membership or resign from the enterprise. The definition of employees was also broadened to include those working a minimum of 18 hours a week. Subsequently, the Worker Protection (Regular Part-Time Employees) Act, 1990 provided that both the worker participation Acts would apply to regular part-time employees with at least 13 weeks' continuous service and those normally expected to work at least eight hours a week.

One important difference in the 1988 Act, compared to the 1986 Bill, was the exclusion of state financial institutions such as the Central Bank, Irish Life, Agricultural Credit Corporation (ACC) and Industrial Credit Corporation (ICC) from the sub-board consultation provisions, reflecting concerns about the confidential nature of their business. About 28 companies have so far established sub-board structures.

THE PRIVATE SECTOR AND THE STIMULUS FROM EUROPE

In spite of the introduction of the 1977 and 1988 Acts, the "spillover" to the private sector has been negligible. Employers continue to oppose any moves to introduce legislation compelling the introduction of participative structures, contending that this would have critical consequences for inward investment.

But faced with increasing demands from the trade unions, during the negotiation of the PESP especially, for some form of participation in the private sector, a joint declaration on employee involvement was published by the FIE and ICTU in June, 1991. The document emerged around the same time as a code of practice on strikes in essential services was being prepared. The employers had been pressing for statutory curbs on strikes in essential services, in the wake of a national strike in the ESB in early 1991. The fact that legislation was not introduced either for the regulation of strikes in essential services or employee involvement in the private sector was in keeping with Ireland's voluntarist traditions but could also be seen as representing a trade-off on such fundamental issues between the employers and the trade unions.

The word "participation" is omitted entirely from the joint declaration; overall, "the document, it has to be said, is rather bland — for the most part it traces developments in worker involvement in Ireland and internationally and outlines broadly the type of voluntary initiatives which might be pursued in the private sector" (Sheehan, 1991). In the same analysis, an ICTU official was quoted as saying the document had to be seen as the first stage in a long term process. Union officials and workers who want to pursue a greater say in their firms, both at the decision making level and in terms of financial involvement "should be able to use the document to get it up and running".

At its annual delegate conference in 1990, ICTU had demanded a say in the boardroom and the development of employee shareholding and profit share schemes. Not surprisingly, the agreed declaration avoided any mention of these issues. The introduction emphasised the company's operating environment, increasing competition and the need for structural changes, more efficiency and a stable industrial relations environment. Developments at EC level and the Social Dialogue had to be seen in the overall context along with the economic and social consensus developed at national level.

The declaration then went on to survey international and national practices and noted that in private sector companies in Ireland, a significant number of enterprises were developing a "range of relevant practices and procedures". These were characterised by their voluntary nature and were clearly designed to relate to individual circumstances, such as the size of the organisation, nature of the business and the level of the development.

The objectives of involvement were detailed: the effective development of the enterprise; the need to maximise competitiveness; increased job satisfaction; closer identification of employees with the organisation; a safe and healthy work environment. Both ICTU and the FIE would have a part to play in publicising and increasing awareness in the development of involvement at company level. The declaration also emphasised the need for appropriate training and suggested roles for the Employer Labour Conference in monitoring employee involvement developments in the private sector and the Irish Productivity Centre in supporting organisations attempting to introduce such developments.

Finally, the declaration noted the wide variety of financial participation initiatives in place: 90 approved schemes covering 80,000 workers introduced since the enactment of the enabling legislation, the 1982 Finance Act. The employers and unions agreed to recommend to Government that further improvements in fiscal incentives should be introduced as a means of encouraging voluntary initiatives. Ironically, the following year's budget introduced by the Minister for Finance, Mr Ahern, initially proposed to remove the tax incentives for employee share schemes entirely. But following an outcry from many and varied interest groups, including the employers and the trade unions, it was eventually decided to simply lower the limit for income tax relief from £5,000 to £2,000. The Department of Finance estimated that between 70 per cent and 80 per cent of existing shareholders would still be eligible for relief under the lower limit.

The appendix to the joint declaration listed the various forms of employee involvement which could be used — including teambriefing, employee reports, newsletters, notice boards and attitude surveys — and the kind of issues on which consultation might take place: health and safety, plant lay-out, incentive schemes, grading, the state of the firm, market performance, personnel practices, technological change and equality. In regard to information sharing, communications and consultation practices, it emphasised confidentiality requirements in relation to commercial sensitivity, contracts, company law and regulations as well as personal privacy.

Throughout the last two decades, the great unknown in regard to employee participation has been the likelihood of legislation arriving from Europe which could have a dramatic effect on practices here. Since the early 1970s, three key proposals have been on the agenda of the European Commission: the proposed regulation for a European Company statute, the proposed 5th Directive on Company Law and the proposed Vredling Directive (procedures for informing and consulting employees).

After years of acrimonious debate, the Commission relaunched the proposed regulation on the European Company statute in 1989, along with a complementing proposed directive covering the involvement of employees in the European Company. The proposals, which require unanimous support for the participation directive to be introduced, effectively offer a trade-off between business and labour by offering companies in different member states the chance to merge or form a holding company or joint subsidiary located in the member state with the most favourable tax regime while workers would benefit by the introduction of formal involvement mechanisms.

The directive suggests several models of participation: a model in which the employees form part of the supervisory board or the administrative board, as the case may be; a model in which the employees are represented by a separate body (for example, works councils); or, other models to be agreed between the management or administrative boards of the founder companies and the employees or their representatives in those companies, the level of information and consultation being the same as in the case of the second model. The general meeting of shareholders could not approve the formation of the European Company unless one of the models of participation outlined had been chosen. Progress on the regulation and directive has so far been negligible.

The second main initiative was the so-called Fifth Directive on the structure of public limited companies inside the EU, which was published in 1972 and was to apply to all public limited liability companies with more than 500 workers. It suggested that such companies would establish a two-tier management board — supervisory to deal with policy direction and management to oversee daily matters — with separate members. The nomination of board members could be along the lines of the German model (one-third worker representatives) or the Dutch model (a balance between worker and employer representatives with an industrial tribunal to resolve rows on the composition).

Faced with intense opposition from employers, the Commission issued a Green Paper in 1975 on the question of employee participation and company structure which offered a more flexible approach, while still proposing two-tier boards. Member states would be offered the choice between dual or unitary board structures for an initial period and employee representation would only be made compulsory after a number of years. Further arguments followed which stalled any progress on the matter.

In 1983, a revised proposal was tabled, which would only apply to companies with more than 1,000 employees and in which the supervisory and management functions would be divided between non-executive and executive members of the Board with the executive members appointed by the non-executive members. It also offered an alternative to employee participation on the Board, allowing employees' representatives to be given regular access to information on the administration, progress and prospects of the company, its competitive position, credit standing, investment plans as well as to information available to the non-executive directors. However, resistance to the idea has continued and the proposal is now effectively in limbo.

In 1991, the European Commission launched what commonly became known as the European Works Council (EWC) directive after the earlier Vredling directive had become irrevocably stalled. The EWC directive envisaged the establishment of EWCs or a similar body in every Community scale undertaking or group of undertakings, on request, normally by employee representatives. The undertakings affected were defined as those with at least 1,000 employees in the Community and at least 100 employees in each of two member states.

Until the enactment of the Transnational Information and Consultation Act, 1996, there had been few attempts to introduce employee participation schemes in private sector companies. As we have already seen, two acts of legislation had been introduced allowing the nomination of worker directors, in addition to sub-board participation, in a wide range of semi-state companies. Therefore, it may not be an exaggeration to describe enactment of the 1996 Act as heralding "a new era in Irish industrial relations", as stated by the mover of the legislation, Ms Eithne Fitzgerald, the Minister for Labour Affairs.

The Act means that employees of EU-based companies which employ at least 1,000 people across the Union (and at least 150 in two of the Member States operating the legislation) will elect representatives to sit at a Works Council or Employees Forum which will inform and consult employees on transnational company matters. The EU information and consultation directive applies to the 14 member states of the EU other than the UK, plus Norway, Iceland and Leichtenstein which are part of the wider European Economic Area. The Act is expected to affect around 200 multinational subsidiaries in Ireland, according to a conservative estimate by the Department of Enterprise and Employment. Around twelve Irish-owned companies are also expected to be affected, such as Smurfits, Roadstone, Independent Newspapers and the Clondalkin Group.

In line with the EU directive, the Act provides for three ways in which transnational information and consultation arrangements can be established. Firstly, predirective agreements could be established where companies which come under the operation of the directive could form agreements on information and consultation procedures, before the legislation came into place across Europe by the end of September, 1996. Such agreements had to be approved by a majority of the employees concerned, a provision which was not in the original directive.

When the legislation was enacted, the latest information suggested that around eighty pre-directive agreements were in place across Europe, of which between 25 and 30 affected employees in Ireland. Secondly, once the legislation came into place, companies covered by it, either at their own initiative or at the request of 1100 employees, could arrange for the election of a special negotiating body which in turn would negotiate the establishment of a European Employees Forum (or works council) for the purposes of information and consultation.

The Act obliges central management and the special negotiating body to negotiate in a spirit of co-operation. Importantly, the Act states that an arrangement for the information and consultation of employees may invoke the establishment of a European Employees' Forum but the parties may also agree to establish one or more information and consultation procedures instead of a forum. One unique feature of the Irish legislation is its provision for the establishment of a European Employees Forum. The real significance of this term and its inclusion is a matter of some contention. Some experts in the area feel mention has been made of such a Forum merely to give a name to what emerges from so-called article six agreements — whatever emerges from negotiations at the special negotiating body. It may be that it is a term which will be seen as less redolent of collective, union orientated bodies and will as such be favoured by non-union companies. Thirdly, if agreement has not been reached within three years, companies are obliged to convene a European Works Council under terms set out in the legislation. If a company fails to do so, it will be guilty of an offence and liable to prosecution. Those failing to comply face fines of up to £10,000 in addition to ongoing fines of £200 for each day of inaction. Managers could also face three years' imprisonment in a "worst case" scenario, though such an eventuality must be considered remote. The Act sets out extra obligations where it is agreed to set up an information and consultation procedure, including placing an obligation to set out the methods by which employees' representatives in the different member states can meet to exchange view on the information conveyed to them. Works Councils or Forums will have to meet at least once a year and employee representatives will have to be briefed on such issues as employment and investment trends, changes in the organisation, proposed transfers of production, cutbacks redundancies and other issues which may impact on the company in the year ahead. In exceptional circumstances, such as relocations, closures or collective redundancies, select committees can also be formed to meet central management. The operating expenses of Works Councils or Forums, and any select committees, are to be borne by central management — the European Commission estimates that a cost in the order of £8 per annum for every employee in a company may arise.

Separate Provisions

The Act includes a number of additional elements which have been added to the directive proposals and which have not been replicated in the legislation giving effect to the directive in other countries. These include provision that any pre-directive agreements have to be agreed with and supported by a majority of the workforce. One of the main trade union criticisms of the earlier drafts of the legislation was acted upon with provision for trade union officials to act as nominees, whether appointed or elected, to the special negotiating bodies which decide the operational ground rules for the works councils. The original directive left it open to each member state to decide on who might be entitled to act as employee representatives to special negotiating bodies, so the Act must be seen as affording trade unions a central role in the overall process.

Union Official's Role

In addition, it has been provided that trade union officials can be appointed as expert advisers on behalf of employees to special negotiating bodies if requested by the workforce of companies. This could mean that companies which have a policy of not recognising trade unions will be obliged to pay the expenses of trade union officials acting as expert advisers to their workforce. The expenses of experts will be borne by the company but funding by central management is to be limited to funding the equivalent of one expert per meeting. In their submissions to the government prior to the publication of the Act, ICTU representatives made it clear that they were not asking that full-time trade union officials would sit on these works councils when established. The Act provides that while trade union officials can be elected or appointed as employee representatives to the initial special negotiating body, only employees of a company can sit on the works council. Each part-time worker meeting the criteria in the existing legislation for part-time workers (those normally expected to work eight hours a week and thirteen weeks in a year) will have a full vote in any elections.

Arbitrator

Companies will be obliged to fully disclose the numbers of employees on their books. Election in Ireland will take place using the system of proportional representation. Employees on works councils will have to be given reasonable time off, with pay, to perform their representative functions. They cannot be dismissed for works council related activities. Irish representatives to a Forum or Works Council will then report back to Irish employees of that company on the activities of the Forum/Council — another provision in the Act which was not in the original directive. The legislation also includes a mechanism for the appointment of an arbitrator in the event of disputes between the parties. If the parties cannot agree on an independent arbitrator, either may apply to the Labour Court to appoint an arbitrator for them, and the verdict of the arbitrator will be legally binding. In some cases this will mean the appointment of an industrial relations expert and perhaps , an expert in company law, depending on the issues in dispute. In line with the forthcoming legislation on freedom of information, an independent arbitrator will decide on disputes over whether or not information being passed on or requested at works council meetings is commercially sensitive. Employees also face criminal sanctions for disclosing commercially sensitive information.

Reactions

The main employers' body, IBEC, was muted in its response to publication of the Bill. With publication of its paper on "Change and Continuous Improvement, Employee Involvement and Communications", earlier in 1996, IBEC criticised works councils as "old fashioned and artificial" in fact Works Councils were not mentioned as an option in the IBEC report. The notion of Works Councils is rooted in the 1960s and 1970s and structural relationships of this type do not improve a company's ability to compete, said IBEC. The speed of business as it affects business today requires companies to communicate change directly to their employees, said the employers' body. The assistant general secretary of ICTU, Mr. Kevin Duffy, welcomed the Bill as "a small first step in recognising employees as stakeholders in the companies where they work". And he said the unions would be pursuing a new stakeholder agenda either inside or outside talks on another national programme.

However, Mr. Des Geraghty of SIPTU said the directive was predicated on the prior existence of works councils, as exist in most other EU member states. The fact that they do not exist even at local level in Ireland was a weakness which had not been addressed by the Act. The unions here had wanted union advisors to special negotiating bodies as an automatic right but this was not accepted. He said there should have been a stronger emphasis on the role of union officials in advising employees on the establishment of works councils. Another feature of the Act was the emphasis on an Employees Forum rather than a Works Council. Works Councils are a distinct entity and the annex to the directive should have been incorporated into the Act, said Mr. Geraghty. No provision is made in regard to Employee Forums for the joint determination of agendas, the rotation of chairmanships or for the arrangement of employee representative meetings the day before the Forum meets, said the SIPTU official. In overall terms, he said a chance had been missed to encourage worker participation in line with the objectives of the Social Charter and the Maastricht Treaty which talk of information, consultation and participation of employees.

Assessment

The Act has to be seen as complying pretty much with the text of the original directive. While trade unions may have secured significant improvements in the Act in the final weeks prior to its publication, the directive itself is widely seen as having better reflected employer priorities and to have had an impact at this initial level is more important. The legislation is faithful to the directive by adds little which, given the fact that Ireland is one of the few European countries without widespread incidence of works councils, is significant. Perceptions of who has done better may be meaningless until the legislation is enacted an put into effect. Already, a number of multinationals which have signalled a willingness to set up information and consultation arrangements, have been giving serious consideration to using Ireland as a base for the purposes of the legislation. Trade unionists may see this as proof that the Irish legislation is more employer-friendly than in other countries but it should be borne in mind that most of these companies are British or American so that fact that English is the everyday language here must also be seen as a factor explaining any such decisions.

Significantly, in her statement marking the publication of the Act, the Minister for Labour Affairs, Ms. Eithne Fitzgerald, said that in nearly every other country, employee representatives to Works Councils would be nominated by their national works councils, "In Ireland we do not, as yet, have works councils at plant or company level". The Minister had already signalled that she intended to build upon the introduction of this works councils legislation, in line with the wishes of the European Commission. In a speech outlining her priorities for the Irish EU presidency, she suggested there would be a strong push for works council type structures to be extended to firms employing at least 50 workers. She was considering an initiative along the lines of the current health and safety laws whereby enterprises would be obliged to draw up a statement on workplace "partnership structures". Precise structures would be left for negotiation at the level of the individual company. These plans follow the publication of a communication by the European Commission at the end of 1995, advocating agreed general frameworks at European level on informing and consulting employees.

IRISH WORKER DIRECTORS: EARLY EXPERIENCES

Prior to the first worker director elections, surveys were carried out which showed employees at all levels to be generally favourable towards the idea of employee participation. However, they had diffuse expectations about the kinds of activities in which worker directors might become involved. Many employees believed worker directors might help directly in the resolution of industrial relations disputes. There was also some confusion about the status of the worker directors — whether they should be completely free agents or act as delegates on behalf of the employees. Although the Acts do not specify or define the worker directors' role, it is generally understood to be an independent one.

To consider how the new system works in practice, we now turn to a review of the experiences of the first group of worker directors. Because of the paucity of relevant work on this subject, and the brevity of the experiment, it is not possible to present an evolutionary assessment. Rather, it is necessary to rely on early studies and interviews to assess the short-term impact of the experiment. In particular, we drew on the only major study carried out in this area, by Murphy and Walsh (1980a). We also used a report issued by a caucus of worker directors from six of the companies, which contains a summary of their combined experiences and responses to the Department of Labour Discussion Paper. We studied various internal company and trade union newspapers, and conducted interviews with seven worker directors from six companies.

During the campaigns leading to the first elections, worker director candidates in several companies detected some resentment or calculated disinterest by senior management. However, this was not widespread and certainly not as offensive as the climate experienced by the new worker directors in the British Steel Corporation experiment (Brannen et al., 1976: 135–8). Irish worker directors quickly found their feet and had little difficulty in becoming involved in board discussions and coming to terms with new procedures (Murphy and Walsh, 1980a: 30). Coming from various trade union activist backgrounds, the new directors were at first startled by certain practices and developments. For the most part decisions were arrived at by consensus, which is not typical of trade union decision-making settings. Frequently the new directors received support for their arguments from other directors (Murphy and Walsh, 1980a: 30). The worker directors were also impressed with the sincerity and commitment of the external directors (appointed by government), a view apparently not widely held at shop-floor level (Murphy and Walsh, 1980a: 30).

The new worker directors had no doubts about their effectiveness and influence in the board rooms. In their own report they wrote unambiguously about their effectiveness in inculcating the employee dimension in decision-making. They also discussed creating improvements in communications between the board and its employees (Department of Labour, 1980: 4). Murphy and Walsh (1980a: 30) confirm these perceptions. There was no indication in any of the companies that worker directors, in their initial stages, failed to secure respect and legitimacy for their new roles from other directors.

The worker directors, while coming from a wide range of occupational backgrounds, took one common attribute to the board. As trade union and staff association activists they had considerable experience in various representational settings and thus brought a further competence in industrial relations to the boards. In Britain, Batstone et al. (1983: 79) found an exceptionally high rate of discussion on industrial relations by the worker-nominated directors on the British Post Office board. This participation clearly reflects an orientation towards worker and trade union interests. This same tendency was evident in the initial Irish experience.

There was some confusion about the appropriateness of this emphasis on industrial relations and also about the onus of responsibility *vis-à-vis* trade union interests. Murphy and Walsh (1980a: 35) point to one company where senior management attempted to declare any discussion by worker directors on industrial relations invalid. Because of the conflict of interest provisions in the Act, it was suggested that where such discussion arose worker directors should withdraw from board meetings. The Irish Congress of Trade Unions rejected this proposition and this was not subsequently contested by other interests.

While worker directors are not prevented from contributing to discussions on industrial relations, they are, however, conscious of the extent to which they should be allowed to intervene. In the Murphy and Walsh study (1980a) there is evidence of an unfailing care by worker directors not to offend established union-company negotiation and communication relationships (Murphy and Walsh, 1980a: 35). In our interviews we found one instance where an explicit instruction was issued by a trade union detailing certain issues which were not to be the subject of discussion. In some companies, particularly where there are inter-union difficulties, there is greater sensitivity about worker directors becoming involved in industrial relations issues. There is undoubtedly a clear appreciation by worker directors of the sensitivity of their roles due to their proximity to collective bargaining affairs.

The relationship between the participative system and the trade union hierarchy is critical to the development and success of worker participation. This is evident both in the initial responses of shop stewards and trade union officials and the behaviour of the worker directors. While shop stewards saw certain benefits they were also critical of the participation initiative. They were concerned about the sufficiency of feedback from worker directors, a point which we will return to later.

Shop stewards were also concerned about how strong their influence would be on the board (Murphy and Walsh, 1980a: 604). They expressed considerable doubt about the capacity of worker directors to influence board decisions in view of their minority position. On the basis of experience, shop stewards claimed they were more effective than worker directors in resolving problems affecting employees.

With trade union officials there was even greater irritation about worker directors. Murphy and Walsh (1980a) interviewed 22 full-time trade union officials on their attitudes toward board participation. Their study detected a more unyielding position than that expressed by shop stewards. While union officials did not dismiss the experiment as irrelevant, their suspicion and caution could not be concealed. Officials were critical of the suggestion that worker directors would bring substantial improvements in industrial relations. They were quick to mark a boundary separating collective-bargaining issues from those concerning company policies (Murphy and Walsh, 1980a: 65). In general, trade union officials seemed to offer support for the idea of participation, but were concerned when it came to application. They expressed doubts and sought to vindicate the pre-eminence of wage and working condition issues.

The worker directors' responses to the shop stewards and full-time trade union officials demonstrate their political pragmatism. They have taken care not to become separated from the trade unions, which were their first sources of power. They clearly recognise the importance of maintaining strong links between the participation and the collective bargaining systems. There is no instance of an attempt by worker directors to compete with, or compromise, the established workplace union organisation. As union activists they show no inclination to pursue an independent course for participation arrangements. All the evidence from our interviews points to a coherent employee and trade union solidarity.

The majority of worker directors are first and foremost trade unionists, and this is reflected in their voting dispositions. Some board decisions are particularly unpalatable from an employee standpoint, for example cases involving the closure of certain uneconomic operations. In these cases worker directors will invariably adopt the expected trade union stance and register their opposition.

Although a partisan posture is ideologically inevitable, the worker directors endeavour to avoid the direct representation of "their own" union policies. All the companies involved have large numbers of trade unions and, at the most, only four can achieve seats. The successful candidates have repeatedly been concerned with showing a united employee front. This avoids acknowledging the validity of existing differences or frictions between the unions in a particular company.

At the outset of the experiment worker directors clearly foresaw the potential for a separation of traditional employee loyalties. Their subsequent behaviour has been directed at maintaining the customary employee bond, although this has required great perceptivity on their part. So far they have managed to avoid disturbing the sensitivities of the vested interests.

The Development of Substructures

Employee representation has had a catalytic effect, evident in the way in which sub-board participative structures have emerged. In some cases these structures are subtly accommodated into existing structures, while in others they have been largely spontaneous and haphazard. Taken together they amount to considerable evidence of progress in sub-board participation.

After the first elections the majority of new worker directors found themselves structurally expressionless. The 1977 Act had failed to provide any guidance on the matter of reporting back to trade unions or communicating with employees. Thus, the worker directors were confronted with the task of legitimising their new roles. This legitimisation had to occur in the context of traditions which were scrupulously guarded by trade unions. Their efforts and success in this task were dictated largely by the traditions and organisational practices then prevailing in the various enterprises.

In reporting the variety of forms of substructure which had emerged in the first decade after the 1977 Act had been enacted, it is useful to divide the developments into two distinct groups. The first group consists of three companies where a long-standing tradition of participation exists. Here, the worker directors were able to continue with existing participation structures and quickly establish direct communication and channels for reporting back.

One of these enterprises (since privatised) was B&I which provides transport services between Ireland, Britain, and Continental Europe. This company has had a works council since 1972. It was initially an information-disclosure mechanism and gradually developed into an employee-management discussion forum (Turner, 1983). By the time the 1977 Worker Participation Act was introduced, the company had already developed employee expertise capable of discussing and contributing to policy debates. The placement of worker directors on the board presented no major obstacles, but rather was viewed as a natural extension of the participation ideal.

Following the first election of worker directors in 1978, the works council structure at B&I was adjusted to accommodate the worker directors. A superior sub-board participation body, known as the Policy Group, included the four worker directors and the other employee and management representatives from various parts of the enterprise. At the Policy Group the worker directors discuss board policy issues and all relevant information is channelled through a network of subcommittees. Thus, the established sub-board mechanism, while retaining an independent purpose, became the primary back-up service and linking structure for the worker directors.

Aer Lingus has also had a comparatively long history of experimenting with participation substructures. However, when the 1977 Act was introduced these had not developed to the extent that they could embrace the company as a whole. By the late 1960s a production department works council had been established, followed by head office and general works councils. However, for the most part these works councils dealt in trivia. In 1976, at the request of the unions, consultants were engaged to assist in the search for appropriate participation structures.

These consultants suggested the formation of a Central Representative Council (CRC). The CRC would become the forum at which all issues — excluding wages, working conditions, and individual grievances — could be discussed. Both management and unions wanted to implement the proposal, but delayed because of industrial conflict and union-staff association friction.

The new participation framework was introduced in 1980 and in the following year the first worker director elections took place. As in B&I, the superior sub-board participation forum, the CRC, became the link which connected the worker directors with trade unions and employees. Worker directors attended meetings of the CRC and it is this channel which carried employee positions and views to the board. The CRC also disseminated the rationale for, and implications of, various board decisions to employees throughout the company.

The enduring characteristic of this first group of companies was the existence of structures, reflecting a custom of dealing in and developing participation ideas. These previous structures were designed to have a purpose independent of the provision of a channel for worker directors. Combining with these bodies proved to be without structural discomfort, and seemed to conform with the developing doctrine of participation within the company.

In the second group of companies no substructures existed at the time worker directors were elected to office. As a consequence there was some confusion concerning the ways in which employees should communicate with directors, and how directors should report on their participation in the board room. In one instance, the worker director experiment directly stimulated the creation of substructures, while others remain without supporting frameworks.

The ESB, although having experimented mildly with some participative structures, had not achieved any measurable progress by the early 1980s. There was considerable scepticism among management about the need for formal structures and the trade unions seemed indifferent to such initiatives (as reported in a 1982 internal discussion document on participation). However, following the first elections under the new Act in 1978, a gradual evolution commenced. Management attitudes toward participation became more positive. The trade unions also recognised the need to create suitable structures to service the new board-level participation. At the beginning of 1983 a joint management-union working party was established to undertake the detailed design and planning of participative structures.

What followed was the introduction of a two-tier Participation Council structure: a Local Council in each of the main branches of the six distribution regions, in power stations and in head office departments, where the staff numbers exceed 50; and a National Council. The Participation Council is specifically concerned with information sharing, co-operation and staff involvement.

In this instance the arrival of the worker directors seems to have been the catalyst which stimulated the creation of substructures. These substructures not only transmit board-level activity but also provide a more inclusive structural arrangement for participation throughout the company.

Other companies where sub-board participation structures were introduced after the enactment of legislation in 1977 include Telecom Éireann, Bord Gais, CERT, Eolas and the Great Southern Hotel group. The Department of Labour published a series of case studies in 1989 detailing the operation of the ESB schemes and the first four of the above named companies (Department of Labour, 1989).

But other major employers in this second group have not experienced such progress in the development of participation structures. No such progress is evident in CIE. Since the first worker director elections in 1981, the national rail and road carrier has remained devoid of organisation-wide substructures. Several distinctive traits may explain the apparent passivity toward participation by all concerned. The company has been the butt of continuous political criticism, mainly due to the enormity of its working capital requirements and allegedly low efficiency levels. The company has had a particularly turbulent industrial relations history and inter-union conflicts have also surfaced from time to time (Kelly and Brannick, 1985). In the second set of elections in 1984 there was a fall-off in the number of employees who voted, down from an 80 per cent turnout to 71 per cent. In such circumstances it is not surprising that employee participation has not become a priority.

The need for a sub-board structure in CIE has long been recognised and discussed. Nevertheless, the four worker directors continue to function at board level and have developed a largely unstructured system for relating with employees. They meet directly with the full-time officials of their parent unions and visit the various facilities throughout the country to address groups of employees. However, the principal means of communication with employees is through the company newspaper on an individual or joint basis. The worker directors provide regular reports to the newspaper on an individual or joint basis. They provide a variety of information on company policies and operations, particularly on employment-related issues.

There is a consensus among worker directors that some form of permanent structure is needed to ensure that the benefits of board representation are realised fully. The state companies covered by the Acts employ a large number of people by Irish standards. All have a multiplicity of trade unions and many of their operations are geographically dispersed. These attributes underline the need for a permanent substructure. This need is supported by experience and observation (Murphy and Walsh, 1980a: 38–46); Department of Labour, 1980: 38; 1981: 9–11). For this reason the development of a permanent substructure found a place in the 1988 legislation which paved the way for the expansion of the worker director system.

The Challenge to Tradition
The research work quoted here, and our interviews, provide evidence of a strong inclination among worker directors to sustain the new system of board level participation. There is no indication to support the assumption that worker directors or employees are in any way naive about the system. However, this predisposition toward participation is not matched by other interests. Trade union officials, and to a lesser extent shop stewards, seem to question the necessity for the new institution. Some form of power struggle seems inevitable if the worker director system is to be integrated successfully into the Irish industrial relations tradition.

Providing for employee representatives on the board of an enterprise results in a shift in the power balance not only between capital and labour but, more importantly, within the representative labour structure itself. It is this latter implication which holds the key to whether the new initiative survives or fails. To predict further developments we need to return to an examination of the historical context in which the experiment has been placed.

In all societies tradition holds a powerful position. The extent to which new initiatives will survive depends on the vigilance displayed by established interests. Also important is the speed with which interests will react to prevent structural changes from taking place. In Ireland the forces of tradition in the industrial, trade union, and collective bargaining structures carry considerable weight. Any attempt to explain or predict outcomes should acknowledge their significance.

As stated, the first 40 years of the new Irish state experienced a sustained stagnation. As Lee observed, this "helped fashion workers' mentalities and led to a reluctance to experiment and a determination to cling to what one has" (Lee, 1980: 12). Irish workers were more concerned with maintaining their positions in the income hierarchy than with questioning the underlying principles of the income structure. The absence of heavy industry inhibited the development of a distinctive class structure and workers did not identify significantly with a working-class political party. The nationalist issue also prevented the development of an industrial working class which might have been conscious of its social and economic interests. There was no political alternative to the traditional authoritarian structure in industry. Ireland had an historical situation of endemic unemployment and emigration. In this context the primary concern of the trade unions was the security of their members' employment and the protection of income levels, even against other groups of workers. In these circumstances, not surprisingly, the notion of employee participation did not assume any significance for workers.

As late as 1958 only 40 organisations outside the public service in Ireland had more than 500 employees. Even today the structure of Irish industry is dominated by a large number of small employments. Although there were dramatic changes in the 1960s, the legacy of the previous half-century lingers on. Irish society is now predominantly urban, but the assimilated labour from rural areas, where nationalist traditions are strongest, remains generally outside the politics of working-class interests (Roche, 1982). Historically, no basis has emerged to ensure a concerted political action for employee participation. The fragmented structure of the trade union movement and the continuous pursuit of sectional interests has made a collective approach to employee participation extremely difficult.

The problems produced by a fragmented and sectionalised trade union movement are well documented in Irish industrial relations literature. The difficulties arising from the trade union structure are a major obstacle to the introduction of any form of organisational democracy. Clearly, the presence of a large number of unions in an enterprise makes it difficult to develop a united representative structure for all employees. Jobs are rigidly defined, which results in continuous demarcation disputes between different groups of workers and serves to further sectionalise the workforce.

An even more divisive element is the competition which exists between unions to expand their respective memberships. Inter-union disputes concerning the recruitment of members erupt occasionally, and often result in protracted bitterness. Introducing a scheme of participation in this environment is likely to be met with considerable difficulty. Compounding these problems is the unions' traditional suspicion of company unions. Many fear that a formal worker representative structure will supplant the union in the negotiation of collective agreements.

The development of participative structures is hindered by more than the organisational and structural problems apparent in the trade union movement. The role of trade unions and employers' associations must be viewed in the wider social and political context. Participation depends not only on the actions of trade unions but also on its acceptance by employers and managers. In Ireland the employers have jealously guarded their prerogative to manage. The activities of the trade unions merely reflect the nature of the wider society, particularly the nature of the industrial relations system. As Whelan (1982: 5) points out, "the strategies which trade unions pursue are not independent of those adopted by other actors in the system". The union's concentration on economic rewards rather than on participation issues reflects the disinclination of employees to make concessions on managerial prerogatives.

It is only on the political level that the trade unions can bring about any fundamental changes in the structure of the enterprise. According to Peillon (1982: 76), the Irish trade union movement lacks the political will necessary to bring about such changes. He notes that Ireland "offers a moderate trade unionism anxious about salaries and working conditions, but not prepared to challenge the authority of the employers in their factories". Although the ICTU has a wide-ranging social and economic program, this remains secondary to the real union activity. The union's primary activity is concerned almost exclusively with improving the standards of living of workers, defending jobs and protecting working conditions' (Peillon, 1982: 73). Finally, the era of national pay agreements in the 1970s resulted in opportunities for political power. These opportunities were not utilised to secure for workers any formal participation in the enterprise. During this period the ICTU was considerably weakened by its lack of influence over many of its affiliated trade unions. The ICTU could not convince unions to exchange short-term market advantages for long-term political and social benefits. Essentially this failure by the ICTU was due to the fragmented and sectional structure of the trade union movement (O'Brien, 1981: 161–2). In turn, the actions of many of the affiliates reflected self-interests which are a legacy of past historical circumstances and the absence of class politics. This constantly shifting environment has been described as inherently unstable in structural terms (Davis and Lawrence, 1977). The task of establishing an employee participation system in this context was clearly a daunting one.

In spite of falling membership the unions consolidated their position through their participation in the tripartite agreements beginning with the Programme for National Recovery (PNR) in 1987. The PNR paved the way for the 1988 Worker Participation Act. The Programme for Economic and Social Progress (PESP) and the Programme for Competitiveness and Work (PCW) contained further commitments to employee participation, with the latter linked to and dependent upon the progress of the EU works council directive.

A survey carried out by the European Foundation for the Improvement of Living and Working Conditions concluded that for Ireland "the extent of participation (in technological change) by employee representatives in the planning stage is almost identical to the overall involvement for the European Community countries" (Frohlich, Gill and Krieger, 1993: 142–9). Around one-third of Irish managers reported that there was no involvement by employee representatives in the planning stage of new technology introduction, whereas just over half of all employee representatives had the same opinion. Similar divergences appeared in relation to information and consultation: 54 per cent of managers claimed this form of participation existed compared to 39 per cent of employee representatives, and 13 per cent of managers said employee involvement took the form of negotiation or joint decision-making compared to 9 per cent of employee representatives. But, overall, the Irish results were "broadly in line with the general European average for the planning stage of technological change". The more remarkable finding was that the Irish appeared to employ greater levels of participation in the implementation stage, though the divergences between the managers and employee representatives' responses was even greater and the authors noted that the results had to be treated with a degree of caution due to the low number of respondents.

Overall, the authors concluded that there were a number of constraints which limited the prospects for greater levels of participation by Irish employees in technological change: the low levels of management and supervisory development; high levels of distrust between management and unions and limited access to information; the multiplicity of trade unions and the rivalry that exists between them; and the absence of flexibility between craft and general functions in manufacturing. Trade union representatives were seen as ambivalent about consultations with management and the acceptance of joint responsibility outside a bargaining situation. Managers were apprehensive about handing over power without any assurance of assistance in completing their tasks.

In terms of specific issues the same survey showed that over 60 per cent of Irish firms respected the consultation objective of the framework directive on health and safety and that Ireland ranks along with Germany and Denmark as among the countries where codetermination is high and no involvement is low in regard to participation in work organisation (Gill, Beaupain, Frohlich and Krieger, 1993).

Ireland was also among the top five countries in terms of participation in product and service quality. And in spite of the responses typified in the above studies in Irish state-owned companies, the European Foundation survey concluded that "the most positive employee representatives in Europe can be found in Ireland. This is another indication that Irish industrial relations is increasingly diverging from the British tradition. Irish workers' representatives and unions are much more positive about participation than their UK counterparts' the authors concluded. Such a finding would receive favourable response in turn from the senior union officials who wholeheartedly endorsed the ICTU policy document on New Forms of Work Organisation — Options for Unions at the Galway biennial conference in 1993.

The report found that the extent of new work organisation initiatives in Ireland is similar to, if not ahead of, the position in other European countries mainly because of the presence of a large number of US multinational subsidiaries. Outright opposition to work organisation changes or the development of their own approaches by employee representatives or local officials are not seen as the best responses. Rather the policy choice should be based on a minimalist approach involving a floor below which the unions would not be prepared to go; a pro-active approach so as to have as much input as possible; and the active promotion of initiatives with the union's own agenda. But, as with the European Foundation survey, the policy issues are confined and there remains scant evidence of employee participation in strategic decision-making where fundamental issues relating to the direction of the business is concerned.

CONCLUSIONS

Ireland has an industrial relations tradition which emphasises voluntarism, with its attendant flexibility, continuous adjustment in collective bargaining boundaries, and comparative absence of legal formalities. Despite this, the experiment with statutory-based employee participation has survived the initial turbulence. In the context of the Irish industrial relations tradition the employee participation experiment represents a discernible change in the mode of policy stimulation. Many threads running through the fabric of Irish industrial relations may be regarded as the products of an unbroken series of historical events. For example, collective bargaining has taken over 100 years to evolve into a widely accepted process for wage determination and grievance handling. The new system for employee participation, on the other hand, was not born out of a similar continuum. For example, the employee participation system in the former Federal Republic of Germany (Furstenberg, 1978: 37) developed from such a continuum. In Ireland, had it not been for legislative intervention, no significant advance in employee participation would have occurred. Thus, the events of the past several years are of considerable import, as they signify a major departure in the field of industrial relations.

It is not possible to provide a complete assessment of the impact or performance of the Irish employee participation system. There is not enough evidence to assess the value of the system to employees, their unions, management, or the organisation. Because of the multidimensional nature of the system we are not yet in a position to comment on the effect of contingency factors. Variables such as enterprise size and location, technology, and the degree of employment concentration, amongst others, may influence the emerging sub-board deliberations.

The trade unions have appeared reticent about the experiment and present some resistance. From the historical collective-bargaining standpoint their position is understandable and predictable. As unambiguous proponents of the collective bargaining process they are inclined to disassociate themselves from the employee participation idea. In practice, many unions view the experiment as the first stage of involvement in the management process. They resist this involvement as they prefer to remain continuously critical of management. The unions are fearful that employee participation will distort the traditional collective bargaining relationships with management.

Another factor explaining the union's stance concerns the matter of a power realignment. All radical institutional developments entail the destruction or adjustment of traditional forms. For trade unions the new employee participation institution conveys the prospect of a redistribution of control. Unions fear they may be possible victims in the new balance of power in the industrial relations environment. However, so far there is no indication of collective bargaining in the board room and the autonomy of the trade unions seems intact. However, we must ask why trade unions have not openly resisted the challenge to their traditions and structures. The answers provide the best clues to the success and future of the employee participation experiment.

From the outset the system was designed to have a strong trade union base. All the companies covered by the 1977 and 1988 Acts are highly unionised, and the trade unions retain substantial influence in the selection of worker directors. Conversely, without the union's support, the experiment surely would have foundered. Another important feature concerns the emergence of a duality in worker directors' roles. This development is regarded as essential by the Bullock Committee (1977: 125) for enhancing the co-ordination of trade union policy. Almost all Irish worker directors have held, or continue to hold, trade union office, which prevents them from becoming isolated from the general industrial relations situation. This linking of collective bargaining with the board participation system provides essential support and legitimacy from the trade unions.

Finally, employee participation is succeeding because it does not contravene any fundamental principles of the trade unions. As the Bullock Committee commented in its prescription for a British model: it simply creates an additional means by which they may influence the managerial process. Particularly those aspects of the process which collective bargaining is inadequate to handle by itself (Bullock Committee, 1977: 125). This is also true in the Irish situation. But if the responses to the most recent survey by the European Foundation for the Improvement of Living and Working Conditions can be seen as typical, we may be seeking a subtle yet significant shift on the part of employee officials and representatives as part of a growing divergence from the British tradition.

The prospects with regard to the future are mixed. The developments described here show that the issue is no longer in the rhetorical provinces but is located on a firm operational basis. There is now a well-defined structure for the implementation of employee participation in public sector enterprises and this can be easily expanded as circumstances demand. The likelihood is that progress will continue in this sector and that sub-structures will continue to develop, especially in view of the impetus provided by the 1988 Act.

The situation regarding the private sector is quiet different. Here there is no evidence of any advance towards the employee participation ideal. Where any government initiates debate, employer interests present a formidable resistance. There is no evidence of any concessions being made with regard to the distribution of power and control within private enterprises. Clearly every effort would be made to defend the rights associated with the ownership of private property (Batstone et al., 1983: 4–5). Because Irish industrial development policy relies on foreign enterprises locating in the country, policies relating to employee participation would be regarded as undesirable. As we have pointed out, the greatest impetus towards participation in the private sector is likely to be the new legislation on Transnational Information and Consultation, though this is confined to a relatively small number of large employers.

References

Batstone, E., Ferner, A. and Terry, M. (1983): *Unions on the Board*, Oxford: Basil Blackwell.

Boyd, A. (1972): *The Rise of the Irish Trade Unions, 1729–1970*, Tralee: Anvil Books.

Brannen, P., Batstone, E., Fatchett, D. and White, P. (1976): *The Worker Directors: A Sociology of Participation*, London: Hutchinson.

Central Statistics Office (1992): *Census of Industrial Production 1989*, Dublin: Central Statistics Office.

Clarkson, J.D. (1925): *Labour and Nationalism in Ireland*, New York: AMS Press.

Committee of Inquiry on Industrial Democracy (1977): *Report of the Committee of Inquiry on Industrial Democracy*, London: HMSO.

Committee of Inquiry on Industrial Relations (1981): *Report of the Committee of Inquiry on Industrial Relations*, Dublin: Government Publications.

Cuffe, C.R. (1969): "Who Makes the Final Decision?" in *Industrial Democracy: A Symposium*, Dublin: Irish Management Institute.

Dachler, H.P. and Wilpert, B. (1978): "Conceptual Dimensions and Boundaries of Participation in Organisations: A Critical Evolution", *Administrative Science Quarterly*, 23(1): 1–39.

Daly, G. (1968): *Industrial Relations: Comparative Aspects with Specific Reference to Ireland*, Dublin: Mercier Press.

Davis, S.M. and Lawrence, P.R. (1977): *Matrix*, Reading, Mass.: Addison-Wesley.

Department of Labour (1975): *Election of Employees to the Boards of State Companies: Proposals by the Minister for Labour*, Dublin: Stationery Office.

Department of Labour (1980): *Worker Participation: A Discussion Paper*, Dublin: Stationery Office.

Department of Labour (1981): *Discussion Paper on Worker Participation: A Response from Worker Directors*, Dublin: Stationery Office.

Department of Labour (1989): *Case Studies in Employee Participation*, Dublin: Stationery Office.

Dickson, I. (1981): "The Relation of Direct and Indirect Participation", *Industrial Relations Journal*, 12: 7–35.

Frohlich, D., Gill, C. and Krieger, H. (1993): *Workplace Involvement in Technological Innovation in the European Community, Volume 1: Roads to Participation*, Dublin: European Foundation for the Improvement of Living and Working Conditions.

Furstenberg, F. (1978): *Worker's Participation in Management in the Federal Republic of Germany*, Geneva: International Institute for Labour Studies.

Gill, C., Beaupain, T., Fohlich, D. and Krieger, H. (1993): *Workplace Involvement in Technological Innovation in the European Community, Volume 2: Issues of Participation*, Dublin: European Foundation for the Improvement of Living and Working Conditions.

Goss, J. (1973): *Industrial Relations and Moves Towards Industrial Democracy in Ireland*, University of Sussex: Centre for Contemporary European Studies.

Gray, E.J. (1969): "Build, not Destroy" in *Industrial Democracy: A Symposium*, Dublin: Irish Management Institute.

Hanlon, R. (1976): *Joint Consultation in Irish Industry*, Dublin: Irish Productivity Centre.

Heller, F.A. (1976): "Decision Processes: An Analysis of Power Sharing at Senior Organisation Levels" in R. Dublin (ed.), *Handbook of Work, Organisation and Society*, Chicago: Rand McNally College.

Hillery, B., Kelly, A. and Marsh, A. (1975): *Trade Union Organisation in Ireland*, Dublin: Irish Productivity Centre.

Hillery, P.I. (1969): "Experiment, Experience and Evolution" in *Industrial Democracy: A Symposium*, Dublin: Irish Management Institute.

Irish Congress of Trade Unions: *Annual Reports, 1965–82*, Dublin: ICTU.

Irish Congress of Trade Unions (1993): *New Forms of Work Organisation: Options for Unions*, Dublin: ICTU.

Kelly, A. and Brannick, T. (1985): *Strikes in the Public Sector*, Working Paper, Dublin: Department of Industrial Relations, University College Dublin.

Lee, J.J. (1980): "Work and Society Since 1945" in D. Nevin (ed.), *Trade Unions and Change in Irish Society*, Dublin: Mercier Press.

McCarthy, C. (1975): "Worker Participation in Ireland: Problems and Strategies", *Administration*, 23(2): 10–9.

McCarthy, C. (1977): *Trade Unions in Ireland, 1894–1960*, Dublin: Institute of Public Administration.

McCarthy, W.E.J. (1967): *The Role of Shop Stewards in British Industrial Relations*, London: HMSO.

Mulvey, C. (1972): *Industrial Democracy: Forms of Employee Representation in Industrial Relations*, Dublin: Federated Union of Employers and Confederation of Irish Industry.

Murphy, T. and Walsh, D. (1978): *National Survey on New Forms of Work Organisation*, Dublin: European Foundation for the Improvement of Living and Working Conditions.

Murphy, T. and Walsh, D. (1980a): *The Worker Director and his Impact on the Enterprise-Expectations, Experience and Effectiveness in Seven Irish Companies*, Dublin: Irish Productivity Centre.

Murphy, T. and Walsh, D. (1980b): *The Worker Director and his Impact on the Enterprise-Expectations, Experience and Effectiveness in Seven Irish Companies: Summary Report*, Dublin: Irish Productivity Centre.

O'Brien, J.F. (1981): *A Study of National Wage Agreements in Ireland*, Dublin: Economic and Social Research Institute.

O'Hara, B. (1981): *Irish Industrial Relations Law and Practice*, Dublin: Folens.

O'Sullivan, H. (1973): "Worker Participation: A Trade Union View", *Management*, April.

Peillon, M. (1982): *Contemporary Irish Society: An Introduction*, Dublin: Gill and Macmillan.

Poole, M. (1979): "Industrial Democracy: A Comparative Analysis", *Industrial Relations*, 18(3): 62–72.

Roche, W.K. (1982): "Social Partnership and Political Control: State Strategy and Industrial Relations in Ireland" in M. Kelly, L. O'Dowd and J. Wickham (eds), *Power, Conflict and Inequality*, Dublin: Turoe Press.

Sheehan, B. (1991): "Employee Involvement in the Private Sector — Draft Declaration Agreed", *Industrial Relations News*, 24: 21–2.

Turner, T. (1983): *An Analysis of Formal Substructures of Participation in the B&I Shipping Company*, (unpublished) M.B.S. dissertation, Dublin: University College Dublin.

Whelan, C.T. (1982): *Worker Priorities, Trust in Management and Prospects for Workers Participation*, Dublin: Economic and Social Research Institute.

CHAPTER 13

COMPETITION AND THE NEW INDUSTRIAL RELATIONS AGENDA

William K. Roche and *Patrick Gunnigle*

Challenges to traditional or established industrial relations practices in Ireland arise from such major forces as intensified international competition, changes to the structure of product and service markets, European integration and new approaches to the management of manufacturing technologies. Their impact is evident in attempts by companies to manage change successfully and with minimum disruption; in efforts by trade unions, employer organisations and international agencies to analyse and control changes in line with their own agendas; and in workplace initiatives aimed at restructuring — sometimes profoundly — production systems and working practices.

In this chapter we examine first, the nature of the major external trends now impacting on the conduct of industrial relations in Ireland, and second, the main lines of management and union response apparent at company and workplace levels.

EXTERNAL CHALLENGES TO ESTABLISHED INDUSTRIAL RELATIONS PRACTICE

The main forces making for change in industrial relations practice in the countries of the European Union originate *outside* the sphere of industrial relations in international, commercial, political and technological trends.

Never before has the analysis of industrial relations practices policies been so closely tied to an appreciation of commercial and national and international political pressures. In the past, the worlds of industrial relations practitioners and academics alike tended to be much more introverted and preoccupied with the internal dynamics of industrial relations systems, agreements and procedures. The professional preoccupations and vocabularies of industrial relations experts tended to revolve around distinctly industrial relations themes: disputes and grievance procedures, anomalies in pay structures, productivity bargaining, inter-union bargaining groups etc. Currently, these concerns, though not altogether displaced, often take second place to such issues as company performance, the union's role in contribution to business success, mission statements and quality standards, business units, employment flexibility and so on.

It may be useful to focus on two major external forces: (a) the intensification of international competition; and (b) changes in governance and the regulation of the public sector.

Intensified Competition

One of the key trends in business of the past two decades has been the globalisation of competition in product, service and capital markets. This has arisen from developments in transport and communications infrastructures, but much more importantly from the liberalisation of world trade. The evolving process of European integration, culminating in the European single market, the liberal trade policy of GATT, the emergence of Japan and the Pacific Rim countries as major trading nations and, latterly, the disintegration of the former Eastern block and increasing integration of former communist-dominated nations into international trade have led to intensified international competition across a range of product and service markets. These developments have been of particular importance for Ireland, given both the "smallness" and the extreme "openness" of the Irish economy. Ireland's reliance on international trade exposes its highly significant exporting sectors to global competition, even allowing that foreign companies dominate Irish industrial exports and that the degree to which competitiveness revolves crucially around cost/price considerations, as distinct from considerations of quality or innovation, varies across product markets and over time (McAleese and Gallagher, 1994; NESC, 1993: ch. 4).

A significant theme in reviews of Irish industrial relations during the 1970s and early 1980s was the apparent willingness of foreign-owned firms to concede wage increases above levels set down in national wage agreements or higher than the norms emerging in decentralised pay rounds (Hardiman, 1988; Roche and Geary, 1994). Given the capacity of foreign-owned firms to absorb labour-cost rises, the major unions often targeted such companies in the early stages of pay rounds. The available evidence for the period since the late 1980s suggests that foreign-owned firms in general, many possibly facing much tougher international price competition, now tend to settle within prevailing wage norms (Roche and Geary, 1994). In many cases this may reflect a change in corporate strategy and organisation in parent companies which involves plants competing against each other for business and new investment. When multinational companies are configured in this way, local plants must have regard to the cost structures of their facility as compared with other plants in the company or even those competing with the company. This provides a direct incentive towards cost control and can lead to tight control of the pay bill, especially in labour-intensive industries. Perhaps related to this development, unions for their part have seemed less able — though in the context of the prevailing national wage programmes they may also have been less willing — to focus their bargaining efforts on major foreign-owned companies to win concessions that might set headlines for other employers.

An illustration of how even high-tech foreign companies in Ireland, not originally competing primarily on cost grounds, can face intensified price competition can be found in the severe competitive squeeze experienced by computer companies like Digital and Ahmdahl in the early 1990s. Another instructive example of price and cost becoming pivotal, with major implications for industrial relations, is provided by Syntex Ireland, which in 1993 faced possible closure following the expiry of the patent on a highly successful drug manufactured by its parent company, the Syntex Corporation. The County Clare plant found itself competing for survival with Syntex plants in other countries. The price of survival was a major overhaul in cost structures and radical changes in industrial relations practices (*IRN*, 1993).

A more recent example is provided by Packard Electric in Tallaght, a subsidiary of General Motors, which faced a competitive threat to its survival emanating from its cost structure relative to other Packard plants in Europe, including a plant located in eastern Germany. At Labour Court hearings into the dispute, Packard management claimed that the Tallaght plant was 20 per cent less efficient than Packard plants in Spain, Portugal and Turkey. Again, survival turned on containing pay costs and accepting changes in working practices, geared to increasing productivity at the Tallaght plant. While the IDA has been urged by the Government to concentrate their job creation efforts in industries not as open to price and cost competition from low-cost European economies as are engineering and electronics, it is clear from the recent industrial history of foreign-owned firms in Ireland that considerations of cost can prove crucial to the survival and growth in Ireland of major companies.

For indigenous Irish companies producing for export markets, cost considerations are usually of greater significance in maintaining competitiveness. This is because indigenous firms more often sell price-sensitive products. The clothing industry provides a particularly stark illustration of the impact on job security of intensified international competition on both export and domestic markets. In this sector, marginal changes in the tax regimes of competing countries, like the UK, or movements in exchange rates, may pose severe competitive pressure on exports. For indigenous exporters the structural features associated with the "smallness" of the Irish economy pose particular problems in the context of intensified competition. Relatively small-scale production units and lack of management expertise in such areas as marketing, may limit the ability of companies to respond to price competition by cutting costs, restrict their scope to diversify markets geographically, or prevent them from seeking to move to less price-sensitive market segments (McAleese and Gallagher, 1994: Kennedy et al., 1988).

Irish firms producing for the domestic market also face intensified competition in which considerations of price are frequently of major importance. It has been pointed out that frequently Irish imports are non-competitive with domestic producers (McAleese and Gallagher, 1994: 25). Nevertheless, in many product markets, particularly consumer markets such as those in food and clothing, domestic producers now face direct competition with products produced throughout the world. Indigenous suppliers of components and related products to foreign-owned companies operating in Ireland must also maintain competitiveness relative to other potential suppliers abroad. With the completion of the Single Market, the coming into force of EU measures to liberalise trade in services will also expose domestic providers of services in areas like banking and financial services to unprecedented levels of competition — adding further to the already intensified domestic competition between providers of such services resulting from the deregulation of these industries during the 1980s. The recent coming into force of EU regulations on the public procurement market also means that domestic suppliers of goods and services to organisations in the Irish public domain must now compete for business with suppliers elsewhere in the EU. The loss by a Smurfit printing subsidiary of the contract to produce directories for Telecom Éireann at the close of 1994 sent shock waves through Irish business. The success of a foreign competitor highlighted the changed competitive conditions facing domestic producers of goods and services for what had long been a protected and stable market. It has been pointed out that the same structural features which limit the competitive performance of Irish exporters pose major competitive challenges for companies in exposed domestic markets (Kennedy et al., 1988: chs. 11–12).

Even in the case of products and markets where pressures on cost are not so intense and competitiveness revolves to a greater degree around considerations of product or service quality (or novelty/ innovation), intensified international competition carries major implications for industrial relations practices.

The strategy of explicitly focusing on the quality or intrinsic features of products or services as a means of securing sustainable competitive advantage, and hence of making competitiveness less sensitive to considerations of price and cost also, is a major international business trend of the past two decades. Competitive postures based on quality and product innovation originated in leading international companies in manufacturing industries like motor manufacturing and electronics and service industries like airline travel. Competing on the basis of quality involves the adoption by companies of exacting manufacturing standards or rigorous criteria of service quality. To realise these standards new approaches to manufacturing and service delivery are adopted, utilising techniques like quality circles, total quality management (TQM) and world-class manufacturing (WCM).

These production techniques frequently dovetail with other innovations more directly focused on cost control, for example, lean production and just-in-time production (JIT). New manufacturing concepts and techniques and new ways of producing services have now diffused well beyond the large international companies in which they were pioneered. In Ireland we find significant developments in these areas in indigenous companies, whether producing for export or domestic markets. Foreign-owned companies will frequently insist that their components and sub-assembly suppliers adopt standards of rigour in monitoring quality similiar to those they themselves apply, putting pressure on small local manufacturing companies to copy the management systems and working practices of leading-edge companies. In industries like retailing, the major foreign-owned and indigenous chains now also tend to insist that suppliers of products adopt rigorous manufacturing and quality standards. The most well-known example of such a strategy is that provided by Marks and Spencer.

The Industrial Policy Review Group (Culliton Committee) (1992) has enshrined in current Irish industrial policy the principle of seeking to make the development of "clusters" the cornerstone of national competitive advantage. This strategy involves giving priority to sectors and networks of companies capable of competing on the basis of indigenous skills and industrial traditions, natural advantages and other aspects of competitive advantage not easily replicable by foreign competitors. While progress towards the achievement of clusters is yet unclear, the thrust of the cluster strategy would seem to imply competing, where possible, on the basis of skills, competencies and distinctive product attributes rather than on the basis of price/cost or the manufacture of products of a generic character, which could be as easily produced in other locations. While there may be no simple correspondence between the cluster strategy and patterns of industrial relations based on high skill, strong employee commitment and flexible work practices, the viability of such a model is likely to be greater in competitive circumstances in which companies are made less vulnerable to ruthless price competition or competition based on ease or replication of product and service attributes (cf. Kochan and Dyer, 1993). If quality and distinctive product/service attributes prove easy for competitors to emulate, competition is then likely to focus on price.

In parallel to such developments in international competition and Irish industrial strategy, a number of commentators have identified a change in the *structure* of competition in a broad range of product and service markets. In place of competition focused on uniform products and services, there has evolved in some markets, or market segments, competition focused on the provision of customised products or services. The *extent* of such a trend in product and service markets remain a matter of considerable controversy in the academic literature (see, for example, Piore and Sabel, 1984; Streeck, 1992; Proctor et al., 1994). Commentators convinced that this represents a major secular trend across a wide range of product and service markets write of the emergence of "post-Fordist" markets and production systems, characterised by extensive product differentiation, rapidly changing product lines, customisation, very versatile production technologies, shorter production cycles, higher levels of skill and more flexible modes of workforce deployment and redeployment. While the extent of such a trend may be debatable, that major consumer product and service markets have changed in this way cannot be doubted. Witness, for example, the remarkable level of product diversification which has occurred in recent years in retail banking and financial services, the diversification and short product life-cycles of cars and many consumer durable goods and the multiplication of product varieties and product variations in retail food markets.

Changes in Governance and the Public Sector

The competitive trends identified above are now beginning to impact in a major way on companies in the public domain. This is due largely to the level of governance shifting in respect of economic policy to the European Community. The effects of such a shift in the governance of markets have been compounded by associated changes in the posture of Irish governments towards commercial and industrial relations problems in the semi-state companies.

Traditionally, the semi-state companies were strongly protected from competition by their status as statutory monopolies. The serious fiscal difficulties faced by Irish governments during the 1980s and early 1990s, combined with the impact of fiscal targets set down in the context of the Maastricht process, represented the first real pressures on the cost structures of semi-state companies and their attendant managerial systems and industrial relations practices. O'Connor (1995) describes the stark situation faced by Bord na Mona in such a climate and the way in which the company's straitened circumstances acted as a catalyst for profound industrial relations change.

With closer European integration and the advent of the Single Market, these protections have been eroded, or stand to be removed with time. Aer Lingus faced increased cost competition on hitherto profitable routes from 1987, triggered by EU attempts to deregulate air travel in the Community. The ESB now faces the prospect of EU-instigated competition in the electricity market. This impending change in the competitive circumstances faced by the Board, combined with the devastating effect of the 1991 electricians' strike, has led to a profound change in the industrial relations ethos of the ESB and its unions. For the first time since the Board was founded, serious joint union–management efforts are being made to move beyond adversarial industrial relations (cf. Hastings, 1994). Telecom Éireann still enjoys a monopoly of the domestic telephone business, but faces stiff competition from domestic foreign competitors providing value-added services other than voice telephony. In the year 2003, the company loses its derogation from European Union regulations on competition in the call services market.

The changed circumstances of Telecom Éireann have also encouraged major initiatives in industrial relations change, this time under the broad rubric of total quality management. Like ESB, Telecom faces the challenge of seeking to recast industrial relations practices, while simultaneously facing job losses of considerable scale. Moreover, the company is also preparing for a strategic alliance with a major international company in the telecommunications industry. The change process at Telecom, like that at ESB, has led to the adoption of non-traditional postures by the company's main union, the Communication Workers' Union. The CWU has sought to influence the debate on Telecom's acquisition of a strategic partner. Specifically, the union has articulated a perspective on the kind of competitive posture best suited to respond to the changing market, while simultaneously supporting an industrial relations culture based on high skill, progressive union–management relations and the preservation of as many jobs as competitive conditions allow (CWU, 1994). Telecom management have shown signs of being prepared to give the union a voice in the process of decision-making on the issue of a strategic alliance.

The shift in governance towards policies shaped at the level of the European Union has thus unleashed competitive forces in markets in which the semi-states long enjoyed a monopoly. Competition has in turn set in train a dynamic of change in industrial relations in the public domain. The main direction of change has been away from the established adversarial model towards the adoption of new concepts of partnership, consensual joint decision-making, work flexibility and product/service quality.

Changes in governance and political regulation, following on from European integration, have also impacted on the traditions of State intervention in public-sector industrial relations crises in Ireland. EU competition policy narrowed the leeway available to the Government to underwrite the survival of Irish Steel and Aer Lingus in the wake of serious commercial and industrial relations crises during 1994.

But the Government's handling of these and other disputes, in particular the dispute at TEAM Aer Lingus, also pointed towards a change in the traditional stance of ministers and politicians towards disputes in public-sector companies. European constraints aside, what emerged in the most serious public-sector disputes of 1994 was an apparent new resolve by ministers to insist that management and unions find solutions to commercial and industrial relations crises through their own efforts in direct bilateral negotiations. The long-familiar dynamic in such disputes was for both parties, but in particular the unions, to appeal to ministers, over the heads of management, to win concessions denied them by the other side. This process of "political exchange" (Ferner, 1988) had coloured the handling of major public sector disputes since the various semi-states were established.

In recent years, while the familiar postures associated with "political exchange" have not altogether disappeared, there has been a new emphasis by governments on public-sector management and unions being responsible for the fate of their companies — even to the degree that their failure to resolve serious crises, like those at Irish Steel and TEAM, might lead to the closure of the companies concerned. Noting the change, Tim Hastings (1994: 42) has written of a "more hands-off approach by Government . . . in which it will leave any direct intervention until the latest possible hour". The fact that intervention at "the latest possible hour" *has* remained a feature of major semi-state disputes, such as those at TEAM and Irish Steel, and even of the Packard dispute in the private sector, indicates that the Government's stance remains ambiguous: more "hands-off" than in the past in operational industrial relations, but "hands-on" if all standard industrial relations procedures have been exhausted and major closures and serious job losses seem imminent. Thus, paradoxically, while some commentators can point to the emergence of a more arm's length and harder commercial stance by governments on industrial relations in the semi-states, other commentators can point in recent years to the "politicisation" of major disputes in the public and even private sector (cf. Sheehan, 1995).

If crisis political intervention becomes a standard feature of major disputes in the public sector, it inevitably threatens to dilute the direct impact of competitive forces on industrial relations restructuring at company and workplace levels. Unions, in particular, will adjust their negotiating stances in anticipation of government intervention to stave off serious job losses and their inevitable political fall-out. The logic of the policy of encouraging management and unions to share ultimate responsibility for the commercial viability of their companies points to a very residual role for governments where serious crises are precipitated. When government do intervene, they must act to underscore rather than dilute competitive priorities — albeit not necessarily taking sides between the specific proposals of the parties in dispute. In the event, this is essentially what occurred in the 1994 Irish Steel and TEAM Aer Lingus disputes in the public sector and the 1994–95 Packard dispute in the private sector. If such a policy gains ground and becomes standard, it will add additional impetus to the impact of competitive pressures on established industrial relations practice in the public (and the private) domain.

New trends in governance are also beginning to put pressure on established industrial relations practice in the public services. While public services, by definition, are insulated most from direct competitive pressures, they are far from being inert to the trends we have been discussing. The fiscal crisis of the Irish state during the 1980s and latterly, the Maastricht process guidelines on the control of public debt, have led to a greater degree of control over public spending. Given that the public service pay bill accounts for about 40 per cent of current government spending, pay determination, work practices and industrial relations generally, inevitably come under the spotlight in a tighter fiscal regime. Thus, for virtually the first time since their inception, the various conciliation and arbitration systems are being reformed, albeit modestly so far. More major changes are under negotiation in public service grading structures and related grades in the health services and local government. While the pace of industrial relations change in these areas is currently far from dramatic, it may be further accelerated by other trends in the public service, such as the implementation of the "strategic management initiative" and wider civil service reform.

Up to now, we have emphasised the challenges to established Irish industrial relations practice posed by international competitive and fiscal pressures associated with the process of European integration. What also bears emphasis, however, is the manner in which European social policy will set the parameters within which managements and unions must respond to these challenges. Possibly the most tangible manifestation of the impact of the EU on Irish industrial relations has been the considerable increase in employment legislation since the 1970s (Fitzgerald, 1995). Key aspects of current Irish employment legislation, such as that on sexual equality, have their origins in European Union directives and actions plans. More recent EU developments in social policy are also likely to impact considerably on the framework of Irish labour law and industrial relations practice. The 1987 Single European Act, aimed at strengthening economic cohesion by removing barriers to competition between member states, attempts to establish a common social policy framework throughout the EU. In 1989, a Charter of Fundamental Social Rights of Workers, the Social Charter, was signed by all member states, except the United Kingdom. The Social Charter (subsequently named the "Social Chapter") was drafted as a response to the objectives set out in the Single European Act of harmonising working conditions in the EU. The attendant Social Action Programme, agreed in 1990, comprises some 49 legally binding directives and recommendations. The Social

Chapter and Action Programme have been supported, with varying degrees of enthusiasm, by the Irish Government, trade unions and employers (Hourihan, 1994).

While aspects of the Social Chapter are already embedded in the Irish legislative framework, the development of EU social policy and its role in regulating labour markets are clearly issues of critical concern for policy makers and industrial relations practitioners. An issue of particular importance for industrial relations is the impact of the Social Chapter on competitiveness (Fitzgerald, 1995). This was a central reason for the United Kingdom seeking to opt out of the Social Chapter prior to the ratification of the Maastricht Treaty. To date, some progress has been made on many of the points contained in the Social Action Programme, with the most important developments occurring with the adoption of directives covering working time, the protection of pregnant workers, the protection of young workers, health and safety, employment contracts and, most recently, on information and consultation. Reviewing the impact of the European Union on Irish industrial relations Hourihan (1994) argues that EU membership has significantly impacted on the nature of national-level collective bargaining in recent years. He suggests we may be witnessing the development of a new facet of the decision-making process affecting industrial relations with the European Commission being afforded a role as "validator" of issues covered in national agreements. Access to EU funding is now being firmly tied to the acceptance or validation of the European Commission of policy decisions achieved at national level bargaining. Increasingly, the use of EU funds may be linked to the adoption of labour market reforms put forward by Brussels. Hourihan (1994) suggests that such developments afford the European Commission an unheralded place in the formation of labour market policies in Ireland and other member states.

THE RESPONSE TO INTENSIFIED COMPETITION: THE NEW INDUSTRIAL RELATIONS AGENDA AT COMPANY AND WORKPLACE LEVELS

Responding to competitive pressure — by emphasising price, quality or distinctive workforce competencies — poses major challenges to established industrial relations practice. In particular, the adoption of new production concepts and techniques, geared to competing on the basis of quality or product diversification — the development path for Ireland set out in current industrial policy — would seem to require a sea-change in traditional postures and practices by each of the social partners. Flexibility becomes of cardinal importance, particularly in the organisation and performance of work; companies must seek employee and union commitment to quality as a primary concern; existing demarcations between crafts and occupations may have to give way to multi-skilled and inter-disciplinary work teams, and employees must be encouraged to participate actively in problem solving at various levels of decision-making. The practical issues that arise in seeking to implement these principles are considered in this section. It bears emphasis that these priorities together effectively constitute a new understanding of "good industrial relations". Traditional industrial relations practice, as emphasised by Pankert (1995) revolved primarily around management and unions jointly regulating working conditions through adversarial collective bargaining. In this understanding of good industrial relations, exemplary practice resided in such things as clear and detailed agreements at company or workplace level covering pay, working conditions, staffing levels, shift arrangements and the many other exigencies of employment. Stable relations between bargaining partners on the union and management sides, which allowed ongoing compromise to ensue, were also integral to this understanding of good industrial relations; collective bargaining was its pivotal practice. The transformation of the established pattern of industrial relations in Ireland, to bring it into line with the more inclusive and demanding understanding of good industrial relations entailed by new market and production trends, will necessitate a high degree of practical consensus regarding change on the part of the social partners — and very considerable skill and resourcefulness in the management of change.

The competitive pressures to which we have alluded have resulted in recent years in a deep and pervasive management-led agenda for industrial relations change. Probably at no point since the Irish industrial relations system was established as a pillar of the economic and political framework of the State have managements felt compelled to seek such degree of change in the conduct of industrial relations across a wide range of industries. The long familiar managerial posture of reacting to union claims and absorbing union pressure has been replaced in many sectors by a new emphasis on industrial relations restructuring. Nor have unions adopted a merely reactive posture in the face of the new managerial agenda. At central level, the ICTU, SIPTU, AEEU, CWU and other unions have engaged in a process of reappraising traditional ways of representing their members' interests. Indeed some unions, in particular the AEEU in manufacturing, claim to be taking the lead in pressing management to adopt new production concepts and associated new industrial relations practices.

Here we present a short examination of some manifestations of change in key aspects of industrial relations postures and practices at the level of organisations. The major issues briefly considered are (a) flexibility, (b) quality management initiatives, (c) employee involvement and participation and (d) the role of trade unions. Our concern in discussing these issues is to identify from the wider literature the major concerns that arise in proceeding with innovations in each area and to draw attention to any relevant existing Irish evidence on the extent and impact of the new initiatives.

Flexibility

A pervasive issue underpinning many contemporary analyses in industrial relations practice is the issue of flexibility. The essential argument is that increased competitive pressures in product markets and changes in consumer behaviour, as discussed above, are forcing organisations to become increasingly flexible in almost all aspects of their operations. Academic research and debate in this area is frequently focused around three distinct types of flexibility (Atkinson, 1984):

1. *Numerical Flexibility*: incorporating extensive use of atypical employment forms which allow the organisation to take on and shed labour flexibly in line with business needs

2. *Functional Flexibility*: incorporating the ability to deploy workers across a range of jobs and tasks

3. *Financial Flexibility*: incorporating the ability of organisations to link decisions on basic pay levels to labour market conditions and to relate decisions on pay increases to employee or company performance.

From an industrial relations perspective the emergence of the "flexible firm" scenario is most commonly associated with the adoption of a so-called "core–periphery employment model" (Atkinson, 1984; Flood, 1990). Within this scenario the "core" is composed of full-time staff who putatively enjoy relatively secure challenging jobs with good pay and employment conditions. In the case of such staff, premium is placed on the achievement of functional flexibility. In contrast the "periphery" is seen to comprise diverse groupings of temporary, part-time and contract workers who have considerably less favourable pay and employment conditions and less job security or training and promotion opportunities. This is seen to reflect an emphasis on numerical and financial flexibility in the management of these categories of staff.

It is now generally accepted that coherent, proactive core–periphery models of industrial relations restructuring are unusual and untypical of general trends. At the same time, the evidence available for Ireland indicates a definite trend towards greater flexibility in a variety of forms (Suttle, 1988; Flood, 1990; Wickham, 1993). However, this development seems to be particularly focused on numerical flexibility.

The growing use of forms of numerical flexibility by employers can probably be explained by the combination of competitive or cost pressures and high unemployment. Chronic high unemployment means that there will be a ready availability of people willing to work in temporary, contract or part-time jobs. A 1990 survey of 200 Irish private sector and commercial semi-state companies, conducted for the European Foundation for the Improvement of Living and Working Conditions, provides the best data available on aspects of the industrial relations of numerical flexibility (Wickham, 1993). The survey found that Ireland has a relatively low incidence of part-time work, fixed-term contract work, Saturday work and evening work, compared with the major European Union countries. However, in companies where such flexible forms of working were used, they generally applied to comparable, or in the specific instance of Saturday working, relatively high, proportions of staff (Wickham, 1993: ch. 3). The survey confirmed that there had been a recent rise in the importance of non-standard employment. However, the responses of managers interviewed suggested that future growth in non-standard employment would be focused around Saturday work and evening work and confined mainly to companies in which non-standard work was already well established (Wickham, 1993:35–7). The study indicated that companies looked to non-standard employment primarily for the direct cost advantages it was seen to bring and placed relatively little emphasis on any advantages it might hold for employees. Evidence of workforce segmentation also emerged from the study; part-time workers and workers on fixed-term contracts occupied a distinct employment tract, with little prospect of movement to full-time or non-contract work (Wickham, 1993: chs. 4–6).

Data released by the IDA Ireland and Forfás point to a sharp rise since the late 1980s in the growth of "atypical" employment in companies supported by both agencies (or until 1994 by the IDA). Between 1987 and 1994 part-time, temporary and sub-contract employment rose by 121 per cent in companies assisted by these agencies. Over the same period permanent employment rose by 10.5 per cent (*IRN Report*, 1994, 48; 1995, 4). Of the total of 20,700 "atypical jobs" at the end of 1994, 60 per cent were in indigenous firms assisted by Forbairt and 40 per cent in overseas firms assisted by IDA Ireland. The rate of growth in atypical employment since 1992 in IDA-assisted firms, however, was in the region of 100 per cent, while that in Forbairt-assisted firms was 38 per cent. For 1994 almost 60 per cent of all employment created in IDA-assisted foreign companies was due to new contract and temporary jobs; by the end of 1994 these jobs accounted for some 10 per cent of all employment in overseas companies and 9 per cent of total employment in foreign and domestic companies assisted by the agencies. The IDA's prognosis was for a continuing increase in the employment share of atypical jobs on the grounds that companies needed "ever greater levels of flexibility in the marketplace" (*IRN Report*, 1994, 48: 11).

Trends in non-standard employment in the public service remain to be determined in detail. However, it seems clear that in response to fiscal pressure and high unemployment there has been a significant rise in the levels of part-time, temporary and contract work. The spread of non-standard employment, including increased resort to sub-contracting, has figured prominently in industrial relations in local authorities, health and education. The use of greater managerial flexibility in making use of non-standard contracts is also on the agenda for negotiations concerning the reform of public service grades and employment practices.

Functional flexibility is defined as the expansion of skills within a workforce, or the ability of firms to reorganise the competencies associated with jobs so that job holders are able and willing to deploy such competencies across a broad range of tasks (Gunnigle et al., 1995). This process can mean employees moving into either higher or lower skill areas or a combination of both. It is sometimes referred to as multi-skilling. The evidence on functional flexibility suggests that this form of flexibility is considerably less common than other forms of flexibility and, thus far, largely confined to tentative initiatives in the manufacturing sector (Suttle, 1988; Gunnigle and Daly, 1992). Some larger organisations have taken a number of initiatives in the area of "multi-skilling", for example, the Electricity Supply Board in the semi-state sector and Krups Engineering and Auginish Alumina in the private sector.

Early case evidence suggests that "add-skilling" or "extra-skilling" are more accurate descriptions of these developments than multi-skilling. This conclusion is based on the evidence that functional flexibility among skilled workers largely involves those categories receiving training in, or agreeing to undertake, a limited range of extra tasks in addition to their traditional trade, for example fitters undertaking some electrical/instrumentation work. There is, of course, evidence of organisations claiming to have total functional flexibility in their operations. However, such flexibility would appear to pertain largely to unskilled assembly-type work where there is a minimal training requirement and it is thus relatively easy to deploy workers across a large range of (simple) tasks as required (Gunnigle and Morley, 1992). A major headline initiative in the area of "complete flexibility" emerged in 1994 out of negotiations between Analog Devices and SIPTU. The "flexibility agreement" concluded at the electronics company was critical in assuring parent-company investment in a new Limerick plant in the face of competition from other Analog plants in the Far East (*IRN Report*, 1995, 2). The agreement provides, *inter alia*, for total flexibility, involving no demarcations between jobs and recognises that all jobs can expand through training and the acquisition of skills. Flexibility is also seen to entail employee involvement in both the direct work process and in preventative maintenance and the handling of breakdowns. The union is also given a voice in the company's business plan.

Financial flexibility incorporates the ability of organisations to adjust pay rates to reflect labour market conditions and to make pay increases contingent on employee performance. Financial flexibility may be used to encourage functional flexibility (Atkinson, 1984; Keenan and Thom, 1988). It is difficult to identify a clear picture for Ireland in the area of financial flexibility. Findings from the Price Waterhouse Cranfield Project suggest a trend towards the increased incidence of financial flexibility through a growth in the use of variable pay systems (Gunnigle et al., 1994; Brewster et al., 1994). However, when the incidence of performance-related pay systems across different employee categories is examined the picture that emerges is much more traditional: the evidence suggesting that performance-related pay systems remain largely confined to managerial and professional categories of employees.

With regard to the second aspect of financial flexibility, namely adjusting base pay levels to product and labour market conditions, a number of developments are notable. First, "two-tier" pay systems have been developed in some major industries. The most prominent examples are found in banking and Aer Lingus (Flood, 1989). These initiatives involved the introduction of a new entry grade at pay levels considerably below levels pertaining to employees who traditionally carried out entry-grade work. Again, the twin pressures of more intense competition and high unemployment explain the origin of two-tier pay systems in these industries. There is little empirical evidence of a widespread incidence of this form of flexibility, although it is apparent that the current state of the Irish labour market facilitates the adoption of such initiatives.

A trend towards greater flexibility in pay was also evident during the period from the early 1980s to 1987, when pay rises negotiated in decentralised pay rounds varied significantly from company to company and sector to sector in response to competitive pressures. In previous periods of free-for-all pay bargaining, "comparability" had come to play an increasingly dominant role in the dynamics of pay determination with the result that pay rises across a wide industrial front were contained within a narrow range. In the early to mid-1980s, the force of "fair comparisons" declined in favour of ability to pay and profitability, resulting in growing wage dispersion (see Roche, 1996). Since the advent of the national programmes in 1987, greater uniformity has been imposed on basic pay round increases. As such, the scope for practising financial flexibility, by basing annual or periodic pay rises on considerations of company performance has been curtailed. Under the Programme for Economic and Social Progress (1991–93), a local bargaining clause permitted negotiations at company level for a 3 per cent pay rise. It appears that the round of local negotiations frequently resulted in pay rises — sometimes well in excess of 3 per cent — linked either to blanket union commitments to "accept or co-operate with flexibility", or to specific flexibility initiatives like multi-skilling and team-working. A SIPTU survey of the union's bargaining units found that 164 companies out of 311 won concessions on flexibility as a *quid pro quo* for conceding pay rises under PESP local bargaining (SIPTU, 1993).

Under the Programme for Competitiveness and Work (1993–96) less explicit scope is permitted for local bargaining. In consequence, the willingness of companies to utilise performance-related pay and other "contingent compensation systems", like skill-based pay and profit sharing, has a major bearing on the practice of financial flexibility. Initiatives in grade and category restructuring can also be used — at least on a once-off basis — as a way of adjusting pay structures to perceived market imperatives.

Much industrial relations activity and many of the most serious industrial disputes of the late 1980s and early 1990s have involved management insisting on the revision of existing agreements and working practices. Indeed, in no other area has the management-led agenda of change been so apparent than in concession bargaining of this type which involves revisions to working conditions without compensation.

While unions across a broad industrial front have been forced to yield significant concessions with respect to working practices and conditions, concession bargaining, involving negotiated pay cuts, or downward pay flexibility, remains unusual in Irish industrial relations. This type of concession bargaining is not, however, unknown. In recent years a number of major companies have concluded agreements with unions incorporating pay cuts and pay freezes in circumstances of serious competitive difficulty. In Waterford Crystal, for example, a pay cut and long-term pay freeze were agreed as part of the company's plan for survival and recovery. Pay cuts have also been agreed in DeBeers and Krups Engineering (craft workers). Cuts were mooted in other major disputes related to restructuring, for example, TEAM and Packard, but disappeared from the negotiating agenda to be replaced by other concessions.

Given the limited incidence, thus far, of concession bargaining focused on downward pay flexibility, it would be invalid to speak of a trend in this type of financial flexibility. However, even the incidences recorded are significant in an industrial relations context long characterised by "real wage resistance", involving staunch union defence of real pay levels. Concession bargaining has become an employer option in circumstances of serious competitive difficulty and unions have been forced to accept wage cuts or freezes long viewed as unattainable in Irish industrial relations. Nor have unions in Ireland usually managed to achieve significant lasting concessions in managerial approaches or policies in return for agreeing wage cuts, or freezes or changes in working practices. Exceptions are Aer Lingus, where employee shareholding was conceded, and Waterford Crystal, where the company committed itself to a "job replacement initiative" based on developing a new packaging project and unions were given a voice in a joint task force established to review margins on products that might be subject to outsourcing.

Overall the research evidence suggests that while all forms of flexibility outlined above are on the increase, this is occurring in a somewhat piecemeal form, in reaction to depressed labour and product market conditions, rather than as part of the planned emergence of the "totally flexible firm". Such apparently expedient responses to environmental conditions may well be sustained when the environment changes and organisations seek to retain the advantage of flexibility in its various forms.

Enhanced Quality Initiatives

Over the last decade one of the most significant issues for many organisations has been a concern to achieve improvements in product quality and service. This focus is largely related to managerial desires to improve the competitive position of their organisations in the face of increased international competition. Some commentators have characterised such developments as a "Japanisation" of work practices, since it appears that the Japanese companies have often been the catalyst for the adoption of many so-called "total quality management" (TQM) or "world-class manufacturing" (WCM) techniques (Blyton and Turnbull, 1992).

In spite of their widespread currency, concepts such as TQM and WCM remain somewhat amorphous and appear to have differing meanings in different organisational contexts. For example, in some organisations TQM simply encompasses the adoption of selected techniques such as Statistical Process Control (SPC) or just-in-time (JIT) production methods. In others, TQM is a much broader concept, encompassing a total re-orientation of managerial strategy, organisational structure and job design, incorporating, for example, increased employee involvement and autonomy.

In its broadest sense, TQM involves such practices as "lean production", "cellular manufacturing", teamwork, autonomous work groups, self-inspection, total preventative maintenance, statistical process control and just-in-time systems of production and service provision (McMahon, 1995). Such systems are generally associated with functional and numerical flexibility, as discussed above. Under a TQM system, greater responsibility for quality is assigned to individual employees. TQM generally encompasses a strong emphasis on achieving continuous improvements in performance (Wilkinson, 1992). Early research evidence suggests that organisations successfully introducing TQM have found that the costs incurred during implementation are outweighed by the eventual cost savings (Hogg, 1990). Particular areas of cost savings include reduced physical costs in terms of lower inventory, reduced recalls and fewer corrections/replacements. It might also be expected that lower labour costs should materialise where organisations are discovering ways of increasing production, or improving service. It has been suggested that

TQM approaches may be associated with more intense work systems and even higher levels of monitoring of employee performance (Blyton and Turnbull, 1992; Geary, 1994; Gunnigle, 1995). Thus, quality enhancement approaches often incorporate a "more with less" focus, whereby organisations seek concurrently to achieve increased productivity and lower employment levels. This has obvious implications for industrial relations. For example, it could mean that employment conditions may deteriorate, while the standards and performance expected from workers increase.

It is suggested that the main distinguishing feature of the "TQM organisation" is that quality is seen as a strategic issue rather than an operational one (McMahon, 1995). Interest in "quality" as a company orientation in Ireland is reflected by the fact that by the end of 1993, over 1,000 companies had been registered to the ISO 9000 standard (an international quality benchmark) by the National Standards Authority of Ireland (EOLAS, 1993). The growing interest of companies in quality may reflect national survey findings which claim that "people regard quality as the most important feature when buying a product" (IQA, 1994). Separate survey findings across a sample of Irish services companies reveal that "quality significantly overshadowed price in competitive pressures" –– 86 per cent affirming the primacy of quality versus 14 per cent affirming the primacy of price (IQA, 1994).

Despite many of the espoused advantages of TQM and related approaches, it appears from the international literature that many organisations which have experimented in this sphere have not been particularly successful. One possible reason is that the majority of organisations which have pursued TQM initiatives have done so on a selective basis by, essentially, "cherry picking" particular techniques, such as SPC, and have found that the overall impact on performance of single techniques has been quite limited (McMahon, 1995). Research evidence in Britain suggests that there are extremely few organisations which adopt a "total" approach to quality management (Wilkinson, 1992; Brewster, 1992). Furthermore, only 8 per cent of British managers surveyed in a 1993 study rated their quality initiatives as totally successful (Wilkinson et al., 1993). Indeed the majority claimed only a moderate degree of success or were neutral about such practices. It is suggested that the main reasons for this are to be found in the challenge posed by TQM to existing corporate cultures. According to Wilkinson, (1992), this is reflected in a preoccupation with: (a) an overly short-term focus; (b) a suggestion that requisite changes in organisational structure are difficult to implement in practice; (c) a lack of management support, particularly in relation to the devolution of autonomy to employees and; (d) a lack of employee support, reflecting low levels of trust between management and employees or trade unions.

Consequently, it is hardly surprising that instances of failed initiatives with "quality" and "new forms of work organisation" have been identified in Ireland in circumstances where "relationships were characterised by low trust and a traditional adversarial approach" (ICTU, 1993). Indeed, given the "strikingly low levels of trust" which characterise worker perceptions of management in many Irish organisations (Whelan, 1982), the successful introduction of TQM approaches poses a considerable challenge to management. From an industrial relations perspective, it is apparent that the pressures created by JIT and TQM towards lower staffing levels and more intensive work systems demand an active and co-operative workforce. For example, given the absence of buffer stocks in the JIT environment, and the focus on continuous improvement under a TQM regime, there is an acute management dependence on labour co-operation. Dependence on labour co-operation is lower when stock levels protect management from short-term production disruptions, or when the same product (or service) can be produced (or supplied) in the same way for years on end, without any real fear of losing market share to higher quality or more effective competitors (Turnbull, 1988; Wilkinson and Oliver, 1990).

There is also considerable debate on the extent to which TQM initiatives impact on employee involvement and autonomy. Some commentators argue that TQM facilitates significantly increased levels of employee involvement through "worker empowerment" and "mutual dependency". However, others argue that these approaches are largely cosmetic and that key decisions are in practice determined by management decree (see, for example, Klein, 1989; Sewell and Wilkinson 1992).

It appears that initial trade union opposition or scepticism towards TQM and related developments has been replaced by a tacit acceptance of their inevitability. It now seems that trade unions internationally and in Ireland are attempting actively to engage these developments through addressing many traditional trade union concerns about increasing industrial democracy and improving the quality of work life. The Irish Congress of Trade Unions' 1993 policy document, *New Forms of Work Organisation*, identified a series of possible trade union responses to quality initiatives and related developments, ranging from outright opposition, through scepticism and pragmatism, to shaping the agenda by entering "partnership" with companies, while safeguarding trade union concerns (ICTU, 1993). The ICTU document concluded that the most effective trade union response was to adopt a "flexible and supportive approach", attempting to optimise the outcome for both workers and their employing organisations. The ICTU strategy further argues for moving, wherever possible, from an adversarial approach, focusing on pay and conditions, to a "new role" as business partner. Such a shift of emphasis clearly requires, and is seen to require, a different trade union orientation. ICTU policy on the union response to quality and related initiatives has been informed by unions' company-level experience of these employer initiatives in practice (ICTU, 1993: ch. 5). While such things as the Q-Mark and ISO standards appear to have diffused widely across Irish industry and services, there is little evidence that the new managerial concern with quality has resulted in any radical restructuring of work and industrial relations practices based on a shared concept of "partnership". Cases like Aer Rianta, where quality initiatives did impact on traditional practices, and Analog Devices, where quality and flexibility are associated with non-traditional forms of industrial relations, remain headlines because they are still so untypical of standard practice.

Employee Involvement and Participation
The above discussion of TQM and developments in work organisation noted that many of these initiatives incorporate a focus on increased employee involvement and participation. Employee involvement and participation range from policies designed to give employees, either individually or in groups, more direct control over the performance of their jobs, to mechanisms designed to increase employee or union input into managerial decision-making (Gunnigle et al., 1995).

The prescriptive industrial relations and human resource management literature suggested that all parties involved in employee relations can benefit from increased employee participation (Beer et al., 1984). For example, it is suggested that employers need a flexible and committed workforce willing to respond to change and perform at high levels of productivity with minimum levels of supervision and that this can best be achieved through employee involvement/ participation initiatives. From an employee perspective it is suggested that the achievement of an input into decisions which affect their working lives, allowing employees greater control and discretion in their jobs, is a widely desired employee goal (Hackman and Oldham, 1980). Even at the macro level, it has been asserted that the

State, the community and macro-economic performance may benefit from positive workplace relations based on trust, open communications, and employee involvement (Beer et al., 1984; Kochan and Osterman, 1994).

However, the achievement of real and effective participation within organisations remains problematic (Marchington and Parker, 1990; Salaman, 1992; Marchington, 1995). Employers, for example, argue that business confidence and managerial control of decision-making must be maintained to encourage investment and expansion. At the same time they are wont to suggest that barriers to worker involvement must be removed and employees given a worthwhile say in decision-making. This perspective is commonly used to encourage employee involvement in shop-floor issues, while legitimising the retention of management prerogative in higher level business decision-making (Gunnigle and Morley, 1992).

Job or work participation encompasses various initiatives to design jobs and work systems which allow for greater individual employee involvement in decisions affecting their jobs and immediate work environment. This appears to be a most practical type of employee participation, but it can be difficult to effect successfully (Marchington, 1995). Increased employee participation in job or work-related decision-making requires effective, two-way communications between management and employees, based on mutual trust. Such initiatives are likely to succeed only where workers feel they have a valuable input to make and where that input is recognised and valued by the organisation's management. It also demands a more flexible and open approach to the management process, with less emphasis on direction and supervision and more on co-ordination and communication. This form of employee participation also involves an element of role reversal with superiors listening to employee comments, discussing these with top management and consulting employees on decisions. Approaches to employee involvement at this level may take a variety of forms such as job enlargement, autonomous work groups, quality circles, suggestion schemes, consultative meetings and "management by objectives".

Employee Participation in the wider process of company decision-making may range from the relatively superficial level of management informing employees of decisions which affect them, to consultation with employees, or their trade union representatives, on major issues of company performance, like product development, work process changes and business plans. Consultation of this kind can be given effect through project teams, consultative committees, works councils and board-level representation. Employee involvement and participation are also conventionally understood to refer to profit sharing and employee equity participation, which we have discussed above under the heading of flexibility.

While instances of all such approaches to employee involvement and participation are to be found in Irish industrial relations, progress in these areas remains piecemeal and the pace of change again appears to be slow. Employee involvement in job and work performance is commonly utilised as part of — as yet confined — initiatives to refashion work practices and industrial relations processes under the broad rubric of TQM or WCM. A study of employee involvement in the introduction of new information technology in 38 Irish establishments, conducted in the late 1980s, established that little involvement other than the basic provision of information or consultation occurred in the planning or implementation phases. Nor did there appear to be any strong desire on the part of managers or employee representatives for more developed types of involvement based on joint decision-making or negotiation (Wallace, 1990). A recent study of the attitudes of the social partners to direct employee involvement in Europe canvassed the opinions of the social partners at central level and in the banking and manufacturing sectors in Ireland (Regalia, 1994). The study seems to point to a positive overall appreciation of "direct participation" at the level of the ICTU, but scepticism as to whether "direct participation" may always be necessary on competitive grounds; concern that direct participation might be used to bypass or weaken collective bargaining; and an awareness that direct participation faces structural and inertial constraints rooted in Irish industrial relations practice and management and employee attitudes. Similar themes recur in interviews conducted in the banking and manufacturing sectors (in manufacturing, however, only one interview was conducted with the AEEU in one US multinational). Differences in union postures also emerge. Employers at central and sectoral levels seem to view the extension of direct participation in a more unequivocally positive light; express a conviction that associated changes in work organisation are essential for competitiveness; and, while underlining the barriers to direct participation, appear committed to supporting its wider introduction (Regalia, 1994).

Instances of greater or lesser degrees of actual or attempted direct union involvement in broader business decision-making can be found, for example, in ESB, Telecom Éireann, Waterford Crystal, TEAM and Analog Devices. But these remain brave experiments in a realm dominated by adversarial collective bargaining and a managerial posture which seeks to marginalise unions from major decisions on company business strategy. Frequently, unions themselves remain satisfied with their marginal status, still viewing their role exclusively in terms of challenging management decisions after they have been made.

The scope for union involvement in business planning may vary as between foreign multinationals, Irish-owned multinationals and indigenous companies. The competitive focus and ultimate fate of multinational branch plants located in Ireland is likely to be determined at corporate level where Irish unions can have little influence. Unions can still become involved in operational business planning and strategy at branch plant, however, as is clear from the new agreement at Analog. The degree of union leverage over Irish-owned multinationals may be somewhat greater to the degree that their Irish based plants enjoy a more pivotal position in company strategy. Thus unions in Waterford Crystal have assumed a role in reviewing products outsourced by the company from European manufactures to determine if their production at Waterford is consistent with similar or higher profit margins. The influence over business plans of unions in foreign or Irish-owned multinationals could be affected by European Union proposals on the establishment of works councils or other similar mechanisms for informing and consulting employees. It is proposed that companies operating in the EU with at least 1,000 employees in all and — in the current draft — at least 150 employees in each of two member states be required to establish a European works council or some other procedure to provide employees with information and a voice in business decision-making. Though assessments of the likely impact of such measures on union influence vary, it has been estimated that about 120 firms in Ireland will fall within the scope of the proposed new arrangements (see Hourihan, this volume).

In the case of indigenous companies, particularly those in the public sector, the scope for direct union involvement in business decision-making would appear to be greater. These companies, whether producing mainly for export or domestic markets, ultimately depend for competitive success on the performance of their Irish plants. Their business strategy will be focused more directly, if not exclusively, on Irish facilities and they may have a high level of dependence on union co-operation with business plans and their industrial relations underpinnings. In the public sector, union involvement in core business decisions can be viewed as consistent with the tradition of adopting best industrial relations practice in publicly-owned companies. Unions, for their part, are not encumbered by the problem of seeking cross-national inter-union co-operation, particularly as unions in different countries are likely to have conflicting interests in company decisions on location and new investment and closures.

A range of public policy documents have discussed the potential benefits of worker participation as far back as the early 1980s and interest in the issue rose again in 1985 when an Advisory Committee on Worker Participation was established (see Department of Labour, 1980; 1986). In the absence of consensus between the social partners on ways of realising worker participation, however, little progress was likely from the government. Unions and management each espouse support for employee involvement and participation initiatives, but with very different slants. Irish employers staunchly resist introducing legislation to support such changes, while unions favour legislation, particularly in the area of works councils. The furthest the parties have been prepared to go on a consensual basis has been to incorporate a joint statement on the desirability of greater employee involvement in private-sector companies into the text of the Programme for Economic and Social Progress and the Programme for Competitiveness and Work. Meanwhile, progress on the ground has been slow.

Greater progress has been made in the public sector. This has reflected less a strategic response to recent international business trends than thinking at European Community level on worker rights. In Ireland the employee participation debate became more intense after entry into the European Community and resulted in much discussion and activity throughout the 1970s and early 1980s. The passing of the Worker Participation (State Enterprises) Act 1977 introduced board-level participation to seven semi-state companies and these provisions were extended to a number of other state organisations under the terms of the Worker Participation (State Enterprises) Act 1988. The 1988 Act also contained provisions for the establishment of sub-board participative structures, but allowed management and unions considerable leeway in tailoring forms of participation to the circumstances of individual companies and agencies. The Act listed 39 semi-state companies and agencies as suited to introducing sub-board structures. By 1994, some 28 of these had established structures (Kelly and Hourihan, 1994). Much of the recent focus of the representative employee participation debate has again reflected developments at European Union level where various policy documents have concentrated on board level participation, disclosure of financial information and participation through works councils.

Informed in part by industrial relations crises in a number of semi-state companies during 1993–94 and the competitive challenges now facing Irish business, the programme of the "Rainbow" Government of Fine Gael, Labour and Democratic Left, which assumed office in late 1994, contains a proposal to establish a unit in the Department of Enterprise and Employment to foster management–union co-operation and employee participation. It remains to be seen whether this initiative will go the way of earlier units and initiatives in the same area or prove to be a more effective agent of change in industrial relations practice.

The Role of Trade Unions

The period from the early to the late 1980s witnessed the most serious and sustained decline in union membership and organisation in Ireland since the 1920s (Roche, 1994b). Over the past decade unions have faced something of a resurgence of employer opposition to recognition in small companies and more sophisticated union substitution strategies in a not inconsiderable number of multinational companies, particularly in the electronics sector (Roche, 1994b; Roche and Turner, 1994). A recent study of employee relations practices in newly established ("greenfield") companies found a high incidence of non-union firms (over 55 per cent) among new start-ups (Gunnigle, 1992; 1995). (Companies establishing greenfield plants and willing to concede union recognition now also seem more likely to insist on single-union recognition agreements.) The incidence of non-unionism in greenfield plants was mainly related to ownership and industrial sector. Indeed non-unionism was predominantly confined to US-owned firms. Most Irish-, European- and Japanese-owned companies recognised trade unions. The study also found that in the case of the great majority of new plants, the decision to pursue the non-union route was determined at corporate headquarters. This research points to the emergence of a vibrant non-union sector among greenfield manufacturing and service companies. It further appears likely that this trend will be accentuated by the increasing numbers and visibility of companies successfully pursuing the non-union route which, in turn, provide useful models for new organisations considering establishing on a non-union basis. Equally, the current industrial policy focus on high technology industries and internationally traded services may reinforce growth in the non-union sector in the Republic of Ireland.

If this trend were to continue, as seems likely given the current thrust of industrial policy, the traditionally significant role of trade unions in manufacturing industry might conceivably be significantly eroded. It remains to be seen if these non-union companies will eventually concede recognition or succumb to unionisation in the face of persistent union-organising efforts, ageing workforce, commercial problems, new trade union approaches to industrial relations, or an improved national economic climate and reduced unemployment levels. Moreover, there remains little solid evidence that new "human resource" strategies, involving innovations in work organisation, new forms of consultation and communication, and greater use of variable pay systems, in themselves critically affect either recognition or levels of organisation in private sector companies (see Roche and Turner, 1994). The fact that a number of well-known companies practice such policies as part of a policy of union avoidance or substitution cannot be taken to mean that in general companies implementing new industrial relations or human resource policies either wish to avoid or maginalise unions, or have succeeded in so doing. It might also be plausibly argued that the continuing legitimacy and acceptance of trade unions, as manifested both in the corporatist structures characteristic of Irish industrial relations and the traditional acceptance of trade unions as legitimate bargaining partners, creates a socio-economic climate conducive to ensuring the maintenance of high levels of trade union recognition and influence among new and established firms (see Roche and Turner, 1994).

For the foreseeable future unions will continue to play a pivotal role in Irish industrial relations and will have a major impact on the outcome of new industrial relations and human resource strategies. But intensified competitive pressures, new managerial strategies for industrial relations and the potential attractiveness to employers of marginalising unions or adopting the non-union option pose for Irish unions arguably their most serious strategic challenge since they became a pillar of Irish industrial relations in the first three decades after Independence.

The problems faced by unions in responding to the new agenda cannot be denied. Union officials and activists have been schooled, in the same way as Irish managers, in a tradition in which adversarial collective bargaining was viewed as the mainspring of industrial relations practice. Competing and meeting commercial challenges were viewed, first and foremost, as concerns of management. Co-operation with company efforts to increase employee commitment to business success is seen to hold risks of reduced commitment to the union. Though unions are being asked to assist with measures to enhance business performance, they must also be capable of challenging managerial decisions and negotiating pay and conditions in collective bargaining. New industrial relations strategies threaten to set in train a pervasive trend towards the decentralisation of industrial relations process possibly reducing the capacity of central trade union organisations to control developments at company level. Competitive pressures may lead in the short or long term to revisions in work organisation and pay regimes which, in the eyes of union members, involve serious disimprovements in working conditions. The expansion of atypical employment also poses problems for trade unions. Unions have long focused their recruiting and organising activities primarily on permanent workers. Recruiting and retaining part-time, temporary and contract workers poses greater difficulties. Representing atypical workers in individual and collective bargaining also poses major challenges. If multi-skilling, employee involvement and enhanced employment security for "core" workers may increasingly involve the parallel development of a "peripheral" work-force composed of atypical workers, unions may have to countenance the prospect of representing a dual work-force in companies. Not surprisingly, these latter features of the new industrial relations agenda are of particular concern to trade unions (see *IRN Report*, 1994, 4: 19).

To the degree, therefore, that unions openly endorse the new agenda of competitiveness, they may thus face particularly acute problems and dilemmas. The ICTU is also subject to such dilemmas of representation. This became clear during 1994 and 1995 when Congress was accused by some sections of membership of adopting an employers' agenda, or of doing the business of the State, when it sought to broker agreements in TEAM and Packard in circumstances of crisis and threatened closure. TQM and WCM may spark frictions or outright convulsions at the interface between different occupational categories and the unions that represent them. These difficulties and uncertainties have come to light in some of the major industrial relations crises of the late 1980s and early 1990s.

A significant aspect of the debate on employee participation in Ireland since the 1970s has concerned the role of trade unions. Traditionally the Irish trade union movement did not seem particularly committed to representative forms of employee participation such as worker directors or works councils (Morrissey, 1989). Reactions to participation through equity holding have been mixed and no discernible trend is evident. Indeed, apart from support for greater disclosure of information, the traditional trade union approach to employee participation has been marked by a considerable degree of apathy. Such apathy has strong links with the doubts many trade unionists harbour about the implications of representative participation for the union's role in collective bargaining.

In recent years Irish unions have begun to face up to and address these and related problems of representation under new industrial relations. The ICTU report, *New Forms of Work Organisation*, suggests that trade unions need to take a more proactive role in influencing the planning and implementation of the new management strategies. In the area of employee participation, the report encourages a particular focus on developing, and actively participating in, employee involvement initiatives at workplace level. This report also identifies key aspects of employee participation which trade unions need to address, particularly the joint monitoring of participation initiatives at workplace level, involvement of trade unions in the internal communications processes of organisations, access to and understanding of business information and involvement in high-level business decision-making.

Some of the major unions have also committed themselves to work "with the grain" of the new managerial agenda. Unions like SIPTU and the AEEU have held seminars and conferences on the implications of world class manufacturing and related techniques.

Unions have sought to enter and even foster "partnership" in a number of major companies. Some such companies, like ESB, Bord na Mona and Telecom (previously Posts and Telegraphs), had long provided textbook cases of adversarial industrial relations at their most highly developed.

In adopting this position, unions are mindful, above all, that working with the new agenda appears the best, or the only, way of ensuring that Ireland responds to increased competitiveness by pursing an industrial and labour market strategy based on high value-added, high skill and high wage employment.

CONCLUSION

This chapter has sought to provide a context for the many changes and challenges currently presented to the conduct of industrial relations in Ireland and the ways in which companies and trade unions have sought to respond. The scope and intensity of the debate currently under way in industrial relations may indicate a growing realisation on the part of the social partners individually and collectively, that the adversarial model and its canons of good industrial relations were suited to a particular historical period of Irish economic and industrial development that has now all but passed. Given the transformation that is occurring in international economic conditions, it seems to be increasingly accepted that the adversarial model no longer provides a viable basis for relations between employees, unions and employers in Ireland.

References

Atkinson, A.J. (1984): *Flexible Manning: The Way Ahead*, London: Institute of Manpower Studies.

Beer, M., Spector, B., Lawrence, P.R., Quinn-Mills, D. and Walton, R.E. (1984): *Managing Human Assets*, New York: The Free Press.

Blyton, P. and Turnbull, P. (1992): *Reassessing Human Resource Management*, London: Sage Publications.

Brewster, C. (1992): "Managing Industrial Relations" in B. Towers (ed.), *A Handbook of Industrial Relations Practice*, London: Kogan Page.

Brewster, C. and Hegewich, A. (1994): *Policy and Practice in European Human Resource Management: The Price Waterhouse Cranfield Survey*, London: Routledge.

Communications Workers' Union (1994): *The Future of the Telecommunications Industry in Ireland*, Dublin: CWU.

Department of Labour (1980): "Worker Participation: A Discussion Document", Dublin: Stationery Office.

Department of Labour (1986): "Advisory Committee on Worker Participation: Report to the Minister of Labour", Dublin: Stationery Office.

EOLAS (1993): "Concluding Statement of the Board", Dublin: EOLAS, The Irish Science and Technology Agency.

Ferner, A. (1988): *Governments, Managers and Industrial Relations, public enterprises and their political environment*, Oxford: Basil Blackwell.

Fitzgerald, G. (1995): "The European Union and Developments in Industrial Relations" in P. Gunnigle, McMahon, G.V. and Fitzgerald, G. (eds.), *Industrial Relations in Ireland: Theory and Practice*, Dublin: Gill and Macmillan.

Flood, P. (1989): "Human Resource Management: Promise, Possibility and Limitations" unpublished research paper, Limerick: University of Limerick.

Flood, P. (1990): "Atypical Employment: Core–Periphery Manpower Strategies — The Implications of Corporate Culture", *Industrial Relations News Report*, 9:16–18;10:17–20.

Geary, J. (1994): "New Forms of Work Organisation: Implications for Employers, Trade Unions and Employees", working paper No. 9, Dublin: Business Research Programme, Graduate School of Business, University College Dublin.

Gunnigle, P. (1992): "Management Approaches to Employee Relations in Greenfield Sites", *Irish Business and Administrative Research*, Vol. 13: 20–36.

Gunnigle, P. (1995): "Collectivism and the Management of Industrial Relations in Greenfield Sites", *Human Resource Management Journal*, 5 (3): 24–40.

Gunnigle, P. and Daly, A. (1992): "Craft Integration and Flexible Work Practices", *Journal of Industrial and Commercial Training*, 24: 10–17.

Gunnigle, P. and Morley, M. (1992): "Something Old, Something New: A Perspective on Industrial Relations in the Republic of Ireland", *Review of Employment Topics* 1: 114–42.

Gunnigle, P., Flood, P., Morley, M. and Turner, T. (1994): *Continuity and Change in Irish Employee Relations*, Dublin: Oak Tree Press.

Gunnigle, P., McMahon, G.V. and Fitzgerald, G. (1995): *Industrial Relations in Ireland: Theory and Practice*, Dublin: Gill and Macmillan.

Hackman, J.R. and Oldham, G.R. (1980): *Work Redesign*, New York: Addison-Wesley.

Hardiman, N. (1988): *Pay, Politics and Economic Performance in Ireland, 1970–1987*, Oxford: Clarendon Press.

Hastings, T. (1994): *Semi-States in Crisis: The Challenge for Industrial Relations in the ESB and Other Major Semi-State Companies*, Dublin: Oak Tree Press.

Hogg, C. (1990): "Total Quality", London: Institute of Personnel Management Factsheet No. 29.

Hourihan, F. (1994): "The European Union and Industrial Relations" in Murphy, T. and Roche, W. K. (eds.) *Irish Industrial Relations in Practice, Dublin*: Oak Tree Press.

Industrial Relations News (1993): "Restructuring and Culture Change to Meet Today's Reality", Industrial Relations Conference Report, Dublin: IRN.

Industrial Relations News Report (1994), 48; (1995), 2;4, Dublin: IRN

Irish Congress of Trade Unions (ICTU) (1993): "New Forms of Work Organisations: Options for Unions", Dublin: ICTU.

Irish Quality Association (IQA) (1994): "Annual Report", Dublin: IQA.

Keenan, J. and Thom, A. (1988): "The Future Through the Keyhole: Some Thoughts on Employment Patterns", *Personnel Review*, 17: 20–4.

Kelly, A. and Hourihan, F. (1994): "Employee Participation" in Murphy, T. and Roche, W.K. (eds.) *Irish Industrial Relations in Practice*, Dublin: Oak Tree Press.

Kennedy, K.A., Giblin, T. and McHugh, D. (1988): *The Economic Development of Ireland in the Twentieth Century*, London: Routledge.

Klein, J. (1989): "The Human Cost of Manufacturing Reform", *Harvard Business Review*, March/April: 60–6.

Kochan, T. and Dyer, L. (1993): "Managing Transformational Change: The Role of Human Resource Professionals", *International Journal of Human Resource Management*, 3: 569–90.

Kochan, T.A. and Osterman, P. (1994): *The Mutual Gains Enterprise, Forging a Winning Partnership among Labor, Management and Government*, Boston: Harvard Business School Press.

Marchington, M. (1995): "Fairy tales and Magic Wands: New Employment Practices in Perspective" *Employee Relations*, Vol. 17 : 151–66.

Marchington, M. and Parker, P. (1990): *Changing Patterns of Employee Relations*, Hemel Hempstead: Harvester Wheatsheaf.

McAleese, D. and Gallagher, M. (1994): "Developments in Irish Trade During the 1980s" in M. Lambkin and T. Meenaghan, (eds.), *Perspectives on Marketing Management in Ireland*, Dublin: Oak Tree Press.

McMahon, G.V. (1995): "New Work Organisation and Quality Initiatives", in P. Gunnigle, G.V. McMahon, and G. Fitzgerald (eds.), *Industrial Relations in Ireland: Theory and Practice*, Dublin: Gill and Macmillan.

Morrissey, T.J. (1989): "Employee Participation at Sub-Board Level", in *Industrial Relations in Ireland: Contemporary Issues and Developments*, Dublin: Department of Industrial Relations, University College Dublin.

National Economic and Social Council (NESC) (1993): No. 96. "A Strategy for Competitiveness, Growth and Employment", Dublin: NESC.

O'Connor, E. (1995): "World Class Manufacturing in a Semi-State Environment: The Case of Bord na Mona" in P. Gunnigle, and W.K. Roche (eds.), *New Challenges to Irish Industrial Relations*, Dublin: Oak Tree Press.

Pankert, A (1995): "Industrial Relations and Adjustment at the Level of the Enterprise" in P. Gunnigle, and W.K. Roche (eds.), *New Challenges to Irish Industrial Relations,* Dublin: Oak Tree Press.

Piore, M. and Sabel, C. (1984): *The Second Industrial Divide: Possibilities for Prosperity*, New York: Basic Books.

Proctor, S.J., Rowlinson, M., McArdle, L., Hassard, J. and Forrester, P. (1994): "Flexibility, Politics and Strategy: In Defence of the Model of the Flexible Firm", *Work, Employment and Society*, 8: 221–42

Regalia, E. (1994): "The Positions of the Social Partners on Direct Participation in Europe", Milano: IRES Lombardia, Employee Direct Participation in Organisational Change — The EPOC Project.

Roche, W.K. (1994a) "Pay Determination, The State and the Politics of Industrial Relations", in T. Murphy, and W.K. Roche (eds.), *Irish Industrial Relations in Practice*, Dublin: Oak Tree Press.

Roche, W.K. (1994b): "The Trend of Unionisation", in T. Murphy, and W.K. Roche (eds.), *Irish Industrial Relations in Practice*, Dublin: Oak Tree Press.

Roche, W.K. and Geary, J. (1994): "The Attenuation of Host-Country Effects? Multinationals, Industrial Relations and Collective Bargaining in Ireland", working paper, Dublin: Business Research Programme, Graduate School of Business, University College Dublin.

Roche, W.K. and Turner, T. (1994): "Testing Alternative Models of Human Resource Policy Effects on Trade Union Recognition in the Republic of Ireland", *International Journal of Human Resource Management*, 5: 721–53.

Salaman, M. (1992): *Industrial Relations: Theory and Practice*, London: Prentice-Hall.

Services, Industrial and Professional Trade Union (SIPTU) (1993): "Discussion Paper Series C", unpublished, Dublin: SIPTU Research Department.

Sewell, G. and Wilkinson, B. (1992): "Employment or Emasculation? Shopfloor Surveillance in a Total Quality Organisation" in P. Blyton and P. Turnbull (eds.), *Reassessing Human Resource Management*, London: Sage.

Sheehan, B. (1995): "Packard 'Reprieve' Poses Wider Questions for the Industrial Relations System", *Industrial Relations News*, 2: 10–3.

Streeck, W. (1992): *Social Institutions and Economic Performance*, London: Sage.

Suttle, S. (1988): "Labour Market Flexibility", *Industrial Relations News Report*, 38: 13–16.

Turnbull, P. (1988): "The Limits To Japanisation — Just-In-Time, Labour Relations and the UK Automotive Industry", *New Technology, Work and Employment*, 3: 7–20

Wallace, J. (1990): "Employee Involvement in New Information Technology in Ireland and the EC", Industrial Relations News Report, 22: 13–16.

Whelan, C. (1982): "Worker Priorities, Trust in Management and Prospects for Worker Participation", Dublin: Economic and Social Research Institute, Paper No. 111.

Wickham, J. (1993): "New Forms of Work in Ireland: An Analysis of the 'New Forms of Work and Activity' Data Set", Dublin: European Foundation for the Improvement of Living and Working Conditions, Working Paper No. WP/93/31/EN.

Wilkinson, A. (1992): "Fitness for Use/Barriers to Full TQM in the UK", *Management Decision* 29(8):46–51.

Wilkinson, A., Redman, T. and Snape, E. (1993): *Quality and the Manager*, London: Institute of Management.

Wilkinson, B. and Oliver, N. (1990): "Obstacles to Japanization: The Case of Ford UK", *Employee Relations*, 12 (1): 17–21.

CHAPTER 14

THE EUROPEAN UNION AND INDUSTRIAL RELATIONS

Fintan Hourihan

Despite recent rows over the level of structural funds, membership of the European Union (EU) is still widely seen as essential in any plan to turn around the Irish economy, providing as it does a ready market of almost 400 million consumers and substantial assistance through the Community Support Framework (CSF) and the common agriculture and fisheries policies. The EU also offers the prospect of harmonising working and living standards, offering the prospect of improved standards in line with those available throughout the 15 member states as part of the EU's so-called "social dimension". This social dimension has been developed in response to a belief that workers and consumers should be allowed to share in the gains more obviously available to business through the creation of free trade. But what does this social dimension entail and how does the EU provide for social policy harmonisation?

This chapter looks at how the EU's social policies are formulated and implemented, examining procedures and institutions such as the European Commission, Council of Ministers, European Parliament and Court of Justice. It also offers a history of social policy, concentrating on the period after Irish accession, and covering crucial milestones including the Single European Act, the Social Charter and the Treaty on European Union negotiated at Maastricht. The debate on social policy is also placed in a conceptual overview and the effects of wider EU developments on the conduct of Irish industrial relations are also considered.

INSTITUTIONS AND PROCEDURES

The European Commission

The European Commission is the EU's executive body, responsible for proposing and implementing Union policy. The Commission is the guardian of the treaties and ensures that the treaty provisions and those adopted by the EU institutions are properly implemented. The Commission can, as a last resort, take member state governments to the European Court of Justice to ensure policy is properly implemented.

The Commission initiates EU policy, a power explicitly entrusted in it by the 1957 Treaty, and presents its legislative proposals initially to the Council of Ministers. It also draws up the budget, which is established by the Council of Ministers and forwarded to the European Parliament. It regularly prepares reports on the economic, social and legal situation in the Union and presents an annual report to the European Parliament.

Commissioners are nominated by the governments of each member state with larger member states allowed to nominate two commissioners while smaller states, such as Ireland, are entitled to nominate one. The current Irish-nominated Commissioner is Mr Padraig Flynn who has responsibility for Social Affairs.

The Council

Sometimes referred to as the Council of Ministers which can lead to confusion as, in practice, there are a number of Councils each of which assemble the ministers from member states corresponding to certain policy areas, for example agriculture, foreign policy, finance, social affairs. The latter is of most relevance to this study and it should be noted that Social Affairs Council meetings could include representation from three Irish government departments as currently structured — Enterprise and Employment, Social Welfare and Equality and Law Reform — while involvement by other departments is not inconceivable.

The Ministers from each of the member states usually attend two formal Social Affairs Council meetings during each six-month presidency of the EU — the presiding member state provides a president to each council whose task it is to set the agenda and to try to gain consensus. Informal Council meetings are also convened regularly and are seen as important in maintaining political contacts, providing for continuity of discussions and in general facilitating progress at later formal gatherings. In the intervening periods, the detailed work necessary to allow progress at Council meetings is undertaken on an almost daily basis at COREPER (Committee of Permanent Representatives) which is composed of civil servants from each member state, including those permanently based in Brussels. Again, for the sake of expediency, various sub-groups are formed according to policy areas — the Social Questions group undertakes the work of most relevance to social policy students.

The European Parliament

Members of the Parliament, whose role within the EU could best be described as supervisory and providing democratic accountability, are directly elected every five years. The Parliament cannot initiate measures but it can amend and, in rare situations, reject measures already considered by the Commission and the Council of Ministers. The new co-operation procedure, introduced as part of the Single European Act, has had a significant effect in increasing the influence of the Parliament by offering it a greater say in the EU's decision making process. Between the period of July 1987 and December 1988, for example, the Commission adopted, in whole or in part, per cent of amendments presented by the Parliament at first reading and the Council adopted 44 per cent in whole or in part. According to the Parliament's own research (1989) in respect of amendments arriving from the second reading, the figures for the Commission and the Council were 58 per cent and 23 per cent respectively. The Parliament's role and influence is now even more important as a result of changes agreed in the Maastricht Treaty, discussed later.

The first direct election to the European Parliament took place in 1979. (At present there is a total of 626 MEPs, most of whom are members of organised groupings — the Republic of Ireland has 15 MEPs.)

The biggest political groups are the Socialist Group (221 MEPs), the Christian Democrats (173 members), the Union for Europe (56 seats), the Liberal, Democratic and Reformist groups (52 members), the European United Left/Nordic Green Left group (31 seats) and the Green Group (25 members). While MEPs tend to vote according to Group allegiances, the party whip would not be applied as strictly as in national parliaments, and it is not impossible for informal alliances to be built where common national interests are at stake.

Almost all of the fifteen Irish MEPs are members of political groups: Fianna Fail (7 MEPs at present) belongs to the Union for Europe group (current total: 20 members and consisting of the Italian Forza and French Gaullist MEPs), Fine Gael (4 MEPs) belongs to the

European Peoples Party, also known as the Christian-Democratic Group (173 members) and which includes the Christian Democrats from Germany and the Conservative Party from Britain. The Irish Labour Party (1 MEP) belongs to the Socialist Group (221 members), the Progressive Democrats (no MEPs at present) belong to the Liberal, Democratic and Reformist Group (46 members). The sole independent MEP, Mr Pat Cox, has attained the unusual and notable distinction of becoming a vice-president within this latter group, in spite of his departure from the Progressive Democrats, for whom he had been an outgoing MEP prior to the last election and a prominent member of the Liberal, Democratic and Reformist Group. The two Green MEPs from Ireland belong to the Greens political group which has 25 MEPs in total. Though there are none at present, a future Democratic Left MEP would probably join the European United Left/Nordic Green Left (31 MEPs).

Most of the Parliament's reports and resolutions are prepared in one of its 19 committees and then debated and adopted when the Parliament meets in plenary session in Strasbourg for one week each month. The committees normally meet in Brussels — those of particular relevance to social policy students are Social Affairs, Employment and the Working Environment and Women's Affairs.

The Court of Justice

The Court is the EU's supreme judicial authority — an independent body which ensures EU law is applied in a uniform manner. It consists of 13 judges and six advocates-general, appointed by common accord by the governments of the member states, and holding office for six years. The Court, which is based in Luxembourg, can, at the request of an EU institution, member state or individual directly concerned, annul any act of the Council or Commission if it is found to be incompatible with the treaties. This power could prove vital if, for example, the legal status of the Protocol on Social Policy, agreed at Maastricht, is ever challenged at the Court as is frequently suggested likely. The Court can also decide that an action or legislative act by a member state infringes the treaties and may require the state concerned to modify or revoke its action.

National courts can ask the Court to rule on the interpretation or assess the validity of EU legislation or, subsequently, a preliminary ruling if there is no remedy under national law. The Court of First Instance, set up to lighten the workload of the Court and provide an intermediate course of redress, can rule on points of law in certain specified areas, particularly those concerning private citizens and businesses. Its judgements can be appealed to the Court of Justice on points of law only. Overall, the Court of Justice has played a vital part in developing case law and many would argue that it has been the most effective instrument of change within the EU. The Court has issued a number of crucial judgements in recent years covering areas such as equality and the transfer of undertakings amongst others. In further developing important case law, the Irish Courts have built upon the Court of Justice's rulings, such as a recent High Court case where it was made clear that the European transfer of undertakings regulations should apply to the contracting out of services (Kerr, 1992).

The relations and dynamics between the various institutions are best understood by examining the legislative process.

The Legislative Process

The 1957 Treaty of Rome, later amended by the 1987 Single European Act, and the Treaty on European Union, or Maastricht Treaty, stand as the EU's constitution. The 1957 Treaty contained articles governing equal pay (article 119), free movement of workers (article 48) and upward harmonisation of social security systems (article 121) plus improved health and safety (article 118), while also establishing the Social Fund (articles 123 and 128). Article 100 contained the legal basis for directives to be introduced which would harmonise member states' legislation affecting the establishment or functioning of the internal market. These directives would require unanimous support, a critical factor which explained a pretty stagnant social policy until the Single European Act offered the Commission new powers to introduce directives covering wider and more explicitly defined areas of competence, including the working environment and health and safety issues.

In order to harmonise the conditions of workers as part of the trade-off whereby the Single European Market offered untold opportunities for business, the Single European Act saw the introduction of articles 118A (health and safety; working environment), 118B (social dialogue) and 130A to 130E (economic and social cohesion). Article 118A contained new clearly defined areas of social policy competence, stating "member states shall pay particular attention to encouraging improvements, especially in the working environment, as regards the health and safety of workers, and shall set as their objective the harmonisation of improvements in this area, while maintaining the improvements made". The great controversy surrounding this particular section related to the scope of the working environment definition, a question which was to be central to the controversial working time directive, as we shall see later. Article 118B charged the Commission with developing dialogue between both sides of industry at European level which could if they so desired lead to relations based on agreement. The aim was to provide an opportunity for management and labour to negotiate directly within the objectives set out in Article 118A, but the vagueness of the terms of Article 118B along with the unpreparedness of both sides to negotiate Euro-wide agreements was to condemn this ambition to futility.

Article 100A offered a new legal basis for directives to approximate laws which have as their objective the establishment and function of the internal market. Such directives would, along with article 118 measures, be the subject of qualified majority voting (QMV), necessitating 70 per cent support at the Council of Ministers, Ireland would have three votes while larger member states such as France, Germany, Italy and the UK would have ten votes each.

With the accession of three new member states (Austria, Finland and Sweden) the voting system has been revised. As a result, where a Council is required to act by qualified majority, the votes of its members is weighted as follows:

Council of Ministers Member States Voting Strength	
Belgium	5 votes
Denmark	3 votes
Germany	10 votes
Greece	5 votes
Spain	8 votes
France	10 votes
Ireland	3 votes
Italy	10 votes
Luxembourg	2 votes
Netherlands	5 votes
Austria	4 votes
Portugal	5 votes
Finland	3 votes
Sweden	4 votes
United Kingdom	10 votes
Total	87 votes

The co-operation procedure enhances the role and influence of the European Parliament but its greatest effect has been to radically quicken the speed with which directives can be debated and finally implemented. The changes envisaged in the Maastricht Treaty promise to build upon the increasingly important role of the EU in regulating workplace affairs and these are examined below in the section devoted to Maastricht.

However, no matter what the fate of the Maastricht Treaty and the protocol on social policy, otherwise known as the Social Chapter, the EU will remain expressly forbidden to involve itself in a number of fundamental industrial relations issues. All member states are agreed that pay determination, union recognition and the right to strike (including the right to impose lock-outs) should be untouched by Brussels and continue to be pursued according to the prevailing practices in each member state, in recognition of the disparate industrial relations cultures across the EU.

As a result of the Single European Act, the Commission could choose from alternative legal bases when introducing social policy measures: directives which would have an effect on the working of the internal market (mainly relating to employment rights or free movement of workers) would be introduced as part of the so-called consultation procedure and require unanimous support. Alternatively, those deemed necessary to the functioning of the internal market such as removing distortions of competition or introduced specifically as health and safety measures, would be introduced according to article 100A or article 118 respectively and require qualified majority support. These would be processed according to what is termed the co-operation procedure.

Following the ratification of the Treaty on European Union, the overall EU decision-making procedure has been extended and significantly changed. As it now stands, social policy measures can be considered under one of three procedures: the consultation procedure, the co-operation procedure or the co-decision procedure. The co-decision procedure gives the European Parliament a limited right to reject legislation. The key to its operation is the establishment of a new conciliation committee in which the Council and the Parliament, with the assistance of the Commission, attempt to reconcile differences on draft legislation.

FIGURE 14.1: CO-OPERATIVE AND CONSULTATION PROCEDURES

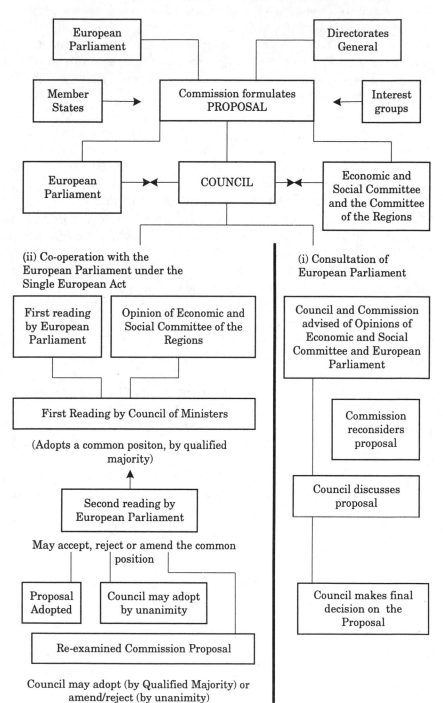

Most key areas in the area of social policy will be dealt with under the co-operation procedure, which allows the Parliament to have the second reading of draft EU legislation and make amendments which, having being submitted to the Commission, can be accepted or rejected by the Council. The co-operation procedure applies to the social policy protocol covering working conditions, information and consultation of workers, equal treatment and integration into the labour market; health and safety at work; social fund implementation decisions; and certain vocational training measures.

Amongst others, the consultation procedure applies to rules on state aids, key aspects of economic and monetary union, taxation, economic and social cohesion and the adoption of specific actions apart from the structural funds, abolition of restrictions on the freedom of establishment and on the provision of services. The new co-decision procedure, established under the Treaty on European Union, applies to the free movement of workers, mutual recognition of diplomas, provisions for the self employed, services, education, internal market harmonisation, the right of establishment, public health, the environment and consumer protection.

In the case of the co-operation and consultation procedures, the initial steps remain the same. The Commission draws up the first draft proposal and then submits it to the Council of Ministers; in the case of social policy the relevant Council is the Social Affairs Council. The Council then considers the proposals supported by working parties including the Social Questions Working Group, made up of each member states' Employment or Labour ministries and COREPER, the committee of permanent representatives to the EU. Each member state has a government office in Brussels, comprising civil servants specialising in different policy areas. At this stage employer and trade union representative organisations offer their opinions along with the Economic and Social Committee (189 representatives from employer, worker, consumer and other interest groups). The European Parliament also offers its opinion as part of its first reading on the matter. The Commission then reviews and revises its proposal, as it deems appropriate.

The legal basis for the measure now comes into play (see Figure 14.1), and the direction of its future progress depends on whether the measure has been submitted under article 100 or articles 100A or 118. Measures submitted under article 100 are simply moved from the Commission to the Council of Ministers where their fate is decided by unanimous vote. The first step in the co-operation procedure is also to send the proposal back to the Council of Ministers. The

Council must then adopt a "common position" through QMV, after which the proposal is sent back to the Parliament. The Parliament then has three months in which to adopt, reject or amend the proposal. If the common position is approved by the Parliament, it will be returned to the Council where again qualified majority support will be necessary to adopt the proposal. If the Parliament rejects the common position, then the Council will have to produce unanimous support for the measure if it is to be implemented. An absolute majority is necessary for the Parliament to amend or reject a common position. If it votes to amend the common position, the proposal is sent back to the Commission within a month. The Commission can then revise the proposal which is sent back to the Council of Ministers within three months. The Council would then have to consider the proposals of both the Parliament and the Commission. It could adopt the Commission proposals by qualified majority, amend them by unanimity or adopt the Parliament's amendments (not approved by the Commission) by unanimity. The co-decision procedure differs from the other two procedures (see Figure 14.2), though it is essentially an upgrading of the co-operation procedure.

Finally, the Maastricht Treaty allowed employers and trade unions, for the first time, the chance to conclude binding agreements on the basis of proposals from the Commission, an issue that is discussed below in the section devoted to the Maastricht Treaty.

For all EU measures, a date for implementation is set when agreement is reached at EU level and it is left to the member states to meet that deadline, under pain of legal enforcement. Up to now, the vast majority have been enacted here through Ministerial regulations but full acts of legislation such as, for example, the Anti-Discrimination (Pay) Act, 1974, and the Employment Equality Act, 1977 have also been employed to give effect to European laws.

A HISTORY OF SOCIAL POLICY

The history of social policy can be divided into four distinct periods: from 1957 to 1974; 1974 to 1987; 1987 to 1993, and from 1993 onwards.

Period 1: The Treaty of Rome and Social Policy (1957–74)

The main social policy provisions contained in the 1957 Treaty of Rome, establishing the Common Market, relate to equal pay (article 119), the establishment of the European Social Fund (articles 123 to

FIGURE 14.2: CO-DECISION PROCEDURE

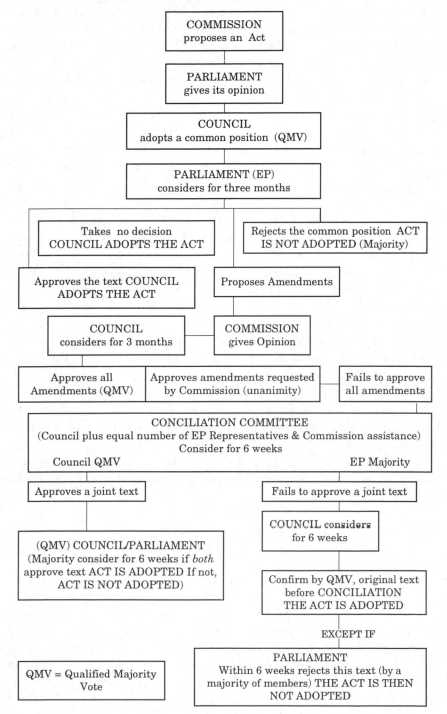

COMMISSION
proposes an Act

PARLIAMENT
gives its opinion

COUNCIL
adopts a common position (QMV)

PARLIAMENT (EP)
considers for three months

Takes no decision
COUNCIL ADOPTS THE ACT

Rejects the common position ACT
IS NOT ADOPTED (Majority)

Approves the text COUNCIL
ADOPTS THE ACT

Proposes Amendments

COUNCIL
considers for 3 months

COMMISSION
gives Opinion

Approves all
Amendments (QMV)

Approves amendments requested
by Commission (unanimity)

Fails to approve
all amendments

CONCILIATION COMMITTEE
(Council plus equal number of EP Representatives & Commission assistance)
Consider for 6 weeks

Council QMV   EP Majority

Approves a joint text

Fails to approve a joint text

COUNCIL considers
for 6 weeks

(QMV) COUNCIL/PARLIAMENT
(Majority consider for 6 weeks if *both*
approve text ACT IS ADOPTED If not,
ACT IS NOT ADOPTED)

Confirm by QMV, original text
before CONCILIATION
THE ACT IS ADOPTED

EXCEPT IF

QMV = Qualified Majority
Vote

PARLIAMENT
Within 6 weeks rejects this text (by a
majority of members) THE ACT IS THEN
NOT ADOPTED

127) and a common vocational training policy (article 128). However, the overriding objective was the creation of the common market, from which it was presumed improved social conditions would follow. The articles providing for the free movement of persons and services were accompanied by labour and social security legislation and there were social policy aspects to transport policy (article 75) and agricultural policy (article 41).

According to Vogel-Polsky (1991) the principal lesson to be drawn from this initial period is that "the theory of social progress being automatic, a result of the functioning of the common market, is inaccurate" and she cites institutional inadequacies and the imbalance of the 1957 Treaty in the social sphere as the main causes of slow progress. She establishes five specific causes: underutilisation or non-achievement of explicit social fields of competence; failure to grasp the potential for drafting operational Community social standards, especially article 119 which provided for equal pay; a failure to integrate fundamental social rights into the Community legal system; a lack of co-operation in the social sphere; and, a lack of automatic or spontaneous development of a Community social policy or co-ordination of the national policies of member states.

There was a recognition in article 117 of a need to promote improved working conditions and standards of living to allow their harmonisation while such improvement is being maintained. But there was no onus put on the various European institutions to achieve this. There was a belief that such improvements would flow from the functioning of the common market and so, in article 118, the tasks of the Commission were confined to promotion of close co-operation between member states in named social areas. The Commission was called upon to make studies, deliver opinions and arrange consultations.

Equal Pay Crisis. There was scope in subsidiary fields of competence (articles 100 and 235) to rectify the reluctance to hand over power to the Community institutions, provided the political will existed — it did not. The unwillingness to bear the social costs associated with the creation of the common market was best illustrated by the near-farcical treatment of article 119 which provided for equal pay among men and women engaged in the same work. The directive was to be fully implemented by the end of 1961 when the first stage of the common market was due to be completed, but in a resolution agreed on December 30, 1961 the various governments postponed the deadline for the first stage of implementing the directive and instead fixed a timetable for the phased reduction of wage differentials up to the end of 1964. It was not until April, 1976 that the Court of Justice found that the December, 1961 resolution was an invalid modification of the original deadline contained in the Treaty. So the principle of equal pay had been delayed for 15 years.

Free Movement of Workers. However, the Community did make progress in other areas, particularly the free movement of workers and in the area of social security. Directives offering the mutual recognition of professional and trade qualifications were adopted for mainly self-employed workers in diverse occupations. Among those to benefit were lawyers, general nurses, midwives, dentists, vets, architects, hairdressers, insurance brokers, doctors and self-employed agents in the retail, catering, food and crafts sectors.

In 1964, agreement was reached on a regulation authorising workers to hold salaried employment in another member state if there were no workers available in national labour markets — it did not apply to seasonal or frontier workers or to non-salaried workers. Various technical and administrative problems were encountered in addition to delicate political sensibilities among various member states, but as Brewster and Teague (1989) make clear, the regulation "established a bridgehead" in an area where the Commission could extend, over time, a body of related legislation.

A further regulation, agreed in 1964, allowed all workers to serve on works councils, provided they had three years' experience in the enterprise, and loosened the national priorities in which "local" workers would be given preference over those from third countries in terms of the length of their work permits and the type of jobs they could fill. Other changes included granting Community workers the right, rather than the authorisation, to salaried employment in another member state, extending the definition of "family" to allow all children, parents and grandparents dependent on the worker to accompany them into another country. And more categories were brought into the regulation's scope, including frontier and seasonal workers.

Agreement was reached on two directives in 1964 liberalising the administration of free movement documentation and stipulating that reasons of "public order, safety and health" could not be cited to bar the entry of workers from other member states. It also stipulated that any proceedings to deny, revoke or refuse renewal of residence permits had to be conducted on an individual basis and that blanket decisions could not be made concerning groups of workers.

Social Security. Further changes were contained in a 1966 regulation, and accompanying 1968 directive, which stipulated that all wage and salary earners in the Community could apply for job vacancies in any member state regardless of their nationality, reside in another state for that purpose, settle there in order to take up employment and be joined there by their families. They would also be eligible to the same working conditions and terms of employment rights as nationals.

The Commission had foreseen the need to co-ordinate social security policies if the free movement of workers was to become a reality. Therefore, one of its first acts was to agree regulations three and four in 1958 which provided for equal treatment for all workers in another member state, the accumulation of benefits acquired by workers in more than one member state, and making benefits exportable to other countries so migrant workers families had to be taken into account in the calculation of benefits. These regulations were revised in 1970 to enable quicker calculation and payment of benefits for migrant workers.

There were social aspects to the common transport and agricultural policies which produced regulations governing the composition of driving crews, the minimum age of drivers, drivers' mates and conductors, limits on continuous driving (4 hours), daily driving (8 hours), weekly driving (48 hours), daily and weekly rest entitlements, and the prohibition of performance bonuses. A further 1973 regulation provided for a need to equip road vehicles with tachographs to monitor work periods.

Agricultural workers benefited from the provisions of a 1972 directive providing for the greater advancement and adaptation of farmers and farm workers, while agreements on the hours of work in agriculture were signed by management and labour in 1968 and 1971, representing the first European collective agreements.

Period 2: Ireland's Accession and the First Social Action Programme (1974–87)

With agreement by the heads of government in The Hague conference of 1969 on a greater push for economic and monetary union, a series of reports such as the Werner report and the Commission's response — its third medium-term economic policy programme — began to recognise the need to harmonise social policies in tandem with economic and monetary union. The Commission then published preliminary guidelines on an EU social policy programme which claimed that if the implementation of social aspects of integration were to lag behind economic and monetary aspects, the success of the process would be compromised. This represented an obvious sea-change from the earlier thinking which saw social policy developments as desirable but contingent upon, and of lesser importance than, the greater goal of a successful common economic market. The Paris summit held in October, 1972 adopted an ambitious programme proposing economic and monetary union by the end of 1980, the establishment of a regional development fund by the end of 1974, and the adoption of the first social action programme by Social Affairs Commissioner, Dr. Patrick Hillery.

In January, 1974 the Council of Ministers adopted a programme of 36 measures to be attained within three years initially, and with three main objectives: full employment and job creation; improvement of living and working conditions giving rise to progress by means of their mutual harmonisation; and, increasing participation of management and labour in economic and social decision making and greater participation of workers in the running of companies. As Vogel-Polsky (1991) makes clear, the programme marked "a watershed, a point of no return in European social legislation". As it stood, Article 118 of the Treaty allowed the Commission to promote close cooperation between member states under various social policy headings by making studies, delivering opinions and arranging consultations. As already stated, there were other legal bases to circumvent such restrictive shackles on the Commission, but the lack of political will left this legal conflict unresolved. In adopting the social action programme, the Council came down in favour of adopting directives in pursuit of social policy objectives. Also, the action programme proposed greater intervention by the Commission for disadvantaged groups: migrants, handicapped people, the elderly and young people as well as other impoverished groups. Such objectives had not been explicitly detailed previously.

Of course, Ireland had become a member of the European Economic Community (EEC), as it was known then, in 1973 along with Britain and Denmark. The Irish referendum returned a massive vote of support for membership, providing a majority of 83 per cent to 17 per cent in a turnout of over 70 per cent. Accession was supported by Fianna Fáil and Fine Gael as well as by the employers and farmers' organisations, but it was opposed by the Labour party and the trade unions. On becoming a member of the EEC, Ireland was obliged to implement the body of legislation already adopted by the Community, or *acquis communitaire* as it is known, so the social policy changes agreed since 1958 applied for Ireland and Irish citizens from 1974. The social policy initiatives, proposed between 1974 and 1987, can be examined under the following headings: equality, employee participation and company organisation, health and safety, protection of employment and regulation of working time.

Equality. There can be little doubt that the greatest advances in the social policy field were in the area of equality. Up to 1987, four equality directives were adopted: the directive on equal pay which implemented the principle of equal pay for men and women engaged in like work or work of equal value; the directive on equal treatment which covered equal treatment as regards access to employment, vocational training, promotion and working conditions; the directive on equal treatment in social security; and the directive on equal treatment in occupational pension schemes. A number of non-binding recommendations and resolutions on equality were also adopted: the recommendation on the promotion of positive action for women; the recommendation on vocational training for women; the resolution on action to combat unemployment among women; the resolution containing an action programme on equal opportunities for girls and boys in education; and the second resolution on the promotion of equal opportunities for women.

The Commission introduced its first equal opportunities programme in 1982, which ran to 1985 and was followed by a second programme running up to 1990. It also established a bevy of Networks on Equal Opportunities, composed of independent experts from each member state, which worked with the Commission on research and the drafting of equal opportunities programmes. Among the specific areas the Networks were established to consider were the application of equality directives, the position of women in the labour market, positive action in enterprises, equal opportunities in broadcasting, childcare, equal opportunities in education and local employment initiatives.

The significance of Ireland's membership of the Community is most clearly illustrated by the controversy surrounding the implementation of the equal pay legislation here on foot of directives from Europe. First, the Fine Gael/Labour coalition government sought but was refused a derogation from the equal pay directive by Commissioner Hillery. The government then proposed to bring only the pay of married female public servants into line with their married male colleagues, thus leaving single workers of both genders at a disadvantage. It was also proposed to phase the changes in over two years after the final implementation date set down by the EEC. Eventually, after three years of fierce campaigning, especially by the ICTU which had threatened to complain to both the European Commission and the International Labour Organisation (ILO), a compromise implementation formula was agreed. But the controversy undoubtedly had the effect of raising awareness of equality and increasing the cohesiveness of equality activists, including newly emerging groups within the trade union movement.

Worker Participation. The equal pay debacle illustrated an ambiguous attitude within Europe, during the first place, to social developments. The failure of the commission's various proposals, during the second period, for the establishment of a European Company and worker participation measures demonstrated Europe's continuing difficulty in achieving consensus on social employment issues. These were described in some detail in the previous chapter.

Information and Consultation. Enjoying a similar fate is the proposed regulation on a European Company statute which would allow companies operating in more than one member state to incorporate as a European company. Employers would benefit from avoiding the conflicting company law systems in different member states and possibly to minimise tax liabilities but in return they would have to inform and consult their employees through one of four options — worker directors, a works council, another equivalent collectively agreed system, or another nationally prevailing system which would meet the directive's broad objectives.

The same fate has befallen the Community's other major initiative in this area, the Vredling Directive, which initially suggested an obligation on companies with over 1,000 workers, including multinationals and their subsidiaries, to supply their workforce with relevant information every six months. Issues such as structure and manning, economic and financial situation, business development plans, projected employment levels, rationalisation plans, work practices, and all procedures and plans likely to affect the workforce were included. This 1980 draft was vehemently opposed by employers, including multinationals based outside Europe, who also drew attention to the apparently inoperable safeguard of confidentiality.

A second draft, published three years later, suggested the directive would only apply to companies with at least 1,000 employees, require information to be transmitted every twelve months, remove the automatic right of workers to consultation and include stricter confidentiality requirements. But the UK vetoed these greatly diluted proposals.

A later series of changes suggesting the incorporation of a system of positive rights for workers to be informed and consulted, rather than an obligation on employers to inform, and excluding parent and subsidiary companies, failed to secure the unanimous support it required. But, as discussed in a separate chapter of this book, the

Commission's ambitions in this area seem set to be realised through the successful operation of the Maastricht social protocol.

Health and Safety. The 1977 directive harmonising safety signs was the first of the health and safety directives agreed during this period and was followed by the 1980 framework directive on chemical, physical and biological agents at work. This spawned further directives concerned with protection against exposure to specific agents: lead, asbestos, noise, and ionising radiation. Another key directive was the so-called Seveso directive which listed requirements to minimise the effects of accidents in dangerous substance industries.

Employment Protection. Also agreed were three important employment protection directives which bestowed further security to workers' rights. The 1975 directive on collective redundancies required employers to offer workers 30 days notice of redundancy and to consult them through their representatives. The 1977 acquired rights directive stipulated that workers' rights and conditions should not be unilaterally diminished in the event of the business ownership being transferred. It also provided that workers could not be dismissed for reasons connected with the transfer.

Finally, in 1980 a directive was enacted protecting workers in the event of their employer becoming insolvent, requiring member states to establish insolvency funds and to meet outstanding wages due to workers where a business collapses.

When agreement was finally reached on a working time directive in late 1993, it represented the end of a long and tortuous attempt to regulate working time in the belief that curbing traditional work and supporting new "atypical" forms of employment such as part-time and temporary work would lead to an overall increase in employment. This thinking has consistently been rejected by British governments which feel it will instead threaten existing employment, and largely explains why there was practically no real reform or regulation of working time during this second phase. Draft directives covering voluntary part-time work and temporary and fixed-term contract workers fell by the wayside, along with recommendations on the reduction and reorganisation of working time, though a recommendation calling on member states to encourage the development of flexible retirement schemes was adopted in 1982.

Considerable progress was also made in promoting the free movement of persons and improving vocational training, the main instrument for which was the European Social Fund. Further advances were made in the mutual recognition of qualifications for road hauliers and pharmacists.

Period 3: The Single European Act and the Social Charter (1987–93)

The Social Charter, signed in Strasbourg in 1989 by member states other than the UK, set out the 12 principles which were to guide the development of social policy, flowing directly from the new obligation under the Single European Act to harmonise working conditions in an upward direction. The Social Charter is a non-legally binding document, of symbolic importance and aspiration in tone, which provided a framework for meeting the objectives spelled out in the Single European Act.

During the Irish presidency in 1990, agreement was reached on a Social Action Programme containing specific measures which would see the aims of the Social Charter realised — effectively, a blueprint for social policy. The 49 proposals contained in the Social Action Programme consisted of legally-binding directives and regulations as well as non-binding opinions and recommendations. Though the UK was not a signatory to the Social Charter, it would be bound to implement all aspects of the Social Action Programme. (The implementation of the programme continues into 1994 and for this reason the chronological distinction in this history of social policy is artificial. However, for the sake of continuity the discussion of the programme's measures is covered in this section.) By the end of 1993 significant progress had been made on the vast majority of these measures in what was an ambitious programme. The most important developments were the adoption of directives covering working time, the protection of pregnant workers, health and safety, and employment contracts. All of the non-binding measures were adopted.

Working Time. The working time directive, adopted in November, 1993, provides for a maximum working week of 48 hours during a 4 month period which can be extended to 6 months for certain categories and to 12 months if agreed through workplace collective bargaining. Workers will be entitled to a daily rest period of 11 consecutive hours in each 24 hour period and a minimum weekly rest period of 35 consecutive hours (this does not preclude Sunday working). A minimum of 4 weeks' annual leave is to be available to workers within 6 years of adoption.

TABLE 14.1: THE TWELVE PRINCIPLES CONTAINED IN THE SOCIAL
CHARTER

1.	The right to work in a member state of one's choice
2.	The freedom to choose and occupation and the right to earn a fair wage.
3.	The right to improved working and living conditions.
4.	The right to social protection under prevailing national system.
5.	The right to freedom of association and collective bargaining.
6.	The right to vocation training.
7.	The right of men and women to equal treatment.
8.	The right of workers to information, consultation and participation.
9.	The right to health protection and safety at work.
10.	The protection of children and adolescents.
11.	A decent standard of living for older people.
12.	Improved social and professional integration for disabled people.

The directive also contains a general limitation of 8 hours' night work on average in each 24 hour period and an absolute limit of 8 hours in any 24 hours in "occupations involving special hazards or heavy physical or mental strain". Night workers will also be entitled to free health assessments at regular intervals and those with health problems connected with night work can be transferred to day work.

The format of the directive perfectly illustrates the degree to which the final effect of directives is still shaped to an important extent by parties within each member state — it remains for governments, possibly in consultation with employers and trade unions, to agree on derogations and the occupations to which the longer averaging period will apply.

Importantly, the directive does not place a blanket ban on working more than 48 hours through its provision for collective negotiation at enterprise level on longer working hours. But the fact that workers cannot in future be coerced into working over 48 hours implies a premium may have to be paid for longer working (Hourihan, 1993a). The night work and leave provisions are set to have the most effect in Ireland — almost 18 per cent of Irish workers work at least half of their hours at night, the highest in the EU, and 12 per cent work more than 46 hours a week on average.

Pregnant Workers' Protection. The Protection of Pregnant Workers' Directive, adopted in 1992, minimises the health risks for pregnant workers but means no improvement in the overall level of pay for workers on maternity leave, thus leaving Ireland to the rear of the EU maternity pay table. The Directive provides that the level of maternity pay for each member state will be no less than its level of statutory sick pay.

The Directive obliges employers to carry out a risk assessment exercise identifying potential hazards for pregnant workers. If the employer cannot remove any identified health risks, the worker will have to be offered alternative work, or as a final alternative, paid leave. Whether the employer or the Department of Social Welfare will have to meet the cost of such leave will be determined when the legislation giving effect to the Directive is enacted in each member state.

The Directive also requires the amendment of current unfair dismissals legislation to ensure the prohibition of dismissal for any pregnancy related reason, that is, indirect dismissal. Finally, the directive offers an entitlement to paid pre-natal leave; again the level of pay and the responsibility for the cost will be decided when the enabling legislation is introduced in the member states.

Health and Safety. Following the adoption of the framework directive on health and safety at work in 1989, many more individual directives have been adopted with further measures at an advanced state. The five "daughter directives" covered the workplace, work equipment, personal protective equipment, manual handling of loads and visual display screens. A directive on the health and safety of temporary and fixed term workers was also adopted in 1989 and was enacted along with the aforementioned in a statutory instrument in 1992. The 1990 directive on carcinogens was also enacted in a statutory instrument in 1993.

Other directives already adopted cover areas such as biological agents, exposure levels for dangerous substances, temporary work sites, health and safety signs, and extractive industries (drilling and non-drilling). Further directives are proposed to cover chemical agents, noise, vibration and optical radiation, the transport and maritime sectors, and disabled workers.

Collective Redundancies. The Contract of Employment Directive, adopted in 1991, provides workers with greater protection against possible infringements of their rights, obliging the employer to notify workers of the essential aspects of their relationship within two months of the contract commencing. Most of the Directive's provisions were already available to Irish workers under the Minimum Notice and Terms of Employment Act, 1973 and the Part-time Workers' Act, 1991.

Similarly, the 1992 directive on collective redundancies means little change in existing Irish legislation — the Protection of Employment Act, 1977 — but will, in future, require undertakings with more than 50 workers to not only inform but also consult workers. Consultation means discussing means of avoiding or minimising redundancies and measures to mitigate the effects on those being made redundant and those remaining in work. Employers will have to supply employee representatives with all relevant information to enable the representatives to formulate constructive proposals. This would include the reasons for the redundancies, the numbers and categories of redundancies, selection criteria, the basis of redundancy payments and the period over which the redundancies are to be effected. The provision for the extension of existing obligations to decision making centres situated in a second member state means that pleas that employers were not notified in time by their bosses abroad in order to comply with notification requirements will no longer be entertained.

Young Workers. The Protection of Young Workers' Directive, adopted in June, 1994, set a minimum working age of 15, with some exceptions, and included a ban on night work (between 8 pm and 6 am) and a weekly limit of 15 hours for schoolgoers and 40 hours for those below 18 and not in full-time education. It also provided health and safety protection measures.

The Commission is considering a review of the acquired rights directive while the directives on parental leave, reversal of the burden of proof in sex discrimination cases, and pensions mobility still remain at an early stage of discussion.

Period 4: Ratification of the Maastricht Treaty and a New Era of EU Social Policy (1993 Onwards)
The difficulties which emerged in negotiating changes to the EU's social policy in the new Treaty on European Union came as little surprise in the wake of the rows which followed the Social Charter and its Social Action Programme. Also, the British opposition to regulation by Brussels had been given a new focus and impetus by the breakdown of talks on the controversial working time directive at the meeting of the Social Affairs Council just days before the Maastricht negotiations began. It was no surprise that given the traditionally strong resistance by British voters to EU membership a scapegoat was found which could divert attention away from so many unpalat-

able and fundamental losses of sovereignty being signed away elsewhere in the talks. What became known as the Social Chapter fitted
the bill perfectly. The social policy impasse threatened the Treaty negotiations and, with so much at stake, it was agreed in an eleventh
hour solution that a protocol on social policy would be signed by the
member states other than the UK. Effectively, this meant that the
existing Treaty provisions remained largely unchanged, apart from
proving a specific legal base for EU initiatives in the fields of education, vocational training and youth (articles 126 and 127). The majority of the proposed social policy changes agreed by the 11 were incorporated into a Protocol, or parallel agreement, whose legal status remains unclear. The Commission insists the social policy protocol (one
of 17 covering diverse subjects) to be an integral part of the Treaty
and there have been suggestions that this will be referred to the
European Court of Justice for clarification.

The British immediately claimed to have won an opt-out from EU
labour regulation and to have gained a major advantage in preventing rising unit labour costs and in seeking to attract inward investment, especially from non-EU countries such as Japan and the US.
Among the EU member states, Britain attracts easily the greatest
amount of investment from outside. In 1992, Britain's share of total
investment into the EU stood at 39 per cent of total Japanese investment and 37.5 per cent of American investment, according to Carson
(1992). And, since 1980, Japanese companies have invested £16 billion in Britain to bring their employment of British workers to over
50,000. *The Economist* (1993) has suggested that as much as 53 per
cent of all Japanese investment into the European Union in 1991
came to Britain. As early as 1985 it was claimed that Ireland's share
of new investment from the US had begun to shrink as countries such
as Britain, Italy and Holland saw their shares rise (Fitzpatrick and
Kelly, 1985). So any perceived advantage gained by a British opt-out
would be enormous in attempting to lure future potential investors.
Already, the British government has sought to capitalise on the perceived advantage it enjoys by advertising in the leading German
business daily, *Handelsblatt*. Readers were told that wages and social
charges in Britain were significantly lower than in Germany and German employers were invited to contact the British consulate in Dus-
seldorf "to find out more about how your firm can profit" (Incomes
Data Services, 1993). Understandably, both the Irish government and
Irish employers expressed great concern at such an advantage being
won as well as the fear that Irish exports could be made less price
competitive in Britain, their single largest market.

The most important feature of the Protocol on Social Policy is that it extends the number of areas which can be dealt with under qualified majority voting (QMV) rather than unanimity. It provides for the 11 member states to "continue along the path laid down in the 1989 Social Charter" employing the institutions, procedures and mechanisms of the Maastricht Treaty. Upon ratification of the Treaty, social policy measures could then be introduced under the Social Chapter and be binding on the 11 and without the voting input of the British. Or they could be implemented in accordance with the existing, unchanged social policy provisions contained in the main Treaty text.

The Social Protocol stipulates that "the Community and the Member States shall have as their objectives the promotion of employment, improved living and working conditions, proper social protection, dialogue between management and labour, the development of human resources with a view to lasting high employment and the combating of exclusion". Measures implemented will have to "take account of the diverse forms of national practices, in particular in the field of contractual relations, and the need to maintain the competitiveness of the European economy". It then goes on to list a number of measures in which the EU will have specific competence and which need QMV support, as well as those requiring unanimous support and those which the Union's competence still does not cover — pay, the right of association, the right to strike or the right to impose lockouts.

In the absence of the British, the Protocol states that 44 votes will be needed to secure support under QMV, a significant change whose effect is to reduce the proportionate number of votes required. From requiring 54 votes from 76 under the existing Treaty provisions, the Protocol merely requires QMV measures to gain the support of 44 of a total of 66 votes. In more practical terms, this means that poorer member states such as Ireland, Spain, Greece and Portugal would not have enough support with 21 votes combined to oppose measures they feel would adversely affect their more fragile economies. With the British included, the combination of Britain's 12 votes and those of the poorer four countries would ensure a blocking minority. Later, the Irish government attempted in vain to have the final version of the Protocol amended to rectify this quirk prior to the Treaty being presented for signature. The fact remains that Ireland has tended to vote with Britain in many social policy debates, if not for the same ideological reasons, and the changed voting arrangements in the Protocol threaten to remove the blocking British shield behind which the Irish have often found it convenient to hide.

According to the Protocol, five different areas require support under QMV: health and safety; working conditions; the information and consultation of workers; equality of men and women with regard to labour market opportunities and treatment at work; and the integration of persons excluded from the labour market. The areas for which unanimous support will be required are also stipulated: social security and protection of workers; protection of workers where their employment contract is terminated; representation and collective defence of the interests of workers and employers, including co-determination; conditions of employment for third-country nationals legally residing in EU territory; and financial contributions for promotion of employment and job creation.

Directives must "avoid imposing administrative, financial and legal constraints in a way which would hold back the creation and development of small and medium-sized undertakings". Article 3 of the Protocol deals with the enhanced powers afforded to management and labour at EU level — the social dialogue. It provides that before submitting social policy proposals, the Commission shall consult management and labour, and if it considers EU action advisable in the social policy field it will again consult both sides of industry. They can offer an opinion or recommendation to the Commission. Alternatively, management and labour can themselves negotiate European-wide agreements in accordance with the procedures and practices specific to management and labour and the member states. The Protocol also allows management and labour to discuss measures expressly covered by the Protocol (under the QMV and unanimity headings) which can be given legal force if the Council of Ministers is agreeable. This new direction in the shaping of social policy is seen as being in keeping with the ill-defined principle of subsidiarity but the 9 month deadline for both sides to complete negotiations means that the Commission is left with the option of pursuing policy measures if the social dialogue becomes deadlocked. This increases the onus on direct negotiations to succeed, especially for the employers who have traditionally sought to minimise interventions by the Commission.

The Maastricht Treaty also provides for significant changes to the European institutions, especially the European Parliament. Its role has been considerably strengthened by granting it the right to reject legislation in a number of areas. The Treaty also extends the areas where the approval of the Parliament is required to take EU action, including the appointment of the Commission, and enhances the Parliament's role in the detailed operation of the EU by giving it a formal right of enquiry, the right to receive petitions and the right to call on the Commission to initiate legislation. Overall, the Treaty is widely seen as representing a fundamental change in European labour law (Bercussen, 1992).

1995–97 Social Action Programme

The 1995–97 social action programme launched by EU Commissioner. Mr. Padraig Flynn, contained a minimum of new legally binding directives, a change which was warmly welcomed by employers.

The plan proposed a public hearing on the Social Charter, which would focus on the UK opt-out from the Maastricht Agreement on Social Policy, or the Social Chapter as it became known. But the Commissioner also signalled that it would examine the feasibility of extending the notion of works councils or information and consultation mechanisms to workers in smaller companies than those Community-scale undertakings covered by the directive adopted in 1994.

The long-standing proposals for a directive on part-time, temporary and fixed terms workers were also tabled again along with a possible directive covering individual dismissals. The programme followed eighteen months of consultation and public debate since the European Commission launched its Green Paper on the future of European Social Policy in 1993. Launching the Programme, Mr. Flynn said that given the achievements of the previous social action programme in 1989 there was less scope or need for a wide ranging programme of new legislative proposals.

Under the heading "Encouraging high labour standards as part of a competitive Europe", the plan proposed that in the first half of 1995, the European Parliament would organise in collaboration with the Commission, a public hearing on the 1989 Social Charter to see whether some or all of its provisions should be incorporated in the future Treaty for the European Union. Obviously, the UK opt-out from the Social Chapter would be one of the key issues for discussion at the hearing. The Commission was keen to build on its success in having the works council directive and wished to see further advances in the information and consultation of workers. The Commission would examine whether, and to what extent, the system of workers' involvement established by the information and consultation directive could help the adoption of the four amended proposals for Regulations concerning the European Company Statute and the Statutes for a European Association, for a European Co-operative and for a European Mutual Society.

The Commission would also initiate consultations with the social partners on the advisability and possible direction of Community action in the field of information and consultation of employees in national undertakings. The Commission would also undertake a study on national legislation and practices concerning the individual rights of workers to be consulted on internal company matters which concern them. Also consultations with the social partners under the Social Chapter would be launched on part-time, fixed-term and temporary work. The social partners would also be consulted for the need for Community level action on individual dismissal.

Discussions with the social partners would continue on how best to ensure that activities and sectors excluded from the directive on the organisation of working time are appropriately covered. The Commission would initiate consultations with the social partners to identify how best to resolve the problems in the field of posting workers abroad in the framework of the provisions of services if no further progress was made in discussions at the Council of Ministers.

A new proposal for a Council Directive on the protection of health and safety of workers at risk from explosive atmosphere would be submitted to the Council of Ministers. Further studies would be launched on work organisation and productivity, including payment systems, working time, reduction of working time, occupational and geographical mobility and stability of employment. The Commission would also consider the scope for a Green Paper on the reduction and reorganisation of working time. A Green Paper on the issue of illegal work would be prepared and the Commission would also adopt a non-binding recommendation on homeworking and present a communication on the social and health impact of telework.

On equality, the Commission would initiate discussion with the social partners on the area of the burden of proof and it would adopt a code of practice for implementation of equal pay for equal value for women and men in the workplace. The Commission would also be taking extensive steps to ensure free movement of labour and propose a draft directive to establish a general framework to protect individual rights acquired or being acquired in occupational or supplementary pension schemes for people who cross national borders. Full details of the 1995–97 Programme are set out in an appendix to this chapter.

EU POLICY AND THE CONDUCT OF IRISH INDUSTRIAL RELATIONS

The debate over the EU's social policy best illustrates the fundamental differences in attitudes to European integration (see Laffan, 1992).

Neo-liberals argue that over-regulation by Brussels has stultified labour market growth and created "Eurosclorosis" while the interventionists, including the European Commission, contend that a higher productivity, high wage economy can only be achieved by the harmonisation of standards through the use of European level institutions and policies.

In arriving at its policy position, the European Commission (1988) rejected what it termed the "normative approach" which relied on binding provisions and the regulation of the main social questions at EU level, as well as the "decentralised approach" which seeks to put an end to further social legislation at EU level apart from minimum health and safety standards. In effect it chose the middle ground and sought to establish a European industrial relations system based on an eventual EU-wide framework of minimum social provisions. The heterogeneous systems of industrial relations and levels of social legislation among the member states would require the EU to initiate proposals which would harmonise protection levels and offer a "fairer playing field". It identified three issues which it was commonly felt would have to be tackled if the internal market was to succeed: the threat of social dumping, illicit work, and wage costs.

Within the systems theory of industrial relations developed by Dunlop (1958), the emergence of new actors such as the European Commission and the European Parliament presents a series of important new questions (Due et al., 1991). Following a decade which has seen record levels of unemployment, trade union membership decline, the widespread decentralisation of pay bargaining, and the introduction of new flexible work practices associated with the growth of human resource management, some union confederations have turned to Europe as their influence has been curtailed by political as well as economic factors. The British Trade Union Congress (TUC) is often cited a classic case in point, though the reasons for its new stance on Europe have been the subject of some debate (see Marsh, 1992; Rosamond, 1993). In many ways, the appearance of this new outside agent has placed both employers and trade unions at a level starting point and offers the unions the opportunity to retrieve some lost ground. For this reason employers are wary of increasing regulation from Brussels, which they see as being led by a Socialist president backed by a Parliament where the Socialists have the biggest numbers. In simple terms the development by the trade unions of an active European agenda could be seen as having an inverse relationship to the level of influence they enjoy within their own national political systems.

Theoretical questions aside, issues such as the emergence of Euro-companies (Marginson et al., 1993), the effect of a single European currency for pay determination (Teague, 1993: 163–77; Marsden, 1992), and the overall implications for models of corporatism (Henley and Tsakalotos, 1992) are part of a new broader industrial relations agenda.

There can be little doubt that European social policy has been an important force in the development of Irish industrial relations, the more obvious results being the sizeable increase in labour legislation, especially in the 1970s, and the less discernible but equally important effect of the judgements from the European Court of Justice, especially in the areas of equality, pensions and the transfer of undertakings. Brewster and Teague (1989) identified four forms of European influence on the British employment system: legal, political, institutional and company, each of which have equal validity for Ireland. The first three are self-evident while the notion of company level influences is "concerned with how Europe has affected company level human resource and personnel policies, and other more general employment related issues in both the public and private sectors". Overall, one obvious effect of membership of the European Union has been a change of focus by employers and trade unions away from the adversarial system of industrial relations inherited from Britain to broader European models. Continental European models of corporatism informed the development of agreements such as the Programme for National Recovery and its successors, the Programme for Economic and Social Progress and the Programme for Competitiveness and Work.

The Irish government has incorporated the bulk of the suggestions of the tripartite NESC (1989: 497–521) which, in its major study on EC membership, called for a positive contribution by Ireland to social policy discussions but similarly recognised the need for centralised European budgeting, while rejecting opportunistic pleas for funding of existing domestic social policy programmes. The Programme for Economic and Social Progress (PESP), to which the Government, employers and trade unions were signatories, committed Ireland to "support Community action geared to promoting social cohesion as an essential basis for the creation of the single market and for sustainable economic integration generally. Ireland will promote Community action directed at the progressive convergence of social policy in an upward direction". This was tied to a recognition of Ireland's "distinctive circumstances and needs, particularly the need to increase viable employment. Ireland will support the practical expression of the rights set out in the Social Charter, through the adoption of Community instruments that respect the overriding employment imperative and the varying practices of the member states" (PESP, 1991: 79–81).

Beyond the narrow confines of the social policy of the EU, other policy areas can be of equal significance for the conduct of industrial relations. The completion of the internal market and economic and monetary union are cases in point. All of the signatories to the proposed Programme for Competitiveness and Work (PCW) fully endorsed the general framework contained in the European Commission's white paper on growth, competitiveness and employment and the ensuing action plan combining measures at national and EU level. According to the PCW, the 1994–1999 national development plan would encompass

- structural measures to help create jobs, including improved education and training systems,

- greater labour market flexibility,

- economically sound reorganisation of work at enterprise level,

- targeted reductions in the indirect costs of labour, especially less-skilled work, and

- better use of public funds set aside for combating unemployment through more active policies to help job seekers.

Clearly, the use of EU funds can be seen as unambiguously tied to labour market reforms largely "imported" from Brussels. Labour market flexibility was a key element of the Irish government's submission to the white paper on growth, competitiveness and employment. Amongst others, the submission called on the Commission to examine ways of increasing labour market flexibility within the framework of existing Community legislation and this was largely acted upon by the Commission (1993). Up to that point there had been little evidence of any moves by any Irish government to reverse the increasingly regulated Irish labour market, possibly reflecting the powerful influence of the Irish trade unions and the reluctance of Irish employers, including the state, to jeopardise the social consensus.

The important point to be noted is that we may be seeing a new facet to the decision making process affecting industrial relations, with the European Commission being afforded a validation role which directly affects the conduct of national level collective bargaining.

The Commission's white paper was largely consistent with the Irish government's submission and this was later incorporated into the proposed Programme for Competitiveness and Work signed by the government, employers and trade unions. The formal backing of the social partners for reforms which may be seen to constitute conditions for financial assistance from Brussels, which has to validate applications for CSF funding, implies a new collective bargaining dimension and affords the European Commission an unheralded place in the formation of labour market policies within individual member states.

The uses to which EU funds are employed also have implications for pay determination in member states. According to Joe McCartin, the Fine Gael MEP, "European money has been misspent in Ireland on current day-to-day expenditure to finance the generous wage increases for the public sector". This claim was based on his assertion that the public capital programme in Ireland fell from £1.85 billion in 1982 to £1.84 billion in 1992, "a reduction of 30 per cent in real terms despite large injections of Euro-cash". But over the same period, current expenditure increased from £5.9 billion to £9.8 billion, leading him to conclude it was an "inescapable fact that European money earmarked for capital expenditure on long term development projects was used in everyday spending, almost as pocket money of the Government, instead of on building on the future" (*Irish Times*, 1993).

The latest Community Support Framework will certainly be the final time assistance of such magnitude will be received here from Brussels. Conscious of this final opportunity to bring Irish capita per head into line with EU norms and of the criteria laid down for entry to the third phase of Economic and Monetary Union (EMU) covering inflation, exchequer debt, convergence of interest rates and debt/GDP ratios, the Irish government is faced with some stark choices in the control of public expenditure in the years ahead. Managing the public sector pay bill will assume critical importance and, in many ways, the impositions of EU membership may prove the decisive push in the long delayed reform of the conciliation and arbitration machinery. This has already been made clear in the proposals for reform of the various schemes where the official side has sought to include new criteria for consideration by the arbitrator — "disciplines imposed on the Government in consequence of the Treaty on European Union" is specifically listed among the new criteria proposed (see Hourihan, 1994).

Ironically, the parsimony in public spending dictated by these guidelines could be seen to have bolstered the government's resolve to curtail the public service pay bill which proved the greatest obstacle to the conclusion of another centralised pay agreement after the Programme for Economic and Social Progress expired and seemed, on the face of it, to come close to jeopardising the new social consensus.

According to the National Economic and Social Council (NESC) report on Ireland in the European Community (1989), the effects of internal market completion per se were likely to be much more prevalent in the services sector than in the manufacturing sector, due to the comparatively low international market penetration in services. Two direct effects of market completion were identified: cost reductions, following the removal of non-tariff barriers, and price reductions resulting from increased competition due to improved market access. These direct effects were thought likely to initiate two processes which would create two substantial indirect effects: exploitation of economies of scale resulting in a major restructuring of industry, and a new stimulus to innovation provided by increased competition. It was considered that the services sector was, with the imminent completion of the internal market, facing the sort of shake-out which took place in the manufacturing sector after Ireland joined the EEC in 1973. Distribution, transport and the financial services sectors were expected to face the most dramatic changes.

The removal of technical barriers will increase the free movement of goods and have particular implications for producers in the following sectors: motor vehicles, tractors and agricultural machines, food processing, pharmaceuticals and chemicals, construction products. The movement towards liberalising public procurement will expose public utilities, such as energy and telecommunications, to new levels of competition while the movement towards a common market for telecommunications services and equipment, spelled out in the European Commission's 1987 green paper, is having added obvious implications for a company such as Telecom Éireann.

The new determination of the European Commission to monitor state aids to industry, reflected in its move to have member states annually submit details of all their existing aid regimes plus a new standardised format for notifying new schemes, has considerable relevance for the state as a supporter of private industry and as shareholder in semi-state enterprises. In the latter category, the recent survival plan negotiated at Aer Lingus, which featured state investment of around £175 million which had to be approved by the Commission, brought home to trade union representatives the unforeseen benefit of this stricter European code. Union officials have made it clear that the unions found a greater willingness to discuss the details of the airline survival package on the part of Commission officials than was evident in contacts with the Irish government and bureaucracy. But the unions' experience in lobbying at Brussels-level was also instructive and, while ultimately successful, displayed the lack of a clear strategy and a failure to fully grasp the potential of opportunities admitted in hindsight.

Overall, the EU-led restructuring taking place within Irish industry clearly has implications for the conduct of collective bargaining and probably means an end to the prospects of a return to the pay determination structures dominant in earlier decades (see McCarthy, 1973), where key trend-setting grades were found in sheltered employments.

As can be clearly seen, the implications of EU membership cannot be confined to social policy developments. The completion of the internal market and the move towards economic and monetary union have equally important, if less obvious implications, for the conduct of Irish industrial relations.

APPENDIX

1995–1997 EU SOCIAL ACTION PROGRAMME

1. Jobs — The Top Priority
Building on the two White Papers on Growth, Competitiveness and Employment and on Social Policy and on the conclusion on the Essen European Council, the Commission will develop a process of surveillance of employment trends and systems in the EU. It will seek to include sections dealing with employment trends and policies in Member States' economic convergence programmes, and will present a report on progress made by the Member States in applying the Essen conclusions to the European Council in December 1995. Annual Employment Reports will focus in turn on the five priorities identified at Essen (1995), the employment potential of the Information Society (1996) and on the emergence of new approaches to work organisation and local employment initiatives (1997).

The Commission's 1996 Report on the Internal Market will include and analysis of the impact on jobs. Regular meetings of Directors General for employment and social security will be organised to forge closer links between national administrations. The Commission will present a proposal to develop a closer and more structured collaboration with the Member States in the field of employment and labour market policy. This proposal will cover the period 1996–98 and incorporate the idea of creating a European Platform to pool experience about local employment initiatives. The Commission will support the exchange and transfer of experience in the field of collective bargaining and other agreements linked to job creation. A first report on national experience will be established by the social partners in the second half of 1995 and could be updated regularly in future years. The role, composition and functioning of the Standing Employment Committee, set up by the Council in 1970, will be reviewed so as to make this Committee the main institutional forum for concentration between the Council, social partners and the Commission. The implementation of the Community support frameworks linked to the Structural Funds will be assessed in the light of the Essen conclusions. The contribution of the Structural Funds to the promotion of equal opportunities between women and men will be reviewed. A first report on this subject will be issued before the end of 1995 and a European Conference will be held in the first half of 1996. The Commission will encourage the active participation of the social partners in European Structural Funds operations. A European Conference will be held in September 1995 in Toulouse to take stock of progress in the implementation of Objective 4 of the Structural Funds, which focuses on the need for firms to develop a better capacity to anticipate industrial and technological change. The Employment, ADAPT and SME Community initiatives will generate 5,000 projects designed to support the process of innovation within key areas of employment and training policies.

2. Education and Training, Key Factors for Social Stability in the Community

The Commission will issue later this year a White Paper on "education and training: the levers of the year 2000". The Commission will outline new proposals including a Community initiative on quality training (1996) and on policies to promote lifelong learning (1996). Debates will be launched on introducing European rules for apprenticeships in the context of mobility. The Commission will publish a Green Paper on the legal, administrative and practical obstacles concerning young people on transnational placement in another member State as part of their vocational training (1995).

3. Building a European Labour Market

The Commission will set up a high level panel on free movement to report on the outstanding obstacles to free movement of persons, and will present a White Paper setting out an integrated strategy including specific proposals aimed at attacking the outstanding problems

(1996). The Commission will propose a draft directive to establish a general framework to protect individual rights acquired or being acquired in occupational or supplementary pension schemes for people who cross national borders. It will bring forward proposals to recast the current legislation concerning rights of residence and extend the general system for recognition of diplomas to professions not yet covered.

The existing proposal on free movement of workers designed to improve the situation of workers as regard family reunion, equality of treatment and residence and consolidate European Court of Justice case-law, will be reviewed. The Commission will issue a memorandum to review progress made in the opening-up of the public sector and propose further measures to promote free movement in this sector. A series of studies, pilot measures and debates will be launched in order to increase the transparency of qualifications (1996). As far as social security for migrant workers is concerned, the Commission will present proposals to codify the regulations already adopted so as to provide a single, up-to-date version, introduce provisions covering early retirement schemes, revise the provisions concerning unemployment benefits, facilitate greater access to cross-border health care and services, extend to third-country nationals the provision of immediate medical care and other limited benefits.

The Commission will also continue to press for the adoption of its 1991 proposal to extend the existing regulations on social security for migrant workers to cover all insured people, students and special schemes for civil servants. On a longer time-scale, a wide-ranging review of existing regulations in the field of social security for migrant workers will be carried out so as to take into account significant changes in national social security systems and simplify the rules. The Commission will present a recommendation inviting Member States to give employment priority to third country nationals permanently and legally residing in another Member State when job vacancies cannot be filled by EU nationals or nationals of third countries legally residing in the Member State concerned. The European employment service EURES will be consolidated and developed. A series of projects are planned for step-by-step implementation of TESS, a transnational telematic system designed to link the Social security institutions in all Member States.

4. Encouraging High Labour Standards as Part of a Competitive Europe

In the first half of 1995, the European Parliament will organise, in collaboration with the Commission, a public hearing on the 1989 Social Charter to see whether there is a need to revised the Charter to extend its scope and whether some or all of its provisions should be incorporated in the future Treaty. Consultations with the social partners under the Agreement on Social Policy will be launched on part-time, fixed term and temporary work. The social partners will also be consulted on the need for Community level action on individual dismissals. Discussions with the social partners will continue on how best to insure that activities and sectors excluded from the directive on the organisation of working time, are appropriately covered. The Commission will present a Communication, including a draft Decision, on the Fourth Programme concerning Safety, Hygiene and Health Protection at Work (1995–2000), including a proposal for a specific programme (SAFE) to promote better awareness of health and safety legislation in small and medium size enterprises.

The Commission will initiate consultations with the social partners to identify how best to resolve the problems in the field of posting of workers in the framework of the provisions of services, if no further progress is made in Council discussions. The Commission is examining whether and to what extent the system of workers' involvement established by the information and consultation directive could help the adoption of the four amended proposal for Regulations concerning the European Company Statutes for a European Association, for a European Co-operative and for a European Mutual Society. The Commission will initiate consultations with the social partners on the advisability and possible direction of Community action in the field of information and consultation of employees in national undertakings.

A new proposal for a Council Directive on the protection of the health and safety of workers at risk from explosive atmosphere will soon be submitted to the Council. The Commission will carry out a study on national legislation and practices concerning the individual rights of workers to be consulted on internal company matters which concern them. Further studies will be launched on work organisation an productivity, including payment systems, working time, reduction of working time, occupational and geographical mobility and stability of employment. The Commission will consider the scope for a Green Paper on the reduction and reorganisation of working time (1996–97). A Green Paper on the issue of illegal work will be prepared. The

Commission will adopt a Recommendation on homeworking and present a Communication on the social and health impact of telework

5. Equality of Opportunity between Women and Men

A medium-term strategy will be launched entailing action on a number of fronts reconciling working and family life, desegregating the labour market and extending the principle of equal treatment and promoting the concept of citizenship for women (gender-balance in decision-making, strengthening of active citizenship). The Commission will present a Communication including a draft Council decision for a Fourth Action Programme on equal opportunities for women and men to come into force in January 1996. It has launched consultations with the social partners to consider the possibility of negotiating an agreement on the reconciliation of professional and family life.

The Commission will launch similar consultations on possible actions in the area of the burden of proof. It will adopt a Code of Practice for the implementation of equal pay for equal value for women and men in the workplace. It will also present a draft Recommendation to the Council defining measures and actions to promote the participation of women in the decision-making process in both the public and private sector. The Commission will relaunch the debate on its proposal designed to complete the Community framework on equal treatment in social security.

6. Social Policy and Social Protection — An Active Society for All

The Commission will launch a debate on the question of fundamental social rights in the EU in the light of the hearing organised with the European Parliament on the 1989 Social Charter, it will consult the European Forum on Social Policy in the first half of 1996 about the possible extension of the Social Charter to cover a wide range of individual rights and responsibilities. The Commission proposes to launch in partnership with the Member States a framework initiative to stimulate a process of joint medium-term reflection on the future of social protection. A common framework for analysis of problems and solutions could be established (1995–96). Common exchanges would be fruitful on topics like the implication of the ageing of the ageing of the European population for our societies.

The Commission will present a Communication of the financing of social security, including an inventory of the benefits that could accrue from increased co-operation in this area, and a Communication assessing the situation and identifying problems and obstacles which complementary insurance schemes may pose to mobility within the European union. A Recommendation may be presented on care insurance for persons becoming dependent (1977). The Commission will continue to press for the urgent adoption by the Council of its proposals on action to combat social exclusion. A European-wide debate will be opened up in 1996 on poverty and social exclusion on the basis for identifying the scopes for concerted action. A report of all relevant Community actions will be presented in 1996, embracing the contributing of the Structural Funds, the Research and Development framework programme etc. . . .

In 1996, the Commission will also focus on the employment of disabled persons. It will launch wide-ranging consultations on possible future Union-level action after the Helios 11 programme ends in 1996. It will present a Recommendation on reciprocal recognition of parking cards for disabled people (1995) and will press for the adoption of the draft directive on transport for workers with motor disabilities. The Commission will prepare a code of good practice on the employment of disabled people within the Commission (1995). It has presented a draft Decision for a series of actions in favour of older people, to run for the period 1996–1999. The Commission will draw up a Communication presenting and action plan against racism. This Communication will include a Council decision to designate 1997 as European year against racism (1996). The Commission will adopt a recommendation on the protection of the rights of migrant workers and their families, encouraging the Member States to adopt the 1990 UN International Convention on this subject.

7. Public Health

The Commission will submit proposals for European Parliament-Council decisions on health data indicators and a programme of action on pollution-related diseases. It will also assess the scope for programmes on accidents and injuries and rare diseases. It will press for adoption of the four pending proposals for EP-Council decisions establishing Community action programmes on cancer, health promotion, prevention, drug dependence and AIDS. In order to prepare this discussion, and building on the joint hearing on the Social Charter (see above), the Commission proposes to establish a "Comite des Sages" to prepare a report. Reports will be presented on the state of health in the EU, as well as on the integration of health requirements into other Community policies.

8. Developing the International Dimension

The Commission will present a framework Communications designed to bring together the different activities under way, to define the role of the Union and procedures for co-operating with international organisations and to propose guidelines for actions in the medium term (1996).

9. For a More Active Society

The Commission will present a Communication on the future development of the social dialogue. It will also present a Communication reviewing and updating the sectoral social dialogue committees (1995). The Commission will periodically convene a European Forum on Social Policy issues involving widest possible range of interested parties. The first meeting of the Forum in February 1996 will discuss the Social Charter. It will present a proposal for a Council decision establishing a permanent consultative forum of disability organisations.

10. Medium-Term Social Policy Analysis and Research

The Commission will develop its capacity to address social policy issues in a medium to long term perspective, and will review, and if necessary, rationalise the different Observations set up in recent years. It will set up a High level Expert Group on the social and societal implications of the information society, and will, drawing on the work of this Group, present a Green Paper (1996).

11. Towards a More Effective Application of European Law

The Commission will produce an annual report on the situation of transposition into national legislation for each directive in the social field. A specific obligation to draw up an implementation report will be inserted in all future directives, which will also contain a specific obligation for Member States to notify implementing measures to the Commission together with a contact point in the respective national administrations. The Commission will adopt a Decision setting up a committee of Senior Labour Inspectors. It will insert in all future legislation a standard clause establishing an obligation for Member States to impose sanction which are effective, proportionate, and dissuasive. The Commission will present a Communication addressing the entire area of implementation of Community directives by collective agreements. It will consider ways and procedures to involve the social partners in the process of control of transposition and enforcement of Community law (1996). A clause concerning implementation by collective agreements will be inserted in all future directives. The

Commission will produce a series of publications and adopt a number of documents aimed at improving monitoring instruments and stimulating further discussions. A series of information and training activities will be carried out by the Commission in 1995 and 1996 in order to provide assistance and guidance in the application of European social legislation to enterprise and individuals through the Euroguichets and EURES networks.

References

Bercussen, B. (1992): "Maastricht: A Fundamental Change in European Labour Law", *Industrial Relations Journal*, 23: 177–90.

Brewster, C. and Teague, P. (1989): *EC Social Policy and Britain*, London: Institute of Personnel Management in association with Academic Press.

Carson, I. (1992): "Oh, those lovely foreigners" in *The World in 1993*, London: Economist Publications.

Due, J., Steen M.J. and Carsten S.J. (1991): "The Social Dimension: Convergence or Diversification of IR in the Single European Market?", *Industrial Relations Journal*, 22: 85–102.

Dunlop, J. (1958): *Industrial Relations Systems*, Cambridge, Mass.: Harvard University Press.

The Economist (1993): "Inward investment: Why Here?", February 27: 40.

European Commission (1988): "The Social Dimension of the Internal Market", *Social Europe (special edition)*, Luxembourg: Office for Official Publications of the European Communities.

European Commission (1993): "Growth, Competitiveness and Employment: The Challenges and Ways Forward into the 21st Century", *Bulletin of the European Communities*, Supplement 6, Luxembourg: Office for Official Publication of the European Communities.

European Parliament (1989): *Ten Years that Changed Europe, 1979–1989*, Luxembourg: European Parliament.

Fitzpatrick, J. and Kelly, J. (eds) (1985): *Perspectives on Irish Industry*, Dublin: Irish Management Institute.

Henley, A. and Tsakalotos, E. (1992): "Corporatism and the European Labour Market after 1992", *British Journal of Industrial Relations*, 30: 567–84.

Hourihan, F. (1993a): "EC Working Time Directive: Leave and Night Work Affected Most", *Industrial Relations News*, 22: 15–7.

Hourihan, F. (1993b): "Works Councils to Cover All EC Countries Despite UK Opt-out?", *Industrial Relations News*, 37: 14–6.

Hourihan, F. (1994): "Uneven Progress in Reform of Education, Local Authority C&A Schemes", *Industrial Relations News*, 9: 18–21.

Incomes Data Services (1993): "Labour Costs: Measuring the Gap" in *IDS Focus: Social Dumping*, 66: 8–12.

Kerr, T. (1992): "Transfer of Undertakings and EC Law", *Industrial Relations News*, 41: 12–3.

Laffan, B. (1992): *Integration and Co-operation in Europe*, London: Routledge/University Association for Contemporary European Studies.

Marginson, P., Buitendam A., Deutschmann, C. and Perulli, P. (1993): "The Emergence of the Euro-company: Towards a European Industrial Relations?", *Industrial Relations Journal*, 24: 182–91.

Marsden, D. (1992): "Incomes Policy for Europe? Or Will Pay Bargaining Destroy the Single European Market?", *British Journal of Industrial Relations*, 30: 585–604.

Marsh, D. (1992): *The New Politics of British Trade Unionism: Unions Power and the Thatcher Legacy*, London: Macmillan.

McCarthy, C. (1973): *The Decade of Upheaval: Irish Trade Unions in the Nineteen Sixties*, Dublin: Institute of Public Administration.

McCartin, J. (1993): "Using Europe's Money", *Letters to the Irish Times*, November 9.

National Economic and Social Council (NESC) (1989): No. 88, Ireland in the European Community: Performance, Prospects and Strategy, Dublin: NESC.

Government Stationery Office (1991): Programme for Economic and Social Progress, Dublin: Stationery Office.

Government Stationery Office (1994): Programme for Competitiveness and Work, Dublin: Stationery Office.

Rosamond, B. (1993): "National Labour Organisations and European Integration: British Trade Unions and 1992", Political Studies, 41: 420–34.

Teague, P. (1993): "Co-ordination or Decentralisation: EC Social Policy and Industrial Relations" in J. Lodge (ed.), *The European Community and the Challenge of the Future*, 2nd edition, London: Pinter Publishers.

Vogel-Polsky, E. (1991): Social Policy in a United Europe, Luxembourg: European Parliament, Social Policy Series, 9.

INDEX